The Quality Yearbook

Yearbook

1996

Also available from McGraw-Hill

McGraw-Hill Encyclopedia of Quality Terms & Concepts (1995)
  James W. Cortada and John A. Woods
QualiTrends: Seven Quality Secrets that Can Change Your Life (1996)
  John A. Woods and James W. Cortada
TQM in Information Systems Management (1995)
  James W. Cortada
TQM in Sales and Marketing Management (1993)
  James W. Cortada

The Quality Yearbook

1996

James W. Cortada
John A. Woods

McGraw-Hill
New York   San Francisco   Washington, D.C.   Auckland   Bogotá
Caracas   Lisbon   London   Madrid   Mexico City   Milan
Montreal   New Delhi   San Juan   Singapore
Sydney   Tokyo   Toronto

McGraw-Hill

A Division of The **McGraw·Hill** *Companies*

Copyright © 1996 by The McGraw-Hill Companies, Inc. All rights reserved. Printed in the United States of America. Except as permitted under the United States Copyright Act of 1976, no part of this publication may be reproduced or distributed in any form or by any means, or stored in a data base or retrieval system, without the prior written permission of the publisher.

1 2 3 4 5 6 7 8 9 0   AGM/AGM   9 0 0 9 8 7 6 5

ISBN: 0-07-024235-6

ISSN: 1072-9135

The sponsoring editor for this book was Philip Ruppel, and the production supervisor was Mary Boss. It was composed at Impressions, a division of Edwards Brothers, Inc.

Printed and bound by Quebecor/Martinsburg.

Contents

Preface

When we started working on this annual anthology and reference in 1993 and published the first edition in January 1994, we hoped we would be delivering articles and information that readers would find useful. It is very gratifying, now that we have completed the 1996 edition, to know that you and many others like you find this a valuable resource. If you are a previous purchaser and are adding this one to your collection, thank you for your continued support. If you are a first-time purchaser, thanks for trying us out. Whether you're a new or a repeat customer, continue reading here. We're going to talk about what we think makes this book special and how this edition is different from earlier editions. The book has two purposes:

1. To provide an *annual documentation* of the most useful ideas, tools, and articles in quality.
2. To serve as an *annual comprehensive reference* for finding information on publications, tools, techniques, and special issues involved in implementing quality management.

We set several goals for ourselves in developing this book. The most important include:

Create a Clearinghouse. Because there is so much coming out in quality, McGraw-Hill and the editors of this book perceived a need for a kind of "clearinghouse" to which people from all different organizations might turn as a starting place to learn about current thinking in quality. *The Quality Yearbook* includes the best and most useful selection of information available. Its utility is founded on this premise, and its success is a continuing testament to how well we fill this need.

Create a Book of Lasting Value. Because it is revised annually, *The Quality Yearbook* focuses on information that has come out in the period immediately preceding its publication. While currency is one of its strengths in this fast-changing field, we also intend each edition to have lasting value. You will find articles throughout the book that will continue to be applicable for several years as you go about implementing quality in your organization or helping others to do this. However, a value of each year's new edition is that it gives you updates on all the book's content areas plus selected new topics that reflect the latest developments in the field.

Develop an Authoritative Review. Yet another goal for *The Quality Yearbook* is to contribute to clearer thinking about and implementation of the principles of quality management. This is a broad field. By providing a comprehensive review of the latest discussions of the applications and extensions of quality principles across many categories, we hope we can provide a way to standardize their study.

Organization

As in the last two years, we have divided the book into four parts:

Part One, Background for Quality, includes two original introductory articles on the idea of value and service in understanding quality and our continuing "Classics in Quality" section, with excerpts from three books that focus attention on the foundation of managing for quality.

Part Two, Quality by Industry, covers TQM as practiced in manufacturing, services, and four different areas of the public sector—government, health care, higher education, and K–12 education.

Part Three, Implementing Quality, presents the best articles and ideas from the past year on the theory and techniques of quality management. We have broken the readings into four categories:

1. Quality Transformation
2. Quality Tools and Techniques
3. Functional Processes
4. Standards and Assessments

Part Three is the longest part of the book and provides a wide spectrum of articles that explain the whys and hows of implementing quality, including many different examples from different industries.

Part Four, Quality References, includes a wide variety of material to help you further your exploration of TQM. Among the content of this part, you will find a comprehensive bibliography of quality articles and books that have come out since in the last edition (this is current through the fall of 1995) and a directory of quality magazines and journals. Use it when you are looking for articles on any of the wide variety of subjects taken up in this yearbook. For reflection and use in preparing speeches and reports, we continue the section that appeared in the last two editions, "Quotes on Quality," with all new quotes this year. We hope this stimulates your thinking on many issues. You will also find a profile of the 1995 Baldrige Award winners in this part and a review of the changes in the 1996 Baldrige Award criteria.

What's New in the 1996 Edition?

An important insight into the effective implementation of quality management is the idea that an organization is a system. We have therefore added a new section in the transforming the organization section of Part Three called "Systems Thinking/Learning Organizations." This includes an original article by Daniel Kim (see below) and three other pieces that we think provide good explanations of this idea. The best review of how to understand what systems thinking means is in Peter M. Senge's book *The Fifth Discipline*. We have received permission to reproduce the chapter from that book that explains how to do this. You'll find this as a new addition in Part Four, Quality References.

ISO 9000 is also an important area of concern for those practicing quality management. We have included an original article "ISO 9000 for Beginners" by Alan Lund, a nationally known consultant in this area. If you want to understand the basics of ISO, this is a good place to start. You'll also find a very practical piece on how to select an ISO registrar that follows the Lund article. Together, these should provide a foundation for exploring ISO 9000 certification.

In the 1995 edition, we included a new section, On-Line Quality Resources. This section is greatly expanded this year. You'll find as comprehensive a listing as is now available in our reference section.

. There is lots more as well. Our objective is to provide you with a tool for keeping up with this expanding field. We want these annual volumes to be the first place you look when you have a question about almost any subject in this field.

Feedback From You

What we put in next year's edition can depend either on our judgment alone or in partnership with you. Please use the feedback form at the back of this book to tell us what you think of this year's edition and what you want in the next one. It only takes a minute, but it allows us to hear your voice, something we take very seriously. You can also write us directly at 3010 Irvington Way, Madison, WI 53713-3414 or by E-mail at jwoods@execpc.com. Let us hear from you. We want *The Quality Yearbook* to do a great job of meeting your needs.

Consulting Editors

As the yearbook has evolved, we have requested and received the assistance of various consulting editors. Their role has been to help us understand their fields, recommend articles we might include, and, most importantly, to contribute an original article themselves. The number of consulting editors has expanded in this edition to 10. We are very happy to have them associated with this book. You'll find that their articles start off the various sections of Part Two and elsewhere. The following profiles these individuals. We include their addresses and phone numbers in case you wish to contact them about their areas of expertise.

- **Robert W. Hall, Manufacturing.** Bob is professor of operations management at Indiana University, Indianapolis and is a founding member of the Association for Manufacturing Excellence and editor-in-chief of their publication, *Target*. Bob was an examiner for the Malcolm Baldrige National Quality Award from 1988 to 1990 and is a certified fellow of the American Production and Inventory Control Society (APICS). He is the author of many articles and the books, *The Soul of Enterprise* and *Measuring Up: Charting Pathways to Manufacturing Excellence*. You can reach Bob at PO Box 309, Mooresville, IN 46158, (317) 839-9829.

- **Ron Zemke, Services.** Ron is president of Performance Research Associates, a Minneapolis-based consulting and training company specializing in service quality audits and service management program. Ron is also senior editor for *Training* magazine and contributing editor to *The Lakewood Report* newsletter. He is the author or co-author of several best-selling business books, including *Service America! Doing Business in the New Economy*, *Managing Knock Your Socks Off Service*, *The Service Edge: 101 Companies that Profit from Customer Care*, and *Sustaining Knock Your Socks Off Service*. Zemke received the 1994 Mobius Award for his contributions to the customer service profession. Ron can be reached at PRA, 821 Marquette Avenue, Suite 1820, Minneapolis, MN 55402, (612) 338-8523.

- **Joe Sensenbrenner, Government.** Joe is president of Sensenbrenner Associates and works in the application of private sector TQM approaches to public-sector service delivery. In 1988, he was recognized as one of the "Ten Most Influential Figures in Quality Improvement." Joe was a three-term mayor of Madison, Wisconsin, serving from 1983 to 1989, during which time he pioneered service improvements in virtually every municipal activity. He is the author of articles that have appeared in the *Harvard Business Review*, *Quality Progress*, and *Nation's Business* in the area of implementing TQM in government. He frequently speaks and gives seminars around the country. You can contact Joe at Sensenbrenner Associates, 818 Prospect Place, Madison, WI 53703, (608) 251-3100.

- **J. Daniel Beckham, Health Care.** Dan is president of the Beckham Company. He is recognized as one of the health care industry's top strategists, with clients from among the most influential health care organizations in the country. He is a contributing editor to *Healthcare Forum* magazine, and his articles are always among the most thoughtful that that magazine publishes. He is the author of *Marketing Your Practice,* a guide for physicians that has sold more than 150,000 copies. Much of his work now focuses on implementing quality management principles in health care facilities of all kinds. You can reach Dan at 1901 E. Cumberland Boulevard, Whitefish Bay, WI 53211, (414) 963-8935.

- **Julie Horine, Education K–12.** Julie is a member of the Department of Educational Leadership at the University of Mississippi, where she teaches and conducts research in quality management and organizational improvement. She annually conducts a national research study that examines the deployment of quality practices in educational systems, both in K–12 and higher education. She serves as the lead training facilitator for the Governor's "Strengthening Quality in Schools" initiative in New Mexico. Julie is also a Malcolm Baldrige National Quality Award examiner and a member of the Baldrige Education Pilot Evaluation Team, which is bringing the Baldrige Award to education. She received her Ph.D. in 1983 from Florida State University. You can reach Julie at Department of Educational Leadership, University of Mississippi, Oxford, MS 38677, (601) 232-5016.

- **Ronald L. Heilmann, Higher Education.** Ron is a member of the school of business faculty at the University of Wisconsin, Milwaukee and head of the Center for Quality, Productivity, and Economic Development at that university. He is also a member of the education committee of Milwaukee: First in Quality (MFIQ) and past president of the MFIQ Executive Committee. Ron is a senior member of the American Society for Quality Control. He is president and founder of the National Educational Quality Initiative, a nonprofit corporation dedicated to improving the quality of the U.S. educational system. You can contact Ron at the Center for Quality and Productivity, University of Wisconsin, PO Box 742, Milwaukee, WI 53201, (414) 229-6259.

- **Daniel Kim, Systems Thinking.** Dan is co-founder and currently the Learning Lab Project Director at the MIT Organizational Learning Center, where he works closely with Peter Senge in putting into practice the five disciplines of the learning organization—shared vision, personal mastery, mental models, team learning, and systems thinking. He has worked with numerous companies, including DuPont, Harley Davidson, Hanover Insurance, CIGNA, Brigham & Women's Hospital, and GE. He has a Ph.D. from MIT Sloan School of Management and is publisher of *The Systems Thinker*™, a newsletter that helps managers apply the power of systems thinking to their organizations. You can reach Dan at MIT Organizational Learning Center, 30 Memorial Drive, E60-372, PO Box 46, Kendall Square, Cambridge, MA 02142-0001, (617) 253-1587.

- **Alan K. Lund, ISO 9000.** Al is mechanical engineer and president of The Ironbridge Group, an ISO 9000 consulting company. He has successfully completed ISO 9000 lead assessor training, conducted by the British Standards Institute, and is certified as an ISO 9000 registrar. He has completed the Chrysler, Ford, and General Motors QS 9000/QSA Registrar training program. He is a highly regarded expert in ISO 9000 certification. You can reach Al at The Ironbridge Group, 9200 Indian Creek Parkway, Building 9, Suite 201, Overland Park, KS 66210, (800) ISO-9001 (476-9001).

- **Leonard L. Berry, Special Contributor.** Len holds the JC Penney Chair of Retailing Studies and is professor of marketing and director of the Center for Retailing Studies at the College of Business Administration, Texas A&M University. He is editor of the *Arthur Andersen Retailing Issues Letter* and former national president of the American Marketing Association. He is author of *On Great Service* and co-author of *Delivering Quality Service: Balancing Customer Perceptions and Expectations*, both published by The Free Press. In a recent study, Len was identified as the most frequent contributor to the services marketing literature in the United States. Len can be reached at the Department of Marketing, College of Business Administration, Texas A&M University, College Station, TX 77843-4112, (409) 845-0804.

Acknowledgments

This book was a big undertaking for us, and we are indebted to many people who have played a role in its coming together. At McGraw-Hill, Phil Ruppel and Danielle Munley have been both supportive and helpful in many ways and have been fine teammates.

We want to thank the editors and publishers of the several magazines, journals, and books from which we drew the articles that make up the heart of this book. All were very forthcoming in supplying the permissions that allowed us to reprint the pieces you see here.

Jan Kosko and Ann Rothgeb at the National Institute of Standards and Technology assisted us by supplying information on the Baldrige award winners and criteria changes for 1996. We thank them for their responsiveness to our needs.

Our production schedule for this book is an extraordinarily quick two months, and at our production house, Impressions, we were fortunate to work on this edition with Mary Boss. Mary's conscientious work made production go very smoothly and finish on schedule. We also want to thank David Nelson, whose skill (and speed) at laying out pages has also been crucial in getting this book completed in a timely fashion.

Our wives, Dora Cortada and Nancy Woods, have been very supportive of our efforts as we shuttle between our houses doing the myriad chores involved in delivering this book to you.

Finally, we want to thank those who have found the 1994 and 1995 editions of this book useful additions to their shelf of quality resources and to those of you who are new buyers this year. Without you, *The Quality Yearbook* wouldn't exist.

Jim Cortada
John Woods

## PART ONE

Background for Quality

Total quality management (TQM) is often misunderstood these days as a buzzword for a set of management techniques that have their place, but there are lots of other management approaches to try as well. People have relegated TQM to the idea of continuous improvement using certain statistical tools to reduce variation in outputs. Certainly that is an important part of TQM, but we believe it is much more than that. It is the most realistic approach to managing organizations when you take the systems view. In managing a system, you must focus on the processes and interrelationships by which any organization transforms inputs into outputs that customers will value and buy. That's what TQM helps you do better than any other management approach.

Delivering value is an important way to articulate the purpose of organizational systems. To do that, of course, it is necessary to understand what value is all about. To help you do that a little better, we are starting the 1996 edition of *The Quality Yearbook* with two articles that explore this issue. The first, by best-selling author and researcher, Professor Leonard Berry, looks at some issues surrounding service excellence. While companies may try to compete on the basis of differentiating product offerings, it is often the services that surround that product that make the difference for customers. The second article, by John Woods, co-editor of *The Quality Yearbook*, reviews the specific components that make up value from the perspective of customers. By managing to get better and better at delivering on these components, you help assure your organization will remain competitive.

The Classics of Quality

In this section of the yearbook, we have sought over the last two editions to bring you seminal writings on TQM. We are especially pleased with the selections we have chosen this time. We start with a chapter from Peter Drucker's 1954 book *The Practice of Management*. In this chapter, he summarizes some basic thoughts he had about management back then. While they do not coincide exactly with the thoughts of the quality gurus, Drucker's piece nevertheless captures many ideas that quality practitioners will recognize. Drucker is always a sage source of sound advice on management practice, and we are happy to bring this piece to your attention.

We are also including a chapter from a 1974 book by Theodore Levitt, one of the pioneering thinkers in marketing and an originator of the "marketing concept." This concept, clearly articulated in his classic 1960 article "Marketing Myopia," states that organizations exist to deliver benefits to customers, as defined by customers. The piece included here clearly lays out a method for analyzing the nature of the relationship a company is building with its customers.

Finally, we have chosen a basic introduction to control charts from AT&T's *Statistical Quality Control Handbook*, which is based on the original work of Walter Shewhart. If Deming had a guru, it was Shewhart.

We hope the material in Part One will deepen your appreciation of the ideas on which quality management is based and give you a sense of its roots.

Leading to Service Excellence

Leonard L. Berry

We are pleased to include this original article by Professor Leonard Berry as the introduction to the 1996 edition of The Quality Yearbook. *Professor Berry has long been helping organizations appreciate the value to customers of good (or even extraordinary) service, one of the cornerstones of the sound practice of quality management. He is the author or co-author of three books published by The Free Press, the most recent being the best-selling* On Great Service: A Framework for Action. *Professor Berry makes one overriding point that cannot be overstated: "All businesses are service businesses." The methods, tools, and principles of TQM become, from this perspective, the best approach to making that truth a reality in every type of organization.*

Premdor is a fast-growing Toronto-based manufacturer of doors. The company's sales growth has been extraordinary, from about $69 million in 1983 to $744 million in 1994. With manufacturing facilities in four countries and inventive marketing that has created a family of door brands such as Safe N Sound, Premwood, and Fast-Fit, service quality seems inconsequential to the company's success. In actuality, service quality is playing a pivotal role. More than perhaps any other door producer in the world, Premdor works closely with its distributors and retailers to help them effectively merchandise the doors. Premdor provides training support for distributor and retailer salespeople, point-of-sale merchandising systems, and a toll-free telephone line staffed by door experts who can advise and answer questions for salespeople or customers. In 1995, Premdor introduced a turnkey, integrated merchandising system for retailers that enables them to stock more door units and offer more variety in less space. One offering to the retailer is an on-site "Door Machine" that in just a few minutes can convert a wood slab into a finished, customized door that meets the customer's precise specifications.

West Point Market is a highly successful specialty food store in Akron, Ohio. By 1993, 57 years after its founding, West Point Market had undergone six expansions and 21 remodels. It is owned and operated by Russ Vernon, son of the founder. At West Point Market, flowers are everywhere: in front of the store, complementing the parking lot, at the store entrance, in the aisles. More than 80 trees are on the property. The delivery truck is painted with dancing vegetables. Merchandise signs are hand drawn in soft colors by the same artist to insure a coordinated look. The exit signs are hand-carved wooden signs. Colorful balloons decorate the store. Information recipe tags on the shelves educate shoppers on how to use the products: "This creamy mild cheese with caraway seeds slices well for ham sandwiches on hearty rye." West Point Market's "Customers of Tomorrow" program includes kiddie shopping carts and cookie credit cards (for children to receive a free cookie on each store visit). The restrooms have classical music, almond soap, indirect lighting, and, of course, fresh flowers.

Product tasting and demonstration events in the store are common. As many as four events may occur simultaneously on a Saturday; for example, there might be one chef cooking pasta, another preparing salsa recipes, and another preparing a cold pasta with a new avocado dressing, and you might find a bread sampling table. Kay Lowe, Director of Public Relations, states: "One of the services we offer is customer education. We don't hesitate to let customers taste a product. Some people come in on a Saturday and eat their way around the store."

Customers visiting the store for the first time receive a personal thank you letter from Russ Vernon and a $2 certificate to use on their next visit. Each cashier in monthly meetings is responsible for reviewing 10 customers by name with the cashier group. "Miss O'Neil comes in every night and always orders croissants. Sometimes she is not feeling well, so we go to the bakery and get them for her." Cindy Yost, the specialty foods buyer, enjoys teaching customers about unfamiliar foods and then following up: "If a customer buys a sauce I recommended, then the next time I see the customer I will ask how the sauce worked out. I don't always remember the customer's name, but I remember the products I sold to that customer."

The West Point Market is not for customers who wish to do their shopping anonymously in utilitarian surroundings. However, for customers who like to cook, who are looking for high-quality and unusual foods, and who enjoy genuinely personalized service, West Point Market is a special place. Russ Vernon comments:

> From the very first day, my father and his partners focused on the customers. They devoted their business life to probing and searching for new and exciting ways to please their customers. This is the kind of retailing that I learned. My competition is not willing to invest in the enhancements. I am.

The Premdor and West Point Market stories powerfully demonstrate the reality that all businesses are service businesses.

The Premdor and West Point Market stories powerfully demonstrate the reality that *all businesses are service businesses.* Premdor, a door manufacturer, and West Point Market, a food store, compete with excellent service, not just with excellent goods. Indeed, these companies use superior service to create strong, enduring bonds with customers. It is difficult to develop strong loyalties with customers by selling them doors or mustard. But when the doors or the mustard is combined with a human face, with a spirit of serving, with a sense of urgency for providing genuine value, then the conditions are in place to build enduring customer relationships.

Value and Service

Great companies compete on value, not solely on price. One of the biggest mistakes many executives make is to assume that value and price mean the same thing to customers. They do not. Price is a part of value, but it is not the equivalent of value.

To customers, value is the benefits received for the burdens endured. Benefits may include product quality, personal service, store atmosphere, convenience, and peace-of-mind. Burdens include both monetary cost (price) and nonmonetary cost. Nonmonetary cost might include long waits in checkout lines, incompetent or rude customer-contact personnel, missed appointments, inability to get through on a busy 800 number, and sloppy workmanship.

Companies become—and stay—successful with a strong benefits-to-burdens offer. They maximize the most important benefits to targeted customers and minimize the most critical burdens. They compete on value, not solely on price—or not on price at all. This is why companies like Premdor and West Point Market can be so successful without offering the lowest available prices. Premdor and West Point Market refuse to market their products as commodities. They sell more than the physical product: They sell fashion; they sell innovative solutions; they sell creativity; they sell personalized attention; they sell a relationship.

Every truly great company, regardless of the nature of its product offerings, emphasizes service excellence. Harley-Davidson, the motorcycle manufacturer that dominates its market, has infused the curriculum of its Harley-Davidson University (attended by dealers) with material on service quality. Southwest Airlines, America's most consistently profitable airline, has developed an unusually motivated and productive workforce that enables the company to be an industry leader in service performance areas such as baggage handling and on-time flights. Roberts Express, a nationwide trucking company that specializes in emergency shipments, picks up most shipments within 90 minutes of the order and delivers 95 percent of them within 15 minutes of the promise time. Roberts Express backs up its service promise by refunding part of its fee if shipments are more than 2 hours late. The company has grown from $3 million in sales in 1982 to more than $200 million in 1994.

Assuming the Mantle of Service Leadership

Excellent service comes from leading, not just managing. Service leadership—at the top of the organization and in its middle—is the make or break quality service issue. With it, great service is possible; without it, great service is a pipe dream. Services are performances, and someone must assume the mantle of leadership to teach, challenge, and inspire the performers. The following are examples of failures in leadership: airline lost-baggage employees who refuse to answer ringing telephones because they are "too busy"; a plumbing firm that shows up at a home four hours late without explanation or regret; a retail store where employees are more interested in discussing their personal lives with one another than serving customers.

To customers, value is the benefits received for the burdens endured.

Every truly great company, regardless of the nature of its product offerings, emphasizes service excellence.

Researchers Warren Bennis and Burt Nanus have identified what they believe is the fundamental difference between leaders and managers. Leaders, they assert, emphasize the emotional and spiritual resources of an organization, such as creativity, commitment, and wisdom. Managers, in contrast, stress the organization's physical resources, such as raw materials, technology, and capital.

Clearly, managing is critical to the success of any organization. However, it is not enough. Only a special form of leadership—service leadership—provides the sustained inspiration and energy required to deliver superior service quality. Service leaders come in all shapes and sizes, but they all possess four essential characteristics:

Service Vision. For a service leader, excellent *service* is the driving force of the business. Regardless of the nature of the business or the type of customers, service leaders visualize quality of service as their foundation.

Good service isn't good enough for a true service leader. Service leaders focus on the details and nuances of performance. They invest in small actions that competitors might consider trivial: thank you notes to loyal customers, a lighted walkway to the store, customer-friendly signs. They believe how the company handles the little things influences how they handle everything. They know that small details add up for customers and differentiate the company from its competitors. Excellent execution of the details ensures that customers receive *more* than they came to buy.

Service leaders define their service vision for the organization. They express it in words, but, more importantly, they model it in daily behavior. They infuse life into their vision. West Point Market's Russ Vernon spends little time in his office. Instead, he is on the sales floor, listening to customers, coaching employees, sometimes even carrying customers' shopping bags to their cars. Joyce Meskis, owner of the highly successful Tattered Cover Bookstore in Denver, teaches a day-long orientation class to all new employees. The subject is the company's vision and values of superior service. Larry Harmon, the owner of De Mar, a Clovis, California, plumbing company, treats incoming calls like a 911 line. The company's core competency is its ability to treat an emergency like an emergency.

These leaders live their vision for the company. And an enlivened vision empowers. From it, service providers receive guidance and aspirations for their own performance. At every level, employees are energized by a service leader with the vision to serve excellently.

Belief in Others. Service leaders intensely believe in the potential of people to achieve. They set a standard of excellence, provide the tools needed for success, and encourage leadership behavior throughout the organization. Service leaders' belief in their employees inspires employees to believe in themselves. Employees nurtured by their leader's belief in them work hard, not because a supervisor monitors them but because they want to work hard, develop their skills and knowledge, be an integral part of the company's success, and justify their leader's belief. Affirmation motivates.

Leaders emphasize the emotional and spiritual resources of an organization, such as creativity, commitment, and wisdom.

At every level, employees are energized by a service leader with the vision to serve excellently.

Mary Kay Ash, the founder of Mary Kay Cosmetics, epitomizes the belief-in-others leadership characteristic. Founded to offer opportunity to women, Mary Kay Cosmetics has created more female millionaires than any other company in the world. Mary Kay Ash believes any woman can be remarkable if she is given the opportunity and sets her sights high. Pink Cadillacs play just a small part in the high motivation levels reflected in so many Mary Kay beauty consultants (sales representatives). The real story is about believing in, trusting, and respecting human beings and inspiring them to rise higher than they ever imagined.

Love of the Business.   The best service leaders love the business they lead. They immerse themselves in its intricacies, welcome the challenges that test them, and bask in the sense of accomplishment after a good day. They love the action. They would rather be running the business than doing anything else. They act from a deep motivation to operate the business well, to make it grow, to create something special.

Love of the business brings to full flower the enthusiasm and ebullience evident in so many service leaders. Their natural fervent spirit and the right setting for its creative expression contribute to the emotional energy of true leadership.

Love of the business motivates service leaders to teach the business and to pass on to others the nuances, secrets, and craft of operating it. Harold Wiesenthal is the founder of Harolds, a highly profitable Houston clothing store in business more than 45 years. Harold Wiesenthal loves the business of helping customers look good. Harold has taught his two sons, Darryl and Michael, and the sales staff the importance of creating "true customers"—customers who are glad they did business with you after the sales transaction is completed. Harold Wiesenthal is the ultimate coach, the ultimate role model, and is constantly on the sales floor teaching the Harolds brand of great service. Below, sons Darryl and Michael relate the retailing lessons they have learned from their father:

1. Customers are the reason we are here. Take care of them. Follow-up. Deliver. Make sure they are happy.
2. Sell customers what they need and what fits. If they need a 44, don't sell them a 46 or a 42.
3. Emphasize quality of merchandise. Do not put anything in the store that you wouldn't be willing to wear yourself.
4. Be on the floor. The floor is everything. If you don't take care of the floor, little else matters. The customer wants to see the owner.
5. Make customers part of the store. Put their pictures on the walls; include them in the TV ads and radio spots; send them thank you letters.
6. Know your stock; know where things are.
7. Show the merchandise. Spend time on the little items, such as the ties to complement the suit and make the customer look good.

8

8. Always smile. The customer wants to see you smile.
9. You sell more than clothes. You sell yourself. People buy from us because they are our friends.
10. Promote the store 24 hours. If you go to the gym, wear a Harolds T-shirt.

Love of the business fosters service leaders' high standards. Service leaders like Harold Wiesenthal not only teach the nitty-gritty of business operations but also exemplify its style, values, and excellence. Service leaders teach service leadership as they model it.

Integrity. Service leaders prize their integrity. They value being fair, consistent, and truthful with customers, employees, suppliers, and other stakeholders, thereby earning the opportunity to lead. Because leaders act from this deep ethical core, both customers and employees trust them.

Personal integrity is the quintessential service leadership characteristic. More than a philosophy, it is the ethical gyroscope of the organization. Out of their integrity, these leaders maintain a true orientation and direction regardless of pressure from other forces. Integrity propels the leader's vision of what the organization must be—internally and externally. Harley-Davidson CEO Richard Teerlink refuses to use alternative channels to market much-in-demand Harley-Davidson insignia products. "We will not compete with our dealers," he says matter-of-factly. Southwest Airlines chief executive Herb Kelleher ignores enticement packages offered by cities hoping to attract the airline. His reasoning: "We will only go into a market where we can make it work on our own. That way we won't have to pull up and leave." Greg Penske is president of Longo Toyota and Lexus in Los Angeles, the largest retail volume Toyota dealership in the United States. Penske teaches his sales staff: "Don't sell customers a car, help them buy a car. Then you make a friend." All Longo salespeople are required to sign a code of ethics.

Much has been written about the broad subject of leadership but less about *service leadership*. Service leaders inspire followers with a vision of service excellence, with a belief in the capacity of the followers to excel, with their love of the business and desire to teach the business's values and craft, and with their integrity. True service leaders engage co-workers in realizing their full capabilities, including their leadership potential.

Companies compete on the basis of the value they offer customers. Quality of service is integral to the creation of value. This is true for all companies. Superior service is rare, but it is not an impossible dream. Leadership is the difference maker. Nurturing service leadership is the single most important step in an organization's service quality journey. Everything else a company might do toward great service follows.

> Service leaders inspire followers with a vision of service excellence, with a belief in the capacity of the followers to excel, with their love of the business and desire to teach the business's values and craft, and with their integrity. True service leaders engage co-workers in realizing their full capabilities, including their leadership potential.

Dr. Leonard L. Berry holds the JCPenney Chair of Retailing Studies at Texas A&M University where he also is Professor of Marketing and Director of the Center for Retailing Studies. He is author of the new book, On Great Service: A Framework for Action *(Free Press, 1995). He also is co-author of earlier books, including* Marketing Services: Competing Through Quality *(Free Press, 1991) and* Delivering Quality Service: Balancing Customer Perceptions and Expectations *(Free Press, 1990).*

Total Quality Management as Total Value Management

John A. Woods

This article, by one of the co-editors of the yearbook, relates quality and value in a concrete manner. When we speak of total quality management (TQM), it often becomes just a phrase that rolls off our tongues in such a way that it almost loses meaning. In this article, you'll see what value is actually all about: utility. And once you understand what utility entails, you can focus on improving your organization's ability to deliver the utility that means real value for customers and profitability and growth for you.

One of the foundation principles of TQM is an unrelenting focus on customer satisfaction. There is a reason for this. The purpose of all companies is to provide customers with products and services that fulfill their needs and wants. This is what attracts the revenue that businesses require to be around tomorrow to continue doing this. Though this idea is at the center of TQM, it remains just a statement of principle until you figure out how to operationalize it. That's what this article is about.

What you want is for customers to gain so much benefit from what you do for them that they willingly pay you enough to cover your costs and profit and that they keep coming back for more. The goal is for you to create a business where customers believe that it is in their best interests to buy from you. And they'll do that because they receive the quality and value they want and expect. Then your goal is to get better and better at doing this.

"Custom-ers"

One way to understand customers is to take the word apart. Its root is the word "custom" as in "customized." It is not an accident that the word customers comes from the word custom. It is the recognition that people value most those items that they believe are customized to meet their personal needs. What happens when you think of those you are trying to sell to as *custom*-ers? It suggests that you customize your offerings as much as you can to conform to their expectations. If your employees also understand this, and you make it part of your business credo (meaning guiding principle), you are taking an important action that will attract *custom*-ers. I am emphasizing this because I want you to appreciate that the absolute foundation of business

It is not an accident that the word customers comes from the word custom.

is serving *custom*-ers. And you must do it in ways that they will appreciate and value.

What Is Value Anyway? Answer: Utility

Customers (I won't keep italicizing *custom* and then adding "ers," but try to remember that anyway) buy what they value. The higher customers value what you offer compared with your competitors, the more likely they are to do business with you. In fact, for the purposes of understanding TQM, the words *value* and *quality* are synonymous. We could call TQM "total value management," and this would not change anything. So, if the term total quality management is making you a bit numb, think about in terms of TVM, and it will keep you focused on what this all about.

The next question, then, is what constitutes *value*? The idea that I think works best to describe value is **utility**. This word reminds us that people value things because they can *use them* in one way or another. Or they value services because these help them achieve some goal they have. *It's your job to make what you sell easy to use and easy to acquire.* Customers always buy the benefits they expect to derive from a purchase and never the item itself. Another way to talk about benefits is utility.

> People value things because they can *use them* in one way or another.

The old saying, people buy holes not drill bits, helps to make this idea concrete. And the more efficiently and effectively particular bits make holes, the more people will value that type over some other one (assuming they know about it and have access to it). Charles Revson, the founder of Revlon, used to say "In the factory we make cosmetics, in the drugstore, we sell hope." The utility of an item tells us something about what it does for someone. In addition, customers derive utility from how easily they can take possession of an item or have access to a service. Think about your business or organization, and do this brief exercise:

> Fill in the blanks to this sentence:
> In our organization, we make _____;
> to our customers we sell _____.

Your organization's mission, or the mission of any business or organization, is to focus on delivering utility to your customers, constituents, or whatever you call them. You want to make it just as easy as possible for these folks to get the performance they want and expect from your offerings. You want to do everything in your power to avoid disappointing them. In fact, what you really want to do is surprise and delight them as often as you can.

The subject of marketing—which, in academic circles, is defined as the study and practice of creating mutually beneficial exchanges—breaks utility up into four components. These components are quite helpful for defining exactly what it is that customers actually buy when they go to the store. The four components of utility are summarized in Figure 1. The word value is in the center of this figure, but I could just as easily have put the word quality. It would be the same thing. What you sell and what your customers will value

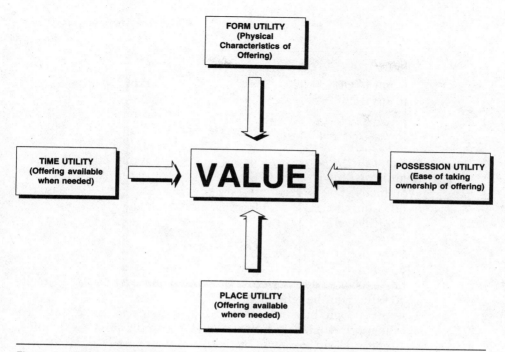

Figure 1. **The components of value and quality.**

and buy from you right now is some combination of these four utilities. Your objective as a manager or business owner is to figure out what that combination is and how you can improve on it to sustain and enhance your competitive position. Below is a more detailed description of each component of utility with examples.

The Four Utilities

When you think about value and utility, consider this quote tossed off by a character in the novel *Polar Star* by Martin Cruz Smith: "Happiness is the maximum agreement of reality with desire." As a business person, this is a good way to think about your responsibility. The four utilities help bring the maximum agreement between reality and desire in the small part of people's lives that your organization affects. These utilities are the ways your organization creates or can create value for your customers. They are the strategic tools you can manipulate to differentiate your offerings from those of your competitors. Understanding these utilities and delivering on them is your purpose as a manager or any level employee and is what will attract and hold customers.

Some companies will emphasize only one or two of these. For example, a discount electronics store may deliver a lot of form utility for a low price, so its focus is on form and possession utility. However, the store may be out

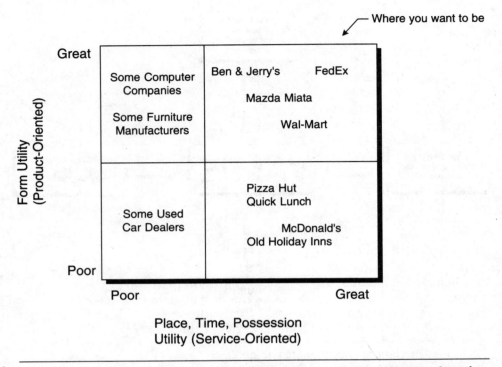

Figure 2.   **This kind of matrix helps position your company's products and services in terms of the utility you deliver.**

of the way, and customers may have to wait if the TV or VCR they want is out of stock. Such stores don't do a good job of delivering time or place utility, but they don't have to. If the prices are low enough and the products are what customers want, then they may accept the inconvenience of going out of their way to find the store and waiting if their selection is out of stock. In fact, they may understand that one of the reasons for low prices is the inconvenient but low-rent location.

Sometimes enhancing your offering in one of these areas is a way to gain an advantage over competitors. Sometimes you must make all of them a priority because that's what your competitors do as well. The four utilities classify in clear, concrete terms what the outputs of your processes should deliver to your customers. If your organization's efforts are not focused on these four areas, then you are undermining your potential in the market. By keeping these utilities in mind, it helps you and your employees become more customer-directed in your decision making.

Finally, it's important to note that three out of the four have to do with *service* to the customer and not much to do with the physical product itself. Many companies will focus only the physical characteristics of their offerings,

The four utilities classify in clear, concrete terms what the outputs of your processes should deliver to your customers.

forgetting that much of what customers value is covered by the other three utilities. That often explains why gee-whiz products fail.

Figure 2 shows how companies should seek to position themselves. The objective is to be in the upper right corner of this matrix, where you are delivering the highest value to your customers. The matrix is set up with the larger boxes representing the service-oriented utilities to emphasize the importance of adding those aspects of value to your offering. The companies located in the boxes are examples of my perception of where they belong based on my experience as a customer. It would be a useful exercise to draw this kind of matrix and position your own organization and your competitors on it in terms of your understanding of your customers' perceptions. It would be an equally useful exercise to query your customers using this matrix to find out where they would position your organization.

Now, let's examine in more detail specifically what the four utilities entail.

Form/Function Utility

This is usually characterized just as form utility, but I think it is important to add function, because the two ideas go together. This utility encompasses the *physical and tangible characteristics* of a product or service that facilitates its use. This type of utility incorporates how well form and function are integrated into the final product or service. It includes such things as how easy a product is to use, how aesthetically pleasing it is to look at, how well it fits, how carefully it is made, the durability of materials used, how good it tastes, how clear the directions for assembly and use are, and whether the product or place where the service is delivered projects an image consistent with the user's self-image. (People make many buying decisions based on whether one product better meets their self-image than another.)

In services delivered, form/function utility includes the courtesy and competence of those delivering the services and the cleanliness, comfort, and atmosphere of the place where the services are delivered. All companies really sell a combination of products and services. They must pay as much attention to these services and how they are delivered as to the products themselves. This part of form utility is sometimes forgotten, opening the door to competitors who realize how valuable customers find the services that surround the basic product.

In services delivered, form/function utility includes the courtesy and competence of those delivering the services.

Examples of form utility:

- Ben & Jerry's New York Fudge Crunch ice cream (unique rich taste).
- Friday's restaurants (good food and attention to the whole family).
- Hotel concierge staff (take care of guest problems quickly and courteously).
- Books with large print for people with poor vision (accommodates disability).
- Component parts that exactly meet manufacturer specifications (simplifies manufacturing).

- Clothes that make overweight people look good (project an attractive appearance).
- Laser printers with easily replaced toner cartridges (simplifies use of technology).
- Training materials that are easy to follow and learn from (saves training time).
- User-friendly software (easy to learn and easy to use).
- Minivans (easy to drive and big capacity).
- High-intensity reading lights (less eye strain when reading).

Think about the form (and function) utility of the products or services your company offers. Does your company do a good job of delivering value in a physical form that your customers really like, or can you improve here? How do your offerings deliver that kind of utility to customers? In thinking about this question, consider such characteristics as appearance, fashion, ease of use, practicality, durability, as well as the atmosphere of the place where the customer purchases your offering and the attitude and behavior of the people who deliver it. And make sure you are thinking about this from the perspective of what customers consider value.

Place Utility

This has to do with *where* the product or service is delivered. If the place where customers go to purchase is a retail store or if they go to a restaurant or a barber shop, delivering place utility means it is easy and convenient to get to these businesses. Mail order companies add place utility by allowing you to shop by phone or by mail from home. Then, when they ship your order the same day they receive it, they add time utility as well. Suppliers to other companies add place utility by having salespeople call at customers' offices and by delivering goods to them.

Examples of place utility:

- Mall of America, with 400 stores and an amusement park all in one place and with parking for thousands of cars.
- Lands' End, with easy catalog shopping from home.
- The drive through at the local fast-food restaurant or bank, making it easy to get in and out.
- Service stations, with easy access off and back onto the freeway.
- Office Depot, with shopping for office supplies, computer supplies, and furniture all in one place.
- FedEx, with easy and reliable pick up of packages from any business or residence.

By being concerned with *where* they deliver their products and services, they add place utility, which people are willing to pay for.

Part of the value of what each of these companies is selling has to do with their use of place to add value to their offering. By being concerned with *where* they deliver their products and services, they add place utility, which people are willing to pay for.

What kind of place utility does your organization offer? Can you say that your current place utility enhances the value of your products or services to your customers? If you are a retailer, is your location convenient? Will your customers be willing to pay extra for your offerings or seek out your business because of easy access to your location or because you go to their place of business? Or does your place of doing business have such low rent that customers will be willing to come because you can offer them substantial discounts because of your location. This is a kind of place utility as well.

If you are a supplier to other businesses, do you have a reliable delivery service? If you offer professional services, do customers have easy access to your business? Note that place utility has nothing to do with the physical form of your offerings. It has value as a *service* to your customers. In making your list, make sure your ideas represent improvements that your customers will actually find valuable—not just things you *think* they might find valuable.

Time Utility

This has to do with delivering your offerings *when* customers want them. This means that stores have the items that customers want in stock. It means that when customers order from their suppliers, they can expect their orders to be available and delivered when needed. This includes just-in-time delivery to customers to help them minimize inventory costs. Here is another way of understanding time utility: Christmas cards lose time utility the day after Christmas, and that is why they are marked down 50 percent or more.

Examples of time utility:

- The 5 minute or less wait for lunch at a local restaurant.
- Same day delivery of supplies to a building site.
- FedEx overnight guaranteed delivery of packages.
- Opening extra cash registers when more than three people are in a line.
- Inventory control that makes sure no item is out of stock for more than a day.
- Early morning opening of an auto repair shop so people can drop cars off for repair before work.
- Airline flights that leave at convenient times and arrive on time.
- Quick turnaround on repairs of products.
- Advertising that lets people know you have what they are looking for now.

Do you pay attention to making sure your customers have access to your products when they want them? Do you have processes in place that allow you to meet your commitments for delivery dates? Does your organization go out of its way to add value by meeting your customers' expectations for the timely receipt of their orders? Did you notice that FedEx is on the list for place and time utility? It is a service company, and while physically it is transporting packages from one place to another, what we value about this company is its reliability in delivering our packages when and where we want them.

If you don't have in stock what your customers want when they want it, you're not delivering time utility. And by not doing so, you are diminishing the value of your offering and your organization to your customers. Again, note that time utility involves *service* to your customers. It has nothing to do with the physical product they are buying, yet it adds value to that offering.

Possession Utility

This has to do with *pricing, payments, and warranties.* Companies deliver possession utility by making it easy for customers to buy their offering. Accepting all credit cards, having special sales, allowing 30 or 60 days for payment, and guaranteeing satisfaction with a purchase are all ways companies make it easy for customers to possess what they are selling. Customers want that transfer to be painless. Further, they want to be sure that what they are buying will function properly with no unanticipated problems. By attending to possession utility, you are adding more value (and quality) to your offering.

Making that transfer of ownership as easy as possible has value to customers.

Examples of possession utility:

- 90 days same as cash for large purchases.
- Sale prices on goods and services of all sorts.
- No-questions-asked guarantee by companies like L.L. Bean, Wal-Mart, and Lands' End.
- Value pricing for used and new cars—no dickering.
- Low interest rates for large purchases.
- Easy set up of credit.
- Tax breaks to companies building plants in particular states.
- 800 numbers and quick response for customers to help solve problems associated with purchase.

How does your organization make it easy for customers to gain possession of your offerings and make sure they continue to be satisfied with their purchases? Remember, making that transfer of ownership as easy as possible has value to customers. This can make the difference between dealing with you and dealing with a competitor. I know a car dealership that has created a complete ceremony of turning over a purchased car to the customer, which includes taking a picture of the purchasers with their new car. This ceremony makes taking possession a memorable event and helps justify the expense to the customer. Further, companies need to be concerned with the satisfaction the owner derives from his or her purchase. Guaranteeing satisfaction helps cement relationships with customers. Customers value this and are willing to pay for it. Part of the success of retailers like Wal-Mart and Lands' End centers on their no-hassle return policies. Finally, note again that this is yet another *service* you provide for your customers. This service has everything to do with increasing value and quality from the customer's perspective and little to do with the physical characteristics of the product itself.

Your job is to manage the resources over which you have control to continuously improve how you combine these four utilities to attract and hold your customers.

Utility and Customer Focus

Understanding these four utilities is central to making sense of the idea of customer focus. We talk about the ideas of value and quality all the time, but the utilities make these abstract ideas concrete. Your job is to manage the resources over which you have control to continuously improve how you combine these four utilities to attract and hold your customers.

The form your products or services take is important. However, it is only a part of what your customers will value about what your business offers. If you don't deliver your products or services where and when your customers want them and make them easy to acquire, you are putting yourself at a disadvantage.

In thinking about these four utilities, consider your own experience. Your suppliers won't last long with you if they don't deliver on all four of them. And if you explore why one company takes business away from others, even from established firms, you will usually find that they have put together a better combination of the four utilities.

Delivering the Four Utilities

Profitably delivering the four utilities requires upstream preparation and management of a company's processes. Management has to get those processes in alignment with delivering products and services in the form customers want, when they want them, at a convenient location, and on easy-to-buy terms. Listen to your customers, and learn from what they have to say. There are always opportunities for improvement, so keep improving.

Of course, this doesn't just happen because we want it to. We must take responsibility for it by making customer satisfaction the driving force of everyone's work. All employees must understand how they add value (form, time, place, and possession utility) to the final output. We should all define our jobs not in terms of function but in terms of the value we each add in the customer satisfaction process.

What about TQM in all this? If we acknowledge that value (as defined by the four utilities) is what you are in business to deliver, it becomes clear that the principles of TQM are about doing just that. TQM includes both a focus on customer satisfaction and concrete methods for organizing and improving an organization's work processes. And this allows you to deliver products and services in a more timely, less costly manner. That helps your company meet and exceed your customers' expectations and even delight them sometimes. It all goes together.

We can summarize what we have covered so far in this article in this way: It is management's responsibility to (1) gather and use information about customers' needs, problems, wants, expectations, and requirements; (2) consider what the company's capabilities are; (3) manage that information and those capabilities; and ultimately (4) satisfy customers, and make the organization prosperous. Figure 3 summarizes this process.

Utility and Your Employees as Customers and as Suppliers   Here is a way to make sure employees understand that their and the organization's fortunes are tied up in customer satisfaction: Use the idea of utility to help define the roles and responsibilities of everyone in the company. Among those who actively practice TQM, we often see the idea of internal customers and internal

Feedback

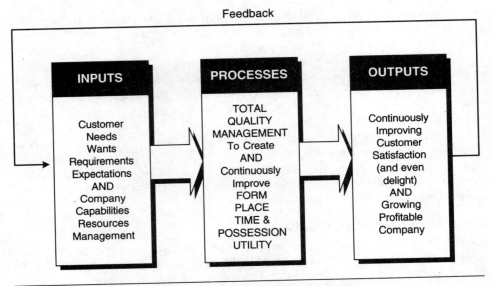

Figure 3.   **The systems view for creating delighted customers.**

suppliers. This idea suggests that all employees are customers of other employees and likewise suppliers to still others. The four utilities—*form, place, time,* and *possession*—are helpful for understanding how to help clarify these relationships and make processes function more smoothly and provide direction for improving them.

Any process is a sequence of steps. When it works well, the steps in delivering a final product or service will incorporate making sure all employees in the process (1) receive a partially finished product or information in a form that makes it easy to execute their steps, (2) receive the product or information where they need it, (3) receive the product or information when they need and expect it, and (4) have the authority to take possession of the product or information and use it to play their roles in delivering the final outputs to customers.

Value, Utility, and TQM

There are many explanations of what TQM is about and how to put it into practice. The idea of the four utilities as a way to understand value and to provide direction for improvement is one such explanation. It is not new. In fact, it is a part of most Marketing 101 courses. However, in the day-to-day focus on process and product problems, we sometimes forget what it is that customers really care about, what it is that actually makes up quality and value from the perspective of the user. The four utilities are a way to remind yourself that organizations exist to deliver value to customers and to help you know exactly what you should focus on to fulfill that service.

CLASSICS IN QUALITY

The Manager and His Work

Peter F. Drucker

Peter Drucker needs no introduction. He is the foremost thinker in management of this century. He has understood the role of managers as facilitating the success of people and the delivery of value to customers and has been writing about this for at least 50 years. This excerpt is from one of his earliest books The Practice of Management, *originally published in 1954 and still in print. To quote from the last sentence in this piece: "The one contribution [the manager] is uniquely expected to make is to give others vision and ability to perform. It is vision and moral responsibility that, in the last analysis, define the manager." Overlooking the use of the male pronoun in this chapter, what we see is that the ideas here are just as relevant today as when they were first published 42 years ago.*

It was Bismarck, I believe, who said: "It's easy enough to find a Minister of Education; all the job needs is a long white beard. But a good cook is different; that requires universal genius."

We have so far in this book discussed what management's job is—to the point where it should be evident that it takes more than a long white beard to discharge it. Clearly to be a manager it is not sufficient to have the title, a big office and other outward symbols of rank. It requires competence and performance of a high order. But is the job, then, one demanding universal genius? Is it done by intuition or by method? How does the manager do his work? And what in his job and work distinguishes the manager from the nonmanager in the business enterprise?

A manager has two specific tasks. Nobody else in the business enterprise discharges these tasks. And everyone charged with them works as a manager.

The manager has the task of creating a true whole that is larger than the sum of its parts, a productive entity that turns out more than the sum of the resources put into it. One analogy is the conductor of a symphony orchestra, through whose effort, vision and leadership individual instrumental parts that are so much noise by themselves become the living whole of music. But the conductor has the composer's score; he is only interpreter. The manager is both composer and conductor.

This task requires the manager to bring out and make effective whatever strength there is in his resources—and above all in the human resources—and neutralize whatever there is of weakness. This is the only way in which a genuine whole can ever be created.

It requires the manager to balance and harmonize three major functions of the business enterprise: managing a business, managing managers and managing worker and work. A decision or action that satisfies a need in one of these functions by weakening performance in another weakens the whole enterprise. One and the same decision or action must always be sound in all three areas.

The task of creating a genuine whole also requires that the manager in every one of his acts consider simultaneously the performance and results of the enterprise as a whole and the diverse activities needed to achieve synchronized performance. It is here, perhaps, that the comparison with the orchestra conductor fits best. A conductor must always hear both the whole orchestra and the second oboe. Similarly, a manager must always consider both the over-all performance of the enterprise and, say, the market-research activity needed. By raising the performance of the whole, he creates scope and challenge for market research. By improving the performance of market research, he makes possible better overall business results. The manager must continuously ask two double-barreled questions in one breath: What better business performance is needed and what does this require of what activities? And: What better performance are the activities capable of and what improvement in business results will it make possible?

The second specific task of the manager is to harmonize in every decision and action the requirements of immediate and long-range future. He cannot sacrifice either without endangering the enterprise. He must, so to speak, keep his nose to the grindstone while lifting his eyes to the hills—which is quite an acrobatic feat, Or, to vary the metaphor, he can neither afford to say: "We will cross this bridge when we come to it," nor "It's the next hundred years that count." He not only has to prepare for crossing distant bridges—he has to build them long before he gets there. And if he does not take care of the next hundred days, there will be no next hundred years; indeed, there may not even be a next five years. Whatever the manager does should be sound in expediency as well as in basic long-range objective and principle. And where he cannot harmonize the two time dimensions, he must at least balance them. He must carefully calculate the sacrifice he imposes on the long-range future of the enterprise to protect its immediate interests, or the sacrifice he makes today for the sake of tomorrow. He must limit either sacrifice as much as possible. And he must repair the damage it inflicts as soon as possible. He lives and acts in two time dimensions, and he is responsible for the performance of the whole enterprise and of his component.

The Work of the Manager

Every manager does many things that are not managing. He may spend most of his time on them. A sales manager makes a statistical analysis or placates an important customer. A foreman repairs a tool or fills in a production report. A manufacturing manager designs a new plant layout or tests new materials. A company president works through the details of a bank loan or negotiates a big contract—or spends dreary hours presiding at a dinner in honor of long-service employees. All these things pertain to a particular function. All are necessary, and have to be done well.

But they are apart from that work which every manager does whatever his function or activity, whatever his rank and position, work which is common to all managers and peculiar to them. The best proof is that we can apply to the job of the manager the systematic analysis of Scientific Management. We can isolate that which a man does because he is a manager. We can divide it into the basic constituent operations. And a man can improve his performance as a manager by improving his performance of these constituent motions.

There are five such basic operations in the work of the manager. Together they result in the integration of resources into a living and growing organism.

A manager, in the first place, *sets objectives*. He determines what the objectives should be. He determines what the goals in each area of objectives should be. He decides what has to be done to reach these objectives. He makes the objectives effective by communicating them to the people whose performance is needed to attain them.

A manager, in the first place, sets objectives.

Secondly, a manager *organizes*. He analyzes the activities, decisions, and relations needed. He classifies the work. He divides it into manageable activities. He further divides the activities into manageable jobs. He groups these units and jobs into an organization structure. He selects people for the management of these units and for the jobs to be done.

A manager analyzes the activities, decisions, and relations needed.

Next a manager *motivates and communicates*. He makes a team out of the people that are responsible for various jobs. He does that through the practices with which he manages. He does it in his own relation to the men he manages. He does it through incentives and rewards for successful work. He does it through his promotion policy. And he does it through constant communication, both from the manager to his subordinate, and from the subordinate to the manager.

He makes a team out of the people that are responsible for various jobs.

The fourth basic element in the work of the manager is *the job of measurement*. The manager establishes measuring yardsticks—and there are few factors as important to the performance of the organization and of every man

The manager
establishes measuring
yardsticks.

in it. He sees to it that each man in the organization has measurements available to him which are focused on the performance of the whole organization and which at the same time focus on the work of the individual and help him do it. He analyzes performance, appraises it and interprets it. And again, as in every other area of his work, he communicates both the meaning of the measurements and their findings to his subordinates as well as to his superiors.

Finally, a manager
develops people.

Finally, a manager *develops people.* Through the way he manages he makes it easy or difficult for them to develop themselves. He directs people or misdirects them. He brings out what is in them or he stifles them. He strengthens their integrity or he corrupts them. He trains them to stand upright and strong or he deforms them.

Every manager does these things when he manages—whether he knows it or not. He may do them well, or he may do them wretchedly. But he always does them.

Every one of these categories can be divided further into sub-categories, and each of the sub-categories could be discussed in a book of its own. The work of the manager, in other words, is complex. And every one of its categories requires different qualities and qualifications.

Setting objectives, for instance, is a problem of balances: a balance between business results and the realization of the principles one believes in; a balance between the immediate needs of the business and those of the future; a balance between desirable ends and available means. Setting objectives therefore requires analytical and synthetizing ability.

Organizing, too, requires analytical ability. For it demands the most economical use of scarce resources. But it deals with human beings; and therefore it also stands under the principle of justice and requires integrity. Both analytical ability and integrity are similarly required for the development of people.

The skill needed for motivating and communicating, however, is primarily social. Instead of analysis, integration and synthesis are needed. Justice dominates as the principle, economy is secondary. And integrity is of much greater importance than analytical ability.

Measuring requires again first and foremost analytical ability. But it also requires that measurement be used to make self-control possible rather than be abused to control people from outside and above, that is, to dominate them. It is the common violation of this principle that largely explains why measurement is the weakest area in the work of the manager today. And as long as measurements are abused as a tool of "control" (as long, for instance, as measurements are used as a weapon of an internal secret policy that supplies audits and critical appraisals of a manager's performance to the boss without even sending a carbon copy to the manager himself) measuring will remain the weakest area in the manager's performance.

Setting objectives, organizing, motivating and communicating, measuring and developing people are formal, classifying categories. Only a manager's experience can bring them to life, concrete and meaningful. But because they are formal, they apply to every manager and to everything he does as a manager. They can therefore be used by every manager to appraise his own skill and performance, and to work systematically on improving himself and his performance as a manager.

Being able to set objectives does not make a man a manager, just as ability to tie a small knot in confined space does not make a man a surgeon. But without ability to set objectives a man cannot be an adequate manager, just as a man cannot do good surgery who cannot tie small knots. And as a surgeon becomes a better surgeon by improving his knot-tying skill, a manager becomes a better manager by improving his skill and performance in all five categories of his work.

Information: The Tool of the Manager

The manager has a specific tool: information. He does not "handle" people; he motivates, guides, organizes people to do their own work. His tool—his only tool—to do all this is the spoken or written word or the language of numbers. No matter whether the manager's job is engineering, accounting or selling, his effectiveness depends on his ability to listen and to read, on his ability to speak and to write. He needs skill in getting his thinking across to other people as well as skill in finding out what other people are after.

The manager has a specific tool: information.

Of all the skills he needs, today's manager possesses least those of reading, writing, speaking and figuring. One look at what is known as "policy language" in large companies will show how illiterate we are. Improvement is not a matter of learning faster reading or public speaking. Managers have to learn to know language, to understand what words are and what they mean. Perhaps most important, they have to acquire respect for language as man's most precious gift and heritage. The manager must understand the meaning of the old definition of rhetoric as "the art which draws men's heart to the love of true knowledge." Without ability to motivate by means of the written and spoken word or the telling number, a manager cannot be successful.

Using His Own Time

Everybody has the problem of time; for of all resources it is the scarcest, the most perishable and the most elusive. But the manager must solve what is a common problem in very specific ways.

Managers are forever pursuing some glittering panacea for their time problem: a course in faster reading, a restriction of reports to one page, a mechanical limitation of interviews to fifteen minutes. All such panaceas are pure quackery and, in the end, a waste of time. It is, however, possible to guide a manager toward an intelligent allocation of his time.

Managers who know how to use time well achieve results by planning. They are willing to think before they act. They spend a great deal of time on thinking through the areas in which objectives should be set, a great deal more on thinking through systematically what to do with recurrent problems.

Most managers spend a large amount of time—in small driblets—on attempts to appraise the performance and quality of the men who work under them. Good time users do not. Instead, they systematically appraise their men once a year. As the result of a few hours' work, they then have the answers for all the decisions—concerning a man's salary, for instance, or his promotion or work assignment—on which judgment is required.

Good time users do not spend a great deal of time on the modification engineering of their products. They sit down once a year—for a few days perhaps—and work out with their sales and manufacturing departments the basic policy, the objectives and the rules for the necessary modifications, determining then how much of it there should be—and assign engineering manpower in advance to the job. In their eyes it is no praise to say: "This year we managed to get through this inventory crisis, thanks to the experience we had acquired last year." If they have a recurrent crisis, they spend the time to find out what causes it so as to prevent its repetition. This may take time, but in the long run it saves more.

The good time users among managers spend many more hours on their communications up than on their communications down. They tend to have good communications down, but they seem to obtain these as an effortless by-product. They do not talk to their men about their own problems, but they know how to make the subordinates talk about theirs. They are, for instance, willing to spend a great deal of their time on the half-yearly Manager Letter, in which each subordinate sets down the objectives of his job, his plans, and what his superior does to help and to hamper him. They may spend a whole day every six months with each of their ten or twelve men going carefully over the Manager Letter—and as a result they do not have to worry much in between about their communications down.

The manager who utilizes his time well also spends a great deal of time on considering his boss's problems, and on thinking what he can do to contribute to the success of his boss, of the whole activity and of the business. He takes responsibility, in other words, for his boss's job—considering this a part of his own job as a manager. As a result, he seems to need no extra time for clearing up the messes that result from a confusion of objectives and viewpoints.

The Manager's Resource: Man

The manager works with a specific resource: man. And the human being is a unique resource requiring peculiar qualities in whoever attempts to work with it.

For man, and man alone, cannot be "worked." There is always a two-way relationship between two men rather than a relationship between man and a resource. It is in the nature of this interrelationship that it changes both parties—whether they are man and wife, father and child, or manager and the man he manages.

If they have a recurrent crisis, they spend the time to find out what causes it so as to prevent its repetition.

There is always a two-way relationship between two men rather than a relationship between man and a resource.

"Working" the human being always means developing him. And the direction this development takes decides whether the human being—both as a man and as a resource—will become more productive or cease, ultimately, to be productive at all. This applies, as cannot be emphasized too strongly, not alone to the man who is being managed, but also to the manager. Whether he develops his subordinates in the right direction, helps them to grow and become bigger and richer persons, will directly determine whether he himself will develop, will grow or whither, become richer or become impoverished, improve or deteriorate.

One can learn certain skills in managing people, for instance, the skill to lead a conference or to conduct an interview. One can set down practices that are conducive to development—in the structure of the relationship between manager and subordinate, in a promotion system, in the rewards and incentives of an organization. But when all is said and done, developing men still requires a basic quality in the manager which cannot be created by supplying skills or by emphasizing the importance of the task. It requires integrity of character.

There is tremendous stress these days on liking people, helping people, getting along with people, as qualifications for a manager. These alone are never enough. In every successful organization there is one boss who does not like people, does not help them, does not get along with them. Cold, unpleasant, demanding, he often teaches and develops more men than anyone else. He commands more respect than the most likeable man ever could. He demands exacting workmanship of himself as well as of his men. He sets high standards and expects that they will be lived up to. He considers only what is right and never who is right. And though usually himself a man of brilliance, he never rates intellectual brilliance above integrity in others. The manager who lacks these qualities of character—no matter how likeable, helpful, or amiable, no matter even how competent or brilliant—is a menace and should be adjudged "unfit to be a Manager and a Gentleman."

It may be argued that every occupation—the doctor, the lawyer, the grocer—requires integrity. But there is a difference. The manager lives with the people he manages, he decides what their work is to be, he directs it, he trains them for it, he appraises it and, often, he decides their future. The relationship of merchant and customer, professional man and client requires honorable dealings. Being a manager, though, is more like being a parent, or a teacher. And in these relationships honorable dealings are not enough; personal integrity is of the essence.

We can now answer the question: Does it require genius, or at least a special talent, to be a manager? Is being a manager an art or an intuition? The answer is: "No." What a manager does can be analyzed systematically. What a manager has to be able to do can be learned (though perhaps not always taught). Yet there is one quality that cannot be learned, one qualification that the manager cannot acquire but must bring with him. It is not genius; it is character.

What Makes a Manager?

The standard definition is that a man is a manager if he is in charge of other people and their work. This is too narrow. The first responsibility of a manager is upward: to the enterprise whose organ he is. And his relations with his superior and with his fellow-managers are as essential to his performance as are his relations and responsibilities to the people under him.

Another definition—though one that is usually implied rather than spelled out—is that importance defines the manager. But in the modern enterprise no one group is more essential than another. The worker at the machine, and the professional employee in the laboratory or the drafting room, are as necessary for the enterprise to function as is the manager. This is the reason why all members of the enterprise have to have the managerial vision. It is not importance but function that differentiates the various groups within the enterprise.

The most common concept of what defines the manager is rank and pay. This is not only wrong, but it is destructive. Even today we find incidentally, so-called rank-and-file workers who have higher incomes than the majority of managers; there are model makers in the automobile industry, for instance, whose annual income exceeds $15,000 and who are yet considered workers and are indeed members of the union's bargaining unit. And unless we can pay professional contributors adequately, can give them promotional opportunities as individual contributors, and can provide for them the status, dignity and self-respect of the true professional, we will simply not be able to manage their ever-increasing numbers.

Altogether the idea that rank and pay define the manager is not much more than a fallacious conclusion from the individual proprietor of yesterday to the manager of today's business enterprise.

Who is a manager can be defined only by a man's function and by the contribution he is expected to make. And the function which distinguishes the manager above all others is his *educational* one. The one contribution he is uniquely expected to make is to give others vision and ability to perform. It is vision and moral responsibility that, in the last analysis, define the manager.

In the modern enterprise no one group is more essential than another.

A Marketing Matrix for a Balanced Business

Theodore Levitt

This is a chapter from Theodore Levitt's book Marketing for Business Growth, *published in 1974. Theodore Levitt is a pioneer in helping organizations understand the importance of focusing on customers. His 1960 article "Marketing Myopia" is one of the most frequently reprinted articles to ever appear in the* Harvard Business Review (HBR). *When Levitt speaks of marketing, he means marketing as the discipline that helps a company create a mutually beneficial relationship between itself and its customers, the folks who give meaning to its existence. This article gives you a tool for evaluating your company's approach to customer satisfaction. It convincingly demonstrates that only those companies that have a clear sense of how to look out for customers and themselves will survive in the competitive marketplace. If you are not already familiar with Levitt's work, this article will get you started. We think it would be worth your time to find more of his writings from the* HBR *and other sources. They are filled with insight.*

A great many marketing executives today are alert, hardhitting, and aggressive. Most of them will quickly admit they wish they got better results. They, like their company presidents above them and their sales managers below them, now fully accept the necessity of being "customer-oriented," not "product-oriented." They agree that the purpose of a business is first to create a customer and then to keep him.

Yet we often deny in deed what we affirm in speech. Robert W. Lear wrote ten years ago that there is "no easy road to market orientation."[1] The translation of that orientation into solidly productive action seems to be an even harder road. Slogans are not enough. They can actually be prophetically dangerous, deceiving their advocates and followers into believing they are doing what they are merely saying. Their companies will get beautifully commendatory headlines—for the resounding speeches of their presidents, for the well-publicized glitter of their marketing programs, for their fetching four-color ads in expensive media, and for their newly revised market-oriented organizational structures. But the narcissistic glare of all this lovely luster can hide

---

1. Robert W. Lear, "No Easy Road to Market Orientation," *Harvard Business Review*, September–October, 1963, pp. 53–60.

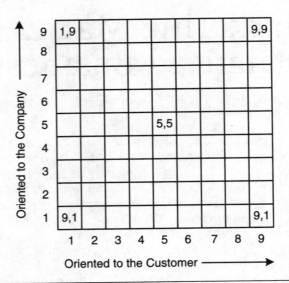

Figure 1. **The marketing matrix.**

an undetected cancer in a company's nerve center. It will confuse form with substance.

Since so many companies have gotten the marketing message—the simple notion that distinguishes between the narrow nexus of selling and the broadly encompassing meaning of marketing—it may be time for them to take a carefully objective look at exactly where they stand in their efforts to implement the marketing concept. Are these companies merely verbal vigilantes, or are they solidly in the mainstream? The manager may ask himself: "Has our company—have I—done what we've preached? If some ultimate computerized arbiter were scoring us, what grade would we get? With rising profits today, but also with rising pressures and demands for high performance in every phase of the business *right now*, have we drifted away in fact from what we've been resolving in speeches? Have we gotten out of phase with our intentions?"

Grading Yourself

Perhaps fortunately, there is no ultimate computerized arbiter to score or grade us. But there is a way we can do it ourselves. Exhibit 1 is a simple mechanism for doing that job. With it we can grade ourselves not on our marketing orientations but, what is more important, on our actions. Indeed, it can help us grade many things, many people, many functions—a corporation's general posture and practices, a marketing vice president, a sales manager, a product manager, a salesman, a manufacturing vice president, a treasurer, or even a receptionist or telephone operator. And with a little imagination and effort it can even help us relate our grade to its potential profitability.

Exhibit 1 shows what may be called the "marketing matrix."[2] The horizontal scale measures an individual's or a company's concern for customers along a nine-point scale: 1 is the lowest ranking or grading it is possible to get; 9 is the highest. The most famous example of a 1 attitude toward customers is Henry Ford's tarnished declaration that people could have any color car they wanted as long as it was black. A 9 attitude might be illustrated by a salesman's telling a customer without qualification or other consideration, "Any size price cut a competitor can make, we'll make a better one." In short, the salesman wants to give the customer what he wants—regardless.

The vertical scale measures concern by the seller for his company or himself. The highest one-sided concern for the company would merit a 9—for example, the scheduling of flights by an airline company in such a way as to avoid the expense of serving meals, an effective cost-reduction program that cuts customer service at the possible expense of continued customer patronage, a drive to raise return on net worth at the expense of developing programs to hold customers under increasingly more competitive conditions, or a market manager's proposal to reduce his product line drastically because competition in some of the products is making his life personally too difficult.

The lowest concern for the company rates a 1—the attitude that any sum of money should be spent to get the desired results, regardless of the fiscal consequences; that the customer should be given anything he wants; that a reorganization of the market department is necessary so that the new marketing vice-president can show that he's energetic and full of ideas, regardless of whether the company or department is ready for it.

Any company long-term policy, action, program, or attitude and any executive's or department's activities can be located in the matrix. Any given action gets a two-number score, one for the extent of concern for the customer which that action represents, and one for the extent of concern for the company or for the implementing executive. The lower right square is a 9,1—an activity, transaction, or attitude that manifests the highest possible concern for the customer but the lowest possible concern for the interests of the company involved in that transaction. A 1,9 manifests the lowest possible concern for the customer but the highest possible concern for the firm. Some possible examples of various ratings follow.

Location 9,1: High Customer, Low Company

1. Use the computer to optimize the customer's use of your product or service—probably raising his consumption with no possibility of future benefit to the seller.

2. The term "marketing matrix" was suggested to me by Mr. Donald G. Moore, then director of marketing, F. W. Means & Co., of Chicago, who developed it in considerable detail as an outgrowth of his exposure to R. R. Blake and Jane S. Mouton, *The Managerial Grid*, Gulf Publishing Company, Houston, 1964. I am happy to acknowledge Mr. Moore's development of the idea and am indebted to his many suggestions regarding its uses.

2. Replace existing company-owned items from service (telephones, leased computers, leased uniforms) as soon as improvements are made, giving the customer the latest improved versions, regardless of the remaining life of the existing items or absence of competitive possibilities and without possible future benefit to the seller.
3. Never charge a lease customer for damages to your equipment, regardless of cost to you.
4. Don't hold the customer to his part of the bargain.
5. Drop everything to answer a customer request, regardless of other commitments.
6. Always keep plenty of extra clerks on the floor in your store in order to give each customer instant service.
7. Put warehouses in every city, town and hamlet for instant delivery.
8. Produce and have available for quick delivery every possible variation of every product that might conceivably fit into your line, regardless of price and cost considerations.
9. Spend a fortune to study every aspect of a customer's needs and wants, and then promise and give him everything.
10. Show the customer that you are on his side by running down your plant and your management. Be his buddy and a big spender. That will solve everything.

Location 1,9: Low Customer, High Company

1. Set your prices on the basis of all the traffic will bear above your costs, regardless of customer-relations consequences.
2. Never tell a customer where he might get a substitute product that would really serve him better than yours.
3. Never try to develop or distribute substitute products for those you now handle (such as plastics for glass, aluminum for steel, nonwoven fabrics for paper, credit cards for checking accounts) if it costs money and is inconvenient.
4. Don't make direct deliveries, even when the customer is willing to pay the expense, if you have to go to the trouble of setting up a delivery system.
5. Have lots of fine-print protective clauses in all customer contracts so that you are sure to win all arguments, regardless of who is to blame.
6. Don't change your invoice dating terms just because the rest of the industry has changed.
7. In running sales meetings, always tell the gathered salesmen that the manufacturing plant is geared up to run at absolute full capacity and ready to roll. Then show your contempt of the customer by enjoining the salesmen to "go out and get the orders,"

making sure you enlist lots of aggressive, warlike phrases like "target the customer," "bang away at the market," "roll out the big guns," "march forward," and "now let's get out and fight."

8. As a company president, make sure all annual plans originate from the top down. Get the manufacturing department to decide what the maximum productive capacity is, or the financial department to decide what revenue is needed, and then tell the sales department to sell the output and deliver the cash.

9. As marketing vice-president, never require the sales organization to break down its sales forecasts by market segments or customer categories. Just look at the totals, and let the field organization assume responsibility for delivering it.

10. If you are a service organization, such as a bank, an insurance company, a public utility, a school, or a computer time-sharing firm, always keep the kind of hours that are convenient for your internal needs. Always be sure to overcome all customer objections to your limited hours by pointing to the "obvious" impossibility of accommodation. Never look for ways to adjust your system to the customer's requisites.

11. When a multidivision customer shifts to centralized purchasing, always hold out for your traditional decentralized way of selling. Don't adjust; it's too troublesome. Always look for ways to justify your *status quo.*

12. When launching a complex new product or material, always insist that the prospect take it "as is." Never try to tailor either the product or your traditional selling methods to his problems.

13. Always use lots of extra chrome and questionable doodads on your kitchen appliances so that they will stand out on the sales floor, even though these cause difficult cleaning and adjustment problems for the housewife.

14. As a television station, cram increasing numbers of commercials into the last hour of the "Late Show," after you've got the viewers hooked.

15. As a railroad, stick to standard-time schedules even though the customers have switched to daylight saving time.

16. As a restaurant operator, insist on seating your customers according to prearranged waitress stations, not according to customer preference.

17. Don't respond to a distant customer's request for technical assistance until you have enough requests from that location to make a trip "worthwhile."

18. Don't make the opening and reclosure features of your package more convenient to the customer if this would require changing your package design or your packaging equipment.

19. Don't list prices and discounts on the same catalog page as your product description. The distributors and customers may like it,

but it creates a lot of problems when you want to change prices and terms.

20. Always show a picture of your plant or headquarters facade on your letterhead, preferably including a picture of the company founder, and never question how the customer reacts to all this.
21. Put lots of salt in the popcorn at your movie theater so that the viewers get up frequently to buy soft drinks and disturb other viewers.
22. Bind all the textbooks you publish in a single standard color so that you don't have to carry a wide color inventory and, as a consequence, so that you will communicate to students how seriously scholarly (and boring) books really are.
23. If you are in the petroleum refining and retail gasoline business, always fight local building codes so that your standard, historic, low-cost matchbox station design will be accepted for all types of neighborhoods.
24. If you run a multinational corporation, always compel your overseas distributors to report to you in English and in your standard domestic format.
25. In setting your company goals, always set the standard in terms of production volume, revenues, profits, and expanded stockholder equity. Never state them also in terms of market factors, customer need fulfillment, customer-service objectives, or market targets.

Location 1,1: Low Customer, Low Company

An executive functioning in this location might be indifferent, hostile, or just incompetent. A company operating in this corner *is* in a corner—suicidal, self-destructive, hopeless. The company may survive for a time by sheer power of product uniqueness or monopoly position. But it is not capable of long-term survival. Such a posture may work for a company that is organized for a one-shot, in-and-out purpose—a quick killing, after which it closes its doors forever.

Location 5,5: Medium Customer, Medium Company

This is the middle-of-the-road situation. Don't stick your neck out. Always let others do the innovating. At best, be a prudent innovator. Let "meeting competition" be your planning guide. Devote the bulk of your effort to prudential fire fighting. It is a sensible policy, but only if it is followed as a result of a conscious decision, not by accident as a result of drift and thoughtlessness.

Location 9,9: High Customer, High Company

A company that values long-term survival at a high level of expanding profits presumably aspires constantly to the 9,9 location in every aspect of its operation. Advocates of the marketing concept argue with conviction and considerable good sense that a company cannot be effectively marketing-oriented unless the marketing viewpoint infuses its every operation and sector. The manufacturing department may have to become more willing to accept shorter production runs and to customize its output to fit particular customer requests. Finance may have to become more willing to support product development expenditures even if the present line of products is perfectly serviceable. Engineering may have to become more willing to respond to marketing's needs for lower-priced, lower-quality products, even though this may offend the engineer's sense of workmanship and professionalism.

What are some of the operational and policy characteristics that would qualify a company for the ideal 9,9 position?

1. When you have a particular resource base (mineral deposits or a plant with a given productive competence or an established distribution network), you try to capitalize on that resource by:

   a. Studying consumer and customer needs for the purpose of seeing how the resource might be modified or augmented so that it would serve customers better.

   b. Expanding the range of services and benefits to customers so that what cannot easily or quickly be changed in, say, the basic material (e.g., steel, natural gas, automotive service stations) can at least be augmented by truly customer-benefiting peripheral services that make it easier and more beneficial for customers to do business with your firm in your industry.

2. Make tie-in arrangements with producers of other products and services in order to provide your prospects with a completed system of benefits, one of which is your specialty. An example is airlines working with computer companies, telephone companies, and freight forwarders to help prospective shippers convert from regional warehousing to direct air cargo.

3. Augment your present generic product line (say, fertilizer raw materials such as phosphate, potash, and superphosphate that you sell to fertilizer mixers and packagers) by helping customers not only with technical services, but also with their forecasting problems, sales-territory planning, sales meetings, sales incentive programs, logistical planning, and even accounting and control problems.

4. Make all your corporate communications integrative, self-reinforcing, and centripetal[3] so that your company is always instantly and easily recognizable, whether it communicates by mail, mass-media advertising, the sign on its buildings, the design and color of its delivery trucks, its annual report, the salesmen's calling cards, its catalog, or its point-of-purchase materials. Hence, give yourself instant identity and, as a result, give the customer the opportunity for instant recognition of your firm.

Advocates of the marketing concept argue with conviction and considerable good sense that a company cannot be effectively marketing-oriented unless the marketing viewpoint infuses its every operation and sector.

---

3. See Theodore Levitt, *Innovation in Marketing*, McGraw-Hill Book Company, New York, 1962, chap. 11.

5. Develop long-term (at least five-year) plans, based both on predictions of external events (competitive practices, customer values and habits, technological developments, government practices) and on assessments of your own internal corporate strengths and weaknesses (manpower, fiscal competence, manufacturing, distribution resources). These audits of the external and internal environments become the basis for determining adaptive changes that are needed to serve properly the existing markets, capitalize on or create new markets, phase out declining products, and provide for the fiscal and organizational resources necessary to do the needed jobs.

The 9,9 Imperative

An appropriate organizational slogan to qualify for a 9,9 ranking is the old but expressive one, "Find a need and fill it." "Find a need" refers to the customer, "and fill it" to the company. The need, of course, has to be a real one, and well understood by the company. Finding it should not consist in identifying things that people could, by hook or by crook, be talked into exchanging for their hard-earned cash. Rather, problem areas, inefficiencies, diluting factors, and opportunities for improving what is valuable to the customer should be identified. In the 9,9 location, not only is the need filled with a high degree of competence, but the competence itself derives from a genuine identification of the seller with his prospect's business and problems. The company makes maximum and efficient use of all its available resources, marshaling them expertly and enthusiastically (not grudgingly) for answering the particular customer need in question. And when the company cannot perform the required function efficiently, or cannot reasonably be expected to develop or help others organize the competence to fill it, either it must price its existing product or service at a level that will weaken, if not cancel, the customer need-satisfaction, or it must consciously sacrifice returns to stockholders and employees. Either of these compromises, (cutting price or forgoing the business entirely) might disqualify the company from its 9,9 position. But that may not be altogether lamentable or wrong. All that really counts is that the disqualification is conscious and planned—the consequence of thoughtful decision instead of thoughtless drift.

> The company makes maximum and efficient use of all its available resources, marshaling them expertly and enthusiastically (not grudgingly) for answering the particular customer need in question.

To qualify for 9,9, there can be no captious compromise. Efficient and competent need filling is essential. In such a selling situation, price is only a secondary part of the consideration. What the seller should attempt to do for the customer would be so significant, in terms of the customer's own operation, that the latter could not afford to be without it. He would feel compelled to do business with that seller without feeling that he was trapped. He would feel compelled to deal with him because he offered the best bundle of value satisfactions.

> The customer would feel compelled to deal with him because he offered the best bundle of value satisfactions.

To qualify for 9,9 can easily cause a company to change the entire character of its business. Indeed, the marketing view of the business process requires that a company organize itself to offer a line of products, product options, and service benefits that are dictated by the requisites of the market rather than the present competence or unbending inclinations of the company.

This uncompromising view of business life can make terrible and sometimes perhaps senseless demands on a company. But whether these demands will really be senseless in the long run depends on more than a quick visceral response to undigested and inadequately analyzed facts and trends. The unhappy fate of America's railroads—their loss of passenger business, their losses to trucks and airlines and pipelines—was not really inevitable, in spite of tight government controls and corporate charter limitations. Railroad companies could indeed have defined themselves as being in the transportation business rather than merely in the railroad business. And they could, in the early days, have gotten into pipelining, trucking, and airlines with a genuinely positive and customer-serving orientation. In short, they could have expanded their product line, the options they offered their customers, and the service mix associated with these operations. The constraints imposed on them by regulatory agencies were largely after-the-fact reactions against predatory maneuvers designed to destroy competing carriers.

To become a 9,9 company ineluctably requires a company to ask the ultimate question: What business are we in? Are we in railroading or transportation; in movies or entertainment; in the tool and die business or the parts fabrication and equipment business; in the linen supply business or the customer-support service business; in the computer business, the computer-assisted problem-solving business, or the data-processing business; in the banking business or the fiduciary management business; in the book business, the knowledge business, or the self-development business; in the publishing business or the information business; in the dry-cleaning business or the product renewal business; in the generator business or the energy business; in the sewer-pipe business or the disposal business; in the retailing business or show business?

To be preoccupied, therefore, with being a 9,9 marketing company is preeminently the preserve of the chief executive and the board of directors, and it is preeminently a preoccupation with the encompassing question of the nature and character of your business. That is why marketing is not just a business function, but a consolidating view of the entire business process. Marketing is not concerned with just the facile arts of promotion and selling, but perhaps more importantly with the involuted issues of corporate product policy—with what is to be offered for sale, with the kind of R & D that is to be emphasized so that the right products and the right services may become available for sale—with, in effect, what kind of company is being and should be created.

The marketing matrix is clearly only a device. There is nothing uniquely substantive about it. But it has certain simple virtues:

1. It structures a way of thinking about the corporate marketing effort that takes into account both company requisites and customer requisites.
2. It is a scaling device that provides a company with a benchmark for helping determine how far along the road it has gone toward

To become a 9,9 company ineluctably requires a company to ask the ultimate question: What business are we in?

achieving a proper balance between serving the customer and serving itself and how much remains for it yet to do.

3. Its use will compel a recognition of the fact that different people in a company and different departments have different kinds of responsibilities and different powers of control—some can best serve the corporate purpose by emphasizing cost control and other directly company-oriented activities, and others by emphasizing sales expansion and directly customer-oriented activities. Seeing more clearly what a particular executive in a particular company can control and what he cannot control, what purpose he can best serve and what he cannot directly serve, makes it easier to judge his performance and easier to direct his efforts for the ultimate best long-term interests of his company.

4. It can be used to stimulate in each job within the organization, and especially at the higher levels, thinking about the appropriate mix in each job of concern for the customer and concern for the company. If the ultimate corporate slogan for a 9,9 operation is "Find a need and fill it," in a small company each key person is likely to be highly involved in both sides of this equation. But in the large company, specialization is inescapable. There will be need finders and need fillers. These will not be the same person. Corporate cupids must exist to make matches between them. Working with the marketing matrix can help individuals within the organization to find where they fit and why, as well as where the "other guy" fits. As a consequence of this structure, people may find that the other guy, who is often viewed as the enemy, may be working toward the same objective and in a not unreasonable, though quite different, manner.

5. Finally, the marketing matrix compels the chief executive to develop a clearer definition of what business his company is in and what directions it must take in product policy, in customer-service activities, in R & D, and in properly orienting the various functional groups and corporate personnel toward making the most meaningful contribution of which they are capable toward the corporation's overall purpose.

Working with the marketing matrix can help individuals within the organization to find where they fit and why, as well as where the "other guy" fits.

Introduction to Control Charts

Western Electric Company

This article comes from the Western Electric Statistical Quality Control Handbook *that tracks its heritage to the work of Walter Shewhart (the originator of statistical control charts) and was first published in 1956. It provides a simple and elegant introduction to control charts and their value. The roots of modern statistical process control are found in books such as this one, which is still available in many bookstores.*

Statistical Phenomena in the World Around Us

Fluctuating Patterns

If data are collected which have a bearing on any problem, any series of events or any manufacturing situation, these data are always found to exhibit variation. Instead of being exactly the same from point to point or from time to time, the numbers vary. If plotted on a piece of graph paper, so the variations can be studied, the numbers always form a fluctuating, zig-zag pattern. Some typical examples of fluctuating patterns are shown in Figures 1–4.

In the first case an operator was assembling spoolheads onto a core. The supervisor kept a record of the percentage of loose spoolhead assemblies made by this operator day after day. He found that the percentages varied. The percentage of loose spoolheads was not the same every day.

Figure 2 is a record obtained from an automatic welding operation. This is an entirely different type of operation from Figure 1. It involves different materials, different facilities, a different operator, different problems. When the supervisor kept a record of the daily percentage of off center welds, he found that the percentages varied in much the same manner as Figure 1. The percentage of off center welds was not the same every day.

The same thing was found on plotting the dimensions of successive parts coming from a screw machine (Figure 3), and also the electrical characteristics of a series of assembled units (Figure 4). Any series of numbers from a process, if plotted in sequence, will form a fluctuating pattern. Even repeat measurements made on the same object will not be exactly the same, time after time or day after day.

Similar variation is found in accounting figures, production figures, records of attendance, temperatures, pressures, medical reports or any other set

If plotted on a piece of graph paper, so the variations can be studied, the numbers always form a fluctuating, zig-zag pattern.

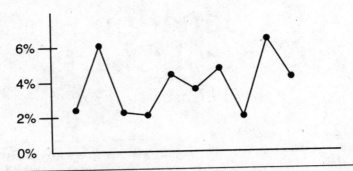

Figure 1.   **Daily percentage of loose spoolheads.**

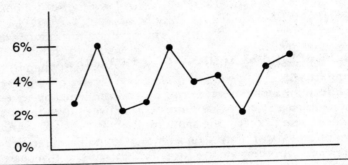

Figure 2.   **Daily percentage of offcenter welds.**

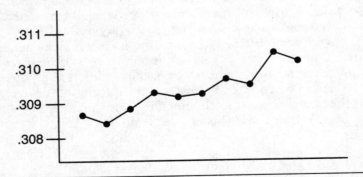

Figure 3.   **Successive parts coming from a screw machine (diameter).**

of numbers from an industrial process. We do not know of any type of man-ufacture in which variation is not present.

What Causes the Fluctuations in a Fluctuating Pattern?
Fluctuations in the data are caused by a large number of minute variations or differences: differences in materials, equipment, the surrounding atmospheric

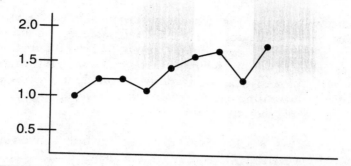

Figure 4.   **Electrical measurement on a series of assemblies (noise level).**

conditions, the physical and mental reactions of people. Most of these differences are extremely small. They cause the pattern to fluctuate in what is known as a "natural" or "normal" manner. Occasionally, however, there will be a large or unusual difference, much more important than all the other differences put together. For example, material is taken from a different batch; the machine setter makes a new setting; an inexperienced operator takes the place of an experienced operator. These large causes make the pattern fluctuate in an "unnatural" or "abnormal" manner.

Fluctuations in the data are caused by a large number of minute variations or differences.

Experience shows that there are definite detectable differences between the "natural" and "unnatural" patterns. It is possible to discover and study these differences by means of simple calculations based on well-known statistical laws.

Once we know that a pattern is unnatural, it is possible to go further and find the *cause* of the unnaturalness. This makes it possible to detect, identify and study the behavior of *causes*.

Distributions

Fluctuations are not the only statistical phenomena which are observable in nature. It has long been known that if we take large numbers of observations on some physical quantity (such as the charge on an electron), or large numbers of measurements on an industrial product (such as the diameter of a wire or shaft), these measurements will tend to group themselves around some central value with a certain amount of variation or "scatter" on either side. The pattern or shape formed by the grouped measurements is called a "frequency distribution." We observe that if the causes which produce the observations or measurements remain essentially unchanged, the distribution tends to have certain distinguishable and stable characteristics. These characteristics become more definite as the number of observations or measurements increases. We conclude from this that, if the cause system is constant, the observed distribution tends to approach, as a statistical limit, some distribution function or "law."

It is possible to make use of statistical limits, derived from distributions, to predict the behavior of a fluctuating pattern when there are no abnormal causes.

This tendency to form a distribution is observed throughout nature. It is one of the most fundamental of all natural laws.

Experience tells us that the two sets of statistical phenomena—distributions and fluctuations—are not separate and unrelated. A distribution can be thought of as a *composite mass of fluctuations*, and the fluctuations can be thought of as *confined within the limits of a distribution*. It is therefore possible to make use of statistical limits, derived from distributions, to predict the behavior of a fluctuating pattern *when there are no abnormal causes*.

This can be stated formally as follows:

Whenever we have a series of events proceeding from a given system of causes, those events will not in general be identical with each other. Instead, they will fluctuate or vary in a manner described as "random." Nevertheless, if the cause system remains unchanged, the frequencies with which the events occur will tend to approach an objective probability, or set of probabilities, as the number of events increases indefinitely.

Translated into industrial terms, this can be stated as follows:

Whenever we have a series of observations or measurements, obtained from a given process, those measurements will not in general be identical with each other. Instead they will vary in such a way as to form a fluctuating pattern. Nevertheless, if nothing disturbs the process, these fluctuating measurements will be held within definite mathematical limits. In the aggregate, a large number of these measurements will tend to form a predictable distribution.

Translated into everyday language, the statements above mean this:

(a) Everything varies.
(b) Individual things are unpredictable.
(c) Groups of things from a constant system of causes tend to be predictable.

Check your understanding of these fundamental concepts by studying the following simple examples:

Example 1
   a. People live to different ages.
   b. No one knows how long he himself will live.
   c. Insurance companies can tell with great accuracy what percentage of people will live to be 60, 65, 70 etc.

Example 2
   a. You cannot write the letter "a" twice in exactly the same way.
   b. You have no way of knowing how your next "a" will differ from the last one.
   c. Nevertheless there is something about your "a's" that makes them recognizably different from my "a's."

Example 3
  a. All patterns fluctuate.
  b. The individual points are unpredictable.
  c. A group or series of points from a constant process will tend to follow a pattern that obeys a fixed law.

These concepts are carefully developed by Shewhart.

Statistical Limits for Fluctuating Patterns

By making use of certain equations, derived from statistical laws, it is possible to calculate "limits" for any given pattern. If a pattern is natural, its fluctuations will fit within these limits. If a pattern is unnatural, its fluctuations will not fit these limits. The following are examples of the calculation of statistical limits.

(1) *Statistical limits for the chart on the spool-head operation (Figure 1).* To calculate limits for this chart, proceed as follows:

  a. First take the percentage of loose spoolheads turned out by the operator, on the average, over a period of time. In this case it was 4%.

  The average percentage is called $\bar{p}$ (pronounced p-bar). The "p" means percentage or proportion, and the bar above it means average.

  b. Then take the average number of spoolheads assembled by this operator during the day. In the example used, this number was 400.

  The number assembled is called n (meaning number).

  c. The equation for the calculation of statistical limits is as follows:

$$\text{Limits of fluctuation} = \pm 3 \sqrt{\frac{\bar{p}(1 - \bar{p})}{n}}$$

$$= \pm 3 \sqrt{\frac{.04\,(.96)}{400}}$$

$$= \pm 3 \times .0098$$

$$= \pm .0294$$

The limits of fluctuation are therefore 2.94% on either side of the average, or 6.94% and 1.06%. The pattern for the spoolhead process should stay inside of these limits.

(2) *Statistical limits for the chart on the welding operation (Figure 2).* To calculate limits for this chart, proceed as follows:
  a. Use the same equation that was used in (1) above.
  b. The average percentage of offcenter welds ($\bar{p}$) was again 4%.
  c. The average number of welds made by the operator per day (n) was in this case 1000.

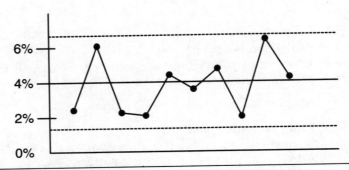

Figure 5. **Control chart for the percentage of loose spoolheads.**

d.

$$\text{Limits of fluctuation} = \pm 3 \sqrt{\frac{\overline{p}(1 - \overline{p})}{n}}$$

$$= \pm 3 \sqrt{\frac{.04\ (.96)}{1000}}$$

$$= \pm 3 \times .0062$$

$$= \pm .0186$$

The limits of fluctuation are therefore 1.86% on either side of the average, or 5.86% and 2.14%. The pattern for the welding process should stay inside of these limits.

(3) *Statistical limits for the charts on (a) screw machine and (b) electrical characteristic.*

Since these involve a different type of data (individual measurements rather than percentages), it is necessary to use a different equation.
Limits of fluctuation around the average of the
$$\text{data} = \pm 2.66\ M\overline{R},$$

where the symbol "$M\overline{R}$" refers to the average difference between successive pairs of measurements.

The limits of fluctuation for the screw machine chart turn out to be .3102 and .3086. The limits of fluctuation for the electrical chart are 1.95 and 0.75. The patterns for these two processes should stay inside of these limits.
In a similar way, limits can be calculated for any other type of data.
When we add the statistical limits to a fluctuating pattern, the result is called a "control chart." The control chart is one of the most sensitive devices known for analyzing data and obtaining information.

Meaning of a Control Chart

The following are control charts for the four operations discussed above.

The statistical limits are drawn in as dotted lines and are called "control limits." The control limits used in this Handbook, unless otherwise stated, are "3 sigma control limits."*

The control limits are used to determine whether the pattern is "natural" or "unnatural." The following procedure is used:

1. Check the fluctuating pattern to see whether it is in conflict with the natural statistical limits. The pattern is in conflict if it (a) jumps outside the control limits or (b) forms unnatural clusters of points inside the control limits.
2. Mark any unnatural points or clusters of points with "x's."
3. If the pattern is not in conflict with the limits (that is, there are no x's), consider it a "natural" pattern. In general, the longer the series of points without evidence of unnaturalness, the stronger is the evidence that this is a natural pattern.

An occasional "x" (perhaps once in a hundred points) may be the result of chance alone, and is not considered to make the pattern unnatural.

4. If the pattern is in conflict with the limits (that is, there are x's), consider the pattern "unnatural" and the process "out of control." The more numerous the x's, in general, the stronger is the evidence of lack of control.

When a pattern is natural, it means that there are no abnormal extraneous causes working in the process. When the pattern is unnatural, it means that outside disturbances are present and are affecting the process.

When a pattern is unnatural, those familiar with the process should investigate to find what the outside disturbances are.

On most control charts, we prefer to have a longer series of points than those shown in Figures 5–8. In the following discussion these charts should be considered as typical portions of a more complete control chart.

Interpretation of Figures 5–8

The chart for the spoolhead operation (Figure 5) is interpreted as follows:

1. There are no x's.
2. There is no evidence that the process is out of control.
3. It is not being disturbed by any unusual, outside causes.

The chart for the welding operation (Figure 6) is interpreted as follows:

1. Four out of the 10 points are marked with x's.
2. There is strong evidence that the process is out of control.
3. It is being disturbed by large and unnecessary outside causes.

When a pattern is unnatural, those familiar with the process should investigate to find what the outside disturbances are.

---

*"Sigma" (usually written σ) is a unit of measure which is used to describe the width or spread of a distribution or pattern. The fluctuations in a "natural" pattern tend to spread about ±3 sigma.

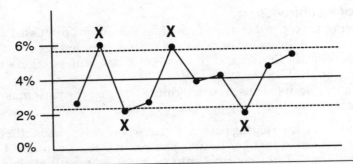

Figure 6.   **Control chart for the percentage of offcenter welds.**

The chart for the screw machine process (Figure 7) is interpreted as follows:

1. Three out of the 10 points are marked with x's.
2. There is strong evidence that the process is out of control.
3. The pattern shows a continuous movement in one direction which, in the presence of x's, indicates a trend.

The chart for the electrical process (Figure 8) is interpreted as follows:

1. There are no x's.
2. There is no evidence that the process is out of control.
3. The pattern appears to show an upward movement, but since there are no x's there is no reason to believe that this is a trend.

Note how this information depends on having a set of control limits. Without the control limits, Figures 1 and 2 look very much the same. With the control limits added, they look entirely different. The same is true of Figure 3 as compared with Figure 4.

This leads to one of the most fundamental principles in statistical quality control, which may be stated as follows:

To interpret data correctly, we must have (a) a pattern and (b) control limits. This is the same as saying: To interpret data correctly, put it on a control chart.

> To interpret data correctly, we must have (a) a pattern and (b) control limits.

Experience as the Basis for Confidence in Control Charts

No one has to accept the evidence of a control chart on faith. It is always possible to make an investigation to see whether the chart is correct. The following is a record of the investigations actually made in connection with Figures 5–8.

1. When the people who had the spoolhead operation made a careful check of all the elements in their process, including the materials, piece parts, tools, fixtures, gages and the activities and habits of the operators and machine setters, they were unable to find anything abnormal or out of order. This agreed with the indications of the control chart.

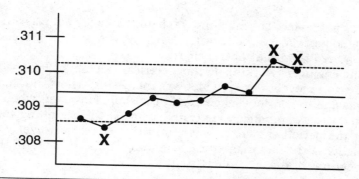

Figure 7.　**Control chart for screw machine parts (diameter).**

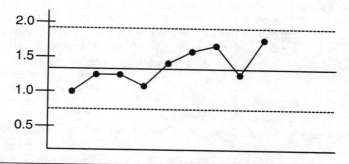

Figure 8.　**Control chart for electrical assemblies (noise level).**

2. When the people who had the welding operation made a careful check of all the elements in their process, including the materials, piece parts, tools etc., they discovered to their surprise the following two conditions:

   a. The method of regulating the voltage supply was not adequate for this job.

   b. Two of the machine setters were being careless in dressing the electrodes.

   When these two conditions were corrected, the chart came into control. The statistical analysis made by the control chart had revealed the presence of "causes" which the people were not aware of.

3. The people who had the screw machine process did not believe that the diameter of the parts could change, since the machine was locked at the beginning of the run and the run was too short to be affected by toolwear. However, when they carefully checked the condition of the machine, they discovered worn threads in the

locking device. The machine was being "locked" but was not stay-ing locked. When the locking device was repaired, the trend dis-appeared from the control chart.

4. The engineers working on the electrical assemblies believed that the noise level of the product was increasing. They said that this was due to poor housekeeping in the shop. However, when large quantities of product were tested, made at the beginning and end of the period shown, it was found that the noise level was no higher at the end than at the beginning. This agreed with the in-dications of the control chart.

This has happened in shops and in laboratories many hundreds of times. Time after time, on chart after chart, investigation and experience have proved that the chart is correct. Anyone can verify this for himself by running a few control charts.

The following evidence is also of direct interest to management:

When large numbers of people in a plant begin to act regularly in accor-dance with control charts, doing what the charts tell them in the details of running their jobs, the plant almost invariably begins to show certain re-markable results:

- Costs are reduced.
- Quality and yields improve rapidly.
- There are major reductions in scrap, rework and the necessary amount of inspection.
- The engineers find their knowledge about the process increasing.
- Experiments are faster and more successful.
- Many design problems vanish.
- Difficult problems having to do with specifications and require-ments are solved easily and economically.

All of this is evidence of the reliability of control charts.

Time after time, on chart after chart, investigation and experience have proved that the chart is correct.

Quality by Industry

While quality management principles remain the same for all types of organizations, different industries apply these principles in ways particular to their businesses. Part Two provides a diverse collection of articles on how quality management is making a difference in various industries. We have clustered this collection around *manufacturing, services*, and *the public sector*. In selecting articles for each sector, we sought to have a balance between principles and applications, with an emphasis on the application of these ideas.

Another goal we have had in gearing up for *The Quality Yearbook* has been to garner the assistance of consulting editors to review and briefly summarize their perspective on the application of quality principles in their areas. We are fortunate this year to have had the assistance of experts in all six areas covered in Part Two. Each of them has written an original article for the 1995 edition. They include Robert W. Hall (editor-in-chief of *Target* magazine published by the Association for Manufacturing Excellence); Ron Zemke (author, consultant, and senior editor at *Training* magazine) for services; Joe Sensenbrenner (consultant and former Madison, Wisconsin mayor) for government; Dan Beckham (a leading consultant to health care institutions and award winning writer) for health care; Julie Horine (a leading researcher, writer, and training consultant in applying Baldrige criteria to education) for K–12 education; and Ron Heilmann (head of the Center for Quality and Productivity at the University of Wisconsin, Milwaukee) for higher education. We commend their articles to you. They provide a wonderful perspective on the value of the quality approach to succeeding in their respective areas.

In the remainder of Part Two, you'll find the following:

Manufacturing

We have chosen three articles, each quite different from the other. The first is a case study on how the company Wiremold went about implementing TQM and the importance of this to their success. The second article is a review of quality practices in American automotive manufacturing and discusses the importance of TQM in turning the industry around. The third introduces the concept of total productive maintenance, an approach to machine and process maintenance that enhances productivity and teamwork.

Services

Besides Ron Zemke's piece, we have selected three other articles for this section, each one exploring a different aspect delivering service quality. The first explores the changing nature of retailing and how different types of retailers, especially small retailers, can compete with the Wal-Marts of the world, by serving customers in special ways. The second article explores the state of service in the banking industry. The third looks at the problems of connecting compensation programs with standards for service to customers at AT&T Universal Card Services.

Public Sector

Organizations of all types are now beginning to appreciate the value of TQM principles for helping them fulfill their mission. For the four areas of the public sector, besides the contributions of our consulting editors, we have selected a variety of pieces that demonstrate how quality management is being applied in government, health care, K–12 education, and higher education. Some articles we especially recommend include Robert Hunt's article on implementing TQM in Incline Village, Nevada, and David Langford's vision for schools, though all are valuable.

*   *   *

For additional material on what is going on by industry, please consult the bibliography in Part Four. It includes a detailed, annotated list of materials across several industries, of which the articles in Part Two are only a small sample.

Vision to Reality

Robert W. Hall

In this article, by consulting editor Robert W. Hall, editor-in-chief of Target *magazine (published by the Association for Manufacturing Excellence), he tells us that while some manufacturing companies have implemented TQM, with good results, they are in the minority. The majority of manufacturing operations have not yet got the message. Hall discusses this and explains how, by adopting quality management prinicples, the vision of a company can be made a reality.*

Despite advances, quality practice in manufacturing generally remains too reactive. True, companies such as Motorola, Solectron, AT&T, and many others are proactive, working toward quality goals that go beyond current customer expectations. However, they are a minority.

Many companies have been compelled to make real improvement through edicts by major customers that "quality is a given," meaning that defect rates that were excused away in 1980 are no longer tolerated. To retain the business of demanding customers, they must demonstrate low defect levels in both products and service and beef up their quality processes. However, much of their improvement activity is to comply with the perceived audit requirements of major customers.

The popularity of ISO 9000 certification is testimony to the current status. To pass a certification, companies create a basically sound system by tightening documentation and corrective action procedures. The quality of output may improve at the price of adding quality staff to handle the paperwork. Although they recognize that better is possible, few companies move far from compliance toward proactive quality.

For example, managements use terms such as total quality to signify commitment to customer satisfaction and launch improvement initiatives—not all successfully—in areas such as team development, streamlining material flows, or preventive maintenance. However, in practice, customer satisfaction is interpreted as adopting quality procedures deemed acceptable by a customer. Improvement processes begun on many fronts stall for lack of time or because enthusiasm is suppressed by the organization's immune system.

Some of the better companies that have performed at a "Baldrige level" also seem to be stalled venturing much beyond where they have been. Achieving customer satisfaction in ways that surprise the customers themselves is by its nature a high-energy push into the unknown.

Joseph Juran has called the concept of product-oriented compliance Small Q, contrasted with Big Q, which emphasizes proactive concern for customer satisfaction and expands the concept of quality to cover all activity in a supply chain directed toward the customers.[1] This terminology is similar to that now heard in manufacturing companies that contrast Small M, meaning production, with Big M, meaning at minimum the complete order fulfillment process, but implying all activity to satisfy customers. While this review of the situation is based on subjective observation of company cases rather than data from a survey, there seems to be two reasons why Big Q and Big M are difficult to expand in practice.

1. Inability to Create a Vision Instead of a Collection of Techniques

It is commonly accepted that implementation difficulties begin with a lack of commitment and leadership by senior management. Descriptions of the phenomenon are loaded with clichés from belief in silver bullets to tree hugging. Lack of commitment begins with a poor concept of what one is committing to. No single program implementation leads to Big Q, and the plethora of programs, often similar in nature but with different labels, makes the picture seem overwhelmingly complex. No one can keep up, especially if they are presently working such extended hours to keep customers satisfied that there is little time to sort anything out.

A vision composed of many bits and pieces is complex, as shown in Figure 1. It is not inspiring either because it does not encompass what "we" will become—whether "we" refers to people in the immediate organization, to customers, or to suppliers. Most vision statements are less complex and slightly more inspiring. They are lofty, but general statements or diagrams of what the organization aspires to become, often couched as obligations to various stakeholders payable, as a matter of faith, by mastering "excellence" or "quality" processes. The authors crunch together whatever they can assimilate. Rarely does anyone flat out state a breakthrough vision, like "We will redefine the X business for both our customers and competitors by . . ."

A vision is a pointer to the future, and it should be integrative without being too detailed in methodology. Scenarios of what we can become are integrative, but need not be very detailed because a long-term future is impossible to project in detail. That is for more immediate planning. Composing an inspiring but workable vision is not easy, but without one, improvement processes run in many different directions.

Improvement processes begun on many fronts stall for lack of time or because enthusiasm is suppressed by the organization's immune system.

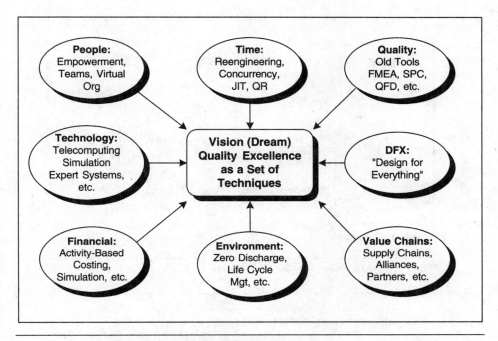

Figure 1. **Seeing quality as a jumble of techniques.**

For example, two of today's music stars come to mind. When young and unknown, both were gripped by the vision of becoming a star. Neither knew exactly the path by which that goal would be reached. But both knew approximately the style they wanted and the types of instruments and skills they needed to master, and they sensed that they could create something that would captivate future listeners. Consequently, they were determined to pay the price and do the detailed preparation, then make and take their breaks. In the beginning, neither seemed to be gifted with talent not possessed by others still in the backwaters of the music industry, but over time, the vision prompted them to pay attention to detailed aspects of performance, like the nuances of a distinctive style show, which contemporaries never pushed very far.

Creating a vision for an enterprise centered on something like mechanical seals is harder than one for musical success. First, people usually become more excited about a public performance than about preventing fluid leaks (unless the leakage trickles on them). Second, the vision has to be articulated and promulgated to inspire people to collective effort in many areas. Single-person stardom cannot realize it.

This integrative nature of a vision is important. Inventors are inspired by the potential of a physical invention, but most inventions never come to much, one reason being that the inventor's vision is shaky on how to test, refine, finance, produce, promote, market, or service their product. A blowout

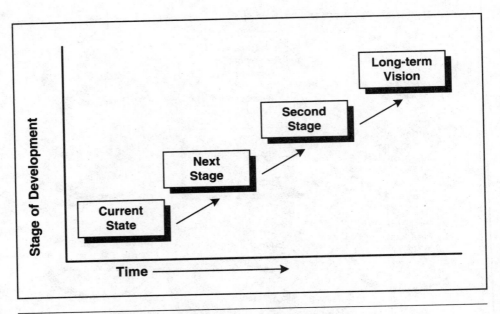

Figure 2.   **Bridging long-term vision to the current reality.**

strategy does not depend on leveraging one advantage. It proposes to create numerous advantages, which taken together establish a position very difficult to duplicate. To be useful, a vision of quality performance, Big Q in Big M, has to be large in scope but also lead to action. Then quality is mastering the details that eventually transform the big vision to reality.

Although hard to do, creating a scenario both integrates a long-term vision, and it sets an easily understood long-term direction. But it is hard to translate to immediate action. For that, an organization needs a more detailed vision of an intermediate stage of development—the next goals to go for.

This general idea is shown in Figure 2. The box called "Current State" suggests that the enterprise should understand how it compares with the competition and with customer expectations today. Unless the organization does regular benchmarking, the assessment of current conditions has big holes in it, a conclusion many companies rapidly reach when they contemplate applying for the Baldrige Award, where examination depends heavily on such data. However, knowledge of current state is never perfect. It just has to be sufficient to suggest the next stage of development and to prompt action to get there. Depending on current state, the next stage may be catch up, or it may go for best-in-class status in areas that count toward the long-term vision.

Developing a long-term vision that is a meaningful guide over, say, 10 years is difficult because projecting developments that far ahead is uncertain. No vision will come about as it was first constructed. Nonetheless, such a vision is important for the development of an organization's most important asset—its people. The second most important asset is its locations. However,

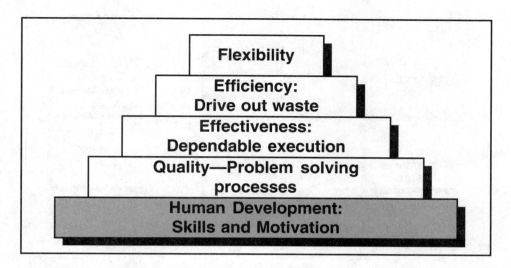

Figure 3.   **Everything depends on a base of human development. That is the point of this figure. For decades, the Japanese have constructed many versions of this to describe their strategic planning for industrial progress. While Japanese tradition honored those who devoted their lives to deepening their skills as artisans doing similar work, the same concept has been applied to developing people to execute innovative concepts. In any culture, the diagram is a good reminder that a core competence that depends on difficult-to-acquire human capabilities is not quickly replicated by a competitor. (Originally from Professor Jinichiro Nakane, Waseda University, Tokyo.**

human development time is becoming the critical factor in opening new locations (Figure 3).

For example, in 1970, Hewlett-Packard opened a division in Singapore, intending to eventually have design capability there. The division began producing parts for the United States, and then the United States designed equipment for the Far East. Two decades later, the issue was how quickly the people there could develop into creating products for Asia, typified by designing and launching an ink jet printer to enter the Japanese home market.[2] The critical long-term question is how human and organizational skills should be developed—and where.

This kind of planning cannot be separated from the development of business strategy (not just an annual budget). In most companies, business strategy seldom adequately incorporates what has been known as manufacturing strategy, and several years ago, manufacturing strategy did not stretch much beyond production strategy: make-buy analyses, plant locations, equipment selection, plant focus, workforce training, and so on. The scope of planning expands when leaders recognize that an organizational culture must evolve in order to reach a long-term vision.

In most companies, business strategy seldom adequately incorporates what has been known as manufacturing strategy.

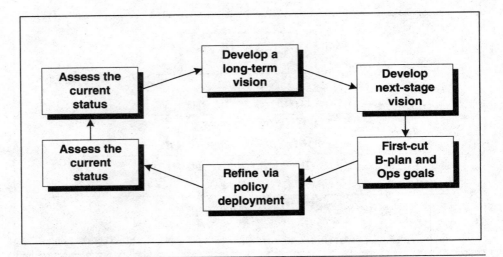

Figure 4. **Overview of developing an improvement strategy to reach a vision.**

Under the concepts of Big Q and Big M, strategy is evolving into something broader, how to develop high-quality core competencies in selected areas and form alliances and partnerships to round out all the capabilities needed to give customers something special. Technology is pushing software into almost every product and process and extending possibilities for geographic interlock. The operations side of strategy is how to develop overall capability for outstanding service to the customer. That is almost the same as the objective of policy deployment, or hoshin kanri, as the Japanese call it.

The number of issues that should be considered in this kind of strategy formulation has multiplied. It is difficult for a single person to encompass them all. One of the needs in strategic planning is the use of affinity diagram exercises and other means to quickly assimilate considerations from many viewpoints and crunch them together into an overall approach (or scenario) and then extend it into planning for improvement. Those who cannot learn to do this is in some fashion are likely to be left looking for techniques to respond to the next round of performance requirements from demanding customers—or they will give up.

An overall view of this approach to strategic planning is shown in Figure 4. The discussion so far has only covered assessment of the current condition to development of the next stage vision. The ability to formulate a long-term plan based on vision is critical. If the pace of change picks up, enterprises that cannot find a stable direction in a sea of techniques have a disadvantage. A trend just beginning is to form alliances or partnerships focused on a target market. In that case, a coalition team will participate in this kind of planning—a process that is in its infancy today. But vision is only one critical need. A second is the ability to stabilize the vision, refine it, and deploy a process to actually get results.

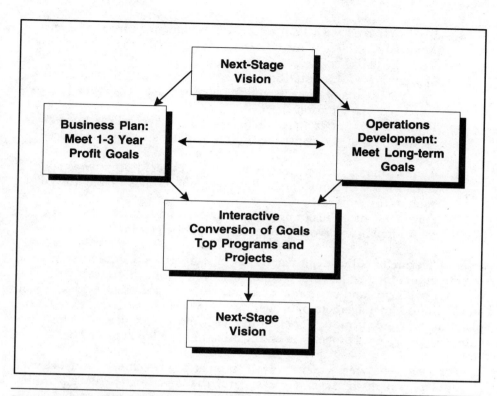

Figure 5. **Goals and objectives to meet a next-stage vision.**

2. Policy Deployment and Improvement Processes

Improvement processes are sloppily divided into (1) continuous improvement (incremental changes primarily carried out by those engaged in the work) and (2) major changes (full-time staff projects and dramatic reengineering). Organizations normally engage in both types of change, and the next-stage vision should instigate both.

Policy deployment has been described in books and articles, but not many companies practice it. Policy deployment starts with management or a core group determining the goals and objectives to meet a next-stage vision and ends with both continuous improvement and major projects aligned to meet the goals. One version of this portion of the process is summarized in Figure 5. The following is a list typical of the steps followed:

1. Identify primary success factors; set primary improvement goals for the relevant planning period, sometimes with priority ratings. (A management team does this.)
2. Disseminate the goals and objectives widely among *all* those affected. (Toss out balls to catch.)

Policy deployment has been described in books and articles, but not many companies practice it.

3. Teams charged with continuous improvement propose specific projects or improvement processes that contribute to the goals. (Toss the balls back.)
4. Appropriate working staff and management evaluate ideas for new and ongoing major projects and make proposals. (Toss back feasibility plans and options.)
5. The management group evaluates the proposals and the budgets for them, often giving priority ratings and considering the budget required.
6. A set of major projects is approved and budgeted. Approvals and adjustments of continuous improvement proposals are tossed back to the workforce.
7. Ongoing continuous improvement activity and major projects are monitored by everyone interested via public posting.

The feature of policy deployment that distinguishes it from conventional top-down planning is "catchball"—the involvement of those who will carry out improvement (and be improved themselves). Proposals are passed back and forth from management or a steering group to those who will execute the plans and who are currently very familiar with operating processes. This takes time, but if executed properly in an organization of a few hundred persons, it works.

For example, Zytec, where everyone is on an improvement team, has used policy deployment for several years. After the goals for the next planning period have been posted, teams have a deadline to send proposals directly to the president, bypassing all intermediaries who might want to filter them. With less than 100 teams, this process consumes time (about two months), but it is worth it for the ingenuity and enthusiasm engendered. Zytec won the Baldrige Award in 1991.

Everywhere along the path from vision to reality, a planning problem is gathering information from many divergent sources and integrating it into first a picture, then action priorities. The process has to be structured to work through a mass of information quickly, attempting to assimilate every important aspect (prioritizing), without burnout and turnoff from information overload. Facilitation methods help to structure group meetings, and messy plans can be compressed using relationship tables, as in QFD.[3]

One reason companies do not engage more people in planning is that it consumes time. Planning seems easier if confined to a few people; however, this method of planning overlooks the head start in implementation when plans are known to the implementers. Then little needs to be explained or "sold" to them.

A great deal of leadership energy must be expended to get everyone in an enterprise making changes in roughly the same direction and in a direction that has great promise. An assumption of policy deployment is that a majority of people in the organization are capable of improving processes and are willing to do so. However, human development is in itself part of the planning

An assumption of policy deployment is that a majority of people in the organization are capable of improving processes and are willing to do so.

process. A key reason for the process is to shape those executing core-competence processes to become the best in the world—so sharp that the organization can successfully convert a "blowout" strategic vision to reality so that it has no competitors left in its class.

Improvement is learned by practice, and practice means contact time. Unless a total workforce becomes accustomed to regularly refining processes down to their value-adding minimums, the planning process comes to nothing—as useless as a game plan for an athletic team that never practices. Dramatic improvement goes by various names—kaizen, reengineering, etc.—but all these need to be stimulated by a regular renewal cycle. Some would call it a learning cycle, like a school semester, for a learning organization. While people are improving their processes on multiple dimensions of performance, they are also improving themselves, and planning for this kind of development is a vital part of converting vision to reality.

Annually retouching the vision and going through policy deployment is one way to ratchet up human capabilities another notch. Some companies have other learning cycles too. For example, Toyota stimulates manufacturing personnel to revise their work stations every month when schedules change and new tact times are calculated. Minor improvements are made then.

In addition, industrial-engineering–type improvements are not the only kind that are important. In some industries, software and technology advancements are coming so fast that improvement cycles can coincide with technology generation turnover. Part of strategy formulation is to master new technology. The challenge is to develop product, service, and order fulfillment technologies so that mastery is within reach of human capabilities, and technical adventure undertaken in one pass is an acceptable risk.

Other improvement cycles can be synchronized with cycles in customer processes, and those may be the most important ones. The winners using blowout strategies will make their own improvement so routine that they can concentrate on improving customer processes, anticipating and stimulating new capabilities for customers. The objective is to work into a position to make this kind of vision a reality.

Notes

1. J.M. Juran, *A History of Managing for Quality* (Milwaukee, Wisconsin: ASQC Quality Press, 1995).

2. "Hewlett-Packard: Singapore (A)," Harvard Business School Case.

3. Relationship tables are used by Delphi Chassis Division of General Motors. See Gerald Jewson and David Edwards, "Proactive Business Planning With Policy Deployment," *Target*, vol. 11, no. 4, July–August, 1995, pp. 18–26. Their software is QFD/Capture Ver. 2.2.1 from International TechneGroup, Inc., Milford, Ohio.

How Wiremold Reinvented Itself with *Kaizen*

Art Byrne

This article explores how Wiremold, the leading U.S. producer of wire management systems (metal and plastic systems that carry power, data, and telephone wiring in buildings of all sorts), decided to completely change its way of operating by implementing the Japanese version of TQM and continuous improvement—Kaizen. Wiremold provides a practical and dramatic case study of the difference TQM can make in a company.

Three years ago, The Wiremold Company was an old-line, unionized manufacturing company. We used traditional batch manufacturing processes, which were organized by function, to make our wire management systems.

At the old Wiremold, a product might take as much as six weeks to make its way from raw material to finished product. We'd make huge quantities of a single component because our changeovers took so long. Often a batch of components would sit gathering dust in our large WIP inventory areas before products could be assembled because the other parts weren't scheduled to be run that week. Finished goods were sent to our 70,000-square-foot warehouse down the road to wait until needed for shipping to a customer. We were cash poor, yet had such large in-process and finished goods inventories that we were shopping for more warehouse space.

We've come a long way since then, reinventing ourselves into a vibrant, growing firm. In just three years, our sales have doubled and our profits have tripled. We've grown our base business by more than 50 percent, and supplemented that internally-generated growth with six acquisitions—five of which we were able to make without borrowing because we had freed up so much cash from inventory reductions.

Our success is not the result of any complex business strategy. Nor is it the fruit of some intensive program of capital investment.

Rather, we turned our company around by turning our manufacturing operation on its head: We adopted kaizen.

Our Results So Far

While the Wiremold experience is certainly not unique, I think the speed with which we've changed the culture of our organization and generated results is encouraging. We still have a long way to go, but our initial success provides us all with positive momentum.

We began to implement our kaizen program of continuous improvement in late 1991. In slightly less than three years, here are some of the changes we've made:

- Productivity has improved 20 percent in each of the last two years.
- Throughput time on products has dropped from four to six weeks to two days or less.
- The defect rate on our products fell by 42 percent in 1993, and by 50 percent in the first half of 1994.
- Inventories have been slashed by 80 percent, resulting in our space needs being cut in half.
- Profit sharing payouts for our employees have more than tripled.
- Equipment changeovers have been reduced dramatically—in some cases from as much as ten hours to less than ten minutes.
- New product development time has been slashed from almost three years to under six months.
- Vendors have been cut from more than 400 to fewer than 100.

And these quantifiable results don't begin to reflect things like the improvement we've seen in the most important areas—like employee attitude.

Getting here wasn't easy. And sustaining our progress is just as tough. But we've learned a few things along the way about what works—and what doesn't—that we're glad to share with others.

Integral to Business Strategy

One ingredient essential to our success has been the way we look at kaizen. At Wiremold, we believe it's a fundamental part of our business strategy. After all, our business delivery systems are what the customer sees.

If we fall behind in quality or on leadtimes, we disappoint our customer and we won't succeed no matter how good our strategy. On the other hand, if our systems can outperform the competition, then we can outrun them.

We've actually made kaizen part of our business strategy: to continually "fix" our base business. We believe that the minute we stop doing so, we'll fall behind.

We've actually made kaizen part of our business strategy: to continually "fix" our base business. We believe that the minute we stop doing so, we'll fall behind.

Getting Started

As an outsider joining Wiremold in late 1991, I realized that we needed to make some fundamental changes in the way we manufactured our products. Something that I had learned by observing other change programs is that it has to be an "all or nothing" proposition. It just won't work unless you make a significant commitment in time and resources and unless you take some risks. It also won't work unless that commitment comes from the top.

So, one of the first things that we did was to completely reorganize our operations.

Historically, our plants had been organized by function—milling here, presses there, assembly in another building, and so on. We began our improvement efforts by completely reorganizing our manufacturing operation into six independent product families (such as Plugmold® Products, Plastic Products, and Tele-Power Pole® Products) and four support teams (tooling and maintenance, administration, shipping and customer service, and the JIT Promotion office). We realigned people and relocated equipment so that each team would have all of the resources necessary to make its product or provide its service.

For example, making our Tele-Power Pole® product requires a number of resources—such as rolling mills, punch presses, painting equipment, and assembly. Historically, each was in a different functional department. The departments were separated by large distances and run by multiple managers. In effect, no person or team was responsible for making the product—only some portion of it.

Our first step was to bring all the necessary equipment together in one area of the plant to create a discrete operating unit. Then we identified a team leader and assigned a team of four salaried and 21 hourly associates to the unit. now our Tele-Power Pole® operation has everything it needs to go from raw materials right to finished goods.

The same is true of our Plugmold® product line. We brought together rolling mills, punch presses, assembly tables, etc. which had been spread across different departments. We staffed the unit with a team leader, a buyer/planner, a shop floor coordinator, several manufacturing engineers, and a group of capable operators.

Bringing Employees "On Board"

While creation of this product-centered organization was certainly important and it helped to get our people closer to their customer, it alone wasn't enough. We needed to make some dramatic changes in the way work was getting done. And that meant changing people's mindset about how to manufacture our products.

We learned that bringing people "on board" is probably the most difficult part of implementing a program. That's because kaizen is "backwards" from everything we've known or practiced about manufacturing here in the United States for the last 100 years. Instead of high-volume "batch" production, kaizen promotes making one piece at a time. High-speed is out, "takt time" is in. Large inventories, long viewed as an asset, were suddenly no good.

We learned that bringing people "on board" is probably the most difficult part of implementing a program.

In effect, we were asking our employees to take everything they had ever learned about manufacturing and turn it around 180 degrees. And, on top of that, we set some tough goals that we expected the organization to achieve. We told our people that we wanted them to:

- turn around every customer order in 48 hours
- cut product defects by half—every year over the prior year
- improve productivity by 20 percent over the prior year—every year

■ increase inventory turns by more than six times what they had been historically.

Naturally, there was skepticism and resistance. In fact, I'm sure most people thought I was totally off my rocker.

Overcoming Resistance

We took a number of steps to help address that skepticism including: establishing a training program, making a commitment to job security, emphasizing the linkage between profit-sharing and productivity improvements, establishing a quarterly recognition and award system, and launching our effort with highly visible projects.

Training Program

Although we had previously done some training in Deming's principles, we initiated an intensive, wide-ranging training program in the principles of JIT and kaizen for our people. We made sure that everyone got lots of training up front, and that they continued to get the training they need to improve their skills.

The training is very action-oriented. We spend a long day in the classroom, followed by four days of doing an improvement project (kaizen) on the shop floor or in the office. People are taken off their regular jobs for the week to focus on kaizen. As a result, we get a combination of training and work improvement/simplification all in one.

Over the past three years, we have done several hundred major, full-week kaizens. Nearly all of our people have participated in at least one, and most have had multiple experiences.

Job Security

One of the errors some companies make is to try to use productivity gains as an excuse to eliminate people. This is fatal. You simply can't expect people to participate in finding ways to improve the work flow if they are afraid that they will improve themselves right out of a job. The objective has to be to use freed-up people to support growth without adding headcount.

We addressed this head-on with a commitment to job security: We promised that no one would lose his or her job because of changes or improvements under kaizen. Instead, we agreed that "freed up" associates would be assigned to kaizen teams to help find more improvements until we need them for new projects or because of increased production. In our particular case, and, for that matter, in all the companies where I have implemented this process, increased volume growth has absorbed all of the associates we have freed up through kaizen. Should our growth slow, we have plenty of in-sourcing opportunities to keep our associates employed.

> We promised that no one would lose his or her job because of changes or improvements under kaizen.

Profit-Sharing

A critical element of bringing our people on board and keeping them motivated is our profit-sharing program. Although Wiremold has had profit-sharing for many years—dating back to 1916—it hadn't been very lucrative for employees in recent years. In fact, the pay-out ratio was about two percent of salary.

As a result, we already had a program that would translate our improvement efforts directly to all of our associates. And it has. Profit-sharing payouts have more than tripled since we started this effort. And we've set a clear kaizen goal of getting profit-sharing to 20 percent of salary.

Associate Recognition

To further support our efforts, we established a quarterly program to recognize associates who demonstrate outstanding commitment to the process of continuous improvement. We call it the President's Award.

Our product team leaders nominate people from their teams who have done an outstanding job of living the values we've taught. We honor two outstanding associates each quarter with a small cash bonus and an additional 12 associates with gift certificates for dinner at a fine restaurant.

While the economical value of this recognition may seem small, being selected for a President's Award has tremendous psychological value and has become a coveted reward in our organization.

Kaizen in Action

Because the Kaizen process is dramatic, just seeing it in action also helped to overcome a lot of employee skepticism and objections. As we've introduced kaizen to each of our operations, we've found that it works best when we begin with a big, visible project to show people we are serious.

At our plant in West Hartford, we selected several high-profile projects for our first kaizen team. Almost right away, employees could see us knocking holes in walls and moving 100-ton presses around—some of which had never been moved before.

Some of our earliest projects involved pursuing major reductions in setup time—and yielded dramatic results: Our first automatic punch press kaizen team reduced setup time from two hours to just five minutes; and our rolling mill setup reduction team went from 14 hours to less than one hour. In both cases, much of those savings were generated by identifying external setup activities that could be completed while the machine was still running. Other savings came from eliminating manual operations and standardizing or simplifying equipment. None came from big capital investment.

In the case of the rolling mill setup, the old way was to wait until one job was completed and the equipment was shut down to select the die and stage the steel for the subsequent job. The kaizen team defined preparatory and planning activities that could be completed while the first job was still running. They also eliminated a number of manual operations and identified opportunities to switch to pneumatic tools to speed up other operations.

The first punch press setup reduction team also identified changeover activities that could be completed while a job was running. They also standardized all of the nuts and bolts used on the equipment (previously there

WIREMOLD KAIZEN GOALS

Wiremold measures itself against six parameters. They are:

- 100 percent customer service
- 50 percent reduction in defects each year
- 20 percent gain in productivity each year
- inventory turns of 20 times
- profit sharing pay-outs equal to 20 percent of salary
- establishing visual control and the 5"S"

were many different sizes, each requiring a different size tool). And they installed quick-change clamping devices to further cut setup time.

The punch press is a good example of continuous improvement. Without understanding the possibilities, many companies would be happy to take a two-hour setup down to one hour—a 50 percent reduction. In our case, we went from 120 minutes to five minutes—a 96 percent reduction on the first kaizen. But we didn't stop there. We kept working at it and got that five minutes down to one minute—an additional 80 percent reduction.

Tackling Monuments

At some plants, we've started by tackling one of the "monuments" in that particular factory. For example, our Walker facility had a huge rotary system with about 150 stations for lacquering certain metal components. The lacquer line had been there for years and consumed about 900 square feet. It was constantly breaking down and was hard to keep clean. It was also located in a key area of the plant that could be better utilized for other operations. But no one questioned whether the lacquer line was the best way to get things done.

The kaizen team that took on the lacquer line started work on a Tuesday morning after a full day of kaizen training. By Thursday, they were tearing the lacquer line down and throwing it away. In its place, they put two 2-foot by 2-foot boxes each containing one lacquer station and serving one assembly line. The new arrangement allowed us to achieve one-piece flow, reduce down time, nearly double output and, most importantly, free up a key part of the plant to give us a better layout with more flexibility.

Sometimes you just have to take a leap of faith. We announced early on to our people in West Hartford that we were going to close our 70,000-square-foot warehouse, which was a separate facility about 15 miles away, and move the warehousing operation back into our main plant. The situation at the time was that both facilities were full to the rafters and material was being stored outside the warehouse facility in about 60 rented tractor trailers. The initial response from our people was "it's not possible." Frankly, I occasionally had doubts, too.

But, after about one year, we not only closed that warehouse—giving our-selves 70,000 square feet of currently empty space—we succeeded in freeing up half of the space at all our locations.

Management Must Lead

Which brings us to the role of senior management. You can't drive the kind of changes required from the bottom up. Without a commitment from top management, you might as well not even start the process because you are doomed to failure. But commitment alone is not enough. Knowledge about the kaizen process and how it works is also necessary—otherwise, you're just a cheerleader.

I believe that to really succeed, the company's leadership must not only be on board, it must lead the effort.

We did a number of things to make sure that everyone at Wiremold un-derstood my level of commitment. First, I wrote a training manual and then led the initial training programs for the first year—personally training about 150 of our people. If that didn't make my commitment clear to everyone, I was a frequent and active participant on kaizen teams. I continue to try to take a highly visible role, serving as the company's kaizen "consultant" as we introduce the process to each of our acquired companies.

Second, we established a sizable JIT promotion office and we started send-ing the members of that team to Japan for a two-week training program. To date, approximately 50 of our associates from various Wiremold companies have been to Japan for training.

Finally, perhaps my most important role in the long-term success of the effort is to never be satisfied, to keep raising the bar and asking, "Why? Why? Why?"

The problem is that, like most American companies, we assume that there is some "right" way of doing a thing. We get trapped by the idea that there has to be some endpoint. Now, with three years of kaizen under our belts, people still ask: "When are we going to be done? We must be almost done."

You want to praise people and tell them they've done a really great job—because, in truth, they have—but you can't stop to take a bow. I think that's one of the hardest elements of kaizen for those of us raised in a traditional manufacturing environment. It's my job to keep reminding people that with continuous improvement, we're always searching for a better way. We never get done!

Sustaining the Effort

Some employees have made continuous improvement an obsession. For ex-ample, the team responsible for punch press could have stopped after their first kaizen, satisfied with that 96 percent improvement in productivity. But they continued to kaizen the process, making gains with each effort.

In general, our people are less resistant to change because they've seen some amazing things happen. Even so, it can be hard to keep the process

We did a number of things to make sure that everyone at Wiremold understood my level of commitment.

moving ahead. We host Kaizen workshops from time to time. Bringing in "outsiders" to participate in a seminar in one of our plants helps generate new ideas and reinvigorates our own program.

Over the long term, the only real way to sustain the process is with a fundamental change in the organization's culture. We've worked hard to make kaizen a part of our culture, and to encourage the values of teamwork, constant change, and constant learning.

This is more than simple platitudes. Our training, job security, and profit-sharing programs all contribute. We also work hard at communication. Everyone in the organization knows what our objectives are and where we stand against them. (See "Goals," box.) Every two weeks, our team leaders present their progress towards these goals to me, my direct reports, and each other.

Over the long term, the only real way to sustain the process is with a fundamental change in the organization's culture.

Three Tips for Getting Started

It's not easy to get started and it's not easy to sustain, but, I think everyone at Wiremold would agree that the results so far are well worth the effort required. The nicest thing of all, however, is that our progress to date is totally attributable to Wiremold's associates. They know it and are proud of it.

We've only scratched the surface, but our expectation of how much further we can go makes our jobs a lot more exciting.

Finally, in summary, here are three "tips" that anyone getting started needs to keep in mind:

1. Changing people's mindset is a critical part of the job. People are naturally skeptical and you have to take dramatic and sustained action to overcome objections. In the long run, you must change the culture of the organization. The "concrete heads" must go.
2. Senior management must "lead the charge." That means not only at the beginning, but throughout, continually putting pressure on the organization. Lack of leadership attention is one of the major reasons that improvement programs die within a year to 18 months.
3. This is a long-term commitment. You have to acknowledge up front that there's no end point. Be prepared for your people to ask, "Are we finished yet?" And be equally prepared to answer, "It's not good yet" . . . even when you think it is.

Arthur P. Byrne is president and chief executive officer of The Wiremold Company. Prior to joining Wiremold in late 1991, he served as group executive of the Danaber Corporation, where he was responsible for eight operating companies. Earlier, Byrne held strategic planning and management positions with the General Electric Corporation.

Quality: A Way of Life in the Motor City

Staff of Quality Magazine

This article provides a nice overview of the role of quality management in the resuscitation of American auto manufacturers. It also provides a brief introduction to QS 9000, the new quality standards developed for the automobile industry.

Less than a decade ago, Detroit's Big Three took such a beating in the marketplace from transplant auto manufacturing operations—Honda, Toyota, Mazda, and Subaru—that they vowed to overhaul their manufacturing operations and recapture market share to the extent that they would never again be embarrassed on their home turf. That promise has been fulfilled beyond the wildest expectations of auto-industry analysts. General Motors, Ford, and Chrysler have posted record profits for 1994, and, in the process, have regained a significant chunk of the market share they had lost in the early '80s.

Ford Motor Co., Dearborn, MI, for example, claims to have been the industry leader in domestic quality, as measured by customer surveys, for more than 15 consecutive years.

Part of this success can be attributed to a fundamental shift in quality inspection practices by both the Big Three and the transplant companies. The domestic manufacturers have embraced Deming's philosophy of a holistic approach to quality inspections, in which the emphasis has been on building the product right from the start instead of inspecting for quality after manufacturing.

The domestic manufacturers have embraced Deming's philosophy of a holistic approach to quality.

Deming's philosophy, coupled with a prime focus on simultaneous, or concurrent, engineering, Taguchi methods for design of experiments (DOE), total quality management (TQM), statistical process control (SPC), and their practical implementation, all have helped the domestic car makers leap ahead in both sales and customer confidence.

"This fundamental shift incorporates the involvement of all the people in the quality process, making quality the responsibility of each employee in the entire operation instead of making quality the responsibility of the inspection department, so that critical inspection occurs at each stage of production," explained David Cole, director, Office of the Study of Automotive Transportation, University of Michigan, Ann Arbor. "Another factor in quality trends is the importance of statistical methods, which are tools to deal with all the data that's associated with quality. Deming's holistic approach emphasizes building the product right instead of inspecting for quality after manufacturing."

"Historically, the industry used to identify quality problems and then rebuild where they found quality problems," Cole said. "That was very expensive. One of the things we used to see in an assembly plant was a very large area where cars were taken after they came off the assembly line to fix problems of one form or another. Today, this is a very small area because the problems are fixed in process rather than waiting for the entire vehicle to be produced."

A Team Approach

"Assembly line workers are responsible for checking their own work to ensure that quality is built-in," said Martha Beard, Ford's director of quality, body, and assembly operations. "The assembly plants use a stop button system that allows key operators to turn the line off when a quality concern is observed. This is part of an overall team approach, which assures that no quality concern leaves a control zone. Special operators are assigned to sections, in some instances to work with groups of employees and repair any concern identified by one of the group members."

For example, in the body construction department, welders check their own welds for integrity, door installers check their own margins and flushness to assure that specifications are met, and final line operators inspect work from prior installations.

Vehicle quality is verified at every point of assembly from incoming material through welding, metal finish, closure panel installation, paint processes, and electrical systems. Finished vehicles are verified for engine electronics, fit and finish, and body sealing. In addition, a final check of everything is made one more time just before the plant releases the vehicle, according to Beard.

"Data accumulated from the in-zone containment, process monitoring, and finished vehicles are measured over time using statistical methods," Beard said. "Broad-based statistical training is widespread within the assembly operations, as evidenced by the use of charts tracking quality performance in every supervisor section. Extensive use is made of control charts, pareto analysis, and various kinds of sampling techniques."

Ford also uses a number of mechanical and electrical devices to enhance its inspection system. These include laser-guided dimensional checking tools in body construction and handheld data collectors. Many of these devices provide real-time statistical data. Examples include paint film thickness, fastener torque readings, in-vehicle electrical systems, and dimensions on finished vehicles and emission systems.

Concurrent Development

Simultaneous, or concurrent, engineering has played a crucial role in enhancing the automotive quality equation. "It has become apparent that about 75%

QS 9000 is structured to enhance a company's quality system and requires a systematic managerial strategy—an area where ISO 9000 appears to be rather thin.

Extensive use is made of control charts, pareto analysis, and various kinds of sampling techniques.

QS 9000: QUALITY REGS FOR SUPPLIERS

The latest frenzy in the quality industry revolves around compliance with the Big Three auto makers' QS 9000 requirements. In August 1994, Ford, Chrysler and General Motors—released Quality System Requirements QS 9000, which will be imposed on the auto industry's suppliers of production and service parts and materials.

QS 9000 incorporates the requirements of Chrysler's Supplier Quality Assurance Manual, Ford's Q-101 Quality System Standard, General Motor's Targets for Excellence, and ISO 9001-1994, verbatim. Chrysler requires that their first-tier suppliers achieve QS 9000 certification by June 30, 1997. The General Motors deadline is Dec. 31, 1997. Ford is requiring its suppliers to comply with QS 9000, but has not established compliance dates.

QS 9000 is structured to enhance a company's quality system and requires a systematic managerial strategy—an area where ISO 9000 appears to be rather thin.

QS 9000 requires that companies maintain both short- and long-term business plans, perform feasibility reviews, maintain control plans from the part prototype through pre-launch to final part production, and adhere to strict process control requirements.

The auto makers' standard also requires that companies establish systems for continuous improvement, identify opportunities for quality and productivity improvements, and incorporate controls to ensure that the current and future expectations of the customer are taken into account. In addition, QS 9000 requires that suppliers monitor customer satisfaction—yet another enhancement over the current 1994 ISO 9000 requirements.

QS 9000 also states that 100% on-time delivery is a mandatory requirement for subcontractors.

With the mutual acceptance of third-party registrations to QS 9000 by the Big Three, more suppliers will move from the traditional second-party assessments to third-party certification performed by registrars. To perform registrations for QS 9000, registrars must have their assessing facility located in the U.S., must hold accreditation with the Registrar Accreditation Board (RAB), National Accreditation Council for Certification Bodies (NACCB), or Raad voor de Certificatie (RvC), and have satisfactorily completed the accreditation body witnessing of a QS 9000 assessment activity. The registrar also must comply with the requirements, Appendix B, of the "The Code of Practice for Quality System Registrars," and the Quality System Requirements (QSA) of QS 9000.

Automotive suppliers will recognize significant benefits from the third-party registration process for QS 9000, particularly in the area of consistency. This has been an area of concern expressed by many companies involved in the ISO 9000 process.

Continued—

QS 9000: Quality Regs for Suppliers (continued)

All members of an assessment team must have successfully passed the QS 9000 training requirements set forth by the Big Three. This training system promotes consistency of interpretation of the QS 9000 requirements between assessment team members and registrars. Also, the assessment team must consist of at least one member with "relevant automotive experience," as established in the registrar's documented quality system.

TE 9000 Lies Ahead

The Big Three have recently released an internal draft of another standard entitled TE 9000 (Tooling and Equipment). This document, which the Big Three expect to impose on approximately 75,000 automotive suppliers, will detail quality system requirements for suppliers of nonproduction equipment such as welding materials, drill bits, stamping presses, electrodes, and capital equipment.

TE 9000 will be similar to QS 9000 (with ISO 9000 contained verbatim in italics). It also is expected that TE 9000 will not contain the production elements of QS 9000 such as the production part approval process, process control capabilities, and charting.

Suppliers should experience the same types of benefits from TE 9000 as from QS 9000. The review and approval cycle for TE 9000 is expected to be much less than that of ISO 9000 or QS 9000. The Big Three anticipate that TE 9000 will be released around July 1995, with supplier compliance tentatively slated for 1997 to 1998.

Stephen Marquedant, operations director and QS 9000 lead assessor, National Quality Assurance, U.S.A., Boxborough, MA

of the cost of manufacturing is defined in the product development process," said University of Michigan's Cole. "I would relate that to quality. Consequently, the design role in the overall production process is crucial. That's one of the reasons that we have seen the emergence of whole areas of considerations like design for manufacturing and assembly. What that really means is that the auto makers have moved the quality people and the design people very upfront in the early stages of engineering. That's what is known as simultaneous engineering or simultaneous development, in which they bring forward into the earlier stages all the people that are involved in the downstream process."

Cole goes on to say that, although the transplant operations in the U.S. had initial advantages of very new employees trained in quality processes,

Auto makers have moved the quality people and the design people very upfront in the early stages of engineering.

along with brand new grassroots facilities and robust designs from Japan, domestic car makers have closed the quality gap. "It's a small gap now, it is nowhere near the magnitude that it was in the early '80s," he said.

Asked about whether the transplanted or the domestic manufacturers have an edge in today's marketplace, Cole said: "Increasingly, because of the cost improvements being made by the domestic auto makers, they may have an edge today. In part, that's because a significant fraction of the transplants' components still come from overseas, particularly from Japan. Because of a number of factors, their costs are very high."

Plant Workers Boost Quality

As with any quality improvement effort, the degree of success is determined by the people who execute the quality practices. This has been the case in the manufacturing of Highland Park, MI-based Chrysler's Dodge and Plymouth Neon sedan. As the new car design moved toward production at Chrysler's Belvidere, IL, plant, operators didn't wait for the line to start up to play their part.

At various stages of the Neon's development, some 1,500 employees—half the plant's work force—went on periodic training trips to the Chrysler Technology Center (CTC) in Auburn Hills, MI. Those involved included workers from the paint shop, body shop, trim, chassis, production control, skilled trades, and the satellite stamping and fascia plants.

Many of the 4,000-plus employee suggestions made during this training period were incorporated into the product itself. For example, two workers suggested changes to the Neon's door installation equipment so that the glass would fit perfectly. Since Neon's design doesn't include an upper door frame to guide the glass, even the slightest gap could cause wind noise or water leaks.

"Employees influenced the design of the setting fixture right from the beginning," said Frank Ewasysshyn, general manager of Large Car and Small Car Assembly Operations. "They changed the handles, the sequence, and almost everything in the early stages. Once a tool is set and handed to the operator, he isn't likely to offer any input, other than that it doesn't work," Ewasysshyn continued. "This time, they were part of the development group, so that they have ownership, which makes a big difference."

Other employees were instrumental in the development of assist arms—ergonomic tools—used to move or load various components or systems into the cars as they travel down the assembly line. "In the past, the instrument panel tooling, for example, would be developed somewhere in the engineering group," Ewasysshyn said. "It would be built and the first time the operator would see it would be the day he or she showed up on the job to use the tool."

"This time, the employees were part of the development process. They worked with the suppliers right from the beginning. They helped us determine the best place for the handles, what the handles should look like, how fast the tool should move, and whether or not it should be motorized. We used their inputs extensively," Ewasysshyn said.

CAD/CAM Sharpens Quality Focus

Chrysler's Neon production also has broken new ground in boosting the accuracy of its parts by using CAD/CAM programs and advanced-composite materials. Carbon-fiber body panels were cut from computer-based tooling very early in the program to produce the first body prototypes.

"On previous projects, stamped body panels would not be available until the 50-week point in a program," commented Chrysler's Robert Dynes, executive engineer, Body-in-White and Exterior for the platform team. "To really appreciate the scope of what that means, consider that previously anyone working on a system that interacted with the body of the car in any way—say a headlamp assembly or door seal—had to work from renderings and blueprints to design and develop the part. There was no way of checking for accuracy or possible problems until a year from production, when an accurate body representation was available."

The Neon engineering team used the Computer Aided Three-Dimensional Interactive Application (CATIA) program, produced by Dassault, a French aerospace company, to create representations of solid components on a computer screen. This model precisely simulated everything from an object's weight to its points of inertia to its structural soundness.

Older CAD/CAM languages allowed objects to be developed and manipulated on screen, but were based on wire graphs that formed the shape of the system or part. While it was possible to mathematically prove a design from points on the graph, it was not possible to accurately represent a true surface.

"This was because the space between the graphed lines could not be represented, so we were never dealing in true surfaces," Dynes said. CATIA is able to mathematically fill in the space between the graphed lines, giving an accurate representation of the surface.

"As good as our traditional CAD/CAM software performed, it was possible to take a design from computer to a clay model and discover that the surface was not linear," said Frank Havasi, manager of the Neon Body-in-White program. "With CATIA, not only can we make a perfect surface, but we can also check the linear form of the surface using simulated light reflections.

"That's a far cry from when our designers would take a wood model, which was developed from a clay model, and eye the surface for imperfections, using a piece of sandpaper to smooth out the flaws. It was from that wood surface that we would get the tooling," he added.

The CATIA-produced carbon-fiber panels used on the Neon were so accurate at the 100-week point before production that they were used to check the hard tooling that was set up by manufacturing to build the metal-bodied prototypes. "This was the first program we've worked on in Chrysler where we didn't have one tooling crash," Havasi said. "Imagine going through clay models, wood models, tooling blueprints, and eventually hard tooling, only to find there is a flaw in the tooling that mandates starting all over again—including all the costs. It's something we simply could not afford under our new way of developing vehicles with the least amount of money required."

Along with cost and time savings have come accuracy and substantially improved quality in the finished product.

CATIA stores every aspect of the Neon design numerically and generates a computerized model with all of its specifications held in a central database, which is available to all engineers working on the program. These specifications are then sent to both in-house and external suppliers by computer for tooling development.

"We aren't exaggerating when we say that no paper was transferred between design, engineering, and the tooling suppliers," Dynes said. "All of the information is available simultaneously to all members of the team. This eliminates untold amounts of time, effort, and error, known in the older system of transferring blueprints and renderings. In addition, it eliminates guesswork early on. Vehicle-build quality early in the program has been outstanding."

Japan's New Advantage: Total Productive Maintenance

David A. Turbide

Total productive maintenance (TPM) aims at reducing the problems that come from improperly maintained machines and work areas. At its heart is the deep involvement of all employees. It can greatly increase productivity and reduce costs while heightening employee commitment to process and quality improvement.

How can a company harness the tremendous power of work teams? Is there a way to encourage production workers to become more involved in quality for the benefit of the company and themselves? The answer to these questions is simple: total productive maintenance (TPM). TPM involves workers taking ownership of their work areas and equipment. In practice, this means that production workers become responsible for routine production-equipment maintenance, including lubrication, adjustments, and minor repairs.

In several Japanese companies I visited, TPM has become a rallying cry for wide-ranging quality improvements. For example, several years ago at Yamato Kogyo, a motorcycle control-cable maker (for Yamaha and other motorcycle manufacturers), business was slow, profits were disappearing, and worker enthusiasm was waning. A previous improvement program got off to an encouraging start but stalled in the second year after modest results. Something had to be done, and it had to be done quickly.

Yamaha convinced Yamato management to use TPM to get Yamato production workers more involved and enthusiastic about quality. Yamato management explained to its workers the problems it faced and how TPM could solve those problems. Five years after Yamato began its TPM program, the firm had improved its productivity by 130%, cut accidents by 90%, reduced defects by 95%, and increased the suggestion rate from 1.3 per employee per month to more than five suggestions per employee per month. Profits recovered, and Yamato received a TPM Award from Yamaha.

> Five years after Yamato began its TPM program, the firm had improved its productivity by 130%, cut accidents by 90%, and reduced defects by 95%.

What Is TPM, and How Can It Be Implemented?

The idea behind TPM is to have production workers take responsibility for the care and routine maintenance of their equipment and work space. Instead of an attitude of "I operate the machines, and someone else fixes them," the approach becomes "I'm responsible for my own equipment." This goes beyond cleaning and oiling. Wherever possible, workers take over simple repairs and more-involved maintenance duties. There is still a maintenance department, but it exists to train production workers, serve as backup for the workers, handle the more-demanding maintenance tasks, and maintain the parts and supplies stock.

Implementing a TPM program starts with training equipment operators so that they are prepared to assume their new duties. The next step is to clean up the work areas. To avoid equipment failure, maintenance activity should be preventive. Preventive maintenance includes watching for early signs of wear, misadjustments, or problems that might be developing. It helps if the area is clean and neatly organized and the floor painted a light color (the better to see oil spatters, errant chips, and loose parts).

There are bound to be improvements needed to help keep the area clean. Typically, splatter guards, hoods, chip collectors, cable conduits, tool racks, and other accessories are installed at this stage.

Workers are intimately involved in the TPM process. They are organized into teams of five to eight people, and the teams develop improvements and implement them on their own, if possible. Yamato regularly held all-company, end-of-the-week meetings that often lasted through the night to develop and review rolling 90-day plans, build enthusiasm, discuss progress, and share ideas.

Yamato's TPM program extended beyond equipment maintenance. Work areas were reorganized for convenient access to tools and materials, and cross-functional teams were developed to provide mutual support. Ultimately, improvement suggestions helped increase efficiency and safety. Worker morale soared.

Due to the program's success, Yamato has become a TPM showcase. Charts, graphs, and posters cover the walls, and awards decorate each department. Visitors to the company will notice white Plexiglas signs hanging overhead with colored stickers that mark achievements: A copper sticker signifies that a basis for improvement has been established, silver means that the goal is in sight, and gold signals that the goal has been achieved.

> Work areas were reorganized for convenient access to tools and materials, and cross-functional teams were developed to provide mutual support.

Why TPM Works

TPM's success stems from its focus on identifying a problem's cause and not merely its effects. Clean-up efforts and intimate worker involvement can lead to the early detection of situations that could result in machines malfunctioning or producing substandard parts. TPM is similar to statistical process control: The goal is prevention rather than correction.

Like Yamato, Somic Ishikawa received an award for its TPM effort, this one from the Japan Institute for Plant Maintenance. In Somic's case, the challenges that led to TPM implementation included difficulty in keeping up with rapid product changes, intense competition, a need to improve quality, price pressure, and too many defects for too long at the new product start-up stage.

Somic makes suspension and steering parts for most of the Japanese automotive companies. This highly competitive industry is extremely cost and quality sensitive. To survive in this market, Somic saw the need to simultaneously outperform its competition and reduce its costs. Somic's TPM program had four phases that led to productivity and quality improvements with reduced costs:

Phase 1. The first activity included organizing small teams to initiate the program by cleaning up the facilities and developing daily maintenance tasks for the workers. The first phase's focus was reducing equipment failures and identifying and reducing primary causes of defects.

Phase 2. The second activity (production preparation) addressed design for manufacturing, improving machine and die design, and establishing a better production management system. In describing this phase, Somic officials pointed to a redesign process for one product that resulted in a 17% reduction in cost, a significant reduction in weight (an important factor to the automotive-industry customer), and significant quality improvements. Perhaps the story's most significant aspect is that Somic proposed the changes to the customer, not the other way around. In Japan, many contracts are written so that the supplier is encouraged (or required) to reduce costs and improve quality every year. A significant redesign initiated at the supplier level must be approved by the customer. Cost savings resulting from supplier-initiated improvements are typically shared between supplier and customer.

During my Somic tour, a number of employee-suggested improvements were highlighted. Typical of these was a set of milling machine fixtures that, for a changeover, required removing three bolts, swapping the fixture, and replacing and tightening the three bolts. In the fixture's improved version, the modified fixture base remained attached to the machine while the detachable top portion was simply slid out and the replacement slipped into the same slot. This improvement was suggested by the machine operator, validated and designed by engineering, and installed for a significant reduction in changeover time.

In another example, an employee suggested that a rack of hand tools be moved from the right side of the work area to another position directly in front of the work area. Not only did this change save time whenever a tool was needed, but it also reduced muscular strain for the worker and reduced the potential for injury and tool damage. This minor change, along with thousands of similar suggestions, has helped transform the Somic workplace.

Phases 3 and 4. The third and fourth activities directed automation improvements in the plant and office. Plant automation is directed at improved productivity and quality. Office automation is an area to which Japanese companies have not paid much attention in the past.

The results of TPM at Somic include a 75% reduction in defects, a significant reduction in defects during the start-up phase of new products (a major concern in a fast-changing industry), 50% higher productivity, 95% reduction in unexpected equipment breakdowns, and reduced manpower requirements, despite a significant increase in business volume.

TPM Unifies the Work Force

At Yamato and Somic, TPM provided a mechanism for focusing the work force's energy and creativity. TPM relies on employee teams to initiate and implement changes, most of which come from worker suggestions. The famous Japanese kaizen suggestion-based continuous improvement process is leveraged in an organized TPM program and directed toward specific strategic targets, such as reduced defects, reduced equipment failures, increased productivity, and cost-reduction goals.

At both companies, specific challenges led to the initiation of TPM programs. But there is much to be gained from TPM, and it shouldn't take a crisis to get it started. The first and most obvious potential benefit is a reduction in machine downtime due to proper routine care. In today's lean-and-mean, just-in-time world, machine breakdowns can be deadly.

Second, making the workers responsible and more involved in the machinery's operation should lead to less abuse and accidental damage. Because they understand the equipment better, the workers will be motivated to take better care of it. This increased involvement, along with management's willingness to listen, can lead to a high volume of improvement suggestions that can improve productivity, raise morale, and positively influence quality. A side benefit is that many TPM improvements don't require large investments. It is often the little things and the small changes that, when added together, generate significant results.

David A. Turbide is a management consultant with Production Solutions, Inc. in Beverly, Massachusetts.

> There is much to be gained from TPM, and it shouldn't take a crisis to get it started.

New Service Quality Challenges Face a New Competitive Era

Ron Zemke

This article by consulting editor Ron Zemke, head of Performance Research Associates and co-author of the "knock your socks off service" series of books, describes the evolving demands of customers for better service and new services never before available. He reminds us that companies can never stand still. Continuous improvement means improvement of products, but it also means improvement, sometimes dramatic improvement, of services, as well. Those, in fact, are likely to be what will give a company its competitive edge. This article explores what that means today and into the future.

Slowly but surely, American organizations are shedding fat and turning themselves into world-class lean, mean, speedy, competitive machines. But every shake and shiver of adjustment, despite the rightness and necessity of it, creates a customer service challenge. Benjamin Schneider, a professor of psychology at the University of Maryland, rightly points out that any and every disruption of an existing, successful, positive customer relationship potentially puts that relationship at risk. Every salesperson who has ever had to deliver bad news to a customer—"I'm sorry to have to tell you this Mr. Jones, but there will be a 5 percent price adjustment in the coming year."—knows the truth and wisdom in Schneider's observation.

Changes in pricing, delivery, packaging, return policy, people assigned to the account—you name it—cause your customers to re-evaluate the business they are doing with you. Today's focus on downsizing, reengineering, new system innovation, and any of a dozen other internally focused efforts—as important and necessary as they may be—nonetheless have inadvertent potential to put accounts at risk. The problem, observes Schneider, is that all productivity improvement efforts are intensely inward focused, and more often than not their effects on short-term customer retention—or disruption—are not thoroughly considered and most certainly seldom managed in a positive, proactive sense.

As customer retention becomes an increasingly important aspect of every organization's success formula, it becomes more important to consider—and manage—every aspect of the customer's experience with your organization, including their perceptions, apprehensions, and the actual results of your internal productivity improvement efforts.

A simple example: Organizations that depend on telephone-bound customer service representatives (reps) to keep day-to-day customer relations running smoothly are routinely challenging the cost-efficiency of one-to-one, personalized rep-to-customer matching. First-come, first-serve queuing is by and large replacing the system of account-dedicated reps. Yet we increasingly hear from customers the lament: "It would be a lot easier to work with your company if I wasn't constantly having to teach your people my business. Every time I get one trained, you lose 'em or move 'em." Such a complaint needs to be taken seriously and not dismissed out of hand with a perfunctory, "They'll get used to the new system."

A study at Marriott Corporation, reported by Reichheld and Sasser, makes the point. An improvement in employee retention of 10 percent directly correlates with a 3 percent improvement in customer retention. Retaining employees and keeping them connected with your business and their customers directly impacts bottom-line results. The lesson—and caution—is that reengineering, downsizing, and a myriad of other unavoidable, necessary efforts create disruptions not only for employees but for customers as well. The effects of those disruptions are often unanticipated—and unmanaged.

Two More Challenges

There are at least two other emerging challenges to service quality and customer retention threatening organizations here in the closing decade of the twentieth century.

- Data management inadequacy, and
- Product availability short fall.

Where's the Info?

Creating customer-pleasing quality service is, increasingly, an information-intensive endeavor. A recent study conducted in the LTL carrier segment of the common carrier trucking business makes the point. In this study, we found that users of LTL freight hauling services routinely expect such companies to have nationally centralized or "1-800" customer service access and that these service access points should be able to provide instant information on pick ups and deliveries, pricing, billings and claims, as well as shipments in transit and the likelihood of on-time arrival or delivery. A significant customer subsegment not only expected these multistop trucking companies to have all this information available at a moment's notice but to proactively, automatically provide customers with this information. The level of proactive automation they expected ranged from daily fax updates on shipments and problems to personal computer access databases of the carrier in question.

Equally impressive (or frightening depending on your point of view) was the expectation that a single person—with access to all this information—should be assigned to their account and should be their account's primary contact for sales, orders, and problem solving. When asked for the source of these remarkable expectations—expectations well beyond any service level currently being delivered in the LTL business—respondents were clear: Federal Express, UPS, and the small-package industry. As one focus group participant put it "these trucking companies can learn a lot from the likes of UPS and Federal Express." This, despite the fact that the small parcel and the common carrier LTL businesses are very different businesses in a multitude of factors. Clearly, the phenomenon of horizontal expectation spread is alive and well.

What makes this set of expectations important is that such information management expectations are prevalent in almost every industry today. But, paradoxically, as more and more customer service functions move toward a data integrated, centralized structure (63 percent of 2,000 companies surveyed by TARP Institute, Washington, D.C., currently use a centralized, "1-800" function for answering customer questions, solving customer problems, and sorting out billing disagreements), the more demanding or "needy" of these services customers are becoming. Satisfying customer information expectations, it seems, simply leads to more expectations.

And to the surprise and dismay of senior managers looking to high-quality service as a strategic advantage, requests—even demands—for database integration and system updating to meet these emerging customer demands are being met with 12- to 20-month delays—in project start dates. In one-to-one interviews of service managers looking to better data management to improve service quality, we were told by a significant proportion (around 15 percent) that their requests for such work were simply out of the question and beyond the scope of their organizations' technical capability.

Typical was an interview with the CEO of a burgeoning cell phone company. When asked what his two biggest customer service problems were, he replied without hesitation: "Incomprehensible bills and our inability to give customers the information they want when they call our customer service center." When asked about the root causes, he was equally clear: "Our computer systems aren't set up to do these things the way customers want them done." And to the logical next question—when will they be?—we received an astonishing answer: "I don't know. My Chief Information Officer informs me that they have a two year back log of projects and aren't sure when they could accommodate something like this."

Where's My Hog?

Success can be an inhibitor of service success. Ask them at Harley-Davidson, where the waiting list for a Harley-Davidson (H-D) street bike is a year and holding. The backorder book, says one industry analyst, was at one time a thousand units deep. One side effect of overdemand for H-D motorcycles has been the development of some interesting free-market dynamics. Many dealers have taken to tacking hefty premiums to Harley's suggested retail prices.

At the same time, individual entrepreneurs have been buying up new and used bikes at a premium, holding them for a few months, then selling them through newspaper want ads at yet another big markup. And smelling opportunity in the vacuum, competitors like Triumph Motors, an English motorcycle manufacturer, are returning to a U.S. market they had formerly ceded to Harley and its Japanese imitators—Yamaha, Suzuki, and Honda.

But Harley-Davidson is hardly the first—or only—company plagued by the bittersweet bane of its own success. In years gone by, Apple, IBM, and Compaq have all been caught short-stocked in the personal computer market, as has Levi Strauss in the clothing biz and most of the automobile manufacturers—Ford with the original Mustang, Mazda with its first RX-7, and General Motors with its currently very popular "Jimmy" sport utility vehicles.

The onset of a supply/demand crunch is usually met with attempts to produce more product. The build more option includes such tactics as 24-hour production; leasing capacity; subcontracting assembly and/or production; and occasionally, loosening quality standards. Eventually, however, there comes a point where the only recourse is to ration the available product in some fashion and work extremely hard to make it, if not ok, at least tolerable to customers.

There are several parsing, rationing, or sharing-the-pain approaches that are traditionally invoked—or negotiated—when demand outpaces supply, and there is no obvious end in sight:

- Straight rationing or limiting the amount of product customers, whether end users or supply chain partners, is allowed. This allocation approach, in use at Harley-Davidson and used traditionally by the auto industry, can be fixed by past sales volume, present need, or invoked on a triage basis.

- First come, first serve is a zero preference approach. It is frequently used in the commercial airplane building business. Boeing Corporation, for instance, puts airline orders for new planes in a fairly simple queue and keeps them there. Leonard Berry, professor of sales and marketing at Texas A & M University, cautions that when a company uses a pure queuing strategy to manage demand, jumping the line has to be policed well. "Allowing line jumping will erode customer loyalty very quickly," he cautions. It also leads to a black market for line positions.

- Rolling queues are, more than anything else, a rationalized first-come, first-serve approach. Four-star restaurants, like Chez Panisse and Quilted Giraffe, world class establishments with multimonth advance reservation lists, routinely require reconfirmation. Office furniture manufacturers frequently utilize rolling queues, reconfirming orders as they move toward custom finishing.

- Segmentation, while not a terribly democratic approach, acknowledges the reality that not all customers are of equal economic value to the organization. When American Airlines establishes different upgrade rules for Platinum card and Gold card frequent flyers, it is applying segmentation to the limited supply of first class cabin upgrades. And can a microelectronic components manufacturer with a long profitable history with the auto industry be second guessed for establishing an allotment rule that reads: "Never shut down a car manufacturer's production line"?

Regardless of the parsing approach invoked, successful rationing depends in no small part on the account management skills of the sales and service staff. Continuous, open communications is a must. Waiting customers wait more patiently when they know what is going on and can chart their progress toward the head of the line. Integral to patience with the process is trust. "Never, ever lie to a customer about product delivery when supply is tight," says Louis Scott, president of Louis Scott Associates, Inc., Rochelle Park, New Jersey.

Emergency planning is also an imperative. Be ready to throw yourself on the mercy of the customers—with your backup plan in hand—if your allocation system breaks down, because your customer is now twice wounded. Buying product from a competitor to fill a customer need when you are in deep recovery should be seen as an acceptable and valid practice.

Allocations situations are, if handled with tack, an opportunity for practicing relationship enhancement, through value-adding activities. When Baxter Healthcare lends an inventory control specialist to a hospital client, with the result being improved usage and decreased inventory, the bonds have been strengthened, and the press of product demand decreased through increased efficiency and better methods.

The Intensive Partnering Option

A more dramatic resolution, one only being used on a small scale so far, is dedicated partnering—specifically, creating an elite customer portfolio, putting a picket fence around these valued clients, and treating them as the priority customer base for the duration (and possibly beyond). But this dedication to a select group of customers requires an unusual degree of openness, information sharing, and transparency from both sides of the partnership. And it requires large amounts of account management time, generally taken from time formerly used for new sales development.

A Continuous Journey

We have become accustomed to hearing that the service quality effort is a journey, not a destination. But it really hasn't been until very recent times that the exact truth of this maxim has been more than an ellipse. Today, however, we are all learning the reality of that admonishment and seeing the importance and impact of the course we are following when we choose to compete for customers on the basis of world-class customer care.

Retailing Looks to a New Century

Meg Whittemore

This article spells out the challenges to retailers to remain competitive in a fast-changing environment. They have to make shopping a more entertaining experience for customers; they have to make it more convenient; they have to take more advantage of technology; they have to open new channels of communication. In other words, they have to be very smart about improving their processes, their selection of niches, and their ability to serve customers.

"Too many retailers are in a real vacuum of innovation and creativity," says D. Lee Carpenter, head of DesignForum, a Dayton, Ohio, store-design firm that describes its mission as "recharging the retail experience." Those retailers, he says, find it easier "to do the same thing over and over again" in the mistaken belief that "what works today will work tomorrow."

Retailing expert Robert A. Peterson says retailers tend to focus "only on their narrow areas of expertise" and fail to commit sufficient resources to monitoring changes in the demographic, technological, political, and economic forces affecting them.

Those might seem to be harsh judgments, but they are shared in varying degrees by a broad range of experts who agree that all is not well in significant areas of a retailing industry on the brink of a new century.

Too many retailers, the critics say, have failed to keep pace with today's customers, employees, and technologies. Those problems are compounded by such factors as an excessive number of retail stores throughout the country and merchandise mixes that are indistinguishable from store to store and region to region.

For smaller retailers in particular, the recommended solutions are not only sweeping changes in the ways they do business but also a sense of urgency in putting new approaches into place.

"To succeed in the year 2000, retailers must recognize that the rate of change will increase geometrically," according to *The Future of Retailing* (Quorum Books), edited by Peterson, a professor at the University of Texas

School of Business Administration and author of more than 100 books and articles.

Peterson and Richard C. Bartlett, president and chief executive officer of Mary Kay Cosmetics, Inc., state in a joint contribution to the book: "The successful retailers of the next century will be those able to develop healthier, psychologically mature, and efficient organizations capable of coping with increasing uncertainty and rapid change."

In discussing the look of the industry in the year 2000 and beyond, retail experts also refer to such concepts as vision, employee empowerment and recognition, interactive technology, the disappearance of purchase orders, experiential shopping, fantasy and entertainment, "co-location," electronic shopping, and even stores with neither inventories nor employees.

The context for these ideas is the evolving environment in which retailers must operate, one in which they find new challenges, new problems, and new opportunities.

Demographics, life-style changes, and the availability of low-cost, high-efficiency technology are driving those changes just as they are driving new approaches in virtually every sector of business.

For example, the baby boomers—those born between 1946 and 1964—were once considered advocates of conspicuous consumption at any price; now, as they move into middle age, their shopping priorities have shifted toward economy, service, and convenience. The result has been the explosive growth of factory-outlet stores, discounters, warehouse clubs, "supercenters," so-called category killers (stores so concentrated on given categories of merchandise that they can "kill" the competition in those categories), catalog shopping, and home shopping. In addition to favorable prices, they are searching for one-stop shopping as a time-saving technique for two-worker families. They also want to avoid delays in checkout lines, and they want products to be in stock.

Edward Cornish, president of the World Future Society, an association based in Bethesda, Md., that tracks future trends, says businesses will find strong support for "ways that will make it easier for people to get or do their daily routine in a hassle-free way."

For smaller retailers, the growth of regional and national chains to meet the desire of today's consumers for hassle-free shopping is bringing intense new competitive pressures. And many entrepreneurs are finding innovative ways to deal with them.

When Don and Gloria Connell heard that Wal-Mart was opening a store half a block away from their small hardware business in Sterling, Colo., they immediately started thinking about survival.

Their store, Mr. D's Ace Hardware, carried a wide selection of housewares, appliances, gifts, sporting goods, and automotive items as well as a small range of traditional hardware products.

Since Wal-Mart carries a similar merchandise mix, the couple decided to face their future competition head-on. The Connells drove to Denver, an hour and a half away, to visit a Wal-Mart store. They spent two days combing the

Businesses will find strong support for "ways that will make it easier for people to get or do their daily routine in a hassle-free way.

aisles, making extensive notes on the store's merchandise, selection, prices, and shelf space.

"The trip back was very depressing," says Don Connell. "We saw what they were doing in our best departments and knew that we didn't stand a chance." Three weeks later, the Connells made a radical decision. They discontinued their strongest departments and became a basic hardware store, selling paint, tools, electrical items, plumbing, carpentry supplies, and lawn and garden supplies—and offering customers advice and instruction on how to use those items.

"The things we dropped were the areas Wal-Mart is really strong in, both in pricing and selection," says Connell. "We kept the departments they were weak in and where we could compete easily." The bottom line: "Our sales have tripled since Wal-Mart moved to town," says Connell.

Tracy Mullin, president of the National Retail Federation, a trade group in Washington, D.C., says that such successful responses are becoming more common. "Instead of being forced out of business by the 'category killers' as predicted," Mullin says, "small retailers are thriving by providing the services and products that larger stores are not able to."

Tom Friedman, publisher of *Retail Systems Alert*, a monthly newsletter in Newton, Mass., that covers automation for retailers, says, "There will be a re-emergence of the independent retailer as a major reaction to the large-format stores that offer very low service.

"Small, high-end retailers with high-quality products and high levels of service will locate near the large-format stores. . . . They will offer added services such as customizing a customer's purchase, which large-format retailers cannot do."

Small, high-end retailers with high-quality products and high levels of service will locate near the large-format stores.

Retailers' strategies for meeting increasingly competitive pressures also include a recognition that appearance and layout of stores are important in attracting and serving customers.

Carpenter, chairman and chief executive officer of DesignForum, says a successful retail environment must recognize the key questions that customers ask: Why buy here? Why buy now?

To persuade those customers to "buy here," Carpenter explains, the store must establish itself as an authority with focused positioning, well-defined offerings, service, and the information the consumer needs to make the right purchase. The "buy now" question is answered, he says, by demonstrating that the store is focused on the consumer, that it is credible, exciting, customer-friendly, and operationally efficient, and that it conveys a sense of urgency and delivers value.

Carpenter says that retailers will serve customer needs and achieve their own goals "when you add value to the retail experience." His firm helps stores do that, he adds, "by creating efficient, exciting, and entertaining environments."

One such approach is evident in the retail stores of Gander Mountain, a regional chain based in Wilmot, Wis.; it sells hunting, fishing, and camping equipment and apparel through 11 retail outlets and by catalog.

The stores' interiors are designed to create a sense of the outdoors. Says David Reirden, president of Gander Mountain's retail operations: "The objective we started out with was to make the avid hunter, fisherman, or camper comfortable immediately upon entering the store." The first thing the customers see, he notes, is a waterfall flowing over rocks, and "the store has an open-beamed ceiling painted blue, giving customers the feeling of the outdoors." Artificial trees surround the waterfall; bird- and animal-hunting trophies are displayed throughout the store; and a track around the apparel area has been given a wooded look with green edging that suggests grass.

On a larger scale, Carpenter's company designed the Incredible Universe stores, which represent a new approach to retailing for the Tandy Corp., known for decades for its Radio Shack stores. The Incredible Universe consumer electronics superstores provide "entertainment and excitement," Carpenter says.

"Customers," he notes, "can participate in product demonstrations, meet celebrities, experience today's technology in multimedia rooms, grab a bite to eat in the food court, or sing along in the karaoke studio. The store is a living, breathing, nonstop event."

While increasingly popular as a part of the growing entertainment factor in retailing, technology also continues to have a major impact on basic areas of retailing, changing the ways things have traditionally been done.

George Kutsunis, owner of Leading Lady, a women's-apparel chain in Geneseo, Ill., recalls that when he went into business 30 years ago, "I operated with what retailers call the little black book." Inventory would be marked off by hand as it went out of the store, and buying decisions were made accordingly.

He moved part way into the high-tech era with a computer that tracked inventory by classification: women's blouses, sweaters, skirts, and so forth. One person entered the codes into a computer from the sales tickets. As sales increased, Kutsunis found that his inventory reports were weeks behind. "I realized I would have to hire two more people just to post the sales tickets," he says. "That's when I faced the fact that I *had* to invest in a better computer software system." It cost him about $150,000 to make the upgrade, but "the payback was there because we had built up our volume enough that we could afford to do it," he says.

But technology continues to evolve. Robert Kahn, a veteran retailer who is now a management consultant and editor of *Retail Trends*, notes there are systems in which retailers' checkout terminals are linked to manufacturers' computers, which are programmed to order production of goods at specified inventory levels. The manufacturer ships the goods with retailers' price tags attached. The shipments might go to a central distribution point where coding on the cartons specifies the store destination, and computerized handling systems move the shipments from the receiving area to trucks at loading bays. At individual stores or central receiving points, scanners identify each carton, the information goes into financial-department computers, and payment is authorized electronically.

"Purchase orders are disappearing," Kahn says, adding that although the most elaborate computerized distribution systems are beyond the reach of most small businesses, there is a good deal of affordable equipment available, and small firms should be taking advantage of it.

Kahn cites a survey by the Arthur Andersen accounting and consulting company showing that 54 percent of the retailers who took part said they do not reorder merchandise until they are out of stock. "It's not a matter of buying power," he says. "It's the system."

Kahn says that today's customers typically have little time to shop and expect a store to have the products they want. Otherwise, he says "they will go to another store. Out-of-stock merchandise remains a constant problem in retailing, and stores that allow it to happen are losing customers. The manual inventory count at the end of every week is no longer acceptable."

Among those seen as major stumbling blocks to success were failure to identify customer needs and expectations, poor merchandising, sloppy inventory controls, and a lack of long-term planning.

Another increasingly important aspect of retail technology comes under the general heading of electronic shopping, particularly those television channels and programs that offer merchandise that viewers can order by calling an 800 telephone number. Once ridiculed as purveyors of garish jewelry, these programs have grown in sophistication and reach, and several major mainstream retailers are turning to that format.

A less extensive yet fast-growing component of electronic shopping is online shopping, in which customers at home use computers to order products. The CompuServe on-line computer service, for example, offers its subscribers access to an Electronic Mall, which now has 125 stores, including JCPenney, Hammacher Schlemmer, Lands' End, and the Shopper's Advantage membership club.

The extent to which electronic shopping will compete with in-store retailers is a subject being debated but one that every retailer must monitor. Watts Wacker, managing partner with Yankelovich Partners of Norfolk, Conn., a consumer trends research firm, forecasts that 40 percent of all U.S. households will have made at least one purchase through a television shopping program or via computer by 1997.

Friedman of *Retail Systems Alert* says: "The Internet will be a platform upon which devices will be built by telephone companies and cable companies in conjunction with retailers. It is very expensive to put products on line, so only high-margin products will be offered, such as apparel, prescription drugs, pet supplies, furniture, and home goods." The Internet is a global online service providing a vast range of information and communications opportunities to computer users.

DesignForum's Carpenter says, however, that electronic shopping will be much less of a factor in retailing than many people expect. The reason, he says, is that retail customers are creatures of habit for whom store shopping is second-nature. They seek, he says, instant gratification when they want to make a purchase, most lack the technological sophistication required for online shopping, and they enjoy the social aspects of visiting malls and stores.

Bonnie Hawley, owner of Hawley's Florist, in downtown Rutland, Vt., says her customers seek social interaction along with the fresh flowers they

SURVIVAL TACTICS

A survey by the Illinois Retail Merchants Association showed that one in five small stores is losing money. And one in four reported pretax income of less than $10,000 in 1992. Moreover, retailers suffering losses were not limited to the smaller stores. Of those recording losses in 1992 (most recent data available), half had net sales of more than $1 million.

The study was part of a lengthy research project conducted by the association in collaboration with the Arthur Andersen accounting and consulting firm. Backed by a grant from the state of Illinois, the study reviewed the current performance of 1,500 retailers and suggested ways for them to improve.

The study identified several reasons why so many small retailers are having so much trouble. Among those seen as major stumbling blocks to success were failure to identify customer needs and expectations, poor merchandising, sloppy inventory controls, and a lack of long-term planning.

Results of the study project were published by the association this year as a 322-page book, *Small Store Survival*. The National Retail Federation calls it one of the most useful sources of survival strategies for small-store independent retailers nationwide.

Small Store Survival lists six best practices for small-store retailers:

- Develop a continuous process to determine what your customers want, and then meet or exceed those expectations at every turn.
- Identify and pursue a distinct customer market. Then offer it unique merchandise or value-added services.
- Design every aspect of store operations to enhance the shopping experience. This includes scheduling employees' hours to maximize productivity and reevaluating the store layout to make sure it maximizes customers' buying opportunities.
- Establish a vision and culture for the store, plan where the company must go, then take the steps needed to get there.
- Be prepared to compete more fiercely than ever for quality employees. Then make empowering, educating, and retaining them a top priority.
- Establish budget controls and cost-containment measures to manage frugally what can be measured, and negotiate more aggressively for favorable terms from vendors and suppliers.

One of the study's participants was George Kutsunis, president of G.W.K. Enterprises, Inc. He operates six women's apparel stores in Illinois and Iowa. He uses the study's findings as a guide for ongoing planning, he says, and his firm enjoys what he calls moderate growth and profitability.

Continued—

Survival Tactics (continued)

Kutsunis credits that growth to a willingness to take steps such as moving to larger locations and investing in a point-of-sale computer system. "The POS enabled us to quickly drop vendors who aren't performing, and to reorder those styles that are doing well," he says.

Using the quick turnaround provided by POS, Kutsunis gives his buyers added ammunition to use on their buying trips and dealings with vendors. "Before [the POS installation] my buyers were being blindsided because they didn't have accurate data," he says.

"The trouble with a lot of small merchants is that they are unwilling to reinvest their profits or their capital into their business to buy into the technology, new fixturing, remodeling their stores, improving their lighting or carpeting," says Kutsunis.

Customers form opinions quickly about a store's level of success by its appearance and layout. He advises retailers to review such things as how merchandise is displayed and how easily customers can reach it.

What is the future for small-store retailers? "It is not getting any easier," says Kutsunis. "It's tough out there, but it's like anything else. The big guys don't get all the business. No one gets all the business."

With that in mind, Kutsunis plans to grow cautiously. But he *does* intend to grow: Two more stores are in the works.

buy when they come into her store. "We get a large lunchtime crowd, and they like the fact that we carry a diverse selection," says Hawley, "and they like to visit when they come in."

Hawley's Florist was designated a 1994 Blue Chip Enterprise Initiative company by the program's co-sponsors, Connecticut Mutual Life Insurance Co., the U.S. Chamber of Commerce, and *Nation's Business.*

"We struggled to bring the business from a negative percentage sales growth in 1991 and 1992 to 9.5 percent growth in sales last year," says Hawley.

She accomplished that by broadening her selection of flowers, affiliating with FTD (an international delivery network used by florists), and computerizing her customer data base for direct-mail advertising. Hawley says she thinks retailing is headed toward more computerization, but "people will always want the experience of walking into a flower shop, smelling the smells, seeing the colors, and making a purchase."

While the debate over high-tech retailing continues and competition between in-store and in-home selling grows, there is one trend that is looking not to future technology but to the past. With most prime suburban locations for shopping mall already developed, the concept of downtown as a retail center is being revived.

The International Council of Shopping Centers, a New York-based trade group, reports that mall developers are looking to downtown areas, warehouse districts, and inner cities for building sites.

Mark Schoifet, the council's director of communications, says: "After World War II, the department stores left the downtown area to follow their customers out to the suburbs. So they abandoned the downtown for the suburban sites. Now we see them coming back downtown and building new stores."

That current trend is an outgrowth of the building of big-city retail complexes such as New York's South Street Seaport and Boston's Quincy Market, which includes historic Faneuil Hall. Both complexes are projects of the Rouse Co., headquartered in Columbia, Md. Many of these intown shopping complexes are tied to themes, such as the sailing-ship museum environment of the South Street Seaport, or a more contemporary approach as in The Lab, a shopping mall in a former Los Angeles factory and warehouse. Its target market consists of consumers in their 20s, and it feature only small retailers whose products appeal to that market.

On the other end of the spectrum is City Walk, a sanitized, two-block indoor version of a city street. Located in Los Angeles, it houses a wide range of stores aimed at appealing to an upscale suburban clientele.

Warehouse Row, in downtown Chattanooga, Tenn., will have 300,000 square feet of renovated space in what was once an area of railroad warehouses. The mixed-use center—both retail and nonretail business tenants—opened in 1989. Earlier this year, Warehouse Row added 26,000 square feet by opening a half-dozen retail outlets in the adjacent Freight Depot, a historic building. The enlarged center now has 35 small retailers.

In Sioux Falls, S.D., 100 small-store retailers joined with banks and professional firms to form the Main Street Association, a nonprofit organization dedicated to the revitalization of the downtown retail center. "If a city is your home, then the downtown is the living room," says Sue Scott, owner of Scotts, Ltd., a women's apparel store in downtown Sioux Falls.

Scott decided to locate downtown 10 years ago despite the influx of regional malls around Sioux Falls. "We could see the downtown coming back, even then," she says.

She credits the Main Street Association with providing a focus for the downtown retailers. There are regularly scheduled events such as outdoor festivals, sporting activities, and community gatherings, all aimed at attracting people who do not usually venture downtown. "While people are here, enjoying the events, they visit our stores," says Scott. "The association has helped broaden our customer base."

Friedman says that regardless of the technology or location of retail operations, the basic competitive factor will be the retailer's ability to recruit, train, and retain qualified employees.

One notable aspect of the discussion about how retailers can best prepare for the new century is the extent to which those concerns about employee motivation are merging into the issue of customer service.

Texas professor Peterson writes in *The Future of Retailing* that "the organization's structure must be redesigned to empower front-line employees, focus on the ultimate consumer, and celebrate the sales force. It must reinforce that people really are human, have strong needs for self-esteem, need a sense of accomplishment, and have a sense of achievement that can be enhanced through motivation and achievement."

He adds that "retail leaders in the year 2000 will have learned to respect the lifetime value of both employees and customers. Without such a philosophy, everything else will be for naught."

> The organization's structure must be redesigned to empower front-line employees, focus on the ultimate consumer, and celebrate the sales force.

Training those employees to provide high-quality customer service is the key to achieving those goals. Colorado hardware-store owner Don Connell says that his employees are the cornerstone of his success, and he puts strong emphasis on training. Ace Hardware, a national chain of neighborhood hardware stores, provides him with videotapes on training in the basics of hardware-store retailing, he notes, but "we supplement that with weekly sessions in each department that concentrate on specific repairs." Sales assistants learn basic plumbing, carpentry, and other skills so they can deal with questions and problems customers bring to the store.

In addition to critical strategies such as training employees to meet customer needs, retailers will be pursuing many other approaches in their drive to remain competitive in the face of the strong challenges they face in this turn-of-the-century era.

Although some of those strategies may be beyond the resources of smaller companies, there may be aspects that they can adapt. Consumer-trends expert Wacker identifies and describes the first two of the following three imaginative approaches to Retailing 2000, and publisher Friedman explains the third:

Stores without Inventory. A customer who goes to buy a bicycle in Japan today from Panasonic enters a store that has no bicycles on display. Instead of sitting on bikes and trying them out, the person is put on a machine that measures the buyer's maximum leg thrust, and an order is written and sent to a factory that makes the bike.

Wacker cites another example of how manufacturing is becoming a service business that creates the inventory-less store: A customer will be able to call Barnes & Noble, name a desired book, describe the quality of their vision, tell where the book will be read, and provide a description of the work he or she does. The store will then send the customer relevant sections of the particular book tailored for the place and time the customer intends to read the material and printed in an appropriate type size.

Such trends are designed to cater to the highly individualized preferences of those in the baby-boom generation.

Stores without Employees. Wacker sees a future in which every block will have a kiosk made up of booths containing the 10 best-selling items on that block. A card key will activate your order for milk, bread, coffee, bath tissue, etc., and charge the purchase to your account.

The kiosk in a neighborhood with a large number of young families, for example, would hold diapers, baby formula, and children's vitamins.

Co-location Retailing.   In this approach, Friedman explains, retail shops will seek locations near compatible businesses, with each helping the other to draw customers. For example, a pizza shop might try to locate next to a video-rental outlet.

More and more such unions will occur between retailers whose products and services are related from the consumer's point of view. Customers want to spend as little time shopping as possible, but they also want to buy complementary products conveniently.

The many elements of today's retail challenges have been consolidated into a formula developed by Daniel M. Bergin, author of "Road Space Map to Successful Retailing in the 90's," an article published in the June 1990 magazine *Drug Topics*. To compete successfully in the 1990s and beyond, he says, a retailer must:

- Invest in technology.
- Find (and exploit) a niche.
- Prize its people.
- Make shopping fun.
- Know its customers.
- Be convenient.
- Know its product offering.
- Widen its vision.

Commenting on those recommendations, retailing authority Peterson says: "Although following Bergin's advice will not guarantee success, not following it will ensure failure. The key to retailing success is constantly to anticipate the future, then to prepare for it by leveraging the firm's distinctive competency."

The Link Between Measurement and Compensation at AT&T Universal Card Services

Robert Davis, Susan Rosegrant, and Michael Watkins

This article profiles the problems and successes AT&T Universal Card Services (UCS) has experienced since its inception, especially with regard to compensating employees in accordance with measures of service to customers. It has been a struggle, but one well worth taking on. UCS earned a Baldrige Award in its third year of business.

When AT&T Universal Card Services (UCS) broke into the highly competitive bank credit card industry in 1990, the company committed itself to delighting customers with its service. To deliver this service and to drive continuous improvement in all operations, UCS designed a multifaceted measurement and compensation system that has become a model of excellence for other service firms.

UCS, a wholly owned subsidiary of AT&T, issues and services VISA and MasterCard credit card accounts. Since its formation, UCS has become the second largest credit card issuer in the United States, servicing 13.6 million accounts and employing more than 3,000 people. In 1992, UCS became the youngest company—and one of just three service firms ever—to win the Malcolm Baldrige National Quality Award. (For more details on why the company won the Baldrige Award, see the sidebar "The Pillars of Quality at Universal Card Services.")

An important element of UCS's quality approach is its world-class measurement and compensation system. While it is not unusual for credit card issuers to monitor aspects of customer service, UCS' system goes beyond the industry norm. The system was designed to locate and address problem processes, assess how well customers are served, and recognize exceptional performance. By linking collective compensation to performance measurement, the company created a culture that continually and cooperatively focuses on

An important element of UCS's quality approach is its world-class measurement and compensation system.

THE PILLARS OF QUALITY AT UNIVERSAL CARD SERVICES

In contrast to many established companies that have struggled to super-impose quality on an existing corporate culture, AT&T Universal Card Services (UCS) had the luxury of establishing quality as an overarching goal from the start. In fact, quality was less a goal than an obsession. UCS's quality system was founded on seven core values: customer delight, continuous improvement, sense of urgency, commitment, trust and integrity, mutual respect, and teamwork. UCS's customer service representatives were carefully selected and extensively trained to provide superior customer service.

To empower employees, the company supports substantial suggestion and recognition systems, sponsoring five companywide recognition programs and more than 40 departmental awards. UCS also provides generous fringe benefits, including on-site fitness and wellness programs and extensive support for continuing education. Employees are involved in decision making from the beginning, sitting side by side with senior managers on teams and deciding issues ranging from what awards the company should bestow to how computer screens should be designed for maximum efficiency.

The programs and activities have paid off. According to annual employee surveys, employees rate UCS significantly higher in such categories as job satisfaction, management leadership, and communication than the average of other high-performing companies.

achieving excellence. This system has been so effective that hundreds of companies have visited UCS to study it since the company won the Baldrige Award.

Concentrating on Continuous Improvement

Despite these successes, UCS is still looking for the best way to measure and compensate its employees. Any measurement system is subject to tensions that must be continually and carefully managed.[1,2] In the case of UCS, the conflicting priorities that must be balanced include:

- Rigor in measurement vs. management of employees' stress levels
- Sensitivity to fluctuations in performance vs. fairness in compensation
- Pursuit of continual improvement vs. stability in employee compensation
- Achievement of daily goals vs. achievement of long-term strategic objectives
- Collective involvement of employees vs. a clear focus on meeting customer needs

- Internal focus on processes vs. external focus on customer satisfaction

The effort that UCS continues to devote to improving its measurement and compensation system demonstrates both the importance and the difficulty of implementing the kinds of innovative and responsive systems that today's learning organizations are often glibly advised to create.

UCS's Measurement and Compensation System

The company's measurement system has two components: external customer satisfaction research and internal process performance measurement. To assess how well it serves its cardholders, UCS uses two sets of external surveys:

1. *UCS-generated customer satisfier survey.* This survey asks UCS's and its competitors' customers to compare organizational performance on a specified set of key customer satisfiers, including price and customer service. An outside market research firm interviews a random sample of 400 competitors' customers and 200 UCS cardmembers monthly.
2. *Customer contact surveys.* Each month, an internal survey team randomly polls more than 5,000 customers who have contacted the company for any of a variety of reasons. The survey team administers up to 15 different contact surveys.

From the information gleaned from the surveys and other sources, UCS assembled a list of more than 100 internal and supplier process measures that critically influence performance. The original list of measures stressed measuring processes that directly influence customers, such as how soon customers receive their credit cards after applying. As UCS gained experience with process measurement, the list expanded to include measures of all key service, production, and support processes, many of which are invisible to customers but, nonetheless, influence them. The expanded measurement system affects all functional groups in the organization, including frontline customer service groups, human resources, accounting, information systems functions, and key external suppliers. (For a list of UCS and supplier processes, see Table 1.)

Measuring Quality Daily

UCS management agrees that the best way to drive quality service and continuous improvement is to measure performance on the key processes daily. Not only does UCS measure process performance, it sets specific standards for each process measure and rewards every employee in the company daily when those standards are met.

To emphasize the importance of quality, UCS links everyone's compensation to overall organizational performance. The conventional wisdom in measurement systems design is that individual or group compensation should be linked to achievement on a compact set of measures that can be directly influenced by the target individual or group. Rejecting that orthodoxy, UCS links everyone's daily bonus to achieving specified standards for the entire list of measures. If the entire company achieves quality standards on 96% of

Table 1. **Key Universal Card Services (UCS) and Supplier Processes**

Key process	Process owner (UCS or supplier)
Business processes	
Strategic and business planning	UCS
Total quality management	UCS
Support services processes	
Collections	UCS
Management of key constituencies	UCS
Customer acquisition management	UCS
Financial management	UCS
Human resource management	UCS
Information and technology management	UCS
Product and service production and delivery processes	
Application processing	UCS/supplier
Authorizations management	Supplier
Billing and statement processing	UCS
Credit card production	UCS
Credit screening	Supplier
Customer acquisition process management (prospective customer list development and management)	Supplier
Customer inquiry management	UCS
Payment processing	UCS
Relationship management (service, communications, and brand management; programs; and promotions)	UCS
Transaction processing	Supplier

Source: Universal Card Services

the measures on a particular day, all nonmanagerial employees "earn quality" for the day. For managers to earn quality, it is also necessary for UCS suppliers to meet standards on key supplier-controlled processes. The measurement-system bonuses represent up to 12% of base salary for nonmanagers and 8% to 12% of base salary for managers.

The logic of this design is obvious: If everyone's bonus depends on everyone's performance, no one group wants to be responsible for sinking it. Moreover, it is in everyone's economic interest to help the weaker performers get better: Collective compensation elicits collective effort. Support services groups, which often escape the discipline imposed on frontline production and service groups, are forced to provide internal customers—in this case,

If everyone's bonus depends on everyone's performance, no one group wants to be responsible for sinking it.

DELIVERING QUALITY CUSTOMER SERVICE AT UNIVERSAL CARD SERVICES

Seventeen process measures are tracked in the general customer service area at Universal Card Services (UCS). The call monitoring system tracks the average speed of answer, number of abandoned calls, number of calls handled by each employee, and average call length. Processing times for all forms of written correspondence with customers are similarly tracked. Customer service representatives are directly monitored by a number of people inside and outside the customer service area. Specially trained monitors listen to 100 calls per day and rate customer service representatives on accuracy, efficiency, and professionalism. Team leaders listen to 10 calls per month for each of the 20 employees in their groups, using the observations to coach and develop representatives. All UCS managers, regardless of their function, are encouraged to monitor at least two hours of calls a month to stay in touch with customers and services. Key groups, such as quality, hold regular monthly listening sessions, followed by discussions, to analyze the quality of employee interactions with customers. Written correspondence undergoes a similar review, with groups of quality monitors evaluating customer correspondence for accuracy and courtesy.

customer-contact employees—with the same level of service that customer-contact employees provide to external customers. Finally, the entire management group becomes strongly interested in supplier performance and has incentives to help improve supplier quality.

At the same time, daily perfection is not expected. Challenging, but achievable, standards are set for each measure (typically, 96% to 100%), and only 96% of these standards must be met on a given day for employees to receive the bonus. At first, this might seem to undermine the intent of the system, which is to make everyone responsible for quality daily. But in practice, it doesn't. It builds a cushion into the system for unavoidable performance lapses and permits groups to have bad days without dragging everyone down. Daily performance reviews and communication of results throughout the corporation ensure that no group is allowed to consistently fail to meet performance expectations.

Organizational Prerequisites

The logic of UCS's measurement and compensation system is straightforward: collective reward for collective performance. There are, however, a number of organizational prerequisites for making such a system work. In particular, a UCS-style measurement and compensation system can only function if everyone has access to complete and accurate information about performance outcomes and if weak performers have the necessary knowledge and resources to rapidly improve their results. At UCS, an extensive system of data collection, analysis, communication, and problem solving provides the necessary underpinning for the measurement and compensation system.

To effectively exert collective pressure to improve, substandard performance must be clearly identified and rapidly communicated to the entire staff. In a system involving more than 100 internal process measures, this means that large volumes of performance information must be collected, analyzed, and disseminated daily. At UCS, significant resources are devoted to collecting and processing this information. In the telephone customer-inquiry area, for example, an automated call-monitoring system collects data on the time required to answer customer calls, the number of customers who abandon calls, and the duration of calls. Customer service representatives get daily printouts that summarize their performance. As part of gathering daily measures, specially trained peer monitors listen to a sample of 100 customer calls per day. The monitors—called quality associates—rate customer service representatives on accuracy, efficiency, and professionalism, using specific criteria that UCS developed for identifying and quantifying the number of negative influences on customers. (For more details, see the sidebar "Delivering Quality Customer Service at Universal Card Services.")

Daily and/or monthly performance results are communicated through video monitors and are posted in office areas and the employee cafeteria. Each morning, the head of operations meets with senior managers to discuss the latest results, identify possible problems, and propose solutions. Employees can access a summary of this meeting via telephone or electronic mail. Performance measures also figure prominently in monthly business meetings, internal Baldrige Award assessments, and other process improvement meetings.

Dealing with Substandard Performance

More than data collection, analysis and dissemination of results are needed to make the UCS measurement and compensation system work. Process owners—the groups responsible for individual process measures—must also take actions that lead to rapid improvements in substandard performance. Without them, collective pressure to improve performance would have no influence, other than demoralizing the low-performing groups. UCS uses a broad array of problem-solving teams and tools that provide the infrastructure for rapid problem identification, diagnosis, and elimination.

In addition, process owners must be capable of sustained periods of high performance for the compensation system to work. Otherwise, meeting standards on 96% of internal processes daily would rarely occur, and the motivational influence of the system would be minimal.

The company's combination of data collection and analysis, communication of results, and problem-solving capabilities forms the basis of a learning organization. UCS's quality system is the result of careful design of an interlocking set of values, capabilities, goals, and incentives. Such systems require

A UCS-style measurement and compensation system can only function if everyone has access to complete and accurate information about performance outcomes.

constant attention and fine-tuning. They are delicate mechanisms that are difficult to create and sustain.

Managing Key Tensions

As UCS gained experience with the measurement and compensation system, the following tensions became apparent.

Rigor in Measurement Vs. Management of Employees' Stress Levels

Performance monitoring for continuous improvement can lead to employee stress. Despite the best efforts to create a positive work environment, stresses inevitably arise from working for a 24-hour customer service operation. Customer service representatives, organized into teams of about 20, spend hours on the phone performing a largely repetitive task. In addition, UCS's culture of continuous improvement imposes its own pressures. For example, managers coach representatives to use improved support technology to shorten the average length of a call, as long as it does not adversely affect quality.

Remote monitoring of employee performance can also generate stress. Early in UCS's history, negative feedback from call monitoring was passed on to team leaders who discussed it individually with the representatives and filed it for use in performance reviews. In addition, customer contact survey results, including verbatim remarks from cardholders, were given to managers in the customer relationships department, who could identify which representative handled a particular call. The combination of high corporate expectations and multiple forms of monitoring and feedback created considerable pressure on representatives to perform well under intense scrutiny.

In response to employee concerns, UCS softened the performance monitoring and feedback systems. UCS made it clear that supervisors and managers were to treat representatives with respect and to view mistakes as opportunities for improvement. For example, if a representative was overheard giving a customer inaccurate information, the team leader was instructed not to rebuke the representative, but to explain the error and, if necessary, provide additional training. Team leaders were trained to give feedback and use monitoring results as a development tool rather than as a club. An experiment began in which representatives critiqued each other rather than relying entirely on team leaders and external monitors. The daily customer relationships quality meeting, which had served as a mistake-reporting session, was transformed into a forum for discussion and learning. Representatives were invited to join the meetings, and the peer monitor position became a rotational position for representatives.

The nature of feedback also changed: Negative reports were no longer placed in employees' files, and team leaders began to publicly compliment employees who provided excellent customer service. The result was significant buy-in from the representatives—so much so that an experiment in withholding individual feedback from daily monitoring was scrapped at the representatives' request.

> UCS made it clear that supervisors and managers were to treat representatives with respect and to view mistakes as opportunities for improvement.

Sensitivity to Fluctuations in Performance Vs. Fairness in Compensation

The measurement system was developed to provide management with responsive feedback on process performance. At the same time, the measurement system was linked to monetary rewards for employees; thus, it had to be stable and reliable. In practice, it has been difficult to achieve both goals. The integrity of the compensation system could easily be undermined by employee doubts about the validity of the performance measures and the sampling process. Suppose, for example, employees believed that many daily changes in the performance measures were due to random variation rather than systematic trends in customer satisfaction. If this resulted in daily variation in compensation, employees' confidence in the system's fairness would be undermined. Actions taken to change employees' work methods, based on daily fluctuations in the measures, would have a similar effect.

Employee confidence could also be undermined by doubts about the validity of sampling procedures. It is not difficult to measure quantitative attributes, such as the average length of a call; it is, however, more difficult to measure qualitative attributes, such as courtesy and accuracy.

UCS attempts to manage this tension by creating buffers between the performance-measurement, problem-solving, and compensation systems. Decisions concerning changes in methods and procedures are made by cross-functional problem-solving teams that track the daily measures. These teams are adept at using their experience and diagnostic skills to assess whether daily fluctuations are due to random variation or adverse trends. A one-day dip in performance measures will not trigger action unless there is independent information that a major process change (e.g., introduction of a new product) has occurred—and then only on the basis of in-depth analysis.

A second type of buffer is built into the compensation system. The organization gets credit for a quality day if standards are met on 96% of the performance measures. This means that standards might be missed on up to 4% of the measures on a given day without negatively affecting employee compensation. In addition, a typical standard for individual process performance might be 97% acceptable calls. This means that 3% of the sample of monitored calls can be unsatisfactory without endangering compensation. As a result, the influence on compensation of daily fluctuations in the more than 100 measures tends to get smoothed out. Individual process owners can have bad days or experience random fluctuations without pulling everyone down.

Concerns about sampling-procedure validity are addressed in two ways. First, the company carefully develops statistically valid sampling plans that ensure expected daily measurement fluctuations do not result in adverse fluctuations in compensation. Much care is also taken in developing detailed scoring templates to guide peer monitors in evaluating qualitative attributes such as courtesy and accuracy. In addition, quality monitors receive regular training aimed at harmonizing group assessments.

UCS continues to refine its existing system while experimenting with other approaches, such as statistical process control (SPC). In the telephone area, UCS uses SPC to chart measures, such as the number of calls handled.

The organization is, however, struggling to apply SPC to qualitative measures. Other difficulties in applying SPC arise because of the explicit link between measurement and compensation. If SPC were adopted, there would have to be significant changes in the way the organization assesses whether it achieved a quality day. Although it seems possible to develop a system that compensates employees when processes stay in control and withholds rewards when processes go out of control, there are considerable practical difficulties in linking performance to incentives when measures are statistical.

Pursuit of Continual Improvement Vs. Stability in Employee Compensation

The strategy of continuous improvement has sometimes run up against employees' and management's desire for stable compensation. This tension is illustrated in UCS's experience in raising the minimum performance standards.

By late 1991, financial analysts had declared UCS a major success for AT&T. Internally, employees were meeting or exceeding standards consistently, achieving at least 25 quality days per month. (See Figure 1 for a summary of employee and management performance.) Despite this stellar performance, the business team–the UCS team responsible for setting the standards and measures—thought it was time to shake things up. The business team raised the minimum performance standards on many performance indicators in early 1992. The move created a triple challenge:

- Standards were raised on 47 indicators in 1992.
- Standards had to be met on a higher percentage of the measures to earn a quality day.
- A number of the indicators were retired and replaced with new measures.

While 15 indicators had been dropped and 26 added in 1991, the plan for 1992 called for the retirement of 48 indicators (many of which were the most consistently achieved) and the addition of 46 new measures. (See Figure 2 for details on changes in the measurement system.) This meant that close to half of the daily performance measures by which employees judged themselves (and were judged) were different.

The result of the changes was immediate. Employees earned only 13 quality days in January 1992 and 16 in the following month. The abrupt performance decline took management by surprise. Employees were concerned about the influence of the changes on compensation. Since UCS was on the verge of logging its first profit, some employees suggested that management had raised the minimum standards as a cost-cutting measure to avoid paying compensation.

In response to these concerns, the business team developed a transitional plan; it was a special incentive program that allowed employees and managers to earn triple bonuses for quality days above 20. For example, if UCS earned 22 quality days in a month, it was credited with 26: two quality days (above

Employee quality days and bonus

Quarter	Number of quality days as percent of total	Bonus as percent of salary
1990-4th quarter	76.1%	6.4%
1991-1st quarter	87.8%	11.4%
1991-2nd quarter	92.3%	9.9%
1991-3rd quarter	96.7%	12.0%
1991-4th quarter	95.7%	11.6%
1992-1st quarter	60%	10.6%
1992-2nd quarter	75.8%	7.5%
1992-3rd quarter	76.1%	7.9%
1992-4th quarter	95.7%	10.8%
1993-1st quarter	84.4%	9.4%

Management quality days and bonus

Quarter	Number of quality days as percent of total	Bonus as percent of salary
1991	87.9%	5.6%
1991	66.1%	4.7%
1993-1st quarter	76.7%	5.6%

Source: Universal Card Services

Figure 1. **Quality days: performance and bonuses.**

20) multiplied by three. The incentive program was successful, but the organizational upset caused by raising the performance standards prompted a closer look at how standards should be raised and which indicators should be added and deleted. In particular, management re-evaluated the process for making changes in the measurement system, opting for fewer, smaller changes, more consultation with employees, longer lead times for communication and preparation, and stricter criteria for determining when standards should be raised and indicators deleted.

Despite these improvements, sustaining increases in performance while maintaining sensitivity to concerns about compensation remains a difficult

UCS learned that a measurement system based on compensation risks becoming an entitlement, which is inconsistent with the basic aim of continuous improvement.

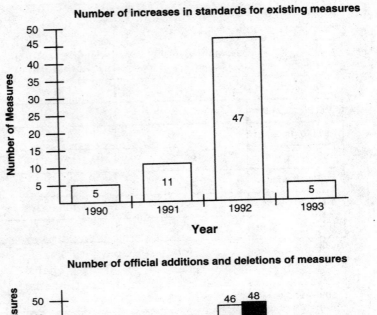

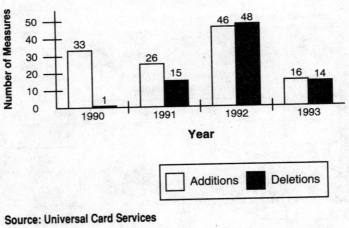

Source: Universal Card Services

Figure 2.   **Changes in standards and measures.**

balancing act. UCS learned that a measurement system based on compensation risks becoming an entitlement, which is inconsistent with the basic aim of continuous improvement. As noted in an internal UCS report on the measurement system: "Danger lies when the primary reason for a measurement system is to adapt to the compensation program rather than to improve the performance of a team or process." Nevertheless, UCS continues to believe that the benefits of linking compensation to performance are worth the costs.

Achievement of Daily Goals Vs. Achievement of Long-Term Strategic Objectives

UCS' system produces a wealth of data on organizational performance daily. Efforts to track and act on these data, combined with the company's cultural emphasis on sense of urgency, could easily lead to a short-term emphasis and a loss of focus on long-term strategic goals.

Consider, for example, the effect of an unexpectedly successful marketing promotion for a new credit card product that leaves an understaffed customer service department unable to keep up with the rush of calls. Although the surge of new business is good for the company, the employees are, through no fault of their own, doubly punished: first, by having to frantically field additional calls, and second, by missing their performance indicators and losing compensation.

UCS tries to avoid making decisions that place employees in such difficult positions. Generally, UCS attempts to balance a short-term, rigorous focus on meeting standards with a long-term emphasis on achieving key strategic objectives, such as the successful introduction of new products. Progress in obtaining a better balance has come through creating comprehensive new product development and strategic planning processes that institutionalize extensive and early consultation with frontline customer service and quality personnel.

Collective Involvement of Employees Vs. a Clear Focus on Meeting Customer Needs

At the core of the UCS measurement system is the principle of collective responsibility for collective performance. UCS is struggling, however, to strike an appropriate balance between supporting collective involvement internally and promoting a narrower focus on meeting external customer needs. In the current system, the list of measures includes indicators for payroll accuracy and a host of other support process measures. It is therefore possible for frontline personnel to fail to earn quality days even when they meet performance standards for all processes that directly influence external customers. Similarly, UCS might fail to meet standards for some key customer processes and still earn a quality day.

Some UCS managers have argued that a smaller set of customer-centered measures might more concretely and powerfully express how the company is serving cardholders. The company has considered moving toward a customer-centered approach, such as the one used by fellow Baldrige Award winner Federal Express. Unlike UCS, Federal Express has just 12 processes that it deems critical to serving customers, and it bases its reward system on those 12 processes.[3] In addition, Federal Express states its measures in terms of the absolute number of customers negatively influenced daily, rather than on the percent of transactions that were handled satisfactorily. That is, rather than reporting a 99.2% success rate, daily reporting would stress that 600 customers were not satisfied.

UCS set up a trial customer-centered measurement system parallel with its existing system in early 1993. This trial yielded some promising results, and UCS continues to experiment with and evaluate alternative approaches.

Internal Focus on Processes Vs. External Focus on Customer Satisfaction

The debates on customer-centered measures bring up another question about the ICS measurement and compensation system: Should compensation be based on internal measures of process performance or external measures of customer satisfaction? The debate surrounding this issue became more heated at UCS after the minimum performance standards were raised in 1992. Although internal process quality results fell off dramatically, customer contact surveys indicated only a slight decline in customer satisfaction. More recently, customer feedback indicated that cardholders viewed employees as somewhat less courteous than before, although the peer monitors had not logged such a change.

Unfortunately, UCS has found that it is very difficult to link performance on internal process measures to external measures of customer satisfaction. In part, this is because customers' attitudes about customer service are influenced by a broad array of factors in addition to the actual service they experience when they call UCS. Competitor image and advertising, plus changes in competitors' service quality, combine to shape customer opinion. As a result, it is difficult to credibly link compensation to external measures of customer satisfaction. UCS continues to struggle to find a way to tighten the link between the external and internal measurement systems.

> Should compensation be based on internal measures of process performance or external measures of customer satisfaction?

The Continuous Search for Excellence

Although UCS's measurement and compensation system has proven to be a great success, management is still working to improve it. In particular, management has struggled to deal with the previously described key tensions. These tensions inevitably arise in any system that attempts to link measurement to compensation. Through careful attention to the needs and concerns of employees, UCS is successfully using collective performance-based rewards to pursue organizational excellence.

References

1. Susan Rosegrant, "A Measure of Delight: The Pursuit of Quality at AT&T Universal Card Services," John F. Kennedy School of Government, cases C16-93-1219.0 and C16-93-1220.0, 1993.
2. AT&T Universal Card Services, "Summary of 1992 Application for Malcolm Baldrige National Quality Award," 1992.
3. Rosegrant, "A Measure of Delight: The Pursuit of Quality at AT&T Universal Card Services."

Robert Davis is a vice president and chief of quality at AT&T Universal Card Services in Jacksonville, Florida.
Susan Rosegrant is a case writer at the John F. Kennedy School of Government at Harvard University in Cambridge, Massachusetts.
Michael Watkins is an assistant professor at the John F. Kennedy School of Government at Harvard University in Cambridge, Massachusetts.

Engineering Products for Customer Value

Patrick T. Harker and Larry W. Hunter

Banks are service businesses. In this article, the authors, professors at the Wharton School, describe the results of a detailed survey they conducted of how well banks are serving the needs of their customers. What they found is that banks do a good job of banking functions, but they have a way to go to understand and meet the service needs of customers. Being close to customers is just as vital for banks as for any other service business. Think about these results in terms of service businesses you might be involved with.

In recent years many companies adopted Total Quality Management (TQM) programs and queued up to qualify for Malcolm Baldridge awards. Banks and other financial-service providers have been among the most enthusiastic supporters of the TQM movement.

Despite the frenzy of quality initiatives, however, is the banking industry more quality-oriented today? Do customers perceive a difference?

Research sponsored by the Wharton Financial Institutions Center suggests that using both technology and human resources effectively can institutionalize quality and create value for customers and for the bank.

Wharton's Bank-Productivity Study

Wharton's research into bank productivity has five parts: interviews with banking-industry leaders (completed); pilot study of seven high-performing retail banks (completed); large-scale survey of top 300 American banks (in progress; target for results is summer 1995); retail distribution project/phase II, non-bank consumer financial-services firms (targeted to begin winter 1995–96); and consumer perspectives (1996).

During the first phases of Wharton's bank-productivity studies, a seven-member Wharton research team—three faculty members and four Ph.D. students—spent 18 months examining how commercial banks create value in retail-delivery systems. The team asked bankers how they: *manage productivity and performance; use technology to support delivery strategies; organize their human-resource practices; and engineer sales-and-service processes to create customer and shareholder value.*

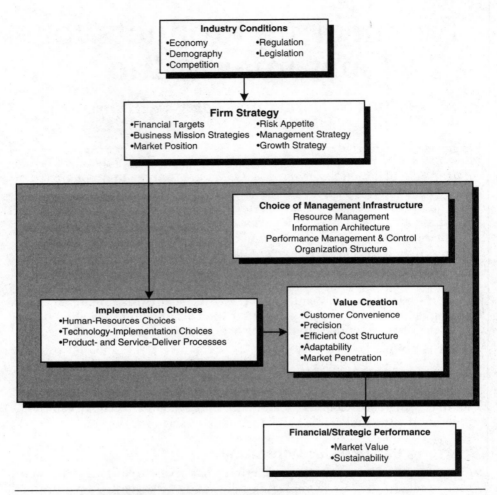

Figure 1. **Implementation choices that create value.**

Our goal was to understand how well banks execute retail-delivery strategies.

Economists use a variety of techniques to explain why some banks are more efficient than others. However, few have identified the silver-bullet strategy that guarantees a consistent 1.5% return on assets, 17% returns on equity, and a 50% expense ratio. Despite economists' sophistication and the in-depth experience of bankers, a major component of performance variances can't be explained by economies of scale or scope, or by silver-bullet strategies.

Instead, implementation expertise—combined with management skill and will—accounts for much of the differences in performance, academics and bankers agree. Academics term thse differences "x-efficiencies."

Wharton set out to examine the causes of these performance differences (see Figure 1).

Delivery Channel	Bank A	Bank B	Bank C	Bank D	Bank E	Bank F	Bank G
Banks	56	56	33	45	40	48	40
Phone Center	168	144	72	not yet completed	66	not yet completed	168
ATM	168	168	168	168	168	168	168
PC from Home	168	not yet completed	168	0	0	0	0
VRU (Voice Recognition Unit)	168	168	168	168	not yet completed	168	168

Figure 2. **Channel availability (average weekly hours)**

Wharton asked retail executives what *value they intended to create for shareholders and customers* with their retail-delivery systems. Five concepts summarize their answers: *convenience in product delivery and access; precision in product functionality (e.g., accuracy, problem resolution); cost-effectiveness in the design of delivery capabilities; adaptability to market and customer needs; and penetration of customer markets and households.*

We then examined the decisions, practices, processes, and policies that banks use that create value in the process of doing business with retail customers. The answers were surprising.

The early results reflect interviews with 12 financial institutions, and a detailed pilot study of seven high-performing retail banks. Banks shared: *standard reports used to manage relationships; types of information available online; how they manage information technology; characteristics of their human resources practices; and overall organization of the retail bank.*

In addition, the research team mapped 17 customer-request processes for five products: home-equity loans, certificates of deposit (CDs), consumer checking, mutual funds, and branch-based small-business loans.

The Value Scorecard

Not surprisingly, many banks scored well in some areas of value creation, while they ignored other factors.

Convenience: To measure convenience, the team examined banks' "open-for-selling" practices, i.e., the hours the bank was available to serve customers. We also identified five distribution channels: visiting the bank in person, contacting a bank phone center, using an automated teller machine (ATM), accessing bank data via a home PC, and accessing via voice recognition units (VRUs) (see Figure 2).

Only one of the seven pilot high-performing banks maximizes the availability of its service channels. Only two others can conduct a broad range of transactions without branches. When we measured *cycle time*—the elapsed

	A	B	C	D	E	F	G	Pilot Average
Cycle Time (min)	6	15	5	6	25	20	5	12
Activity Time (min)	8	15	5	6	25	20	5	12
Customer Time (min)	5	13	5	4	25	6	5	9
# of People	4	2	2	4	1	2	2	3
# of Departments	4	2	1	4	2	2	2	2
# of Approvals	0	0	0	0	0	0	0	0
# of Handoffs	3	1	2	3	1	1	1	2
# of Applications	1	1	1	1	1	1	1	1
# of Screens	4	3	2	3	2	2	4	3

Figure 3. **Process profile (CD redemption)**

time from customer request to product usage—the differences among participants were dramatic (see Figure 3). The involvement required by the customer varied considerably as well.

Cycle times vary among banks for a variety of reasons, both good and bad. Nonetheless, not all of the differences seemed well-reasoned. While banks *say* it is important that customers have easy access to products, not all banks have mastered the customer-oriented approach to convenience.

Precision: Banks assess risk factors—credit, market, and operating—quite precisely and extensively, using loan-loss rates, interest-rate gap analyses, failed transaction counts, and other measurements.

However, they measure the risk of losing a dissatisfied customer only anecdotally, if at all. Only one bank could measure customer complaints fielded through branch networks. We uncovered *no* management reports focused on macro evaluations of error rates and rework requirements. The results sound difficult to believe, yet the facts speak for themselves.

Efficient Cost Structure: In evaluating cost structure, we tried to compare costs by customer segment and delivery channel. Unfortunately, most institutions' performance-measurement systems aren't adequate for this approach. In fact, many institutions have difficulty measuring even total retail business performance at the overall bank level.

Next we compared pricing practices of the seven banks in our pilot study to their markets' rates. We wanted to determine what, if any, relationships exist between a bank's commitment to service quality and its pricing power. We found good news for market leaders. On average, financially high-performing institutions paid less for deposits and charged more for loans than did local competitors.

While banks *say* it is important that customers have easy access to products, not all banks have mastered the customer-oriented approach to convenience. We uncovered *no* management reports focused on macro evaluations of error rates and rework requirements.

Participants made important distinctions between an *efficient* cost structure and the *lowest* cost structure. All agree that costs must be as low as possible. At the same time, however, for most banks the challenge is to arrive at a cost structure that matches the business' value-creation objectives.

Adaptability: We examined banks' ability to change risk tolerances and pricing levels in local markets. Again, the variances were large. A few banks give branch managers the power to make exceptions on CD rates, and to negotiate rates and waive fees on home-equity and small-business loans.

Only those institutions with credit-scoring models believe they change risk-tolerance levels effectively and quickly throughout their networks. However, in local markets, adaptability measures must go beyond pricing. In the next study phase, we will expand our research to evaluate banks' capacity to spot new product or pricing opportunities. We also will report on banks' ability to set new product strategies and to implement them.

Market Penetration: Banks vary considerably in their capacity to measure market and household penetration. While all participants have MCIF (marketing central information file) systems, few have standardized management reports, and fewer still have on-line point-of-sale access to MCIF information. Few banks match resource alternatives to segment goals. Thus, while banks like to *say* they are customer-oriented, few actually measure and report market performance.

Research Scorecard: Based on the pilot results, we give the bank industry a C+ in execution and an A− for good intentions. *Bankers talk the customer game, but their systems and practices are littered with inconsistencies and gaps.* A number of factors cause these gaps. Among them are affordability and earnings' pressures, timing and resource conflicts, and the need to manage a broad range of change factors.

> Based on the pilot results, we give the bank industry a C+ in execution and an A− for good intentions.

Nonetheless, preliminary results suggest the industry faces an important strategic challenge: Can banks manage the degree of change required to remain competitive? And, can they do it while at the same time generating sustainable earnings and restructuring their companies to be able to succeed in the financial-services industry for the next decade?

The answer isn't clear. We believe successful banks will focus on activities that truly create value—value for the bank and for their customers. To do this, banks need to pay more attention to an important area: customer-driven product engineering.

Customer Sales-and-Service Processes

We analyzed 17 customer-request processes and uncovered dramatic differences among pilot institutions. Executives recognize they no longer can save their way to prosperity and shareholder value. Today they look for new ways to sell and manage key businesses. Consequently, re-engineering is in the hearts—and on the lips—of most CEOs.

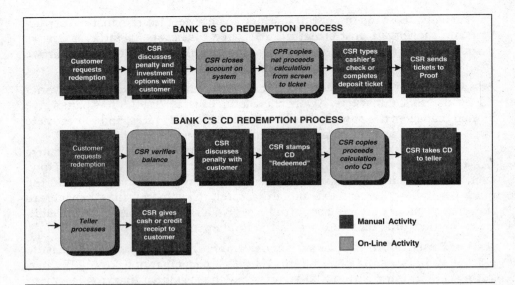

Figure 4. **Customer request process**

Re-engineering often is a code word for cost reduction. But, when applied to banking practices, re-engineering seems to be an oxymoron. Of the 17 product processes we reviewed, few were engineered at the outset. In fact, none of the seven pilot institutions had process maps for the 17 transactions we analyzed.

Engineering is important because the engineering of the product process creates value for customers and shareholders. A simple process we examined was premature redemption of CDs. Figure 3 shows the bank variations in *activity time* (how much staff time is spent doing a task) and the number of hand-offs in processing this simple transaction.

Meanwhile, Figure 4 shows a flowchart of two banks' CD-redemption processes. Reviewing Figure 4, we see that Bank B's sales/service representative drafts the check for the customer. In contrast, virtually all of the other banks handle the transaction similarly to Bank C's process, with the sales rep walking the paperwork over to the teller who then drafts the check.

Which process is better? *Better for whom* is the better question. From *the bank's perspective,* risk controls may be better with Bank C's process. In addition, Bank C avoids having high-priced sales talent completing clerical tasks. However, it probably takes the sales rep just as long to walk the transaction to the teller and wait for the check to be created as it does to type the check himself or herself.

Now let's consider which is more satisfying from the *customer perspective.* We believe most consumers would prefer the Bank-B approach. They would like to have a single person handle the transaction from start to finish.

You'll notice that Bank B's cycle time is longer. However, that's because Bank B built a cross-selling activity into its redemption process. Thus, while

Bank B's process may be longer, it is more satisfying for the customer. And, because of the cross-selling built in, it is more profitable for the bank.

One problem with process maps is that they don't reveal what information-technology (IT) and human-resource practices a bank uses. Both elements are critical in design of product processes. And a bank must tightly coordinate its technology and human resources to maximize benefits for both the customer and bank.

Can we say which IT or human-resource strategies and practices are better? Research will show the link among strategies, practices, and value expectations. For most banks, *best practices* depend on the value outcomes the banks seek, and preferences of the customer markets. Understanding these relationships is the first step in evaluating the costs and benefits of human-resources strategy choices.

Future Prescriptions

We have now finished testing our research methodology in our pilot study of seven high-performing banks, and have moved well into our large-scale survey of America's top 300 banks. Already, more than 115 banks have responded.

Based upon the pilot and survey responses to date, Wharton offers these observations:

Several banks are moving aggressively to align practices, policies, procedures, and information-technology architecture with value-creation outcomes.

Banks must define the value outcomes they seek and then use those outcomes as the templates to assess the management choices and implementation practices the company adopts. Starting with value-creation objectives assures that every decision will work toward achieving desired results.

For example, banks believing local market adaptability and agility are key to meeting national competition give their local market managers the authority and capacity to customize product pricing and delivery to the *specific* needs of their customers. They may use sales teams and high-involvement workplace practices to maximize customer satisfaction at the point of sale.

Alternatively, banks for which low-cost distribution is the driving factor in retail-delivery performance will standardize pricing, operating practices, and human-resource policies to capture greater economies of scale in processing areas, eliminate variation in product sets between markets, and drive for consistent quality.

Build the customer's perspective into product processes.

Some products are more important to one customer segment than to others. Banks committed to segment-driven management practices should extend segment standards to product-process design. Would customers rather have the sales rep or teller draw up the CD redemption check? *Why speculate about it? Instead, ask your customers.* Cultivating customer involvement in process design needn't extend to every product and process at the outset. However, starting with products most important to each customer segment seems to be a logical place to begin.

> For most banks, *best practices* depend on the value outcomes the banks seek, and preferences of the customer markets.

> Would customers rather have the sales rep or teller draw up the CD redemption check? *Why speculate about it? Instead, ask your customers.*

For example, for some high-net-worth segments the first interaction with a new bank is a jumbo mortgage product. Consumer research suggests that these customers want no fee, large-dollar mortgages, minimum documentation, and quick turn-around on decisions. Banks interested in building high-net-worth relationships will ask these segments which of these features (and others) are the most important . . . then engineer their mortgage-origination process accordingly.

Align human-resources practices with value-creation objectives.

Much is said about the benefits of high-involvement workplace practices in manufacturing. But do these practices work in retail banking? Wharton's research team will answer that question when the results of its large-scale survey are analyzed and announced this summer.

We know today, though, that job design and incentive programs for individuals must be consistent with and support the bank's value-creation goals. If they aren't and don't, the reengineering benefits will be diffused. Our field experience indicates that bank employees have a good feel for customer preferences and how bank processes can be streamlined to improve customer service. Accordingly, banks should use employee input as a primary intelligence source in developing re-engineering products.

Manage product processes with classical product life-cycle techniques.

A bank's portfolio of product processes has evolved over many years. Restructuring of the financial-services industry and dramatic improvements in technology and software applications have helped redefine these processes in recent years. Pressures from competition and regulatory agencies also have helped shape processes, as has the legacy of past bank decisions.

In the early days of deregulation, for example, banks learned to fashion "new" deposit and savings products almost monthly. The ability to offer a competitive product rapidly was critical to survival. Not surprisingly, product processes were cobbled together—but with only smoke-and-mirror benefits for customers. Manual back-office processes were the norm, and not the exception.

Telephone bill-paying is yet another example. Early on, bank promoters gave the impression of providing automated paying services—but for most, early "automated" answering services fronted for a large, and mostly manual, clerical back office that cut checks and mailed them.

Today's pace is even faster. Protecting a customer base means adding product capabilities and enhancements quickly. At the same time, most banks also must manage their enormous investments in new operating capabilities and technologies.

We don't recommend that banks throw out their current processes and start again. Instead, we recommend that banks manage product processes as they would any other resource investment. A process should have a life cycle and present value based on its expected utility and the investment made. If a bank wants to maintain a cost-effective customer-oriented product line, it should apply that same life-cycle discipline to all its product processes.

> Banks should use employee input as a primary intelligence source in developing re-engineering products.

Summary

There is no panacea to the customer-value puzzle. Creating customer value, building a high-performing organization, and embracing a commitment to quality take hard work and attention to detail. Continuing research can help identify high-performance characteristics and alternative approaches. Managing customer sales-and-service processes effectively is an important element of a comprehensive commitment to creating value for customers and shareholders.

Patrick T. Harker headed the Wharton Financial Institutions Center research team that conducted the banking-systems study. He is now chairman of the Department of Systems Engineering in the University of Pennsylvania's School of Engineering and Applied Science. Larry W. Hunter is assistant professor of management at the Wharton School.

Fundamental Change in 1995; Bigger Change in 1996

Joe Sensenbrenner

This original article by consulting editor Joe Sensenbrenner summarizes the state of quality management in government operations at various levels. He relates how the implementation of TQM and its attendant disciplines is spreading in governments of every kind and how learning is being shared among states at different conferences that are growing in participation every year.

During 1995, the predominant question posed to public quality improvement practitioners changed radically. For most of the preceding decade, the growing usefulness of these techniques had been recognized and channeled by underlying questions like: How can we improve this process? How can we get to know and respond to our customers better? How can I get those to whom I report to understand and use these methods more? These are not easy questions in any sector. They are, however, fundamentally important, and quality leaders pursued them in an informed way by drawing on learnings from other sectors.

All that changed in 1995. Driven by the election results that altered the political balance in Washington and in state houses across the country, apparently in tune with the corporate "downsizing," and fueled by the dismal public opinion of the effectiveness of large, long-standing government programs, the question became: Tell me, what can be done with, say, 20% less money and 25% fewer workers? In many cases, it wasn't really a question: The answer was not sought to shape the final decision; the answer was the bottom-line cutback. Quality practitioners were not so much seen as part of a long-term strategy to improve performance—time was too short—but as possibly crafty cost cutters or sources of cover for other agendas. The change was occasionally subtle in its expression, it was rarely not noticed by the organization.

Further, there were specific "solutions" that came from the campaign trail and paralleled strategies used in the private sector. They included contracting out, privatizing, using temporary employees (with fewer benefits), and "de-layering" organizations. These practices were often proscribed with little study of the circumstances of the organization intended to be improved or the substantive work the agency was established to accomplish. The practiced rhetoric of the newly elected official was frequently taken up by incumbents as elements of a national movement emerged: It was time to cut back and discontinue quite a few things that weren't working very well.

This turn of events was not well anticipated by many who had been work-ing in quality improvement. This was the case for several reasons. First, such workers by and large believe that good deeds merit good rewards. It takes some kind of optimist to undertake the personal and organizational path toward public inquiry and improvement. This personality often has a heightened sense of fairness and belief in some sort of progress. Such persons also often have less acute peripheral vision for those coming from another perspective, and they are less watchful.

These circumstances have led many public workers to hunker down and prepare to be less involved in what will be the principal agendas of their gov-ernments. The sense of quality leaders that they were being let down was accompanied by the sense of many in the rest of the organization that they were being betrayed. And the implication was that the quality leaders may have been partially or knowingly involved in their being "used."

This feeling of blame and scapegoating has other causes, also. One is that the current cutbacks are not the result of poor program administration, i.e., errors of those doing the work. It is in almost every case the result of problems caused by the very program design itself. That is, the deficits and lack of program success are more accurately described as dissatisfaction with the in-evitable consequences of careful execution of prior political decisions. Mis-takes were at a policy level in Medicare, Medicaid, K–12 education, welfare payments, farm subsidies, crime fighting, and the like. They are not the failure of individual police officers, caseworkers, teachers, and average bureaucrats. Yet, often, the cutbacks organizationally fall on those[1] who have been faith-fully attempting to carry out the new intentions of the policy makers who have more recently been elected or, frequently, changed their minds.

Another source of the quality activists' feeling let down is the fact that the results of their efforts during the last five years have been, almost without exception, very positive. When asked by the Council of State Governments

Quality practitioners were not so much seen as part of a long-term strategy to improve performance but as possibly crafty cost cutters or sources of cover for other agendas.

(CSG) in late 1994 about the outcome of quality programs across the country, the results were summarized: "During the next few years, the new management philosophy is likely to be embraced by more executive branch agencies across the states. All but one respondent that returned the CSG survey questionnaire said TQM activities in their states were likely to increase during the next five years. Reasons for the anticipated increase cited by the survey include successful TQM activities in their states or in other states."[2] While new full-time or expanded programs were initiated in a dozen states in 1995, none, to my knowledge, were eliminated or substantially cut back. And individual annual reports from Arizona to Georgia to New York and Ohio detail real improvements and dollars saved.

These facts were reflected in quite positive national press. *Governing* magazine entitled its survey "TQM—Surviving the Cynics" and noted, "After years of experience, it's clear that TQM can be adapted to the public sector. And not only has it lasted, but it continues to grow, and rapidly. The number of states and localities involved in TQM is no longer in the dozens as it was a few years ago. It is in the hundreds."[3] And a correspondent for *U.S. News & World Report* wrote about Clinton's federal quality improvement efforts in *The New Republic* as the initiative "that might save his presidency."[4]

In these circumstances, it is all the more important to look at what is working and what are potential areas for increased contribution to public service delivery.

Two current strategies appear to be most successful. The first is to reiterate that these practices are nonpartisan. As new administrations took office, the usefulness of private sector business councils and other partnering activities gave programs a neutral coloration rather than being tainted by the prior administration. This long-term survival strategy continues to be one of the most valuable improvement strategies. As noted in *Training* magazine, "Exiling TQM to . . . the nether parts . . . may be just the protection it needs—to shield it from political heat and hide it from politicians clamoring for simple solutions."[5]

The second strategy involves government improvement activists engaging in peer learning. Such learning includes the following attributes:

- Case studies solely from the public sector
- Presentations solely by public sector employees
- Long-term perspective
- A nonjudgmental setting in which to learn
- Honest answers to tough questions
- Continuing contact between participants
- Learning free or of minimal cost

Learning with these attributes promotes both the initiation and sustainability of improvement efforts. Training efforts encompassing many of the elements have been initiated in Madison, Wisconsin,[6] Austin, Texas,[7] and Columbia, South Carolina.[8]

Two examples of these learning principles are particularly noteworthy. Both the Minnesota Quality Conferences and the South Carolina–based First States' Quality Forum currently represent the two best-known efforts at initiating and sustaining dramatic public improvement.

Minnesota Quality Conferences

In 1989, quality practitioners in Minnesota state government organized a conference for 150 of their co-workers. They determined the content, rented the hall, and selected the speakers: they invited only people who could talk knowledgeably at an operational level, speakers who knew what they were talking about. From this small initial sponsorship, the Minnesota Quality Initiative has seen growth in both its own activities and the number of volunteers who make the conference happen.

The Minnesota Quality Initiative's mission is "to grow the quality movement in the public sector in Minnesota." It has held a conference each year since 1989 with attendance increasing significantly each year. The original 150 in 1989 became 1,200 in 1994. The primary audience continues to be state employees with participation by city, county, and other public sector individuals growing each year.

The Minnesota Quality Initiative accomplishes the equivalent of a major national conference without the benefit of either staff or separate appropriations. All of its activities are carried out by public employees.

Significantly , the election of a new governor or a shift in majority in the state legislature has had no substantial adverse impact. Improvement has no party label. The organizers have made it "their show."

The First States' Quality Forum

The First States' Quality Forum initiated by South Carolina Quality Coordinator, Nathan Strong, provides a second model of effectiveness. Strong took $8,000 earmarked for statewide quality improvement and attracted other states' quality coordinators who found the practical content engaging enough to pay their own way. That was no accident: Strong developed the program by going to his potential customers, the hands-on coordinators in the states of Washington, Arkansas, Iowa, and New York. Together they developed a set of topics, solicited presenters from other states, and limited invitations to states with three years of experience and centralized quality coordination.

The four-day program in Columbia, South Carolina, May 2–4, 1993, drew 45 civil servants from 15 states whose responsibilities included organizational development and training in continuous improvement. The exchange among participants was candid and the free admission of mistakes/learnings was more forthcoming than in any conference I had previously attended.

Three hundred civil servants from South Carolina state government attended parts of the program on the third and fourth days. The best presenters from the visiting states presented their experiences to their hosts. First-class learning accelerated at minimal marginal cost. Programs included public sector use of loaned private sector executives. Officers who had spent a full year

The exchange among participants was candid and the free admission of mistakes/learnings was more forthcoming than in any conference I had previously attended.

as loaned executives to the governors of New York, Ohio, and Arkansas joined the discussion.[9] Such dialogue helped bridge some of the private-public gap in preferred leadership practices.

A Second States' Quality Forum was held in Little Rock Arkansas April 10–12, 1994, with 25 states in attendance. Because the number of attendees had reached the point where the interaction among the participants was reduced, regional meetings were established in 1995 to increase ownership and participation. Regional meetings were held in Phoenix, Arizona, on April 7, 1995, and in Columbia, South Carolina, on March 27–28, 1995, and in conjunction with the Minnesota Quality Conference on September 28–31, 1995.

Looking Ahead

If these areas are where the energy in government quality is currently going, where are the sources of learning that might be next? To respond to this question, it is appropriate, as in the years preceding government use of the present techniques, to look to the private sector and academia. There appear to be several areas of particular promise. Each may make a substantial contribution to government in the coming decade.

Organizational Learning: Pioneered by academic practitioners at MIT Learning Center, Innovation Associates, Inc., and others, this set of questions and practices looks to understand the ways organizations communicate and improve to develop methods to accelerate that learning.

Systems Thinking: Popularized by such authors as Peter Senge, Daniel Kim, and Margaret Wheatley, this ancient and holistic way of thinking and acting can enable people to understand their organizational circumstances in new ways and increase their understanding of their environment.

Interactive Management: Developed by Russell Ackoff for nation building and private sector improvement, these design and implementation practices are best suited for "clean slate" development in government of an Idealized Design.

Dialogue: Most recently articulated in the West by physicist David Bohm, this specialized practice of deep, group communication can surface group wisdom while building community.

Community-Wide Activities Around Alignment: Large-scale processes around "life-long learning" (Greenwood, South Carolina), community improvement (Wilmington, North Carolina), and "learning community" (Jackson, Michigan) are testing the use of Future Search (Weisbord, *et al.*), Community "civic" Development (M. Scott Peck), and Asset Development (John McKnight), among others.

The Once-in-a-Generation Circumstances Confronting Quality in 1996

Looking ahead, 1996 will present quality practitioners with their greatest challenge and opportunity. In fact, it is a once-in-a-generation context change.

The federal government will radically change how it allocates approximately $200 billion in "block grants." When whole programs get swept aside and whole areas of social policy—for example, health care for the needy and elderly, child development, employment, and training—are open for redesigning, new technologies are needed. Only by focusing on improving systems can government be able to do either the same or more with less. Whether public quality advocates continue to be relegated largely to the ongoing work of incrementally improving existing processes or whether players are in the most important public policy issue of the last of the twentieth century is the practitioner's question of the moment.

The outcome will largely determine the direction of the public quality movement. New technologies including those mentioned here are available. To undertake using and learning about these methods and ways of thinking not previously applied to the public sector will require initiative, courage, and a strong sense of purpose. Leaders in the quality movement were in this "place" before as they appraised the potential for TQM in the 1980s. The stakes are, perhaps, even higher now. Having demonstrated our capacity to learn and improve and lead, do we have the ability to lift the planning/design efforts of the 1990s from the traditional trade-offs to new, systemic thinking? The answer may be the key to continuously learning and contributing to America's quality future.

Notes

1. This is not to suggest that the greatest unfairness or suffering from program discontinuance falls on the bureaucrats. It does not. The purpose of this article is to suggest some of the special character of the year 1995 as it affected those involved in the quality movement.

2. *State Trends and Forecasts*, vol. 3, issue 2, October 1994 (Lexington, KY: The Council of State Governments, p. 16).

3. Jonathan Walters, *Governing*, September 1994, p. 40.

4. *The New Republic*, November 21, 1994.

5. Marc Hequet, "TQM at City Hall," *Training*, March 1995, pp. 58–64.

6. The Academy for Continuous Improvement is a collaborative effort involving the City of Madison, Madison Area Technical College, Madison Metropolitan School District, the Vocational Technical and Adult Educational Department, State Government, and the University of Wisconsin, established 1994.

7. The Texas Quality Forum is a collaborative effort including the City of Austin, the State of Texas, and the University of Texas, established September 1993.

8. The South Carolina State Government Quality Network includes the State government and several "community of excellence" programs, established June 1993.

9. Arkansas Eastman Chemical Company, Xerox Corporation, IBM, and Met Life loaned executives.

Joe Sensenbrenner is the principal of Sensenbrenner Associates of Madison, Wisconsin, a consulting company specializing in quality in government issues. He is the former mayor of Madison and has an extensive background in the problems of governing and the value of TQM and the idea of the "learning organization" in making governments work better.

Whether public quality advocates continue to be relegated largely to the ongoing work of incrementally improving existing processes or whether players are in the most important public policy issue of the last of the twentieth century is the practitioner's question of the moment.

How Quality-Oriented Have State and Local Governments Really Become?

Michael E. Milakovich

When considering the implementation of quality-improvement (QI) strate-gies, public-sector organizations must grapple with a host of economic and political concerns that do not generally affect their private-sector counter-parts. This article examines the diffusion of quality initiatives in state and local governments within the context of several models of change. It also discusses the role of leadership and employee empowerment in removing barriers to high performance in the public sector.

Once considered bastions of parochialism, stubbornness, and resistance to change, governments are now deregulating outmoded laws, empowering employees, privatizing nonessential services, and streamlining procurement processes to act in the citizen/taxpayer/customer's best interest. Responding to customer needs as suppliers of essential services for millions of people who cannot or will not purchase them from private providers, many public agen-cies are using various quality and productivity improvement approaches to achieve these breakthroughs.

But despite some preliminary evidence of success, state and local govern-ments still lack relevant case studies, consistent leadership, meaningful em-pirical examples, and useful theory-based models to guide their quality im-provement (QI) efforts. Anecdotal evidence is readily available from consultants, but there is very little comparative analysis of the many QI al-ternatives available. As a result, there is often more talk about the "need to improve quality" than actual efforts to change organizational cultures, elim-inate barriers, and apply various QI theories in government. Often, decisions to improve the quality of government services are made in a politicized en-vironment of profound cynicism and distrust. Diminished public confidence in political leadership neither encourages the maintenance of democratic pro-cesses nor promotes effective management of government.

Often, decisions to improve the quality of government ser-vices are made in a politicized environ-ment of profound cynicism and distrust.

Barriers to the implementation of public-sector QI include maintenance of individual reward systems, rigid vertical hierarchies, lack of genuine employee empowerment, outmoded performance appraisal systems, and management practices that impede the acceptance of team-based solutions to customer-defined problems. To overcome these barriers, many state and local governments are delayering hierarchical pyramids of unnecessary authority, investing in training to empower employees, and redesigning systems to better serve customers' needs. In many cases, these changes are measurable and subject to objective evaluation and continuous improvement. In others, neutral assessment of progress is very difficult, because as has often been said, in politics even the facts are debatable.

Competing Models for Quality Improvement

There are several often competing models used by state and local governments to guide QI efforts. They can generally be classified on a scale from less to more bureaucratic in terms of power relationships, the amount of discretion to make decisions, the extent of employee participation, and rule-making authority held by private or public entities. When applied to public agencies, QI models are limited by:

- The absence of market-driven competitive rewards
- The complexity of our decentralized federal system of over 87,000 legally autonomous governments
- Rapid turnover of political leadership
- Fundamental disagreements over the roles of citizens as "owners" or "customers" of democratic institutions

These models can be described as:

Privatized—Emphasizing practice of *contracting out* government services to private contractors or independent consultants who provide designated goods or services to government agencies for an agreed-upon fee.

Deregulated—Allowing natural market forces of supply and demand to determine policy designed to lessen the regulatory burden on private businesses by reducing government authority to make and enforce economic and social regulations.

Entrepreneurial/Competitive Market-Driven—Most recently associated with the best-selling book *Reinventing Government* by David Osborne and Ted Graebl, arguing for customer-oriented, decentralized, and "demonopolized" public service markets.

Customer Service Quality-Oriented—Emphasizing the Clinton Administration's *National Performance Review*, which encouraged federal agencies to become more customer-focused and results-driven.

Participatory—Recognizing the role of bureaucracy and decentralization in policy making and attempting to involve as many of those affected by decisions in the policy-making process as possible.

Traditional Administrative—(commonly known as the Weberian "bureaucratic" model) relying on hierarchies of centralized public employees with specific job responsibilities and regulatory authority to make and enforce public policies.

Calls for privatization and deregulation of the public sector have been heard and various efforts have already succeeded in that direction. Numerous factors will determine whether that trend continues, although questions about it are more likely to center on the *extent* to which we should privatize and deregulate, rather than on whether we should do so at all.

There is also growing interest in and changing perspectives on administrative discretion. Public administration literature generally supports the position that discretion should not be restricted and that public servants should exercise discretion in the public interest. This is one way to counterbalance the influence of private interests who know where they are likely to obtain the most favorable decisions. Those representing business and industry have come to view Congress and other representative institutions as generally more favorably disposed to their interests than the bureaucracy. The unrestricted use of administrative discretion would obviously be perceived more favorably if civil servants acted more often in the broad public interest. On the contrary, private business interests are more likely to support privatization, deregulation, or entrepreneurial models that diminish the administrative authority of public agencies.

Management techniques accompanying the diffusion of total quality management (TQM), continuous quality improvement (CQI), and other productivity-enhancement efforts have contributed to more sophisticated and systematic administration of public programs. One dimension involves the growing use of quantitative methods and computers as well as project management techniques designed to more efficiently manage individual projects. At the same time, they discourage participation and have a centralizing effect on decision and policy making.

> There is growing interest in the possibility of pursuing alternatives to direct regulation using government agency performance as a yardstick against which to measure private-sector performance.

Another trend is the movement toward deregulation, though how fast, how far, and in how many areas of economic activity are questions yet to be resolved. The issue of cutting red tape also relates to unnecessary regulation of private interests. It runs counter to demands for protection and risk reduction in our daily lives, which have accounted in large part for twentieth-century regulatory growth. How far we as a nation should *try* to go in reducing risks and ensuring public health, welfare, and safety are topics endlessly debated in Congress. Some have argued that we should strive for a "no-risk" society; others feel that such a goal is not only futile but also detrimental to other private functions in society (such as private-sector productivity). There is growing interest in the possibility of pursuing alternatives to direct regulation using government agency performance as a yardstick against which to measure private-sector performance. Recent federal legislation, including the

Government Performance and Results Act (GPRA) of 1993, attempts to re-orient federal executive agencies in the direction of better results and performance monitoring.

Government Performance and Results Act

GPRA is one step that the federal government has already taken to shift the focus of government officials from program inputs to program execution and measurement of results. To bring about this shift in focus, the GPRA sets out requirements for defining long-term general goals, setting specific annual performance targets that are derived from general policy goals, and annual reporting of actual performance compared to the targets. As federal managers are held more accountable for achieving *measurable* results, they are also given more discretion in how to manage programs for optimum outcomes. The legislation establishes various performance and budgeting concepts, and sets up pilot projects that will operate through fiscal year 1999. Two sets of pilot projects are required over the next several years to test and demonstrate annual performance plans, strengthen program performance reporting, and encourage managerial accountability and flexibility. Full-scale, government-wide implementation of strategic planning, annual program goal-setting, and annual program reporting of expenditures begins for all federal agencies in 1997. These tests will be evaluated with the goal of optimizing resources ultimately allocated for results. The legislation is characterized by the following policy-making principles:

1. Defining an agency's mission and setting general goals and objectives are viewed as budget and policy issues that involve broad groups of agency, Congressional, and public stakeholders.
2. Annual performance goals should correspond to requests for program resources and be linked to budget requests.
3. There should be emphasis on agencies' identification of performance measures so that performance goals can be properly set.
4. With implementation ultimately an executive agency responsibility, administrators must take a leadership and coordinative role during the pilot phase, in preparation for full-scale implementation.
5. Agencies will have substantial discretion in defining annual goals and performance measures.
6. Prescriptive directives or guidance, such as how-to instructions from the Office of Management and Budget (OMB), will be limited.
7. Implementation should be limited to existing agency resources as much as possible, applying existing systems and processes.
8. The (1994–1996) pilot phase will be used as a "lessons learned" opportunity to identify and resolve problems.

With the full implementation of the GPRA, greater emphasis should be placed on the execution of programs (outcomes, outputs, and results) rather than on traditional regulatory policy analysis. This could lead to demonstration projects in state and local governments, as well as more effective expenditures as ineffective programs are either improved or terminated.

In increasing numbers, state and local governments are striving to learn and implement the most effective practices to achieve customer-driven high-performance status. Evidence suggests, however, that there is little, if any, exchange of management techniques between levels of government. The impetus for high-performance quality and productivity improvement at the state and local level comes from other governments at the same level and, to a lesser extent, from the private sector. Despite some successes in government, more is known about how to achieve high performance in the private sector.

Learning from Private Industry

Over the last decade there has been a profound restructuring of many of our basic productive industries. Using TQM and CQI principles, large multinational enterprises literally reinvented themselves from the inside out. To establish closer working relationships with customers and suppliers, many broke up into smaller, more manageable, decentralized units. But given the sheer size and scope of the effort, mistakes were inevitable.

In some instances, the principles of TQM, CQI, or business process reengineering (BPR) were misunderstood and misapplied. Deploying innovative QI strategies in the 1980s raised product quality and productivity, but did little to forestall the downsizing of labor forces in many U.S. companies. In other industries, unrealistic expectations and controversial quality bureaucracies were created. For a variety of reasons, a TQM backlash has dampened enthusiasm and limited applications in service organizations. The lack of theory-driven, empirical, case-based research has limited acceptance of QI programs in the public sector as well. A question frequently heard in local commission meetings is, What can the CEO of Chrysler or Ford tell us about how to improve schools, fight crime, or collect the garbage?

At the same time, a new national quality consciousness successfully promoted the Malcolm Baldrige National Quality Award, raised hopes for restoring American industry, and spawned the growth of numerous quality consulting firms with expertise in applying "brand-name" QI theories to both the manufacturing and services sectors. (Unfortunately, the desire to provide better product quality and customer service often did not match the motivation or capacity to consistently meet customer expectations.) Such private-sector firms as AT&T, Federal Express, Ford, Metlife, Motorola, Ritz-Carlton, USAA, and Xerox mandated that *their suppliers* demonstrate service quality commitment by insisting on a higher standard and showing enhanced responsiveness to customer quality requirements. As the quality circle expanded, public agencies responded by learning how to become more competitive and customer-driven. The service quality revolution is affecting the daily operations of public and nonprofit agencies, as well as private organizations. According to David Osborne and Ted Gaebler, massive changes are required and the effort will be "catalyzed and guided" by national policy and action.

In increasing numbers, state and local governments are striving to learn and implement the most effective practices to achieve customer-driven high-performance status.

The trend is accelerating worldwide as attention is focused on recommendations for change and success stories from a wide range of public agencies and private industries.

This theme is the basis for Vice President Albert Gore's 1993 Presidential Report, *From Red Tape to Results: Creating a Government that Works Better and Costs Less,* which outlined the blueprint for reinventing the federal government. Another promising spillover is that several state governments, including Florida, New York, North Carolina, Minnesota, Missouri, and Texas, have modeled their own quality awards after the Baldrige criteria, broadening the base of the emerging national quality constituency.

Quality and the New Economic and Political Realities

Providers of critical public, private, and nonprofit services, such as corrections, education, health care, and public safety, realize that a new economic reality exists. At the same time, many still lack the knowledge, motivation, and political support to make the changes necessary to implement QI in their organizations. In the private service sector, training is available, markets are well-defined, and quality improvement is often rewarded with a share of bottom-line profit. By contrast, many governments serve a broader base of citizens (*not* clients) and interests, have conflicting missions, and lack incentives to become more efficient. Decision making is more complex, a greater number of interests are affected, rewards tend to be less immediate, and leadership is less stable. Many elected boards, commissions, and legislatures suffer from a paralysis of pluralism in which numerous public- and private-interest groups compete for a greater share of shrinking government budgets.

Nearly all governments are still budget-, rather than customer quality-driven. So, even when efforts are made to become more efficient, elected legislatures have responded to tax cut fever by reducing agency operating budgets. The focus of public budgeting and financial accounting is on inputs, or appropriations, rather than on outputs, or results. Therefore, legislatures become the dominant customers of budget-driven public agencies. There is, in short, no equivalent to the bottom-line market determination of quality progress in the public sector. Regardless of the model or models deployed, government agencies must develop new ways to measure customer-driven service quality and monitor results.

Nearly all governments are still budget-, rather than customer quality-driven.

Traditionally, noncompetitive regulated service monopolies have had fewer incentives to become customer friendly. Often protected by quotas, tariffs, or (their own) regulations, they are isolated from the rigors of do-or-die competition in domestic and international markets. Without competition, inefficiencies in service delivery processes are protected, costs increase, and customer complaints are more likely to be ignored. But despite the relative security of regulated local markets, many service managers are increasingly aware that *their* jobs, as well as *their* organizations, could disappear overnight as rules change and world markets continue to merge. (Think of the changes that have occurred in Europe since 1992 and in Latin America since the passage of the North American Free Trade Agreement.)

During the past decade, administrators of public agencies accustomed to successive increases in operating budgets have had to adjust to new economic and political realities. At all levels of government, increasing attention is now paid to the need for doing more with less. The political environment in this respect has turned hostile toward "big government," partly out of economic necessity, if not always due to direct public animosity. The long-term consequences of this change may prove to be both permanent and fundamental in their impact on administrative operations in general and on quality improvement in particular.

Many governments are now actively seeking to link budgets, customers, missions, providers, and systems to improve quality in a regulated, nonmarket service delivery environment. Budget constraints and deregulation have created opportunities requiring a commitment to change and the need to acquire new skills, learn systems thinking, and practice leadership for customer service quality improvement. There are concerns about the range of acceptable employee empowerment, the new roles of elected and appointed leaders, performance appraisal, systems improvement, and the definition of customers in state and local governments.

In the past, it was assumed that competitive service quality standards aimed at delighting the customer were inapplicable to public or non-profit agencies—especially where services are not purchased on the open market or where regulatory, law enforcement, evaluative, or authority relationships exist. On the contrary, recent research suggests that customer-driven quality definitions need not assume a competitive market or multiple providers of goods or services. Indeed, it is precisely in nonvoluntary compliance agencies, such as state and local police departments, state bureaus, and the U.S. Internal Revenue Service, where extraordinary progress is being made in the application of service quality principles.

Despite the lack of relevant cases and empirical theory, state and local governments have begun to apply customer service and total quality concepts. Many of these applications apply QI concepts loosely and do not follow strict or orthodox theories. Public administration expert James Swiss has argued that pure quality initiatives are ill-suited for public sector organizations because:

1. Governments have difficulty defining their customers.
2. They are service- rather than product-oriented.
3. They are input- rather than output-oriented.
4. Politics works against long-term leadership and constancy of mission.

Others have suggested that governments are primarily small service organizations which can respond to customers if investments in training, appropriate rewards, and systems changes are made. In today's tax-conscious political climate, however, such investments are very difficult for political leaders to make. Responding to a survey of quality applications in local government conducted in the summer of 1994, a city manager was careful not to

> Budget constraints and deregulation have created opportunities requiring a commitment to change and the need to acquire new skills, learn systems thinking, and practice leadership for customer service quality improvement.

describe his QI effort as a formal program. Rather, he said he was "using selected techniques with an extremely low profile. [The] public would support the concept so long as it *didn't cost money* or take people away from their jobs."

The results of a national survey of quality improvement in state and local government published in July 1993 found that an estimated 25 percent of all cities with a population over 25,000 reported the use of QI techniques in at least one functional area. Quality-improvement and customer-service strategies are most often used in police, parks and recreation, personnel administration, and financial reporting. Nearly 60 percent of all states were applying quality management principles in one or more functional areas; 34 percent implement TQM in five or more service functions. Functional applications include corrections, education, health care, transportation, and welfare assistance. Most of the state agencies began their QI journeys since 1992 and many still characterize their efforts as "in the beginning stages" and judge success as "too early to tell." Among the internal and external factors that drive the quality efforts of states: the governor's and agency director's interest, public complaints about service, and the need for statewide strategic planning. Key methodological issues remain. Case studies should be conducted to better understand why some organizations are further along in their TQM implementation plans than others. Case studies would also help identify implementation strategies currently in use.

Quality Improvement Vs. Democratic Participation

Trends toward more participation and more systematic management methods may conflict, but that has not prevented many governments from pursuing both. Requirements for broader participation may conflict with the need for quality management systems. Efforts to promote quality and productivity in government are an extension of the human relations and participatory models of management. Since the 1960s, there has been a far wider range of participation in and demands for new forms of direct involvement. Calls for greater *internal* participation in decision making by agency employees (empowerment) as well as *external* participation by affected clients (citizen-customers) came from what is usually known as the liberal side of the political spectrum. Internal forces, such as budget pressures and the personal interest and insistence of city and county managers, combined with external forces, such as voter demands and public complaints, are driving the movement for better management of local government.

These participatory theories were far more popular with democratic, usually more liberal, politicians in the 1970s and 1980s. Under the Reagan Administration, with its policy of block grants, a major new shift began to devolve federal government program responsibilities to state and local governments. This "New Federalism" doctrine was consistent with conservative ideology of local control and decentralization of political and administrative authority.

In the 1990s, however, both participation in government and devolution of intergovernment authority have been taken up by others whose politics are decidedly not liberal. Transfer of national government functions back to state and local governments has been more recently espoused by high-level Clinton Administration appointees, including Alice Rivlin, director of the OMB. The potential long-term significance of this shift is immense, politically and administratively. Demands for greater participation and for devolution respond to feelings of powerlessness among the customers of public agencies. Both manifest a distrust of big government and represent an attempt to regain control of decisions affecting vital personal, economic, political, and social concerns. These countertrends raise the important question, Can quality and productivity improvement models based on the corporate, centralized, rational, open-market approach coexist with the democratic, decentralized, participatory ideology common at the state and local levels of government?

Wanted: Additional Analysis of Quality in the Public Sector

There is little systematic knowledge about best practices and what works in various units of state and local government. County-level organizations nationwide are particularly understudied. There is a need to test theories of organizational change and document the extent, nature, and impact of quality-related activity in other local governments, such as special-purpose districts. Some preliminary efforts have been made to identify and compare governmental organizations having different levels of TQM-related activity. By doing so and collecting data on independent and other control variables—for example, population size, geographic region, form of government, service area, leadership style, organizational culture, driving and restraining forces, action strategies in local governments, and some of these variables plus department structure, longevity of program, and centralization vs. decentralization in state governments—factors that contribute to higher levels of activity can be identified and a generalizable knowledge base can be established.

To determine an individual unit's level of TQM activity, a multidimensional construct must be used. For example, in the case of quality, such a construct might include:

- Commitment to customer-driven quality
- Employee participation in quality improvement
- Actions based on facts, data, and analysis
- Commitment to continuous improvement
- Systemic perspective as a starting point

Accurate and reliable comparisons can only be made on a case study basis.

To date, an emphasis on both efficiency and accountability (of processes) and effectiveness (of results) of administrative agencies has led to numerous adjustments in relationships among political institutions. Emphasis on reinventing government, service quality, employee empowerment, and measurement of results has only reinforced this trend. Among the areas affected by these changes are the politics of structure, bureaucratic neutrality versus advocacy, altered budget procedures, changes in intergovernmental relations, and new initiatives in public personnel administration. All these were controversial areas in the national government during the 1970s, and became more significant in the Reagan-Bush era, and remain important today.

These conflicts have spawned related debates over the very nature of the changes being proposed in the early and mid-1990s. For one, efforts to reinvent the federal government have been criticized on various grounds. Public administration scholar Charles Goodsell, for example, has suggested that in their book *Re-Inventing Government* David Osborne and Ted Gaebler recounted numerous anecdotes and drew large-scale conclusions from those anecdotes, but failed to identify meaningful empirical patterns of administrative behavior that might be used as a justification for large-scale governmental reform. Also, it has been argued that accepting without question the underlying assumptions of "reinventing" government means willingly substituting the entrepreneurial model for the administrative management paradigm that has been in use for more than a century—with consequences that are impossible to predict. Presidential efforts to reform the bureaucracy seem to overlook the fact that custodial responsibility for American public agencies is shared between the chief executive and the legislature. Thus, unilateral efforts to impose new systems and procedures often run afoul of legislative prerogatives, as well as of administrative procedures.

Furthermore, tension arises because the consumer is considered both a customer of government agencies/services, and a citizen of the republic. The former clearly implies that *service provision* is a primary concern of government, and serving the customer must necessarily be a high priority for all those involved in that endeavor—including legislators and chief executives, as well as administrators. The latter, by contrast, suggests a very different relationship between the individual and his/her government, one in which the citizen is an integral part of the governmental *system*, and not *only* a consumer of government *services*. This is especially important in the application of QI, since most customers do not directly pay for the services they receive.

A related concern also exists in the privatized, market-driven or deregulated models: the contrast between public-oriented vs. private-oriented conceptions of government. If government, acting in an entrepreneurial manner, simply serves customers, then what is its unique role as distinct from the activities—and purposes—of private-sector businesses? Few, if any, of those advocating higher quality in the provision of public services or arguing the need for reinventing government would quarrel for a moment with the concepts of citizenship that are at the foundation of the republic, or would hesitate to defend the basic *political* relationships that are defined in the Constitution. But the important point is this: What is emphasized about our government processes reflects what is important, at the moment, about government, and it may influence attitudes in the years ahead as well. In other words, we could end up moving in a direction that causes us—intentionally

If government, acting in an entrepreneurial manner, simply serves customers, then what is its unique role as distinct from the activities—and purposes—of private-sector businesses?

or not—to redefine what sort of *broader* governmental system we will have. In short, if we focus so heavily on reinvention, productivity improvement, quality, or empowerment that we lose sight of some of the traditional assumptions and concepts underlying the political system, we may have made some useful short-term gains, but in the process we might trade off (or trade *in*) more fundamental notions of who we are as a polity.

To reiterate, citizens have both rights and responsibilities because they are purchasing a good or service on the open market; customers have few if any of the latter. Perhaps the rise of the customer is a sign of the times, in this nation, where more attention has been paid to individual rights and liability issues in recent decades. Some say that this has occurred at the expense of proper attention to collective responsibilities. Only as we exercise responsible citizenship will we be in a position to improve the quality of government services available to us as customers.

Michael E. Milakovich, Ph.D., is a professor of political science in the School of Business Administration at the University of Miami in Coral Gables, Florida.

Self-Directed Work Teams Untax the IRS

Mathew J. Ferrero

This article profiles the process one large office of the IRS has gone through in initiating and carrying out initiatives in TQM and CQI. It includes good accounts of their start-up procedures and problems, how they have progressed, and continuing challenges. The IRS continues to be a leader in the implementation of TQM in government.

Customer service at the Internal Revenue Service? Most people would argue that's an oxymoron. But to the IRS, customer service over the past seven years has become a strategic business objective. If any governmental agency has benefited from a total quality management environment, it's this one.

Seven years ago, the IRS and the National Treasury Employees Union (NTEU) formed the IRS-NTEU Joint Quality Improvement Process (JQIP). The JQIP was based on material from the Wilton, Connecticut-based Juran Institute, which provides training and consulting for total quality management.

In order to transform the IRS into a total quality organization, then-Commissioner of Internal Revenue Larry Gibbs recognized the need for human resources support. The agency's HR specialists were asked to negotiate with the union and help implement the joint quality improvement agreement. They also were responsible for explaining the agreement to the employees and setting up the training program for managers.

As a result, more than 400 cross-functional teams have been developed in the government agency, which includes seven regions, 10 service centers and 63 district offices. Some of their improvements included:

- An automated data-base program in Anchorage, Alaska, that identified taxpayers whose state benefits would be withheld if they were still liable for federal taxes.
- An employee handbook developed in Sacramento, California, for preparing various tax adjustments. The improvement helped employees follow a case step-by-step in an otherwise complicated procedure. It also reduced the number of errors and processing time.

■ Extensive changes to Form 1065 (U.S. Partnership Return of Income) in the Laguna Niguel, California, district. The time to prepare an average return was reduced by 41%, significantly reducing the taxpayers' burden.

In addition to these tangible savings and an improved customer focus, the IRS-NTEU project teams also have improved the agency's internal communication. Consequently, many district offices and service centers have reported a greater ability to settle labor-relations disputes informally. Despite its achievements, however, the agency still wanted to get more of its front-line managers and employees involved with improving work systems. But instituting a total quality organization (TQO) among managers and employees is difficult. In fact, many quality-improvement programs fail because organizations don't know what total quality involves or don't know how to attain it. Although the Juran-style teams were formed, the most vital work systems for improvement weren't always selected. For example, one district wanted to solve a parking problem. This issue certainly affects employees' morale. But how does that issue affect collecting taxes and serving customers? Moreover, the majority of projects were being assigned bureaucratically by the joint quality councils formed in each region, district and service center. Many projects were too ambitious, and systems couldn't be easily changed at the local level. As a result, productivity gains dipped. Not surprisingly, interest in quality improvement among front-line managers and employees also declined during this period.

IRS Urges Regions to Experiment with Different Team-Based Approaches.
In 1991, the agency decided to reinvigorate the process. The strategic objectives were to meet or exceed customer expectations and to move from simple problem solving to continuous improvement. In addition, the IRS wanted to empower employees by creating an environment in which they could exert more control over their work and also take more responsibility for their decisions. What follows are two examples in which one district in Laguna Niguel, California, and a collection division in San Francisco successfully responded to the call for reinvigoration.

With about 2,200 employees, the IRS Laguna Niguel District Office is one of the largest districts in the United States. It administers tax laws and serves approximately 4.5 million taxpayers in Orange, Riverside, San Bernardino, San Diego and Imperial counties of Southern California. In addition, it serves Southwestern Los Angeles County (in and around the city of Long Beach). Over a year's period, the district's two automated collection sites receive an average of 7,000 phone calls a week. The objectives of promoting employee involvement, enhancing communication and improving work processes in such a large business entity is daunting. However, in 1992, the District Joint Quality Council (JQC), which monitors the quality improvement program, was determined to succeed.

The JQC basic premise was that front-line employees and managers have the best understanding of the work processes for meeting or exceeding business objectives and customer expectations. Therefore, team activity should

> The IRS wanted to empower employees by creating an environment in which they could exert more control over their work and also take more responsibility for their decisions.

be emphasized in individual work units, most of which are defined by functions. For example, some work units specialize in tax assessment; others in tax collection. Through training in small group dynamics, the work units slowly transformed from a group of individuals to a work team.

Again, HR specialists were pivotal because they helped to identify which managers would make good team leaders. The criteria included verbal and listening skills and the ability to encourage participation. All of the team leaders were selected from within the agency based on division chiefs' recommendations. The JQC made the final decisions. Those selected then attended a two-week training class on team leadership and facilitation skills during the 1987 to 1991 period. It was important to proceed very slowly to ensure that the team leaders were well qualified.

The district JQC and HR specialists decided to pilot only four *impact teams* and assess their progress over an eight-month period. Impact teams are entities designed to help drive the district's transition to a total quality culture. At that time, a decision to alter, expand or abandon the impact-team concept would be made. Each team was composed of approximately 12 individuals, including a manager. They were determined by division functions such as collection, examination and criminal investigation.

Initially, the union chapter presidents weren't enthusiastic supporters of the concept. The joint quality improvement agreement required consensus decision making. In addition, the union wanted to see a periodic rotation of team leaders, rather than having only the group manager in that role. But after a lively dialogue, the union was won over, and the JQC developed the following impact-team prototype:

- The group manager is the team leader.
- A structured decision-making model is required. Consensus is encouraged, but not mandatory. Each impact team could make its own choice about how it would make decisions, including a majority-minority rule.
- Each team is assigned a facilitator.

The impact teams will focus on their own work processes to identify opportunities for improvement, develop solutions, test solutions and monitor results.

Managers had to change their mindsets about how to lead. The selection process for impact teams was primarily based on the group manager's ability to adapt his or her style as a team leader. In the past, IRS managers operated in a top-down fashion. The managers supposedly knew all the answers and told the employees what to do. Now, managers were required to employ better listening skills, solicit diverse opinions, focus on tasks instead of personalities and help resolve disputes. The goal was to model team behavior in several offices and among different types of employees. The pilot teams selected were two work groups in the Laguna Niguel office and two others in the San Francisco area.

Managers were required to employ better listening skills, solicit diverse opinions, focus on tasks instead of personalities and help resolve disputes.

After completing two weeks of training on small-group dynamics conducted by line management and HR personnel, the team leaders and facilitators began adopting ground rules, operating procedures and a decision-making model. They also learned how to use different types of quality tools such as brainstorming, selection matrices, flow charts and statistical tabulations. Then the teams began to critically examine specific work processes that merited improvement.

However, team members soon realized that the awareness training didn't stick because opportunities to practice the theory weren't available. To remedy the problem, team leaders and facilitators now train team members in using quality tools on a just-in-time basis. The primary text for this training is the *Juran Institute Quality Improvement Tools Desk Guide.* Just-in-time training allows team members to immediately learn, practice and apply such tools as flow diagrams and brainstorming in a real work setting. The key objective, according to Peter Senge's book "The Fifth Discipline," is to promote learning "through a continual movement between practice and performance, practice, performance, practice again, performance again." In short, each team is expected to be innovative and flexible by using the most suitable methods available. The ultimate goals are to encourage communication and collaboration.

Impact Teams Conduct Self-Assessment.   Eight months after initiating the impact teams, the IRS used a questionnaire to measure the progress in effective small-group dynamics and communication and in the use of quality tools. The team leader and facilitator wrote a narrative assessing their team's strengths, weaknesses and specific accomplishments. Three of the four teams were pleased that their structures enhanced their ability to communicate effectively. Over a period of months, most team members felt very comfortable discussing their work problems. Most team members felt they were learning to think critically. Moreover, they felt they could question a work procedure in a safe and supportive environment. One team produced a video on its own time. The educational aid explained how the team functioned and the value of a team approach in promoting effective communication. In short, most team members said that being able to ask questions was crucial for team formation.

Those teams that first targeted small projects were the most successful. For example, a team of tax examiners who service taxpayers in a high-volume phone center ensured that breaks and lunches were taken on time by synchronizing the office clocks every two weeks. They also developed a better method for prioritizing the numerous technical and administrative tasks. In the past, a manager would distribute several memos without first evaluating their relative importance. Now, managers prioritize memos, and employees know what to review immediately.

A special agent team, which conducts investigations of alleged criminal tax violations, initially rearranged office furniture to increase its efficiency. Later, the team revised the summons process. It also improved the structure

Those teams that first targeted small projects were the most successful.

of their search-warrant kit and developed a guide for various procedures used during field investigations. Most recently, it identified two criminal cases for investigation by the team rather than one special agent. The objective was to determine if the team approach reduced the investigative period and enhanced quality. The initial results were encouraging. The team invested 60 staff hours on the cases over three weeks and were prepared to arrest the suspects. Normal cycle time for one special agent conducting similar investigations is 120 to 180 staff hours over six to eight months.

On the other hand, another team used a very structured approach (brainstorming, data collection, selection matrices) to identify their key problems. However, they discovered that none of the recommended solutions for the root problem could be implemented locally. Regulations in the Federal Personnel Manual and district-negotiated agreements with the union precluded their adoption. The lesson was that management must take a proactive and supportive role for each team, especially in its early development stages. This includes ensuring that teams remain focused on work processes that can be changed or reinvented locally. In addition, this type of assistance, when given properly, demonstrates mid- and upper-management's interest in the teams. Communications must be horizontal and vertical.

Another issue was trust between team leaders and team members. The transformation from a group of individuals to a true team called for major changes in behavior. Employees now were expected to consistently and directly contribute ideas about how to improve quality and productivity. They were encouraged strongly to express their feelings about the work environment and team interaction openly and honestly, even if the disclosure pertained to the team leader's behavior. For example, did the manager listen well, encourage participation and focus on tasks? Some employees worried about being disciplined for their candor. But one team leader addressed this concern directly. She said that the team leader must state that any unethical use of the appraisal process is unacceptable. If it did occur, the team concept could never survive. The team leader must model behavior and attitudes that fully support team development.

The transformation from a group of individuals to a true team called for major changes in behavior.

Lastly, the teams learned that management must market the successes of any team-based approach. One of the district's goals was to have the impact teams sell themselves by word of mouth. This included encouraging team leaders and members to make presentations to other work groups and for mid-level managers to discuss team progress at employee forums. As the marketing proceeded in April and May 1993, approximately 25 managers applied for team-leader facilitation training. Two years earlier, only three managers were involved actively in quality team activities. Today, the Laguna Niguel District Office has 16 impact teams and six cross-functional teams. Thus, the district JQC and HR personnel believe a natural migration of impact teams is under way.

Cultural Change Begins to Take Hold.

The following benefits from the initial impact teams were evident in the self-assessments and from informal observations made by branch managers:

- Group decision making and the ability to select their own projects made the use of quality tools relevant to business goals.
- Honest and open communication between team members and the team leader increased.
- Team members more willingly shared information and technical skills with each other. The trust level significantly increased.
- The teams began viewing work from a process perspective in order to achieve business goals.

The overall feedback from team leaders, team members and facilitators was very positive. Currently, all major offices in the Laguna Niguel district have at least one impact team. In June 1993, the district's mid-level managers recommended that all district managers attend team-leader facilitation training and follow the impact team model—the linchpin for a successful transition to a total quality culture. Similar to the Laguna Niguel district employees, the San Francisco Collection Division employees also were dissatisfied with the old system. Their experiment focused on work groups in the context of their particular function. Collection-division compliance officers contact taxpayers—individuals and businesses—that owe back taxes or have not filed their returns. They must collect the money and returns under difficult and adversarial circumstances. Nevertheless, there are signs of improvement in customer focus, employee satisfaction, quality of work and productivity.

The division implemented the self-directed work teams in three of its 12 field-collection groups. The new work system integrated teams of compliance officers and support personnel to work on a centralized case inventory. This procedure was a major change from the traditional method of handling cases. In the past, compliance officers worked on their cases individually and were evaluated on individual ability and performance. With self-directed work teams, performance is based on the accomplishments of the team.

This is how the work teams were implemented:

In the past, compliance officers worked on their cases individually and were evaluated on individual ability and performance. With self-directed work teams, performance is based on the accomplishments of the team.

- Define the purpose and goal.
- Form the sponsor group and the steering committee.
- Form and train the design team.
- Study the current work system and define the work-system requirements.
- Redesign the work system.
- Write a comprehensive guide.

Over a six-month period, the design team (one manager, one secretary and five compliance officers) wrote a comprehensive guide known as the *Big Book*. It provided a detailed account of the new work system that included job descriptions, team-member rules and responsibilities, employee evaluation criteria, a promotion and recognition system, physical office design and overall working-environment suggestions.

The design team's work resulted in a combined union-management work-system redesign for the collection division. A steering committee, composed of three collection managers, four union officials, one management analyst and the chief of labor relations, was responsible for overseeing the implementation.

The first step was to select the team. Teams were composed of volunteers. However, some tests were conducted to determine which employees were best suited to work together. The teams were provided with three days of Juran quality-team training and the 250-page *Big Book*. Approximately 50% of the employees in one of the two collection field branches participated in the test. Four teams are located in the district headquarters in San Francisco. Two teams are located in San Mateo, an office 20 miles south of the headquarters. Those that didn't participate in the work teams were used as control groups. Their location was similar to the teams to ensure an equitable distribution and makeup of cases.

Several measures were used to compare the work teams' productivity with that of the control groups. Among them were return on investment, salary-based operating costs, number of tax returns secured and overall productivity. The quality measures focused on the number of errors that were made and the additional work required for processing different types of cases. The teams assessed their progress every six months and—depending on the budget—an organizational-development specialist might be enlisted to identify barriers and make recommendations.

After the first year, it was evident that the startup costs were high. Initially, the work teams showed little or no improvement in quality or productivity. After 18 months, an employee-development specialist and an outside consultant were brought in to troubleshoot the test. This is what the analysis revealed:

- Although some training had been conducted on quality tools, the sessions overlooked interpersonal skills and communication training. Moreover, conflict resolution and facilitation skills had not been sufficiently addressed.
- Even though the design team's Big Book clearly addressed team-member roles, members did not adhere to those roles.
- Evaluations were sporadic. When information was provided, it was difficult to understand.
- Management applied their hands-off philosophy too prematurely. Management needed to be more involved and supportive in the beginning stages.
- Major changes, such as an evaluation procedure, should have been considered only after a total buy-in of team members.

By May of 1992, the collection division in San Francisco took several steps to refocus their goals. They identified four areas that needed to be monitored: quality, productivity, customer satisfaction and job satisfaction. Quality is determined by the quality assurance division's review of the teams' case work. Customer satisfaction is determined by contacting taxpayers who have worked with the compliance officers. Their feedback on the professionalism, timeliness and overall quality of the contact is rated by a telephone interview. And job satisfaction is determined by a monthly employee survey conducted for each team. Each team meets weekly for one or two hours to evaluate its progress. Rather than just being compared with control groups, the teams also emphasize continuous improvement of their own work.

Since 1993, the IRS has continued to make progress on its journey toward total quality. For example, the agency and the union entered into a partnership that focuses on improvements in four major areas: systems management, employee empowerment, labor relations and quality of work life. Each individual IRS office also is expected to complete a self-assessment of its current quality culture; negotiate an agreement with the local NTEU chapter on how to better involve the union in a total quality culture; and develop a multi-year action plan for continuous improvement in the four areas.

Both the Laguna Niguel and San Francisco districts will complete their self-assessment, NTEU agreement and multi-year action plan by August. This careful planning process and the implementation of goals will continue to require the active support of HR specialists. They will have to lead the change in defining new job descriptions and training managers to approach their responsibilities differently. The future for the IRS holds both challenge and promise. By involving all of our employees in the total quality process, the team concept shouldn't overtax individuals unfairly.

Mathew J. Ferrero is the Internal Revenue Service district quality coordinator in Laguna Niguel, California.

On the Road to Quality, Watch Out for the Bumps

Robert A. Hunt

Incline Village is a small but popular town in the Sierra mountains at the northern edge of Lake Tahoe. Like many other local governments, they have had to do more with less. This down-to-earth article explains, from the perspective of the general manager, how this town went about implementing TQM to better serve citizens and make their work more personally rewarding.

When I attended my first full-fledged quality seminar in 1990, TQM seemed a perfect fit for our organization. Operating a ski resort and golf courses as well as water and sewer systems, the Incline Village General Improvement District was hardly a typical government operation. While most public officials were forming partnerships with the private sector, we headed in the opposite direction:

- In 1986, the District entered the food/beverage business when our elected Board decided not to renew the private concessionaire's contract . . .
- In 1987, we doubled the size of our ski resort, renaming it Diamond Peak to reflect a new, more aggressive image . . .
- In 1989, the golf lease was terminated, and soon we were managing two courses, one ranked by *Golf Digest* among the nation's top 50 . . .
- By 1990, we were well into design of a new recreation center, a 36,000 square foot facility with indoor pool, gym, aerobics studio and exercise equipment that would sell memberships like most private health clubs. We had a merchandising manager and marketing director; we reported financial results in terms of profit and loss.

Growing pains . . : While priding ourselves on a business-like approach to management, we suffered many of the symptoms of any newly entrepreneurial organization, public or private. Our vision too often exceeded our grasp.

The upsized ski resort opened for business as this century's worst drought gripped the Sierras. Cutbacks in ski management proved insufficient to stem the red ink from dwindling skiers and scant snow. At golf, we promised to *restore the masterpiece* by installing a new irrigation system; the resulting scars caused disgruntled golfers to nickname the design, *Robert Trench Jones.*

The highly visible recreation projects left too many people, both inside and outside of the Village, thinking our mission was growth. That is a dangerous notion for any public agency, especially one located in a basically fiscally conservative community accustomed to changing political directions every four years.

Learn to do things better, not bigger . . . Even in 1990, when much of the growth still lay ahead, the handwriting was on the wall. By mid-decade, we would need a new direction. With no more big projects on the drawing boards, we'd have to become adept at doing things better, not bigger. Unless we could become more disciplined, our econometric models suggested that the recent large gains in revenue would be overtaken by runaway costs. And unless we improved our sometimes erratic service, our lucrative base of upscale customers was also threatened.

Let's Try TQM, Whatever That Is   It was in this setting that we invited our staff, board, customers, and owners (the public) to help us frame a mission statement.

Afterwards, we held senior staff retreats to hammer out how we were going to meet our pledge of *service, value and people.* We invited a consultant to introduce the executive team to total quality, and after a lengthy and confusing discussion we committed ourselves to it. At this point we were not yet quite sure what it (TQM) was, but it sounded like something we could use.

At this point we were not yet quite sure what it (TQM) was, but it sounded like something we could use.

Progress by Mid-1994   As we approached the middle of last year, we had made some progress to be proud of:

- A new ski manager challenged his supervisory team to reinvent the business, and they did, from outside in.
- Focusing on families as the core market, every operating assumption has been challenged. Visits are up, costs are down and the ski area has posted its fourth consecutive profitable season.
- The championship golf course is now green from one to eighteen, even during the hot summer months which used to sizzle it brown.

The new irrigation system was an important ingredient in the transformation, but the technology proved inadequate until we reorganized ourselves to make better use of it. The solution involved a classic merger of technical and human systems.

Quality is driven by learning from errors . . . While our more glamorous recreation operations stole the spotlight, our utility staff was quietly (sometimes noisily) rebuilding itself around principles of teamwork. A *peer feedback* process replaced the traditional *evaluation-by-your-manager* approach, with dramatic results. Productivity rose, supplies expense fell, and maintenance refocused on prevention instead of correction.

While it is easy to herald the successes, we must not forget our failures, because that is where the most learning occurred. I offer here a few of the bumps we've encountered on the road to quality. Perhaps this will help others to chart a path around them. Rest assured, no one can miss them all. But would we want to, even if we could? Bumps make for a thrilling ride—and can launch us into some very scenic detours. No one said the journey couldn't be fun—especially if it is at Lake Tahoe!

The Executive Bump

Perhaps one of the hardest lessons for me was discovering that I was part of the problem. As general manager I was insulated from grumbling in the ranks. I had nurtured a strong self-image as an enlightened manager. Little did I know that the perception was not shared by many on the front lines.

Fortunately for all of us, a teambuilding consultant, retained before we ever heard of TQM, had the guts to share with me the feedback he'd received from work crews. Their description of me was something I couldn't even recognize. I resolved to do something about it, and within three months hosted a day long class on leadership for my direct reports. I assigned each manager a chapter from a leadership text, which they were responsible for teaching to the rest of the class. By the end of the day, we had adopted a new approach to management that used less *direct-and-control* and more *reward-and-recognition*.

Reverse evaluations . . . The visible changes I made in my personal style inspired others to make changes of their own. It also gave me the confidence to demand changes from authoritarian supervisors, who did not want to hear the feedback they were hearing from others. They were aided by *reverse* evaluations, in which managers were rated by subordinates.

My personal changes also helped me lead the organization in unfamiliar directions. When I became comfortable not having all the answers, I found that many of them were available from those around me.

The Expertise Bump

Because so much of TQM was new territory for us, we were tempted to rely on consultants. While they provided us much-needed wisdom during the start up, we were fortunate that budget constraints prevented us from using them heavily. That made us trust our own instincts. We found that when changes resulted from our own efforts, we worked harder to make them succeed.

Partnering for learning . . . To overcome our limited knowledge, we tapped as many sources as we could.

- I set an objective for each of our senior managers to attend at least one comprehensive TQM seminar.
- We joined various networking groups, such as AQP, and encouraged our people to attend their meetings.

> When I became comfortable not having all the answers, I found that many of them were available from those around me.

As one of the rewards for graduation from leadership classes, each participant received a coffee mug, encouraging them to *do it* if it met these three criteria.

1. Will it improve service?

2. Will it add value to the customer? and

3. Will it respect people?

Figure 1.   **How to know when to *just-do-it*.**

- We also linked up with private companies already well along the quality journey.

When these quality firms were in our own backyard, we invited their leaders in to visit with our people: when farther away, we sometimes sent a team to visit. To break down communication barriers, these teams were ad hoc—involving people from different departments and all levels of Incline Village that did not normally work together. Many of our new found experts were in industries very different from our own: office furniture and flight simulators to name just two. Nevertheless, we found we shared many things in common.

The "Just Do It" Bump

To drive home the message of empowerment, we expanded our first-phase leadership classes to include all supervisory personnel. I personally facilitated these sessions. As one of the rewards for graduation, each participant received a coffee mug, encouraging them to *"Do it!"* if it met three criteria which flowed from our three tenet mission (Figure 1).

A bit of chaos and more learning from errors . . . Unfortunately, this message worked almost too well. Coupled with the entrepreneurial spirit that already prevailed within the Village, the *Just do it!* campaign sent people flying in all directions. While this had the desirable attribute of creating momentum, it also created a lot of confusion and more than a little conflict. Teams were formed to tackle some long-standing problems. No particular process was observed to charter the teams and team members received virtually no training.
    In hindsight, the results were predictable:

- Teams jumped to solutions before adequately defining problems, and fought over which solutions made the most sense . . .
- There was scarce analysis . . .
- Little was accomplished and much time was wasted . . .

- The most serious problem was that it created a credibility gap for the overall change effort.

The Training Bump

We got over *just do it* by *bumping* into training. We decided it was time to roll out a more systematic approach to quality, so we retained an experienced firm to help us assemble a training program.

- A cross-section of Incline Village's natural leaders were selected to receive train-the-trainer instruction . . .
- All full time employees received an orientation in continuous improvement and other basic concepts . . .
- To overcome some of our teamwork problems, everyone also received skill training in communications and supporting others . . .
- Managers received skill training in empowerment.

Unwarranted training expectations . . . We got generally good marks from participants about the raining, but it was hard to tell whether much of it was being used on the job. Our expectations were probably too high; some people thought that training alone would change things. Some even thought that the training program was TQM!

Learning works best at the moment it's needed . . . We quickly revised our training to focus natural workteams on real work problems. The training now focuses more on skills in continuous improvement techniques and team mechanics, delivered *just-in-time* so it can be applied immediately. That seems to be when people are most able to learn.

The training now focuses more on skills in continuous improvement techniques and team mechanics, delivered just-in-time so it can be applied immediately.

The Democracy Bump

Despite our best efforts to explain empowerment, it was sometimes perceived as *us first-democratization*. Some were tempted to use new authority for the team's benefit at the customer's expense. The choices were not necessarily bad; work areas were sometimes an impediment to work (such as bad lighting that caused eye strain). Occasionally, personal benefit could turn into a business detriment (such as closing the office for lunch, when customers wanted to transact business).

Do your really mean it! testing . . . Often these first decisions seemed as much a test of management as a test of employees:

- Does management believe in this empowerment thing enough to allow us to make a decision that is different than they would make?
- Do they really value us as people enough to invest in something that makes us feel better about our jobs?
- Are they really listening?

Yes we do (we said a little anxiously) . . . To pass this test, we swallowed hard and accepted teams' first decisions. We reasoned that, even if the decisions were off target, they would provide valuable opportunities to learn that outweighed any potential harm. As employees acquired a taste for authority, we salted it with responsibility. We were entrusting them to make decisions on behalf of our customers. If they could do so in a way that also made work-life easier, so much the better.

In any event, we found that pre-occupation with personal work issues tended to be temporary, if effective teamwork was taking hold in the work unit. As teams began to focus on critical work issues, less attention was paid to peripheral concerns. Most teams became good judges of this distinction.

The Too Much to Do Bump

As continuous improvement ramped up, so did the level of stress. Budget cutbacks were already causing us to ask everyone to do more with less—now we were asking them to do with less and catch lots of new concepts we were throwing at them. When the pressure was on, the tendency was to revert back to old ways.

The strong temptation was to say, "I don't have enough time to do my regular job, let alone, all of this TQM stuff!" We tackled the fallacy that quality was not part of the regular job. We attempted to show people how lack of concern for quality created more work and compounded the time crunch. But we also realized that our approach was part of the problem. We were not being clear enough about priorities. In response, we invested more time in planning and organizing the improvement process and surveying customers. We also sharpened the focus on eliminating non-value adding work, freeing up resources for newly added tasks.

We tackled the fallacy that quality was not part of the regular job.

The Buy-in Bump

Any organization attempting to make the basic cultural changes we undertook runs into problems with buy-in. People appear to be working from the new text, mouthing the new lingo, but nothing substantive really changes. We felt that the longer this problem existed the more corrosive it would become to our change effort. We dealt with it through a large number of small ways.

Unequivocal about Our Expectations We established responsibilities which everyone in the organization shared, from general manager to janitor:

- The *duty to learn,* involving the continuous improvement of personal skills, work habits, and work systems . . .
- Find a way every day to improve and share it.

In many one-on-one encounters and in groups, I shared with people what I was doing to do my own job better. I tried to stress that the responsibility to improve was a personal one, not something that just happened in teams.

Each of us had to find a way, every day, to do the job better than it was done the day before.

- Each of our jobs is contingent on improvement:
  —Salary increases had to be earned by becoming more productive . . .
  —The very existence of our jobs depended upon making ourselves more valuable to our customers.

If comments about the necessity to improve were idle threats, they would have backfired. But since our people understood them to be true, they were accepted as straight talk.

Many other people involved in the change effort delivered similar messages, and we worked hard to turn up the heat on those who were not responding. We hosted a performance improvement workshop for our management team, helping them identify and confront individual performance problems head-on.

One-on-one victories and a few losses . . . This guerrilla approach to quality indoctrination is still claiming victories one-by-one. Several people we considered beyond reach have recently made improvements. Others have quit, been fired, or reassigned. The remaining hold-outs are becoming the exception, rather than the rule. Incline Village is now revising new employee orientation and performance evaluation processes, to ensure these tools reinforce our quality goals.

Bump to the Future

Looking back at the course we travelled, I doubt that we could have steered clear of the ruts. On occasion we may have spun our wheels a bit more than necessary, but usually we emerged a little wiser and with deeper resolve. Looking ahead to tomorrow's bumps, perhaps our people are better prepared to absorb them. As we develop the habit of seeing opportunity beyond each obstacle, the journey becomes more of a jaunt and less a struggle for survival.

Robert A. Hunt was general manager of Incline Village General Improvement District from 1984 through 1993.

Each of us had to find a way, every day, to do the job better than it was done the day before.

HEALTH CARE

Health Care's Slow Progress

Dan Beckham

This review of the implementation of quality practices in health care, prepared by consulting editor Dan Beckham, states that the industry has a long way to go. The belief that America has the finest health care in the world seems to be a roadblock. We're already good, so we don't need this quality improvement stuff. There is hope, though, as health care facilities find themselves competing with each other, quality and customer service may emerge at the way these facilities differentiate themselves.

The truth is that the consistency and statistical orientation that so much characterizes modern quality improvement have been largely absent in health care.

It is a great irony that the quality movement found its way to health care late. Long after American companies like Motorola and Ford had made quality a fundamental business focus, a small group of health care professionals began to advocate the quality philosophies and practices of W. Edwards Deming, Joseph Juran, and Philip Crosby. Few industries in America would have been expected to have done so little with the tools of quality improvement than had health care. Certainly no industry had as great an imperative for quality as health care. After all, the stakes were exceedingly high. The truth is that the consistency and statistical orientation that so much characterizes modern quality improvement have been largely absent in health care. Instead, health care has been a hotbed of professional independence and adhocracy.

Although a few pioneering physicians like Donald Berwick and Paul Batalden have made great contributions to the body of thinking on quality in health care, that thinking has been largely lost on their colleagues. It's not that physicians are uncommitted to quality. But their notion of what comprises and contributes to quality is much at odds with accepted thinking in other industries.

Physicians are highly oriented toward professional independence. Even those employed in group practices are imbued with a strong sense of clinical autonomy. As a result, American medicine and the health care industry that has been built on it are amazingly devoid of best practices, protocols, and meaningful data about results. The still dominant fragmentation of medicine into specialties makes the management of holistic processes relevant to an entire patient almost impossible.

Quality improvement efforts in other industries have been described as having gone through a necessary evolution from a focus on the internal to a focus on the external, particularly the needs of the customer. Many of the quality initiatives launched in health care suffered from this same myopia. Unfortunately, a smooth evolution to customer focus has been more problematic in health care than in other industries. Health care professionals, including physicians and nurses, dislike the term "customer." (This may be one of the few things on which doctors and nurses agree.) To them, customer implies a commercialization of the patient. It also threatens to debase their roles as professionals with a privileged relationship with the patient (indeed, a relationship secured by legal license). Further, the notion of a customer who must be catered to and who is capable of making choices based on market considerations assaults the health care professional's altruistic and paternalistic position "as the one who knows best."

Finally, there has been an accepted belief that the quality of health care in America was "just fine, thank you." Indeed, the whole industry has been well satisfied with its oft repeated claim to be "the best health care system in the world." Any discussion of efforts to improve the quality of care have been widely regarded as an affront to an industry unwilling to accept the notion that there was any room for additional improvement. It continues to cling to this notion despite competing evidence that suggests the life expectancy of the American population is no higher than that of Italy and that it has the highest infant mortality rate among the major industrialized nations. For this middling performance, it spends roughly 50 percent more per capita than Canada and fully 100 percent more than Japan.

Many of the most visible and highly touted quality improvement efforts in health care have proceeded with no active input from customers. Instead, quality improvement teams have assumed they understood fully the needs and expectations of patients and other direct customers. At many hospitals, this fuzzy approach has been further clouded by designation of health care professionals and workers as "internal customers." At one large hospital in Nashville, confusion over who the real customer was played itself out in loud complaints from nurses offended that they, the organization's most important

The still dominant fragmentation of medicine into specialties makes the management of holistic processes relevant to an entire patient almost impossible.

internal customers, were going to be forced to give up their parking spaces so external customers could park closer to the outpatient treatment center.

Health care, fortunately, attracts a higher percentage of altruistic workers than other industries. One of the reasons these folks end up in health care is that they have a greater need for meaning and meaningful work. The strong Judeo-Christian traditions underlying the teachings of W. Edwards Deming hold strong natural appeal to these individuals. Quality improvement holds the very real promise of fulling the workplace with greater meaning. Unfortunately, in some health care organizations, quality improvement has transcended from pragmatism to a crusade with almost religious overtones. As in other crusades, some quality disciples have displayed an intolerance for those cut from a different cloth. Deming's teachings in particular seem to have evoked a "take it or leave it" militancy that has had a chilling effect on honest skepticism and intellectual freedom in some health care organizations.

Just as it has in other industries, quality improvement in health care has recently run into a buzz saw of less enlightened movements, most notably, reengineering and radical cost cutting. Impatient with the 10-year transformations that Deming insisted were essential to a true transition to continuous quality improvement culture, health care executives have decided to cut costs today and improve tomorrow. These cost-cutting initiatives have preceded without regard to previous organizations' commitments to the philosophical tenets of quality improvement. Organizations that before had committed to "driving out fear" instead inoculated it into confused organizations by sweeping out thousands of full-time employees through cost-reduction efforts.

Whether health care will embrace quality improvement to the extent leaders in other industries have remains in my mind an open question. Even if a large percentage of American hospitals were to adopt quality improvement, the effect on physicians would be negligible. Doctors still do not dance to the hospital's tune in this country. There's a good chance they never will. On the other hand, wholesale adherence to quality principles by the managed care industry might cause a significant response among physicians. Increasingly, physician incomes rely on these managed care plans. If participation in a quality improvement effort becomes a condition of full reimbursement, physicians will probably comply, albeit grudgingly.

Even more than hospitals, managed care plans are locked in a battle with each other as they attempt to differentiate themselves on characteristics of importance to the marketplace. To date, that differentiation has been largely derived from pricing. But as competitive pressures push health plans ever closer to the same price points, the need to be able to differentiate based on quality increases. Unfortunately, health plans have relied on the established reputations of the hospitals and doctors they contract with to supply the plan with its reputation for quality. In the future, mere reputation will be insufficient. The health plan and its panels of hospitals and doctors will have to demonstrate that they have a clear quality advantage. Already, some health plans have recognized this and are adopting quality initiatives targeted toward

> Just as it has in other industries, quality improvement in health care has recently run into a buzz saw of less enlightened movements, most notably, reengineering and radical cost cutting.

demonstrating results. It is likely, then, that quality have a second coming in health care. It may stick this time.

Dan Beckham is president of The Beckham Company. He is recognized as one of the health care industry's top strategists. He has received numerous awards, including the Steuart Henderson Britt Award from the American Marketing Association, an honor he shares with such recipients as Ray Kroc of McDonald's. He is a contributing editor to Healthcare Forum, *where he writes some very.*

Making Improvements in Good Samaritan Hospital's Orthopedic Unit

Judy L. Womack, Carol S. Wasyk,
and Marilyn Conner

This article provides a case study of how one unit of a hospital went about implementing continuous quality improvement. Their goal was to improve patient care, reduce the length of hospital stay, and reduce costs. By using various quality tools and initiating teams and teamwork, they have made solid improvements. Pay special attention in this article to the part of bringing people together from many different areas in the hospital: nurses, physical therapists, pharmacists, and physicians. Without this teamwork, they would not be succeeding.

Improving quality and reducing cost is clearly the mandate for the health-care industry of today. Like many hospitals, Good Samaritan Hospital (GSH) in Dayton, Ohio, first looked at reducing the length of the patient stay and making more effective use of its resources. However, these cost-reduction tactics addressed only one part of the equation. It became clear that concentrating on cost reduction would not necessarily lead to improved quality. The challenge was to find methods that would streamline the structure and process of delivering patient care.

In 1990, the hospital instituted a clinical assessment and cost accounting system to help analyze the resources used to provide care to specific patient populations with specific diagnoses. The first available information clearly identified orthopedic services as a target; utilization of resources for these procedures exceeded reimbursement payments.

An orthopedic task force was established in July 1991 to analyze the financial data and develop recommendations for providing orthopedic services in a cost-effective manner that would be competitive in the Dayton market. The task force members included representatives from administration, cost accounting, orthopedic nursing, physical therapy, orthopedic surgery, management engineering, and peri-operative nursing. A review of the cost accounting data covering fiscal year July 1, 1990, through June 31, 1991, led the task force to focus on major joint procedures, which accounted for 44 percent of the 397 orthopedic procedures performed. The average length of stay for these procedures was 11.8 days, and the total cost, including fixed and variable costs, exceeded net revenue. The major goal was to reduce the length of hospital stay from 11.8 to seven days, which would result in a decrease in cost per procedure. The major recommendations from the orthopedic task force to achieve this goal included:

1. Develop a pre-operative educational program that would include pre-admission testing, physical therapy evaluation, nursing assessment, patient teaching, anesthesia assessment, and cognitive assessment.
2. Deliver physical therapy services on the weekend, which would provide patients with physical therapy seven days a week.
3. Reduce operating room costs by developing a program to match hardware selection with patient need.
4. Consider adopting nursing case management to expedite inpatient care, and develop a plan for outpatient services.
5. Develop a plan for efficient transfer to an extended skill facility for patients unable to be managed in the home following discharge.

Of Critical Pathways and Continuous Improvement

At the same time, nursing administration was evaluating nursing case management as a practice model. The model developed at the New England Medical Center, which uses a case management plan and critical pathway, was selected for use. The GSH case management plan was designed as a multidisciplinary tool with three distinct categories:

1. Identification of a nursing diagnosis that reflects patient clinical problems.
2. Articulation of patient goals and clinical outcomes
3. Selection of specific interventions necessary to achieve established goals and outcomes within specific timeframes

The critical pathway describes key events in the process of patient care that, if performed as described, would produce the most desirable clinical outcomes.

The critical pathway, a case management tool, is an abbreviated version of the multidisciplinary process identified in the case management plan. The critical pathway describes key events in the process of patient care that, if performed as described, would produce the most desirable clinical outcomes in the most efficient and effective manner. The critical pathway is kept at the bedside for documentation purposes and becomes a part of the permanent record. With these tools and a structure identified, orthopedic joint replacement was selected as the trial for case management.

Concurrently, the hospital was exploring the development of a continuous quality improvement (CQI) program. To learn more about CQI, a management group attended educational programs on the subject and conducted a literature search to review current programs being used within the healthcare industry. In evaluating GSH's readiness to implement continuous quality improvement, hospital managers determined that a program would be needed to provide administrators, directors, and team leaders with specific analytical skills. The organizational development department staff assumed responsibility for evaluating suitable training programs. In July 1992, GSH administrative staff selected the Improving Process Performance Program (IPP) developed by Prism Performance Systems of Farmington Hills, Michigan, for pilot evaluation. Eventually, the program was chosen as the basic instructional vehicle to educate various GSH groups in CQI efforts. The next step was to identify opportunities where IPP concepts could be applied.

GSH's vice president and nursing director responsible for orthopedics were active participants in the orthopedic task force, the nursing case management planning, and the IPP evaluation. They recognized that IPP could be used to develop a critical pathway that would address the hospital's orthopedic joint replacement issues.

Administrative staff selected participants who would represent all three shifts from both orthopedic units on two four-person teams that would be charged with initiating improvement efforts. Team members included nursing team leaders, a physical therapist who specialized in the therapy of total joint replacements, and the orthopedic nursing coordinator.

A representative from organizational development also joined each team to assure that the teams remained focused on their assigned task. The goal of one team, the Hippies, was to develop a critical pathway for total hip replacement. The other team, the Knee Highs, was charged with developing a critical pathway for total knee replacement. The physical therapist floated between the teams, providing input. The teams were given two months to complete the project. A chairperson was assigned to report back to the vice president and director.

Improving Process Performance (IPP)

Improving Process Performance has four major components: scanning, defining the gap, resolving the gap, and implementation (see Exhibit 1). The teams began a structured, twenty-four-hour IPP training program during which they were taught IPP concepts and were given the opportunity to apply the ideas immediately by working together on a hypothetical process in need of improvement. Between sessions scheduled every other week, the team worked on their own "real" process to further apply their knowledge.

Scanning   The look and select steps of the scanning phase had been accomplished by the GSH management group. They used brainstorming techniques to identify which processes in the hospital needed improvement. Then, they prioritized those processes based on the criteria they wanted to be met. The criteria were:

Phase 1. Scan	Phase 3. Resolve Gap
• Look • Select • Describe	• Find the "Why" • Identify Solution • Develop Plan

Phase 2. Define Gap	Phase 4. Implement
• Identify Requirements • Measure Process • Display Results • Identify Gap	• Take Action • Institutionalize

Exhibit 1. **IPP components.**

- Increase customer satisfaction
- Improve quality
- Increase productivity
- Reduce cycle time

The Hippies and Knee Highs began the project by learning to describe their process for total hip and total knee replacement. The teams accomplished this by developing a process map, which outlines the steps of a process in detail and presents a pictorial view of the process. First, all the events that occur each day are listed in the order in which they occur. Then, the relationships among these events are identified by using symbols, such as diamonds, rectangles, and arrows to describe decisions, actions, and directions of the process. By developing a process map, the teams could visualize what they do for total hip and total knee replacement patients from the day of surgery through the day of discharge from the hospital. It also enabled them to identify the materials and resources required for the process.

Defining the Gap   Once the teams described the process in need of improvement, they needed to identify who their customers were and what their customers wanted or needed from that process. They identified their customers as the patients who experienced total knee and total hip surgery.

The teams learned to develop questionnaires to help them identify customer requirements and measure process performance. Customers were asked about aspects of the care they had received during their hospitalization for total hip or total knee surgery. A brief questionnaire sent to the customers' homes asked questions about their physical therapy, pain management, discharge and admission preparation, support systems, and knowledge of insurance coverage for hospitalization. Some of the significant findings were:

- 60 percent of total hip patients were not aware of insurance coverage related to length of stay in the hospital.
- 47 percent of total knee patients did not have a support person attend physical therapy with them.

- 50 percent of total hip patients were not aware that short-term placement in an extended care facility might be needed after surgery.

To further identify customer requirements, team members conducted a retrospective chart review. Information such as age, sex, and health history was obtained from the medical charts to develop a patient profile and identify special needs. Data were collected about types of pain medicine used and when physical therapy was initiated after surgery. This information was analyzed in relationship to length of hospital stay. The data were displayed as graphs and pie charts, which were presented to the nursing staff, orthopedic physicians, and other groups. With all this information collected and organized, the teams could now identify the gaps in their process.

The formula for identifying the gap is: Customer Requirement − Process Performance = Gap. When all the information was reviewed, other gaps were identified:

The formula for identifying the gap is: Customer Requirement − Process Performance = Gap.

- Need for improved pain relief
- Need to increase patient mobility on the orthopedic nursing unit
- Need for earlier discharge planning
- Need for more staff/patient education to provide continuity on all three shifts
- Need for daily physical therapy
- Need for better coordination of care so that physical therapy sessions are not missed

Resolving the Gap Now that the teams had identified their customers' needs and expectations, it was time to improve their process of care by resolving the gaps. The team members had to first ask why the gaps were occurring. They used a brainstorming technique to list possible causes of the gaps, then categorized their responses. A cause-and-effect, or fishbone, diagram was developed to further identify causes, which again helped team members and others visualize the process (see **Exhibit 2**).

After causes and effects were considered and the patient questionnaires were analyzed, a new plan of care was developed—the critical pathway. Since the critical pathway lists key processes and clinical outcomes, its use can be measured continuously. If an outcome is not achieved, it is classified as a variance or deviation from the standard and analyzed. When the variances indicate a trend, a change in the process may be indicated.

Implementation   This involves introducing a plan of action and institutionalizing it. Implementation of the critical pathways for total hip and total knee procedures formally began with the introduction of the case management concept to the orthopedic nursing staff, orthopedic physicians, and the other disciplines involved in the care of these patients. A conference room in the patient care area was designated for staff education. The staff and physicians were provided with handouts to share data collected from patient questionnaires. In-service education was provided for the orthopedic nursing staff to

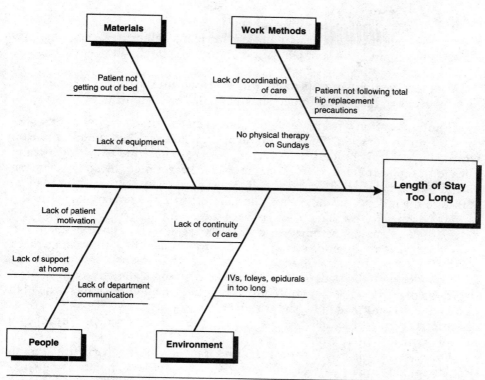

Exhibit 2.   **Fishbone diagram.**

explain the process used to develop the critical pathway. A story-board approach was effective in displaying the work done by the orthopedic team leaders. Brightly colored posters were also used to display the steps of the IPP process. A process map and the critical pathway were used to compare the proposed changes. Staff members were asked for suggestions to include in the critical pathway and were asked to complete a brief questionnaire that measured their knowledge of the initial critical pathway. The plan for introducing the critical pathway was very successful.

An orthopedic case manager was selected to direct a multidisciplinary case management team to monitor the new process and develop improvement projects. This team consisted of representatives from pre-admission testing, physical therapy, occupational therapy, pharmacy, nursing, nutrition services, utilization review, and discharge planning, as well as the geriatric clinical nurse specialist. The multidisciplinary team met monthly to discuss clinical and financial outcomes, variance trends, patient and provider satisfaction, and goals and objectives for future planning and quality improvement. Customer data were continuously monitored, measured, and interpreted to analyze gaps and to determine which changes would be institutionalized. Improvement projects that have been developed include:

- Update of pre-op teaching program
- Refinement of the case management plans and critical pathway
- Development of staff education materials related to case management
- Development of a plan to improve communication of patient needs to home health agencies/extended care facilities

Communication with key stakeholders is an essential component for successful implementation. The communication plan described the information required by all stakeholders involved in the care of patients requiring hip and knee joint replacement. The orthopedic case manager met with physicians on an individual basis to share the goals of case management and the plan to facilitate the process. In the orthopedic nursing unit, the case manager makes rounds with the physicians to see the total hip and knee patients. This provides an excellent opportunity to discuss questions and concerns about an individual patient's plan of care, as well as to discuss the case management plans. The case manager attends the orthopedic physicians' section meeting and provides periodic updates on orthopedic case management. Formal presentations of clinical data and outcomes are provided and revisions to the plan of care are recommended by the orthopedic surgeons. The section meetings are interactive and productive; case management has helped the orthopedic section focus on quality improvements in care.

> The communication plan described the information required by all stakeholders involved in the care of patients requiring hip and knee joint replacement.

The case manager has been instrumental in working with the staff to implement case management and the critical pathways. The on-going communication plan for the nursing staff includes newsletters, staff meetings, and one-on-one interactions with staff members. Involved with the nurses on a daily basis, the case manager is highly visible and accessible to them as a resource person not only for the total hip and total knee patients, but also for other orthopedic patients.

The case manager visits the patients and assesses their understanding of the process and how they perceive their progress. The goal is to identify potential and actual problems immediately and to coordinate care so that delays in treatment can be avoided. During hospitalization the case manager coordinates the planning of care with the discharge planner, utilization review nurse, physical therapist, occupational therapist, dietitians, and geriatric clinical nurse specialist as needed. Communication with the patient does not end at discharge. The case manager uses telephone surveys to conduct clinical follow-ups and to clarify patient questions or concerns.

Process Improvement Yields Healthy Results

The IPP process in orthopedics produced positive financial and clinical outcomes, as well as improved internal working relationships.

Clinical Outcomes Effective pain management is essential to provide patient comfort, facilitate early ambulation, and prevent vascular complications. The pharmacy staff helped explore options that would provide the patient with more effective pain management. Clinical trials for continuous analgesia as well as the use of patient-controlled analgesia have been effective in minimizing discomfort.

The orthopedic surgeons asked for pharmacy assistance in improving the regime for anticoagulant therapy, which is necessary to prevent vascular complications, such as deep vein thrombosis. Initially a pharmacist was involved on a daily basis to recommend therapeutic doses of Coumadin, an anticoagulant. In late 1993, Lovenox became available on the market and has proven to be more appropriate for this group of patients. The advantages of this product include:

1. The elimination of daily anticoagulant lab testing.
2. The elimination of the need for anticoagulant therapy after discharge from the hospital.
3. A more immediate therapeutic effect because it is administered by injection, compared to other anticoagulants in tablet form, which took two to three days to take effect.

A demographic review of patients requiring joint replacement revealed that the average patient age was sixty-nine years and 32 percent of patients were seventy-five years or older. Specific assessment for the elderly patient seventy-five years or older has been helpful in identifying risk factors associated with patients' response to a surgical procedure. The geriatric clinical nurse specialist provided guidance in developing a plan to minimize postoperative disorientation and loss of function related to activities of daily living. A shorter hospital stay for the elderly patient has reduced the risk of complications, as well as loss of function.

Early ambulation was identified as a key element in reducing complication risks, as well as facilitating patients' recovery. Prior to the development of the critical pathway, ambulation was limited to daily physical therapy initiated on the second day after surgery. The following steps were implemented to encourage early ambulation:

1. A video on proper patient transfer was developed and used to educate nursing staff. Consistency in the technique of transferring patients improved patient safety and increased patients' sense of security and competence with ambulation.
2. After the physical therapy evaluation, patients are encouraged to walk to use the bathroom instead of using a bedpan. This increased opportunity for ambulation builds patient confidence and increases muscle tone and endurance.
3. Physical therapy services have been expanded to provide service on Sunday for patients who have less than four days post-op experience.
4. A satellite physical therapy exercise area was installed in the orthopedic area. This increases the opportunity for staff to work with patients to improve ambulation skills. In addition, it eliminates the unproductive time it takes to place patients in a wheelchair and transfer them to physical therapy, which is located on another floor.

An interdisciplinary study was done before to IPP to determine the nutritional requirements of total hip and total knee patients. It was found that 95 percent of patients experienced an iron deficiency after surgery. Total hip and total knee patients also experience a decrease in protein levels in their blood after surgery. Dietary staff now educate preoperatively about these specific nutritional needs and monitor and treat these patients while in the hospital.

A significant finding from the patient questionnaire was that patients are not adequately prepared for the surgical procedure. A multidisciplinary planning group designed a pre-admission educational program to specifically meet the needs of these patients. Patients are scheduled for a pre-admission visit to the hospital two weeks before the scheduled procedure. During the visit the pre-operative lab work, chest x-ray, and EKG are obtained. An in-depth assessment is obtained and includes the following components:

1. Nursing history and assessment
2. Pre-surgery mobility and functional status
3. Cognitive geriatric testing for patients seventy-five years and older
4. Assessment of support in home for discharge care

This patient data is then utilized to develop an individualized plan of care for the patient. Patients are provided with information about their surgical procedure and post-operative care. For example, patients are taught exercises, precautions, and ambulation techniques that will be required after their surgery. Patients who are knowledgeable about the care they are to receive are able to directly participate in their care and achieve better outcomes. Pre-operative education has been shown to decrease patients' anxiety and improve their ability to perform after surgery.

Customer Satisfaction   Patients who attend the pre-operative teaching program express their gratitude for having the opportunity to get an idea of what they are getting into before surgery. They also appreciate the follow-up phone calls. The case management process also offers the total hip and total knee patients an individualized plan of care, since they have a multidisciplinary team watching over them. Patients like to know that someone is monitoring their progress.

Financial Outcomes   The change in length of stay (LOS) for hip and knee joint replacements has been very favorable (see **Exhibit 3**). There is appreciable decrease in the LOS for each procedure associated with joint replacements when comparing fiscal years '92, '93, and '94. The actual LOS savings can best be demonstrated by reviewing the procedures as two separate entities. All hip joint replacement procedures achieved a 3.71 day decrease from fiscal year '92 to fiscal year '94. All knee joint replacement procedures achieved a decrease of 3.45 days over the same timeframe.

Internal Working Relationships   The IPP program enabled the nursing team leaders from two orthopedic units to work together on a common goal. They

PROCEDURE	LOS FY '92	LOS FY '93	LOS FY '94
Total Hip Replacement	11.3	8.7	7.0
Partial Hip Replacement	12.4	10.0	9.6
Revision of Hip Replacement	12.0	7.9	7.8
Total Knee Replacement	10.2	7.6	6.9
Revision of Knee Replacement	7.0	7.5	5.6

Exhibit 3.   **Average length of stay in days by procedure.**

found that differences in how they cared for the same types of patients could be resolved, improving overall quality of care. They became excited about how they care for their patients and about their ability to make a difference for them.

GSH's experience in developing a process focus using quality management tools was complicated by the many professional disciplines involved in the care of patients with joint replacements. In the past, each discipline provided care in an autonomous manner, and there was little opportunity for collaboration. A major benefit of this effort was eliminating barriers to enhance interdisciplinary planning and collaboration to achieve common goals for this patient population. The various disciplines now have more ownership of this process and continue to meet at regular intervals to plan further efforts for continuous quality improvement.

Key Lessons Learned

An evaluation of GSH's continuous quality improvement effort for orthopedics reveals important success factors as well as pitfalls to be avoided in future projects. First of all, the best candidates to participate on a team effort are staff members who know the process best. Also, it is important for the organization to provide appropriate paid time for staff to engage in this type of activity. At GSH, education for CQI was provided on a just-in-time basis. That is, only those teams working on specified CQI efforts were given extra education.

Administrative support is required in other areas as well. At GSH, an administrative sponsor is required for all projects. The role of sponsor involves finding appropriate resources to support the team effort, as well as providing consultative services when requested by the team. In addition, the team will occasionally require encouragement, particularly when it is facing a roadblock or barrier within the institution. When possible, the administrator will participate in the process without disrupting the efforts of the group.

In the past, many decisions at GSH were made intuitively, based upon whatever information was available. Improving process performance requires

A major benefit of this effort was eliminating barriers to enhance interdisciplinary planning and collaboration to achieve common goals for this patient population.

a careful measurement and analysis before developing solutions. GSH staff learned to be patient and to avoid the natural response to develop solutions before they had all the necessary data in hand.

The orthopedic teams benefited greatly from having a facilitator from the organizational development department who was able to educate and guide the staff through the IPP process. In addition, the facilitator was invaluable in helping the teams focus on the process in a productive manner.

Physician support is critical when a process to be modified involves physician practice. The orthopedic teams were very successful in engaging a key orthopedic surgeon who was supportive of the efforts to streamline the cycle time for hip and knee joint replacements. In addition, this surgeon assumed personal responsibility for communicating with the other orthopedic surgeons to gain their support for the proposed changes. Involving physicians in this process is essential and yet problematic because of the necessary time commitment. Therefore, creative ways have to be developed to find opportunities for physician participation that will not be a burden on their time.

One of the pitfalls experienced was a lack of staff experience in developing questionnaires and analyzing and displaying data. Additional resources needed to be available to support these learning needs. For example, the display of data was greatly simplified with the availability of Harvard Graphics software. This, in turn, required additional education for staff less experienced in computer usage.

Establishing very specific boundaries for each process is critical. The orthopedic teams experienced frustration due to the breadth of the project and their desire to "fix it all." Successive teams have been guided to narrow their focus to a more manageable segment of any process.

The orthopedic case is but GSH's first step in a journey toward continuous quality. Institutional performance improvement is more than a program. Ultimately, it will change the culture that defines how GSH operates as an organization.

Judy L. Womack, RN, is vice president of operations and chief nurse executive at Good Samaritan Hospital in Dayton, Ohio. Carol S. Wasyk, RN, is the director of nursing at Good Samaritan Hospital. Marilyn Conner, RN, is the orthopedic case manager at Good Samaritan Hospital.

Quality Improvement OrNda Style

J. Kelley Avery, M.D.

This article documents the efforts of one hospital to reduce medical malpractice lawsuits by implementing some basic quality control procedures. These included categorizing problems as to type and frequency of occurrence and the development of preventive measures. The author believes this approach improves quality of care and has reduced the accidents that prompt lawsuits. The important point of this article is that quality management techniques have the additional benefit (besides improving care) of reducing lawsuits and, in the long run, the cost of malpractice insurance.

In the delivery of health care, when there is a true quality issue, there is also a risk management issue. The converse is not true: there are many risk issues that have little or no relation to the quality of care given. Falls in the parking lot, for example, or slips and falls in the corridors—those can be and are very expensive claims to settle. But the loss of a patient from an anesthetic or surgical accident, the untimely delay in performing a cesarean section, and other unfortunate clinical outcomes take on an entirely different dimension in the real world of torts and can spell financial disaster for both the hospital and the physician.

Loss of Control

When in the early 1970s there began to be a significant increase in the number of lawsuits filed against members of health care teams, and when jury awards against a hospital or physician were no longer a rarity, insurers began to lose control of their ability to predict the future with any degree of certainty.

This loss of the ability to realistically underwrite their product led many insurers to leave the medical malpractice insurance market. In some states there was simply no market for physicians and hospitals to go to for this kind of coverage, and the crisis of medical malpractice insurance began. A variety of means was used to confront this serious problem, but they are not the focus of this article.

Prior to this time of crisis, the risk management function in the average hospital was the responsibility of an individual who, among other duties usually unrelated, was assigned to make sure that the casualty insurance that protected the institution was current (financially) and in force. The risk management personnel made themselves available to assist in the processing of any event that occurred requiring the participation of the insurance company involved. Most often that participation consisted of writing a check to cover whatever damage might have occurred. Little attention was given by risk management to the investigation of the particulars of the event, and they paid almost no attention to trying to prevent a recurrence. Thus, the explosion of malpractice litigation and traditional low-key risk management practices in institutions made a more structured response essential on the part of hospitals and physicians.

I am sure that many systems evolved to deal with what was happening to OrNda HealthCorp at that time, but I will briefly deal with the elements of the one with which I was involved.

"Needle Stick" Problem

The time-honored "Incident Report" began to receive far more attention than it had previously. The reports were categorized so that with some attention one could approach a prevention strategy more precisely. This system was managed manually at first, but soon computerized programs were developed that greatly assisted in the classification of events. The tracking and trending of this information was important in our effort to devise risk management education pointed toward the prevention of injury to personnel and patients.

With this new tool in hand, teams of people representing the different departments of the institution could develop the educational approach necessary to reduce the risk.

For example, I remember, vividly, the "needle stick" problem that came to light in the team I worked with. It was determined over time that the increased number of needle sticks in scrubbed-in surgical professionals occurred in the cardiac surgery department. The problem was further narrowed to a certain cardiac surgeon who insisted on using the same assistants for all of his cases. The majority of the sticks were reported by the same assistant. Upon investigation, the surgical nurse from that department informed us that this particular surgical assistant had unusually large hands. With closer observation, it was determined that these "sticks" occurred more often during the closure of the chest incision by the same two assistants, who always began their closure at the ends of the incision and worked toward the center. The number of sticks were significantly reduced when these two assistants were advised to begin their closure in the center and work toward the ends of the surgical incision. There were numerous similar experiences with that one team.

It is common knowledge that when the hospital is sued, a physician is almost always a part of the claim. The converse is also true: a physician in one of our hospitals is almost never the target of litigation without the hospital also being named. For this reason, it was felt that it would be very helpful if a committee of physicians was formed to examine the overall quality of medical practice in the hospital from the standpoint of possible litigation.

Given the constant threat of malpractice lawsuits, it was not hard to find a senior physician from the most suit-prone specialties to lead in the formation of this committee. Ultimately, a group of extremely talented physicians adopted the principle stated above, that every true quality issue in the care of a patient is, in fact, a potential lawsuit.

Concurrent Review

During the same time frame, the quality assurance/utilization management (QA/UM) department was moving toward house-wide concurrent review. This group of dedicated nurses already was identifying the quality issues that were being taken to physician advisers for comment/action. The Joint Commission on Accreditation of Healthcare Organizations (JCAHO) began to advise close cooperation between the QA/UM activity and the risk management people. The screens already in use were expanded only slightly to include other indicators—for example, unplanned returns to the emergency department. As time went on, more outcome indicators were added to the screens.

On a monthly basis, the cases that were identified by this screening activity were taken to the chairman of the physician committee, and those cases where the quality issue could have been perceived as the cause of an undesirable outcome were brought forward to the physician group for review.

The physician committee set its own ground rules. The only non-physician in the room was the chairperson of the QA/UM department. The hospital attorney was not a member of the committee, because it was feared that the presence of a lawyer might make full discussion of the clinical issues involved less likely to occur. The cases were assigned to a committee member of the same specialty when possible, and a full review of the clinical management of the case was carried out. Physicians were on their honor not to reveal the identity of the treating physician. When the treating physician was a member of the committee, he/she was notified in advance of the meeting and was given the option of attending or taking an excused absence. If he/she elected to attend, which most did, his/her identity was not to be revealed. A full, sometimes heated, discussion often occurred. Action was taken on consensus, and appropriate follow-up was designed by the committee. The action could range from a discussion with the chief of the service—the most common—to threatened loss of privileges membership. When the committee found a quality concern that adversely affected the results of treatment, the patient and family were counseled and fully informed. We believed that this approach usually prevented legal action. And when litigation did occur, the case was much more easily brought to closure.

Elements of Integration

There are four key elements of our approach to the integration of risk management into the overall Quality and Utilization Management program:

1. A core committee of physicians dedicated to the study of quality issues in the care of hospitalized patients and the relationship of these issues to potential malpractice charges.

2. Integrating risk management review concurrently with the quality and utilization review, usually by the same personnel.
3. Tracking and trending of Incident Report information, such as medication errors or needle sticks.
4. Ongoing targeted risk management/loss prevention education specific to hospital departments and/or the medical staff and based on the actual experience in the institution.

Clearly, physicians are interested in and concerned about the threat of malpractice lawsuits, and it should not be difficult to channel that interest into this kind of prevention activity.

Did this approach improve quality? We believe we can show that it did in the practice of certain physicians and hospital departments. Did it prevent litigation against the hospital and/or the physician? We believe it did, but proof would be difficult. Also, in my years of experience this was the only time when physicians asked for an opportunity to serve on a committee. Clearly, physicians are interested in and concerned about the threat of malpractice lawsuits, and it should not be difficult to channel that interest into this kind of prevention activity.

Our total team effort, which included active participation by a physician committee, along with hospital-wide awareness, has been the logical foundation for the effective, ongoing quality improvement program.

J. Kelley Avery is chief medical officer for OrNda HealthCorp, Nashville, Tennessee.

9 Lessons of Value-Driven Leadership

William W. Arnold

This article summarizes what one health care executive has learned about allowing values to drive management effort. Indeed, it emphasizes the importance of values in implementing quality management in a health care facility. These lessons are equally applicable to any organization.

To be value-driven leaders today, we must be willing to take risks and support positions that may be unpopular with the status quo. Hesitancy on the part of a leader can mean the difference between the success or failure of an organization—particularly when external issues are accelerating and an organization is unprepared to address change. A leader must be primed to champion the goals of an organization, work to achieve short-term financial success, and build an infrastructure to support long-term results that are sustainable and measurable.

The question is: How do we position our organizations for success while maintaining our values? Based on my experience as senior vice president of Franciscan Health System in Tacoma, Wash., I have developed the following nine lessons for value-driven leadership. Perhaps they will offer you some direction.

Lesson 1
Focus on Doing a Few Things Extremely Well
I have taped to my desk six strategic objectives that comprise the focus of my work. They are:

1. Improve quality, identify major waste, and reduce costs
2. Develop a primary care network and position the organization to effectively operate and contract in a managed care environment
3. Develop key partnerships
4. Achieve clinical integration
5. Meet budget and operating plan goals
6. Continue to orient myself to the values of our Franciscan organization and to focus my leadership skills on repositioning our regional system for success

Value-driven leaders must understand what results their organizations expect in both the short and long term. Also, to achieve these results, their personal values must be in synergy with organizational values.

In August 1993, Franciscan Health System CEO Ron Aldrich, FACHE, revised the system's vision and goals. Now, FHS's vision is "to be a healing influence in the communities we serve. We will improve health status, create easy access, and establish a cost-effective, quality health system." That vision is supported by Beth O'Brien, CHE, executive vice president/chief operating officer, and her goal of "90-day deliverables," which calls for focused work through focused, productive relationships.

When I joined FHS in May 1994, the following strategic goals had already been established. My job was to help staff meet them.

GOAL 1: *Advance the healing mission of the Sisters of St. Francis.*
- Support a shared vision and holistic healing
- Encourage communication, expansion, and full integration of values
- Address ethical issues
- Support public policy leadership

GOAL 2: *Create a culture of continuous improvement in leadership, quality, and innovation that demonstrates cost-effectiveness and customer value.*
- Reduce waste and costs
- Improve customer value and satisfaction
- Support problem-solving and systems thinking
- Benchmark
- Support experimentation and innovation

GOAL 3: *Create an organizational environment that values, empowers, enriches, and supports those with whom we work.*
- Support change management and retraining
- Develop reward and recognition systems
- Support open communication
- Support education
- Encourage diversity

GOAL 4: *Develop an affordable integrated delivery system through partnerships that provide a continuum of care in the communities we serve.*
- Form an integrated delivery system
- Reorganize care
- Develop primary and specialty care networks
- Develop financing mechanisms and manage care
- Develop sophisticated information systems

The FHS leadership has set a superb tone and pace for our system that make achieving these objectives realistic not only on the national level, but on the local level as well.

Lesson 2
There Is No Substitute for Good Business Practices

At times, we may feel torn between accepted business practices and our personal values. We should never let this happen. Telling the truth, looking people in the eye, and being true to oneself is essential to value-driven leadership. Our organizations must enrich us as people and provide us with a sense of well-being as we develop business goals into action plans.

At FHS, regional office executives, hospital executives, and vice presidents met to develop a set of working values. Based on our collective years of work experience, we developed the following team ground rules:

- Be responsive
- Respect the time of others
- Be honest
- Help others feel safe
- Over communicate
- Be flexible
- Show an eagerness to learn
- Ask for help
- Care for others

Like many of my co-workers, I carry the values in my wallet and pull out the card every so often to remind myself how we should do business and interact with each other.

Value-driven leaders believe they have a social contract to respond to community health needs. It is based on an essential respect for their fellow man and makes them accountable to the people they serve. Their word becomes their bond, and they loose tolerance for games and politics.

Telling the truth, looking people in the eye, and being true to oneself is essential to value-driven leadership.

Lesson 3
Create an Environment for Teamwork

In our regional facility, all offices are open; no one has a door. Members of our hand-picked regional team are selected for their ability to build relationships. They do not depend on a "large office power trip" infrastructure to get results. In about a 4,500 square foot area we have our vice presidents of finance, managed care, legal services, marketing and communications, human resources, information systems, and mission and sponsorship as well as myself. My office is plain and simple—no frills—which helps me maintain a clear focus on FHS's mission and key strategies.

To achieve this open-office architecture, we recently relocated our offices to one of the area hospitals. The move allowed us to trim expenses by $4 million and introduce a leadership style that enables us to better serve our customers. We use voice mail to address issues more quickly and get business done in a rapid manner. Our dedication and loyalty to each other is real—we are mutually accountable to each other.

Members of our hand-picked regional team are selected for their ability to build relationships. They do not depend on a "large office power trip" infrastructure to get results.

These objectives—simplicity and well-organized work—are essential elements of value-driven leadership. When distractions are minimized and the focus is on achieving organizational goals, the results are crisp and effective.

Lesson 4
Make Long Work Short

When a leader is integrated personally and professionally, work that once took years to complete becomes amazingly compressed into much shorter cycle times. In three months, we relocated our regional FHS office, integrated three hospitals into a single managed care contracting entity, and organized ourselves as an integrated delivery system.

In 11 months, we developed the structure for a new regional board, nationally introduced a program for developing community health councils, and reduced costs by $28 million. We also created a physician-hospital network and a limited liability corporation in cooperation with another healthcare provider, creating a network of 220 primary care physicians that is expected to grow to 400 in two years.

In the same time frame, we developed a framework for clinical integration and launched several information system initiatives to analyze costs for DRG-related resource utilization. Our cost per adjusted admission has declined 11 percent in less than a year, and we now have a financial model in place to calculate risk absorption based on our managed care contracting.

Lesson 5
Don't Be Afraid of Failure

A major downfall of healthcare systems around the country is hesitancy. Everybody watches everybody else before deciding to move forward. Value-driven leaders can only succeed in organizations that are not suffering from identity crises. Initiatives for action must be clear and targeted at success, not survival. Staff must be urged to apply their talents, to take accountability for their departments as cost centers, and to provide services that are quality measured and value-provider based.

Value-driven leaders are not out to win popularity contests. They must be willing to make unpopular decisions and be motivated by a commitment to serving their organizations, rather than promises of personal gain, especially when those gains come at the expense of the organization. A physician I know sold out his group for personal gain. At first everyone thought it was a brilliant scheme, but after a year the venture failed. Value-driven leaders cannot afford to have a part succeed at the expense of the whole.

Relationships should never be viewed only as business transactions, but as long-term investments that must be nourished and developed. Rather than look at their positions as a "right," value-driven leaders must be committed to those they serve and candid about the services they are providing in an effort to meet their organizations' missions. While value-driven leaders are not perfect, they are honest and willing to work harder than anybody else. They earn trust through their results and the predictability of their actions.

Value-driven leaders must be willing to make unpopular decisions and be motivated by a commitment to serving their organizations, rather than promises of personal gain.

Lesson 6

Take Responsibility for Your Work and Require Others to Do so as Well

I can't tell you how many times staff people have asked me to explain FHS's strategy. It's been distributed, discussed, and continuously referenced; it's even typed and taped to my desk. After a number of such requests, I abbreviated my explanation:

> You must exercise your leadership and be accountable for your job. Continual confusion is not an excuse for not developing and doing real work. Today's value-driven leaders talk straight and in a manner that is firm, yet respectful.

Value-driven leaders must recognize, however painful, that some staff members may not want the organization to succeed. They may perpetuate confusion and establish work agendas that further their own careers rather than the organization. Unfortunately, that's the nature of organizations everywhere, so why not address the problem at the outset? Value-driven leaders should focus on the same objectives as everyone else. They should ground themselves in the core mission and business objectives of their organizations and not allow themselves to be distracted.

Lesson 7

Live with Details

Value-driven leaders live with the details and understand the operational dynamics of their organizations. Many years ago, a well-known healthcare leader with whom I worked looked at his office coffee table, loaded with reports, and said to me, "Bill, I've lost the details. I've gotten away from the details of the organization and somehow I need to get back."

It is impossible for leaders to immerse themselves in all the details of everything, but they should always know the details of key strategic objectives. Value-driven leaders should be able to apply the standards of CQI and be fluent in ratios and market share percentages. They should know how to read trend graphs and understand variance.

Leaders' time is limited, so they should focus on those goals that are most important. For value-driven leaders, the potential for burnout is real because they must overcome a number of obstacles to get work done in a more effective manner. Value-driven leaders must ask hard questions, track work, and remember detail. They must set the pace, tone, and direction.

Value-driven leaders should be able to apply the standards of CQI and be fluent in ratios and market share percentages.

Lesson 8

Maintain Balance in Your Personal and Professional Life

Leading in a value-driven manner is difficult. Value-driven leaders are tenacious and willing to "die on the mountain" they're climbing. This tenacity is deeply tied to leaders' belief systems and world views—they must be positive change agents.

Staying physically fit is essential to meeting the demands of value-driven leadership. Taking the time to lead a balanced life is also key. Value-driven leaders must learn to say "No," even when it means displeasing others.

Lesson 9
You Can't Always Celebrate Your Successes

Value-driven leaders should never take credit or wait for a thank-you. The world is not kind to these leaders—they force accountability for results and confront organizational truths. Often, after many years of work, the value-driven leader moves on to a new position, leaving those left behind to celebrate and congratulate themselves for their wise leadership. While this experience might be painful for many, value-driven leaders relish the journey and not its completion. They enjoy developing strategy and establishing values for an organization.

William W. Arnold, CHE, is senior vice president of Franciscan Health System in Tacoma, Wash.

Quality Management in Schools: 1995

Julie Horine

This article, by Julie Horine, consulting editor in K–12, highlights national initiatives that are providing a foundation for fostering quality management efforts in K–12 schools. The article profiles how a growing number of partnerships between schools, businesses, communities, and government agencies are resulting in improvements in the educational system and suggests how the Malcolm Baldrige National Quality Award criteria for education may provide a comprehensive framework for assessing quality excellence.

In the past five years, a growing number of American schools, faced with public demand for accountability, state mandates, and national reform efforts, have sought improved school performance by joining industry in adapting the quality principles and tools espoused by quality authorities such as W. Edwards Deming and J. M. Juran. At least 140 school districts are actively implementing quality principles through a combination of business-education partnerships, school improvement teams, classroom initiatives, and administrative efforts.[1] The wide-spread interest by educators at all levels in continuous quality improvement is evidenced through the proliferation of networks, conferences, books, and articles on the applicability of quality management principles in schools.

In 1995, educators participated in a variety of quality conferences such as the Fourth Annual National Governor's Conference for Quality in Education in Albuquerque, New Mexico, attended by approximately 900 K–12 teachers, students, administrators, business partners, and policy makers from 44 states, Canada, and Spain. In addition, thousands of educators joined quality networks, such as the American Association for School Administrator's Total

Quality Network, the Association for Supervision and Curriculum Development TQM Education Network, and the American Society for Quality Control's Education Division (see resource listing at the end of this article).

Quality Innovators

Public school districts are using a variety of quality management results ranging from classroom learning improvements to school-wide improvement efforts.[2] Of the 140 public school districts actively implementing quality principles, 85 percent have identified key customer groups, 76 percent of the districts have defined critical processes, and 70 percent have flowcharted some of their critical processes. Districts report a wide range of successful school-wide quality improvement projects such as reducing "student movement in the halls" to decreasing "unscheduled parent classroom visitations."

School districts are using quality principles to improve classroom learning, either through teams or through individual teachers and students. For example, team projects deal with classroom initiatives like improving the "mastery of algebra concepts" and increasing the "amount of completed homework." Results of selected quality initiatives from the 140 districts are summarized in Table 1.

Research suggests that while quality management efforts are producing some significant results in schools in a variety of areas, results still appear to be isolated and not interconnected.

Systems Thinking and Partnerships

Despite the flurry of interest among educators in quality management principles, most of the nation's roughly 15,000 public school districts are still in the early stages of developing sound, systematic approaches for deploying quality principles throughout the school system. Research suggests that while quality management efforts are producing some significant results in schools in a variety of areas, results still appear to be isolated and not interconnected.[3] Perceiving a school as a system represents a paradigm shift for most educators. The ability to see interrelationships rather than linear cause-and-effect chains was initially discussed by Deming in 1950 and more recently popularized by Peter Senge as "systems thinking." School systems represent a set of interrelated entities that work together to achieve a common purpose, driven by customer needs and requirements. At a community level, for example, Deming suggests that city schools, including public and private schools, trade schools, and colleges, represent components that ought to work together as a system for education.[4]

From a system's perspective, quality improvement in education must ultimately involve all levels of America's educational infrastructure.

As the concepts of quality management gain greater acceptance among educators, there is growing recognition that sustained progress and breakthrough learning requires collaborative partnerships both within and outside the educational system. More than two-thirds (71 percent) of the 135 K–12 school districts participating in *Quality Progress'* 1994 survey report business partnerships that support their quality improvement efforts.[5] Many states, such as Minnesota, New Mexico, and New Jersey, have formed statewide coalitions between education, business, and government leaders interested in promoting quality throughout the state. Pennsylvania's Lehigh Valley currently has 17 partnerships between schools and businesses working together

Table 1.   **Selected Quality Improvement Results from 140 School Districts**

Improvement Project	**Results**
Algebra I class	Increased percentage of students mastering more material and receiving top grades to 80 percent
Discipline	Reduced office referrals by 40 percent
District-wide records of absences and releases	Increased accuracy of data by 85 percent through standardization
Elementary science lab kits	Reduced lost boxes from 20 percent of total delivered to 9 percent and reduced damaged items by 50 percent
Electronic ordering	Increased the number of people who order from central supply electronically by 30 percent; decreased the time required to place orders electronically by 7 percent
Employee absence forms	Reduced processing time of employee absence reports and revised format to reduce printing costs
Homework study	90 percent of the staff changed the homework study process
Lunch operations	Reduced lunch operation cost by 10 percent and provided healthier lunches
Maintenance	Increased work order completions 100 percent from 800 monthly in 1993 to 1600 monthly in 1994 with no increase in personnel
Parent satisfaction	Increased parent satisfaction to 90 percent (district met or exceeded expectations)
School-wide discipline	Reduced number of discipline referrals by 40 percent
Special education assessments	Increased the percentage of assessments completed within deadlines from 30 percent ('92–'93) to 85 percent ('93–'94)
Student movement in halls	Reduced student movement in halls by 90 percent
Student portfolio usage	Increased student portfolio usage from 10 to 50 percent in one year
Unscheduled parent classroom visitations	Decreased unscheduled visitations by 90 percent

to transfer quality improvement methods to the educational system. From a system's perspective, quality improvement in education must ultimately involve all levels of America's educational infrastructure, from grade schools to the universities, as well as business, state agencies, community social systems, and family units.

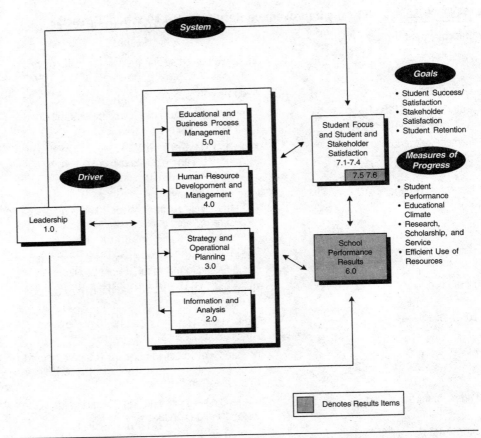

Figure 1. **Educational pilot criteria framework: dynamic relationships.**

A Framework for Quality Excellence

While all school systems profess to have quality programs, there is less agreement among educators when asked, "How do you know that your school system is providing ever-increasing value to students and stakeholders?" Educators find themselves caught up in a swirl of "quality" rhetoric devoid of a common definition of what constitutes quality excellence. Diagnostic self-assessment tools such as the Malcolm Baldrige National Quality Award education pilot criteria[6] may represent the necessary integrated framework to connect processes with performance results and provide a national standard for assessing quality excellence.

The Baldrige Award, initially enacted into public law in 1987 to stimulate American companies to improve quality and productivity, provides organizations with a rigorous evaluation process to systematically assesses performance and improve effectiveness. Over a million copies of the criteria have been requested and disseminated since 1988 to business and, more recently, to education and health care organizations. The criteria are a set of interrelated, results-oriented requirements linked to organizational excellence defined through seven categories and 28 items (see Figure 1). Category components work together as a system to achieve the goals of the organization. Organizations that fail to build category linkages end up with "disconnects" or systems that are out of alignment. For example, a school system might identify key measures for tracking educational progress (category 2.0) but then fail to set goals for these measures (category 3.0) or fail to show trend data results (category 6.0) for most of the key measures.

With the introduction of the education version of the Baldrige criteria in 1995, school systems have shown increased interest in using the Baldrige criteria to assess school performance. For example, in 1995, 19 educational systems (nine K–12 systems and 10 higher education systems) assessed their organizations using the Baldrige education criteria and submitted their assessments to the national board of evaluators for feedback (the pilot does not include awards) as part of the national education pilot program. In addition, 35 states have implemented their own state quality awards patterned after the national Baldrige criteria, many with award categories in education. At least five states have recognized K–12 school systems as award recipients at various award levels for their quality efforts, including the following: Florida: Pinellas County School District (1993); New York: Kenmore-Town of Tonawanda Union Free School District (1992), Pearl River School District (1994); New Mexico: Del Norte High School (1995); Pennsylvania: Millcreek Township School District (1992); and Virginia: Danville City Schools (1993).

Conclusions

As increasing public pressure for accountability and cost containment requires education systems to address how they are delivering ever-improving value to students, the Baldrige criteria may provide schools with a meaningful framework for answering this challenge. Without prescribing "how" to improve performance, the Baldrige criteria foster a systematic self-examination process leading to comprehensive performance improvement opportunities. With its emphasis on connecting process with results, sharing of best practices, and partnership development, the Baldrige criteria could become a significant catalyst in promoting systemic change in education.

Notes

1. Julie E. Horine, William A. Hailey, and Robert O. Edmister, "Quality Management Practices and Business Partnerships" in *America's Schools, Planning and Changing,* Fall/Winter 1994, vol. 25, no. 3/4, pp. 233–240.

2. Ibid.

3. Ibid.

4. W. Edwards Deming, *Foundation for Management of Quality in the Western World,* paper presented at the meeting of the Institute of Management Sciences, July 24, 1989, pp. 1–30.

5. Laura Rubach, "Fourth Annual Quality in Education Listing," *Quality Progress,* July 1995, vol. 27, no. 9, pp. 27–79.

6. United States Department of Commerce, *Malcolm Baldrige National Quality Award 1995 Education Pilot Criteria* (Gaithersburg, Maryland, 1995; phone: 301-975-2036).

Resource List of K–12 Networks

The Center for Schools of Quality
    Association for Supervision and Curriculum Development (ASCD)
    Publishes quarterly newsletter: *Quality Success Stories*
    Contact: John Jay Bonstingl, P.O. Box 810, Columbia, Maryland 21044
    Phone: 410-997-7555; Fax: 410-997-2345

Total Quality Network
    American Association of School Administrators (AASA)
    Publishes bimonthly newsletter: *Quality Network News*
    Contact: AASA: 1801 N. Moore St., Arlington, Virginia 22209
    Phone: 703-875-0764; Fax: 703-528-2146

Education Division
    The American Society for Quality Control (ASQC)
    Publishes quarterly newsletter: *QED News*
    Contact: ASQC, P.O. Box 3066, Milwaukee, Wisconsin 53201
    Phone: 800-248-1946; Fax: 414-272-1734

Dr. Horine is a faculty member at the University of Mississippi in the Department of Educational Leadership. She is a two-year Malcolm Baldrige National Quality Award Examiner and a two-year member of the Malcolm Baldrige National Education Pilot Evaluation Team.

A Vision for Schools

David P. Langford and Barbara A. Cleary

This article is really the last chapter in the book Orchestrating Learning with Quality. *It provides some real insight into why quality management principles make sense in education, not only in managing schools and the classroom but equally importantly as ways to facilitate learning. The ideas presented here represent innovative thinking about learning and affirm the wisdom of the tools of quality management to enhance our understanding and our performance.*

School reform efforts, from the first attempt at modernizing schools even to the most recent emphases on outcome-based education and site-based management, have often adopted language that quickly evolved into jargon and then passed into history as the reform movement was abandoned. Is quality learning another example of a movement that will become dated, and then outdated?

While the language of quality has its limitations (educators will perhaps never feel comfortable with *customers* or *outputs* in describing what they do), the concepts of quality learning are timeless because they do not represent a single program or movement. Instead, they provide a framework within which improvement of all kinds can take place. They are not a template to be imitated or applied, but instead represent a way of thinking. Quality learning is not a reform program, but a way of seeing all aspects of education as they relate to each other and to their customers.

Building a New House

Quality learning represents a way of seeing. Its language is of vision, purpose, and improvement. It is in this sense theoretical. The theory of quality learning is embodied in the principles that recognize systems (perhaps the most fundamental of the principles), customers, human behavior (including the psychology of learning), and change. Making these principles into concrete realities is the challenge of each organization.

To envision an educational system grounded in these principles provides an opportunity for what Russell Ackoff (1993) calls "idealized redesign." This strategy involves thinking about the system as if there were no system already in place—the kind of thinking home owners would engage in by imagining that their house has burned down and they must start over. They would have

> The theory of quality learning is embodied in the principles that recognize systems (perhaps the most fundamental of the principles), customers, human behavior (including the psychology of learning), and change.

an opportunity to change the things they never liked about the original house and to develop new features that were not possible with old constraints. This kind of thinking is useful even if the house does not burn down, because it represents an opportunity to refocus the problem with new thinking. This chapter will offer an opportunity to dream about the new house but then to return to the reality of the situation. We are not starting from scratch, but must renovate what we have. By imagining the ideal school, we can indeed create the schools we want.

What is the ideal classroom? There may be more agreement on this than we realize. Even without a consensus about purpose, for example, many can envision an environment that is active, where students and teachers are engaged in the learning process, and where young people are given support for their learning. A quality classroom, like a quality product or service, is hard to define, but easily recognized. Or as John Guaspari (1985) suggests in the title of his book, *I Know It When I See It*. Some of the classrooms we know already represent this ideal; others demand change.

Theory alone is not enough to bring about change. It must be supported by processes and tools that are consistent with that theory in order to put it into practice. Nonetheless, the theory must provide clear direction for the change. We need to be very sure that we understand the same theory, or no two of us will design the same house even if we have to live in it together.

Processes, though highly individual to school settings, contribute to the sense of purpose that is fostered by system thinking. The processes of learning about dinosaurs, of gaining confidence in speaking and writing, of creating papier-mâché replicas of the Roman Coliseum, of applying formulas to mathematical problems, and of preparing drama productions, all contribute to the purpose of a system of education. This contribution comes about not because of specific content alone, but by virtue of providing opportunities to develop suitable skills of understanding, analyzing, synthesizing, clarifying, and so on. In this sense, it does not really matter whether students understand everything about the Paleozoic Age, for example, It is critical, however, that students know how to find out about the Paleozoic Age, and, of course, how it is related both to dinosaurs and to student life in the twentieth century—and to have some excitement about it, one hopes. It is thinking skills, not the specific content, that characterizes real learning.

Each level of learning provides its own appropriate depth and breadth of understanding. Thus, content directives and must-read book lists cannot be seen as the answer to what ails our schools. If students' interests are aroused, through a sense of purpose; if precision is developed, with the vocabulary and tools necessary for understanding and communication; and if the ability to generalize and apply is fostered, through authentic learning tasks, it makes little difference whether students read *The House of the Seven Gables* or *The Scarlet Letter*. The important outcome is the students' abilities to apply what is learned—ideas, skills, and knowledge—to new situations. These situations include meeting new characters in literature or new people in life, pursuing further reading, and simply living daily life with openness and joy in learning.

Schools of the Future

Among those who are trying to "reinvent the future of school" is Seymour Papert, director of the Epistomology and Learning Group at the Massachusetts Institute of Technology (Hill, 1994). Papert points out that while the world has experienced "megachange" in communications, health care, transportation, and recreation, the classroom has evolved very little since the turn of the century. Educators remain largely committed to educational philosophies developed in the nineteenth century and in the early part of this century. Since they are unable to change the system within which they find themselves, individual students—or "yearners" as Papert calls them—and their parents simply find ways to get around schools. Among these methods are home schooling or alternative schools. Teachers, too, find ways to develop learning centers in their classrooms that have little to do with the school community within which they find themselves. It is to be remembered that these approaches represent beginnings; they do not fundamentally change the school system as a whole. Nonetheless, they support the aim of the school, to develop learning.

In assessing reform in school, Papert urges those who share his vision of the future to simply abandon the present system of education and form their own "little schools," characterized by shared vision and "authentic personal beliefs." While this alternative is appealing to many, it is clear that it reflects a deeply shared belief that the public schools cannot really improve, and that the best hope is to build smaller systems of schooling that can be more responsive to students' needs.

We may picture such little schools as isolated units of learning, each with its own purpose. This vision, however, is not necessarily one of fragmentation. Even with much smaller units of schooling, each of which has defined its own vision, a sense of larger system can invigorate these units and give them connectedness to the society within which they operate. Understanding the customer, in the largest meaning of that term, suggests that all schools ultimately respond to the same customer—students as well as future generations that will depend on current school populations for the leadership and problem-solving skills to assure survival.

But they'd better hurry. As a high school senior announced on a microphone at a Global Awareness Day sponsored by AFS Intercultural Programs in Ohio, "I suddenly realize that if we don't address some of these [environmental] problems, our children won't even have a *chance* to solve them." The same observation might be made of our schools, which are on the brink of tremendous change—even, some would assert, of destruction.

The challenge facing school reformers, then, may be one of accommodating specific needs of internal customers within a large framework of external customers, both present and perhaps especially those of the future. Generations of private and independent schools have balanced this accommodation nicely. While they may have been educating students for a particular or specialized need (vocational skills, religious values, or academic concentration),

Educators remain largely committed to educational philosophies developed in the nineteenth century and in the early part of this century.

they have, for the most part, not operated outside the general system of society and the educational system that serves it. Just because students educated in parochial schools, for example, have had the advantage of the moral and religious training, which they and their families sought, does not mean that they cannot also be prepared for good citizenship in a world that does not share their religious orientations. Schools can have their own narrowly defined purposes and visions and yet support the purpose and vision of the large system of education.

When schools recognize that they are all in the business of preparing graduates to function as citizens in large communities with pluralistic values, the relationship of one school to another can be one of support, not competition. A private school with 100 students can do quite different things from a public school with 2500, but the reverse is also true. Quality education prepares students for a world with a variety of threats and challenges, and each type of education and each individual classroom can support this aim.

The school of the future—for that matter, the workplace and the home of the future—will have an emphasis on technology that we cannot immediately envision. In the same way, schools of the 1930s could not have foreseen the impact of broadcast media on student learning, nor, might it be argued, did they adequately prepare their students to deal with this dramatic change in their lives. Our schools cannot provide or even anticipate precise technological developments of the mid-twenty-first century. Most cannot afford even the technology that is currently available. The challenge is to prepare students to critically evaluate and use whatever technology will be available in their lives. This is like walking in a dark tunnel, to be sure. But by continuing to prepare students to think and learn, rather than only to do, educational systems will produce graduates who are ready for whatever comes. Like students who attend a school with a specialized purpose, all students must learn to live in environments that do not always mirror their own comfortable experiences. The ideal school will prepare them for this expanded world.

Quality as a Framework

Systems thinking, and its understanding of the dynamic needs of customers, support a variety of school models because they identify the interconnectedness of systems. The needs of internal customers do not have to be seen as a source of conflict with those of external customers, for the two can interface positively even within a diverse range of small-school models. The key is in identifying the large system and its purpose, as well as the small unit's contribution to this purpose.

Quality learning, with its framework for seeing schools anew, provides a sense of connectedness among various components of the system of education. It also gives an essential foundation for the necessary interactions between schools and society. Customer needs are fundamental to understanding purpose.

Systems thinking, and its understanding of the dynamic needs of customers, support a variety of school models because they identify the interconnectedness of systems.

It is within this framework that a number of current reforms in education can be placed, demonstrating how quality learning does not contradict or supersede thoughtful changes that have already been made, but indeed places these changes within the system of education and its purpose. Site-based management, for example, represents a potentially powerful strategy to transfer ownership of school issues to schools themselves and to bring decision making close to those directly involved in educational processes. Seeing this approach against larger issues of purpose and vision, variation in systems, and customer needs provides a way of reaffirming purpose while evaluating the specific strategy itself. A question that arises from systems thinking relates to suboptimization: Is the school placing an inordinate number of its resources, for example, into assuring the success of site-based management without understanding how this management contributes to its larger purposes? Any specific strategy, program, or solution can take on a life of its own when it is not placed with a context. Quality learning provides this context.

The network of never-ending contexts is somewhat like a mirror held up to another mirror, the same objects repeatedly reproduced in the two reflected images. Interdependence between the individual component and its larger environment represents an aspect of systems thinking that is particularly vital to schools. In quantum physics, this interdependency is called contextualism; in art, T.S. Eliot observes something like it in "Tradition and the Individual Talent." While the scientific principle of contextualism has been improperly construed to suggest that things have meaning only with respect to their contexts, it seems more accurate to say that things are what they apparently are because of the multiple interactions and relationships that they experience. This is at least how we know them.

Small Steps

Within the context of theory, a number of steps can be taken to interact with the present system in order to create a new one. Translating quality theory into concrete reality means recognizing that the individuals in the system cannot change the entire system all at once. When managers of the entire school system are not ready to begin the quality improvement process, however, individual educators can effect change and begin the steps toward improving the system. There must be first steps in any change.

Situations where individual teachers are using quality learning to improve their classrooms even without the support of their leaders are legion. When they are introduced to quality learning principles, educators' frequent response is, "This may make a lot of sense, but my principal [superintendent/board of education/department head] will never support it." It is important to understand that there are ways to introduce this new way of thinking, one person at a time. Concentrating on their own circle of control, teachers can begin to change the system in small increments. Examples of these incremental improvements are easy to find.

Concentrating on their own circle of control, teachers can begin to change the system in small increments.

- When they must give grades, teachers can minimize the competitive impact of these grades by using alternative assessments and conferences to enhance student opportunities to evaluate their own work and even determine criteria for assigning their own grades.
- Tools of quality management can be adapted for application to classroom use. Cause-and-effect diagrams, flowcharts, histograms, and other analytical tools will reinforce the importance of data in decision making and clarify thought processes. Before students begin a lab experiment, they can create a flowchart of the process; when they study the Civil War, a cause-and-effect diagram will help clarify their thinking about the big picture of the war; a language class can create a histogram related to verb usage; and so on.
- Students can be introduced to systems thinking and understanding of variation as they examine classroom processes. This thinking will ultimately become a new way of seeing with respect to other processes in their lives. This is true even in supposedly terrible schools, with problems so complex they defy solution, for it gives students and teachers a sense of control over their own destinies. Knowing about the learning process (metacognition) enfranchises learners and provides them with choices about their learning lives. The approach can be aligned with the curriculum and can provide a sense of integration to otherwise fragmented 50-minute increments of learning. Systems thinking can be integrated into the smallest events; when a child spills a pot of tempera paint in the first-grade classroom, the class can focus on ways to design the system of organizing art supplies so they will be less likely to fall from the edge of a table.
- In small ways and large, teachers can begin to work to transfer the ownership of the learning process to students. It is not hard to imagine students evaluating their own work, reviewing their portfolios, articulating the purpose of particular activities in the classroom, and creating choices within which they can learn. It is already happening, as has been noted.
- Using theory as a framework for processes and tools, teachers can engage students in meaningful activities that reflect sound principles of learning and brain function. Students can be encouraged to understand how they learn when teachers share these principles with them, and students can develop their own methods for demonstrating how well they know something.
- Making decisions on the basis of data rather than on subjective interpretations and perceived information reinforces skills of analysis and promises improved outcomes of decision making at all levels. Remember that "a fact may blossom into a truth," as Thoreau pointed out. Data can lead to information, which can

become knowledge, understanding, and ultimately wisdom, as Ackoff asserts (1990).

The list can go on. While quality learning may seem complex because it demands understanding of systems, it is important to see that this understanding applies to the smallest system as well as to the largest. Third-grade students can understand how applying spelling rules can be seen as a system, subject to variation and serving the needs of a customer. Teachers who want to introduce fine art works to a historical study of industrialization understand how this method has purpose. The teachers are able to relate it not only to a goal of learning about industrialization, but also to the ways in which it reinforces learning styles and brain connections.

A useful approach to understanding the impact that quality learning can have on the classroom is to examine the first steps that educators have taken, and to reflect on how these steps represent not just new techniques, but also genuine change in thinking. Teachers in school districts from Texas to Ohio respond to an "I used to . . . now I . . ." framework for the changes they have made.

- "I used to think in terms of remediation; now I understand variation." (High school teacher)
- "I used to insist on finishing the book no matter what; now I focus more deeply on learning." (High school history teacher)
- "I used to give students just one shot at a test; now I allow them to continue learning concepts they missed, and improve their grades." (High school math teacher)
- "I used to use the word *change*; now I use *improve*." (Superintendent)
- "I used to give all the rules for the semester on the first day of class; now I brainstorm with students about how we will work together." (Sixth-grade teacher)
- "I used to decide on my room arrangement; now I have students do an affinity exercise and nominal group technique to select the best location for things. Instead of my classroom, it's becoming *our* classroom." (Fifth-grade teacher)
- "I used to threaten with grades; now I spend more time in feedback sessions addressed to improvement." (High school science teacher)
- "I used to think I should know how to do everything myself; now I ask my colleagues and students for suggestions." (High school math teacher)
- "I used to be relieved when someone did poorly on my tests, since it validated the difficulty of the exam; now I know that tests are only a way to see what has to happen next." (High school English teacher)
- "I used to keep supplies locked up so that students couldn't get to them unless I distributed them; now I have students who 'own' the supply process." (Fourth-grade teacher)

■ "I used to have the art teacher come to my history class and lecture about art from a particular era; now students do this themselves." (High school history teacher)

Imitation Won't Work

Latching on to any of these before-and-after statements as a way of explaining quality learning is dangerous and inaccurate, of course. Each technique or approach represents behaviors that have been translated by individual teachers from a large concept of the learning process. As noted, imitating what others do without understanding this context will not bring about lasting improvement. Ralph Waldo Emerson (1842) urged this lesson: "Insist on yourself; never imitate." It may be no more important anywhere than it is in education. A Shakespeare will never be made, Emerson emphasized, by simply imitating Shakespeare. Each classroom and school is unique and can create its own approach to quality learning.

At the heart of the improvement process is the plan-do-study-act (PDSA) cycle. Even the smallest of processes can be approached with this technique. A drama class that is preparing a production can begin by flowcharting the tasks that need to be done, brainstorming about ways in which these tasks can be approached, collecting data about rehearsals, charting progress with respect to memorizing lines, and developing theory about how to improve the process. A school where violence is part of each day's expectations, or where absences preclude learning for many students, may have further to go toward developing the vision of a quality school, but it can begin tiny steps even with these serious problems. For example, while some may think of Mt. Edgecumbe High School in Sitka, Alaska, as a selective program in a bucolic setting where officials can deny admission to many students, it is, in fact, a school for students from cultures that face many of the complexities that are seen in inner-city schools: poverty, lack of parental support, learning disabilities, drug- and alcohol-related problems, and a diverse ethnic makeup. The PDSA cycle and the emphasis on quality learning can improve any learning environment—residential and day programs, and private and public schools with college preparatory and vocational emphases.

To approach the task in small, step-by-step ways requires no additional school district resources or levy support, but it immediately engages students in the learning process. As the drama class proceeds with its preparations, students will monitor and study not only the drama that they are producing, but also the ways in which they are learning it. In a science class, children not only see how the lima bean grows in the soft wet cotton, but also observe and record that growth. And in the final phase of the cycle, after the stage production is over and the set has been struck, the drama students can record the ways in which the process can be standardized. If early-morning rehearsals had better attendance than after-school sessions, that strategy can be adopted for future stage productions. The students' purposes in staging a dramatic production might have included demonstrating their acting and set design

To approach the task in small, step-by-step ways requires no additional school district resources or levy support, but it immediately engages students in the learning process.

skills, interpreting a dramatic work, learning more about characterization, or a variety of other aims that can be accomplished in the process of producing a play. Agreeing on their purpose before launching into the hours of rehearsal that are demanded will give a sense of wholeness to the effort and a vision of the outcome that each participant can hold onto.

Each improvement, when seen within the context of purpose and broad customer needs, leads inexorably to creating a new way to work together to achieve different results. The real measure of learning is how well newly acquired knowledge can be put to use in a new situation. Students are not likely to discover that they need to be able to dissect every frog that they meet on a walk in the woods. But by dissecting the frog in the artificial atmosphere of the classroom laboratory, they can understand "frogness" when they meet it, and know, for example, that the bullfrog on the rock is not a creature to be feared or reviled (or dissected), but instead one to be understood and appreciated. Students can begin to use their knowledge of the frog in new ways—metaphorically, for example, to enrich their communication about a variety of things. The best poems about frogs are undoubtedly rooted in complex understanding about the creatures. In this sense, the laboratory experience of dissection is an authentic learning experience, whose purpose supports the larger one of education.

If students learn history with the clear purpose of understanding the time in which they live, they may be able to apply some of the lessons that history teaches, and even avoid the calamities that recur without this knowledge. When they learn history only for its own sake, or for the purpose of pleasing teachers, such knowledge occurs in a vacuum, with little application to life. How can we expect such students to become responsive, interested citizens who take their voting responsibilities seriously, if their exposure to history and government has taken place in such a vacuum? This is what Thomas Jefferson meant when he noted that an enlightened citizenry is an educated one.

A View of Learning

Organizations such as schools have their own identities and purposes, but by responding and contributing to other organizations and to the larger system, they evolve. No system is permanently fixed, for it must exist in a dynamic world with increasingly complex relationships and interdependencies. Schools of the future will not result from single-minded reform, but from careful evolution.

Quality learning provides a framework within which to view the learning process. Since it is not easy to describe the entire framework in only a few words, *TQM* or *quality learning* becomes a kind of label, used to summarize that framework in general terms, and to distinguish it from other approaches. Let us not be misled by our own need to simplify in this way. Because it represents a new way of thinking, quality learning cannot be encapsulated in an educational acronym nor fully understood outside its fundamental principles. In the last analysis, understanding the theory, process, and tools that

Schools of the future will not result from single-minded reform, but from careful evolution.

are known as quality represents a new way of seeing—one that identifies the rich connections between prior knowledge and new learning, among processes that are in place to deliver learning opportunities, and ultimately with the larger world in which students and teachers live and function.

Notes

Ackoff, Russell L. 1993. Rethinking education. *Journal of Management Consulting* (fall):4.

————. 1990. *A theory of a system for educators and managers.* Produced by Clare Crawford-Mason. Written by Lloyd Dobyns. 30 min. Films, Inc. Deming Library, tape XXI.

Emerson, Ralph Waldo. [1842] 1950. Self-reliance. In *Selected Writings of Ralph Waldo Emerson*, edited by Brooks Atkinson. New York: Modern Library Editions.

Guaspari, John. 1985. *I know it when I see it: A modern fable about quality.* New York: AMACOM, a division of the American Management Association.

Hill, D. 1994. Professor Papert and his learning machine. *Teacher Magazine* (January): 16–19.

David Langford was a teacher at Mt. Edgecumbe High School in Sitka, Alaska, where he pioneered implementing quality concepts into school management and the learning process, beginning in 1988. Barbara Cleary is currently a teacher at the Miami Valley Day School in Dayton, Ohio and is also corporate vice president of Productivity–Quality Systems, Inc.

New Unionism Defined

Doug Tuthill

Doug Tuthill believes strongly in the value of TQM as the only way schools can meet the many challenges that education faces in an increasingly diverse and economic disparate society. This article talks about the importance of using TQM to bring teacher unions and school districts together with constancy of purpose and the continuous improvement of education to the benefit of all stakeholders.

It is an all too typical phone call. A second year teacher working in an inner-city Pinellas County elementary school receives a poor evaluation, is told she's being terminated, and tells her story to a sympathetic staff person at the Pinellas Classroom Teachers Association.

"I know I haven't done a good job," the young teacher says crying, "but I'm doing the best I can. I get up every morning and think today is going to be better, but these kids have so many problems. I just don't know where to begin. I've never worked with these types of children before. The school I interned in was nothing like this. What am I going to do?"

Three weeks later, the district's termination decision has been reversed, and the teacher has been transferred to a school in the suburbs where "she can be more successful." Our highly competent, well trained staff have done their jobs well. We saved another one.

This story illustrates both the strengths and weaknesses of our union. The teacher in this story is the victim of a series of dysfunctional systems. She was poorly trained, improperly placed given her training, not adequately supported once she was placed, and then blamed for the failures of these systems. These dysfunctional systems caused this young teacher to be abused; nothing gives me more pride than knowing my union helped her.

This is the strength of our union. We do a wonderful job in protecting our members from being abused by dysfunctional systems. Our weakness is that we seldom do anything to change these dysfunctional systems. We are great at treating symptoms of the disease, but we do little to affect the disease itself.

Our critics accuse us of perpetuating dysfunctional education systems for our own gain. They say that poorly trained, poorly placed, poorly managed teachers are easy prey for our "fear-based" membership pitch. "Without us you have no protection," we say. "You are a fool to work in this system without our liability insurance. Do you really want to stand alone when your time comes?"

Our critics are wrong when they question our motives. We are not greedy or self-centered people, but I do agree that we need to do more to change the education systems our members work in. These systems are putting our members, their students, and our society at risk. They must be changed, and we have a moral obligation to lead the reformation.

In Pinellas County, we have concluded that our education Association has two major tasks: (1) To protect our members from being abused by the dysfunctional systems they currently work in and (2) to begin transforming these systems so that our members no longer need to fear being abused.

Our goal is to create a school district free of fear, where no employee needs protection, and where coming to work is a joy. Our experiences over the last 10 years have convinced us that we cannot achieve this goal without Total Quality Management.

A Question of Existence

In Pinellas County, we are convinced that there will be two types of school districts and education associations in the 21st century—those that are organized around the principles of Total Quality Management, and those that don't exist. We intend to exist.

We are convinced that there will be two types of school districts and education associations in the 21st century—those that are organized around the principles of Total Quality Management, and those that don't exist.

TQM is a theory of organizational learning that enables organizations to continually improve their ability to meet and exceed their customers' expectations. If implemented properly, TQM processes enable organizations to become effective, life-long learners. I know of no other theory of organizational learning that is as powerful as TQM, or as widely misunderstood.

The TQM orientation seminar in Pinellas County lasts three 12-hour days and always begins with the following exercise.

Imagine nine chairs in a neat circle, all facing outward. In eight of the chairs "willing workers" are squirming in their seats, nervously playing with the brown paper bags in their laps, while in the ninth chair a stoic "inspector" waits patiently. Inside the circle, the "manager" paces. Surrounding the circle, 50 or 60 Pinellas County educators begin to press forward in anticipation. Most of the seminar participants have heard about the "tinker toy" exercise and don't want to miss the fun. The seminar leader quiets the audience and gives the 10 players their final instructions.

"Remember," she says sternly, "we are in the barbell business to make money. The manager is responsible for ensuring that you work fast and efficiently. I don't want any talking or fooling around on the assembly line. Do you understand, Mr. Manager?" The manager frowns and nods.

"Okay, the inspector is in charge of quality control. If any of your barbells do not meet specifications, she will yell 'rework' and send the defective barbell around again. I don't like rework. It costs money. Do you willing workers understand?" The willing workers cast their eyes downward and nod.

"Now when I say begin, you take a toy part from your bag and pass it to the willing worker on your right. When you receive the part from your left, you either add a piece or take a piece off, then pass it on to your right. And remember, no talking or goofing around. Our production quota is five barbells in three minutes. Ready, begin!"

As the willing workers begin fumbling through the randomly placed toy parts in their paper bags, the manager immediately starts yelling, "Make barbells! Faster! More barbells! Faster!"

One of the many problems the workers have is that only the inspector knows what an acceptable barbell looks like. Consequently, the manager's exhortations are quickly joined by the inspector's shouts of "Rework!" Soon a pattern emerges.

The inspector's shouts of "Rework!" cause the manager to shout louder, "Faster! Faster!," which in turn causes the workers to work faster, which causes the inspector to shout "Rework!" more often, which causes the manager to shout louder, "Make more barbells! Faster!," which causes the workers to work faster. And so on.

Chaos Ensues

The assembly line process seldom lasts the full three minutes. Invariably, one of the willing workers turns around and tells the manager to "Shut up!" This causes the manager to respond, "Be quiet and work faster." A shouting match ensues, signaling to the seminar leader that it is time to stop the activity.

After a brief cooling off period, the seminar leader guides the entire group through a debriefing process. "Was this process capable of producing five acceptable barbells in three minutes?" The group, usually lead by the former willing workers, answers loudly in unison, "NO!"

"Would offering the workers merit pay improve their productivity?" "NO!" "Why not?" "Because this system is not capable of producing five barbells in three minutes and offering the workers merit pay won't change that. If you want to improve productivity, you have to change the system."

"Was the manager's 'encouragement' helpful?" "NO!" "Why not?" "His yelling did nothing to help us improve the system."

"Would a kinder, gentler manager have helped?" "Yes, but it would not have changed the outcome." "Why not?" "The system was not capable of producing five acceptable barbells in three minutes, and a kinder, gentler manager would not have helped us improve the system."

"Did the inspector help?" "NO!" "Why not?" "Her shouting 'rework' did not let us know what was wrong or how to improve. All she did was increase our frustration. She did nothing to help us improve the system."

"Perhaps the system was underfunded. Would doubling the number of people on the assembly line have helped?" "NO! More people would not have improved the system. In fact, it may have made things worse."

Change the System

At this point, the seminar leader summarizes the group's conclusions. "So, let me get this straight. There is nothing I can do to the workers, inspector, or manager in this activity that will improve the workers' ability to make acceptable barbells. The only way to improve productivity is to change the system? "YES!," the group says confidently.

The seminar leader then asks the seminar participants to "list the changes we need to make in this process to ensure the willing workers are capable of producing five acceptable barbells in three minutes or less."

We have done this activity with about 100 different groups, and the list of process improvements is always the same. They include:

- letting the workers see an acceptable finished barbell,
- turning the chairs inward and allowing the workers to communicate and help one another,
- changing the manager's role from intimidator to facilitator,
- eliminating the inspection process.

After generating this list, the 10 barbell participants are allowed to turn their chairs around, look at an acceptable barbell, design a new process that is capable of producing five acceptable barbells in three minutes, and begin again. This second time they always produce five acceptable barbells in 15 seconds or less, and the larger group gives them a much deserved round of applause.

Next, the seminar leaders asks the participants to describe the similarities between the barbell activity and our public schools. Forty hands always shoot up at once. This second list usually includes:

- the inability of teachers to regularly communicate with their colleagues,
- a hierarchical management system that controls people (especially students) through fear and coercion,
- state standardized inspections (i.e., tests) that do not improve teaching or learning,
- pressure to push students through the material whether they have learned it or not.

The seminar leader ends the barbell activity debriefing by asking the group a final series of questions. "Is it fair to conclude that we will never significantly improve student learning until we significantly change our system of education?" This question is usually met with silent stares.

"Will adding 30 days to our current school year greatly improve student achievement?" "Probably not," a few scattered voices say softly.

"Assuming we make no other changes in the system, will lowering your class sizes by 25 percent lead to dramatic gains in student achievement?" "No," they say louder. "Will teaching all the teachers and principals in our school system to be kinder and gentler enhance student learning?" Everyone laughs and answers, "NO!"

"Correct," the seminar leader responds. "The barbell activity illustrates one of the most important tenets of Total Quality Management. About 94 percent of the production capacity in any organization comes from the organization's systems and processes—not its people.

"Blaming people did not improve your ability to make barbells, and it will not improve your ability to teach children. The only way to significantly improve student achievement in Pinellas County is by significantly changing our systems of education. Everything else is just useless, and often times, harmful rhetoric."

The Implications

The barbell exercise illustrates a few of the implications TQM has for the NEA and its affiliates. First, we need to stop using our collective power to blame people and start using it to improve systems. The blame game creates adversarial relationships, breaks down communications and trust, and diverts attention from systems improvement.

I have never met a teacher, support person, principal, student, school board member or superintendent who gets up in the morning and says, "Today I want to be a failure." Given the choice, most people would rather be successful than unsuccessful. Unfortunately, as the barbell example illustrates, many of us are not given the choice. Everyone in education is victimized by dysfunctional systems, and everyone has a stake in seeing these systems improved.

Sharpening the Vision

After "turning the chairs around" and agreeing not to blame people, the next step in system improvement is the creation of a "constancy of purpose." A constancy of purpose refers to a shared organizational vision.

In the barbell activity, a constancy of purpose was created when everyone saw the picture of an acceptable barbell. Much of the day-to-day conflict we encounter as Association leaders stems from a lack of organizational constancy of purpose.

For example, suppose a local school board asks for the union's help in initiating a new magnet school program. Should the union support this program? Without a clearly defined, widely agreed upon constancy of purpose, the union has no way of properly deciding what position to take.

If, for example, our members want desegregated schools with minimal political controversy, then supporting more magnet schools is probably a good idea. If, on the other hand, our members believe that all students deserve an equal education, then a new magnet school program is problematic since, by definition, magnet schools provide some students with different educational opportunities than others. (It is this unequal education that enables magnets to "attract" students.)

The magnet school scenario shows why it's important that the union and school district also share a constancy of purpose. Without an agreement on where they are going, the union and school district will have difficulty agreeing on how to get there.

About 94 percent of the production capacity in any organization comes from the organization's systems and processes—not its people.

Without an agreement on where they are going, the union and school district will have difficulty agreeing on how to get there.

Magnet schools are designed to achieve a particular goal. If the union and school district do not share a commitment to this goal, then they will not agree on whether more magnet schools are appropriate.

All roads are good roads if you don't know where you're going. And as we saw in the first barbell exercise, when all roads are good roads, chaos, conflict, and frustration abound. The lack of clearly defined, jointly held constancy of purpose accounts for about 90 percent of today's labor/management conflicts.

The new TQM-oriented collective bargaining process in Pinellas County illustrates how local Associations and school boards can begin to use existing processes to develop a constancy of purpose and facilitate systems improvement.

The big project this fall involves phasing out the existing employee evaluation system and replacing it with a system that assesses processes and systems, not individuals.

Two years ago, we merged the teacher, support person, and school board bargaining teams into a single team—we're hoping to add parent representatives this year. After receiving training in TQM and group process skills, the team's first task was to develop a group mission statement that reflected its constancy of purpose.

The mission statement, which is part of our collective bargaining agreement, reads:

"Consistent with the District's vision and the values of mutual trust, respect, and openness, the mission of the collective bargaining team is to create a quality education environment for all stakeholders by using a collaborative approach through Total Quality Management."

The team and its various subcommittees meet year round to work on systems improvement. The big project this fall involves phasing out the existing employee evaluation system and replacing it with a system that assesses processes and systems, not individuals.

Introducing a New Culture

NEA affiliates that choose to turn their organizations and school districts into learning organizations through TQM will find all aspects of their work culture changed. TQM is a culture. It is not a new program. Committing to change an organization through TQM is tantamount to committing to engage in a cultural revolution.

TQM is a culture. It is not a new program.

While change of this magnitude is difficult, we in Pinellas County have concluded that we have no choice. We have participated in virtually every NEA sponsored reform effort imaginable over the last 10 years.

We experimented with site-based decision making through the Mastery-In-Learning Program. We initiated districtwide reforms through the Learning Lab Project. We received an Operation Rescue grant through NEA's foundation—the National Foundation for the Improvement of Education. We participated in statewide accountability networks. And we have spent a small fortune attending national conferences and symposiums.

These programs have been created and implemented by good people with good intentions, but all of them have had no sustained effect on student learning in Pinellas County. These initiatives, many of which I helped design and implement, failed to make a significant difference because they were not embedded in the context of TQM. I am convinced.

A political coalition is now forming in Pinellas County around the idea (or constancy of purpose) that all students—regardless of their race, ethnicity, economic class, or family condition—can meet rigorous academic and vocational standards. The members of this coalition include progressive members of our business and religious communities, our teacher and support personnel unions, and our civil rights community.

The motivations behind this coalition are moral and economic. The enlightened business community has decided that it can no longer afford the costs of undereducating large numbers of low-income and minority students. We are building prison beds in Florida at unprecedented rates, and what we are finding is that "if we build them they will come."

The future tax increases necessary to support these prisons is going to cripple Florida's economy, and bankrupt many of our businesses. The progressive elements of our business community know that something other than prison construction needs to be done, and that something is public education.

"Moral Outrage"

Our civil rights and progressive religious communities are morally outraged by what our dysfunctional education systems are doing to low-income children. They believe this "waste" of human potential—and the hopelessness, despair, and violence that result—are sins and should be stopped.

Our union's motivation is both self-serving and altruistic. Increased welfare costs and "get tough" crime measures are draining state dollars from public education. Ten years ago, 62 percent of state general revenues in Florida went to public education. Today the figure is 48 percent.

As this trend continues, and it will continue, pressures to increase class sizes and reduce employee compensation will intensify. Our members and their students will inevitably be hurt.

While the kind of coalition we are forming in Pinellas County is not unique, it is fragile. Our other partners are skeptical about the union's commitment to significant systemic change, and given our track record, their skepticism is understandable.

We used the power of our union to help the second-year elementary teacher I described at the beginning of this essay, but we did nothing to help the students she left behind. We protected our member from being abused by a dysfunctional system, but we left the students to fend for themselves.

They, unfortunately, don't have a union, and unlike their more affluent peers in the suburbs, they lack the resources and political power to help themselves. Until our actions show that we have expanded the scope of our union from protecting our members from dysfunctional systems to transforming these dysfunctional systems, our partners in these fledgling coalitions will remain justifiably skeptical.

My fear is that the NEA and its affiliates won't expand their scope, causing our coalition partners to abandon us and public education.

Many in the civil rights community are starting to figure out that the victory they won in the 1954 *Brown v. Board of Education* case was a partial victory at best.

De Facto Segregation

While legal segregation does not exist, the promise of equal educational opportunity for all children is still a distant dream.

Today, we allow children of all races and creeds to walk through the schoolhouse door only to track them and resegregate them as they enter their classrooms. No wonder many in the civil rights community are bitter and increasingly angry toward public schools and public school unions.

Forming partnerships with progressive people in our business and civic communities around the idea that all students can meet high performance standards is meaningless, and probably destructive, if we lack a strategy for achieving this shared vision.

We need to develop educational strategies that are powerful enough to overcome the negative effects of poverty and dysfunctional families, and we think that is only possible through TQM.

Perhaps we in Pinellas County are mistaken. Perhaps there is a theory of organizational learning out there that is more powerful than TQM, and if there is, we'd like to hear about it.

But what I don't think we are mistaken about is the need for the NEA and its affiliates to begin using their collective resources to help create education systems that are capable of ensuring that all students graduate capable of meeting and exceeding world-class performance standards.

Using our influence only to protect our members from being abused is no longer acceptable. We have a moral obligation to do more.

Doug Tuthill is the president of the Pinellas County (Florida) Teachers Association.

Pennsylvania Builds Tomorrow's Work Force

Connie R. Faylor

This article spells out how the "Koalaty Kid" program was established in the Lehigh Valley schools as a partnership between businesses and schools. It has been very successful, leading to students who understand and use systems thinking and quality tools right from kindergarten on up. It provides another example of the ideas discussed in the Langford/Cleary article.

Transferring quality improvement methods to the educational system through school-business partnerships contributes to improvements in school systems, builds community responsibility, and offers both partners the opportunity to share visions and strategies. The strategic effort builds the foundation for a work force that will be prepared to meet the competitive challenges of the global economy.

Since the introduction of a quality improvement program in 1991, schools and businesses in Pennsylvania's Lehigh Valley have been working together to apply the theory, process, and tools of quality improvement as an outgrowth of the Koalaty Kid program, an idea that was piloted by ASQC. There are currently 17 partnerships between schools and businesses and one partnership between a business and a child care center in Lehigh Valley.

Ben Franklin Lends a Hand

Quality improvement training has been delivered through the Ben Franklin Technology Center, a state-sponsored economic development program, for the past six years in Lehigh Valley organizations. Both business and service organizations use the team-based, project-by-project implementation approach to bring the quality process to life in Lehigh Valley. This training process was first used by Lehigh Valley elementary schools in 1991. The Ben Franklin approach was adapted from ASQC and Corning, Inc.'s original Koalaty Kid process, which was started at Carder Elementary School in Corning, NY, in the 1970s.

The original Koalaty Kid program was developed to help children:

- Achieve a healthy sense of self-esteem and pride

- Develop a sense of responsibility toward themselves, their work, and their school
- Acquire a habit of excellence and make each effort their best
- Influence and contribute to the school by participating in a team of school administrators, teachers, sponsors, parents, and others
- Become motivated in reading and other learning areas

There is great value in these student-centered objectives. Based on industry models, however, successful quality improvement implementation occurs through a project-by-project improvement approach that is implemented by school staff members. By using cross-functional project teams, the Ben Franklin Koalaty Kid model builds on the original approach, forming partnerships to develop the skills and culture needed to focus on customers and systems. The Ben Franklin Koalaty Kid process coordinates partnerships between elementary schools that are interested in learning and applying continuous improvement and business partners who are proven leaders in implementing the quality process in their organizations.

The Ben Franklin Koalaty Kid process coordinates partnerships between elementary schools and business partners who are proven leaders in implementing the quality process in their organizations.

Five Schools Get Started

Ben Franklin's pilot Koalaty Kid process started in the fall of 1991 with five schools representing three of the 17 Lehigh Valley school districts. The Ben Franklin Center matched schools with business partners that had successful continuous improvement processes. The businesses' quality professionals shared their expertise to help the schools develop pilot project teams. The objectives of the process were to help teachers learn, promote, and apply quality methods; to help students develop the skills they will need to succeed in the workplace; and to allow business to play a strong role in the community's educational process and contribute to future employee development. The partnership provided both parties with the opportunity to learn and share new ideas: Schools learned quality improvement theory and methods, and businesses learned how to manage a school.

The Koalaty Kid partnership began by identifying schools and business partners that had an interest in the process. Based on the success of the Ben Franklin quality improvement training for business clients, the same training process was used for the educational sector. For the pilot program, adaptations were made to accommodate educational terms and applications.

Each school and its business partner formed a pilot project team based on an opportunity for improvement. The team members participated in an application-based training process, using PQ Systems' Total Quality Transformation Training System. (PQ Systems is a firm in Dayton, OH, that is dedicated to helping organizations continuously improve themselves; its comprehensive network of products and services is designed to improve the quality, productivity, and profitability of all industries.) Whenever they learned a new problem-solving step or a new tool, they applied it to their project.

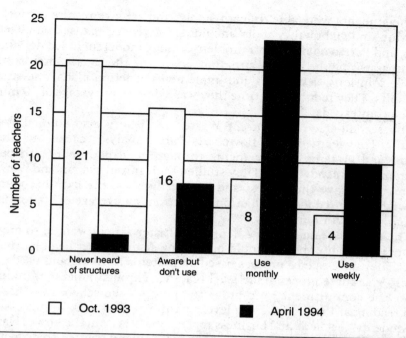

Figure 1. **Knowledge and use of cooperative learning structures.**

Quality Improvement Projects Get Results

The following examples illustrate the variety of projects and results that the schools have achieved through the improvement process.

A project conducted by Salisbury Township's Western Salisbury Elementary School and its business partner, Stanley-Vidmar, sought to increase for teachers the number of opportunities to use cooperative learning strategies with students while also receiving training in new cooperative learning strategies. Although some teachers had been trained in using cooperative learning in the classroom, not all had the opportunity to train due to their schedules.

A team was developed to introduce cooperative learning to teachers at monthly faculty meetings. Between meetings, the teachers implemented the new strategies in the classroom. If a teacher didn't have success, he or she worked with a team member until success was obtained.

As a result of the project, the number of teachers who were unfamiliar with cooperative learning structures decreased and the frequency with which these structures were implemented in the classroom increased (see Figure 1). The faculty team showed a 280% increase in the use of cooperative learning in the classroom.

While the teachers were working on the cooperative learning project, third graders in the same school were writing technical manuals to document quality tools, including the problem-solving process, and working on an improvement project to decrease the amount of time they waste during the day.

The faculty team showed a 280% increase in the use of cooperative learning in the classroom.

The students were able to learn, apply, and achieve results through systems thinking and quality tools, including flowcharts, cause-and-effect diagrams, and Pareto charts. Their problem-solving model included defining the system, assessing the current situation, analyzing the causes, brainstorming possible solutions, developing and implementing action plans, and studying the results. They reduced the time they wasted from an average of 10 minutes to two minutes a day.

The second-grade students at Western Salisbury also studied systems thinking. They learned about flowcharts, Pareto analysis, cause-and-effect diagrams, and systems improvements through an experiment with peanut-butter-and-jelly sandwiches. They studied their initial system and worked as a team to improve the process and reduce the time needed to produce the sandwich. They reduced production times from an average of approximately three minutes to 1.4 minutes.

The principal and staff of Allentown's Ritter School wanted to provide a guarantee that all children would be reading at the proper level by the third grade. They developed a process based on systems thinking and used quality tools to guarantee proper grade-level reading. Through process thinking and having the commitment to improve the process, the school now has every child reading at the proper grade level by third grade—a 100% success rate.

Students, teachers, and business representatives from the Lower Nazareth Elementary School and the Martin Guitar Company wanted to decrease the number of behavior problems in the cafeteria. All of the process stakeholders, including the cafeteria workers, were included in the process. The project team gathered baseline data, identified improvement strategies, and implemented the new ideas. The behavior problems, which included shouting, running, and exiting the building, decreased by 56%.

The Lower Nazareth team also initiated a homework assignment improvement project during the 1992–93 school year. The baseline data collection process revealed that an average of 358 nonconformances occurred in fifth-grade homework assignments over a two-month period. The nonconformances were identified using the quality criteria that had been established for homework. The improvement strategies included clearly communicating expectations from teacher to teacher and from teacher to student. This process resulted in revised in-class presentation of assignments and the use of homework assignment books. (The purchase of the books was co-sponsored by the Parent Teacher Association and the Martin Guitar Company.) Since improvement was shown at the fifth-grade level, the improvement process and the assignment books are now being used in all grade levels.

Cleveland Elementary, an Allentown grade school, wanted to create a positive learning environment by increasing positive interactions as measured by the number of social skills learned and the number of remaining negative interactions. The project team included members of the staff, the school principal, and a Pennsylvania Power & Light (PP&L) quality professional. The team assessed the current situation using run charts and control charts, then gathered and analyzed data using run charts, control charts, and Pareto charts.

The result was the development of a new system to help students and parents with the process of increasing positive interactions.

Cleveland Elementary's business partner, PP&L's nuclear department, assisted the school by encouraging risk taking, facilitating the problem-solving process, and helping the team avoid obstacles. Last year, this partnership devoted its efforts to examining its problem-solving process, building its team, and collecting baseline data. Both partners have demonstrated a true commitment to the process and to mutual communication.

Improving the Ben Franklin Koalaty Kid Training Process

The Ben Franklin Technology Center uses the quality process to improve coordination of the Koalaty Kid approach and training. A checklist has been created to help both the school and business partners determine their readiness for the commitment. The approach uses education-related simulation to teach participants the theory, process, and tools related to the improvement process. Since training was too disruptive for teachers during the school year, a three-day summer training program was designed.

During training, the Ben Franklin Technology Center introduces schools to strategic quality planning. The center works with the faculty members, parents, and students to develop a vision, a mission, and long-range objectives and measurements for the school. The business partners have been extremely valuable in implementing this part of the process.

Quarterly network meetings for the Lehigh Valley partnerships have also been established based on the philosophy of ASQC President David Luther, former senior vice president of quality at Corning and one of the national Koalaty Kid founders. These meetings provide a forum for the partners to share results of their strategies and improvement projects, to learn about specific activities that are being conducted through the business partners, and to build on the success of others. The meetings are held at different school sites to encourage additional participation.

The Ben Franklin Koalaty Kid effort will continue to be improved. Based on the plan-do-check-act cycle, improvement areas including coordination, training and education, and the design of methods to help the schools become independent and discover ways to share their strengths with their business partners.

Because of the successful activities and documented results in these Lehigh Valley schools, the ASQC Koalaty Kid program adopted the same training model for the national pilot program that was launched in May 1994. Joelene Puotinen, manager of ASQC's Koalaty Kid department, is coordinating the national effort. Eleven teams representing schools, business partners, and local ASQC sections from across the United States and Canada will begin to transform their organizations through the quality improvement process.

Encouraging Caring, Sharing, and Daring

"Change through the quality process is a positive experience for every employee in my company and can provide the same experience for every student, teacher, and administrator," Dick Donati, manager of employee involvement at Stanley-Vidmar, told staff members at Western Salisbury Elementary School. "We want the children to understand the value of working in teams and the value of using data for decision making. We want to help the faculty identify ways to implement the process in the classroom as well as in administrative and maintenance areas." Donati and Jack Vass, Western Salisbury's principal, are working together to make the changes that will encourage students, teachers, and parents to practice fundamentals of quality improvement: caring, sharing, and daring. Vass said, "As we help our students to care, share, and dare, we help them develop the quality foundations of commitment, teamwork, and continuous improvement."

The Koalaty Kid training and project improvement process have shown positive benefits for all participants. The teachers learned quickly and have begun applying the process and tools in the classroom. Children in every grade, including kindergarten, are familiar with systems thinking and understand the importance of focusing on the customer. Students are doing things right the first time, and business partners are motivated to initiate more quality-related activities at their companies.

The Ben Franklin Koalaty Kid approach uses methods that have proven to be successful in business and industry. The approach strives to form partnerships that promote and apply quality principles. The success of the process will be determined by Koalaty Kids developing an understanding of systems and a desire to never settle for systems that are just good enough. Systems thinking, self-monitoring, and improvement are foundations for their futures.

The new ASQC national Koalaty Kid pilot will also continue to demonstrate the value of implementing the quality improvement process through staff development and the project-by-project approach.

Connie R. Faylor is the manager for quality partnerships at the Ben Franklin Technology Center in Bethlehem, Pennsylvania.

> Children in every grade, including kindergarten, are familiar with systems thinking and understand the importance of focusing on the customer.

HIGHER EDUCATION

TQM in Higher Education: 1995

Ronald L. Heilmann

This article by higher education consulting editor Ronald Heilmann reviews some of the progress that has taken place over the past year in implementing TQM not just in college and university administration but also in the classroom. The so-called writing off of quality management in higher education is premature, to say the least, as Heilmann documents here.

Looking back on TQM, or continuous quality improvement (CQI) developments in higher education during 1995 reveals mixed signals. There is some evidence of slippage mainly resulting from two sources. The first is budget constraints that many institutions of higher learning faced and will continue to face for at least the near future. The cutbacks have eliminated seed capital from startup initiatives or have eliminated support before sufficient internal knowledge resources could be developed to enable an initiative to be self-sustaining.

The second source of slippage is attributed to the lessons learned from the business media that during recent years has focused attention on failed initiatives of TQM or related activities such as reengineering. Story after story of these failures has appeared providing ample evidence for doubters to feel secure in their reluctance to support or participate in TQM activities. Unfortunately, writers of these stories have failed to distinguish between a failure of the concept and a failure of its implementation. These are clearly separable issues. As a result, they have done a disservice to the total quality movement in both the business and higher educational communities. However, it has been more acutely felt in the educational community because of the shorter history and lower level of momentum existing therein relative to the business community.

Unfortunately, writers of these stories have failed to distinguish between a failure of the concept and a failure of its implementation. These are clearly separable issues.

Despite the setbacks described above, 1995 will also be viewed as a break-through year in the evolution of TQM in higher education because TQM made the leap from administrative applications to academic applications. The pioneers in this effort, most of whom experimented in obscurity, collectively "came out of the closet" with the publication of a book entitled *Academic Initiatives in Total Quality for Higher Education* edited by Professor Harry V. Roberts of the University of Chicago Graduate School of Business. The book, published by ASQC Quality Press, consists of a collection of over 30 papers. Most describe specific classroom initiatives (primarily experiments in delivery rather than new courses in total quality) taken by individual professors in their classes in an effort to put total quality, or continuous improvement, into practice in the classroom. Thus, as Professor Roberts points out in the Introduction section of the book, "[This book] is about the faculty and student sides of total quality." Professor Roberts argues persuasively that the evolution of this dimension of the total quality in higher education can be accelerated by an appeal to faculty self-interest. He states:

> The potential gains from total quality come not from working harder, but from rooting out the wastes that pervade organizational and individual work processes, *including teaching and research processes.* Waste includes process flows and mistakes, and process steps that are unnecessary.

Roberts goes on to hold out the carrot of possibilities that total quality can bring to higher education. For example, he suggests the following possibilities for the application of total quality to faculty research:

- Freed-up time for research by application of principles of personal quality: total quality applied to ordinary job duties. The amount of time is not trivial. For many faculty members, I would suggest two hours per day as a reasonably attainable gain within a relatively short time. Improvement of research processes, especially by waste reduction.
- Reduction of wasteful faculty administrative activities with consequent freeing of time for actual research.
- Facilitation of team research by application of total quality experiences with effective use of teams.

Roberts sites the following improvement possibilities when total quality is applied to the teaching of a course:

- The possibility of teaching more in a given course (or the same course in less time).
- Cutting out unnecessary topics that contribute little or nothing to the course, or unifying concepts that are now treated separately.
- Continually making the course content more up-to-date and valuable.

- Continually removing obstacles to student understanding while finding better ways of helping students reinforce learning by doing.
- Several papers in this book show that total quality lends itself to doing this by means of real-world, real-time student quality improvement projects.

As a specific example of improving teaching, Roberts presents several papers, plus reinforcements from his own experience, on two-way fast feedback. In this technique, a professor employs simple questionnaires to get fast feedback from students at class sessions on class content and delivery issues and then provides prompt feedback, usually before or at the beginning of the next class session, on their feedback. This new channel of ongoing dialog between professor and student leads to continuing improvement of teaching and learning—a clear win-win experience.

The papers included in Roberts' collection range from an overview of the total quality philosophy applied to higher education to specific descriptive pieces on classroom experiments. Myron Tribus, in a philosophical paper with the innocuous title "Total Quality Management in Schools of Business and Engineering," contains the best definition of quality in education: "Quality in education is what makes learning a pleasure and a joy." Tribus goes on to point that joy is ever changing as students grow and mature, raising a challenge to professors ". . . to be ever alert to engage students in a discussion of what constitutes a quality experience. The negotiations and discussions are never done. It takes constant engagement to wed a student to learning."

Tribus also emphasizes the principles of learning that "people learn best when they feel the need to know." This theme is picked up in a subsequent paper by Bateman and Roberts, "Real-World Total Quality Projects for Statistics Courses." The chain of logic leading to this change in the teaching of statistics by Professors Bateman and Roberts was as follows:

- Statistics students cannot learn statistics without doing data analysis.
- Only by having students do statistics could they most be motivated to learn about underlying statistical theory.
- Data analysis is more meaningful when it is directed to applications that students can relate to, which means the projects should involve the students collecting their own data.

Bateman and Roberts list 60 student projects they have overseen involving real-world quality improvement applications in the following diverse categories:

Health Care
Manufacturing Industry and Processes
Chemical Industry
Improving Work Processes
Information and Work Flow

Information Technology and Systems
Financial Systems and Services
Marketing and Business Development
Sales and Professional Services
Human Resources
Food Services
Theater

Every project involved a real problem in an operating enterprise and thus bridging the gap between education and the world of work. Their most important findings after all of these projects were

- The same students who do only mediocre work on statistics course examinations that stress statistical theory can do outstanding work on applied data analysis in projects of their own choosing.
- The applied student projects can be focused on quality improvement, and real-world quality improvement can be achieved as a by-product of a statistics course.

The paper in *Academic Initiatives* that issues the greatest challenge to the reader is entitled "Using Total Quality Education to Prepare Globally Competitive Citizens: The Perspective of Motorola University" by Brenda B. Sumberg. In this paper, she describes Motorola University as an "industrial university" in a transition to a "lifelong learning institution"; that is, she portrays an institution with a long-range vision of education as it will have to be in the future. She challenges readers, assuming them to be in higher education, with a series of questions and shares either the Motorola University current initiative responding to a question or thoughts on necessary steps to develop an appropriate response. A small sampling of the questions follows:

- Are you identifying changes occurring in institutions of higher learning around the world that might be appropriate for your own institution?
- Are you thinking of trying to reduce cycle time in your college or university?
- How well do your students understand different cultures and different meaning of ethics around the world?
- Will [your students] be able to handle empowerment or be able to provide appropriate leadership to an empowered workforce?
- Are your students becoming adept at applying what they are learning?
- Do your students know how to continue to learn?

Roberts' best summary of that which appears in *Academic Initiatives* is actually found in a separate briefing review he authored for ASQC entitled "Making Total Quality Work in Higher Education." Here he states:

Total quality principles can be thought of as **improvement knowl-edge**: knowledge bearing on the improvement of any work process. Improvement knowledge is to be distinguished from **professional knowledge**: what faculty know and continually learn more about in their own specialized fields. It is surprising but true that one can be very strong in professional knowledge but almost unaware of improvement knowledge. Improvement knowledge can lead to never-ending and substantial improvement in everything that faculty does and value.

Thus, it is in distinguishing the concept of improvement knowledge that Roberts finds the key to continuing the transition of TQM from administrative to academic applications where the greatest long run and societal gains are to be made. The papers he includes in *Academic Initiatives* should serve to stimulate many more in higher education to seek out improvement knowledge for their own benefit and thus accelerate the improvement of higher education.

A personal footnote may help to persuade those who continue to doubt the benefits that can flow from the application of TQM to an academic activity. In 1984, I initiated a compensated internship program for graduate students in business or engineering at the University of Wisconsin-Milwaukee (UW-M). This program, administered through the Center for Quality, Productivity & Economic Development (a joint entity of the School of Business Administration and the College of Engineering and Applied Science), contracts with area firms to undertake improvement projects to enable students to learn by doing. Since its inception, over 100 placements (a graduate student for a semester or summer) have been made generating over $600,000 to supplement scarce student support funds. However, the most rewarding aspect of the program has been the intensified learning. Comments such as "I have learned more in the past two months on this project than in the past two years in the classroom" have not been uncommon.

During 1995, I had an opportunity to return to classroom teaching and chose to experiment with some of the techniques described in *Academic Initiatives*, including two-way fast feedback. The excerpt below, received in a letter from a graduating senior, constitutes my reward for a willingness to experiment. "This was an *excellent* class. Some of the most useful things I learned in college came out of this class."

Needless to say, with feedback like this, I am motivated to continue to improve any and every class I offer. And, as has been learned at leading companies around the world, the effort invested in earning such feedback is not viewed as extra work; rather it is an investment leading to the recognition that *quality pays*. As more faculty recognize the potential benefits in achieving the benefits of improvement knowledge, the 1995 breakthrough in TQM in higher education referenced herein will pay huge returns for years to come.

TQM: What's in It for Academics?

Richard J. Schonberger

This article provides an overview of the value of TQM in a variety of the applied academic disciplines. The idea is to show that it has relevance in every discipline and can help students better understand theory and put it to use.

Big Business wants to hire university graduates who are literate in total quality management. Six mega-companies—American Express, Ford, IBM, Motorola, Procter & Gamble, and Xerox—said so in an open letter published in 1991 in the *Harvard Business Review*. Five of these companies and three others joined forces with several universities to charter and fund six TQM working councils charged with bringing total quality to higher education.

It may not be easy. Total quality management is, in some ways, contrary to instruction and research practices in the university. TQM is team-based. Faculty members, however, are notorious independents. So are students: it's dog-eat-dog in the classroom. Also, TQM calls for cross-functional thinking, planning, and doing. Faculties and curricula, however, are highly specialized, and professors avidly protect their turf. We might add that universities are tradition-bound, whereas TQM trumps for continuous change.

Despite these gloomy-sounding assessments, TQM initiatives are appearing here and there in academia. There are a few good reasons why this may continue, though perhaps fitfully. They have to do with opportunities to innovate and explore new instructional and research horizons, which have strong appeal for most academics. Business, economics, engineering, and related tool disciplines (information systems and mathematics/statistics), plus other professional schools, are particularly affected by total quality management.

Business and Economics

Colleges of business and economics include specializations in operations management, marketing, business policy and strategy, management accounting, corporate finance, financial accounting and auditing, human resource

Reprinted with permission from *Business Horizons*, January/February 1995. Copyright © 1995 by the Foundation for the School of Business at Indiana University. All rights reserved.

management, organizational behavior, and economics. TQM offers differing challenges and attractions for each.

Operations Management (OM). TQM affects nearly all of the OM agenda. A primary focus on modeling for efficiency gives way, under TQM, to planning and doing for and with the customer. The customer outlook, in turn, calls for major overhauls in the OM approach to scheduling, equipment selection, facility layout, maintenance, inventory management, and quality assurance. Briefly, schedules, equipment, layout, and inventory management must be geared for quick reaction to customer needs, not just to efficiency and utilization; and process control must replace breakdown maintenance and delayed inspection.

OM professors have a special reason for heeding the call of TQM. They had failed to stay abreast of an important OM movement called materials requirements planning (MRP) that emerged in industry in the 1970s. The MRP juggernaut had become OM's leading edge in the real world of manufacturing, but for a decade OM textbooks and journals said little or nothing about it. To catch up and stay caught up, OM professors, in droves, joined the professional societies, where they could keep an eye on fast-changing developments. And they began publishing heavily in practitioner periodicals, which they fought to elevate to tenure-class status. Then, when TQM and related topics made their appearance, OM faculties were not far behind.

Marketing. In TQM thinking, the customer is the object. Which university specialty has charge of customers? Marketing. TQM concepts load easily into topic outlines in marketing courses and into marketing research hypotheses.

In practice, marketers and salespeople have carried the burden of having to cover up for their organizations' defects, late completions, and other customer service failings. As TQM kicks in with continuous improvements in quality, timeliness, and so on, the burden is lifted somewhat. Each improvement is marketable—in proposals, in advertising, in sales promotions. For example, Ford Motor Company's slogan, now a decade old, is, "Quality Is Job One." Putting a more positive face on their function holds appeal for marketing professors and students as well as practicing marketers.

TQM concepts load easily into topic outlines in marketing courses.

Business Policy and Strategy. Such important TQM-oriented topics as benchmarking, quality function deployment, and customer-centered strategic principles need an academic home. These topics seem general enough to find their way into instruction in several disciplines. However, they deal specifically with matters central to the business policy/strategy area: directing internal resources toward enhanced competitiveness and customer retention. To a certain extent, total quality becomes strategy—and perhaps should be taught that way.

Management Accounting. TQM does not permit cost, efficiency, and resource use to remain as primary operational measures of performance. Quality—in all of its dimensions—dominates. Because management accountants have been the guardians of performance measurement, the challenge of reinventing performance management is largely theirs. Thus, a decade ago leading management accounting professors, notably Harvard professor Robert Kaplan, began arguing that performance should be measured in nonfinancial terms, including quality, inventory levels, and deliverability.

Although some academics in management accounting may not welcome the idea of nonmonetary measures, most have been easily caught up in the excitement of activity-based costing (ABC). ABC arose because just-in-time (JIT) production—the quick-response component of TQM—throws conventional costing into a tailspin. The old costing system favored filling stockrooms, even with wrong models and substandard quality, to absorb overhead costs. JIT, however, puts the damper on stockroom filling, and total quality shrinks the production of lesser-quality goods. Such improvements show up perversely as bad performance (negative cost variances) in monthly cost reports. So ABC comes to the rescue. If done right, ABC will assign less overhead cost (rework, scrap, stock management, and so on) to products undergoing continuous improvement—especially in cycle time.

A few management accounting professors are finding still another challenge to pursue: working out ways of putting the cost of quality into financial statements. I have raised questions on the wisdom of this (Schonberger 1994).

Corporate Finance.   A related area ripe for research is how to give quality, responsiveness, flexibility, and customer satisfaction their due in capital budgeting—instead of relegating such factors to the last page of the capital expenditure proposal under the heading "Intangibles."

Financial Accounting and Auditing.   In this TQM era, the financial side of accounting has not generated the same degree of dynamism as the management accounting side. This does not mean there is no awareness of deficiencies. Income statements and balance sheets have not served investors well. Too often yesterday's buy list becomes tomorrow's basket cases. The "financials," as required by generally accepted accounting principles, simply do not distinguish between the firm whose quality-related competitiveness is deteriorating and its continuously improving competitor. Though many academics, and legions of securities analysts, continually seek better ways of assessing the strength of a business, breakthrough ideas that recognize quality-centered competitiveness are not yet forthcoming.

Human Resource Management (HRM).   Human resource policies have traditionally favored specialization. Their aim is to narrowly specify jobs through division of labor, then hire people to fill the jobs, give them scant training, and keep them in that specialty for life. HRM has been taught that way and practiced that way. TQM, on the other hand, requires cross-training, job switching, and breadth of vision. Otherwise people on improvement teams will not know enough about the full process to improve it, or even communicate about it. Labor, long blamed for protection of work rules, is generally proving not to be the obstacle to their removal. One reason is that cross-training and learning add lines to one's resumé, which is the key to work-life security (of greater concern today than mere job security). HR departments in superior companies are making the transition toward TQM-based practices featuring never-ending training and development for all employees. HRM textbooks and courses are slowly catching up.

Organizational Behavior (OB). At first, the community of OB scholars watched in amazement as TQM and JIT achieved high levels of teamwork without their help. Since the factory floor was the initial action arena, non-technically oriented OBers kept their distance. However, when TQM hit the back office—and then the entire service sector—the stampede began. Today, treatises on new TQM-related topics have become common in OB academic journals. For example, *Organizational Dynamics* devoted its entire Spring 1992 issue to the theme. These topics include employee involvement and empowerment (versus participation); non-hierarchical, non-functional organization structures; and debates about motivating continuous improvement (accommodating, perhaps, Deming's warnings against performance evaluation). An additional pursuit is reformulation of conventional OB concepts—such as team building, conflict resolution, and equity theory—for use in TQM implementation.

Economics. In the early years of JIT, economists thought it an anomaly that inventories kept falling instead of following the economic cycle. Now it is clear that the pattern is broken. Continuous improvement reduces the need for inventory protection, so inventories just go down. Economists have much to do to revise their models.

More significantly, economists may need to expand their world view. In conventional economic thought management has no role; economic activity is a function of fiscal and monetary policies of government and business. Tinkering with taxation, spending, and a few other money-denominated factors explains everything.

No more. Economists must accept that management can make a difference. Japan's fixation on quality management is especially convincing, and now the same story repeats itself in other countries.

Tool Disciplines

Information systems and mathematics/statistics, indispensable tools for the aforementioned academic areas, are also affected by TQM.

Information Systems (IS). IS practitioners can play an important role in their employers' partners-in-quality efforts with customers and suppliers. Computer-aided design networks, external bar-coding, point-of-sale scanning, electronic data interchange, automatic funds transfers, and satellite communication with freight haulers are among the IS devices that help link firms with suppliers and customers. These expanded uses of IS will naturally interest information systems academics.

Total quality internal to the organization can, however, have opposite effects on IS—which call for changes in academic instruction and research. Organizations typically have a full plate of out-of-control problems. Conventional, non-TQM controls rely on inspectors, counters, dispatchers, and expediters who fill data communications channels with transactions detailing

HR departments in superior companies are making the transition toward TQM-based practices featuring never-ending training and development for all employees.

what's going wrong. Transactions generate reports, which generate computer-produced corrective plans—and the cycle continues expansively. TQM-based controls—on process variation, defects, rework, delays, and complaints—shrink the armies of inspectors and controllers, and the need for internal transactions and reports drops commensurably.

Mathematics/Statistics.   Near the core of TQM is a set of tools known as statistical process control (SPC). At the low end of the SPC methods are the "seven basic tools"—easy to learn and, some say, essential in the daily work of every employee. For a time, universities looked the other way while the community colleges—1,400 strong in the U.S. and Canada—put together training courses in SPC for business and industry. Now SPC is fully covered in operations management and industrial engineering textbooks, plus texts in management accounting, marketing, and general management.

At the high end—drawing in the mathematics and statistics academics—are advanced statistical methods, especially design of experiments and the related methods of Genichi Taguchi. Eminent statisticians such as George Box at the University of Wisconsin and Harry Roberts at the University of Chicago are already recognized leaders in the world quality movement.

Professional Schools

All the professions—from engineering to law—have a mission to provide quality services. The management of the professions also must have quality as its mission.

Engineering.   Quality control and reliability engineering are traditional teaching and research specialties in industrial engineering departments. IE professors have their hands full propagating the old message (sometimes called little q) as well as expanded, new TQM concepts (big Q).

Besides that, every department in the engineering school has the same twofold challenge: (1) teach team design, in which engineers work on project teams with other engineers, customers, suppliers, business functionaries, and the frontline employees who produce the engineered products; (2) teach the principles of design-for-quality and design-for-manufacture (DFM) and its derivatives. Related fertile research areas include design for safety, disassembly, and the environment; quick design-to-market; and elimination of disruptive post-production engineering changes. Some engineering professors and graduate students are already absorbed in these topics.

Public Administration, Teachers College, Medical School, Dental School, Veterinary School, Library School, and Law School.   In each of the other professional schools, quality is—or should be—the foremost concern. All of the professional schools in the university can benefit from adding TQM as an instructional and research topic.

What about all the remaining academic areas? The opinion of the late W. Edwards Deming is instructive. Dr. Deming agreed to allow his name to be attached to Columbia University's Deming Center for Quality Management. A condition, however, was that the center be multi-disciplinary. The project proceeded when the School of Engineering and Applied Science and the Department of Statistics joined the Graduate School of Business in the endeavor. "Actually," according to Professor Peter Kolesar of Columbia's business school, "[Deming] wanted the whole university involved and didn't understand why all departments didn't do so at once."

References

"An Open Letter: TQM on the Campus," *Harvard Business Review*, November–December 1991, pp. 94–95.

"A Report of the Total Quality Leadership Steering Committee and Working Councils," printed by the Procter & Gamble Company, November 1992; definition of total quality developed by Core Body of Knowledge Working Council, p. 2–2.

Robert S. Kaplan, "Yesterday's Accounting Undermines Production," *Harvard Business Review*, July–August 1984, pp. 95–101.

Peter J. Kolesar, "Hats Off to Quality: W. Edwards Deming at Columbia," *Quality Progress*, March 1994, p. 35.

Richard J. Schonberger, "Less Scorekeeping as TQM Takes Root," *Journal of Cost Management*, Summer 1994, pp. 3–4.

"Shaping America's Future: Total Quality Management in Higher Education," *Quality Progress*, October 1993, pp. 41–60.

Richard J. Schonberger is president of Schonberger & Associates, Inc., and a professor of management science at the University of Washington in Seattle.

Arthur Taylor:
Taking TQM to School

Mary Mihaly

Arthur Taylor, former president of CBS and dean of the business school at Fordham University, has taken on the presidency of Muhlenberg College, a small liberal arts school in Allentown, Pennsylvania. This article relates some of the actions he has taken to rejuvenate the college using the principles of TQM.

He looks as though he belongs here, a balding, bespectacled, 59-year-old administrator in suspenders, making his way home for lunch across the 70-acre Muhlenberg College campus. There is no swagger in his step; the uninformed eye would see a modest intellectual, presumably just another inhabitant of the ivory tower.

But look again. Arthur Taylor, president of Muhlenberg since August 1992, is no ordinary scholar. Although one of his titles is "Distinguished Professor," in fact, he never completed the classwork for his doctoral degree. What he does bring to this one-time Lutheran seminary is more compelling than an advanced degree: Arthur Taylor's students are being schooled in Total Quality Management (TQM), boldly applied to every facet of campus life from faculty training to student recruitment, fundraising, and career counseling.

Mr. Taylor became a TQM devotee in 1985. Charged with saving Fordham University's business school, he had to find a focus for the programs under him. He consulted with the late Dr. W. Edwards Deming and his teaching staff began studying TQM with the quality expert. Within five years the school was saved. Dr. Deming's method, well known in industry, is based on 14 principles, the most important being to "drive out fear."

That premise resulted in the historic Muhlenberg Plan-In. On Feb. 3, 1993, classes were canceled for the day and every student, professor, secretary, gardener, technician, and other employee of the college was invited to the planning marathon. More than 1,000 attended, breaking into 32 concurrent sessions addressing such diverse concerns as new facilities versus green space, nurturing quality teaching, the college's role in students' social lives, internationalizing the curriculum, and environmental literacy.

"It was quite a *tour de force*," Mr. Taylor recalls. "Deming always said, 'If you listen to the people doing the job, they will tell you how to do the job best.' So we invited them to do just that, and it was quite efficient—eliminated a lot of constant conferencing and consulting. In one day we knew what was on everyone's mind."

Mr. Taylor had taken a few detours on his way to being named Muhlenberg's president, making his mark as an expert in international finance and then in 1972 becoming the youngest-ever head of CBS. A few years later, he purchased a 30-day option on 50,000 hours of quality programming from the British Broadcasting Co. and founded the Arts & Entertainment Network. However, Mr. Taylor says, Muhlenberg's presidency "is the only job I ever asked for." His relationship with Muhlenberg began in 1992 when the school's trustees called him, among other consultants, for advice: With declining enrollments and escalating costs creating panic at private colleges across the country, Muhlenberg's leaders needed a plan. The college has been solvent for the last four decades, but its trustees had done little to position the school for the future.

Mr. Taylor, then in his seventh year as a dean at Fordham, expected merely to perform an objective assessment for Muhlenberg; instead, he fell in love with the challenge and with the school. Mr. Taylor has taken responsibility not only for Muhlenberg's financial future, but also for excellence in all areas. He presented his four-part mission in his inaugural speech two years ago—his plan to make Muhlenberg "truly distinctive among colleges":

Continuous Improvement in Student Focus.   Under Mr. Taylor's plan, TQM transforms students into "customers" and ensures the quality of the academic "product" they've purchased. Their dorms, their security, even their relationships with each other are affected. "TQM is a religion," Mr. Taylor says. "It's a philosophy. It's not a technique."

Academic policies have been redesigned to encourage rather than inhibit student responsibility, recognizing alternatives to classroom learning as valid educational experiences. A student community-service initiative is being developed, faculty-student interaction is emphasized through new events created to foster such communication, and a climate of ownership of one's academic goals and efforts is being fostered, among other changes.

Staff has been restructured to make way for a new Dean for Academic Life, a position equal to the Dean for Faculty. "This says we're as concerned about one as the other," says James Steffy, vice president of planning and administration.

Mr. Taylor has made it known that students need not schedule an appointment to see him, that they can knock on his door—at the office or at home—whenever they need to talk to him. "And they do," he says, "at 3 a.m. sometimes. If they're troubled or afraid of something, we want them to know they don't have to worry, we'll push them forward."

Mr. Taylor and his wife, Kathryn Pelgrift Taylor—a principal in Women Broadcasters Inc. and a consultant for radio station investors and other entrepreneurs—host up to 40 students, visitors, and other dinner guests at least five nights a week. (She also has been a senior vice president of strategic planning for RCA Corp. and treasurer of Philip Morris Inc.)

"Deming always said, 'If you listen to the people doing the job, they will tell you how to do the job best.'"

Academic policies have been redesigned to encourage rather than inhibit student responsibility, recognizing alternatives to classroom learning as valid educational experiences.

Continuous Improvement in the Global Experience of Faculty and Students. Muhlenberg's faculty this year includes Visiting Prof. Gennadi Gerasimov, Russian ambassador to Portugal and former spokesman for Mikhail Gorbachev. He has appeared on television many times, including a dozen appearances on "Nightline." Mr. Taylor invited him to visit Muhlenberg, and they became friends.

"This shows that we're serious about globalization," says Chris Hooker-Haring, admissions dean, "and that's something that makes Muhlenberg a much more compelling experience. We can tell students, 'You can take a course with Gennadi Gerasimov.' For some students, that's a big deal."

Mr. Taylor has pledged to be creative about globalizing Muhlenberg. To that end, in addition to increased faculty and student experiences abroad, Mr. Taylor has created the College of Asian & Western Learning—a "college within a college." The unique program is another direct outcome of the Plan-In. As many as 400 students will receive an intense international education, including a full year of study in Japan. Graduates will be able to "live thoughtfully and work effectively in both cultures," he says, so that they can work toward international solutions to global problems.

Continuous Improvement in the Supremacy of Teaching. TQM has profoundly affected faculty life at Muhlenberg as well, most notably in the creation of the Faculty Center for Teaching. Conceived by the faculty at one of their own seminars, the new center is a place where they can immerse themselves in "the scholarship of teaching," says Kathryn Wixon, associate professor of foreign languages and literatures. The center will be operated and governed by faculty. "But," adds psychology department head Kathleen Haring, "we can do this because we get so much support from the administration."

Teaching methods are traditionally a minor, haphazardly presented aspect of teachers' training, especially at the college level. "We are immersed in our disciplines, then come here and are expected to be great teachers," Prof. Haring says. "Now, I'm thinking more about the consequences of my actions in the classroom."

Business Prof. Fred Norling agrees. "I've seen a lot more discipline," he says, "showing awareness on the part of the faculty that Muhlenberg's not going to survive if it continues dog-paddling."

Continuous Improvement in Financial Strength. "Admissions counselors can be fairly gloomy when they get together," says Dean Hooker-Haring.

They have cause for worry—especially in the Northeast, where the college-age population has shrunk by 22% since 1989. At high-cost private colleges—such as Muhlenberg, where tuition and feeds for its 1,700 students reached $16,975 this year—expenditures per full-time student have risen 38% in the last 10 years.

Muhlenberg's endowment is relatively small, about $38 million; nearly 87% of the college's $39.5 million budget comes from tuition and fees. The region has begun to see a gradual rebound in the number of college-age people, but the growth is in populations at socioeconomic levels.

In one attempt to harvest as many funding sources as possible, Muhlenberg's evening college will expand from slightly more than 400 students to about 1,000 in the next four years. "Small colleges often are not where adults are," Vice President Steffy explains. Muhlenberg is fortunate in that, instead of sitting in a small college town, it's located at the western end of Allentown, a city of some 200,000 people—and Philadelphia is an hour's drive to the south. To attract older students, Saturday-morning classes and library privileges for the entire family will be instituted—strategies for "making them feel a part of the place."

A nearly total turnover in board-of-trustees membership in two years also has improved finances. "When I came here, I found a very tired board of trustees who had given and given," he says. "We needed new people with fresh enthusiasm and fresh funds." The rewards from that move were almost immediate: Alumni contributions are up 20% from last year, foundation funds have increased by 50%, and trustee giving has tripled. Within the next year, Mr. Taylor will establish a true capital campaign. When Mr. Taylor first arrived at Muhlenberg, he recalls, "not one basic thing had been done in development. [The college] had never gone to the Ford or Mellon Foundations—basic things that should have been done 20 years ago."

Although the setting is a world away from Mr. Taylor's high-powered corporate past, the strategies are the same as when, after his time at CBS, he helped found an investment-banking firm with Nelson Rockefeller and retired World Bank chairman George Woods.

Mr. Taylor's "goal is to leave Muhlenberg so that it has a forecastable future well into the next century. I want to see this little college . . . well into the placid waters—and I want to make sure she sails well and sound."

Mary Mihaly is a correspondent for Industry Week *magazine.*

Defining the Customer

Jacob R. Wambsganss and Danny Kennett

This article explores who the customer is for college courses. It is often seen as the student, but these authors suggest that an equally valid selection is the companies who will employ students. If the courses do not prepare students to meet employers' needs, then they may be failing in delivering a quality education. The article discusses this in the context of accounting departments, but the idea is equally valid across the curriculum. Whether employers are the customers of colleges would be controversial, but it is worth considering.

Total quality management (TQM) has had a major success in industry, and now its use in education is being advocated. TQM can produce improvements in accounting education, but only if prevailing definitions of "customer" and "quality" are examined.

Ivancevich and Ivancevich say the "first step in applying TQM is to view the student as a customer who must be served."[1] Their view of the student as a customer is recognized widely but not accepted universally. As Dean L. Hubbard, president of Northwest Missouri State University, explains, "We concluded that in the classroom, the student, along with the instructor, are 'suppliers' producing a 'product' (knowledge) that a future 'customer' (employer or graduate school) will evaluate."[2]

In a study sponsored jointly by the Institute of Management Accountants (IMA) and the Financial Executives Institute (FEI) that attempts to determine the needs of Corporate America relating to qualifications of entry-level accountants, Siegel and Sorensen present their findings as a "customer perspective."[3] Julian Freedman, director of research at the IMA, states that " . . . these corporations are one of the most important customers for colleges and universities."[4]

Identifying the Customer

The first step in applying TQM is to identify the customer and determine the customer's quality needs. Traditionally, students are viewed as the customer because they "pay the bill" (tuition) and receive the service offered (education). The university or department does not exist without them. TQM, however, is not a traditional concept. Deming warns "there are curious exceptions" to the supposition that a person who pays the bill is the customer to be served. He says the end user should be the focus of the organization.[5]

Why do students pursue an accounting major—or any business-related major for that matter? What are students' expectations of their college education? Few students pursue a degree in accounting as the ultimate objective. Most accounting majors are pragmatic and are drawn to accounting because of the career opportunities. Before applying for admission to college, students and their families frequently want to know an accounting department's relationship with the profession.

Accounting departments develop relationships with employers based on their alumni's successes. Employers, in turn, monitor accounting departments' program improvement and communicate their future recruiting qualifications. As employers affiliate with accounting departments for recruiting and students seek admission to departments with strong connections with the profession, it may be the employers who actually pull students to and through an accounting department.

Employers who recruit an accounting department's graduates, therefore, serve its continued existence in three ways. First, they encourage prospective students to apply for admission, thus providing the quantity and quality of students necessary for the continued existence of the department from an administrative and fiscal viewpoint. Second, they validate the accounting department's educational process through their hiring practices. For example, students see the rewards for their efforts when interacting with alumni in positions of responsibility. Third, alumni—especially those who perform at or above employer expectations—provide a justification for the firms' continued affiliation and recruiting efforts with the accounting department. Clearly the long-term success of an accounting department depends on the quantity and quality of employer affiliation.

Problems with Considering Students the Primary Customer

Placing the student as the focus of the accounting department and its curriculum may sound appropriate or even politically correct, but there are major problems with this focus and its outcomes. The term "student" is difficult to define in accounting departments, especially those with minimal or no admission standards. There is substantial diversity regarding abilities, determination, and ambition. This diversity becomes a problem when a department is developing a focus. Should the department direct its attentions to the "best and brightest" or concentrate on those students in the lower achievement categories?

In the TQM environment, "customers' needs" and "quality" refer to end users and the degree of satisfaction end users receive from the product or service, respectively. When the student is viewed as the customer, a dilemma arises. For students, "needs" may be described more accurately as "immediate concerns," such as earning good grades on tests and in courses, graduating, or perhaps passing a certifying examination. Students cannot determine "customer needs" effectively because they are not cognizant at that moment of the types of skills or level of achievement expected by the end user.

The course evaluation is the formal instrument used by students for assessing an accounting department. Ideally, students could base their evaluation of departmental and course quality on the difference between the "facts" known at the beginning and the end of the period. The greater the difference between "fact" levels, the better the education. Unfortunately, with students' relatively narrow perception of what the accounting profession encompasses, skills such as communication, problem solving, and computer literacy may be overlooked as vital for a successful career. Focusing on the student for an effective accounting program evaluation may substantially overestimate or underestimate its quality to the detriment of the university, department, employers, and current and future students.

Considering the student as the customer may lead an accounting department, mistakenly, to recognize the importance of exam pass rates and also to present course material in a traditionally structured lecture and problem-solving format. Unfortunately for these schools, the "Big 6" public accounting firms reject the traditional accounting curriculum as irrelevant and the traditional "lecture-routine-problem" presentation as ineffective.[6] Major changes are occurring in curricula, presentation, and learning skills in accounting education, but this trend does not mean that every accounting department is changing. The extent of change is affected by various factors, one of which is student resistance. Conflicting with many students' "needs" is the shift in emphasis toward writing, unstructured problems, critical thinking exercises, and nonaccounting courses—with less emphasis on accounting rules and certifying exams.

For example, suppose an accounting department considers adding a nonaccounting course to the required curriculum. The course is recommended widely by employers but opposed by students because it is too difficult, time-consuming, and unrelated to accounting. If students are considered the accounting department's customers, the department may respond to their opposition by offering the course initially as an elective. The department would take the only step it feels is necessary, that is, to communicate to students the value of the course. The long-term benefit of this optional course would be lost to many students and eventually to those who will employ them.

Looking at students' preferences, however, is only one part of the total picture. What happens to the overall integrity of the accounting program and the working relationship with employers? What happens to the reputation of the accounting program and to job prospects of future graduates when these new professionals find out *on the job* that they made a mistake in not taking that recommended course (and probably other courses as well)? Considering the course requirement decision as internal and affecting only some students is shortsighted and dangerous.

Employers are not ignored by those who contend that students are customers. Generally, however, the customer role of employers is implied or of a secondary nature. Ivancevich and Ivancevich, for example, treat employers as secondary customers when they state, "Accounting faculty should strive to listen to the impressions, needs, goals, and suggestions provided by students and *business leaders* for improving the quality of the departmental

The customer role of employers is implied or of a secondary nature.

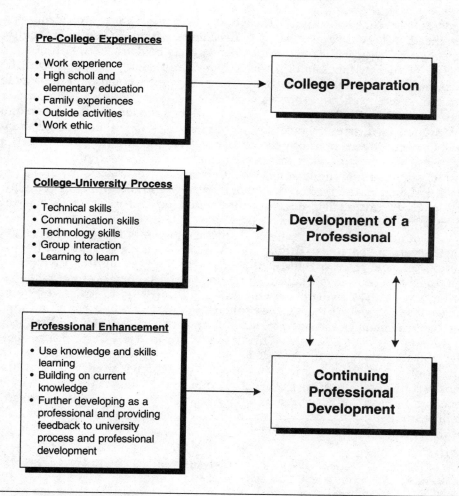

Pre-College Experiences

- Work experience
- High scholl and elementary education
- Family experiences
- Outside activities
- Work ethic

College Preparation

College-University Process

- Technical skills
- Communication skills
- Technology skills
- Group interaction
- Learning to learn

Development of a Professional

Professional Enhancement

- Use knowledge and skills learning
- Building on current knowledge
- Further developing as a professional and providing feedback to university process and professional development

Continuing Professional Development

Figure 1. **Educational process.**

courses and degree programs."[7] (Emphasis added.) Fay, Ferrara, and Stryker state that "Measuring teaching excellence must include a system of evaluation by current students."[8] Individuals who focus on the student do not consider the inevitable conflict between the two different perspectives (at least at that moment in time) and the resulting definition of quality. Quality based on current student acceptance may not be the same as quality defined by the end user of the graduates—the employer.

Quality based on current student acceptance may not be the same as quality defined by the end user of the graduates—the employer.

Employers as the Primary Customer

When students fail to have qualifications employers seek, the accounting department provides a disservice to both students and employers. Students leave the accounting program believing they are prepared for the profession when, in fact, they realize upon joining the workforce they are not equipped for what lies ahead. In this circumstance, better students, albeit with some difficulty, may succeed. Other students, unfortunately, may be doomed to failure.

If a program's focus is on people in the profession, instructors will be encouraged to maintain contact with practicing professionals and to become familiar with current and future practice needs. (See Figure 1.) This contact may diminish the stereotypes associated with the accounting profession and give students a different perspective on various tracks including public, management, and government accounting. Course content would give students a more realistic view of what lies beyond the academic environment. For example, students may understand why they are asked to perform classroom tasks assigned by the instructor. Students also would recognize that employers are their future customers and that education is a process of preparing them to meet their customers' needs.

Accounting firms, companies, and other employers of accounting graduates act like "good customers" if they communicate their expectations of qualifications for new professionals. In fact, many leading accounting departments are recognizing employers (although not explicitly) as their customers and are acting like "good suppliers" by changing their curricula to meet employers' needs. If employers are recognized explicitly as customers of both the accounting department and accounting students, then both parties are focused on meeting the needs of one customer. This unitary focus fosters a long-term perspective and a constancy of purpose that results in clearly defined objectives.

Continuous improvement in an accounting department's curriculum means continually meeting the needs of employer-established quality criteria. Accounting faculty also can improve the learning process as it relates to students. Student input, however, should be considered secondary to the needs of the profession.

Notes

1. Daniel M. Ivancevich and Susan H. Ivancevich, "TQM in the Classroom," MANAGEMENT ACCOUNTING®, October 1992, pp.14–15.

2. Dean L. Hubbard, *Continuous Quality Improvement: Making the Transition to Education*, Prescott Publishing Co., Marysville, Mo., 1993.

3. Gary Siegel and James E. Sorensen, "What Corporate America Wants in Entry-Level Accountants," MANAGEMENT ACCOUNTING®, September 1994, pp. 26–31.

4. *Ibid.*, p.31.

5. W. Edwards Deming, *Out of the Crisis*, MIT Press, Cambridge, Mass., 1986.

6. *Perspectives on Education: Capabilities for Success in the Accounting Profession*, Arthur Andersen & Co., Arthur Young, Coopers & Lybrand, Deloitte Haskins & Sells, Ernst & Whinney, Peat Marwick Main & Co., Price Waterhouse, and Touche Ross [former "Big 8"], New York, N.Y., 1989.

7. Ivancevich and Ivancevich, *op. cit.*, pp. 14–15.

8. Jack R. Fay, William L. Ferrara, and Judson P. Stryker, "The Quest for Quality in Business Schools," MANAGEMENT ACCOUNTING®, December 1993, pp.48–50.

Jacob R. Wambsganss, Ph.D., is associate professor of accounting, Department of Accounting and Business Law, College of Business and Public Administration, University of North Dakota, Grand Forks, North Dakota. Danny Kennett, DBA, is associate professor of accounting, Division of Accounting and Computer Information Systems, School of Business, Emporia State University, Emporia, Kansas.

Implementing Quality

Part Three presents a collection of articles and excerpts from books, almost all published in 1995, that deal with the strategic and tactical issues surrounding the implementation of total quality management. Reflecting what organizations have learned over the past several years, we have organized the material in this part into four logical groupings: *Quality Transformation, Quality Tools and Techniques, Functional Processes,* and *Standards and Assessments.* Within each of these groups, you will find ideas, practical advice, and techniques relevant to all types of organizations.

Quality Transformation

Quality management is **not** just a set of techniques to add to your management repertoire (as we discussed in the article that opens this book). It requires a long-term commitment at the top and a disciplined, informed transformation of company culture. Managers **must** focus on supporting and developing the people who carry out the interrelated processes that characterize organizational work. This section includes an array of articles on *leadership, cultural change, customer focus, training, teams and teamwork, systems thinking/learning organizations,* and *communication.* Our selection is designed to give you a clear sense of the attitudes and practices that can help you make the transition to a culture that supports continuous improvement of processes and quality for customers. It is not easy to build a culture based on the values of quality management. It takes long-term commitment and discipline. But it's worth it, because it creates an organization that is vibrant and supportive of employees, that continually becomes more efficient, and that will have a sustainable competitive advantage.

You may note that the section on systems thinking/learning organizations is new to this edition. We are pleased to have Daniel Kim as a consulting editor and to have his original article introduce this section. Daniel Kim is co-founder and currently the Learning Lab Research Project Director at the MIT Organizational Learning Center, where he works closely with Peter Senge. Kim is also publisher of *The Systems Thinker* newsletter and a popular and in-demand speaker on issues regarding learning organizations and systems thinking. Understanding organizations as systems is an important foundation of total quality management and continuous improvement, and we are putting an emphasis on this area in the 1996 yearbook. Besides Kim's piece, you will also find articles by other prominent thinkers in this area.

Quality Tools and Techniques

In the 1996 edition of *The Quality Yearbook*, we are also emphasizing process management; the three subsections here, *Process Reengineering, Benchmarking,* and *Process Management Measurement,* include a variety of practical articles to assist you in thinking about these issues. For example, see the Roger Rupp and James Russell article, "The Golden Rules of Process Redesign." If you are in the midst of process improvement or redesign, this article can help you avoid mistakes and pitfalls.

You'll also find an intriguing piece on what to avoid when undertaking a benchmarking project in Irving DeToro's "The 10 Pitfalls of Benchmarking." Joseph Kelada's article "Is Reengineering Replacing Total Quality?" answers that question by demonstrating that reengineering is part of quality management, not a replacement for it. The other pieces also include valuable advice and observations about the practice of process management.

Functional Processes

Important work is underway in many industries at the functional level (for example, accounting, purchasing, and human resources), making it possible to begin documenting their successes and procedures. We have noted this and chosen to highlight four areas: *suppliers and purchasing, information technology, accounting and finance,* and *human resources.* Our guideline here was thoughtful practicality, and these articles describe how quality principles can help shape and improve practices in all these areas.

Standards and Assessments

We conclude Part Three with three articles that look at the issues surrounding ISO 9000 and the Baldrige Award. The Eugenia Brumm article "Managing Records for ISO 9000 Compliance" is a great introduction to this important part of becoming certified. And the piece by Mike Herrington on using the Baldrige criteria to do a self-assessment highlights what is perhaps the most valuable feature of the Baldrige Award: standards for judging how well you are doing even if you never apply for the award.

*   *   *

We again want to refer you to the detailed bibliography in Part Four. You'll find an extensive listing of current articles and books covering all the topics taken up in Part Three.

How to Prevent the Coming Failure of Quality

Rita E. Numerof and Michael N. Abrams

As the title suggests, this article profiles an all-too-common set of events in organizations that seek to implement quality management but that just don't understand that this is not a "program." Quality bureaucracies, silos, lack of union buy-in—these are some of the problems companies encounter when they approach TQM as business as usual. Only when top management gets intimately involved over the long haul can organizations get the results that TQM promises.

Quality is dead at the XYZ Corporation. The last of the quality facilitators are packing their things and heading off to new assignments—some to corporate planning, others to corporate training, and still others to outplacement services. After many years of enthusiasm, commitment, exploding growth, newsletters, training, teams, posters, meetings, and all the attendant hoopla and financial backing, quality at XYZ is dead. It's even been taken out of the latest labor contract. No union employee will be expected or encouraged to participate in any quality improvement team activity for the duration of the contract.

What happened at XYZ isn't, unfortunately, an isolated situation. What began in earnest as an attempt to improve quality and performance in a major corporation has ended in frustration and disillusion. The lessons, however, are significant. And they point to the direction corporate America must take if it's serious about maintaining its position as a global competitor.

Typical Responses to the Quality Imperative

Across industries, there tends to be a general understanding of what quality should look like (i.e., zero defects and meeting customer requirements) but a massive misunderstanding about how to achieve quality and continuous improvement. The most common response to the quality imperative is a structured and often comprehensive training effort, kicked off with substantial fanfare, pomp, and circumstance.

In the case of XYZ, about eights year ago, an energetic young manager with a record of success in industrial quality assurance in the company was given the green light by the chief executive officer (CEO) to establish a corporate quality improvement division. Forty-five full-time quality facilitators were selected for the initial events. Technically expert in their fields, these enthusiastic and committed facilitators were sent out to convert the corporate masses to the ways and whys of corporate quality. With messianic zeal, they preached about the merits of quality, quality tools, and statistical process control (SPC). They had a fully functioning corporate structure to support them.

The structure reflected all of the right components, and it was evident to the casual observer that XYZ had done its homework to implement a successful quality effort. The quality director reported to the CEO to ensure visibility and communicate the message that senior leadership was committed to this "quality stuff." Two steering committees were established to approve ideas suggested by quality improvement teams (groups of people working together for an hour or two each week to improve the quality of their products and services). One committee was a senior management group that reviewed and approved improvement suggestions with cross-functional implications. The other committee was at the division level, and it approved and prioritized suggestions with functional implications. XYZ had set up a quality structure that had its own hierarchy and decision-making review process and was tied directly to top management.

Phase I of the quality effort focused on corporate communication and building awareness. The CEO addressed groups about the quality program, signed his name to newsletter columns and annual reports, and spoke of employee involvement and customer satisfaction—all new ideas in an industry that hadn't really known competition before. Enthusiasm and skepticism walked side by side.

Quality improvement facilitators (QIFs) headed up massive training efforts to teach the quality improvement process that would enable employees to work in quality improvement teams (QITs). Teams were assigned facilitators to help them manage their processes and to make sure that managers didn't subvert the nascent involvement process.

Mavericks who wanted to follow their own quality processes were brought in line with the quality-correct ways of doing things. Forms to ensure consistency and replication across teams were introduced. It wasn't long before walls were papered with Pareto charts, histograms, and control charts. On certain days, one could get the sense that Walter Shewhart himself was walking the halls.

By the year's end, 100 teams were operative—a critical measure of success, according to the quality director. Enthusiasm ran high. The quality newsletter talked about commitment, quality, and involvement. Year two sparked the training of 100 part-time QIFs. The QIFs, XYZ's most enthusiastic and technically proficient employees, began complaining about the dinosaurs. Dinosaurs were managers with extended tenure at XYZ (15 to 25 years) who were seen as resisting the quality effort. Resistance manifested itself in a number of ways, most frequently in the form of naysaying and doubt. A less common but nonetheless annoying form of resistance was subtle subversion and failure to implement. Specifically, quality language and the quality process weren't used. Some managers insisted on using their own language and wouldn't use the appropriate charts and graphs for reporting progress and results. In other cases, managers asked for marketing and process assessments but never used the results even though the studies were performed with rigor and quality.

Year three continued much the same as year two, only now more teams were operative. Increased frustration was apparent among all but a handful of QIFs. One source of their frustration was the lack of compliance. The QIFs felt helpless to force managers to change. Teams were beginning to resent seeing managers act one way in team meetings and revert to autocratic styles outside the groups. But most frustrating was the fact that presentations for improvement changes were made to the appropriate committees and then not approved. Grumbling among the committed was heard more and more.

The quality effort still had its official champions. Senior management still spoke at meetings about quality, increased competition, and change. The CEO applauded the efforts of the quality director, QITs, and QIFs. Indeed, XYZ was seen as a model of innovation and change. The CEO and the quality director were finding that requests for their presence on the speaker circuit were increasing. This was a sure sign of their success.

The fact that no clear monetary gains could be identified as a result of the effort was seen as a non-issue. Many believed that expecting financial results at this stage in the process was unrealistic. The fact that anomalies existed was regarded as an inevitable part of the changes XYZ had to manage. One such anomaly occurred with the promotion of a department head to vice president. This particular young engineer was abrasive and rude, despite his technological brilliance. Under the new rules of quality, management was expected to be managerially responsive first and technically astute second. This man's promotion was clearly inconsistent with XYZ's new philosophy.

In year five, the quality director ceased to report to the CEO. The official word was that quality had sufficient visibility and could now be incorporated into XYZ's mainstream. In year seven, XYZ's union leadership made, as part of its contract, the stipulation that no union employee would be asked or expected to participate in teams until management changed. Teams quickly

> On certain days, one could get the sense that Walter Shewhart himself was walking the halls.

> Most frustrating was the fact that presentations for improvement changes were made to the appropriate committees and then not approved.

and quietly disbanded. The unofficial word was that quality at XYZ had died. Officially, the word was that there was no longer any need for a separate division and that the union no longer supported participation. Quality was now going back to the line.

Examining the Pitfalls: What Went Wrong at XYZ

How can the demise of the quality effort at XYZ be explained, especially after its apparently auspicious start? Some of the pitfalls XYZ encountered were:

Parallel Process.   As with quality efforts at other companies, XYZ established a parallel process. A quality bureaucracy was created with its own reporting mechanisms, staff, processes, rewards, and accountabilities that ran parallel to the rest of the organization. Its mission was to train all XYZ personnel in quality improvement. The operating assumption was that if people were trained to use quality tools and techniques, they would behave differently. The QIFs, armed with their new language, training, idealism, commitment, and ostensible executive support, were to create a new way of doing business because it was the right thing to do. And yet, the effort was doomed to failure from the beginning.

XYZ neglected to change the balance in the way work and organizational power were distributed, failed to change what was organizationally rewarded through the line structure, and failed to change the distribution of rewards. Without modifying at least two of these basic elements, no lasting organizational change could be feasible. At XYZ, the basic power structure and accountability and reward systems remained intact. Quality was never integrated within the line structure.

XYZ neglected to change the balance in the way work and organizational power were distributed.

Means-ends Inversion.   In addition to running a parallel system that held no one in the line accountable, XYZ made another common error. It mistook inputs for outputs, confused processes with outcomes, and accepted activity as a proxy for results. It assumed that if it did enough of the right improvement activities, improved performance would result. Activities such as training and building employee involvement weren't tied to specific results. Nor were they seen as the means to a specifically defined end. They were accepted instead as measures of success, and it was assumed that they would result in changed behavior and desired outcomes. The number of people trained and satisfaction with the training were seen as acceptable measures. The operational changes that training effected were never evaluated.

Lack of Strategic Focus and Cross-Functional Integration.   This common error contributed to and was a result of the means-ends inversion just described. XYZ neglected to define a narrow range of three or four strategic business issues to address systematically. By failing to identify a limited number of strategically relevant variables, XYZ left its teams to charge off on their own—doing good in the name of quality and creating a state of energized chaos. The absence of clearly defined, measurable indicators gave XYZ no baseline from which it could measure sustained progress to a goal. The lack of common focus also exacerbated XYZ's historic (and common) struggles

There are a number of ways you can help ensure the failure of quality at your organization. Many were detailed in the story of XYZ Corporation. Below are additional problematic and erroneous quality assumptions (in italics) that are easy traps in which to fall, followed by the correct action. When planning your quality journey, keep these false assumptions in mind:

- *Staff teams can solve significant quality problems at a weekly meeting.* Significant quality problems require more than one to two hours per week if organizations are serious about eliminating them. Focused and concentrated efforts are required to attack each component of a problem systematically. Employee involvement is absolutely critical to problem identification, analysis, and resolution. Isolated chunks of time won't be sufficient to warrant speedy changes necessary to remain competitive.

- *Staff teams can solve quality problems in the absence of changes in managerial performance and accountability.* Staff teams quickly become energized in the face of opportunity for meaningful input. But disillusion sets in when the old rewards get reenacted and attempts at innovation and challenging the status quo go without response or get punished.

- *Training can result in behavior change even if accountability for new skills application isn't ensured.* Training can help those whose personal quest for excellence is beyond any external sources of motivation. Unfortunately and predictably, people engage in those behaviors that get rewarded and reinforced. New behaviors (learned in training situations) will go dormant if they aren't recognized or given the opportunity to be expressed. Quite simply, organizations get the behavior they expect and reward.

- *Quality and continuous improvement efforts can be successfully instituted without management involvement.* At the most important level, quality and continuous improvement entail a new way in which managers and employees do business together. Long-term success in quality and continuous improvement must bring about real partnerships between managers and their employees.

- *Employee-customer behaviors can be changed without examining underlying employee-organization relationships.* Employee identification with the goals, values, and objectives of the organization is the link that makes quality and continuous improvement possible. Every employee must identify strategically, beyond the daily tasks of the immediate job, the broader perspective on the meaning that job has for overall organizational performance. It's management's job to articulate this link and to hold the work force accountable for performance consistent with it. Without organizational trust, integrity, and fairness, employee identification will never be more than loyalty to the next paycheck.

with divisional functionalization—each operating unit seeing itself as a separate entity rather than an important part of a unified and integrated whole. Relatedly, XYZ failed to identify that work is a continuous process with a myriad of internal and external customer interfaces that must be managed as part of that process.

The Unspecified Role of Management.   Perhaps as a reflection of the parallel process, XYZ failed to define a specific role for its management team. This was the fatal error. Delegating quality to the work force at large, while an obvious problem in specifying accountability, also sets the stage for massive confusion and resistance. XYZ's effort, like that of so many others, emphasized the role of participation and employee involvement, not as a means to an improved end, but as an end in itself. The fact that no one could adequately define what this meant operationally seemed irrelevant. Managers who tended to involve staff prior to the quality emphasis used the process to support the work of their areas and continued to be successful. These heroes, unfortunately, were inadequately recognized. XYZ was unable (or unwilling) to learn from their successes.

Unfortunately, most managers at XYZ, rewarded for bureaucratic management, were hard pressed to change direction. Some didn't have the skills to change, others lacked the will, and some lacked both. Often, QITs worked around management, believing that the just cause would get approval after much data collection, research, and presentation to management. But proposals from QITs were frequently turned down—sometimes because the proposals lacked strategic relevance, and sometimes because they were great ideas that hadn't gotten management's support. It was about here in the process that disillusionment and frustration became widespread—and the war between the dinosaurs and the QITs escalated. The dinosaurs still held the power, and no one bothered to inform the QITs just what the limits to their involvement were. The discrepancy between expectation and reality fueled frustration.

The failure to adequately structure participation, define the limits of involvement under certain conditions, and clearly define the critical role of management under the new rules of engagement was clearly problematic.

The Employee-Organization Interface.   This error was a failure to recognize that improved relations with employees provide a foundation for, and tend to result in, improved relations with the customer. When employees identify with the goals of the company, understand how they can make a difference in achieving strategic goals, and are knowledgeable about the business and its competition, they can solve problems before managers even know they exist. The development of a solid strategic foundation must begin with strong employee identification with the organization. This identification allows employees to build on and improve their relationships with their customers for the benefit of all.

The Complexity of Change.   The demise of XYZ's quality effort can also be explained by another factor: inadequate understanding of the complex process

XYZ failed to define a specific role for its management team. This was the fatal error.

of organizational change itself. Resistance, a natural by-product of any change, must be understood and managed. By merely naming and blaming the resisters (the dinosaurs), the QIFs were unable to manage resistance and deal with understandable and deep-seated issues.

In addition, XYZ opted for a "revolutionary" approach to organizational change. The choice to enthusiastically break the ties with the old and start fresh, without acknowledging and integrating what already existed, doomed the effort to failure. In reality, the revolution existed only in words: the basic organizational underpinnings remained constant. XYZ failed to weave change into the fabric of the organization. In essence, it neglected to modify the reward, compensation, and performance management systems to support desired behavioral change.

Finally, XYZ failed to manage the revolutionary-evolutionary change continuum. The revolutionary pressures, coming from real, dramatic changes in the business environment, were never tied to the enduring values that led XYZ to its success in the first place. For some at XYZ, it was quality that had led to their success, and these people believed that quality was already reflected in their current operations. Thus, there was no need to change.

Doing It Right the First Time

The continuous improvement effort that XYZ embarked on was doomed to failure from the outset. But how can it be done right the first time?

Beginning right at the beginning means framing the continuous improvement effort as a targeted response to increased and dynamic marketplace demands and pressures and as a requirement for continued organizational viability and competitiveness. All members of the organization must understand strategic context—the environmental opportunities and constraints that drive business decisions. While an understanding of how an individual fits in and ultimately can make a difference is essential, it's insufficient to achieve results. A structured, systematic, and focused effort to improve selected business processes must be in place. The improvement effort must be linked with relevant activities that have gone before it.

Most organizations are concerned with improving operations, enhancing service, and developing more-responsive systems. To introduce quality and continuous improvement as something new implies that whatever was done before wasn't quality. Regardless of the relative veracity of whether quality was or wasn't in existence before, a turbulent business environment renders present processes obsolete quickly. Today's quality initiative might work well today, but it will probably be inadequate tomorrow. Continuous improvement and continuously matching up expectations are necessary for survival.

Demystifying Quality and Continuous Improvement

At its core, a quality effort isn't the mystical, time-consuming, resource-intensive process that it's made out to be. In fact, the steps involved are fairly straightforward:

Business goals must
be articulated by
senior management
in light of external
opportunities and
constraints.

1. Business goals must be articulated by senior management in light
    of external opportunities and constraints.
2. These goals must be communicated consistently, effectively, and
    frequently to the entire work force so that people can relate per-
    sonally and enthusiastically to them. It is dangerous—and falla-
    cious—to assume that people know what the company's goals are
    merely because they work there. As is true for any new product
    introduction to market (or for an existing product into a new mar-
    ket), success depends in part on the ability to communicate.
3. Internal and external customers (critical to the success of business
    goals) must be identified.
4. A systematic process to gather meaningful data about the percep-
    tions, expectations, and requirements of each critical constitu-
    ency must be implemented. Included should be an assessment of
    the key processes used to achieve the business goals.
5. Data should be analyzed to identify and prioritize gaps between
    perceptions and expectations and to identify process barriers.
6. Problem-solving tools should be applied to key processes associ-
    ated with these gaps to understand contributing factors and po-
    tential solutions.
7. Universal education without immediate structured application is
    costly and doesn't achieve results. Viable solutions should be se-
    lected and implemented just in time in a way that's consistent
    with principles of effective change management.
8. Management must ensure that the organizational culture sup-
    ports quality improvement initiatives through a process of system
    integration and alignment.

At a bare bones level, these steps identify important business goals in
relation to key constituencies, pinpoint what the constituencies really need
and want, and systematically address the gaps. AS simple as these steps seem,
there are many quality efforts that have failed or are currently headed for
failure. The failures highlighted in the case of XYZ aren't unique. They are
repeated across companies and across industries. An outline of the underlying
assumptions—both critical to success and problematic—will help other organizations avoid potholes along the quality road.

Building Successful Quality Efforts

There are several critical principles that a company must understand before
it can transform itself into a successful quality organization:

■   Change will not occur without a specific and clear focus, clearly
    defined expectations, measurable objectives, accountability, feed-
    back, monitoring, and follow-through.
■   Performance improvement must be an important part of every-
    one's job every day—not something that's addressed one or two
    hours a week.

- Any successful quality improvement effort must be built into daily line structure and accountability. It must be tied to the organization's enduring values and what has gone before, or the quality effort will appear to be just another program.
- Although each manager is held accountable for budget responsibility, separate groups can't be solely responsible for achieving corporate quality objectives.
- Specifying performance improvement or quality improvement indicators and achieving desirable results within defined time lines should be the responsibility of all managers.
- The focus, strategic relevance, responsibility, and accountability for results rests with senior management. As with financial indicators and human resources management, centralized and decentralized systems need to work together. Quality bureaucracies are guaranteed to kill the flexibility, responsiveness, innovation, and ownership that's necessary for continuous improvement and success. On the other hand, a consistent lack of cross-functional integration and lack of attention to strategic initiatives will result in chaos, frustration, and the failure of otherwise good intentions.
- Too many organizations get caught up in the technology of SPC and other problem-solving modalities for their own sake, mistaking the tool for the solution. Others become trapped in analysis paralysis, gathering so much data that action is choked or the problem has changed by the time action arrives.

> The focus, strategic relevance, responsibility, and accountability for results rests with senior management.

Focus Quality Efforts

A quality implementation mistake many organizations make is embarking simultaneously on several quality efforts. Their thought is that if one structured approach to quality is good, two or three must be even better. In the name of participation, this approach argues, operating units should be entitled to choose the quality philosophy that they believe is the best fit for them.

While rigidity isn't useful, a common conceptual framework is an absolute necessity. It's important that different components of the improvement effort be united by a continuous philosophical approach. The power to mobilize is achieved when people working together have a common understanding of the challenge, the process, and the necessary tools to do the job. Only in this integrated fashion will the journey along the path to continuous improvement be continuous.

Rita E. Numerof is the president of Numerof and Associates, Inc., in St. Louis, Missouri.
Michael N. Abrams is the vice president of Numerof and Associates, Inc., in St. Louis, Missouri.

Vision: How Leaders Develop It, Share It, and Sustain It

Joseph V. Quiqley

This article lays out the important role of leaders in articulating a vision for an organization and then leading so as to make that vision come true. The importance of developing a shared vision in the implementation of TQM is very important and a primary responsibility of organization leaders.

Although the concept of vision is highly topical, not one in 20 corporations has what could pass as a vision statement inside or outside the company. Fewer than one in 100 has a vision statement that has been effectively communicated to its people.

Vision has been discussed by other authors, but there has been little definition of content. No one has described how to develop vision that encompasses broad-based commitment. Equally important, little has been written on how to communicate vision, how to renew it, and how to sustain it over long periods.

A distinctive element of the process of conveying and maintaining vision is that it is more collegial or group-oriented than other planning processes, which are more leader-oriented or hierarchical. A collegial process does not mean a democratic one. Listening to and respecting individual opinions are built into the process. There are no votes unless the leader asks for one. The leader has the final responsibility and the final word.

Vision: The Fundamental Source of Power

Leaders understand that life is a process of competition and selection. They compete for the minds and hearts of those who would join or follow them. A leader's vision implies an understanding of the past and present. More important, it offers a road map to the future and suggests guidelines to those in a given enterprise—how people are to act and interact to attain what they regard as desirable. A leader's vision may be intuitive or highly structured, but it is the bedrock for success in meeting the twin tests of competition and selection.

> A leader's vision offers a road map to the future and suggests guidelines to those in a given enterprise—how people are to act and interact to attain what they regard as desirable.

Some of the earliest and strongest visions were religious in nature. The visions of Buddha, Moses, Christ, and Mohammed still compel followers throughout the world.

The peoples of leading nations have always had a strong sense of vision. Sixteen years after the end of World War II, John Gardner laid out in his book *Excellence* what he called the "shared aims of a free people." His view of the American vision was peace with justice, freedom, the dignity and worth of the individual, the opportunity for all people to achieve the best that is in them, and equality before the law. Gardner pointed out that this list is not exhaustive, but is certainly indicative of the shared values of the American people.

Neither leaders nor followers are always able to move in a straight line toward the achievement of their vision. Lincoln Kirstein, artistic director of the New York City Ballet, when commenting on his namesake, Abraham Lincoln, said, "We see the Lincolnian self, capable of delay, double-talk, maneuver, hesitancy, compromise, in order that one prime aim of his own era be effected: preservation of Federal union" (Bennis and Nanus 1985).

The Corporation as an Institution

Philosophers and historians have only begun to assess the role of the large supranational corporation in the West. A brief comparison to other major institutions, such as the church, state, and family, is appropriate.

Churches in the West are struggling to remain vital and keep their members actively involved. They are fortunate to receive one hour per week from most of their members. The nation and state receive even less of our time directly. Although our tax bite may be large, we pay our taxes by mail and thus seldom come into direct contact with our state or nation as an institution. The role of the family in our society also seems to be declining. The typical family has become highly mobile, its members often preoccupied with their own concerns and their significant interactions limited to an evening meal, if that.

The corporation, on the other hand, is the focal point of many people's lives for 40 to 60 hours per week. It is the institution with which they have the most contact and with which they are most familiar.

An effective case can be made for the significant role corporations have played in the post-World War II peace among the developed nations. A firm's suppliers today are often global in scope, and their markets and customers are widely distributed. It is not customary for corporations to wage war with their customers and suppliers. They must treat them with care and respect, as partners in success. When the Berlin Wall finally tumbled down as a symbol of division between East and West, communism and capitalism, it was the supranational corporations—IBM, GM, GE, PepsiCo—that moved in immediately and closed the first big deals. To better appreciate the size of these supranational corporations, one must realize that their annual budgets surpass those of most member countries of the United Nations.

VISION VERSUS RUNNING THE BUSINESS: A CONTEMPORARY DEBATE

R.J. Eaton, the newly appointed chairman of Chrysler, has said that inside Chrysler they don't use the word "vision." They focus on quantifiable short-term results—things everyone can understand and count.

Louis Gerstner, chairman and CEO of IBM, has said that a vision is the last thing IBM needs right now. And William Gates, CEO of Microsoft, said he believed being a visionary is trivial.

Those are strong words. None of these CEOs seem to think the "vision thing" is very important. What they also seem to be saying is that the day-to-day running of the business is what is really important. And it is. But it is not enough.

There are some strong arguments on the other side of the vision debate that need to be heard. Alfred P. Sloan, Jr., said that both William C. Durant and Henry Ford had unusual vision and foresight. They gambled on the future of the automobile when fewer were sold in a year than are now made in a few days, and both men created lasting organizations.

More recently, Jack Welch, CEO of General Electric, said that leaders must articulate a vision and the rationale for it and find a mechanism to engage the whole organization in achieving it.

Max DePree, former CEO of Herman Miller, the smallest company ever elected to *Fortune's* most admired companies, has written two best-selling books on general management. He asks, "How does the company connect with its history? Most important, perhaps, what is their vision of the future? Where are they going? What do they want to become?"

On a broader level, Korn/Ferry International asked 1,500 senior leaders from 20 different countries around the world to describe the key traits desirable for a CEO today and in the year 2000. The dominant personal behavior trait identified by 98 percent of the leaders was a "strong sense of vision."

The debate seems to be engaged. But it is not a case of one or the other, vision or running the business day-to-day. To be outstanding, a company needs both a vision and a high level of attention to running the daily business. They can be embodied in the same person, the CEO, or as a CEO/COO combination. In fact, it is even better if the corporate vision is a product of the whole leadership group. That way they all own the vision and have a high degree of commitment to it.

Continued—

Vision versus Running the Business: A Contemporary Debate (continued)

Some executives seem to have difficulty with the concept involved in the word vision. Bob Eaton, Chrysler's chairman, alludes to it as "some esoteric thing no one can quantify." That is understandable. It is a softer word than some like. Many of these same executives see *corporate reengineering* as good, hard stuff with measurable results. But three important points can be made about the relationships between vision and reengineering:

- Reengineering focuses on operations. Only vision and strategy dictate what operations matter.
- Reengineering without vision or strategy is simply cost cutting. It can maim. If the only goal is cost cutting, you will not energize the work force. Dramatically increasing value must be the goal.
- The power of reengineering is that it can turn vision into fact.

In short, vision precedes reengineering in time and concept. Vision guides reengineering, and some element of the vision must be the goal of reengineering.

I define a corporation's vision as the most fundamental statement of its values, aspirations, and goals. It is an appeal to its members' *hearts* and *minds*. It represents a clear understanding of where the organization is *today* and where it wants to be *tomorrow*, and offers a road map of how to get there. A firm's vision is *the foundation of its culture*. It must be simple, understandable, and desirable, and must motivate the firm's members.

In the final analysis, a high level of skill in running the business is required for *survival*, to keep the business alive and well. At the same time, sustained vision is required to achieve continuing *growth* and *renewal*, and to make a real contribution to the local, national, or global economies.

For the highly successful CEO, vision and running the business are complimentary, not opposing, skills.

The Corporate Vision

The vision of the corporation is the most fundamental statement of its values, aspirations, and goals, an appeal to its members' hearts and minds. It must indicate a clear understanding of where the corporation is today and offer a road map for the future. Because the corporation is so very important in our lives, we as members want to know its:

Values: what distinctive or fundamental beliefs it stands for;
Mission: what it is today and what it aspires to be;
Goals: what it is committed to and where it is going.

> The vision of the corporation is the most fundamental statement of its values, aspirations, and goals, an appeal to its members' hearts and minds.

FREQUENT QUESTIONS REGARDING *VISION*

Since publication of the author's book Vision: How Leaders Develop It, Share It, and Sustain It, *he has been asked certain questions in interviews or following speeches. Below are some of the most frequently asked questions and his answers to them.*

1. Why should an organization or a corporation have a vision? What difference is it going to make?

The leader's vision is the primary source of organizational energy, both the energy that empowers others and the energy that results in superior performance.

Empirical evidence of this performance has been supplied by Harvard Business School professors John Kotter and James Heskett in their new book, *Corporate Culture and Performance* (1992). In a four-year study of nine to ten firms in each of 20 industries, they found that firms with a strong corporate culture based on a foundation of shared values outperformed the other firms by a huge margin:

- Their revenue grew more than four times faster.
- Job creation was seven times higher.
- Their stock price grew 12 times faster.
- Their profit performance was 750 percent higher.

Performance follows vision. Without vision a firm may be profitable, but its competitive performance will suffer significantly.

2. If profit goals are clear and understood, why is vision needed? How do values fit with profitability?

I define values as the guidelines by which the organization expects its members to conduct themselves. As a corporation becomes an institution, and thus a society in itself, a set of values and beliefs becomes a necessity.

It is critically important to see values and profits in their proper perspective—as partners and not opponents. Profit is viewed with disdain by many who fail to understand its role in the economy at large. The inclination to disparage the profit motives seems to originate from the medieval concept that one person's profit must always entail another person's loss.

Values are the primary drivers or motivators, profit is the reward. Leaders need to make values and profits work together toward business success. Neither one can get it done alone.

In short, an organization's vision should be as clear as its profit goals. Profit alone is not enough to motivate employees.

Continued—

Frequent Questions Regarding Vision *(continued)*

3. How will vision affect employees? What is the difference from an employee's point of view between working for a company that has a vision and one that does not?

Organizations with vision and values offer their employees strong opportunities for personal growth as corporate revenue and profits grow. In addition, employees can enjoy increased responsibility and compensation and a strong possibility of greater personal wealth as the value of their ownership in company stock appreciates. This combination of company growth and individual growth creates a winning attitude that permeates corporate cultures.

Employees who work for a corporation with a well-defined and motivating vision and who buy into values such as customer service, superior quality, integrity, and excellence are more apt to derive satisfaction from their work. They tend to approach their jobs with a sense of pride, and strive constantly for excellence and superiority.

Profit and profit goals are not significant motivators for many employees. Often they view profit as something that their hard work and sacrifice earn for their employer, who then takes it and distributes it to shareholders. Therefore, reliance on profit alone may not be enough to get employees to work at their very best. But vision combined with profit can be tremendously motivational.

4. What do you mean by the phrase, "vision rollout"?

Rollout refers to the leader's responsibility to communicate the corporate vision and values throughout the organization. It is based on the understanding that the work of the leadership group will be meaningless unless those leaders pass on their vision effectively to their people.

Leaders must provide people with the opportunity to see, hear, question, and discuss the vision for the future. Consensus and commitment generally fall off the deeper one goes into the organization. The vision must be conveyed to everyone in the company. Simplicity and focus will be two of the key criteria regarding successful rollout: focus in the vision, focus in the implementation plan, focus in communications and operations.

Continued—

The answers to these questions form the essential elements of the vision, with shared values as the foundation. The vision should be viewed as open-ended rather than closed. This definition is not intended to exclude the leader's creativity. But the fundamental vision questions must be answered in a way that stimulates the organization.

Frequent Questions Regarding Vision *(continued)*

5.   Have you personally worked with any of these companies recognized for their outstanding vision?

Yes, I have: IBM and SmithKline. I worked with IBM in the days of Tom Watson, Jr. This was in the 1960s, when IBM was clearly the most valuable company in the world. I also worked with SmithKline in the early 1970s in the creation of its vision—which took it from a $400 million company to a $4 billion company in ten years.

But most of my assignments are with corporations or organizations that face or have just faced a strategic crisis. Sometimes that crisis is survival itself, or renewed growth after a period of drift, or the development of a new vision and aspirations. Outboard Marine Corporation, Briggs & Stratton, and Browning-Ferris Industries are companies I have worked for in some phase of crisis.

Sometimes the crisis is evident and sometimes it is visible only to the leader or leaders. Our usual assignment is to serve the leader and the leadership group as a catalyst or counsel in addressing that strategic crisis.

Vision is not just something for the corporate legends and *Fortune* 500 companies. It is for all organizations, large and small, that aspire to dramatically improve their performance and make work meaningful to their people. And any organization can create such a vision.

Some will argue that profit, not vision, is the primary corporate motivator. But profit alone is not enough to motivate people. Profit is perceived negatively by many in corporations. Employees often see it as something they earn that management then takes and passes on to shareholders. Although this perception may be distressing to management, it clearly indicates that twin motivators—profit *and* vision—are required to get the most out of a corporation's people.

Although employees may not understand profit or may even be alienated by the notion of it, almost all will buy into the concepts of customer service, superior quality, integrity, and excellence if the corporation makes a serious effort to live up to these values. A statement of *vision* must be provided by the firm's leaders, particularly the CEO. This is because, as Warren Bennis and Burt Nanus state in their book *Leaders* (1985), "A business corporation is not only an economic entity but a community, possibly the central community of our times. . . . What the leader hopes to do is to unite the people in the organization into a 'responsible community.'"

The vision statement is not a closed proposition. It may also contain a slogan, a diagram, a picture—whatever grabs attention. The aim is to capture the essence of the more formal parts of the vision in a few words that are easily remembered yet evoke the spirit of the entire vision statement. In its

20-year-plus battle with Xerox, Canon's slogan or battle cry was: "Beat Xerox." Toyota's is just as brief, but more broadly based: "To Win." Motorola's slogan is "Total Customer Satisfaction." Outboard Marine Corporation's slogan is "To Take the World Boating." Chevron strives "To Become Better Than the Best."

Vision as the Key Leadership Attribute

Korn/Ferry International recently reported on a survey of 1,500 senior leaders, 870 of them CEOs, from 20 different countries, including representatives from Japan, the United States, Western Europe, and Latin America (Korn 1989). The leaders were asked to describe the key traits or talents desirable for a CEO today and important for a CEO in the year 2000. The dominant personal behavior trait most frequently mentioned, both for now and for the future, was that the CEO convey a "strong sense of vision." A rather amazing 98 percent saw that trait as most important for the year 2000. When the leaders were asked to cite key knowledge and skills for CEOs of the present and future, "strategy formulation" to achieve a vision was seen as the most important skill—by a margin of 25 percent over any other.

The Leader's Vision as the Source of Power

The leader who offers a clear vision that is both coherent and credible, and who lives by a set of values that inspire imitation, has a fundamental source of power. Power can be defined as "the ability to get things done, to mobilize resources, to get and use whatever it is that a person needs for the goals he or she is attempting to meet" (Kanter 1977). This is an excellent working definition of power for operating people in an organization. It looks at power in terms of the structures and processes of the corporation, essentially from an inside perspective.

A broader definition of power is "the basic energy to initiate and sustain action translating intention into reality" (Bennis and Nanus 1985). This definition is more appropriate for the visionary, the leader, the CEO. It recognizes not only a corporation's *internal* constituencies—managers, employees, and so forth—but also its other constituencies: the board, shareholders, customers, and suppliers. Working from this latter definition, then, I contend that *a leader's power is the capacity to translate a vision and supporting values into reality and sustain them.*

Power flows from vision. The leader's power is suboptimized unless it empowers others. According to Tom Peters and Robert Waterman (1982), "The leader arouses confidence in his followers. The followers feel better able to accomplish whatever goals he and they share." In other words, the leader *pulls* rather than *pushes* people on.

Robert Greenleaf, author of *Servant Leadership* (1979), explains this further in a comparison between servant power and coercive power:

> In a complex, institution-centered society, which ours is likely to be into the indefinite future, there will be large and small concentrations

A leader's power is the capacity to translate a vision and supporting values into reality and sustain them.

Table 1   **The Role of Culture in Corporate Performance**

	Average growth for firms with performance-enhancing culture (%)	Average growth for firms without performance-enhancing culture (%)
Revenue	682	166
Employment	282	36
Stock Price	901	74
Profit	756	1

Source: Kotter and Heskett (1992)

of power. Sometimes it will be a servant's power of persuasion and example. Sometimes it will be coercive power used to dominate and manipulate people. The difference is that, in the former, power is used to create opportunity and alternatives so that the individuals may choose and build autonomy. In the latter, individuals are coerced into a predetermined path.

Ultimately, a leader's vision-based power must result in superior competitive performance. This is not a wish or a desire; it is an imperative. Speaking of society at large and the individual in particular, John Gardner makes the point both more expansively and more personally: "Our society cannot achieve greatness unless individuals at many levels of ability accept the need for high standards of performance and strive to achieve those standards."

Holding high standards of performance means expecting to be the best. A leader's power can be maintained and enhanced only through performance—progress toward achieving the goals implied in the leader's vision.

For many years there was little empirical evidence that a firm with a strong sense of vision and shared values also demonstrated superior performance in the marketplace. That evidence has now been supplied by Harvard Business School professors John Kotter and James Heskett in their book, *Corporate Culture and Performance* (1992). In a four-year study that focused on nine to ten firms in each of 20 industries, the authors found that those with a strong corporate culture, based on a foundation of shared values, outperformed the others by a huge margin. The cultures of the winning firms emphasized three key constituencies: customers, employees, and shareholders. The differences in performance in the two sets of companies is summarized in the Table.

The Kotter and Heskett thesis is quantitatively supported and by no means simplistic. It stresses that a strong corporate culture alone is not enough; it must be combined with an appropriate business strategy for the industry. This strong and strategically appropriate culture must go hand in hand with a highly adaptive approach to change in the external world. A final and necessary ingredient is strong leadership at all levels of the organization, not just at the top.

References

Warren Bennis and Burt Nanus, *Leaders: The Strategies for Taking Charge* (New York: Harper & Row, 1985).

Max DePree, *Leadership Is an Art* (New York: Free Press, 1990).

John W. Gardner, *Excellence* (New York: Harper &: Row, 1961).

Robert K. Greenleaf, *Servant Leadership* (Mahwah, NJ: Paulist Press, 1979).

Rosabeth Moss Kanter, *Men and Women of the Corporation* (New York: Basic Books, 1977).

Lester B. Korn, "How the Next CEO Will Be Different," *Fortune,* May 22, 1989, p. 157.

John Kotter and James Heskett, *Corporate Culture and Performance* (New York: Free Press, 1992).

Thomas J. Peters and Robert H. Waterman, Jr., *In Search of Excellence* (New York: HarperCollins, 1982).

Joseph V. Quigley is the president of Quigley & Associates, a Houston-based management consulting firm. This article is a summary of the core theme of his book, Vision: How Leaders Develop It, Share It, and Sustain It *(McGraw-Hill, 1993).*

Motorola Trains VPs to Become Growth Leaders

Debra Eller

Leadership is not left to chance at Motorola. The company has developed a special Vice President Institute to foster leadership that helps the company maintain its 15% annual growth. This article profiles Motorola's approach to this training. Note that leadership training is different from management training. It isn't surprising that Motorola would have such a program. It has one of the strongest commitments to training of any American company.

In the Vice President Institute (VPI), a leadership development program for new vice presidents, top executives of Motorola Inc. pitch challenging questions to start the VPs on the path to professional growth.

- What will our organizational structure look like in 2025?
- How does our structure need to be different to support our vision?
- What new technologies will be needed?
- What skills will our managers need for the growth we are experiencing and the world changes we are encountering?
- How can we attract the worldwide talent needed for this outstanding growth?

Because Motorola has exceeded its targeted annual growth rate of 15 percent per year for the past few years, the newly appointed VPs have an unusual challenge—how to sustain the growth of their already expanding corporation.

Leading growth in new directions using new methods is the theme of the five-day institute, which has the backing and commitment of top management. Gary Tooker, CEO and vice chairman of the board, opens the program. Bob Galvin, chairman of the executive committee; Chris Galvin, president and chief operating officer; and Bill Weisz, chairman of the board, also spend significant time with the participants. Debby King, then-director of executive education, had a major part in developing the program.

Besides interaction with the CEO and other top executives, the institute offers constant networking with colleagues, seminars with experts on creativity and globalization, and individual assessment and leadership coaching. So far, about 200 new vice presidents have participated in the VPI since the pilot session in May 1992.

Leading growth in new directions using new methods is the theme of the five-day institute, which has the backing and commitment of top management.

The Motorola vice presidents participate in a two-year process, which begins with the five-day seminar program. This training program is followed by a series of alumni events designed to sustain learning, introduce new tools and continue the networking opportunities.

Setup and Goals of the VPI

King introduced the institute—a new model for Motorola executive education—to the office of the CEO in 1991 as a way to promote networking and to develop leadership abilities. Previous training presented one topic per year to all vice presidents, challenging them to address that particular issue within their own business unit or function. As Motorola decentralized many of its operations, the company's executives realized they needed to foster more connections among the vice presidents who head individual business units.

King's program identifies critical issues that span several business units or functions, providing a forum to bring together the VPs responsible for those areas. The VPs then create working teams of executives to address the issues, and the teams build new networks aimed at changing Motorola's business to meet the demands of worldwide growth.

In developing the VPI, Motorola established three overall aims. First, to teach the vice presidents about the company's unique heritage so they understood why the company has outstripped its competition and is uniquely positioned to grow. Galvin explains the significance of this growth in the past and the basis it provides for Motorola's continued renewal.

Second, to help the vice presidents explore ways to invent new technologies and businesses—not just new products. To those ends, the VPI focuses on innovation, globalization and communication. Finally, to foster networking among vice presidents from different countries, cultures and genders by carefully selecting participants.

Program planners set specific goals to carry out those aims. To complete the program, the VPs must be able to

- Identify the company's key leadership success factors.
- Discuss the CEO's leadership expectations for this decade and the next.
- Examine their personal impact in the organization and leverage their natural leadership skills.
- Build stronger networks across all sectors, groups and functions.
- Initiate an 18-month process for achieving personal development.

After collaborating with the office of the CEO to define and refine these VPI objectives, King brought in Struxor Inc. of Scottsdale, Ariz., a consulting firm specializing in executive education, to identify and clarify the learning processes necessary to meet the VPI objectives and develop a training program. As a part of the development process, Struxor interviewed Motorola executives at all levels of experience to validate the objectives.

Developing Leaders

CEO Gary Tooker starts the program by discussing Motorola's leadership profile, his views on the growing corporation and the need to have well-rounded leaders. He also makes it clear that this group of leaders is expected to be accountable for the company's future. On the final training day Tooker comes back to listen to the vice presidents' presentations on globalization and new business ideas. He talks with them about issues that they've raised and often charters teams to take on the issues as personal responsibilities.

"The true role of a leader is to lead people in new directions," says Chairman Galvin. To spark this kind of leadership, Motorola brings in exciting outside speakers to lead discussions of issues and teach skills the VPs will need.

Renowned globalization expert Charles Hampden Turner of Cambridge University leads a day of sessions on how to deal with different cultures when trying to grow a business. VPI participants discuss the varied systems of values, motivations and expectations that affect business decisions and processes across cultural boundaries. They learn about flexible management systems and procedures for optimum use of cultural variety in building organizational capability.

William Miller of Global Creativity Corp. in Austin conducts working sessions on creativity and innovation. He teaches the VPs four innovation styles and other tools such as scenario-based planning. They apply the four styles as part of the Creative Journey. This process is designed to generate a 30-year strategy for inventing new industries, grooming new and existing businesses, and developing an organization that can consistently generate a high level of innovation.

Another important VPI component is communication skills. Marty Stoller, from the Kellogg School at Northwestern University, teaches the VPs how to handle crisis communication in a positive way. Participants analyze videotaped segments from news programs and press releases to determine whether the message was effectively communicated. This session concludes with a mock press conference for practice in high-pressure communication.

A key characteristic of the VPI is flexibility, King says. "We're constantly redesigning program modules based on the feedback we receive from the vice presidents who have attended," she explains. "We sit down and listen to feedback from the vice presidents each day of the program, and we also ask them to evaluate it for us at the end of the week so we can make adjustments before the next class."

VPI Alumni Program

"It is very important that we support the networks developed during the first week of VPI, by providing further education and an opportunity for the vice presidents to meet again," King emphasizes in describing the follow-up program.

For example, one alumni event focused on scenario-based planning skills. The event also provided a detailed overview of the opportunities and challenges for Motorola in Latin America. Combining those two topics ensured

> They learn about flexible management systems and procedures for optimum use of cultural variety in building organizational capability.

that the VPs were using the scenario-based planning tools to address an important emerging market for the company.

The two-year process also includes several opportunities for individualized personal development. Implementing a personal success plan includes linking personal development to the key success factors of global leaders; examining potential inconsistencies in current skills; and designing a resolution plan necessary to gain new skills, leverage natural strengths and expand awareness of overall organizational impact.

Results from the VPI

The VPI has provided a much-needed connection for busy, geographically scattered vice presidents. The institute recognizes and builds on the belief that new businesses grow out of the crossroads of technology and it puts vice presidents on paths that cross, thus encouraging new business development. To encourage further networking, VPI classes are combined at regular alumni events. New business opportunities and partnerships develop regularly out of the VPI.

One example of such synergy is a new relationship between a Japanese and a Malaysian Motorola facility. S.K. Ko was general manager of a Malaysian facility operating with excess capacity. That changed after she met Ian McCrae, the company's managing director and deputy general manager of Motorola in Japan, at the VPI. McCrae was sending all the way to an American Motorola plant for the manufacture of a part that he and Ko determined her facility could produce. The American plant was overburdened, so transferring production to Ko's closer facility not only lowered McCrae's cost, but it also improved the flow in both places.

For Joann Piccolo, vice president and director of Federal Legislation Relations, the VPI was a chance to explain to other vice presidents how her office could help them. "I found that few of the other vice presidents knew what my department did. Once I was able to explain this, we found a lot of areas where we could work together. I'm now also able to call upon them to help me better understand pending legislative issues and help me with grassroots efforts," she says.

Similarly, Rose Gibson, vice president and chief software engineer with the Government and System Technology Group, found the program to be an invaluable source of networking. "I formed an action plan with four other vice presidents to take a more global view of software initiatives that has led to much stronger relationships between different corporate areas. As Motorola is establishing software centers in different countries, we also did a global analysis of software capabilities in different countries," Gibson explains.

Benefits for Entire Company

The VPI has had a cumulative effect on Motorola. Vice presidents leave the program with new relationships with each other that may grow into new businesses or technologies, an assessment consultant to guide them through a highly personalized development process, face-to-face coaching from the

CEO and senior staff, and a host of experts to draw on for additional training for themselves and their staffs. The VPs bring fresh ideas to their staffs, who in turn participate in training to implement the new ideas. Meanwhile, the executive education office continues to look for new topics, experts and consultants to add to the VPI. The entire company benefits from this continual training and career development.

Debra Eller is president of Struxor Inc., a Scottsdale, Arizona, consulting firm specializing in customized leadership development and executive education.

CULTURAL TRANSFORMATION

Transforming the Organization

Francis J. Gouillart and James N. Kelly

This is an excerpt from a book with the same title as the excerpt. It uses a biological model to help readers understand what an organization is and how to best manage it. The biological model suggests the holistic, systems view of an organization, but it also suggests that it is a living entity that will survive and prosper based on how well it adapts to and contributes to the world of which it is a part. This excerpt explains the authors' basic premise and the role of leadership in shaping a culture that can take advantage of these insights.

The need for Business Transformation represents a fundamental shift in the relationship of the corporation to individuals and to society as a whole. Simply put, corporations need to reconnect with the people that comprise them.

Born in the Industrial Age, our model of business has been a mechanistic one. Corporations have been economic agents in an efficient market system, parts of an every expanding, ever more complex machine. Caught now in the Communications Age, we have stretched the models of the Industrial Age to the limits of implosion. It is time to replace our mechanistic view of business with a more organic one, and to endow the recently discovered biological

---

nature of our corporations with a new spirituality that recognizes the sanctity of individual human life and has compassion for individuals.

We have moved beyond the Industrial Age, but our business model is still rooted there. Some say that the ability to manage the flow of information represents the basis for the new business model of the Communications Age. We submit, however, that more is involved than that. The communications revolution is merely the facilitator of a more fundamental social and business influence: an unstoppable trend toward *increased connectivity*. As more and more parts of the machine have learned to talk to each other, connectivity has become the dominant feature of modern business. As the trend continues, the role of corporations within society must change.

The entire history of civilization, and therefore of business, is one of increased connectivity. Verbal and written communication represented the level of connectivity needed to form the earliest civilizations. Gutenberg's printing press raised connectivity to a new level, spreading knowledge that would eventually undermine the simple tyrannies of church and monarch. The rights of church and monarch were displaced by the rights of individuals, giving birth to the democratic movement and culminating in the great revolutions of the eighteenth century.

The age ushered in by the Industrial Revolution and lasting until our own time was largely driven by technology, but its most important manifestations were social. It freed us from drudgery and physical isolation, and led to urbanization. The rhythm of life changed profoundly, and because the spirit of the Industrial Age was mechanical, the qualities of the social institutions it created (bureaucracy, hierarchy, command-and-control systems, and specialization) were machine-like as well. The line worker became a cog in a wheel, with no sense of personal connection to the company and often with no sense of communion with the environment.

And so the Communications Age is upon us, replacing the Industrial Age. As was true of earlier social transformations, this one is increasing the level of social complexity and leading to profound changes in society, to which the company—the dominant institutional creature of the Industrial Age—must adapt.

Viewed from the perspective of the individual, speech, writing, printing, telephones, radios, and televisions all represented technological advances that increased the size and scope of our connectivity networks. Now we can fax, videoconference, and computer-network with all parts of the world, on demand. Our networks are growing inexorably in both size and complexity, and that growth probably will continue.

What is true at the individual level is also true for corporations. Companies are forming alliances and partnerships with their suppliers and customers, becoming parts of networks, even networks of networks. The physical and financial boundaries between companies are blurring, and the trend probably will continue.

But while the individual networks expand, and while *business* networks become *knowledge* networks, there is a human element that warrants careful attention and nurturing. Connectivity can be a double-edged sword, triggering either greater individual isolation or a greater sense of community, depending on the role companies choose for themselves in the future.

On the pessimistic side, increased connectivity of the electronic variety may cause a loss of genuine human contact. We will continue to lose our ability to feel and touch each other. Encounters become simulations, contrived by electronics. We don't touch, smell, or feel emotional about the things and people we interact with, because they are not *there*. A credit card doesn't have the feel of a gold coin; talking to your boss on the phone isn't the same as playing golf with him on weekends; and electronically swapping production schedules with a supplier isn't the same as doing it over a beer in the pub. We used to have *physical* experiences when on the job. We have fewer and fewer of them now, and we miss them.

The economic logic of business has taken over. Old social contracts have expired, and they are being replaced by more Darwinian models of individual survival. The rural textile plant in the southern United States now competes with Taiwan. The wider the network becomes, the greater the need for a new compassion, because there are human voices to be heard, crying out in the emotional silence.

Another more optimistic scenario is possible, the one we encourage in this book. Corporations *can* provide the new caring that so many seek. This will not happen in the paternalistic fashion of the previous generation, and we are not likely to see a return to guaranteed employment. But it *will* happen in different forms.

Successful corporations will develop a new role built around the invention of a new social contract. We believe we will see corporations taking responsibility for the renewal of individuals, helping them to acquire new skills. We will see corporations redefine the boundary of their responsibility, accepting accountability for the way they use resources and contribute to the environment. Corporations probably will play a major role in the renewal of education in many countries, and become involved in the solution of major societal ailments. Most importantly, they will build a new pride in the people who are part of them.

> We believe we will see corporations taking responsibility for the renewal of individuals, helping them to acquire new skills.

This book is a first attempt to define this new *spirituality of business.*

Business Transformation

Our work with some of the world's largest corporations has convinced us that *Business Transformation is now the central management challenge and the primary, if not the sole, task of business leaders.*

The program of Business Transformation presented in the pages that follow is not a theoretical model based on a few new insights and hypotheses about how firms change. It is a tried-and-tested system, a proven and powerful agent of corporate evolution in industries ranging from chemicals, electronics, pharmaceuticals, and auto-making, to telecommunications, aerospace, railways, and financial services.

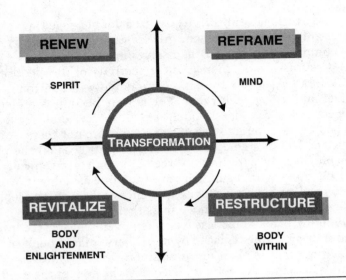

Figure 1. **The four R's of transformation.**

It is a living methodology. Each day we learn more and more about business transformation—about what works, and what leads to dead-ends; about how strategies and visions can be translated into action programs at every level of an organization; and about the role of business leadership in the alchemy of transformation.

The biological model of Business Transformation that we shall be exploring in this book consist of four broad categories of therapy, what we call The Four R's of Transformation (see Figure 1):

Reframing
Restructuring
Revitalization
Renewal

We define Business Transformation as *the orchestrated redesign of the genetic architecture of the corporation, achieved by working simultaneously—although at different speeds—along the four dimensions of Reframing, Restructuring, Revitalization and Renewal.*

Reframing addresses the corporate mind.

The four R's are to the biological corporation what the "three R's" of Reading, wRiting, and aRithmetic are to schoolchildren: the life skills it needs if it is to survive and thrive.

Reframing is the shifting of the company's conception of what it is and what it can achieve. It addresses the corporate *mind.* Corporations often get stuck in a certain way of thinking, and lose the ability to develop fresh mental models of what they are and what they could become. Reframing opens the corporate mind and infuses it with new visions and a new resolve.

Restructuring deals with the body of the corporation.

Restructuring is a girding of the corporate loins, getting it to achieve a competitive level of performance. It deals with the *body* of the corporation, and competitiveness—the need to be lean and fit—is the primary consideration. Restructuring is the domain where payoffs are fastest and cultural difficulties are greatest, often making layoffs and the anxieties associated with them an unavoidable side effect. The payoffs, however, if invested in revitalization and renewal, can be used to heal the wounds, if not lessen their severity. Many companies stop at restructuring, cajoled into contentment by their "quick wins." But they won't gain true health unless they use those wins to fuel longer-term transformation programs.

Revitalization is about igniting growth by *linking the corporate body to the environment*. Everybody wants to grow, but the sources of growth often are elusive, making the process of achieving growth more challenging and protracted than restructuring. Of all the four R's, revitalization is the single greatest factor that clearly distinguishes transformation from mere downsizing.

Renewal deals with the people side of the transformation, and with the *spirit* of the company. It is about investing individuals with new skills and new purposes, thus allowing the company to regenerate itself. It involves creating a new kind of metabolism, the rapid dissemination of knowledge inside the firm, and it involves the cultivation of a reflex of adaptation to environmental changes. Renewal is the most subtle and difficult, the least explored, and potentially the most powerful of transformation's dimensions.

Companies are living organisms. Like people they need holistic medicine, not organ-by-organ treatments. In this book we hope to show, as we have already shown in our work, that the four-R model represents a uniquely powerful way to tap a company's hidden reserves of energy, and transform it into something far better than it had ever dreamed of being.

Revitalization is about igniting growth.

Renewal is about investing individuals with new skills and

From Chromosomes to Biocorporate Systems.

The essential physical, mental, and perhaps even the spiritual quality of each human being can be traced back to a unique human genome and its 23 sets of chromosomes. The structure of this book is based on our proposal that 12 "chromosomes" comprise the biocorporate genome, three for each of the four R's. Each chromosome spawns a *biocorporate system*, and one chapter is devoted to each of them.

Together, these 12 corporate chromosomes represent the integrated "software" that governs biocorporate life. Each chromosome and its corresponding system can be considered independently, but no one acts independently of the others. For example, the mobilization chromosome is most vigorous when the vision and market focus chromosomes vigorously exchange their genetic code. Similarly, organizational development must reflect the firm's vision, its system of goals and measures, and its work architecture.

In other words, *each cell within the biological corporation carries the imprint, or genome, of all 12 corporate chromosomes*. It is therefore important to bear in mind that, although each chapter of this book is dedicated to only one chromosome, it is really the same story told again, but from the stand-point of a different protagonist.

The role of the CEO and the leadership team is to act as *the genetic architects of the corporation.* As such, they are not concerned with the minutiae of corporate life, but with splicing the right genes, of the right chromosomes, at the right time, and in the right place to enable the 12 biocorporate systems to interact with each other in the best possible way. In other words, it is leaderships' job to create the unique genetic architecture that comprises the biocorporate genome, not to construct and control every cell within the corporate body.

It is tempting for leaders to get involved with the details, but the details can obscure the view of the business or corporation as a whole. For example, CEOs should design the mobilization process, but not the composition of individual teams; they should create a vision, but let each line of business develop a strategy consistent with the vision; they should articulate an operations strategy, but leave it to others to decide whether to shut down a particular plant; and they should encourage business units to share knowledge among themselves, but not supervise individual, cross-business initiatives.

As genetic architect, the leader's job is essentially that of programming the "code" of the corporation. Viewed from this perspective, each chromosome and its corresponding biocorporate system may be translated to a high-level leadership task (see Figure 2, and the following section).

The Three Reframing Chromosomes

1. *Achieve mobilization.* Mobilization is the process of mustering the mental energy needed to feed the transformation process. It involves expanding the realm of motivation and commitment from the level of the individual to the team, and finally to the entire organization. In human terms, it musters and liberates the *mental energy* needed to feed the transformation process.

    When Don Petersen unleashed Employee Involvement at Ford, when Jack Welch created the Work-Out process at General Electric, they were mobilizing their companies for major change.

2. *Create the vision.* Mobilization creates potential in an organization; it prepares it to create a better future. Vision provides a shared mental framework that gives form to that future. It must be challenging, representing a significant *stretch* from current reality, becoming the firm's new raison d'être, its most passionate aspiration. In human terms, it creates a sense of purpose.

    Bill Gates' vision of the computer business—in essence, that software, not hardware, is the name of the game—is one example of a powerful vision. Another is Ted Turner's vision of a global news network, which he realized with CNN; another, Sam Walton's vision of discount retailing, manifested in the resounding success of Wal-Mart.

3. *Build a measurement system.* Once the company has been mobilized, and armed with an inspiring vision, leadership must translate the vision into

The role of the CEO and the leadership team is to act as the genetic architects of the corporation.

Figure 2. **Transforming the organization.**

a set of measures and targets, and define the actions needed to reach the targets. In human terms, the measurement system creates a *sense of commitment*.

Motorola used the quality process and metrics to drive its transformation; Xerox used a combination of benchmarks, particularly vis-à-vis Japanese competitors, and a quality process to regain its competitiveness; Taco Bell's transformation was driven by customer service measurements.

The Three Restructuring Chromosomes

4. *Construct an economic model.* Constructing an economic model involves the systematic, top-down disaggregation of a corporation in financial terms, from shareholder value considerations to activity-based costing and service-level assessment. It gives the company a detailed view of where and how value is created (or destroyed) in the firm. The economic

model is to the corporate body what the cardiovascular system is to the human body. Just as the cardiovascular system supplies oxygen and other vital nutrients wherever they are needed throughout the body, so the economic model transports resources to where they are most needed inside the corporation.

AT&T, Hanson, and Coca-Cola are examples of successful companies that are strongly driven by shareholder value considerations.

5. *Align the physical infrastructure.* The redesign of a corporation's physical infrastructure is one of the most visible and telling measures of the overall health and strategic direction of a company. It is the corporate equivalent of the skeletal system, the network of facilities and other assets—plants, warehouses, trucks, barges, machines, etc.—upon which work processes, the muscles of the business, depend. Like bones, the physical assets of a company are relatively fixed and rigid, resisting movement beyond their design. Some are like the spine—when they fall out of alignment, they pinch vital nerves, causing pain and partial paralysis. Others may fracture under stress, immobilizing whole sections of the corporate body and requiring mechanical realignment to allow the healing process to occur.

Johnson Controls and Hewlett-Packard, for example, continuously reconfigure their physical facilities according to their "focused factories" strategy.

6. *Redesign the work architecture.* In the corporation, work gets done through a complex network of processes, the *work architecture*. Work processes are the vehicle of business life, the biocorporate equivalent of muscles. Like muscles, they can be considered in isolation, but are in fact so interconnected that a change in one may affect them all. Also like muscles, they must continuously adapt to the demands placed on them or fall into atrophy from lack of stimulation. If properly configured and aligned, and if properly orchestrated by an integrated set of goals and measures, they produce a symphony of value creation so fluid that process boundaries seem to disappear.

The first two genes of redesigning the work architecture involve principles of classic reengineering. The third gene brings reengineering into the realm of *bioreengineering.*

The dramatic reductions Hallmark Cards achieved in its design and printing cycle time demonstrated the power of reengineering. The success of Detroit's Big Three auto makers in shrinking new model development time enabled them to catchup with their Japanese competitors.

The Three Revitalization Systems

7. *Achieve market focus.* Revitalization implies growth, and focusing on customers is a good place to start, for providing the benefits customers seek—often new, as yet undiscovered benefits—is what leads to business growth. Market focus is to the corporation what the *senses* are to the

human body, connecting the corporate mind and body to its environment.

Rubbermaid has shown how identifying customer needs and quickly designing products around those needs can revitalize a company even in an industry as prosaic as rubber goods. Johnson and Johnson is another company that has sustained its customer-driven creativity over the years.

8. *Invent new businesses.* Growth also comes by starting new businesses from scratch. This requires the cross-fertilization of capabilities that are often scattered throughout a firm's business portfolio, and the creative assembling of them to develop new offerings. In many cases the capabilities of other firms are required, spawning alliances, partnerships, mergers, or acquisitions. Inventing new businesses brings new life to the corporation; it is the corporate equivalent of the human *reproductive system*.

Canon leveraged its optical and small-motor knowhow into a strong global position in copiers; NEC was one of the first companies to exploit the convergence of computing and telecommunications.

9. *Change the rules through information technology.* Technology can often provide the basis of new ways to compete. Information technology, in particular, can redefine the rules of the game in an industry. Technology is the equivalent of the *nervous system* in the human body, connecting all parts of the body and allowing it to experience sensations produced by the environment.

Federal Express's ability to track packages was a powerful service differentiator in the courier business. Progressive Insurance's ability to settle claims on-line with centrally connected, hand-held devices rewrote the competitive rules in the insurance industry.

The Three Renewal Systems

10. *Create a reward structure.* Rewards aren't the only motivators of people, but they are very powerful ones. When they are misaligned with corporate objectives, they can be equally powerful demotivators. The compensation system should reward risk-takers, and encourage people to link their own futures to the transformation of the company. The reward structure builds a *sense of gratification* among individuals in the corporation.

Goldman Sachs, in the investment banking field, Coca-Cola in soft drinks, and Heinz in the food business, are examples of companies in which rewards are strongly linked to performance.

11. *Build individual learning.* There can be no corporate transformation without the transformation of a large number of individuals. Companies must commit themselves to the development of their people by encouraging the acquisition of skills and by cultivating mutual learning. Individual learning promotes *self-actualization* in the individuals who make up the company.

Federal Express has always understood the link between customer loyalty and the service-orientation of its drivers, and invests heavily in increasing employee skills with sophisticated electronic learning systems.

12. *Develop the organization.* Companies need to organize themselves for learning, so that they can adapt, constantly, to their changing environments. Developing the organization fosters a *sense of community* among individuals.

Dow Chemicals was one of the first companies to adopt the controversial matrix structure, but has now abandoned it in favor of a spider's-web arrangement, in which multifunctional teams periodically coalesce around customer applications, quite independently of formal, reporting relationships. Asea Brown Boveri's CEO, Percy Barnevik, uses organization design to combat bureaucracy and force ABB's business units to remain small.

Corporate Evolution

The 12 biocorporate systems don't exist in isolation. They are perpetually being challenged to adapt to changes in their environment (such as the arrival of new competitors and technologies), shifts in the attitudes of customers and regulators, and signs of the impending extinction of their industries. Gestetner almost expired when xerography destroyed the duplicator market it had invented. Wang was rocked to its foundations when the word-processing hardware market it had dominated was colonized by general-purpose PCs. The mechanical "one-armed bandit" was rendered obsolete by microprocessors and video games.

An ability to sense environmental change, and whether it carries threats or opportunities, is essential for survival, because the biological corporation is always evolving. Rewards systems are changing, work architectures are being redefined, visions are being refreshed. We once assumed that corporate evolution consists of long periods of stasis, punctuated by periodic adaptations, but the pace of change is too fast for that now. Now, the company needs to adapt every day.

In the natural world, evolution is driven by chance mutations and natural selection. Very occasionally, the DNA replication system makes a minor mistake. Almost invariably, these errors are harmful, killing the mutant life-form before it can breed. An infinitesimally small proportion of errors are advantageous, and the mistake is passed on. Malaria kills over a million people each year. Hemoglobin S is a mutant hemoglobin gene, which happened to protect its carrier against malaria. A tiny copying error, the odds against which were astronomical, has lifted the threat of a deadly disease from millions of people.

A company need not wait to get lucky. Armed with a map of its genome, its leaders can splice a few processes and change its systems to adapt to environmental change.

Francis J. Gouillar is an authority on business strategy and reengineering and a leading specialist in business transformation. He is a senior vice president of Gemini Consulting. James N. Kelly is an expert in the area of managing large complex organizations. He is co-chairman of Gemini Consulting.

In Search of the Future

Tom Broersma

In this article, you'll find a thoughtful review that contrasts the old assumptions about managing in a changing world with the new assumptions, which incorporate the principles of quality management: systems view, customer focus, empowered teams, and statistical process control. It summarizes many of the new ideas floating around in a succinct and readable fashion. The case study is especially interesting.

> If you realize that all things change, there is nothing you will try to hold onto. If you aren't afraid of dying, there is nothing you can't achieve.
>
> Trying to control the future is like trying to take the master carpenter's place. When you handle the master carpenter's tools, chances are that you'll cut your hand.
>
> Lao-tsu
Tao Te Ching

Do you work in the belly of an organization dinosaur? The average U.S business survives only about 40 years. Many government agencies, though technically alive, function as though they folded years before. Now, complex and rapid changes in the world's economic and social climates heighten the threat to organizations' survival. Organizations that don't adapt to these changes will die.

Organizations that learn to search creatively for the future can transform themselves when they confront the chaos of constant change. Such organizations create sustainable futures by building visions, systems, and structures that not only weather change, but thrive on it.

All organized entities—businesses, government agencies, service organizations, and communities—confront the challenge of searching for a sustainable future. As organizations transform themselves, they will have to address the following issues:

Organizational structure. The traditional organization is vertically organized. Power vests at the top and spreads ever thinner through descending layers of management, staff, and—at the bottom, with the least power of all—frontline workers.

The new organization pushes power down and out among fewer, wider layers. Frontline workers play new roles as decision makers.

Empowered workers and teams.   In the traditional organization, each employee performs only discrete tasks. Workers must meet minimum standards of performance.

In the new organization, cross-functional, self-managing teams design, produce, and deliver products or services. All team members share leadership roles and responsibilities. Workers perform multiple tasks. Teams set production goals and schedules, order their own materials, and hire new workers. Workers must meet world-class standards of performance.

Systems thinking.   The traditional organization emphasizes bureaucracy, hierarchy, narrow job descriptions, policies and procedures, and distinct departments. The new organization emphasizes systems. It organizes work in ways that minimize bureaucracy and maximize performance. Workers eliminate inefficiencies through continuous-improvement processes. Engineers, planners, and accountants work side-by-side with production workers to facilitate quick solutions to problems and ensure high performance.

Ecosystem management.   The traditional organization tended to view the ecosystem as a source of unlimited resources, and thought little about protecting the environment. The new organization views the natural environment as a partner and considers environmental sustainability essential to the future.

Quality focus.   In the traditional organization, engineers and experts inspect the quality of the finished product. Organizations choose external suppliers based on price rather than quality.

In the new organization, quality control takes place at all stages of the production process. Workers evaluate and continuously improve the quality of their work. Organizations cultivate long-term relationships with suppliers who deliver top-quality goods and services.

Customer service.   In the traditional organization, only employees who had contact with customers were expected to provide customer service. Most employees did not serve any customers, beyond their bosses.

In the new organization, everyone learns who all of his or her customers are and how to meet their needs. Internal customers receive the same level of service as external customers. External customers often help the company develop and improve its products and services.

Flexibility.   The traditional organization produced standardized products and services. New-product development was a lengthy and laborious process. The new organization speedily develops and delivers products and services, often tailoring them to customers' desires. Organizations replace their traditional stockpiles of inventory with just-in-time production methods.

Rewards.   The traditional organization bases pay on length of service and views labor as a cost. Annual evaluations are formalities. They precede annual

CREATING THE FUTURE: HOW ORGANIZATIONS ARE MEETING THE CHALLENGE

As global change increases in speed and complexity, all organizations confront the challenge of creating their futures. Here are some examples of ways organizations are meeting this challenge:

- A leading U.S. defense-research organization responded to dramatic post-Cold War challenges by transforming itself into a more flexible and participative organization and shifting its focus from the laboratory to the marketplace.
- Costa Rica used a management development program to transform its old, bureaucratic health-care delivery system to one based on teams, systems thinking, and continuous quality improvement.
- Primorski Sugar Corporation, a newly privatized Siberian sugar refinery, had a discouraging history of chronic problems, antiquated equipment, low employee productivity, and little leadership. A new director, selected by employees from outside the company, challenged entrenched managers and employees to create a true private enterprise or leave. Most left. Today, a new leadership team is transforming the old Soviet plant into a diversified world-class organization.
- The U.S. Department of Health and Human Services, with 140,000 employees and the third largest budget of all federal agencies, used strategic planning to prompt its employees to explore the value they place on their role as public servants, the responsibilities of public stewardship, and their capacity to influence the future direction of the agency.
- Brigham Young University's business school invented a new curriculum using a future-search conference in which major stakeholders participated. Faculty members usually resist new programs. But this time, the faculty voted to approve the new curriculum, with few abstentions and no opposition.
- Maliwada, an ancient, once-wealthy village in India, was impoverished. A team of community-development practitioners met with the village leaders to help them discover a shared vision for the future of their community. As villagers learned to reinvent their community, they started to let go of old class and cultural differences. With grassroots support, the community acquired a bank loan and government grant to build a dam, a brick factory, and a health clinic. Today, with the community once again prospering, Maliwada is teaching other villages how to replicate its model of development.

raises and often promotions as well. Employees do not own companies and rarely share in profits.

The new organization pays people based on their knowledge and skills and views labor as a competitive advantage. Teams evaluate their members based on their performance, and performance determines advancement and compensation.

Organizational learning.   The traditional organization emphasizes technical training and directs most training at managers and professionals. Line workers receive only basic training on equipment operations. The new organization views the capacity to learn as a competitive advantage and views training as an investment strategy.

Organizational Learning

In new organizations, individuals learn a wide range of technical and interactive skills and pursue continuous personal development. Similarly, work groups learn a wide range of skills for planning, organizing, and controlling their work. They also learn ways to interact with other work groups. The organization as a whole learns to think and act strategically in response to the ever-changing environment.

Systems thinker and futurist Eric Jantsch characterizes organizations that search for the future as learning organizations. In *The Self-Organizing Universe* (Pergamon Press, 1980), he writes that organizations do not learn by importing "strange knowledge" into their systems. Instead, the processes for learning are inherent within organizations; by learning to mobilize these processes, organizations can adapt to changes in the environment.

To create sustainable futures, organizations must master three interrelated types of learning processes: operational learning, systematic learning, and "transformative" learning.

Operational learning.   Chris Argyris and Donald Schon describe operational learning as "single-loop learning." Operational learning forms the foundation of any work organization. Operational learning springs from an organization's efforts to improve its basic work processes. Put simply, we learn operationally when we try to do the best job possible for our customers and correct our mistakes. Today, many companies use continuous quality-improvement processes to develop employees' operational learning skills.

J. Redding and R. Catalanello, in *Strategic Readiness: The Making of the Learning Organization* (Jossey-Bass, 1994), offer a case study of operational learning at Motorola. This Baldrige-award-winning electronics manufacturer is approaching a milestone, the achievement of "six sigma"—less than 3.4 defects per million opportunities for error. It took Motorola 14 years to achieve this level of quality.

Recently, the company studied six sigma as a process of organization learning, noting key milestones, breakthroughs, and roadblocks. With new insights into its own learning processes, Motorola aims to reduce its corporate learning process by one half (from 14 years to 7) as it undertakes two new

---

The new organization pays people based on their knowledge and skills and views labor as a competitive advantage.

We learn operationally when we try to do the best job possible for our customers and correct our mistakes.

strategic initiatives: becoming a leader in integrating hardware and software, and entering the Eastern European market.

Systemic learning.   Systemic learning focuses on the organization as a complex of interacting systems. Argyris and Schon describe systemic learning as "double-loop learning," because the learning addresses not only the work itself, but the fundamental assumptions that underpin the organization's systems and structures.

Systemic learning occurs when organizations detect and fix errors by modifying not only work procedures, but also organizational norms, policies, or objectives. Systemic learning also encompasses people's ability to reflect critically on the interaction of organizational systems and to focus on improving the performance of the whole organization rather than on improving single systems in isolation from one another.

Redding and Catalanello's case study of Royal Dutch/Shell offers an example of systemic learning. During the 1970s, Shell was considered a weak link in the petroleum industry. Several years ago, as part of its efforts to survive despite the uncertainties of the petroleum industry, the century-old Shell conducted a landmark study to discover how organizations can weather changes in their environments. The study looked carefully at 30 companies, all of which were founded more than 75 years ago. The study concluded that the firms persevered because of their capacities to absorb environmental activities and to respond appropriately.

As a result of this study, Shell decided that thriving in its own changing and even chaotic environment would depend on developing similar capacities. Shell aggressively took steps to transform its learning abilities into a competitive advantage. The company gains an advantage through a process that enables its management teams to share their mental models of their company, their markets, and their competitors, and to alter these models as appropriate.

Arie P. de Geus, Shell's former head of planning, asserts that, "for this reason, we think of planning as learning and of corporate planning as institutional learning." Shell's strategy for organizational learning seems to work. In 1990, the company surpassed Exxon in total revenues to become the world's largest oil company.

Transformative learning.   Transformative learning is the process of continuous development of the whole organization. Transformative learning incorporates operational and systemic learning into an ongoing process of evolutionary change. Argyris and Schon describe this as "deutero-learning":

"When an organization engages in deutero-learning, its members . . . reflect on and inquire into previous episodes of organizational learning, or failure to learn. They discover what they did that facilitated or inhibited learning, they invent new strategies for learning, they produce these strategies, and they evaluate and generalize what they have produced. The results become encoded in individual images and maps and are reflected in organizational learning practice."

(For a snapshot of transformative learning in action, see box "The Transformation of JK Fibre.")

THE TRANSFORMATION OF JK FIBRE

When the JK Fibre plant opened in 1989 in Jhalawar, India, to manufacture acrylic fiber, it was the realization of plant director Rampati Singhania's vision. Singhania wanted to create a company culture of openness, equitable relationships, and minimal bureaucracy, writes J. Troxel in *Participation Works: Business Cases From Around the World.*

Consultants helped Singhania design a plant that put into practice new thinking about open organizations and participative management.

Singhania introduced these organizational concepts into a traditional Indian work culture deeply and firmly rooted in hierarchy, guardedness, and bureaucracy. His informal yet professional style set the tone for the whole organization.

The new plant featured open work space, with cubicles instead of closed offices. Departments flowed together, not divided by walls. Managers—including Singhania—sat in cubicles at the center of their teams' work spaces, giving all employees access to them. As in Japan, work teams started every morning with physical exercises. And everyone ate in the cafeteria, regardless of rank.

Employees were responsible for their own quality inspection, maintenance, and housekeeping. The managers filled out their own forms and kept their own files. As much as possible, communication took place face-to-face, with few memos and little paper.

Openness extended even to the compensation system, with salaries posted on public bulletin boards. Most radical of all for an Indian company was the gain-sharing incentive plan Singhania introduced for all employees. At the close of each quarter, an independent agency conducted a survey asking customers to rate JK Fibre's performance on each factor. Each employee received a gain-sharing award based on the results. The awards accounted for a large part of employees' salaries.

Did the forward-looking JK Fibre become a role model for Indian companies to emulate? It did not, reports Troxel. Two-and-a-half years after the plant's opening, production was at 50 percent of capacity, quality was poor, and morale was abysmal. Worst of all, customers were leaving in droves. JK Fibre was losing money fast, and its parent company was about to cut its losses in this apparently failed experiment. In January 1992. the plant literally ground to a halt, and the managers despaired.

After talking with JK Fibre managers and staff and reflecting on the situation, the consultants who helped with the plant's original design presented the managers with a proposal for a whole-system transformation of JK Fibre. The management team accepted the proposal and spent five days with the consultants to form a coordinated plan of action.

During the retreat, consultants led the managers on a comprehensive search for a sustainable future, incorporating organizational planning, team building, and personal development.

Continued—

The Transformation of JK Fibre (continued)

The first challenge facing the managers was coming up with a way to get the plant running again. The parent company would not provide any more capital, and no banks would lend to the plant. Working with the consultants, the managers eventually devised a far-fetched but intriguing plan: The managers would seek financing from their customers—the very customers who complained about poor quality and late deliveries.

"Can you imagine what it was like to go back to our customers and now ask for money?" recalled one manager. But it was their only hope. The managers decided to convince their customers that it was a new day for JK Fibre and that they had a strategic development plan they could and would deliver on. In groups of two and three they visited every customer.

It worked. With just enough cash advances to purchase raw materials, they started up the plant two weeks to the day after creating the plan.

By May, the plant was producing an average of 30 tons a day, about the level of production before the January shutdown. Quality was uneven, but it was improving. By midyear, the plant was producing more than 50 tons a day, and quality was still improving. In October, the plant reached full capacity, producing 60 tons a day. Quality was at an all-time high.

Spontaneous dancing broke out on the shop floor when people heard the news. The managers ordered an ice-cream truck into the factory for a celebration. The truck remained for 24 hours, time enough for all three shifts to celebrate.

How did JK Fibre produce such a dramatic turnaround in just seven months? In that five-day planning session, the managers went through a process of deep reflection to discover the mental models that were preventing them from achieving success. Once the managers recognized the contradictions that blocked their success, they were able to transform the company and achieve their vision using a three-pronged strategy:

- corrective-action teams
- communication
- leadership development.

Corrective-action teams.   Management set up corrective-action teams to improve plant operations. A CAT is an eight- to 12-member cross-functional team that is designed to solve quality and systems problems quickly.

A CAT would meet for a day or two to analyze a specific problem such as excessive moisture in the fiber or the frequent breakdown of electronic control systems. After determining the root cause of the problem, the team would identify at least four possible solutions, create a plan, assign tasks, and begin solving the problem.

Employees enjoyed serving on CATs because of the satisfaction they got from solving long-standing problems.

Continued—

The Transformation of JK Fibre (continued)

Communications. The communications strategy was a systematic learning strategy designed to improve the interaction of departments, functions, and systems. From the beginning of JK Fibre, communication was encouraged. Now it was essential.

Once a month, managers had always invited all employees to speak with them openly about factory problems and to suggest solutions. Now, managers started meeting daily instead of monthly.

The increased discussion helped break down invisible walls between departments. Managers started to understand the interrelatedness of their functions. Decisions made collectively took into account the needs and requirements of all departments. Before, managers were preoccupied with the performance of their own departments. Now, they concentrated on coordinating activities with other departments to achieve optimal company-wide performance.

At monthly review forums, senior managers reported on accomplishments, issues, and ideas in relation to the overall action plan.

Leadership development. The company invested the most financially in leadership development—a transformative learning strategy—to turn the company around. Managers, supervisors, and team coordinators participated in learning laboratories to cultivate transformational leadership styles. In addition, they learned to incorporate personal development into their leadership.

In the leadership-development program, people learned the skills they needed to make the open-organization system work, including the facilitation skills that enable them to solve problems as part of a team and to help create a better work environment.

Many managers reported that the personal development training not only improved their leadership skills, but also produced more peace and harmony within their families!

Once every three months the core leadership team at JK Fibre sets aside two days to continue developing its members' leadership skills and to help them work on their personal development.

Nine months after JK Fibre set out to transform itself, the market for acrylic fiber collapsed in India. The market collapse resulted from political unrest in the country, the introduction of cheaper imported fiber, and an oversupply of fiber.

JK Fibre now must develop new market strategies to respond to this upheaval. The company will push its burgeoning organizational learning skills—operational, systemic, and transformational—to meet these new and unexpected challenges from its changing environment.

Evolutionary Self-Organization

New scientific discoveries about the way living systems evolve offer some practical guidelines for transformative organizational learning.

The laws of thermodynamics say that systems inevitably reach a state of static equilibrium. Then, entropy sets in. Think of a child's spinning top as it slows and eventually falls over. For the top to spin again someone has to twist it.

Likewise, organizations gravitate to a state of equilibrium. As entropy takes hold, an organization spends more and more energy just maintaining the status quo, leaving less and less energy free for productive work.

But entropy does not seem to govern living systems. We see plants, animals, and whole ecosystems that have evolved over millions of years. Some human cultures have existed continuously for thousands of years. Why are they not trapped by entropy?

The theory of evolutionary self-organization offers some clues as to why living systems thrive while nonliving, mechanistic systems die. Nobel Laureate Ilya Prigogine discovered that living systems continuously renew themselves through processes of "spontaneous structuration." Information from the environment floods a living system, jarring it out of its state of equilibrium. The living system becomes disorganized and reconfigures itself into a more complex state that is better suited to the changed environment.

Three elements that lead to evolutionary self-organization are openness, non-equilibrium, and autocatalysis.

Openness.   Living systems overcome entropy by developing a partnership with the environment—they import energy and export entropy, similar to the way plants breathe out oxygen and breathe in carbon dioxide.

In *Developing and Managing Open Organizations*, authors O. Mink, J. Schultz, and B. Mink (University Associates, 1979), describe the components of organizational openness as external responsiveness, internal responsiveness, and unity. An open organization adapts to both internal and external environments while maintaining its own identity. Closed organizations, in contrast, maintain their identity by resisting change in their environments. And entropy is the price they pay.

This does not mean that living systems are randomly driven by environmental changes. In *Leadership and the New Science* (Berrett-Koehler, 1992), Margaret Wheatley notes that openness to the environment paradoxically creates a greater sense of identity. Over time, what dominates the system is not the environment but the self-organizing dynamics of the system itself.

Environmental fluctuations may originate randomly, but the changes the fluctuations cause within the system are not purely random. When environmental disturbances signal a need for change, the system changes in a way that sustains its consistency. This self-reference is what facilitates orderly change in turbulent environments. "In human organizations, a clear sense of identity—of the values, traditions, aspirations, competencies, and culture that guide the operation—is the real source of independence from the environment," Wheatley writes.

An open organization adapts to both internal and external environments while maintaining its own identity.

Royal Dutch/Shell, in its commitment to organizational learning, stresses openness to the environment. Shell intentionally devised learning strategies that enable the company to respond quickly and effectively to changes in local operating environments. "While its chief competitors, such as the giant Exxon corporation, have become increasingly centralized, Shell has systematically given more and more autonomy to its 260 operating divisions, promoting quick action and experimentation," note Redding and Catalanello.

Non-equilibrium. Nonliving systems become trapped by entropy because they achieve equilibrium. Living systems, in contrast, thrive in a state of non-equilibrium—they constantly respond to local fluctuations in their environment. Paradoxically, over the long haul, the instability of living systems produces stability.

Destabilization, then, holds the key to breaking free of equilibrium. Environmental disturbances create disequilibrium, and disequilibrium leads to renewal. By maintaining fluid connections between the disequilibrium in their internal and external environments, living systems change, but survive. Conversely, systems that try to maintain their equilibrium in a changing environment protect themselves in the short term but ultimately invite entropy to set in.

Consider the difficulties of IBM. With its rigid corporate structure and culture, IBM dominated the computer industry for many years. What happened? IBM learned late that stability does not represent a strategic advantage in a changing environment.

More nimble upstarts, in contrast, continuously reinvented themselves in response to their industry's constant mutations.

Shell continuously renews itself by purposefully fostering internal disequilibrium. For instance, by changing its planning process from time to time, the company promotes new ways of thinking. Shell also uses a method called the "management challenge," in which managers question their peers about the assumptions that underlie their business plans and operations.

Autocatalysis. A system's natural response is to quell small disturbances to its structures. But when autocatalysis occurs, the disturbance survives the system's attempt at suppression and feeds back on itself, becoming amplified in the process to the point where the system must respond. This phenomenon "supports some current ideas that organizational change, even in large systems, can be created by a small group of committed individuals or champions," writes Wheatley.

As Margaret Mead observed, "A small group of thoughtful, concerned citizens can change the world. Indeed, it is the only thing that ever has."

The movement against the war in Vietnam offers a historical example of the effects of autocatalysis. At first, just a few individuals and small groups spoke out against the war. As the war escalated, protests amplified to a point where the governmental system had to respond.

An Evolutionary Spirit

Bombarded by constant change, organizations must transform themselves in response to the complex, competing, and contradictory demands of their external and internal environments. The ability to make that transformation is perhaps their most important competence. By using organizational learning to foster evolutionary self-organization, businesses and other entities can create and sustain their futures.

In self-sustaining organizations, leaders no longer must provide all the answers. Instead, the leaders provide others with the opportunity to reinvent their enterprise collectively and continuously.

As Jantsch writes, "To live in an evolutionary spirit means to engage with full ambition and without any reserve in the structure of the present, and yet to let go and flow into a new structure when the right time has come."

Tom Broersma is a consultant specializing in developing high-performance learning organizations.

The Collaborative Workplace

Edward M. Marshall

Marshall puts his own spin on the idea of understanding the organization from holistic perspective, suggesting that the successful organization of the future will be characterized as collaborative. In this article, excerpted from his book Transforming the Way We Work, *he talks about the culture of the collaborative workplace.*

After a large financial services firm spent $25 million on a quality improvement program, it decided to reorganize. It moved the boxes around and renamed key business functions. The silos, however, remained, as did the hierarchical structure that had worked so well for the past two generations. To further reduce costs, it decided to reengineer eight key business processes. While stripping out 20 percent of its financial costs, its human costs were extraordinary.

Top managers and their direct reports were still trying to figure out where their new offices were and what they were supposed to be doing. After three downsizings in two year, most of them were worried about their jobs and were working 70-hour weeks in a frenzy to demonstrate their added value. Stress and tension were off the charts. Many were looking for new jobs, thinking it might be different elsewhere. They wanted to be loyal and wanted the programs to succeed, but they were not sure they would. Too much change, too fast. What would happen next?

All across America, businesses are undergoing their most profound transformation since the Industrial Revolution. But what are we transforming into? Chaos and instability infect many of our organizations, leaving us wondering what the future may hold. We know we must realign the fundamental essence of how we lead and manage the business organization, but to what?

Hierarchy, the cultural principle by which we have led and managed business for at least the past century, no longer seems practical or relevant. The basic covenant we have had with our organizations is broken. Jobs are being eliminated or totally redesigned. Employees are expected to behave in new and different ways, but often lack the skills to do so. The rungs on the career ladder are no longer well-defined. In fact, many employees wonder whether the concept of a career ladder even exists anymore. In the meantime, the cultural framework in which business operates continues to evolve. Where is it heading? What is the new cultural foundation that will guide us into the 21st century?

What is the new cultural foundation that will guide us into the 21st century?

Everyone is familiar with the litany of external marketplace factors causing this chaos—global competition, technology, demographic and political changes. These forces have resulted in the elimination of millions of jobs, drastic restructuring and new business relationships. What we are much less clear about is what is going on with our people *inside* our companies and how we must now work together to face the new realities. How are our employees handling this chaos? How can we regain their loyalty, confidence, energy and productivity? And assuming we get that energy back, how will we sustain their commitment as our companies continue to face unrelenting change?

The senior vice president of a high-technology firm put it this way: "We have been through it all in the last five years—TQM, executive education, facilitator training, empowerment workshops, restructuring and now reengineering. But nothing in my company has really changed, except we have fewer people and more work. In fact, the net net at the end of the day is that we have lost trust, mutual respect and candor. What can we do?"

Increasingly, people are recognizing that programs-of-the-month will not rescue them from all this chaos. These programs are designed to change the structure of our workplaces, but not their essence. One round of structural change often leads to another with a focus almost exclusively on the cost side of the ledger. In fact, these structural changes often produce precisely the opposite result than was intended by increasing instability and fear, and reducing productivity. Other programs such as self-directed work teams have improved work processes, but in most instances the underlying values by which these organizations are led have not changed. Management often does not walk the talk, and thereby undercuts the value and impact of these process-focused programs.

There is no silver bullet that will solve the complex organizational issues we face. Without fundamental cultural change and the adoption of a new approach to leading and managing, American businesses will continue to experience significant difficulties in sustaining competitive advantage.

The 21st Century Workplace

We have always looked to the future with a fairly high degree of hope and anticipation that things will get better. This may not be the case now. We know that the 21st Century workplace will be totally different from what it is now. We know we need a new cultural framework to guide us in the design and creation of that workplace. The workforce must be able to do more with less and adapt quickly to or anticipate change. It must be nonbureaucratic and passionately focused on the customer. The workforce must be aligned with and own the strategic direction of the business, have trust-based work relationships, and be able to build value with each other and their customers. Leadership in the new workplace must be seen as a function, not a job. It is

The workforce must be aligned with and own the strategic direction of the business.

THE BENEFITS OF COLLABORATION

When the principles of collaboration have been adopted, we have seen extraordinary results. Here are a few examples:

- The cycle time for a real estate development company in concluding its deals was reduced by 9,000 percent.
- When a 25 percent reduction in force in one part of the manufacturing company was needed, the members of that group did it themselves, in three days, with no backlash and full ownership.
- The customer satisfaction ratings for an internally focused information systems group doubled as they built "full value partnerships" with their clients.
- The quality and number of strategic decisions made by this executive doubled after they put their operating agreements into effect, learned how to trust each other and tell the truth about the business.
- The productive capacity of a customer service organization doubled in the six months after it began its collaborative team-based organization.

based not on power and authority, but on principles, new people skills and the ability to engage people in coming to consensus about critical decisions and solutions to problems. The resulting trust and productivity provide the enterprise a clear competitive advantage.

We have been trained expertly to focus on organizational structure, systems and programs, while most of us would admit that at least 70 percent of all our problems in business are people-related or culturally based. By not focusing on the workplace culture as the source for transforming the business, we have missed the proverbial forest for the trees. That culture reflects the values and beliefs that drive our actions and behaviors and influence our relationships. As an output, culture shows up in powerful ways as results, commitment, quality, loyalty and pride. Moreover, it creates the standards, work style and expectations by which our companies are defined. Our job is to engage that culture so that those values emerge and flourish.

When I go into any organization, I always ask people what type of work environment they would like to have. Regardless of the type of business, the answers are uniformly the same.

The Missing Ingredient

To create the 21st century workplace, the organization as a whole must create a cultural framework that will be powerful enough to replace hierarchy. What is this new cultural framework? What can this new workplace look like? How can we go about creating and sustaining it?

When I go into any organization, I always ask people what type of work environment they would like to have. Regardless of the type of business, the answers are uniformly the same. They want to work in an organization where there is trust, candor, honesty and integrity. They want to "own" their jobs, and work in a way that is aligned with the strategic direction of the business. They want to make decisions by consensus, not compromise or "can live with . . . " They want to be entrusted with responsibility, held accountable and rewarded for their contributions. They want to learn and grow. They want to work in businesses where there is honor, dignity and respect. These are the core values of collaboration. In fact, based on more than 20 years of work with hundreds of companies of all kinds, I have concluded that collaboration is how people naturally want to work.

As a leadership principle, I have seen collaboration work in a wide range of tough business and organizational situations, from strategic alliances and mergers that were breaking up, to internal mergers between departments; from companies in high-tech industries to those in the service sector; from senior executives to front-line managers. This principle provides the basis for significant and permanent change for people as well as organizations. Collaboration provides the cornerstone for the creation and enhancement of the 21st century workplace.

Collaboration is the premier candidate to replace hierarchy as the organizing principle for leading and managing the 21st century workplace. It is a way of life, a values-based framework that enables us to meet our fundamental needs for self-esteem, respect, trust and integrity in the workplace.

It is *not* a program or a course. It is not a quick fix, silver bullet or magic solution to organizational challenges. It does not have a shelf life of two years. There is a natural tendency in how we think about new approaches to business to categorize, classify and pigeonhole them, give them a label, and then dismiss them when they show the least imperfection. This would be a mistake given the real value that collaboration has to offer every business.

More specifically, collaboration is a principle-based process of working together that produces trust, integrity and breakthrough results by building true consensus, ownership and alignment in all aspects of the organization. Here are several other ways to think about collaboration:

- **A decision-making framework:** Collaboration provides a basis for making business and organizational decisions based on principle rather than power or personality, whether that decision is about strategy, customers, people or systems. Collaboration helps us decide when and how to use any particular program or technique to improve performance, and how to engage the workforce in its implementation. It is just as concerned with relationships and the company's reputation as it is with bottom-line results.
- **A common denominator for relationships:** Collaboration provides the common denominator for engaging all members of the workforce since its core values and beliefs are the basis for building trust-based relationships.
- **A business transformation methodology:** It is a way to transform the way we work, complete with the methods, tools and processes that help the workforce become aligned, take ownership of and

responsibility for the success of the enterprise, and build an organizational system that produces sustained high performance. It is a total shift in the way we think about transforming ourselves.

- **An organizational gyroscope:** Collaboration helps us manage our way through the paradoxes of change. In the face of extraordinary pressures from both outside and inside our companies, it helps us maintain balance and focus.
- **A new work ethic:** Collaboration provides long-term stability for the workplace because it is a work ethic that recognizes that work gets done through people, that people want and need to be valued, and that any change must be owned by those implementing if it is to be successful.

The Collaborative Design

Think of your own organization and how it presently operates. If we were to take each major component of that organization and redesign it in accordance with the principle and values of collaboration, we would call that new organization a collaborative workplace. There are five core components:

- **A collaborative culture:** A set of core values that shapes the behaviors and conduct of the business.
- **Collaborative leadership:** Leadership is a shared function and is situational, rather than a position. Consequently, it involves everyone in the organization.
- **A strategic vision:** A customer-driven organization that is internally aligned, and strategically focused on its unique and value-added role in the market.
- **Collaborative team processes:** A flat, nonbureaucratic set of collaborative work processes managed by teams of aligned professionals who have taken full responsibility for their success. Team members also learn new skills that enable them to become self-sufficient.
- **A collaborative structure:** The business and support systems in the organization, especially information systems and human resources, are realigned to ensure the success of the collaborative workplace. Members of these internally focused groups see the rest of the organization as customers, and focus on quality in all aspects of their work.

Creating a New Workplace

What precipitates an organization moving toward collaboration? Here's one real-life example: The new leadership at a technology-based company knew that the board had very high expectations of them. Financially, the company had just been through a devastating three years. They knew they had to either reduce costs by 30 percent or increase productivity by 25 percent to get back in the game. Their financial and organizational pain was great. A major change process was needed.

The leaders, however, had watched other companies tackle similar challenges by instituting drastic cost reductions, reengineering and downsizing, flattening the hierarchy and stripping out thousands of jobs. The loyalty and productivity of their people had been damaged. These leaders did not want to repeat those mistakes. They also did not quite know how they were going to create this change, but they believed that if they invested in their people, there was untapped productive energy they could engage to leapfrog the competition.

They also knew that in using this investment approach to change, they would make mistakes. Even so, they decided to bet on their people. They thought it was worth it to try another approach so they could retain the intellectual assets, loyalty and productivity of their people. They decided to try an approach based on the principle of collaboration that would engage the workforce directly in the change process and open up the possibility of a different outcome. They had little to lose and a lot to gain They could always slash and burn.

The application of the collaborative method to transform an organization's culture and business process begins by shifting the organization's culture rather than its structure. First we need to get alignment on the core values that will be used to lead and manage the organization as a whole. Second, since we know that organizational change is evolutionary rather than revolutionary, we will create a process that gives people the time they need to change their mind-sets and behaviors. When change is "done to" people or "for" them, it will not take hold; it must be done by them. Once this "culture-first" approach has been initiated, there are five arenas where you can begin to apply the principle of collaboration.

1. **Strategic business alignment:** Using collaborative tools, leadership defines the unique and value-added role of the business in the marketplace, and provides a clear strategic direction. They then actively engage members of the company to ensure clear understanding of the business focus, and ownership of the direction and its implementation.

2. **Collaborative team-based organization:** Leadership commits to a flatter, cross-functional organization based on teams, not silos, which are driven by specific results and meeting customer requirements. The teams are formed using a critical set of collaborative governance processes, including operating agreements, charters, critical success factors and action plans.

3. **Full-value partnerships:** Whether it is with customers, strategic alliance partners, suppliers or other business relationships, leadership can commit to the development of work relationships based on mutual respect, win-win, clear behavior agreements and realistic expectations where each partner receives "full value" from the relationship.

4. **Culture assessment:** The culture of an organization includes the values, principles, beliefs, customs, mores, habits, language, energy, pride, commitment and loyalty of its workforce. The workplace culture drives the organization's productivity. Using a unique tool called the Workplace Culture Index, leadership can benchmark the quality of the work environment and periodically assess it, using the data to make interventions and improvements.

5. **Self-sufficiency:** To remain competitive, businesses must become proactive in their transformation. Rather than relying on outside consultants, leadership can invest in building the capacity of their own people, particularly the line leaders and managers who can become the internal cadre who will self-resource the ongoing change process.

Beginning the Journey

The race to create the successful 21st century workplace will need to be a victory of the human spirit over chaotic change and our own self-imposed limitations.

Creating a collaborative workplace is a commitment to a new way of working together. It is not a quick fix. It is not a simple process. It is not for everyone. But transforming the way we work to collaboration is the right thing to do to restore the honor, respect and vitality of our workplaces. We live in extraordinary time that require extraordinary solutions to increasingly complex problems. The change programs and techniques we have tried to date have been helpful as far as they have gone. But now we must go much further in our thinking and behaving. We need to evolve organizationally at a rate much faster than the market and our competition, which may be faster than our people may be willing to let us. We really have little choice.

The race to create the successful 21st century workplace will need to be a victory of the human spirit over chaotic change and our own self-imposed limitations. To win this race, let us appreciate the most important asset we have: the values that already reside in each one of us and the people we work with. The real task of leadership is to create a work environment where these values can begin driving the enterprise.

If American businesses want to thrive in the 21st century, they must seriously consider whether they are willing to detach themselves from the culture and comforts of the past to meet this challenge. The leaders and companies who do are more likely to win. Those who don't—won't.

Edward M. Marshall, Ph.D., is president of The Marshall Group Inc. in Chapel, Hill, North Carolina.

Retooling People and Processes

Barbara Ettore

This is a case study of the changes that took place at one company in a reasonably obscure business—sequins—when the president made the decision to fully implement the ideas of W. Edwards Deming and other quality thinkers. All the indicators, including an enthusiastic work force, indicate that the changes have garnered the results they were looking for.

Funny thing about sequins. Apparel makers don't think about them much. But when they need them, darling, they *need* them.

This dilemma is nothing new for sequin manufacturers. The demand for sequins has always been cyclical, dependent on longer-term fashion trends. (Sequins were first handmade hundreds of years ago from gelatin and, later, from thin metal, even gold and silver foil. Now, they're machine-made from rolls of plastic.) The dress-down chic of the 1960s, for instance, wasn't kind to sequin manufacturers. Business got better during the Reagan years, when conspicuous consumption, big parties and big gowns were the rage. In the 1990s the trend has continued, as buffed bodies show off slinky, elegant, sequined apparel. Even Oscar night is more glittery these days. So are weddings.

When demand is down in the lean years, sometimes it is only the likes of the Ice Capades, Las Vegas, Mardi Gras, ballet companies and brides that can bring a smile to a sequin maker's face. (But there are always orders from Europe, where sequins have *never* lost their allure.)

The making of sequins and trimmings—and the sewing of these products onto fabrics in designs of varying complexity—is a specialized niche. As such, only a handful of sequin manufacturers exist in the United States. A major player is Sequins International Inc., located in an 85,000-square-foot factory in Woodside, a quiet neighborhood in the Queens borough of New York City, and in a small (6,000-square-foot) factory in Englewood, N.J.

Sequins International is meeting intense foreign and domestic competition head-on by using modern management ideas. And, it is training its largely Spanish-speaking workforce to be proficient in everything from English to statistical process control.

The company faces a formidable task in besting the competition, particularly its Chinese and Indian counterparts. The sequins-on-fabric industry in

Sequins International is meeting intense foreign and domestic competition head-on by using modern management ideas.

China and India conservatively produces at least $100 million at wholesale, according to textile experts. In China alone, an estimated 500,000 women and children hand-sew sequins into strands during off-hours at home, getting paid a pittance for each bagful of raw sequins they use.

Thus, the sheer number of low-paid workers allows foreign companies to compete effectively with sequin producers in developed countries, which, despite automation, have high labor and operating costs. Sequins International is banking on the idea that automation plus training, efficiencies and quality will give it enough of an edge to take on Asian competition handily.

Book Learning

The ideas propelling the company forward today came to management's mind less than two years ago. In mid-1993, Lawrence "Larry" Gladstone became president and CEO of Sequins International Inc., formed when two companies merged into a family partnership.

Gladstone had been president and CEO of an earlier entity also called Sequins International, which he acquired at the end of 1987. Then, his company merged with Quality Braid, a firm headed by his father, Frank. Quality Braid was a respected trimming manufacturer founded in 1941 by Frank Gladstone's Polish immigrant parents, who came to Brooklyn via Manchester, England.

The present-day company is, thoroughly, a Gladstone family enterprise. Frank Gladstone is now chief financial officer. Larry's Uncle David is chief operating officer. His sister Lisa is vice president. And his cousin Jeff is treasurer. They wear white jackets with words from W. Edwards Deming embroidered on the pocket—in Spanish because 80 percent of the company's 350 employees are Hispanic. The message: "You don't have to please the boss. You have to please the customer."

The seeds of this message were planted in 1993, when Larry Gladstone was concerned about his plant's rising material and labor costs while on Christmas vacation in the Cayman Islands with his wife and twin sons. He engaged in atypical beach reading: just-in-time case studies from the Japanese automaker Toyota. Inspired, he returned home and enthusiastically soaked up ideas from 40 books—reengineering, Japanese quality circles and team building, Zapp empowerment ideas from William C. Byham, TQM, quality and customer service concepts from J.M. Juran and Deming, and management advice from Peter Drucker. The books are piled on shelves in Gladstone's ramshackle office.

"I would say the culture here is Deming," he says, rummaging through a sea of order forms, management articles, trimming samples, crumpled notes, lunch bags and other paraphernalia at the large oval table that serves as his desk. "We have team meetings here," he says proudly. "This is my leadership desk." Sitting in a corner, dressed in a vest and handmade glasses, is a giant teddy bear given to Gladstone by his employees. Gladstone records a visitor's office number in his hand-held, computerized office organizer, yet scratches appointments and phone dates in minuscule notations on a wall calendar.

Gladstone may be casual in his office comportment, but he is all business on the production floor. His company does about $30 million in revenues, and he wants to take it to $40 million by 1996–1997, an ambitious goal in an entrenched industry.

The good news is that sequin-making produces practically no waste. Besides yielding sequins, a role of plastic raw material produces glitter (the sequin holes) and arts and crafts materials (ribbons of circular holes from cut-out sequins). The whole process conspires to generate riotous colors. The plant is an extravagance of color—scores of different-colored rolls of plastic piled everywhere; long ropes of sequins sewn in strands; enormous bolts of fabric stretched on machines that apply sequins in layers; and dozens of spools of colorful thread on knitting machines that sew sequins and trims to cloth or knit the cloth itself. Sequins and spools of thread are everywhere—jumbled in boxes, on the floor, draped around machinery, on file cabinets. Machine operators sweep up during lulls.

Sequin-making machinery, for the most part, dates from the 1940s. The German process of putting sequins onto string, called *schlung*, has been around since the 1800s. The noise from the machinery is ear-splitting. Chopping machines stamp out the sequins and line them up on string. Braiding machines and spooling machines take those strings and, via five strands of polyester thread, speedily roll out delicate ropes of sequins, ready to be affixed to fabric or sold in large spools. Schiffli embroidering machines from Switzerland and Austria turn out intricate designs on fabric.

Getting Going

The machines are the bane of a sequin maker's existence. The repetitive motions used to shepherd sequins from initial cutting through final sewing can produce an array of muscle pains and carpal tunnel syndrome. The pre-merger Sequins International began to attack this problem in 1992 with a machine redesign, using a small grant it received from the Ergonomics Project, a program administered by employers and the International Ladies' Garment Workers Union (ILGWU) for apparel makers based in the Northeast and committed to improving their operations ergonomically. (Local 62-32 of the ILGWU is the company's union.) The machine redesign project at Sequins International eventually cost around $20,000—$13,000 from the company, $7,000 from the program.

Employees have had significant input in how the machines operate today. For example, every inch of sequin strands must be inspected for defects and improper stitching, and 100 employees used to be engaged in this effort manually. Reconfigured spooling machines, built in the plant, automated the inspection process and integrated it into production, eliminating it as a separate function in another room. The inspectors were laid off due to the project—the only lay-offs planned. Gladstone is reluctant to discuss the tooling modifications, but operators gladly show how it's done.

Employees have had significant input in how the machines operate today.

The ergonomics effort marked the first step in Sequins International's improvement strategy: Because it cannot summon enormous resources of its own, the company has been aggressive in seeking out grants and other forms of aid to train its workers and to make itself competitive. Some examples:

- The empty, 1,500-square-foot space where the laid-off inspectors once worked is being turned into a classroom. This spring, the Consortium for Worker Education will provide the company with a teacher for English as a second language. Instructions in mathematics and statistical process control will help employees become proficient in a variety of tasks.

- Textile Clothing Technology, a nonprofit consortium of private firms, apparel workers' unions and large manufacturers, funded by federal government grants, will help Sequins International supply interactive training on computer stations to teach employees how to operate chopping and threading machines. Interactive "yes" and "no" questions, presented via script and video, will take employees through the training. The computers are expected to be on the factory floor by the end of this year.

- The company is in partnership with the Trade Adjustment Assistance program through the Department of Commerce. A package of federal and state grants (75 percent of the total) and Sequins International's own funds (25 percent) will kick off a comprehensive, top-to-bottom factory project—involving process mapping, teams and quality control—intended to retain jobs and produce measurable results in quality.

To qualify for the program, the company had to present a workable plan. "Eventually, we'll spend $250,000, but we'll have an edge on competition," Gladstone says. Accordingly, Coopers & Lybrand consulted on the company's technology and computer systems, including computer-aided-design (CAD) stations. Working with it customers, Sequins International will be able to computerize all phases of its operations, from the making of raw sequins to the design of patterns, textiles and fabrics for its trims. This system is expected to be in place by June 1996.

All That Glitters

Along with training over the past year, Sequins International has adopted a new operational structure, one that incorporates teams and opens lines of communication between management and workers.

By December 1994, the company had reduced the cost of producing a unit of goods by 30 percent and had seen concomitant 30 percent cuts in cycle time, inventory, overhead and floor space. According to Frank Gladstone, product development time has been accelerated by at least 30 percent: "Because of all this [cycle-time] reduction, we can develop new line and samples much quicker," he notes.

In fact, the company resorts to a primitive but effective method to get orders out the same day they are received. A bucket containing an order is lowered from the customer service staff upstairs to the shipping room downstairs.

The essence of the company's operational changes come from two "M" teams, one for product satisfaction, the other for customer support. Each has a team leader in manpower, machines, method and material, and each leader wears a color-coded jacket.

As a result, cross-functional expertise and shared knowledge have become components of Sequins International's newly emerging culture. A case in point is the 15-minute overlap between the day shift and the night shift, each eight hours long, so that employees can communicate and act upon new developments.

Craig Wagner, a facilitator on the product satisfaction team (yellow jacket), discusses a tooling project focused on the dust that accumulates from chopping sequins: "We wanted to prevent that powder from making the sequins stick together." The company constantly looks for better ways to operate through internal benchmarking, he adds.

Sal Mateo (yellow jacket) has been teaching *schlung* machine operators to use a brass screwdriver-shaped implement to make a time-saving minor adjustment on a small plate. In the past, an operator would have to stop the machine and turn on a light above, signaling a mechanical breakdown.

"We're involving the front-line operators in maintenance, tooling and quality improvements," says Keith Wernicke, group leader of product development and R&D (no jacket). He adds that over the next year, the plant will reconfigure its tool-making area—where machines are modified—for more efficiency.

Ray Kootz, group leader in the knitting area (ditto, no jacket), which employs 150 workers, offers one example of how the company has used technology to improve operations. Kootz notes that the cumbersome CAM chains on the knitting machines are difficult to maintain and often break down. "It would take a good mechanic four to five days to fix this one," he says, pointing to a black, gleaming—and particularly intimidating—web of chains and gears. But as part of its retooling, Sequins International now has 16 knitting machines hooked up to computers, enabling the company to work with customers in designing 1,000 styles. Eventually, the entire knitting floor and design process will be computerized.

If all this seems like so much cheerleading and team spirit, the floor workers clearly like the new culture. "The whole system has changed for the better, with better quality," says Ampero Guisao. Adds Ruby Osorio, "With cross-training, we can do three jobs now: chopping, *schlung* and spotting [inspection]." Employees in several areas of the plant say they feel management is listening to them more than ever before. Several of them remark that they are looking forward to the free English classes, which will be offered at lunch for three hours every week.

Luz Lopez (orange jacket) is manpower team leader on the machine team. She was a supervisor in the inspection area when she was offered a job in the new organization if she could make the shift to an empowered workforce.

Employees in several areas of the plant say they feel management is listening to them more than ever before.

"There is more closeness and communication between workers and management now, and less waste," says Lopez. She notes that absenteeism in her area is down by two-and-one-half times.

The fervor at Sequins International has spread to all levels, including management—a process Larry Gladstone calls "grabbing leadership in." And Jeff Gladstone, for his part, recalls coming to the office one Saturday and being regaled by an employee for 40 minutes. "He was so enthusiastic, showing me what he was doing," he says. "That employee got me pumped up. He got me going."

Barbara Ettore is a writer with Management Review *Magazine.*

VOICE OF THE CUSTOMER

Is Quality Compatible with a Passive Customer?

Robert W. Hall

This article, a second original by our consulting editor in manufacturing, explains the importance of involving customers in all aspects of managing your business. Actively involved customers are more likely to get what they want and much more likely to buy it from you.

Dictionaries still define quality as "the essential character of something" or "degree and grade of excellence." The definitions primarily describe goods and infer a single dimension of quality measurement, such as the purity of an inert gold bar. Applied to people, "quality" suggests high social position or a polite, reliable character.

These historic definitions are insufficient to capture the implications of quality today. Products and processes have become much more complex than in the early 1800s, when quality was achieved by craftsmanship and "inspecting it in." Commercial law presumed caveat emptor because the average person could knowledgeably examine most items he purchased. In this century, the principle of caveat emptor weakened because no one understands in depth the complex products and services on which they depend nor the processes that bring them about. Suppliers now bear more responsibility to "get it right" themselves and to help their customers do the same.

Today product quality refers to features, ease of use, maintainability, reliability, and other attributes—and to the service accompanying the product. Service quality implies a totally satisfactory experience to the customer,

Product-Oriented Quality ("Objective," but remote)	Customer-Satisfaction Quality ("Subjective," but closer to customer)
Physical phenomena or condition	Reaction to experience—emotion
Process separate from customer	Customer participates in process (service)
Indirect feedback from customer	Processes themselves depend on customer cues

Figure 1. **Product-oriented versus customer-oriented quality.**

whether in conjunction with a manufactured product or otherwise. Thus, the quality movement came to define quality as customer satisfaction—now embedded in the Baldrige Award criteria. Then attention turned to quality of processes, for only these deliver quality products and services.

From the notion of quality processes to deliver customer satisfaction, "quality" has become a modifier for everything—quality leadership, quality strategy, quality education, quality deployment, even quality layout—all of which make sense in the context of a multidimensional, process view of excellent performance. Considering this broadly, quality approaches the status of a philosophy, which it is, but a pragmatic one, because the field has created an array of methodologies to reduce quality intentions to practice. However, quality is not merely a set of techniques applied to business as usual, and it is certainly more than an attitude that produces remarkable results only through human dedication.

Joseph Juran refers to the expanding concept of quality as Big Q, and Q keeps getting bigger.[1] It is becoming so large that qualityphiles are beginning to describe nearly all human experience through quality vision, which is somewhat disconcerting to those with other views of the world. However, it is this expansion of vision that pushes us to see our next steps in progress. By defining quality as customer satisfaction and then defining the customer satisfaction process, we arrive at the conclusion that the limit to quality is us.

It is becoming so large that qualityphiles are beginning to describe nearly all human experience through quality vision.

Customer-Oriented Quality

Most quality assurance practices deal with how to execute and deliver what was promised to a customer. Moving beyond that, we have begun to improve the process of determining what customers want to design quality products and processes using methods such as quality function deployment (QFD). However, if quality is defined as customer satisfaction, it follows that quality is achieved through processes that serve customers, some of which may include design and production of physical goods, and at least a few of which include the customers themselves (see Figure 1). This "Big Q" version of quality can self-expand as far as the mind can stretch—well beyond where current practice has taken us. This definition begs those who adopt it to ask basic questions: Who are the customers? What are the customer's real needs? (Not necessarily the same as what at first they think they need.) How can these needs be met? By what processes can we answer the first three questions—actually achieve customer satisfaction?

Asking these questions afresh with intent to find superior answers produces quality innovation. Although most of us only adapt established methodology to our own applications, rather than invent new, by answering the fundamental questions for ourselves, we avoid just going through the motions.

Who Is the Customer?

The notion of an internal customer is that the next person in a process is the customer of the preceding step. Therefore, anyone working should try to please the internal customer. This idea has merit, but is inadequate, as many companies trying it have found.

First, internal processes are all intended to serve external customers, and the external customers are not always well served by a chain of internal customers all satisfying the next in line. Second, in more complex processes, there are a large number of both internal and external customers, each of whom may have a different relationship to the process.

One external customer may be someone who makes a buying decision but does not use the product or service personally. In that case, the buyer is only one customer. For example, when the Oregon Cutting Systems division first began to employ quality function deployment to guide the design of the chain saw blade, they were initially stymied because their customers of record were buyers and purchasing agents. To learn about the realities of blade use, the company had to organize a method to talk to loggers and others who personally use chain saws and capture the data. This effort sounds simpler than it is because designers can easily assume that they personally understand how a product is used, or base their design on data interpreted by others, without gaining insight into the experience of real users in different environments.

The difficulty of identifying the customer is illustrated by the quandary of a hospital floor nursing staff determining who their customers are. The patients themselves? The patients' families? Third-party payers? Medical doctors? Accreditation agencies? All are customers with various types and degrees of interest in a nursing staff's overall performance.

In the same sense, there are many customers for complex products such as automobiles: drivers, buyers, dealers, mechanics, financiers, insurers, police, traffic engineers—including workers who at some point must deal with the vehicle at the end of its useful life. Even the general public is a customer if one considers noise, pollution, and the roads and parking space needed for automobiles to operate.

The difficulty with identifying almost everyone as a customer is loss of organizational concentration on a defined, primary customer's needs.

Type	Customers	Suppliers
External	Final buyers or users of the product and services. Payments usually received. Separated by a monetary transaction boundary.	Providers of products and services. Payments usually sent. Separated by a monetary transaction boundary.
Internal	Next person or step in the chain of operations or in the process. No monetary transaction boundary.	Preceding person or step in the chain of operations or in the process. No monetary transaction boundary.
Primary	Firsthand users experiencing the product or service.	Persons performing the operations that directly provide the product or service.
Secondary	Agents, dealers, franchisees, enablers, service persons, etc.	Second tier and indirect suppliers.
Tertiary	General public affected by the product or service.	Schools or supporting communities.

Figure 2. **Different types of customers and suppliers.**

The difficulty with identifying almost everyone as a customer is loss of organizational concentration on a defined, primary customer's needs. Big Q is a challenge because conceiving of customers in multiples is useful only too the extent that an operable process can deal with the needs of each one. With more customers, more extensive and complex quality processes would seem necessary, and yet the challenge of quality is to simplify complex, ill-defined processes until they are predictable. Big Q is something to grow into.

On the other hand, the Big Q concept of suppliers is as partners in a quality process of serving customers—fellow problem solvers. It does not take long to conclude that an essential for having good problem-solving partners is participating in the problem solving with them, and of course, suppliers have needs too. The Big Q ideal is to organize a multiparty quality network focused on the problems of a set of customers.

Some of the notions of customer-supplier relations from the current rhetoric about quality are summarized in Figure 2. However, today's reality is that while this vision exists, incentives to compete rather than cooperate limit the degree of cooperation.

Scientists in laboratories that compete for funding and recognition do not totally cooperate with colleagues in other institutions, so it's hard to imagine

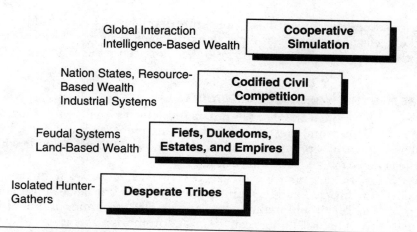

Figure 3. **Organizational stages of progression in Big Q.**

profit-driven commercial competitors totally embracing problem-solving teamwork among themselves to achieve an ecstatic level of customer satisfaction.

Despite the friction of negotiating payments, external suppliers may be superior to internal ones, possibly because the supplier's incentive to serve an external customer is stronger than the one to serve an internal customer. Companies today are outsourcing work. One reason is lower cost, but another is that companies increasingly find it difficult to manage a large set of core competencies. GM, IBM, and Xerox are only three companies that have made the news for shedding operations. On the supplier side, Manpower has become one of the largest "indirect" suppliers in the United States, and its employees in the financial sense frequently participate as team members with their "customers" on the job.

Optimistically, the business world is heading in the direction summarized in Figure 3, although it is presumptuous to assume that quality practice will cause a major shift to "cooperative stimulation" in how human institutions work. However, in complex operations, the need to integrate various specialties in solving the problems necessary for satisfaction of primary, secondary, and tertiary customers has become one reason to modify business organization. The business world is moving into teams, supply chains, value-adding networks, and so on, but it is confused because most business units are still more focused on cost reduction and market expansion than on overall performance improvement.

In any case, Motorola, among many other companies, has found that associates of a company must give attention to the needs of identified external customers, not just their internal customers. Likewise, if a network of people affiliated with different companies is to achieve quality performance, they all need to focus on the customers of their processes, not just on another member of the network. In the aircraft industry and several others, progress has been

The business world is moving into teams, supply chains, value-adding networks, and so on, but it is confused because most business units are still more focused on cost reduction and market expansion than on overall performance improvement.

made for several years identifying the nature of product use over full life cycle and the needs of various customers along the way. However, in most industries, that thought either is unknown or has not been reduced to practice.

What Are the Needs of Customers?

Customers have likes and dislikes but cannot always know what they need. If they did, they would prescribe their own treatments without consulting a physician. In turn, a physician's medical diagnosis is more difficult when a patient is incapable of communication.

With experience, many of us can describe what we want in technical terms or even engage in do-it-yourself satisfaction of our needs, for instance, by performing repair and maintenance to vehicles (becoming more difficult because of complexity). Others can describe automotive operations only with such naïveté that it is humorous, as on the radio show, "Car Talk," but the needs of the naive are no less real than those of the experts who respond to them. Indeed, one major customer need is to better understand what is happening without prolonged effort.

"Chinese menu" problems are old hat in marketing. So many choices are available that customers have no intention of making an exhaustive search. A major objective of marketing is to first determine what offering should attract a selected segment of potential customers, then stun them into paying attention to it amidst an ocean of information.

This constitutes a "push system" of marketing, contrasted with a "pull system," teaming with a customer to determine what he needs and then as nearly as possible, creating it—a consultation approach to marketing. Professional services use it with varying degrees of customer satisfaction. Here and there, consulting is making inroads into push system marketing.

Two examples of this shift are from Japan. One is in housing. Sekisui Housing Division is one of five Japanese companies that factory-build customized houses from standard-sized room modules, and many of them are wired as "smart houses." These houses are designed using CAD, and 80 percent of the work is completed in only three days. About 20 percent of new Japanese houses are built by such a system. Japanese housing starts roughly equal the number of starts in the United States, despite having only half the population.[2]

Throughout the house, dimensional tolerances are held to 1 mm so that craft work trimming and fitting is almost eliminated. The associated quality system is more like that used in mass production factories than in construction.

However, the most interesting aspect of Sekisui's operation is working with the customer to design the house. The number of hours of consultation with the customer to design the house is about equal to the number of hours needed to assemble the room modules before they are transported to the building site for erection—significant. After erection, about 30 days elapse before the house is ready to move in. Some of the delay is waiting for agency inspections, but some of the time is also making adjustments because the owners do not like all features of the finished product even though they designed it and specified the features themselves.

One of the problems, familiar to house builders everywhere, is that customers have varying degrees of difficulty trying to visualize what a house will look like from drawings and computerized models and also how they will use various features even after they have experienced a demo of them. And some simply have fickle tastes.

A key success factor of Sekisui's business is efficiently assisting customers through an educational experience. Part of this is guiding customers into discovery of what they really need instead of what at first they think they need. When a customer wants something unusual, both the customer and Sekisui have a mutual learning experience.

Mayekawa Manufacturing Co., Ltd. is the second example. This company designs and manufactures heavy refrigeration systems for commercial customers, mostly in the food industry, but the core of the business is helping customers to create a high-quality process in their own environment, thus expanding their capabilities beyond anything they would have imagined unassisted. That is the real value Mayekawa adds to their customers. They call this the production of quality results—for the customer. Naturally, to have quality results, the physical system must be high quality in operation and come from a quality process that minimizes defects, but all that is only the basic foundation for creating quality results.[3]

To do this, Mayekawa concentrates on small niche markets consisting of a total chain of supply. For example, it formed a cooperative arrangement with a fishing cooperative that began with a machine to freeze scallops in line rather than in batches. The program soon spread to fishermen, distributors, and other parties in the chain that brings scallops from the sea to the consumer's mouth. The objective was to minimize waste and improve taste by carefully controlling the thermal history and other attributes of each scallop from the point of harvest to the point of consumption. Done in conjunction with many customer partners, the program has greatly improved the quality, efficiency, and productivity of a small, but important segment of the food industry in Japan.

That is truly improving quality by asking basic questions about a process from beginning to end. It was only accomplished because the various partners in a supply chain first visualized an accomplishment that was beyond any of them acting alone, then joined in overcoming a series of issues that stood between them and their vision. (They are still at work improving the process.)

A key part of this story, and others like it, is that no one really understood what was needed when they began. By asking fundamental questions and applying basic problem solving (and advanced technology) over time, every party to this process improved their capabilities beyond any level that they would have imagined only a few years ago.

How to Meet the Customers' Real Needs

One approach to meeting customer needs is also illustrated by the Mayekawa example. To promote intimate problem solving with the various parties in each supply-chain niche market, Mayekawa has evolved a unique organization. Each customer's unique issues are addressed by small legally independent companies while R&D is operated centrally. Each plant is a separate independent company that serves the small field companies. However, everyone in one of these units can move temporarily between them. They may assist in building apparatus in a plant, deal directly with an R&D specialist, or work directly in a customer's operations for a time. It takes about 10 years for most people to learn how to function effectively in this milieu.

In this way, a small field group can mount a cooperative effort to identify and overcome customer problems and personally follow the implementation of solutions from beginning to end. Interestingly, this approach to organization has resulted in a very flexible problem-solving approach, unencumbered by the usual bureaucracy of large organizations or by the suspicions that hinder cooperation between entrepreneurs, each trying to dominate something, and unfamiliar with each other.

Mayekawa deals with numerous small niche markets. At first review, most have some mundane challenges—like how to improve scallops. Some problem solutions involve advanced technology; many do not.

A limitation of this approach is whether consumer customers would seriously participate in solving problems as mundane as what kind of pencil they might like, or simply follow the course presently taken most of the time—briefly shop for something off the shelf that looks attractive at the right price. The time and effort spent solving one's own problems are significant, and impatience with search time is an issue well known in mass marketing. Few people are likely to engage in personal pencil design unless the process were made very easy and attractive to them.

However, hundreds or thousands of problem-solving methodologies exist, some more popular than others. The trick is to make them easy to use and to create the mutual confidence that allows them to be used effectively.

Involvement of the Customer

The Industry Week Best Plants application form asks whether the applicant receives ratings from their own suppliers on what kind of customer they are. One would suspect that few companies do this, but many of the Industry Week Best Plant winners do.

Xerox, Motorola, Honda, Toyota, and other companies have become industrial customers well-known for development of suppliers. First they developed quality practices themselves before they had much to offer suppliers. Then they improved the quality of their participation as partners with suppliers—and became better customers.

A good customer puts effort into overcoming his own problems and will work through a problem-solving process with a supplier. Improvement partners are far from docile—buy, pay, and go away. If not easy to serve, they at least make rational demands. If consumers, they will at least fill out the comment cards. Good commercial customers help suppliers improve processes that belong to both partners.

Sometimes the need for a customer to be active in improving quality is obvious. Suppose the customer is buying education. A passive student does not improve much, no matter what method of education is used. Student engagement in the process is a two-way street, and one can argue such issues as how much positive and negative reinforcement, or "entertainment," should be provided to maintain enthusiasm. Appropriate methods depend on the maturity of the student. Disagreement about both the goals and the results are common. But when the process is successful, both student and instructor learn.

However, if the customer is buying something as inert as a load of bricks, all this is much less obvious, but even then, the customer wants service and sometimes a little know-how on what to do with the bricks. Many modern products and services have a much stronger educational component associated with them than bricks. For example, an experienced driver entering a strange rental car must find the readouts and controls and learn to use them. If this learning process takes more than a minute or two, the customer is likely to be irritated.

Software is a prime example of customer-participation issues. Features considered user-friendly by a novice are considered annoying by an expert, so that satisfaction depends on the prior experience of the customer. Because software is starting to become embedded in almost any operative product, one of the major goals is to extend or enhance the capabilities of customers to have a satisfactory do-it-yourself experience.

Here, customer satisfaction depends on both the prior experience and expectations of the customer. (The now-popular objective of "delighting" customers becomes more difficult as customers become jaded. For example, the earliest Xerox customers were surprised and delighted by any plain-paper copy, but expectations are far different today. The concept of "delight" has been attacked using the puckish observation that by severely depressing their prior expectations, leery customers might turn giddy with delight.) As the concept of Big Q continues to expand in an information age, better definitions of customer satisfaction are needed.

This issue was addressed by the committee that designed the 1995 Education Pilot Criteria based on the Malcolm Baldrige National Quality Award. Recognizing that everyone should gain from an educational process, the heavily weighted category called "Customer Focus and Satisfaction" for commercial enterprises was replaced by "Student Focus and Student and Stakeholder Satisfaction." A subcategory called "Future Student Needs and Satisfaction" ask applicants to stretch their concept of long-term added value to their customers. Literally responding to this request requires looking several decades ahead. Although the headlights mostly reflect fog that far out, the request is a good one.

What adds long-term value for many people has been asked in some form

As the concept of Big Q continues to expand in an information age, better definitions of customer satisfaction are needed.

many times for ages. Pyramids and temples are monuments to answers given by bygone civilizations. In an age when secondary and tertiary customers can be considered, the question applies to seemingly mundane businesses such as weed killers and facial tissues that on second thought are not so simple. The challenge is how to do it.

Considering the customers is the first step in a business plan, the first step in policy deployment (by whatever name), and the first in quality function deployment. But understanding the real, long-term needs of an extended set of customers is challenging. So is the integration of those needs into products and processes. It probes the unknowns of life cycles and the processes of distant partners.

Interpreting customer needs is often an exercise in statistically dissecting survey data on primary users and sometimes merely customer buying habits. Lost in the unexplained variance are the insights that come from direct study of customer processes. Study of real customer processes in depth and detail costs time and money, and it annoys customers. (Have you ever conscientiously filled out a survey a day, much less done a detailed study of, say, everything you do to shave your face, including how you dispose of the materials?)

Analysis tools have been developed. They may not be simple enough to make process capture easy, but what is missing is building customer-supplier partnerships to achieve customer satisfaction Without it, our current processes to improve quality run into themselves as their own limitations.

Notes

1. J. M. Juran, *A History of Managing for Quality* (Milwaukee, WI: ASQC Quality Press, 1995). See Table 18.7.

2. Robert W. Hall and Yoshinori Yamada, "Sekisui's Three-Day House," *Target*, Association for Manufacturing Excellence, vol. 9, no. 4, July–August, 1993, pp. 6–11.

3. Yoshio Iwasaki and Jinichiro Nakane, "Downscaling to Adapt to Your Environment," Mayekawa Manufacturing Company, Ltd.," *Target*, Association for Manufacturing Excellence, vol. 11, no. 4, July–August, 1995, pp. 9–17.

Balancing Conflicting Stakeholder Requirements

Guy W. Wallace

The author of this article reminds us that while customers are important, they are only one of the stakeholders that organizations must serve and seek to satisfy. There will always be some trade-offs that managers must make to balance the often conflicting needs of different stakeholders.

The slogans of many total quality management efforts state emphatically: The customer is king! Customer satisfaction reigns supreme! Meet the customer requirements! Exceed the customer requirements! Delight the customer! This overly simplistic view ought to cause many an executive to lose sleep and quiver with fear at the thought that if they follow their peers' lead, push the total quality management into their organizations, then everyone on the payroll might take the slogans literally and act accordingly. Very, very scary.

One question: Are you/we willing to meet the customer's requirements at any cost?

In a word, your answer ought to be: No!

The reason for the *No!* answer—nothing in business (or anywhere else) is really that simple. There are more stakeholders than just the customer. And more often than not, there is no *one* customer, just as there is often no *one* right answer as to what the requirements are. Nor is there any point in ignoring one of the key considerations in making a business decision—cost. The truth is that there are always a number of complex trade-offs in business decision making.

Too many TQM advocates have done a poor job of convincing management that they understand these trade-offs and, as a result, TQM sometimes sounds naive about business.

Are all requirements created equal? Often the requirements of the various stakeholders are in conflict with each other. Then we have to answer questions such as:

- How do we balance the requirements and determine where trade-offs can be made?

> The truth is that there are always a number of complex trade-offs in business decision making.

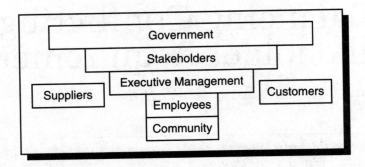

Figure 1. **Stakeholder hierarchy.**

- How do we evaluate them to determine how to create a *win-win* solution for everyone?
- How do we decide whether *win-win* for everyone is feasible and not just a pie in the sky goal in a world of variability?

Both sides have a point . . . TQM advocates have a point when they try to move the focus away from "profit as a goal" toward "profit as a result of competent, fair service." And executives need a way to get the message out that the company exists at the will of its customers but that competitiveness can only come by *profitably* meeting customer needs better than their competition.

The problem: slogans are incomplete . . . If all you want is to generate some results through a lot of activity, then management might just as well run around shouting:

- *Empowerment to the people!*
- *Delight the customer!*
- *Improve all processes everywhere continuously!*

Perhaps Deming had a point after all . . . Without a sound business evaluation, the results may be nothing more than increased costs. Maybe that is why one of Deming's *14 Points* is to eliminate slogans, exhortations, and targets. But management's problem still remains, what is the right message to send to employees? Try this one for starters: the customer is not the only one whose requirements we must consider.

Other groups *hold* a stake in our decisions. Effective decisions must balance the requirements of a number of disparate stakeholders. Let's take a look at who these *stakeholders* are, what their requirements typically are, and how much *clout* they carry.

Stakeholders and Requirements

There are at least seven basic stakeholder categories, each with different types of people in each of them (Figure 1):

What is the right message to send to employees? Try this one for starters: the customer is not the only one whose requirements we must consider.

- Government
- Shareholders
- Executive management
- Customers
- Employees
- Suppliers
- Community

Government —The government represents the most formal and powerful stakeholder. This stakeholder embodies the laws and regulations which guard the interests of the public and business. The laws provide the guidelines for conducting business. In addition, there are a wide variety of regulatory agencies at the federal, state and local levels whose purpose is to control the business practices in particular industries. Whether the entity is a publicly owned business, or a family business, the Girl Scouts of America, the National Football League, or a religious organization, various laws and regulations ensure that the public interests are protected and served.

Requirements . . . As a stakeholder, their interests and requirements supersede all others. It doesn't matter that the customer may require a bribe to do business, or that they want an unfair price, or they require you to act unethically and illegally and dump toxic wastes. The government(s) requirements will take precedence, under the penalty of law for non-compliance.

The government represents the most formal and powerful stakeholder.

Shareholders Shareholders are the owners, whether they are the members of a non-profit society, a closely held or publicly traded company. Their shares represent capital invested in the firm with an expectation for an equitable return.

Requirements . . . Their goals are typically long-term growth in equity or short-term income through dividends, but can include other goals such as societal enhancement, environmental protection, etc.

Management is responsible to shareholders for business results. If the management group does not achieve shareholder financial performance goals, they will either be replaced or investors will withdraw their capital and invest it elsewhere.

Executive management Executive management stakeholders are those responsible for the operations and results of the entity. They may be *partners* who contributed and own all the capital of the entity and run the business, or they could be an elected board of directors responsible to all the owners and the overseeing of daily business operations.

Requirements . . . As a matter of law, the managers of a publicly held corporation have a fiduciary responsibility to the shareholders for all operating decisions made. Their decisions could be determined to be unlawful/fraudulent, and they may be liable for their actions within the context of the law. They must always balance the (conflicting) interests of various stakeholder groups when determining the course of action for the organization.

Customers Customers are typically a diverse group. There are numerous methods used to analyze them as distinct groups to gain insights into their situations, problems, and needs.

Requirements . . . In some cases, such as with large-scale contracting businesses (aircraft or information systems), many customer requirements are specifically defined. Even in this type situation, there are many different customer requirements, such as those from technical experts, business management, contracts management, etc. Each of these may have unique, and sometimes conflicting requirements.

In other types of businesses, the provider has to generalize the requirements of the entire marketplace to create the right product. And in either of these situations, customers may not really know exactly what they want or what is available to help them with their problems/opportunities. One thing is certain however: customers will generally demand a quality product at a competitive price.

We need to listen to customers to understand their requirements fully and consider those in light of what our competition is doing. This allows us to responsibly determine which customer requirements we will choose to pursue. And in choosing those, we have to carefully consider pursuing only those that meet the requirements of other critical stakeholders.

Employees This stakeholder group includes all ranks of employees below the executive management level: upper-middle management, middle management, supervisors, individual contributors and employees with union representation.

Requirements . . . At the heart of all employee requirements is a safe workplace and financial security but other needs exist as well:

- Some employees want the opportunity for career growth and advancement . . .
- Others want a work situation where they can use their intellect and creativity . . .
- Still others may simply want an un-demanding set of tasks to do before they head home each day.

> At the heart of all employee requirements is a safe workplace and financial security.

Each set of needs is as different as the individual doing the job. Global assumptions, such as: everyone wants to be a team player, may only lead to a population of dissatisfied employees. Organizations need to listen carefully to all their employees.

Suppliers Suppliers (both internal and external) are also a key stakeholder group. To promote a long-term arrangement with particular suppliers, one needs to be aware of how your business decisions impact their businesses.

Requirements . . . Supplier requirements typically include the following:

- Clear/stable specifications for their products and services . . .
- Stable demand, or accurately forecast demand . . .
- Prices that enable a growth in *their* shareholders' equity.

Win-win collaboration with targeted suppliers helps to ensure a stable inflow of goods and services which will efficiently meet the needs of our own process and business requirements. It's not just a nice theory; it's a good business practice.

A supplier sub-category . . . Another potential stakeholder constituency is made up of various organizations that establish standards for technical and business practices. Though their requirements are similar to governmental regulations, they do not have the *power of law* to enforce their points of view; they may have the *power of the marketplace* via consumer confidence in their standards. A standards stakeholder may also generate requirements of your business such as packaging/labeling, purity, recyclability, percentage of parts manufactured domestically, et cetera. In addition, they may address the processes within your company, such as the implementation of your quality management system, hiring and recruitment processes, and so on.

Community Community stakeholders, although a less formal group, remain important through the influence they can have on our businesses. Church groups, neighborhood action committees, service clubs and such can exact as consequence if ignored. The various stakeholders in the community can choose to support our business or, if they do not agree with the ways in which your operations are run, bring it to the attention of the greater public.

Requirements . . . Their interests primarily lie in community and environmental safety, jobs and cooperation with or donation to community interests/causes. Community members can be a nuisance or a powerful base of support, depending upon the effort put into establishing and nurturing the relationship.

Balancing Stakeholder Requirements

It would seem, given the extent of the list of stakeholders and requirements, there are really three problems:

1. Identifying specifically who our stakeholders are in any given situation . . .
2. Understanding their requirements and priorities to be placed on those requirements . . .
3. Balancing requirements that are in conflict. Balancing requirements means making tough trade-offs on which needs will be exceeded, met, or not met (at least in today's view).

We make similar trade-offs in our personal lives every day:

- How do you decide which set of in-laws wins the first holiday visit to see the new grandchildren?
- Whose career will take precedence when the next opportunity knocks?
- Do you buy a quart of oil every week for $2.00 to drive the old beast to the job, or rebuild the engine for $3,000?

	Government			Shareholders		Shareholders		Customers		Employees		Employees	
	1.1	1.2	1.3	2.1	2.2	3.1	3.2	4.2	4.3	5.1	5.2	6.1	6.2
1. Government													
1.1													
1.2													
1.3													
2. Shareholder													
2.1 Regular dividends													
2.2 Long-term growth													
3. Executives													
3.1 Low-cost volume strategy													
3.2													
4. Customers													
4.1 Custom orders						3							
4.2 Interchangeability						2				1			
5. Employees													
5.1 Avoid last-minute scrambling								1					
5.2 Overtime													1
6. Suppliers								3					
6.1 Stable market for components								2					
6.2 Low inventory requirements													

Figure 2.   **Stakeholder requirements matrix.**

Step one in balancing stakeholder requirements is simply knowing what the requirements are and who is making them. The many and different types of requirements can be made more manageable by using a decision matrix.

A stakeholder requirements matrix can help organize the requirements definition and balancing process, especially when you are trying to develop a consensus view across a team. It gives you a starting point for a list of stakeholders and for their individual requirements. The specific needs involved in your own decision or process may well require you to expand or reduce this list.

Stakeholder requirements matrix   Basically, the matrix shows key requirements of each of the primary categories of stakeholder. The requirements are general but can be made more specific as needed (Figure 2).

For example, instead of a general heading of *suppliers* you may be able to list the individual companies and note that *supplier A* wants to provide a broader range of services while *supplier B* is more concerned with a stable volume of orders. To be sure you have the full range of requirements covered, use the general items as a checklist.

One way to use the matrix for your own situation could be to identify individuals who represent each stakeholder group and ask directly for their perspective. In situations where you don't want to discuss things with the actual stakeholder groups, internal experts in areas relevant to the stakeholder groups could role play their interests. For simple decisions, you may find that this general requirements list is sufficient.

Resolving stakeholder conflicts   Identifying where requirements conflict is really the most important step but the hard part is figuring out how to resolve it. To resolve the conflict, you need to decide if there is an alternative that will somehow meet both requirements or, what will more likely be the case, is a decision on which set of requirements takes precedence.

Using the hierarchy and "clout" as a measure . . . Typically, the higher the group in the stakeholder hierarchy, the more *clout* they have and the more complex their requirements will be. In some situations, the specific requirement of a lower-placed stakeholder may seem to take precedence over higher-level stakeholder, but usually, the hierarchy is kept intact. However, saying the hierarchy is usually not violated is not the same as saying there aren't honest differences of opinion on how requirements should be met. For example, some of the shareholders requirements might not be fully met for some reasonable amount of time to enable the enterprise to invest in R&D for a new product or settle for a slimmer short term ROI to attract new customers.

Using the matrix . . . So, how do you balance the requirements of such a diverse set of stakeholders? The stakeholder requirements matrix will help to organize your information and prepare you to speak with the various constituencies involved in the decision about all the requirements, conflicts, and trade-offs, but it will not give you an answer.

The matrix will steer you toward the real key: truly understanding the *whys* behind the stakeholders' requirements.

Then, when and if a compromise is necessary, you will be better able to choose the least offensive alternative and defend it rationally. Understanding the *whys* will also lead you to the real requirements and away from *nice to haves.* In the example, the employees would know why management might overrule a recommendation to make the product more *customizable.*

Those furthest from one stakeholder and closest to another may upset your balancing act . . . Overlooked stakeholders are usually those farthest removed from those making the decision. If employees only consider *end-use customer* needs when working on continuous improvement efforts, product development teams, or even during front-line customer contacts, they run the risk of missing and/or conflicting with requirements of other important stakeholders.

Decisions made by employees, unaware of more distant shareholder requirements, may result in a waste of shareholder equity in chasing requirements that customers aren't willing to pay for, that don't fit the standards of the industry, or are outside the company's strategic direction.

If management reverses decisions made by newly empowered employees, waste may be avoided but employees may begin to distrust management. Management may well then be seen as not walking the talk and as *duck walking*—ducking the issues. TQM may then be viewed as just another management whim or fad from the consulting quacks. What they don't see is that

> Typically, the higher the group in the stakeholder hierarchy, the more *clout* they have.

the real driving force behind all business decisions is the overall good of the business—the slogans didn't communicate the full message.

What we all need to understand is that meeting customer needs is yet another instance where there is a series of trade-offs and compromises. Business decisions are inherently complex due to the conflicting demands of a variety of stakeholders. The message that needs to be communicated is that everyone in the enterprise has to apply sound logic in making business decisions and remember that often not all stakeholder requirements will be met to their entire satisfaction.

> *Business decisions are inherently complex due to the conflicting demands of a variety of stakeholders.*

Some Closing Thoughts

All of us must try to understand the requirements of all stakeholders involved with the business. The closest customer cannot reign above all other stakeholders. Stakeholder requirements must be understood and balanced within the context of their legitimate hierarchical relationship and the firm's basic need for profitability.

The basic message to all employees should include the following:

- Your immediate customer's demands should not be met at all costs . . .
- There may be situations in which it is better to lose a client than to jeopardize the business . . .

All employees need to understand the range of stakeholder segments, typical requirements, and the hierarchy so they may understand:

- Which requirements take precedence when conflict arises . . .
- What customer requirements should not be met now, and/or later, and why?

Armed with such information, employees can, when appropriate, inform the customer why a particular need cannot be met.

But questions such as those above can only be answered when all the requirements are uncovered and judged in relation one to another so as to reveal the full implications of any decision. The long and the short of it is this: there are no simple answers; business decisions are inherently complex and take time, effort, and frequently involve trade-offs.

Good luck. And may the balance of requirements be in your favor.

Guy W. Wallace is a partner at SWI · Svenson and Wallace, Inc. Wallace's major areas of expertise include the development of performance-based curriculum frameworks, customer training programs, and project management.

A Cure for Initiative Burnout

John Guaspari

In this insightful article, the author clearly explains that the idea of value can provide the motivation and direction to keep a company on its toes and improving. Guaspari takes a slightly different approach to this idea from the article early in this book by co-editor John Woods, which explores value in terms of utility. The two articles together provide a "valuable" foundation for understanding this important idea.

If you ask me, there's a plot masterminded by the powerful coffee mug and one-size-fits-all baseball cap lobby. Otherwise how do you explain the need for all those corporate initiatives, complete with companywide meetings, executive pronunciamentos, special edition newsletters and somewhat clever slogans festooning the aforementioned mugs and caps?

However well-intended, all of this activity has some serious side effects. Large numbers of people in large numbers of companies are suffering from "initiative burnout." Whether it's total quality management, cycle-time reduction, business process reengineering, empowerment, customer focus, or you-name-it, people feel that something new is coming around the corner every day. And with each new initiative there is more work to do, less time to do it in and fewer people to do it with.

Employees do not consider this feeling to be a pleasant one. Under the circumstances, the last thing that anyone would seem to need is yet another concept around which to orchestrate yet another initiative.

Which leads me to the notion of "value." These days, it's hard not to bump up against it as one strives to deliver value to customers, drive out non-value-adding steps from processes, and otherwise do what one has to do to compete in the 1990s, a.k.a., "The Value Decade."

Value and Context

The fact is that people's eyes begin to glaze over when the talk turns to value. This is most unfortunate, because the notion of value differs in kind from the other notions emblazoned on the row of coffee mugs lined up neatly on the shelf in your office. Not because it's a panacea or because it can offer a quick fix. It's not, and it can't.

The real value of value is this: *It can provide context.* It can help people to understand—and management to communicate—that things aren't quite as random and chaotic as they might feel. It can help take all of those seemingly disparate pieces an integrate them into a logical, compelling whole that meets the needs of the business to perform at a higher level and the needs of individuals to work to a higher purpose.

Herewith, four propositions about value that help provide the context that is much needed and, all things considered, quite valuable in treating initiative burnout.

Proposition 1: Value is the only thing that causes customers to buy.

- You're in the market for a new car: Do you by the Chevy or the Porsche?
- You feel like eating out: Will it be McDonald's or The Four Seasons?
- You're tired of paying rent: Do you buy a house or a condominium?

In all three cases, the answer is, "It depends." If you're looking for basic transportation, you buy the Chevy. If you're looking to make heads turn as you drive by, you go with the Porsche. Twenty-fifth wedding anniversary? Book a table at The Four Seasons. Quick bite on the way to the movies? McDonald's. Do you have small children? A house on a cul de sac with a nice yard might be best. Don't want to be a slave to painting and yard work? Go condo.

Customers go through the same process whenever they buy something— whether they do it consciously or not. They line up the various options, consider the plusses and minuses, and choose the best combination thereof. Think of this as the ratio of "What the Customer GOT" to "What it COST the Customer," and you get a usefully simple definition of value: VALUE = what-the-customer-GOT/what-it-COST-the-customer, or VALUE = GOT/COST.

In this definition, GOT includes the product, plus service, plus intangibles (such as the head-turning reaction that the Porsche had better induce if it's going to be worth the extra money spent). Similarly, COST includes money, plus time, plus intangibles (such as the rocky start you're bound to get off to in year 26 if you celebrate your silver anniversary with a Big Mac and fries). Customers always do this GOT/COST calculation and buy from whoever can give them the best ratio.

"To maximize value" is the only reason that anybody has ever bought anything in any industry at any time. To the extent that you want customers to buy from you rather than the other guy, this is a useful point you need to drive home to all your employees.

Proposition 2: All company initiatives are, fundamentally, about creating more value.

The real value of value is this: It can provide context.

"To maximize value" is the only reason that anybody has ever bought anything in any industry at any time.

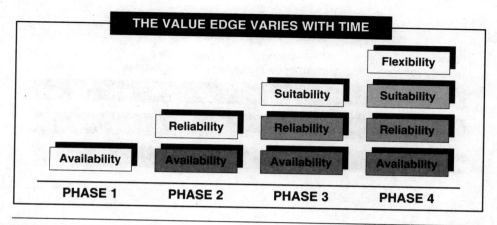

THE VALUE EDGE VARIES WITH TIME

PHASE 1	PHASE 2	PHASE 3	PHASE 4
			Flexibility
		Suitability	Suitability
	Reliability	Reliability	Reliability
Availability	Availability	Availability	Availability

Figure 1.

To say that customers buy on value is not to describe a new phenomenon. Customers have always bought on value. What differs over time is what it is that constitutes value.

When an industry is in its infancy, there may be only a small number of suppliers that offer a particular product or service. The offering may be less than ideal, but the mere fact that a customer can get the product or service is decisive. In this first value phase, "availability" is the value attribute that provides the decisive edge.

Before long, though, competitors enter the picture, and customers find that they have a broad range of choices. Simply offering a product or service is no longer enough. Now it is essential that your product or service works as it was designed to work. Availability no longer produces the value edge. In phase 2, "reliability" does.

Over time, many suppliers are able to offer reliable products or services, and customers begin to take reliability for granted: "Of course it had better work! I paid good money for it!" Consequently customers can be choosier, selecting the product or service that is just right for them. The phase 3 value edge now comes from "suitability."

By the time the industry reaches value phase 4, there are plenty of suitable products and services for customers to choose from. As a result, suitability is no longer enough to stand out. Customers are no longer simply asking, "Do you have what I need?" In effect, the question becomes, "Will you do what I need you to do to customize your offering for me?" There is now a greater premium on "flexibility"; that's where the phase 4 value edge resides.

In all four cases, customers bought from whichever company was able to provide them with that incremental bit of value. As shown in the figure below, the particular attributes that make up that value edge vary over time, with today's value attributes becoming tomorrow's base line attributes. But the dynamic is always the same. Company X figures out a way to offer its

The particular attributes that make up that value edge vary over time, with today's value attributes becoming tomorrow's base line attributes.

VALUE PHASES		
Customer buying motive	Differentiating performance attribute	Discipline to be mastered
Maximum value	Reliability	Conformance quality
Maximum value	Suitability	Customer-focused quality
Maximum value	Flexibility	Time-based process improvement

Figure 2.

customers a better GOT/COST ratio—that is, more value. Smart competitors recognize that they too must offer that level of value. As more suppliers perform at the new, higher level, possessing this value attribute ceases to be unique. Other smart competitors will figure out ways to offer a still higher level of value, and the cycle will begin again.

All of which raises an interesting set of questions. What happens between phases 1 and 2 that enables organizations to provide more reliable products/services? How, during phase 3, can suppliers offer a higher degree of suitability? What does a company have to do to possess the kind of flexibility characteristic of phase 4 performance?

To move from providing "availability" to "reliability," an organization needs processes that are under control and able to produce the desired outcomes reliably and repeatably. In short, it must have a mastery of "conformance quality": the ability to make things that work.

When reliability gives way to suitability, a premium is placed on being in touch with the marketplace, and successful companies—those providing the value edge—have to be practitioners of "customer-focused quality." No longer are internally generated standards enough. Requirements are framed in customer terms and aimed at meeting customer needs.

And in a climate where "flexibility" is king, time is, quite literally, of the essence, and mastery of "time-based process improvement" must be achieved.

So while the differentiating performance attribute will vary from phase to phase, and the disciplines to be mastered will change accordingly, the fundamental buying motive is always unchanged. It is always "to maximize value."

This means that the walk through the litany of change initiatives—quality, customer focus, cycle-time reduction, etc.—has not been a random one. They've all been about increasing GOTs and decreasing COSTs. Fundamentally, they've all been about creating more customer value.

In a world where change is a way of life, that can be reassuring indeed.

In a climate where "flexibility" is king, time is, quite literally, of the essence, and mastery of "time-based process improvement" must be achieved.

Proposition 3: Value is not the same thing as quality.

When Philip Crosby defined quality as "conformance to requirements," he rendered an extraordinarily important service to us all. The power of Crosby's definition resides in its characterization of quality as a binary phenomenon. That is, the act of checking for quality, properly understood, becomes a yes/no question: "Did we do what we intended to do?" As such, quality is asking about the mastery of internal processes.

Focusing on value has the effect of asking a very different question, namely: "Is what we're doing useful enough that someone will pay good money for it?" As such, it positions you to address a number of issues that often arise during change efforts. Consider:

- Since the concept of value only makes sense from the customer's vantage point, it *necessarily* puts you in the customer's shoes. The concept makes no sense from any other point of view. The same cannot be said of quality, which ultimately forces an inside-out perspective, in that quality efforts are fundamentally about answering the question, "Have we done what we set out to do?" (This should not be interpreted as a shortcoming of quality. In fact, quality's scrupulous quest for conformance to requirements—no compromises, no rationalizations—is its strength.)

- It avoids the "How do we link our quality initiatives to the mainstream of the business?" problem. In fact, it's impossible to work value issues and not be in the mainstream. (The act of creating value for customers should *define* the mainstream of the business.)

- It can help anchor "soft" activities, such as the development of a common vision, in business realities. The notion of being in the business of serving customers is evocative enough to touch people at an extra-rational, emotional level. The notion of creating value in order to gain a hard, competitive business advantage will make the activity feel more substantial. This is not the case when visioning activities become free-form and inwardly focused discussions about "the kind of environment we want to work in."

> Since the concept of value only makes sense from the customer's vantage point, it *necessarily* puts you in the customer's shoes.

A major obstacle to gaining broad-based buy-in to quality efforts is that they are inevitably viewed as being negative. Try as you might, it's difficult to dissuade people from the belief that, fundamentally, the study of quality is about figuring out ways to mess up less often. (The reason it's so hard to dissuade people from that belief is that, fundamentally, the study of quality *is* about figuring out ways to mess up less often.) Creating value for customers, on the other hand, is a more positive, more affirming focus that is nicely congruent with the natural human affinity for initiatives driven by such notions as creativity, opportunity, initiative and breakthrough results.

Value provides a positive platform for change. People are more inclined to buy in. This may be its most important characteristic of all.

Proposition 4:   The timing is now right to shift to a focus on value.

If, as has been argued here, value has always been the issue, why elevate it to such special status now? Why haven't we been talking about value all along?

That's a fair question, best answered by analogy.

My 10-year-old son has recently taken up the saxophone. One could say that the ultimate objective of this activity is for him "to make music." At this point in the process, though, "making music" is a rather lofty description of what he's doing. He's still at the stage of rote memorization of fingerings, struggling to understand the difference between quarter rests and half notes, and making sure that the reed is on right-side-up. The assorted sounds that emanate from the sax when he blows into it can be described in many ways, but the word "music" is not one that leaps to mind.

If he stays with it, this will change over time. He'll take lessons, practice, play in the junior high school band. Take more lessons, practice some more, play in the high school band. Still more lessons and practice, maybe start a band with his friends. At some point along the way, the sounds wafting down from his room as he practices will begin to sound suspiciously like . . . music. And at that point, playing the sax will fundamentally change for him. No longer will it be about practicing scales and not hitting wrong notes. Now it will be about something evocative, something more sublime. It will be about making music.

The evolution from quality, to various other corporate initiatives, to value is like that. While it's true that value has been the goal all along, it's also true that until a certain level of mastery has been attained, until some basic process capabilities have been reached, until people have learned to work with each other in new ways, exhorting people to create value will be fruitless at best, dispiriting at worst. (It would be roughly equivalent to me trying to motivate my son by bursting in on him while he's practicing and saying, "You call that *music?!?*")

Warding Off Burnout

Enormous progress has been made. Processes are under control, reliable and repeatable. Customers are at the forefront of people's thinking. Organizations are more flexible and nimble. People are working together in new and different ways.

And in spite of being somewhat burned out on corporate initiatives, those same people are still willing and able to meet significant new challenges. What's missing for many of them, though, is a context for all the change and disruption. Something that's valid on the face of it. Something that's compelling. Something that can help them make sense of it all.

The notion of value—uniquely—can provide it. And the organization that best understands and most clearly communicates this fact will have gone a long way toward immunizing itself from the next outbreak of initiative burnout.

John Guaspari, vice president at Lexington, Massachusetts-based Rath Strong Inc., is author of four AMA-COM books and six AMA videos on quality and customer value.

Quality Transformation
TRAINING

Quality Training at FedEx

Bill Wilson

This brief article overviews the Quality Academy, the training division of FedEx. The company believes in its people and in quality management and has made a large and long-term commitment to continuously training its people.

Federal Express has long been the leader in the delivery of time-sensitive packages and documents. Employee training has played a large part in the reputation Federal Express has earned during the years as one of the premier customer-oriented companies in the United States.

When the quality effort spread across the country in the mid-1980s, Federal Express was already ahead of the game, cultivating an employee-centered environment.

Chairman Fred Smith summarizes the corporate philosophy of "People, Service, Profit" this way, "When people are placed first, they will provide the highest possible service, and profits will follow." PSP is a system of three interrelated elements, all of which share equal importance in the company's long-term success.

In other words, a company that treats its employees well can expect its employees to treat their internal and external customers well, thus the company will be successful.

One of the ways Federal Express has lived up to the "people first" pledge is by providing top-notch training to all of its 100,000+ employees. When Federal Express became the first service company to win the Malcolm Baldrige

National Quality Award in 1990, its commitment to employee training was cited as a major plus. This commitment has created one of the most professional and knowledgeable work forces in corporate America.

Federal Express established the Quality Academy in 1991 to design corporate quality courses, ensure consistent instruction and consult with various employee groups regarding quality educational topics. The Quality Academy offers numerous methods to support its training efforts and its support for quality improvement.

Federal Express established the Quality Academy in 1991 to design corporate quality courses.

Satellite Training

Using the Federal Express television network, employees may take courses such as *Benchmarking* and *Fast Cycle*. This medium allows employees to take a just-in-time program at their work site in a short period of time. These courses usually take an hour-and-a-half and are normally offered to management.

Multimedia

Federal Express offers its basic six-hour quality course titled *The Journey Toward Quality* on its interactive video network. This network consists of 1,200 work stations at more than 700 locations. The corporate mainframe links each work station. Because of this link, the Quality Academy can track module test scores, pass rate sand time on the machine. The interactive medium also provides a great cost savings to the company because it involves no travel costs or trainer salaries. Federal Express has found that multimedia can compress training time by 50 percent when compared to traditional instruction.

Self-Paced Instruction

The Quality Academy offers more than 2,000 course titles through self-paced instruction. Partnering with National Education Training Group, the Quality Academy offers video/workbook course titles such as: *Reengineering, Empowerment, Quality Improvement* and *Team Building*. In addition to quality programs, we offer leadership, management, career development, literacy, computer training, customer service and sales courses.

These programs are just a toll-free phone call away. Employees select a course from a catalog, and shipment occurs the next day at the employee work site via Federal Express, of course. Many courses are offered in multiple foreign languages.

Computer-Based Instruction

The Quality Academy uses the QUEST 2000 system to deliver quality programs to its customers. QUEST 2000 is an internal, computer-based program linked to the Federal Express mainframe. The Quality Academy uses it as a testing and tracking tool.

In the future, many internally developed quality courses will require employees to pass a competency test within 30 days of class completion in order

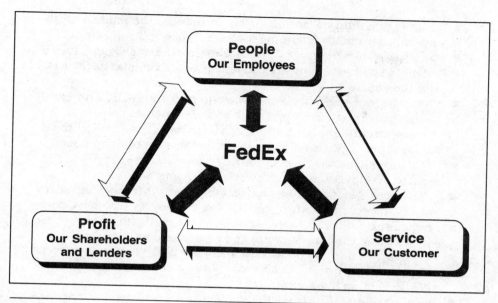

Figure 1.

to receive course credit. The QUEST 2000 system will deliver the test, which can be taken at the employee's local computer terminal.

Competency testing for Quality Academy courses will guarantee that student knowledge stays consistent throughout the company. This method also will ensure active vs. passive student involvement.

Competency tests for selected quality courses are computer-assisted, open-book and timed. They consist of 25 multiple-choice questions that are randomly accessed from a pool of 50 questions. The courses have a 90-percent pass rate for credit, with unlimited chances to test. QUEST 2000 also allows the Quality Academy to conduct corporatewide surveys on-line. In addition to the QUEST system, the Quality Academy broadcasts monthly information to more than 100 quality professionals worldwide using electronic mail.

Stand-up Instruction

For courses requiring more in-depth training, the Quality Academy provides scheduled classroom instruction at its corporate headquarters or dedicated regional programs in the following courses:

- *Blueprint for Systematic Quality* provides management with planning techniques using the seven Baldrige categories as the primary focus.
- *Quality Principles and Applications* provides the basics for understanding the quality philosophy at Federal Express.
- *Quality Action Teams Revised* analyzes work-group problem-solving methods.

- *Strategic Quality Planning Tools* introduces the student to the seven basic quality-planning tools, their use and application.
- *Workshop for Practical Applications* teaches managers quality-planning techniques, using real operational examples as the basis for the course.
- *Benchmarking* teaches employees how to internally and externally benchmark best practices and incorporate enhanced processes into their organizations. The Federal Express satellite television network also offers a shortened version of this program.
- *Measurement and Process Control* teaches statistical process control to employees in a nonthreatening manner.
- *Advanced Measurement and Process Control* teaches advanced statistical process control concepts to employees who have completed the basic course, possess advanced math skills and whose jobs require them to measure and report productivity data.
- *Leading Teams* introduces to the potential team leader techniques that will assist in accomplishing group tasks and fostering positive group dynamics.
- *Facilitation Skills* assists the student in learning classroom and/or quality action team facilitation skills.

All Quality Academy instructor-led courses occur on a quarterly basis. Employees can register for these courses by using an automated system known as Electronic System Employee Enrollment. The Quality Academy can track registration, class size and student cancellations using this system. It also displays course descriptions, prerequisites, course times, locations and special instructions.

Another on-line system called System Managing and Reporting Training allows each division within the company to set its own required course curriculum and monitor compliance. Both systems are linked to the mainframe in Memphis, Tennessee, and can be accessed at Federal Express locations.

Other Educational Efforts

The biannual Quality Academy lecture series brings in a well-known speaker in the field of quality, human resources or training to address Federal Express employees.

For those divisions in the company that wish to teach their own quality courses, the Quality Academy offers train-the-trainer programs for all of its courses.

The Quality Academy also responds to individual department and divisional needs by providing internal consulting and research services related to specific quality educational needs.

Benchmarking

Another way we ensure success in the quality-training effort is through benchmarking. Our goal is to benchmark with 20 companies per year regarding courses offered, new training breakthroughs and quality organizational structure.

For those divisions in the company that wish to teach their own quality courses, the Quality Academy offers train-the-trainer programs for all of its courses.

The mission of the Quality Academy is to provide direction for the corporation's quality education effort by:

- Recommending, implementing and maintaining the corporation's quality curriculum,
- Offering worldwide, state-of-the-art consulting, research and instructional services related to quality education that will enhance the quality-improvement process.

The Quality Academy believes in taking a cafeteria approach to quality-training efforts. We believe this approach allows divisions the opportunity to select training that is specific to their diverse work groups and their individual needs. The Quality Academy also recognizes that employees learn in different ways. We believe that by offering training media such as multimedia, classroom instruction, self-paced learning, computer-based training and satellite courses, we can be very flexible in our approach to employee quality-training needs.

We are confident that the Federal Express approach to quality training will continue to support the corporation in its goal of providing outstanding service 100 percent of the time. By creating numerous avenues for employees to receive training, the Quality Academy strives to communicate the quality message and, in turn, ensures that each employee has received the appropriate quality tools to promote 100-percent customer satisfaction. In 1990, Federal Express became the first service company to win the Baldrige Award. In 1994, Federal Express was awarded ISO 9001 certification, the most comprehensive of the ISO 9000 standards. We believe our methods work.

Bill Wilson is the manager of the Quality Academy at Federal Express. He has been in management for 13 years and has managed in both staff and operation units.

Guerrilla Learning: Continuous Education on a Tight Budget

Theodore B. Kinni

There are many ways to get training underway in small and medium-sized organizations. Even when the training budget is small, it is vital that training be ongoing. This article describes how to make sure that happens.

Once upon a time we went to school, and afterward, diploma in hand, we went to work. First we learned, then we worked, and rarely the twain did meet. No more. Today there is a widespread understanding that success depends on continuous, lifelong learning. Further, individual learning is not enough; companies must also learn.

The "learning organization," best described by Peter Senge in his book, *The Fifth Discipline*, is a place where capabilities are continuously expanded, new ways of thinking are nurtured, assumptions are constantly challenged, people learn together, and collective aspiration is set free. The result is a smart company—a creative force in its industry, a fast responder to innovation, and an embracer of change as the only external constant that can be depended upon.

The paragons of the corporate world have adopted the vision of a learning organization with a vengeance. The intensity of their commitment is directly reflected in their investment in workforce education. Last year, for instance, the American Society for Training & Development, Alexandria, Va., estimated that corporate training budgets had topped $30 billion annually. "There have been some studies done that show companies are investing 2.5% to 4% of their payrolls in training," says Jack Zenger, president of the Times Mirror Training Cos. and cofounder of Zenger-Miller Inc. "Certainly, that is higher than average, but that is what the best are doing."

Small businesses must also support their superstructures with organization-wide learning. Although establishing their own in-house university like Motorola or providing instant start-up financing for every new employee idea

---

like 3M may be out of the question, employee training and education must nevertheless become a strategic priority. The question is: How can this priority be pursued effectively and cost-efficiently? Happily, there are a number of viable options for the smaller enterprise.

CEO networks: A commitment to continuous learning, like every other corporate value, starts at the top. The leader as learner is a primary tenet of most leadership-development theories and is well illustrated by small-business leaders such as Jennifer Closshey, president of Plant City, Fla.-based Crystals International Inc. She devotes 10% of her time and resources to learning, calling education a "never-ending process" (see "The Empowered Workforce," IW, Sept. 19, Page 37).

CEO networks and semiformal gatherings of local business leaders are a good way to expose what Dr. Dan Tobin, author of *Re-Educating the Corporation* (Oliver Wight), calls unconscious ignorance. "One of the biggest challenges small-business leaders face is uncovering their areas of unconscious ignorance," says the Framingham, Mass.-based consultant. "Before you can learn, you must first figure out what you don't know and what you need to know."

Since 1986 Oklahoma's Tulsa-based Meridian Technological Center's Management Development Group has been hosting a CEO network consisting of the heads of eight local manufacturing companies every six weeks. "The thrust is to provide those who participate with a safe environment to share peer to peer," explains Meridian's Kristi Treadwell. No direct competitors participate in the group, which meets for two hours including lunch to discuss issues and receive training in specific areas of their own choosing.

Meridian's CEO network also supports other educational activities. Twice a year the CEOs choose noted business speakers, such as Steven Covey and Joel Barker, for engagements at the center. They each commit ahead of time to a minimum number of seats, thus underwriting the cost. By acting together, they gain access to resources that might otherwise be out of reach.

Business/education partnerships: The small business may not be able to afford an in-house university, but it can almost always have one in-town. Colleges and universities, especially community colleges, have jumped into the corporate-training market in a big way in recent years, and they offer substantial savings versus the cost of developing in-house training programs. In fact, local educational institutions often offer the prepackaged training programs of consulting firms well under the direct purchase cost.

"We have over 450 educational institutions offering our 'Frontline Leadership' and 'Working' programs to the business community," explains Leo Presley of Zenger-Miller's Education & Economic Development Div. "Generally speaking, the cost of getting our training from them is anywhere from 20% to 50% cheaper than doing it on our own." Why? Community colleges do not operate under the same pricing constraints as private firms, and, because the same training can be offered to many different companies, economies of scale apply.

A commitment to continuous learning, like every other corporate value, starts at the top.

Tulsa-based Centrifugal Casting Machine Co. Inc. has used a local educational consortium called Quest to help train its workforce. "They put together four or five small companies," says Tom McKee, president and owner, "and gave Zenger-Miller courses to all of us at the same time. We got several benefits: cost reductions based on the number of people enrolled and interaction with people from other companies."

What should small companies look for in a partnership with local educators? Mr. Presley offers the following tips:

- *Look for an institution with a dedicated technical-training center—a strong indicator of commitment to workforce education.*
- *Expect a professional approach and a soft-sell—all consultations should focus on company needs.*
- *Look for a staff with a strong business background—traditional academics don't always translate well to workforce training.*
- *Check how pricing is fixed—a cost-recovery basis is the usual standard for public institutions and offers the best value.*
- *Beware of brand loyalty—training should be needs-driven, not product-driven.*

Customer/supplier training.   Perhaps the most common low-cost training, especially among manufacturers, is that provided by a small business' customers and suppliers. "Work with larger customers," urges Dr. Tobin. They "will respond to suppliers who ask them for help. In California, for example, a group of prime contractors in the aerospace industry put together a supplier-improvement program that includes training in TQM, SPC, JIT, etc. It may take some research to find these programs, but it is worth the effort."

The growing concern with supplier quality can prove a boon to smaller vendors. At Tennant Co. in Minneapolis, for instance, conferences, seminars, and other meetings with suppliers are regularly scheduled. The company sends its own engineers to suppliers' plants and offers quality-control-process training. In *Managing Supplier Quality* (Monochrome Press), company officials explain: "Training allows us to work more closely with suppliers. Also, it's often a help to small companies. One of our Wisconsin suppliers has sent dozens of people to Minneapolis for training; the company is too small to have a training staff, and they like the training we provide."

Elsag Inc.'s Bailey Controls Co., Wickliffe, Ohio, offers its primary suppliers help with their ISO 9000 registration efforts. Bailey's in-house auditors conduct executive overviews and perform detailed audits of quality systems and manuals. "The cost," explains Bailey's QA Director Ed Mahoney, "is usually offset by the savings on the ongoing quality audits we would otherwise have to perform."

Expecting customers to foot the entire training bill is, however, unrealistic. "Because of budgetary constraints, it is increasingly more difficult to continue to train suppliers," cautions Mr. Mahoney. "This kind of help is restricted to the strategic suppliers with whom we need to build long-term relationships, and that list gets smaller and smaller as our procurement-quality efforts continue."

The growing concern with supplier quality can prove a boon to smaller vendors.

Internal expertise: There is a rich and often overlooked source of expert knowledge readily available for training purposes in every company—employees themselves. The same skills employees are taught in empowerment efforts and team implementations can help them become effective trainers. "There is already a lot of knowledge and skills in companies that are not being used," maintains Dr. Tobin. "Use internal resources whenever possible."

The idea that employees can make effective trainers is not unproven. Westborough, Mass.-based Web Industries taps employees from all levels of the organization to help teach the company's 20-hour new-employee-orientation course. Front-line customer-service representatives, machine operators, and maintenance employees, as well as plant and general management, teach the one-hour modules.

In addition to bringing practice to bear on theory, conducting training helps crystalize the teacher's skills. "We try to get everyone involved in teaching," President Donald Romine explained at Goal/QPC's 1993 annual conference. "'As they teach others, using outlines we provide, they are also teaching themselves."

At Winchester, Va.-based American Woodmark Corp., level-to-level training was utilized to ensure that everyone in the company was working from the same script. In *The Fifth Discipline Fieldbook* (Doubleday), President Bill Brandt describes how he personally scripted four two-hour training modules used to impart the core values of the organization.

After review, critique, and rewrite sessions, Mr. Brandt taught those courses to the senior-management team, who, in turn, taught them to their respective teams and so on down the organizational chart. As the lessons moved level-to-level, the process of learning, practicing, and teaching resulted in increased buy-in and greater competency at all levels.

Other methods.   Training assessments are available from many of the more than 30 state-based Manufacturing Technology Centers.

Other organizations—such as Manpower Inc., a Milwaukee-based temporary-help firm, which recently announced its successful registration to the ISO 9000 quality standards—are also looking for opportunities to develop training programs in partnership with local businesses.

Simple ideas can also pay big dividends. Web Industries, for example, uses reading groups to stimulate creative thinking and explore new ideas. In addition to offering inexpensive access to expert thinking, books serve as a neutral forum for what otherwise might be controversial dialogues. *Workforce Training News* reports that Appleton, Wis.-based AAL Capital Management Corp. has gone so far as to start a formal "Business Book of the Month Club," which caters a discussion luncheon four weeks after each book is assigned. Employees who read all 12 books each year receive $50 gift certificates to a local bookstore and are entered in a drawing for a getaway weekend.

No matter what size the budget, companies that invest wisely in the education and training of employees are going to reap the largest returns.

Theodore B. Kinni is a correspondent for Industry Week *Magazine.*

There is a rich and often overlooked source of expert knowledge readily available for training purposes in every company—employees themselves.

Training for Effective Continuous Quality Improvement

John C. Anderson, Kevin Dooley,
and Manus Rungtusanatham

This article reviews the state of training in U.S. businesses. It is especially valuable for its breakdown of topics covered in training and the main objectives for each of these areas.

For architects of training and educational programs in continuous quality improvement, these are challenging times. On one hand, the fundamental nature of work is changing; a recent study by McKinsey & Company's Amsterdam office estimated that, by the year 2000, 70% of all jobs in Europe will require cerebral skills rather than manual ones. (In the United States, the figure is expected to be 80%.)[1] On the other hand, there have been substantial changes in the way employees must learn to manage and improve their work. Robert Hayes, Steven Wheelwright, and Kim Clark note in their book *Dynamic Manufacturing* that long-term success for an organization is not the same as simple survival; success requires developing an organization that builds and continually renews its competitiveness in all functions.[2]

An article in *FORTUNE* magazine suggests that the most successful corporation of the 1990s will be the "learning organization," in which knowledge is widespread.[3] It will no longer be sufficient for management solely to do the learning for the organization.[4] Only those who learn can identify and pursue opportunities for continuous quality improvement.

The need for learning has not gone unnoticed by global and domestic industries. Effective design and delivery of training and education, however, requires careful assessment and planning. This article explores the content of the training and education needed for continuous improvement, draws conclusions from a study of training and education programs, and suggests a structure that can serve as a starting point.

What Issues Should Be Covered?

Training and education should provide incoming employees with an orientation to the organization and give them the skills needed to fulfill their responsibilities. In addition to training in particular work tasks, areas such as statistical process control (SPC), problem solving, decision making, team building, communication, and leadership have become common components of training programs. W. Edwards Deming advocated developing employee proficiency in a number of knowledge elements, including systems, theory, theory of variation, theory of knowledge, and psychology.[5] Instruction in these knowledge elements, collectively referred to by Deming as the concept of profound knowledge, should supplement the domain-specific skills needed for efficient task execution. An understanding of and ability to apply the elements of profound knowledge, Deming argues, is imperative to the adoption of his 14 points. John C. Anderson, Kevin J. Dooley, and Susan A. Misterek's parallel synthesis of Deming's profound knowledge elements resulted in a similar taxonomy that incorporates the knowledge areas of cognitive psychology, organizational theory and behavior, statistical theory, and systems theory.[6] Not only is a collective knowledge of these four areas crucial to embracing Deming's 14 points, it represents the "know-how" needed to nurture an organization's efforts in continuously improving its processes, products, and services.

Two kinds of knowledge—domain and nondomain—play an important role in organizational improvement. Domain knowledge is the knowledge of how to conduct specific work-related tasks. This kind of knowledge has historically been the backbone of employee training, enabling employees to complete their task responsibilities accurately. The training involved with domain knowledge, while perhaps following uniform approaches, is often unique to the particular needs and environment involved. Nondomain knowledge, on the other hand, is the requisite knowledge that enables ongoing learning and continuous improvement. This is the area that creates the greatest challenge and opportunity.

Two kinds of knowledge—domain and nondomain—play an important role in organizational improvement.

Observations of Current Practice

A recent unpublished study, by the authors, of current practice in training in the requisite knowledge areas for continuous quality improvement leads to five observations:

1. *More organizations are providing training and education related to quality improvement.* Despite depressing economic conditions in the United States, many organizations have not cut back expenditures in employee training and education. Between 1988 and 1991, U.S. organizations committed an average of $40 billion annually to formal employee training. While the average dollar expenditure earmarked for training has remained relatively stable, noticeable differences in both the recipients and areas of

emphasis of such formal training have become apparent. For example, 47% more firms reported providing quality improvement training in 1991 than in 1988. At Motorola, 40% of an approximately $120 million training budget is devoted to quality improvement training efforts. In the manufacturing facility of another large, high-technology organization, each employee participated in 58 hours of quality-related training in 1991.[7]

2. *Current employee training and education efforts place strong emphasis on statistical topics.* Organizations have been enticed by the methodological tools of quality improvement. Training in such statistical topics as SPC, design of experiments, reliability, and, to some extent, the concept of six sigma appears to have widespread popularity. Training employees in acceptance sampling, once a core quality control course, has been minimized.

Current employee training in quality improvement at Motorola, for example, centers on understanding six sigma.[8] Issues such as the universal applicability of six sigma; the tools, steps, and calculations used to achieve it; selection of products for analysis; and questions developed to determine customer requirements are core to this key area. Another example is a midsize division of a technological company, with approximately 700 employees, that has developed plans to expose all of its employees to either SPC or continuous process improvement. Its SPC course encompasses the seven quality control tools, process capability, team dynamics, and Deming's 14 points and is targeted at all engineers in the organization. The continuous process improvement course is directed toward nonengineers throughout the organization but also covers the seven quality control tools and several of the "new" quality control planning tools that have an emphasis on team projects.

There is some indication of increasing interest in the more advanced statistical tools of experimental design and Taguchi Methods, especially in technological firms. In fact, firms that emphasize design and assembly, rather than fabrication, seem to be focusing attention more on design of experiments than SPC. Coverage of these statistical topics, however, tends to address application, not theory. While this emphasis on application might fulfill an immediate need for organizationwide immersion into using control charts or designing experiments for quality improvement, it deprives employees of a better understanding of why these statistical methods are useful and how powerful they can be in the pursuit of continuous quality improvement.

3. *Planning and design tools receive increased attention under current employee training and education efforts.* Observational findings show expanded coverage of the seven planning tools (including affinity diagrams and matrix diagrams), quality function deployment, strategic planning (hoshin planning), and design for manufacturability (including assembly, testability, and maintainability). This trend parallels the increasing emphasis on planning and design within organizations, especially with respect to total quality efforts. Such tools generally tend to be systems anal-

ysis methods that help organize and analyze complex systems by breaking them down into their constituent components.

While systems thinking might pervade some individual instructors and their course content, formal training in systems thinking, such as soft systems and causal loop diagrams, rarely occurs. As with the case of statistical topics, the benefits derived from training employees in systems theory should outweigh the cost, especially if the knowledge of systems theory can be taught through actual application.

4. *Coverage of the requisite knowledge areas of organization theory and behavior and cognitive psychology appears to be scattered.* While employee training in the methods and tools affiliated with statistical theory and systems theory has only recently taken a strong foothold, the requisite area of organization theory and behavior infiltrated the practice of employee training much earlier. This infiltration began in the 1950s as organizations realized that the promotion of employees to supervisory positions necessitated training in areas such as leadership and delegation. Given the wealth of knowledge accumulated in this requisite area, however, its coverage in current employee training activities is limited. Coverage tends to be on team dynamics and the organizational change process, including leadership and interpersonal skills. Such training, while extremely valuable in supporting organizational behavior issues, does not provide a comprehensive, in-depth treatment of the relevant knowledge in this area. Furthermore, as in the requisite areas of statistical theory and systems theory, training is typically focused on implementation. Other areas of organization theory and behavior—such as goal setting, rewards systems, and motivation—receive little attention, aside from the unilateral, common-sense coverage by quality leaders.

By far, the area with the least coverage is the requisite area of cognitive psychology. Some organizations, such as the manufacturing facility alluded to earlier, offer experimental design courses that discuss issues in cognition, such as the bias of the experimenter, belief in small sample sizes, and causality vs. correlation, but overall, coverage is generally limited. Some emphasis is placed on demonstrating to employees how knowledge is generated via the scientific method, and models such as the plan-do-study-act cycle and the quality journal are taught. Informal observations indicate a lack of integration of the problem-solving methodology with the rest of the training material. In fact, problem solving tends to be taught as a stand-alone topic with little carry over as employees move from one training session to another.

5. *A comprehensive, integrated employee training and education program is needed to develop employee proficiency in the requisite knowledge areas.* Current practices in employee training and education can and should be strengthened to aid the pursuit of continuous quality improvement. Particularly, comprehensive and well-integrated employee training efforts are needed so that skills and knowledge are not developed in pockets and adequate attention is dedicated equally to all four requisite knowl-

Current practices in employee training and education can and should be strengthened to aid the pursuit of continuous quality improvement.

Table 1.   **Requisite Knowledge for Continuous Improvement:
            Cognitive Psychology**

Concept	Learning Objective
Perception	Describe the process of perception and frame of reference and productively change or use alternative perceptual models.
Individual motivation	Identify controllable factors and deal effectively with uncontrollable factors affecting personal or human motivation.
Cognitive constraints	Recognize and deal effectively with human constraints to turn them from hidden limitations into informative structures, with judicious selection of analysis and/or intuition.
Bias or judgment	Identify, predict, and overcome bias and judgment error.
Bounded rationality	Discuss the advantages and disadvantages of bounded rationality and use tools and methods to overcome its limitations.
Problem finding	Engage in problem finding and choose correct models and measurement to discover problems and opportunities for improvement.
Problem formulation	Employ intuition and conscious thought in the formulation of problems and opportunities involved in process improvement.
Problem representation	Use alternative methods of problem representation for effective analysis and action of process improvement.
Lines of reasoning	Choose and deploy various lines of reasoning, including classification tools, cause-and-effect reasoning, systems representations, and creative methods.
Learning and knowledge	Recognize the importance of learning and knowledge in quality and continuous improvement and engage in continuous learning in daily work.
Scientific method	Apply the scientific method in quality and continuous improvement and use the plan-do-study-act cycle in the course of personal daily work.

edge areas. Employee training and education initiatives must be designed to capitalize on the base theory available in each area. They must go beyond the training goal of creating awareness and procedural capability to the educational goal of a more fundamental understanding of what is needed for continuous quality improvement in the learning organization.

Improving Employee Training and Education Programs

As a first step toward improving employee training programs, it is useful to recognize the unique, yet complementary, contributions that each requisite knowledge area makes to the pursuit of continuous quality improvement.

Table 2. **Requisite Knowledge for Continuous Improvement: Organizational Behavior**

Concept	Learning Objective
Quality strategy	Describe the strategic effect of quality and continuous improvement on the organization.
Economics of quality	Identify and measure cost of quality and its effect on the performance of the organization.
Quality culture and values	Specify and evaluate the characteristics of the organization's culture and encourage verbal and written communication behaviors that nurture a culture for quality.
Organizational reward systems	Describe organizational reward systems and effectively conduct continuous improvement efforts within these systems.
Organizational change	Promote organizational change and remove the barriers to its implementation.
Quality leadership	Describe the role of leadership in quality and continuous improvement and communicate expectations regarding this role.
Organization for quality	Describe the organization for quality in terms of resources, capabilities, and relationships.
Situational leadership	Describe and choose leadership styles to address contingencies in the system.
Group process	Describe and effectively participate in the prescribed team approach to process improvement for the organization.
Effective communication	Describe the communication process and its barriers and listen, verbalize, and energize that process.
Work group constraints	Recognize group constraints and effectively employ methodology and tools to overcome these constraints.
Organizational motivation	Identify and overcome functional and dysfunctional group behaviors that affect group motivation and performance.

Cognitive psychology examines how individuals identify, think about, and resolve issues and problems. Organizational theory and behavior examines how people behave individually and in groups within organizations and how organizations as entities behave among themselves. Systems theory deals with how processes and organizations should be structured and viewed in terms of their purposes, elemental parts, and functional interactions among these parts. Statistical theory deals with how variation or uncertainty in data and information should be handled. The knowledge areas of cognitive psychology and organizational theory and behavior help people deal effectively with themselves, others, and their organizations for continuous quality improvement. Statistical theory and systems theory offer logical and analytical

Table 3. **Requisite Knowledge for Continuous Improvement: Statistics**

Concept	Learning Objective
Common and special causes	Categorize sources of process variation as common or special causes using control charts and other diagnostic methods.
Analytical and enumerative studies	Identify whether a specific statistical study calls for an analytical or enumerative statistical method.
Probability	Determine objective probabilities and translate subjective statements of belief into probability and vice versa.
Operational definition	Write operational definitions for any quality characteristic of interest.
Sampling strategy	Design a sampling strategy and quantify the relative effect of sampling strategies on uncertainty in decision making.
Data collection	Design and conduct effective process data collection.
Data analysis	Explain tendencies, patterns, and trends in data, using simple exploratory statistical tools (histograms, Pareto charts, run charts, etc.).
Generalizing	Explain the assumptions behind these simple exploratory tools and the effect of these assumptions.
Statistical hypothesis	Translate a problem into a specific hypothesis.
Statistical hypothesis test	Formulate a plan of action given a statistical hypothesis.
Designed experiments	Specify a designed experiment that maximizes information in a minimum number of tests, given a hypothesis and learning objectives, and analyze and summarize subsequent data.
Statistical control and statistical capability	Specify and contrast the purpose, design, assumptions, and use of control limits vs. design specification limits.
Dependence and independence	Demonstrate, using examples, the difference between dependence and independence.
Causation and correlation	Demonstrate, using examples, the difference between causation and correlation and differentiate the two in a process.

structures to appropriately guide and conduct continuous quality improvements in processes, products, and services.

While requisite knowledge is useful and research foundations are informative, it is also important to identify clearly the specific concepts within each area and outline learning objectives for these concepts. The identification of relevant concepts and specification of learning objectives provide guideposts for both the design and evaluation of employee training and education initiatives. Tables 1, 2, 3, and 4 provide a list of concepts involved in each requisite knowledge area. This identification is a starting point for introspection, not a normative statement of what defines each requisite knowledge area. Its primary purpose is to illustrate—to provide a provocative set of concepts for design and evaluation. It is in no way intended to be a topical listing for

Table 4. **Requisite Knowledge for Continuous Improvement: Systems**

Concept	Learning Objective
Systems thinking	Define problems and opportunities in the context of a system/process view.
Systems elements	Identify inputs, outputs, customers, suppliers, resources, and environment for any system under different levels of scope and complexity.
System hierarchy	Visualize relevant levels of systems involved in continuous process improvement and choose the most appropriate level for analysis and action.
System functionality	Define functional, as opposed to causal, relationships and specifically define structures and functions within a system under different levels of scope and complexity.
Causal reasoning	Demonstrate causal thinking involving complex interactions of time and space (hierarchy) and demonstrate effective use of many different methods that enable causal thinking and creativity.
Multiple causation	Identify multiple causes, as opposed to a single cause, of system behavior.
Complexity	Identify requisite variety, as opposed to undue complication, and visualize systems with reduced complexity.
Feedback	Design conceptual feedback mechanisms within a system.
Socio-technical systems	Specify whether a problem or issue is primarily a social, technical, or socio-technical interaction.
Interaction	Identify when interactions are present in a system and make appropriate decisions in light of interactions.
System archetypes	Demonstrate interactions using examples of different system archetypes and apply these archetypes in continuous improvement efforts.

immediate inclusion within curriculum; to do so would contradict the need for thoughtful, holistic, and well-integrated design of training initiatives for continuous quality improvement.

Each concept is complemented with a learning objectives statement, which forces instructors to make the expected behavior an explicit result of the learning that takes place.[9] The use of learning objectives has proven to be an effective tool in design and development programs at all educational levels and has increasingly been employed in adult education. The learning objectives shown in the tables have been written in the form of an observable action, as prescribed by Benjamin Bloom.[10] Like the concepts themselves, the learning objectives provide a starting point for the design and evaluation of training and education initiatives for the pursuit of continuous quality improvement.

Emphasis on Nondomain Knowledge Is Increasing

Despite up-and-down economic conditions in the United States, it is encouraging to see that investments in employee training and education have remained relatively stable over the years. While domain-specific training efforts remain a major theme, training and educational programs related to nondomain knowledge and skills are increasingly emphasized for the pursuit of continuous improvement. This trend should continue, based on the attention given to the development of the learning organization and the necessity of investing in organizational knowledge as a new form of human capital.[11]

The extent of each of the four areas of requisite knowledge varies, and the nature of their inclusion in training errs on the side of application, as opposed to fundamental understanding. Significant opportunities exist to improve both the content and delivery of employee training in the requisite knowledge areas. The theoretical concepts identified for each area and the specific learning objectives for these concepts should be evaluated, not to the extent that they are normative, but rather as a starting point for organizations in developing training and education efforts that are applicable to their unique settings.

References

1. McKinsey & Company, quote from an unpublished study, McKinsey Amsterdam Office, 1986.
2. Robert Hayes, Steven Wheelwright, and Kim Clark, *Dynamic Manufacturing* (New York, NY: Free Press, 1988).
3. T. A. Stewart, "Brainpower," *FORTUNE*, June 3, 1991, pp. 44–62.
4. Peter Senge, *The Fifth Discipline: The Art and Practice of the Learning Organization* (New York, NY: Doubleday, 1990).
5. W. Edwards Deming, comments from a speech given at the Institute of Management Sciences in Osaka, Japan, on July 1989. Also see W. Edwards Deming, "A System of Profound Knowledge," *ActionLine*, August 1990, pp. 20–26.
6. John C. Anderson, Kevin J. Dooley, and S. A. Misterek, "The Role of Profound Knowledge in the Continual Improvement of Quality," *Human Systems Management*, vol. 10, no. 4, pp. 243–259.
7. Kheki R. Bhote, "Motorola's Long March to the Malcolm Baldrige National Quality Award," *National Productivity Review*, Autumn 1989, pp. 365–375.
8. Ibid.
9. B. S. Bloom, G. F. Madaus, and J. T. Hastings, *Evaluation to Improve Learning* (New York, NY: McGraw-Hill Book Company, 1981).
10. B. S. Bloom, *Taxonomy of Educational Objectives: The Classification of Educational Goals—Handbook I: Cognitive Domain* (New York, NY: David McKay Company, Inc., 1956).
11. M. Zeleny, "Knowledge as a New Form of Capital—Part 1: Division and Reintegration of Knowledge," *Human Systems Management*, vol. 8, no. 1, pp. 45–58.

John C. Anderson is an associate professor of operations management at the University of Minnesota in Minneapolis. He received a doctorate in production operations management from the University of Minnesota in Minneapolis. Kevin Dooley is an associate professor of industrial engineering at the University of Minnesota in Minneapolis. He received a doctorate in mechanical engineering from the University of Illinois in Urbana-Champaign. Manus Rungtusanatham is a doctoral candidate at the University of Minnesota in Minneapolis. He received a bachelor's degree in business administration from Birmingham-Southern College in Alabama.

Challenges to Implementing Self-Managing Teams

Henry P. Sims Jr. and Charles C. Manz

These authors of SuperLeadership *and* Business Without Bosses *explain in detail the problems companies encounter in implementing teams, especially self-managed teams, and how to deal with these problems. This is a practical and informative piece by two people who have been there.*

There seems to be a great deal more written about the benefits and advantages of teams, than is written about the problems and challenges they raise, especially during the implementation phase. We have been fortunate to have had an inside look at teams in a variety of workplaces, and a diverse set of companies. We have also seen the difficulties and challenges created by these work systems, which, after all, are created by and for imperfect human beings. Here, we realistically summarize the challenges that teams must deal with. We will also include some prescriptions that emerged from the lessons we uncovered in the various team systems (Figure 1).

Challenges to implementing self-managed teams...

Many expect too much too soon...

...Things often get worse before they get better

.......Managers/supervisors sense of power and control is threatened

.........Some employees initially feel like losers

............Need expanded technical and behavioral skills

.........The fallacy of sink or swim implementations

......Integration of teams with total quality management

...Greenfield sites easer than retrofit changes

Teams are difficult to diffuse throughout the organization

Implementing self-managing teams

Start here **X**

Figure 1.

Challenges to Implementing Successful Self-Managing Teams

Many expect too much too soon   Perhaps the notion of teams is now achieving fad status. From our viewpoint, a new approach to management becomes a fad when managers expect easy implementation, and immediate results.

Actually, the view of some managers can be characterized as "expecting too much, too soon." For example, at IDS Corporation executives expected it would take about 3½ months to create the design necessary for team implementation. It actually took 8½ months.

Fortunately, in the IDS story, management had the patience and the staying power to absorb the frustration of this extended planning period. Their patience paid off with a very successful start-up. In fact, 8 months is much more typical than 3 months for team design.

We have encountered managers who severely underestimate the effort necessary to launch teams successfully. Their attitude seems to be *Decide it . . . say it . . . and it will be done!* They are setting up their organizations for failure.

Sometimes, the initial baseline when launching a team is less productive than the traditional organizational system it replaces.

Things sometimes get worse before they get better   Like any new innovation, teams follow a learning curve. Sometimes, the initial baseline when launching a team is less productive than the traditional organizational system it replaces. In practical terms, it is not unusual for teams to suffer short term reductions in effectiveness as they start up. Some consultants believe that team productivity will initially decrease, and may take a year to regain former levels. Significant increases in productivity may not become evident for almost 18 months.

Why the falloff in effectiveness? This falloff in effectiveness may occur as team members learn new behaviors, new responsibilities, and especially struggle to find the path for internal organization that works for them. Many employees have no real practical experience with self-management strategies such as self goal setting, self feed back, designing their own information system, etc.

Can this temporary falloff in productivity be eliminated, or, at least reduced? Some say yes and note that an appropriate lead time for planning the changeover to teams is necessary. But more importantly, intensive up-front training can be an important vehicle in which team members learn to adjust and succeed with the new system. In the Lake Superior Paper Company case (reported later here) they not only provided training, but *seeded* their teams with workers experienced with *state of the art* technology. (See box).

Testing, testing: Is this for real? Management should be aware that employees will sometimes *test the system* to see if management really has moved to a self-management philosophy. The testing may show up as some employees occasionally make decisions that they know are contrary to management preferences, and then wait to see if *they step in* and revoke the decision making authority.

This is a critical time in any team implementation, because the naysayers will be saying "I told you so!", and management begins to feel lack of control and total organizational effectiveness seems to be threatened.

Our experience is that teams do go through a period where they test management, but rapidly move on to a higher level of trust and sense of responsibility. Once through this period, and confident of management's commitment/support, they are typically inclined to take on some of the challenges of improving quality and productivity that make a real difference to the bottom line.

Managers/Supervisors' Sense of Power and Control Is Threatened

Frequently, it's the middle managers and the supervisors who feel (at least at first) they are the big losers in a transition to team systems. This was a recurring theme in the stories we report in our book. In one sense, this fear is based on reality, since the raw numbers of managers and supervisors is typically reduced with the introduction of a team system. In fact, one of the typical sources of savings that derives from a team system is a *delayering* of management and supervisors.

Our experience is that teams do go through a period where they test management, but rapidly move on to a higher level of trust and sense of responsibility.

Well what is your commitment to us? When changing to teams, its critical to make a commitment to managers and supervisors that none will lose their job because of the team system. (However, not everyone will be guaranteed that they will be doing the same job or performing the same duties. Also, the commitment does not typically cover job loss due to declining economic factors.)

Typically, managers or supervisors who are *displaced* are either reassigned to more technical specialized positions, or covered over a longer period of time through normal attrition.

At Texas Instruments in Malaysia . . . In making the changeover to teams, the Texas Instruments Plant in Malaysia reassigned many former supervisors to training or technical troubleshooting responsibilities.

The important point, however, is that management needs to make an upfront commitment to managers and supervisors that no one will be out of a job because of the team system.

It was supposed to be my turn, wasn't it? A more insidious and difficult challenge is dealing with the *psychological* loss of control that is sometimes experienced by supervisors and middle managers. They have *grown up* under a system where the manager is a boss who gives orders, and employees carry out those orders. They have *served their time* as one who *follows* orders and now enjoy the satisfaction of *giving* orders. They find satisfaction through the power they exercise as the boss.

Most of all, these individuals just don't know how to behave in a team system. How can they get others to carry out their work, if it's no longer legitimate to give orders and instructions—if they can no longer discipline? All of a sudden, the world has turned upside down, and they are indeed frustrated and confused.

I'll show them! If left to themselves, some of these individuals can be a severe threat to the team system, mainly because:

- They might attempt to deny a team the opportunity to actually become self-managing . . .
- They reverse team decisions if they feel a mistake has been made, or, if they believe that team decisions are too self-serving . . .
- Or, perhaps more subtly, they quietly set out to sabotage a team launch. They look for team mistakes and errors, and pounce on these as definitive evidence that this team stuff will never work!

Can traditional supervisors be converted to team facilitator or coordinator? Clearly, this change requires both new attitudes and new behaviors. Many are incapable or unwilling to learn these new behaviors. Our experience is that the capability to make this transition is difficult to predict:

- We have seen the traditional *bull o' the woods* become the most ardent supporter of the team concept . . .
- We have seen others who are unable to make the transition, and were moved to more technical or specialized functions . . .

- We have seen some retire or quit rather than accommodate themselves to a team system. In a few cases, top management has asked a supervisor or manager to leave the organization, because they cannot adjust.

The important conclusion from all this is that middle managers and supervisors cannot be ignored when launching a team system. They have the power and capacity to severely retard or cause the transition to fail. They must become part of the solution, not part of the problem.

Training and orientation are a critical part of the process . . . Sometimes, training is almost exclusively focused on the teams themselves, and supervisors are left out. Supervisors and managers must be involved early with orientation, information sharing, and question and answer sessions. Mainly, they want answers to the question, *"What's going to happen to me?"*

Eventually, they must walk on their own . . . Managers and executives responsible for a transition to teams should prepare themselves for the inevitable: despite all the training and orientation, despite best efforts, supervisors will be anxious, and one can never totally satisfy supervisors in transition—their appetite for reassurance and support, some might call it hand holding, is insatiable. Their being upset is a part of the change and must be patiently endured and dealt with.

The important conclusion from all this is that middle managers and supervisors cannot be ignored when launching a team system.

Some High Status Employees Initially Feel Like Losers

Just like supervisors, some other employees also feel like losers. Who are the ones likely to feel this way? In our experience, we can generalize some characteristics of employees who are likely to have negative feelings about the change:

1. Employees who currently enjoy some privilege because of seniority may feel the loss of that privilege.

Teams tend to reward and value people more on the basis of performance and contribution, rather than seniority.

2. Employees who have achieved a special position such as specializing in a job with status derived from special knowledge or experience are more likely to feel loss of rank.

Special clerks in the transition at the IDS Corporation felt resentful because virtually every team member would be trained in their expertise. Their special niche based on expertise was no longer going to be special. Technicians *(techs)* in the Lake Superior paper mill start-up wanted to maintain their special status, and resented the team system.

3. No one should make the assumption that every employee or category of employee will embrace the team concept with equal, great enthusiasm.

LAKE SUPERIOR PAPER COMPANY: LESSONS FROM A START-UP . . .

In a major start-up effort using teams, Lake Superior Paper got some things right the first time, had to revise others, still kept refining others and continued on despite setbacks. What is atypical about the Lake Superior Paper story, is that it introduced, from the first day of operation, a system that was designed to evolve into team self-management. At that early stage, no one could predict whether the system would last.

Productivity issues . . . The mill's productivity was exceptional but self-managed teams were not the only success factor: Superior Paper had a highly automated continuous mill, at a greenfield site which had no history of traditional labor/management conflicts to overcome. *(Self-managed team systems can take five to eight years to overcome all their glitches. Superior Paper is now in its sixth year of operation.)*

Start-up When Lake Superior Paper opened its mill in 1987, it formed 20 self-managed teams to cover all mill operations. A vice president explained that not moving to self-management in this industry would have been an aberration; all of the ten most recently opened of Lake Superior's US paper mills using new technology have opted for this type of system. Clearly, self-managing teams were tremendously productive from a technical standpoint. However since most workers have never been introduced to this form of management before, progress in social behaviors was lower.

Manager's lament and fears . . . Some managers, for example, who were training workers to become better at self-managing worried that they were *managing themselves out of a job.* Top management tried to reassure them that another mill would be opened soon, but they protested that it wasn't fair that their reward for building an exceptional team was to start all over again with a new workforce in another area.

Technician's lament and fears . . . Technical specialists also questioned management's fairness. As more self-managed team workers completed training and were compensated through a *pay for knowledge* policy, salary gaps between technical and non-technical workers shrank. The *techs* objected to the pay-for-knowledge component of the self-managed system, which rewarded workers with weak skills and knowledge for completing training. They also protested when they were called upon to do tasks they considered below their status (responsibilities under the traditional system they most likely would have escaped).

Continued—

Lessons From a Start-up . . . (continued)

Worker's impatience for rapid progress . . . Other plant workers grew impatient. They thought management could achieve its goal of full-fledged self-management in less than five years and complained that progress was slow because meetings were called too frequently. In addition, many accused management of deliberately running a lean operation.

Still in all: the start up was a success . . . Despite these challenges, the workforce delivered: the start-up was a definite success. Among other reasons for success, training for a workforce, not yet influenced by traditional management is more efficient because it can be solely dedicated to learning, instead of unlearning and relearning. A year into the operation, the mill was described as the most successful start-up in the paper industry's history, churning out over a quarter of a million tons of paper annually.

The Picture in 1993

External economic restraints . . . Four years ago, Superior Paper suffered mild cutbacks as the paper industry faced keener competition from local and European enterprises that have grown capacities. Added to that, the company saw diminishing demand for the particular kind of paper it produces. Market conditions pushed the company into a downturn and a proposed addition to the plant was delayed.

Those who couldn't get along, moved along . . . The workforce has changed significantly from what it was.

- Dissatisfied technicians moved on. This category of workers is usually mobile and generally prefers seeking out new opportunities.
- Managers who remained found what top management had earlier tried to explain: the pace of development for full-fledged self-management was slower than originally anticipated.

An overall success   Jack Lavoy, Superior Paper's vice-president, reported that:

- Absenteeism at Superior Paper was 75 percent below the industry average, turnover 83 percent below, and critical machine efficiency rate was 86 percent (placing the company on the top 10 percent list in the industry).
- Superior Paper has stayed with, promoted, and endorsed the self-management system despite the economic downturn.

Continued—

Lessons From a Start-up . . . (continued)

More recently, *The New York Times* announced that Superior Paper opened a $76 million recycled pulp mill in Duluth.

(The original investigation of this story took place during the second year of business.)

Emphasis on individuality In the US, we have a strong political and personal tradition of individual freedom that, at times, run counter to the collective nature of teamwork. For both managerial and non-managerial employees, an emphasis on team values threatens not only their traditional views of work, it threatens their approach to life. As an interesting counterpoint, it is also difficult for many employees to adjust to the idea of working without a traditional boss or supervisor after so many years of dependence. We recently learned of a case where a large burly production worker, after learning about his company's move to SMTs, banged his fist on a table and demanded his right to have a boss to tell him what to do.

Distrust With a history of management-induced fads and poor management of industrial relations, some companies don't have sufficient credibility with first-line employees, especially unionized employees, to earn the trust needed to implement team processes. If management sees team development as an expense rather than an investment, and employees see teams as another attempt to co-opt employees to management's views, the shift to team values and work will likely fail.

It is not surprising that many stories of successful team efforts have come from threatened companies or industries, where workers and management were forced to confront and discard traditional distrust in favor of teams. In one General Motors assembly plant, traditionally independent quality control functions were turned over to production teams, only to have the decision reversed when quality problems persisted.

At a paper mill, teams were created after a lengthy collective bargaining process, only to result in the union representatives being voted out of power within a year of signing the agreement.

The big squeeze of middle management For managers, a shift to teams and to the corresponding flatter organizations reduces their opportunities for advancement in the traditional organizational hierarchy, if only because there is no longer much of a hierarchy. But there are economic factors, not just a movement to teams, that have threatened the career prospects and aspirations of many managers. Downsizing and delayering will continue whether teams are used or not.

Lack of empathy and understanding Management of self-managed teams requires the ability to listen, to change views, to empathize and to change basic behavior patterns.

Continued—

Lessons From a Start-up . . . (continued)

Without an adequate investment in the training and development of new social skills, team development will be retarded, or thwarted. In the GM case mentioned above, turning over the quality control responsibility to the production teams reduced quality; training was needed but not provided.

Managerial resistance Managers who have been trained to actively manage in a forceful, even threatening way, may not readily accept the concept of teams, based mostly on a combination of the four previous points. The change to a team approach results in a variety of disincentives to the traditional, hard-charger manager.

During the planning stage, it may be advisable to conduct an analysis to identify whether some employees have special stakes in the existing system that they may be reluctant to part with.

How should these sensitive employees be handled?   One way is to bluntly force the change upon them. The likely result will be resentful employees.

Sometimes, these employees leave the system, and other times they cause distress to the team implementation. Another approach is to involve them in the transition planning process, and attempt to deal with their concerns. Sometimes, their special status or pay might be *grandfathered* into the new system.

Most of all, it's important for management to realize that not all employees will see a transition to teams as a winning proposition, and these employees can cause considerable damage to the transition.

Need Expanded Technical and Behavioral Skills

Multi-tasking issues . . . Added responsibility and expanded autonomy means that both the technical and behavioral skill competencies of employees must be expended. One of the fundamental changes typically accompanying a team implementation is the notion that a team member becomes capable of most, if not all, of the tasks required of a team. Typically, task or technical oriented training is required to assure that team members develop these skills.

Group/team skills and issues . . . Perhaps more important and not as well understood is the idea that team members must also develop their individual and group self-leadership capabilities. This entails the development of new organizational, planning, interpersonal, and self-direction skills:

- They must learn how to set goals and interpret feedback systems . . .

- They must learn how to lead and participate in meetings, conflict resolution skills are a must . . .

- They must learn how to initiate problem solving on their own, rather than automatically shifting the burden to a now nonexisting supervisor.

Development of all of these behaviors requires training, since few employees have had this experience prior to their employment.

The Fallacy of *Sink or Swim* Implementations

Recently, we have heard of cases where organizations form teams by removing the supervisor, and making a grand pronouncement that the work-groups are now teams!—no training, no design, no organizational change strategy. Overnight, workgroups are magically transformed into teams. Sometimes this might work, but we see a high probability for failure.

The general logic behind an implementation strategy like this is that teams that are really self-managing will also be able to self-manager the implementation. The flaw in this logic is provided by the rubber band metaphor: a rubber band can absorb a limited amount of stress by stretching. However, too much, too soon, and the rubber band breaks. Self-managing teams can also break—they can fail.

Teams need to be trained in fundamental social processes.

Typically, this failure comes because teams are given total responsibility without resources to carry out the assignment. Resources include both technical and social knowledge and skills. Teams need to be trained in fundamental social processes like learning to lead a meeting, how to generate creativity, how to conduct a problem solving session, how to engage in conflict resolution, and, most of all, how to develop the special self-management and leadership skills that are required.

We've already mentioned the special skills involved in *SuperLeadership*—leading others to lead themselves. These special leadership skills also extend to the team members themselves. Employees need to learn effective techniques and strategies for managing and leading themselves under the highly autonomous conditions that teams create. For example, the book, *Mastering Self-Leadership: Empowering Yourself for Personal Excellence* provides a detailed description of how these self-leadership skills can be developed.

The team system cannot be partial or voluntary, or superimposed on a traditional top-down type of leadership philosophy.

Integration of Teams with Total Quality Management

Often, a TQM program is implemented mainly as a technical innovation, and the critical social skills are ignored. Many such programs try to place a quality overlay on an existing traditional management/leadership system, with no fundamental change to the hierarchical approach.

As Texas Instruments Malaysia discovered, sooner or later, to take TQM to its logical end, some type of team system is necessary. We don't think this team system can be partial or voluntary, or superimposed on a traditional top-down type of leadership philosophy. A fundamental change is needed.

In many applications, we see TQM as the quality circle fad of the 90s! If it does not include real changes to the fundamental way of doing business, then the prospects for failure are high. On the other hand, if it is integrated with a true self-managing system, the two can work hand-in-hand to move the organization to competitiveness.

Greenfield Sites Are Easier Than Retrofit Changes

Of course, by greenfield, we mean a start-up situation, where the team system is tightly integrated into the organizational structure from the very beginning.

A retrofit *(brownfield)* means an organizational change where an existing traditional organization is changed over to a team system.

Retrofit problems In a retrofit change, the challenges of implementation are considerably more intense. A significant amount of *unlearning* must take place, before the *new learning* can replace the old.

One of the main issues is the behavior of supervisors . . . Many have years of experience with a particular pattern of leadership (typically top-down). To become a facilitator or coordinator, a supervisor must act in ways that are directly contrary to years of prior experience. This is difficult indeed. In one of our book chapters, we traced the difficult transition of managers in a warehouse operation. These managers were ultimately successful, but this transition consumed time and emotional energy.

Also, in a greenfield situation, the managerial tool of selection is available. That is, the management team can devise tests and selection mechanisms to evaluate a person's potential cooperation and team skills. For greenfield sites, this selection perspective is an important part of success. In contrast, in a retrofit implementation, selection is not available. The personnel that staff the current traditional organization are the same that must staff the self-management system. Needless to say, these currently employed personnel may not be the most suitably experienced or tempered to succeed in a team system.

But retrofit we must We find the greenfield versus retrofit challenge to be a troubling paradox. While greenfields have a higher probability for success, we suspect the 80 percent of the need for self-managing teams is with existing organizations.

It's neither feasible, practical, nor ethically defensible to launch a wave of old-plant closings because greenfield sites are easier to manage. The simple truth is that over the next decade, the vast majority of team applications will be retrofits rather than greenfield applications.

Retrofitting can be done, quite well . . . We do not wish to be pessimistic about the potential of changing existing organizations. We have personally observed many successful retrofit applications, and indeed, many of the stories contained in our books are retrofits.

It's not necessary to stand around bemoaning that we have to work with retrofits rather than greenfield sites. It's important to accept this reality, and then further develop and hone our technology of change so that a retrofit to a team system becomes more certain and routine.

It's neither feasible, practical, nor ethically defensible to launch a wave of old-plant closings because greenfield sites are easier to manage.

Teams Are Difficult to Diffuse throughout the Organization

Several years ago, Richard Walton wrote about how difficult it is to diffuse the team concept throughout a total organization. Success with teams at one location does not necessarily mean that teams will be implemented at another location. Walton's writing focused on the Gaines pet food plant at Topeka, a well known innovator of the team concept. Walton speculated about how the team concept seemed to threaten other managers, and even seemed to be resented by other parts of the organization.

As another example, one of us visited a food manufacturing plant that had been extremely successful with teams for over a dozen years. The plant was a constant contributor to corporate profits, and was also well known for its creativity and innovation. Yet, over a half-dozen other plants in the same company had not yet moved to a team system.

Why this failure to diffuse?   Perhaps one simple explanation is the so-called *not invented here syndrome*—"if we didn't invent it, then it must not be any good." We encountered this attitude at Ford, when one manager exclaimed, "If it's any good, then someone else would have done it and written it up!" He had a very difficult time seeing that everything has to be done first somewhere, sometime, at least once. Unless this manager changes his thinking he is doomed to being an imitator for all of his life.

You can't learn IT by just reading about IT . . . Learning about teams is not something that can be completely accomplished in the abstract: by reading about teams, for example. Real learning takes place only when teams are experienced. Our own best learning has taken place through hours and weeks of observation of teams. Further, we also experience teams in our own universities where faculty are typically grouped into areas or departments to accomplish their teaching, service, and research objectives as a team.

Go out and experience teams!   We recommend that if you are really serious about learning about teams, get out and visit other sites with teams. We especially recommend talking to team members. Sometimes they may not be able to write, speak or report as a junior executive might, but quiet conversations about their personal team experience is extraordinarily revealing.

Get over lack of faith and belief in your employees   In the long run, we suspect that diffusion of teams is mainly impeded by the difficulty many managers have in really understanding and having faith that ordinary workers are actually capable and willing to undertake the responsibilities that teams require. We continually encounter this perspective in workshops.

To be fair, however, the percentage of executive workshop participants pessimistic about teams has significantly decreased over the 12 year period that we have been doing training in this area. As more and more organizations become successful with teams, and, as more and more articles about teams appear in *Fortune* and *Business Week*, top management's perspectives on teams will continue to change.

Summing Up

Self-managing teams do pose many challenges that need to be addressed if they are to succeed. In part three of this series, we will discuss some of the payoffs that make the challenge of doing business without bosses through teams worthwhile. We will also address the special issue of team leadership.

References

Manz, Charles C., *Mastering Self-Leadership: Empowering Yourself for Personal Excellence.* Prentice-Hall, 1992.

Manz, Charles C. and Sims, Henry P., Jr., *Business Without Bosses,* Wiley, 1993.

Manz, Charles C. and Sims, Henry P, Jr., "Business without bosses: how self-managing teams are creating a competitive revolution . . . Tyrannosaurus Rex: the boss as corporate dinosaur," *The Journal for Quality and Participation,* Sept., 1994.

Walton, R.E., "The Diffusion of New Work Structures: Explaining Why Success Didn't Take." *Organizational Dynamics,* Winter 1975, pg. 3–22.

Dr. Charles Manz is an associate professor of management at Arizona State University in Tempe, Arizona. He is co-author with Henry Sims, Jr. of SuperLeadership: Leading Others To Lead Themselves. *Dr. Henry P. Sims, Jr. is a professor of management and organization at University of Maryland–College Park. In addition to having over 90 articles published, Manz co-authored* The New Leadership Paradigm *(with Peter Lorenz) in 1992 and* The Thinking Organization *(with Dennis Gioia) in 1986.*

Virtual Teams

Beverly Geber

Technology and the necessity of having people work together who live in different locations has made virtual teams possible. However, the best way to manage these teams is still emerging. This article discusses the advantages and disadvantages of virtual teams and how various companies are making them work.

Most of the time, Barbara Recchia likes being a "remote" member of her work team. Although she is a communications program manager in the corporate human resources department of Hewlett Packard Co. In Palo Alto, CA, Recchia lives and works in Santa Rosa, CA, a large town woven into the wine country north of San Francisco.

Each day, Recchia fiendishly works the phones and the company's e-mail system to cement herself with her team members. Yet sometimes, in staff meetings she attends in person, it's clear how isolated she is. Someone makes a sly comment and everybody but Recchia giggles, wise to the joke that only insiders would appreciate.

"Sometimes you just feel really lonely and disconnected," Recchia says.

Not that she would consider abandoning the river across the street from her house to move to the "urbanized" environs of Silicon Valley, where the rest of her teammates live and work. Santa Rosa suits her lifestyle and satisfies her yearnings for a quieter, more outdoorsy existence. So she tries hard to make things work even though she faces obstacles that might not exist if she were in the same building as the rest of her teammates.

Recchia may be lonely but she is not alone. She has plenty of kindred colleagues across the country as companies try to get work done through distributed work groups, a more formal title for what many call virtual teams. Virtual teams are groups of people working closely together even though they may be separated by many miles, even continents. Sometimes, as in Recchia's case, the teams are intact work groups whose members stick together indefinitely. Other times the teams are cross-functional groups brought together for a finite time to tackle a project.

They are connected by all the modern appurtenances we take for granted in the 1990s' workplace and some we're still getting used to: telephones, fax machines, e-mail and videoconferencing. Often, they are linked as well by

> Virtual teams are groups of people working closely together even though they may be separated by many miles, even continents.

groupware, a powerful new class of project-management software that electronically links workers and allows them instantly to trade and manipulate project information.

The rise of virtual teams is a relatively recent phenomenon, brought about in part by the invention of groupware and the reluctance of many workers like Recchia to relocate for a new job. But virtual teams are a benefit and a necessity for companies too, and are bound to become more prevalent, says Lee Sproull, a professor of management at Boston University.

The reason, Sproull says, has to do with the global nature of marketplaces, the need to get projects done as quickly as possible in order to get new products to those global markets, and the necessity of tapping the best brains for those projects no matter where those brains may be.

A company may prefer to devise a new product by pulling together a group of people in one spot for the duration of the project, but that's impractical if the project will last less than a year or if the product needs to be simultaneously recast for markets around the world. In the latter case, it's a certainty that the workers needed for the project are scattered across a wide geographic expanse.

"Even though the barriers are enormous, companies have no choice," Sproull says. "If you say to a bunch of executives, 'Would you prefer to have this project done face-to-face or by computer?' nine out of 10 would say, 'Face-to-face.' But if you were to ask them if they wanted to do the project by computer or not at all, there wouldn't really be a choice."

To illustrate, she cites a U.S. aircraft manufacturer that recently designed a new-generation jet plane, its most technologically advanced product ever. The project bound together myriad subcontractor teams from around the world, each lending its obscure expertise to the design of a complex new machine. Since it was impractical to assemble all those people in one place, much of the work took place through electronic links, particularly computer networks, Sproull says.

Although the technical challenges of such a project were enormous, one of the thorniest problems this company faced was how to get all those individuals working together compatibly and productively, even though face-to-face contact was limited and communication was confined almost exclusively to phone, fax and computer. Companies that use virtual teams are finding that tending to the human factors of the arrangement is one of the savviest things they can do to ensure the success of the teams' projects.

In the case of the aircraft manufacturer, Sproull says company officials brought many of the "remote" team members to its headquarters for at least six months and up to 18 months so they could get to know other team members face-to-face while learning how to work within the company's project-management system.

Some people maintain that it's not necessary to sponsor bonding fests before asking people to work in virtual teams. Sheldon Laube, national director of information and technology for Price Waterhouse in Menlo Park, CA, says his company seldom does so. That's despite the fact that the accounting and consulting firm is a heavy user of groupware and frequently uses virtual teams.

Some virtual teams at Price Waterhouse work together for just a week or two preparing work for a particular client, Laube says. It would be unrealistic to put everyone on a plane for a get-together when all the necessary information can be coalesced quickly on networked computers. Considering that Price Waterhouse has 45,000 employees in 120 countries, people often work on projects without benefit of having met in person. But Laube maintains that the company's set methodology and common language for conducting audits eases collaboration. Also, he adds, there is a strong unspoken expectation within the company that colleagues share information freely with one another.

But in some companies, in which projects may be of long duration and even include members from other firms, such as suppliers or subcontractors, forming a team without face-to-face meetings may be courting disaster.

At the very least, it's necessary to have a one-day videoconference so the team members can see one another, says Chris Newell, executive director of the Lotus Institute, the research and education arm of Lotus Development Corp., in Cambridge, MA. The company makes Lotus Notes, the most widely used groupware product. Newell says the introductions are crucial because "it's important to develop some level of trust and relationship before you can move into electronic communication."

Others maintain that a brief videoconference is too minimal to be of any help in warding off the interpersonal problems that might arise among people who work closely together without ever being together—especially if the team is going to be together for many months, even years, and particularly if the team members face language and cultural differences.

John Spencer, worldwide manager for the design and development of single-use cameras for Eastman Kodak Co. in Rochester, NY, recently pulled together a product-development team to design a new product that hasn't been announced yet. Although the interior workings of the product will be the same worldwide, Kodak wants to adapt the exterior and the features for the European market.

Since the company didn't want to do a mere cosmetic makeover of the product, it was necessary to involve German design engineers from the start. So Spencer brought two German engineers to the United States for the initial six months of the project.

Why such a long engagement? "The most important part of the project is the up-front time," says Spencer, who doesn't believe that a long-term virtual team can be successful without that personal contact. During the six months, personalities gelled, friendships formed, and the members got used to one another's work styles and temperaments. That's the time for finding out, for instance, that when Kurt says no, he's adamant about it and doesn't tolerate jawboning. Trying to fathom personality quirks like that via computer is much more difficult and time-consuming, and can damage the rapport of the team if tensions develop into flame wars via e-mail.

> It would be unrealistic to put everyone on a plane for a get-together when all the necessary information can be coalesced quickly on networked computers.

Often, says Spencer, extracurricular activities do more to cement a team than a passel of team meetings or team-building sessions. The two German engineers who stayed for six months ended up socializing on weekends with their U.S. counterparts, a factor that helped secure their bond. To keep the team members connected, Spencer is also sending U.S. engineers to work in Germany for brief periods of time.

The importance of personal contact and socializing can't be overestimated, says HP's Recchia. In the early months of her remote work arrangement, she visited the HP headquarters just once a month and felt hopelessly out of touch with her colleagues.

"It was a very odd feeling walking in and knowing you weren't exactly connected," she says. She found that she had to curb her hard-driving, let's-get-on-with-it style to sit down and "neighbor" with teammates each time she visited Palo Alto. Eventually, she decided that she needed to drop in once a week instead of once a month in order to maintain her connection to the team.

A lot can be missed when communication is carried on long-distance, Recchia says. Subtle tones and meanings slip away. Recently Recchia's group had been asked to give a presentation on its work to another section of HP. It wasn't really necessary for Recchia to make an extra trip to be there; someone else could describe what she did. But while her boss told her this in a face-to-face meeting, Recchia sense that the boss really wanted her to come. When she asked, her boss said yes, it would be nice if the entire group could be there.

Would Recchia have picked up the clue during a phone call? She thinks not. "She's kind of hard to read sometimes," she says of her boss. So Recchia attended the presentation, which was followed by an informal luncheon that Recchia says was one of the most enjoyable times she's spent with her team.

Often, the most valuable "team-building" sessions are the informal ones, arranged outside business hours and without the company's imprimatur. Lotus' Newell works in a virtual team whose members are spread across much of New England. Two months ago, they all went off on a ski weekend "because we decided it was important to do some social things together a couple of times a year," Newell says.

Vince Anderson, director of environmental programs for Whirlpool Corp.'s North American Appliance Group in Evansville, IN, oversaw a two-year project using a virtual team that developed a chlorofluorocarbon-free refrigerator. The expertise came from sites in the United States, Brazil and Italy.

The team met every four months or so to discuss the project, but Anderson found that some of the most valuable events during those visits were the informal get-togethers, including a backyard cookout and volleyball game Anderson hosted at his house.

Informal meetings help team members size up others, a task that would be protracted, if not impossible, on-line. How to tell, for instance, which team member is easily crushed by criticism, especially if criticism makes her clam up? Are any of the teammates devious, likely to manipulate others in order

A lot can be missed when communication is carried on long-distance.

to advance a hidden agenda? Who's power hungry? Who likes handholding? Is anybody downright malicious?

Not all the answers to these questions become apparent during a backyard barbecue, of course, but the informal gatherings go a long way toward developing the understanding and personal trust that individual team members must develop in each other to weather the conflicts that inevitably arise during the course of work.

There is another kind of trust that must be present for teams to work smoothly, says Sproull. It's trust that springs from competence. "Trust comes from performance," she says. "If I see this person is going to do a first-rate job with the information I provide, that he won't undercut it, won't embarrass me, then I'm more likely to trust him."

Building this kind of trust is more difficult to accomplish among cross-functional teams that spring up for a spurt of time to complete a project. "If you take people from finance and marketing and manufacturing and give them the same paragraph to read, you'll get three different interpretations," Sproull says. That may not be as much of a problem if team members are all on-site and meeting frequently to hash out differences. But completing a project by using groupware means that the members are more isolated from one another and the chances for misinterpretation are greater.

Groupware allows information about a project to be fed into a huge, structured database that can be accessed by all team members. You can always tell when a virtual team isn't working well together, Sproull says, because the database doesn't hold all the latest information. People hoard what they know and share it only with teammates they trust. You might get design engineers sharing information only with design engineers and not with their teammates from finance or manufacturing.

Lotus' Newell says trust is a crucial factor in a well-oiled team, but the degree of trust that's needed may depend on the type of project. If a Price Waterhouse accountant needs some information from several colleagues scattered around the world for a client presentation due next month, the task can probably be completed without undue angst or bickering. The need for trust is more pressing in a cross-functional team tackling a difficult long-term project that will require negotiation and compromise.

Newell believes that organizations in general have created cultures in which information-hoarding is rewarded. The task for companies using virtual teams is to get team members to break that habit. Newell knows of one large consulting group that has changed its performance-appraisal system to reward individuals who share information. If a piece of information a consultant puts into the shared database gets accessed a certain number of times by others, the end-of-year bonus for that consultant grows.

Amid all the carping about the difficulties of using distributed work teams, it's easy to lose sight of the fact that there are a few special advantages that electronic distance affords. For one thing, it's a particular boon to shy people, says Newell. Extroverts may resist the isolation of electronic communication, but shy people often thrive on it. For many people, writing is

You can always tell when a virtual team isn't working well together, because the database doesn't hold all the latest information.

Extroverts may resist the isolation of electronic communication, but shy people often thrive on it.

easier than speaking. "Some people like the barrier. Their interpersonal style lends itself to it," says Recchia. She recalls having many delightful telephone conversations and computer communications with a woman she eagerly anticipated meeting in person. When it finally happened, Recchia was disappointed. She realized the individual dealt with others much better if she was doing it from behind a screen.

There may be formidable interpersonal barriers to overcome in making virtual teams click, but that doesn't mean it can't be done, according to those who have managed them. A few sensible rules apply.

For one thing, says Sproull, a manager needs to fight for the budget to get team members together periodically. It may be hard to justify that need to executives who have invested considerable money in new-fangled electronic communications. Therefore, it's best to use the synergy ploy. Remind executives that often a company's best ideas are born out of chance encounters in a hallway or around a watercooler. Letting virtual team members get together sometimes for extended watercooler discussions improves the chances for serendipity.

Paradoxically, virtual work teams require *more* formal communications, not fewer, says Susan Sowers, manager of the Hewlett Packard corporate client computing group in Palo Alto. Sowers manages a distributed work team of 21 people spread over three U.S. sites.

Precisely because there is less informal chatter among team members, the kind that takes place during birthday gatherings or coffee-machine chats, Sowers finds that she must change her previously informal approach to managing. "I have to do things differently. I can't just walk around to supervise people and call a meeting whenever I think one is needed," she says. To do so would favor the team members who work in her own office and would eventually alienate those at other sites. Sowers tries to make sure the team members in Atlanta and Fort Collins, CO, feel as though they have the same information as someone who works in the office next to Sowers.

The cohesion of the group can be broken when someone new joins, Sowers says. That's why it's particularly important to make sure that nearly all communications are kept in the shared database, so that a historical document of the group's work is available for the new person to peruse.

Whirlpool's Anderson says it's essential to use rigorous project-management principles. Make sure to be as specific and direct as possible in determining who will do what by when. This is especially important if the team is a global one, wrestling with language and cultural differences.

Lotus' Newell recommends that each team establish a mission for what it intends to accomplish. Along with this, team members need to come up with a list of norms and agreements about how the team will operate and how it will handle the technological aspects of its interactions. All this gets written down and stored in the same database that contains the project information, Newell says.

Team norms can be anything that team members feel is important for everyone to commit to doing. For instance, says Newell, a team norm might

Team members need to come up with a list of norms and agreements about how the team will operate and how it will handle the technological aspects of its interactions.

be that everyone check into the database once a day to monitor the progress of the project, even if he has no new information to add. Other norms might deal with the way information is handled. Which kinds of issues are discussed by the team as a whole, and how often do they get discussed? Does everyone have access to all information, or is some of it restricted?

Other agreed-upon practices might cover ways to deal with conflict. Teams sometimes enforce a rule that if one team member has a conflict with another, it can't be dealt with electronically; one person has to telephone the other, or the two must meet in person.

Newell also recommends that virtual teams have both a team leader (formerly called a manager) and a team facilitator. The facilitator is a member of the team who is assigned to monitor the way in which the team works. For instance, if two team members are having frequent conflicts, the facilitator is the first to intervene to try to smooth things out. In a way, she's like a team conscience.

Eastman Kodak's Spencer believes you can improve the chances of fielding a successful team if you choose members carefully. Select people who are comfortable sharing information and working with computers, he says, but also make sure they're people with strong personalities who can assert themselves in an electronic medium.

Sproull says team members should be chosen in part for their empathic abilities. "You can be the world's best hydraulic engineer, but if you can't put yourself in the shoes of an electrical engineer, it would be problematic," she says. "You can't all sit around a table for the life of a project to hash things out."

And of course, that, in a nutshell, is why virtual teams may become less an oddity than a common—if challenging—way to work.

Why Work Teams Flop—And What Can Be Done About It

Barrie Richardson

This article includes some basic truths that we need to be continuously reminded of: There has to be a supportive culture, people need training in teamwork, there have to be leaders who can facilitate teamwork, and so on. Teams don't just happen. You have to prepare people to work together, have shared values and procedures, and have a sense of purpose that drives the team forward together.

Human beings have a special ability. They can sit around a table and envision a situation that does not exist. This is amazing if you think about it. No computer can do this. People can dream in the daylight, and their dreams can energize them to make things happen. A group of people can initiate, plan, organize, and monitor programs and projects. They can redesign work stations and introduce new procedures. They can rework curricula to make it more meaningful to students. They can remodel a church kitchen to feed hungry people. In each of these examples, the quality of the decisions made by the group might be superior to those made individually by its members. Human minds stimulate one another, generating novel and effective solutions. Furthermore, the process of working together as a voluntary group can increase the probability that tasks will get done. With an increase in ownership comes an increase in concern for results, which increases the probability of success.

Work groups, which can appear in many forms—task groups, problem solving teams, quality circles, committees, etc.—can significantly improve the effectiveness of an organization. Indeed, high-performing improvement teams are the driving force of total quality management programs in all types of organizations. The issue is not whether people ought to work cooperatively in groups. Rather, the question is, How can organizations make these teams more productive? Why is it that so many of us participate in team meetings that we consider a waste of time? Why does so much energy often yield so little? Apparently, good people who come together with good intentions do not automatically produce significant results. What can be done to improve the effectiveness of an organization's teams? The first step is to examine the three main reasons why work teams flop.

Reason 1: The Team Operates in a Hostile or Demotivating Environment

All groups operate in an organizational culture. Every school, church, and business over time has developed its own way of doing things. Herman Miller has a culture much different from Steelcase, and General Motors' culture is different from that of Volvo.

An organization's culture is difficult to change. Think about it. How easy would it be to adopt the values, morals, and communication style of a contemporary of yours who lives in another country, say France? But we do not have to look at another country to make the point. Doesn't the family across the street from you have a different culture than yours? If it's hard to change a family's culture, think how difficult it is to change a larger organization. Imagine an organization that:

- Operates in a stable environment with few outside threats so that management feels secure.
- Has an environment where people are extremely conscious of status and power.
- Considers people who challenge other people's assumptions or positions, particularly the bosses', as radical or as troublemakers.

Is your organization like this? If so, it will be extremely difficult for both individuals and teams to initiate change. In the past, public utilities, commercial banks, universities, and government agencies have had cultures with these characteristics and were, therefore, highly resistant to change.

Reason 2: The Participants on the Team Lack the Skills Needed for Success

It's easy to blame the company or boss for the low performance of a team. But often it is the ineffectiveness of the team members themselves that causes the team to flop.

We as individuals may not only lack the analytical and creative thinking skills needed to develop better group decisions; we also have the bad habit of looking to an authority figure for solutions. Good students please teachers, and good children please their parents. We want to be liked by the boss, and we are reluctant to question or challenge him or her. We also want our peers to like us, so we do not question their assumptions, facts, or conclusions.

When working on a team, we often make quick decisions, rather than following the technique used by judges of suspending judgment until they are sure they have the facts. We also tend to have a selective vision problem—that is, we tend to see what we believe is true, and this problem is further compounded when team members all see the situation the same way. "Group think" creates social pressure for conformance and inhibits hardheaded and passionate debate.

> If it's hard to change a family's culture, think how difficult it is to change a larger organization.

Furthermore, most of us worry that people will either laugh at us or give us a funny look if we ask a dumb question or challenge what everyone else thinks is obvious. We have been programmed at home, church, school, and work for low levels of confrontation and challenge. One reason teams flop is because we have not learned how to think and behave the way team members on high-performing teams do. High-performing teams are not status-conscious groups. People openly debate an challenge one another. Consensus comes out of the lively exchanges of competing ideas. This is a foreign way of thinking and behaving for most of us.

High-performing teams are not status-conscious groups.

Reason 3: The Team Has Poor Leadership

Let's assume that you are sitting in on a team's meeting and this is what you observe:

1. The tasks and objectives of the meeting are not clear.
2. People do not listen to one another.
3. A few people dominate the meeting.
4. People talk to the boss and look for approval from the boss.
5. There seems to be little sense of priority.
6. Novel ideas are frowned upon.
7. There is little open disagreement.
8. Decisions are made without challenge or confrontation.
9. Team members demonstrate little passion or enthusiasm. They seem to have no sense of being involved in something that is both important and worthy.

Do these observations sound a lot like the meetings you attend? Each team needs a strong leader to help its members stay on track while encouraging lively participation, so that the team can generate the information it needs to meet its goals.

Teams that flop are found in organizations that do not support innovation. Team members on ineffective teams do not know how to openly disagree or ask for facts or challenge their superior's ideas. Finally, low-performing teams are both poorly led and poorly managed.

No one wants to be part of an ineffective team. Who wants to waste time, be bored, or feel impotent? But low-performing teams, even those operating in conservative cultures, can be more effective if they take the following steps:

A newly formed team or committee should invest in the time it takes for the team to develop both a value statement and rules of conduct.

Step 1: Establish a set of values and a code of conduct.   Team leaders must establish a more productive environment in which everyone on the team feels that his or her ideas are valued by others. This is an ongoing task in which mutual trust is developed and everyone on the team believes that they are working on something significant.

Team leaders and team members need to be clear about what kinds of behaviors are permissible and what behaviors are not acceptable. If it is a newly formed team or committee, the leader should invest in the time it takes for the team to develop both a value statement and rules of conduct. This may take several hours to accomplish. It is worth it. If this step is bypassed, there will be trouble.

The values that the team agrees on ought to be made explicit to everyone. They should be printed and distributed. Everyone on the team ought to know, for example, that the team respects moral courage, individuality, questioning, and the honest search for the truth, and that meetings should build members' self-confidence and self-esteem, not destroy them. These are the values listed by AT&T for its teams:

- Respect for individuals
- Dedication to helping customers
- Highest standards of integrity
- Innovation
- Teamwork
- Accountability
- Excellence

After a value statement is produced, the team should develop some rules of conduct. Here is an example of the team rules used by a Boston bank:

- Respect each person.
- Share responsibility.
- Criticize only ideas, not people.
- Keep an open mind.
- Question and participate.
- Attend all meetings.
- Listen constructively.
- Make decisions by consensus.
- Start on time, end on time.
- Remember that what's said here stays here.
- Leave your stripes at the door.
- Encourage laughter.

Step 2: The team needs to spell out, preferably in writing, the responsibilities of team members and the team leader.   This will help define what it means to be part of a high-performing team. For example, team members are expected to show up on time and be fully prepared to participate; they are expected to listen to others and not interrupt; they are expected to actively participate, serve on subcommittees, and so on. Team leaders may have the responsibility of encouraging participation, developing the agenda, and acting as both coach and cop at the meetings and being the team's representative at council meetings.

Step 3: Clearly define the team's purpose and objectives.   Everyone needs to know the purpose of the group. This seems obvious, but when you observe how much time and energy most teams spend on irrelevant or trivial concerns, it's not so obvious. The overall mission could be one that seems large and difficult to achieve.

Teams also need short-term objectives. How else can they feel successful? Ideally, these objectives should to be specific, attainable, and challenging. Team members also need to find ways to monitor and measure their progress. Bar charts and graphs displayed in the work area are a good way to make success visible to everyone.

Step 4: Make provisions to have a rotating gadfly.
The role of the gadfly (or devil's advocate) is to challenge anyone who makes statements without sufficient facts, evidence, or data. Assertions such as, "The absentee rate is rising," "Our products are selling better than last year," "Women are better than men on this type of job," should be challenged by the gadfly.

When someone proposes a solution, the gadfly will ask "Why?" The gadfly may even ask this more than once, which will make those making a recommendation rethink their proposal or broaden their perspective. This tactic slows down the problem-solving process, but it can also improve the quality of the recommendations. How many decisions have you been involved in the last year that might have been made differently if you or your team had asked "Why?" at least three times?

Finally, the gadfly can help the leader of the team. If team members are talking to the boss and not to the group, the gadfly will stop the discussion and ask this person why he or she is addressing the boss. If someone is personally attacking another person rather than the issue, the gadfly will stop the process and get the discussion back on track. In this way the gadfly is also an umpire. The gadfly's position should be a rotating one. Everyone should have this responsibility over the course of the year.

Step 5: Celebrate victories.
Effective teams always celebrate their victories. Celebration is a way to stop and acknowledge a job well done, and the celebration itself will pull the team closer together. Success breeds success.

Even though they operate in a cautious, bureaucratic organization, strong team leaders can develop a high-performing work team. To do so, they must be fearless, determined, and passionate about their own vision and have the capacity to develop an environment in which the other team members feel they are respected and needed.

Barrie Richardson, D.B.A., is dean of the Forest School of Business at Centerary College of Louisiana in Shreveport. He is also the author of The +10% Principle: How To Get Extraordinary Results From Ordinary People *(Pfeiffer, 1993).*

> Bar charts and graphs displayed in the work area are a good way to make success visible to everyone.

SYSTEMS THINKING/ LEARNING ORGANIZATIONS

Sytemic Quality Management

Daniel H. Kim

In this original article, consulting editor Daniel Kim explains the relation between total quality management and systems thinking. Each informs the other, and only by viewing the two together can we truly implement TQM for long-term continuous improvement of processes and customer satisfaction. Kim—editor of The Systems Thinker *newsletter, consultant, and teacher—explains that one of the reasons for the seeming failure of TQM efforts in many companies is not really TQM failing but a profound misunderstanding of the organization as a whole entity, a system. Only by viewing it in that way can you use TQM's tools and methods to optimize the whole rather than the individual parts.*

Total quality management (TQM) has been instrumental in reshaping the competitive landscape of business in the 1980s by making quality improvement a *necessary* (not a high-priced option) way of conducting business. Many companies have benefited from quality crusades in their organizations that have shaved millions of dollars in costs and shrunk cycle times by factors of 10 or more. But not everyone has fared so well in their TQM efforts. Some studies have shown that many quality programs are discontinued after several years of effort because of disappointing results.[1] One study revealed a number of common themes[2] that resulted in implementation "false starts". A common characteristic of the themes identified was that they were organizational, not technical or methodological, in nature.

Organizational "Messes"

Many companies that experience dramatic improvements in their TQM efforts initially benefit from harvesting low-hanging fruits—problems that are relatively easy to identify and solve. As they gobble up such low-hanging fruit, however, the problems become increasingly more difficult as they require a more sophisticated understanding of the larger organizational system than was previously needed. As the organizational complexity of the issues increases, the current set of TQM tools and methods may grow increasingly inadequate. In particular, TQM may be ill-equipped for tackling a class of problems that Russell Ackoff labels as a *mess*:

> I am going to call this thing a mess. Then we say that what reality consists of are messes, not problems.
>
> Now what is a problem? Let's take a mess for a moment, which is what you're confronted with in the morning when you come to work, and let's analyze it. Remember what analysis is—to take something apart. So if we take a mess and start to break it up into its components, what do we find that those parts are? The parts are problems. Therefore, a problem is an abstraction obtained by analyzing a mess.
>
> Then what is a mess? That's the significant thing—a mess is a system of problems. Now, the significance of this is that the traditional way of managing is to take a mess and break it up into problems and solve each problem separately, with the assumption that the mess is solved if we solve each part of it.
>
> But remember . . . if you break a system into parts and make every part behave as effectively as possible, the whole will not behave as effectively as possible. Therefore, the solution to a mess does *not* consist of the sum of the solutions to the problems that make it up. And that is absolutely fundamental.[3]

Figure 1 is an attempt to classify "organizational messes" into a matrix based on Organizational Complexity (the number of units and level of complexity of their inter-connections) and Time Lags of Process (current cycle time of projects).

Organizational complexity. Many of the initial improvements gained in most companies come rapidly and with relative ease, either because the situation was so bad that almost *any* concerted effort would have yielded quick results or most of the early projects revolved around single functional units requiring minimal cross-functional cooperation. These initial projects are often part of a bootstrapping strategy where other functional units in the organization slowly buy into the TQM philosophy after its value has been proven.

Many companies that experience dramatic improvements in their TQM efforts initially benefit from harvesting low-hanging fruits—problems that are relatively easy to identify and solve.

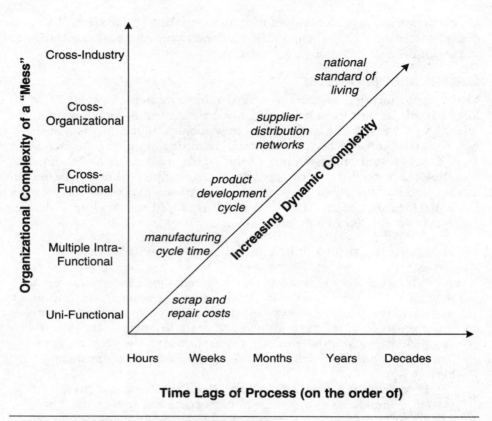

Figure 1.   **Complexity and time lags of organizational "messes."**

This buy-in process progresses at a slow pace, taking longer and longer as it involves increasing levels of cross-functional cooperation. One study shows that the rate of improvement in a wide range of TQM projects is *primarily a function of the organizational complexity* of the project, not the specifics of the project itself.[4]

Time lags.   Another attribute of early TQM projects is that the time delays within those systems are relatively short. For example, reducing defects at a specific production step means getting real-time data and analyzing it to see what the data has to say. The process step usually takes minutes or hours, not days or months. Thus, it is feasible to collect data and be confident about causal conclusions drawn from the data. When the time delays of a project are extremely long, such as a product development process that takes several years, running real-time experiments becomes impractical and current data are of limited usefulness. One can tweak individual steps within the process but cannot gain much insight about their implications on the process as a whole.

Organizational issues that involve a high degree of organizational complexity and long time delays can be characterized to be high in *dynamic complexity*—where cause and effect relationships are nonobvious and not close in time and space—may require additional tools and methods for continued improvements. In such situations, a systemic approach can augment the traditional TQM approach by providing a complementary set of principles and methods that are particularly well-suited for dealing with dynamic complexity.

A Systemic Perspective

Systems thinking[5] (ST) approaches problems from the basis of the whole, rather than breaking up the whole into its individual pieces and trying to understand each part. Where TQM focuses on *analysis* of the separate parts that make up the whole, ST strives for *synthesis* of the constituent parts. System dynamics, the theoretical underpinning of systems thinking, allows us to articulate causal interconnections so that we can take high-leverage actions instead of being paralyzed by complexity. Grounded in feedback systems and control theory, system dynamics provides a set of tools and methods for making sense of complex interconnections—similar to how TQM helps us understand variation through statistical theory.

> Systems thinking approaches problems from the basis of the whole, rather than breaking up the whole into its individual pieces and trying to understand each part.

According to ST, if a system is decomposed into its components and each component is optimized, the system as a whole can be guaranteed not to be optimal. A common characteristic of many complex systems is that they are often designed with the intention of optimizing the parts rather than the whole. Each function or department in an organization striving to optimize its own performance often leads to functional gridlock leaving the organization as a whole grossly suboptimized.

Systems thinking can help break through functional walls of isolation by providing the framework and tools for understanding the importance of managing the interconnections between the various functions. ST provides a methodology for thinking about the ways in which prevailing mental models may restrict learning, gaining deeper insights into the nature of complex systems, finding high-leverage points in the system and testing one's assumptions about the efficacy of various policy choices.

> A common characteristic of many complex systems is that they are often designed with the intention of optimizing the parts rather than the whole.

Integrating TQM and Systems Thinking

The TQM mission is not just about improving production steps and reducing cycle times; *TQM is a thought revolution in management.*[6] Rephrasing the statement, I would state that TQM is about *changing the mental models of management in order to enhance an organization's capability to determine its own future.* This change requires more than a one-time shift in thinking; it means continually re-evaluating the way managers think. Sustaining this thought revolution requires not only continual improvement activities in which many firms are engaged but also changing the common knowledge and mental models shared within an organization; it requires *organizational learning.*

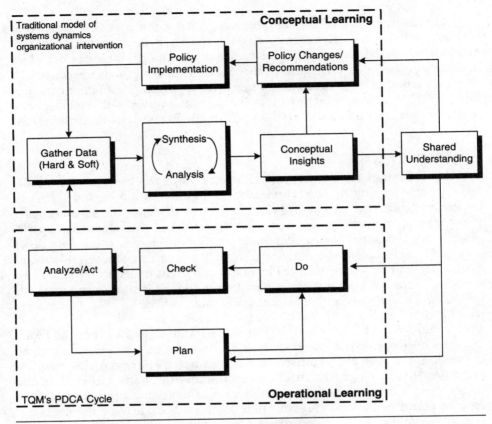

Figure 2. **Systemic quality management model.**

With respect to learning, TQM is particularly strong in operational learning—building greater understanding of *how* to do things—while systems thinking is relatively strong in conceptual learning—developing richer theories about *why* things work the way they do. The seven tools of TQM (pareto chart, cause-and-effect diagram, stratification, check sheet, histogram, scatter diagram, and control charts) are relatively easy to understand with well-defined guidelines for the use of each tool. Through the use of control charts and pareto analysis, for example, operators can understand and improve their production steps. At the heart of this learning process is Deming's PDCA (Plan-Do-Check-Action) cycle, which promotes continual improvement by cycling through the PDCA problem-solving loop. Transfer of learning from individual to organizations is managed through an organization-wide TQM effort that is designed to facilitate the sharing of learning in one setting with the rest of the organization.

Integrating TQM and systems thinking[7] can accelerate organizational learning beyond the current capabilities of traditional TQM methods. The two approaches form a synergistic pair whose individual strengths complement

Integrating TQM and systems thinking can accelerate organizational learning beyond the current capabilities of traditional TQM methods.

each other and provide a balance of operational and conceptual learning (see Figure 2). Each process informs and enhances the other. Together, they advance organizational learning by helping to build a shared understanding of conceptual insights and operational processes and create a powerful new model of systemic quality management (SQM).

In the SQM model diagram, the top dashed box represents the traditional system dynamics approach of gathering data, conceptualizing, building a model, running simulation analyses, and proposing policy changes. An implicit assumption of this process is that the insights alone would be compelling enough to produce action. In reality, however, such policy change recommendations are seldom implemented since building shared understanding traditionally has not been a part of the process. Clearly, more could be done on the implementation side of things.

The bottom dashed box represents a typical TQM process of making quality improvements, the PDCA (Plan-Do-Check-Act) cycle, which should be carried out at every level of an organization. Requests from a higher level are interpreted and translated into a plan of action with the appropriate check points identified for monitoring progress relative to the plan. The plans are incorporated into the budgetary cycle and implemented. The check points identified earlier are tracked, and deviations are observed. The data are then analyzed and actions are taken to correct any discrepancies. Although the PDCA cycle can work very well in implementing new requests given from above and in maintaining control over current processes, it is relatively weak on identifying the high-leverage areas to drive the whole process.

Combining these two processes means integrating conceptual learning with operational learning by blending the two into a seamless process. For example, building shared understanding through the use of systems thinking tools and methods can enhance the *planning* and *doing* steps by providing a common base of conceptual models. Having greater shared understanding can also facilitate the "buy-in" process on policy change recommendations. Conceptual insights such as "eroding goals" and "worse before better behavior" can help those involved in the *doing* to see how their specific actions relate to the overall system. The analysis and action produced through the PDCA cycle should generate new data that would feed into the data gathering process as well as the next cycle of the *plan*.

Managers' New Roles as Researcher and Theory Builder

The next stage of evolution for the TQM movement is to redefine the traditional role of managers to become researchers and theory builders within their own organizations.[8] Just as the initial quality improvement efforts empowered the frontline workers to become *de facto* researchers on their own processes, managers must assume a similar role in approaching their managerial responsibilities.

The dichotomy between manager and researcher must end because the pace of change is such that one can no longer separate the two functions—managers must wear both hats simultaneously. As theory builders, managers must have an intimate knowledge of how their organization works together as a whole. It is no longer sufficient to apply generic theories and frameworks like bandages to one's own specific issues. They must create new frameworks within which they continually test their strategies, policies, and decisions to inform them of improvements on the organization's design. Integrating systems thinking with traditional TQM can help organizations continue to gain superior results through their improvement efforts.

Notes

1. "The Cracks in Quality," The Economist, April 18, 1992; "Where Did They Go Wrong?" *Business Week*, October 25, 1991.

2. Jim Brown and Scott S. F. Tse, "A System Dynamics Analysis of Total Quality Management Implementation False Starts," Unpublished master's thesis, MIT Sloan School of Management, Cambridge, Massachusetts. A summary of their themes is contained in "TQM Implementation: An Uphill Battle," by Colleen Lannon-Kim, *The Systems Thinker*, June/July 1992, vol. 3, No. 5.

3. This is taken from an essay by Russell Ackoff entitled "The Second Industrial Revolution."

4. A.M. Schneiderman, "Setting Quality Goals," April 1988, pp. 51–57.

5. Although there is no universally accepted definition of what is meant by systems thinking, the term will be used to represent a school of thought whose focus is more on the whole system rather than the individual parts. Specifically, the tools and methodologies of systems dynamics constitute the core of what is referred to as systems thinking in this paper.

6. K. Ishikawa (1985). Masayoshi Ozawa, *Total Quality Control and Management* (Tokyo: JUSE Press, 1988).

7. For a more extensive treatment of this topic, see Daniel H. Kim, "Toward Learning Organizations: Integrating Total Quality Control and Systems Thinking," (Cambridge, MA: Pegasus Communications, 1990).

8. See "TQM and Systems Thinking as Theory-Building Tools," by Daniel H. Kim, *The Systems Thinker*, March 1994, Vol. 5., No. 2.

Breathing Life into Organizations

Margaret J. Wheatley and Myron Kellner-Rogers

The message of this article is that organizations are living systems, and to manage them as if they were machines means that you will compromise the quality of the outputs and undermine the motivation of people to perform up to their full capabilities. We need to understand the dynamic nature of living systems to self-organize to solve problems and achieve goals. When we do, things work better because this approach takes advantage of what is: the living, breathing nature of human organizations. Compare the ideas in this article with those in the piece by Gouillart and Kelly, "Transforming the Organization."

Many of us have begun to think about the world differently. In many fields of inquiry, people are discovering a new world view. We are rediscovering that the world is not a machine. We are rediscovering that we, as human beings, are not machines.

Without the mechanistic blinders of the past, we are encouraged to inquire about entirely different questions. We now can ask about work and meaning, work and wholeness, work and spirit. We are free to talk about love, compassion, meaning—the whole host of human emotions and experience.

In this emerging view, we are rediscovering that the world is supportive of who we are as human beings. We are free to rediscover what it means to be human, and what it means to work together in organizations. We can develop new beliefs about work and organizations and the human beings who try to make life different by their labors. Such new beliefs make life in organizations much more interesting to think about.

The world of the past several centuries was alien to us as humans

Beginning three centuries ago, scientists and philosophers stated that the world was a great machine. In one of the strangest twists of thinking in the history of ideas, this mechanistic image of the world was turned back on ourselves and we came to believe that humans too were machines.

This is the world most of us in Western society grew up in. From such mechanistic imagery, we developed our sense of self, others, and organizations. It was a very strange world view. We shredded the world into pieces

TINKERING THE WORLD INTO EXISTENCE . . .

We do not have language to convey the processes life uses to organize itself and the words of machine efficiency don't apply. Yet any of the words that describe the emergent processes of life—tinkering, groping, experimenting—sound soft or irreverent.

Biologist Francisco Valera describes evolution this way: "Many paths of change are possible . . . in a path of continuous tinkering." The tinkering concept appears in the work of other revolutionary biologists to describe the creative, evolving nature of life. Nothing is fixed, not even the rules of evolution. We are all making it up as we go along. We need to become better tinkerers, able to make quick assessments of what resources are available, what's possible right now. Strategic plans get replaced by organizations of distributed discovery and workplaces filled with many tinkerers.

and then reconstructed it. Piece by piece we built work tasks, departments, functions, and specializations.

We focused on creating organizations as well-oiled machines designed by bright engineers. Organizational leaders, or teams, could figure it all out ahead of time. If they were smart, the machine worked well. If their design failed, they simply went looking for another solution to impose upon us.

Trying to engineer the world into existence, we became isolated, lonely individuals who couldn't talk with one another about what really mattered. Instead of exploring what it was to be human, we suppressed those questions. We could not acknowledge who we were. The rules of machine efficiency smothered the deeper realms of experience, the feelings and desires that make us human:

Trying to engineer the world into existence, we became isolated, lonely individuals who couldn't talk with one another about what really mattered.

- We spent all our time constructing organizations according to machine logic . . .
- We focused exclusively on how best to analyze, assemble, and carefully control the world—nothing else mattered . . .
- Our most important task was to engineer the world into existence.
- The world itself was dead, incapable of creating anything for itself.

This machine world ignored us as living systems . . . Machines have no innate desires, motivations, or intelligence. Everything must be built into them, imposed from the outside. In our organizations, questions about our effort, commitment, motivation, and quality were answered mechanistically. It was thought that the only way to motivate us was from the outside. Leaders were charged with making us work. They needed to find the right benefit or salary or threat. Without these external coercions, we wouldn't work. We, like the world, were assumed to be dead, incapable of creating anything from ourselves.

The impact of machine thinking . . . As the machine image took over so much of our thinking, human nature receded from view. Human concerns evaporated in the wake of relentless mechanistic forces. We couldn't talk about our passions, our families, our spirits, or our true selves because these had nothing to do with the efficiency concerns of machines. Because we could not find ourselves in this world, it became more and more fearsome. We often seek to control what we fear. Having created an alien world, we could only hope to grow more skillful in dominating it. We sought to harness and control everything: nature, one another, the future. Command and control became our only hope to fend off this hostile world. The machinery of organizations grinded on. Work became more deadly and more deadening. Our fear increased. The heart and spirit of being human disappeared from organizations. It is this deadening world view that is coming to an end.

We are rediscovering that the world is alive, that we are alive. This world welcomes back our most human qualities, our creativity and passion and spirit. As we leave behind the machine images, we recover a world that is supportive of us in the full expression of our humanity. The world supports our efforts to organize, to accomplish, to find meaning, more than we could have hoped.

> We are rediscovering that the world is alive, that we are alive. This world welcomes back our most human qualities, our creativity and passion and spirit.

Our Personal Exploration of Living Systems

For the past few years, we personally have been exploring the world through these new eyes of living systems. We learned a great deal from the work of scientists who study complex systems, the cosmos, the origins of life. While many of their findings seem startlingly new, mostly their work echoes in a different voice what philosophers and spiritual leaders have been saying for many long centuries.

Our exploration has led us to a new set of beliefs about people and organizations. We share them here as a work in progress. Although some of them will undoubtedly change, the fundamental shift in perception they represent has changed forever our view of work, organizations, and human endeavor. We personally have discovered a world that has respirited our own work and given us not only new understandings, but new hope.

Living systems learn constantly They change when necessary. But they adapt by *tinkering*. The world is not as harsh as we have made it out to be. Living systems tinker in their environments, exploring new possibilities, new forms of creative self-expression. In tinkering, they make do with what is at hand—a solution doesn't have to be right, it just has to work. When it stops working, they tinker their way into another solution. Their ability to learn, adapt, and create is fed by information. They maintain acute awareness of what is occurring around them. They are webbed with information from all directions. Such information and acuity allows them to be responsive and creative when the situation requires a change.

Living systems are self-organizing They have the innate capacity to create structures and processes that respond to the needs of the moment. Their organizing tendency shows up as temporary patterns and structures. These emerge without plans or supervision or directive leadership. Everywhere in the universe, we observe this self-organizing capacity. The complex structures of life emerge from many local self-organizing efforts, not from a master plan or blueprint.

Life is systems seeking   life seeks to affiliate with other life. Such affiliation makes more life possible. Systems of relationships develop because systems make life more sustainable for their individual members. From these networks of support, a global system emerges that is more stable and less affected by changes. Such a stable system provides the conditions for more diversity. More varieties of life can maintain themselves because they have aligned with differing partners.

Life is attracted to order, but it uses messes to get there   The processes of life have nothing to do with machine efficiencies. They are fuzzy, redundant, and messy. Many solutions are sought in parallel, many individuals are involved in experimentation about the same dilemma. There is no straight line of logic or process that leads to a perfect solution. Instead, there is a great deal of tinkering till someone discovers something that works for now. But the messy processes and fuzzy logic lead to orderly solutions because it is the nature of life to evolve towards more complex and effective systems.

The processes of life have nothing to do with machine efficiencies. They are fuzzy, redundant, and messy.

Organizations are living systems   As living systems, organizations possess all of the creative, self-organizing capacities of other forms of life. The people within all organizations are capable of change, growth, and adaptation—they do not require outside engineering or detailed design. People are capable of creating structures and responses that work, and then moving into new ones when required. We possess natural capacities to work with change in a creative and effective way.

Because we are living systems, most people are intelligent, creative, adaptive, and self-organizing   We want to organize to learn, to do quality work, to contribute, to find meaning. We do not need to impose these attributes on one another. We merely need to learn how to evoke them.

Our Emerging Beliefs about Organizations

Our emerging beliefs create new questions, new ways of thinking about organizations. This set of beliefs, which we like to think captures some elements of an emerging world view, influences every aspect of our own thinking about organizations.

So many efforts in the past have been focused on how to create learning, or create motivation, or create structures, i.e. how to get the machine to work. We are finding that as our own world view shifts, we are asking a different set of questions. If organizations are living systems, then they have many innate capacities, perhaps some we never expected. In looking for these innate abilities, we've become curious about asking:

- Where does organization come from?
- Where does learning come from?

■   Where does quality come from?

If organizations are living systems, then even these characteristics are innate. We don't have to impress or train or bribe people into organizing, or learning, or doing quality work. We don't even have to structure organizations into existence.

Creating supportive conditions for self-organization   Most people want to express their quality, their learning, their self-organization. They want to figure out the best response, the best structure for a given situation. The question becomes whether we can create the organizational conditions that allow people to express these innate desires and abilities. The primary condition we need to create is:

> An organizational community that is clear about its intent, knows what it wants to accomplish and knows what its purpose is.

If people have enough clarity about intent and direction, then they can effectively self-organize into temporary but appropriate structures for fulfilling that intent. They know the self that they need to organize around. Two other conditions also are essential to creating a purposeful organizational community:

> Living systems are webbed with feedback, information available from all directions.

If people have enough clarity about intent and direction, then they can effectively self-organize into temporary but appropriate structures for fulfilling that intent.

This is true for organizations as well. Information is the nourishment of the organization; the system cannot adapt or change if it is starved to learn what is happening. It cannot be adaptive without access to information about its situation. The organization loses its adaptability whenever anyone goes hungry for information.

> Living systems also are webbed with connections; individual members have access to the whole system.

In networks of living organizations, people need to know that they can reach anywhere in the system as a particular need or opportunity arises. They need to be able to seek out skills, experience, information from anyone in the system in order to respond intelligently to a particular situation.

If we focus on creating these conditions, we find that most of what we have spent our time on—designing, structuring, planning, motivating—becomes unnecessary. These things will be done by the organization as it *tinkers* in its environment, as it seeks to find the best system or solution for the demands of the times.

What would be different if we supported self-organization?   Think about how quality efforts would differ in a living system. What would be different, if we really believed that most people have a deep desire to do quality work, want to make things work better and want to develop sustaining relationships beyond narrow self-interest.

It seems to us that if we believed in such innate capacities, we wouldn't be investing nearly as much in training programs, motivational efforts, contests or awards. We'd spend much more time in thinking about how to engage people in figuring out how to resolve quality issues. We would focus on providing better resources to support their inquiry, rather than limiting that inquiry to particular metrics or measures imposed from outside.

We would support many more solution-seeking processes, many more sources of feedback. We would support a whole conglomeration of quality efforts that operated in parallel rather than hoping to find the one perfect program or measures. We also would understand that meaningful relationships with customers are a natural desire of most humans. We would give up trying to implant customer service through trite slogans or campaigns, and instead support our employees to seek out the relationships with customers that they discover they need. We could expect that they would create diverse but effective responses.

If organizations are living systems, then quality is not tools, or diagnostics, or particular process modifications. Quality, we believe is a deeply ingrained desire to make our lives mean something, to contribute to others. We do this by weaving ourselves together into systems that can sustain us. We know that we cannot do it alone.

> Quality, we believe is a deeply ingrained desire to make our lives mean something, to contribute to others.

In the later years of his life, Dr. Deming urged us to look more deeply into quality, to understand what it was, truly. He stated simply that quality was about the human spirit. Spirit is the Latin word for breath, breath as a symbol of life.

As many of us inquire into respiriting work, we literally are breathing life back into our organizations. As we understand more about the qualities and capacities of living beings, we naturally will create organizations that nourish and respect our extraordinary human spirits.

Margaret J. Wheatley and Myron Kellner-Rogers have been exploring and applying the discoveries of chaos and complexity science to organizations for several years. With their clients an seminar participants, they are learning to create organizations that know how to change continuously because they engage the intelligence of all their people. Through this collaborative inquiry, they are discovering the conditions that support self-organizing in today's organizations. Their inquiry into science is combined with more than twenty-years of consulting, line management and academic research. Wheatley's book Leadership and the New Science *(winner of many awards, including "Best Management Book of 1992," in Industry Week Magazine) marked one stage in their inquiry. Their current thinking, reflected, in part of this article, will be shared in their forthcoming book* A Simpler Way, *due to be published in the Spring of 1996 by Berrett-Koehler Publishers, Inc.*

Understanding Organizations as Learning Systems

Edwin C. Nevis, Anthony J. DiBella,
and Janet M. Gould

This is the longest article in this book. It will take some time to get through, so block out an hour or two before you sit down with this one. We have included it because it is a very good overview of what is involved in helping everyone in an organization become more focused on learning that can contribute to the company's continual improvement. There is an extensive listing of references at the end that should provide you with additional resources on this important subject.

With the decline of some well-established firms, the diminishing competitive power of many companies in a burgeoning world market, and the need for organizational renewal and transformation, interest in organizational learning has grown. Senior managers in many organizations are convinced of the importance of improving learning in their organizations. This growth in awareness has raised many unanswered questions: What is a learning organization? What determines the characteristics of a good learning organization (or are all learning organizations good by definition)? How can organizations improve their learning? In the literature in this area, authors have used different definitions or models of organizational learning or have not defined their terms.[1] Executives have frequently greeted us with comments like these:

- "How would I know a learning organization if I stumbled over it?"
- "You academics have some great ideas, but what do I do with a mature, large organization on Monday morning?"
- "I'm not sure what a good learning organization is, but you should not study us because we are a bad learning organization."

Our research is dedicated to helping organizations become better learning systems. We define organizational learning as the capacity or processes

---

within an organization to maintain or improve performance based on experience. Learning is a systems-level phenomenon because it stays within the organization, even if individuals change. One of our assumptions is that organizations learn as they produce. Learning is as much a task as the production and delivery of goods and services. We do not imply that organizations should sacrifice the speed and quality of production in order to learn, but, rather, that production systems be viewed as learning systems. While companies do not usually regard learning as a function of production, our research on successful firms indicates that three learning-related factors are important for their success:

We define organizational learning as the capacity or processes within an organization to maintain or improve performance based on experience.

1. Well-developed core competencies that serve as launch points for new products and services. (Canon has made significant investments over time in developing knowledge in eight core competencies applied in the creation of more than thirty products.)

2. An attitude that supports continuous improvement in the business's value-added chain. (Wal-Mart conducts ongoing experiments in its stores.)

3. The ability to fundamentally renew or revitalize. (Motorola has a long history of renewing itself through its products by periodically exiting old lines and entering new ones.)

These factors identify some of the qualities of an effective learning organization that diligently pursues a constantly enhanced knowledge base. This knowledge allows for the development of competencies and incremental or transformational change. In these instances, there is assimilation and utilization of knowledge and some kind of integrated learning system to support such "actionable learning." Indeed, an organization's ability to survive and grow is based on advantages that stem from core competencies that represent collective learning.[2]

As a corollary to this assumption, we assume that all organizations engage in some form of collective learning as part of their development.[3] The creation of culture and the socialization of members in the culture rely on learning processes to ensure an institutionalized reality.[4] In this sense, it may be redundant to talk of "learning organizations." On the other hand, all learning is not the same; some learning is dysfunctional, and some insights or skills that might lead to useful new actions are often hard to attain. The current concern with the learning organization focuses on the gaps in organizational learning capacity and does not negate the usefulness of those learning processes that organizations may do well, even though they have a learning disability. Thus Argyris and Schön emphasize double-loop learning (generative) as an important, often missing, level of learning in contrast with single-loop learning (corrective), which they have found to be more common.[5] Similarly, Senge makes a highly persuasive case for generative learning, "as contrasted with adaptive learning," which he sees as more prevalent.[6] The focus for these theorists is on the learning required to make transformational changes—

Some learning is dysfunctional, and some insights or skills that might lead to useful new actions are often hard to attain.

changes in basic assumptions—that organizations need in today's fast-moving, often chaotic environment. Their approach does not negate the value of everyday incremental "fixes"; it provides a more complete model for observing and developing organizational learning. After periods of significant discontinuous change, incremental, adaptive learning may be just the thing to help consolidate transformational or generative learning.

Another assumption we make is that the value chain of any organization is a domain of integrated learning. To think of the value chain as an integrated learning system is to think of the work in each major step, beginning with strategic decisions through to customer service, as a subsystem for learning experiments. Structures and processes to achieve outcomes can be seen simultaneously as operational tasks and learning exercises; this holds for discrete functions and for cross-functional activities, such as new product development. The organization encompasses each value-added stage as a step in doing business, not as a fixed classification scheme. Most organizations do not think this way, but it is useful for handling complexity. With this "chunking," we are able to study learning better and to see how integration is achieved at the macro-organizational level. This viewpoint is consistent with a definition of organizations as *complex arrangements of people in which learning takes place.*

While we have not looked at organizations' full value-added chains, we selected our research sites so that we could examine learning in different organizational subsets. In addition, we gathered data indicating preferences or biases in investments in learning at different points of the chain and to understand how learning builds, maintains, improves, or shifts core competencies. Do organizations see certain stages of the chain where significant investment is more desirable than at others?

Our last assumption is that the learning process has identifiable stages. Following Huber, whose comprehensive review of the literature presented four steps in an organizational learning process, we arrived at a three-stage model:

1. Knowledge acquisition—The development or creation of skills, insights, relationships.
2. Knowledge sharing—The dissemination of what has been learned.
3. Knowledge utilization—The integration of learning so it is broadly available and can be generalized to new situations.[7]

Most studies of organizational learning have been concerned with the acquisition of knowledge and, to a lesser extent, with the sharing or dissemination of the acquired knowledge (knowledge transfer). Less is known about the assimilation process, the stage in which knowledge becomes institutionally available, as opposed to being the property of select individuals or groups. Huber refers to the assimilation and utilization process as "organizational memory." While this is an important aspect of knowledge utilization, it is limited and works better when discussing information, as distinct from knowledge. True knowledge is more than information; it includes the meaning or interpretation of the information, and a lot of intangibles such as the tacit knowledge of experienced people that is not well articulated but often determines collective organizational competence. Studies of organizational learning must be concerned with all three stages in the process.

Early in our research, it became clear that organizational learning does not always occur in the linear fashion implied by any stage model. Learning may take place in planned or informal, often unintended, ways. Moreover, knowledge and skill acquisition takes place in the sharing and utilization stages. It is not something that occurs simply by organizing an "acquisition effort." With this in mind, we shifted our emphasis to look for a more fluid and chaotic learning environment, seeking less-defined, more subtle embodiments.

The first phase of our research was based on intensive field observations in four companies, Motorola Corporation, Mutual Investment Corporation (MIC), Electricité de France (EDF), and Fiat Auto Company.[8] We wanted to have both service and manufacturing settings in U.S. and European environments. We chose two sites where we had access to very senior management and two where we were able to study lower levels. We selected Motorola as an example of a good learning organization; we were able to observe organizational learning during its fourteen-year quality improvement effort.

We did not attempt to study entire firms or to concentrate on any single work units in these four organizations. For example, at Motorola, we began by studying two senior management teams of twenty to twenty-five executives each from all parts of the corporation. Each team focuses on a critical issue defined by the CEO and COO, to whom the groups report. The teams' structures were designed as executive education interventions and vehicles for "real-time" problem solving. Our objective was to see how these teams reflected and utilized organizational learning at Motorola.

From our interview data, we identified what organizational members claimed they had learned and why. We wrote case descriptions of the learning processes in their organizations, which we shared with the organizations to ensure their accuracy. Using a grounded analysis, we identified categories that reflected learning orientations and then constructed a two-part model of the critical factors that describe organizations as learning systems.[9] We have since tested this model in data-gathering workshops with personnel from more than twenty *Fortune* "500" companies. Our testing led us to revise some of the model's components, while retaining its overall framework.

Core Themes

Next we discuss the core themes that emerged from our research and provided a basis for our model.

All Organizations Are Learning Systems

All the sites we studied function as learning systems. All have formal and informal processes and structures for the acquisition, sharing, and utilization of knowledge and skills. Members communicated broadly and assimilated values, norms, procedures, and outcome data, starting with early socialization and continuing through group communications, both formal and informal. We talked with staff people in some firms who claimed that their companies were not good learning organizations, but, in each, we were able to identify one or more core competencies that could exist only if there were learning investments in those areas. Some type of structure or process would have to support the informed experience and formal educational interventions required for knowledge acquisition, sharing, and utilization. We found this in both our field sites and other firms. For example, one firm that considers itself to be a poor learning organization because of its difficulty in changing some dysfunction has a reputation in its industry for superior field marketing. It is clear that this group has well-developed recruiting, socialization, training and development, and rotating assignment policies that support its cadre of respecting marketing people. Obviously, some learning has been assimilated at a fairly deep level.

Learning Conforms to Culture

The nature of learning and the way in which it occurs are determined by the organization's culture or subcultures. For example, the entrepreneurial style of MIC's investment funds group results in a learning approach in which information is made available to fund managers and analysts, but its use is at the managers' discretion. In addition, there is a good deal of leeway in how fund managers make their investments; some are intuitive, some rely heavily on past performance, and a few use sophisticated computer programs. Thus the fund managers' use or application of learning is largely informal, not dictated by formal, firmwide programs. Meanwhile, the culture of MIC's marketing groups is more collaborative; learning is derived more from interaction within and between cross-functional work groups and from improved communication.

The nature of learning and the way in which it occurs are determined by the organization's culture or subcultures.

In contrast, there is no question that a great deal of organizational learning about quality has occurred at Motorola, but its emphasis on engineering and technical concerns resulted in an earlier, complete embrace of total quality by product manufacturing groups. In a culture that heavily rewards product group performance, total quality in products and processes that require integrated, intergroup action lags behind, particularly in the marketing of systems that cut across divisions.

Style Varies between Learning Systems

There are a variety of ways in which organizations create and maximize their learning. Basic assumptions about the culture lead to learning values and investments that produce a different learning style from a culture with another pattern of values and investments. These style variations are based on a series of learning orientations (dimensions of learning) that members of the organization may not see. We have identified seven learning orientations, which we see as bipolar variables.

For example, each of two distinct groups at both Motorola and MIC had different approaches to the way it accrued and utilized knowledge and skills. One Motorola group had great concern for specifying the metrics to define and measure the targeted learning. The other group was less concerned with very specific measures but, instead, stressed broad objectives. In the two groups at MIC, the methods for sharing and utilizing knowledge were very different; one was informal, and the other more formal and collaborative. From these variations, we concluded that the pattern of the learning orientations largely makes up an organizational learning system. The pattern may not tell us how *well* learning is promoted but tells a lot about what is learned and where it occurs.

Generic Processes Facilitate Learning

How well an organization maximizes learning within its chosen style does not occur haphazardly. Our data suggest that talking about "the learning organization" is partially effective; some policies, structures, and processes do seem to make a difference. The difference is in how easy or hard it is for useful learning to happen, and in how effective the organization is in "working its style." By analyzing why learning took place in the companies we studied, we identified ten facilitating factors that induced or supported learning. While we did not observe all the factors at each site, we saw most of them and at other sites as well. Thus we view them as generic factors that any organization can benefit from, regardless of its learning style. For example, scanning, in which benchmarking plays an important role, was so central to learning at Motorola that it is now an integral, ongoing aspect of every important initiative in the company. Although MIC tends to create knowledge and skill internally, it maintains an ongoing vigilance toward its external environment. On the negative side, the absence of solid, ongoing external scanning in other organizations is an important factor in their economic difficulties.

By analyzing why learning took place in the companies we studied, we identified ten facilitating factors that induced or supported learning.

A Model of Organizations as Learning Systems

Our two-part model describes organizations as learning systems (see Figure 1). First, *learning orientations* are the values and practices that reflect where learning takes place and the nature of what is learned. These orientations form a pattern that defines a given organization's "learning style." In this sense, they are descriptive factors that help us to understand without making value judgments. Second, *facilitating factors* are the structures and processes that affect how easy or hard it is for learning to occur and the amount of effective learning that takes place. These are standards based on best practice in dealing with generic issues. (See the sidebar for definitions of the learning orientations and facilitating factors we identified.)

Both parts of the model are required to understand an organization as a learning system; one without the other provides an incomplete picture. In addition, separating the parts enables organizations to see that they do indeed function as learning systems of some kind, and that their task is to understand better what they do well or poorly. (The idea of assessing what exists is more

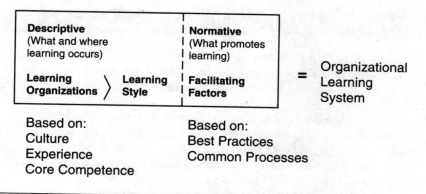

Figure 1. **A model of organizations as learning systems.**

useful than the pejorative notion that there is only one good way to be a learning organization.) Finally, a refined, detailed list of factors related to organizational learning may help companies select areas for learning improvement that do not demand drastic culture change but, rather, can lead to incremental change over time.

Learning Orientations

In the next section, we expand on the definitions of the seven learning orientations and provide examples of each.

1. Knowledge source. To what extent does the organization develop new knowledge internally or seek inspiration in external ideas? This distinction is seen as the difference between innovation and adaptation—or imitation. In the United States, there is a tendency to value innovativeness more highly and look down on "copiers." American critiques of Japanese businesses often mention that the Japanese are good imitators but not good innovators. In our opinion, both of these approaches have great merit as opposing styles rather than as normative or negative behaviors.

Although our data show a tendency in organizations to prefer one mode over the other, the distinction is not clear-cut. While MIC does scan its environment, it prefers to innovate in responding to customer needs and problems and has been a leader in developing new financial products and services. EDF modeled its nuclear power plants on U.S. technology. Motorola appears to be equally vigorous in innovation and in reflective imitation; it has been innovative in developing new products and adroit at adapting others' processes, such as benchmarking and TQM procedures. Among firms not in this study, American Airlines, Wal-Mart, Merck, and Rubbermaid appear to be innovative in producing knowledge. And American Home Products is a good example of a highly successful, reflective imitator, as are AT&T's Universal Credit Card, Tyco Toys (a Lego "copier"), and Lexus and Infiniti automobiles.

2. Product-process focus. Does the organization prefer to accumulate knowledge about product and service outcomes or about the basic processes

DEFINITIONS OF THE ORIENTATIONS AND FACTORS

Seven Learning Orientations

1. **Knowledge Source: Internal—External.** Preference for developing knowledge internally versus preference for acquiring knowledge developed externally.
2. **Product-Process Focus: What?—How?** Emphasis on accumulation of knowledge about what products/services are versus how organization develops, makes, and delivers its products/services.
3. **Documentation Mode: Personal—Public.** Knowledge is something individuals possess versus publicly available knowhow.
4. **Dissemination Mode: Formal—Informal.** Formal, prescribed, organization-wide methods of sharing learning versus informal methods, such as role modeling and casual daily interaction.
5. **Learning Focus: Incremental—Transformative.** Incremental or corrective learning versus transformative or radical learning.
6. **Value-Chain Focus: Design—Deliver.** Emphasis on learning investments in engineering/production activities ("design and make" functions) versus sales/service activities ("market and deliver" functions).
7. **Skill Development Focus: Individual—Group.** Development of individuals' skills versus team or group skills.

Ten Facilitating Factors

1. **Scanning Imperative.** Information gathering about conditions and practices outside the unit; awareness of the environment; curiosity about the external environment in contrast to the internal environment.
2. **Performance Gap.** Shared perception of a gap between actual and desired state of performance; performance shortfalls seen as opportunities for learning.
3. **Concern for Measurement.** Considerable effort spent on defining and measuring key factors when venturing into new areas; striving for specific, quantifiable measures; discussion of metrics as a learning activity.
4. **Experimental Mind-set.** Support for trying new things; curiosity about how things work; ability to "play" with things; "failures" are accepted, not punished; changes in work processes, policies, and structures are a continuous series of learning opportunities.
5. **Climate of Openness.** Accessibility of information; open communications within the organization; problems/errors/lessons are shared, not hidden; debate and conflict are acceptable ways to solve problems.

Continued—

Definitions of the Orientations and Factors (continued)

6. **Continuous Education.** Ongoing commitment to education at all levels of the organization; clear support for all members' growth and development.

7. **Operational Variety.** Variety of methods, procedures, and systems; appreciation of diversity; pluralistic rather than singular definition of valued competencies.

8. **Multiple Advocates.** New ideas and methods advanced by employees at all levels; more than one champion.

9. **Involved Leadership.** Leaders articulate vision, are engaged in its implementation; frequently interact with members; become actively involved in educational programs.

10. **Systems Perspective.** Interdependence of organizational units; problems and solutions seen in terms of systemic relationships among processes; connection between the unit's needs and goals and the company's.

---

underlying various products? Many observers have stated that one reason Japanese companies are so competitive is that they make considerably more investments in process technologies in comparison to U.S. companies. The difference is between interest in "getting product out the door" and curiosity about the steps in the processes. All organizations give some attention to each side; the issue is to organize for learning in both domains.

Motorola makes learning investments on both sides. The executives we observed spent roughly equal amounts of time in collaborative learning about processes and outcomes. They paid less attention to "people processes" than to "hard" or technical processes, but many of them accepted the importance of process issues. MIC, EDF, and Fiat have traditionally focused almost exclusively on product issues but are now making greater learning investments in process issues.

3. Documentation mode. Do attitudes vary as to what constitutes knowledge and where knowledge resides? At one pole, knowledge is seen in personal terms, as something an individual possesses by virtue of education or experience. This kind of knowledge is lost when a long-time employee leaves an organization; processes and insights evaporate because they were not shared or made a part of collective memory. At the other pole, knowledge is defined in more objective, social terms, as being a consensually supported result of information processing. This attitude emphasizes organizational memory or a publicly documented body of knowledge.

MIC's investment funds group focuses on a personal documentation style, eschewing policy statements and procedure manuals. In keeping with its entrepreneurial orientation, MIC makes it possible for individuals to learn a great deal, but there is little pressure to codify this. Though engaged in a business that values "hard data," the group supports subjective, tacit knowledge in decision-making processes. And at Fiat's Direzione Technica, where the individual has historically been the repository of knowledge, efforts are being made to establish a *memoria technica*, or engineering knowledge bank. Motorola shows evidence of both approaches but works hard to make knowledge explicit and broadly available.

4. Dissemination mode. Has the organization established an atmosphere in which learning evolves or in which a more structured, controlled approach induces learning? In the more structured approach, the company decides that valuable insights or methods should be shared and used by others across the organization. It uses written communication and formal educational methods or certifies learning through writing the procedures down. In the more informal approach, learning is spread through encounters between role models and gatekeepers who compellingly reinforce learning. In another approach, learning occurs when members of an occupational group or work team share their experiences in ongoing dialogue.[10]

MIC's investment funds group clearly prefers informal dissemination in which learning develops and is shared in loosely organized interactions. This method occurs in other MIC areas, although the marketing groups are becoming more structured in their dissemination. Motorola supports both approaches, though it invests heavily in structured, firmwide programs when senior management wants a basic value or method institutionalized. It considered quality so critical that it now includes vendors and customers in its dissemination. (Recently, some vendors were told that they had to compete for the Malcolm Baldrige Quality Award in order to be on the company's approved vendor list.) EDF prefers formal modes, emphasizing documented procedures that all share. Fiat's Direzione Technica formally spreads knowledge by accumulating it in specialist departments and then disseminating it to cross-functional design teams.

5. Learning focus. Is learning concentrated on methods and tools to improve what is already being done or on testing the assumptions underlying what is being done? Argyris and Schön call the former "single-loop learning" and the latter "double-loop learning."[11] They have rightfully argued that organizational performance problems are more likely due to a lack of awareness and inability to articulate and check underlying assumptions than to a function of poor efficiency. In our opinion, these learning capabilities reinforce each other. Organizations may have a preference for one mode over the other, but a sound learning system can benefit from good work in both areas.

Our research sites displayed a range of behavior. EDF is primarily focused on incremental issues and does not question its basic assumptions. It prides itself on being the world's major nuclear power utility and devotes significant resources to being the most efficient, safe operator through small improvements rather than transformations. Though similar, Fiat's Direzione Technica is beginning to question assumptions about its new product development process. Since 1987, MIC has been in a transformational mode, particularly in the way that its marketing groups have focused on a questioning learning style. Motorola is fairly well balanced in its orientation; the founding family has historically accepted the concept of organizational renewal, which has led to far-reaching changes in the company's product lines through the years and to an inquisitive style. On the other hand, its strong dedication to efficiency learning often precludes questioning basic assumptions.

6. Value-chain focus. Which core competencies and learning investments does the organization value and support? By learning investments, we mean all allocations of personnel and money to develop knowledge and skill over time, including training and education, pilot projects, developmental assignments, available resources, and so on. If a particular organization is "engineering focused" or "marketing driven," it is biased in favor of substantial learning investments in those areas. We divided the value chain into two categories: internally directed activities of a "design and make" nature, and those more externally focused of a "sell and deliver" nature. The former include R&D, engineering, and manufacturing. The latter are sales, distribution, and service activities. Although this does some disservice to the value chain concept, the breakdown easily accounts for our observations.

At MIC, the investment funds group focuses on the design and make side. While this is balanced by learning investments on the deliver side in the MIC marketing groups, there is a strong boundary between these groups, and the fund management side is regarded as the organization's core. Motorola's total quality effort clearly recognizes the importance of value-added at both sides, but "design and make" is significantly ahead of "deliver" in learning investments in quality. Fiat's Direzione Technica is clearly oriented toward design and make, although its new system of simultaneous engineering is balancing its approach with increased sensitivity to the deliver side. EDF nuclear operations focuses squarely on efficient production. While not in our study, Digital Equipment Corporation's learning investments traditionally were much more heavily focused on "design and make" than on "deliver."

7. Skill development focus. Does the organization develop both individual and group skills? We believe it helps to view this as a stylistic choice, as opposed to seeing it in normative terms. In this way, an organization can assess how it is doing and improve either one. It can also develop better ways of integrating individual learning programs with team needs by taking a harder look at the value of group development.

MIC designed the investment funds group to promote individual learning, which seems to fit with its culture and reward system. Heavy investment in team learning would probably improve its performance. On the other hand, MIC's marketing groups, more supportive of collective learning, are now investing in team development as one way to improve its total effectiveness. Fiat's Direzione Technica has been oriented toward more individual development, but, with its new reliance on cross-functional work teams, group development is increasingly more important. Recently, Motorola has become more team oriented and is making heavier investments in collaborative learning. It designed the two executive groups we observed to foster collective

If a particular organization is "engineering focused" or "marketing driven," it is biased in favor of substantial learning investments in those areas.

learning on two strategic issues affecting the entire company. EDF develops both individual and group skills, especially in control-room teams. All EDF employees follow individual training programs for certification or promotion. Control-room teams also learn, in groups, by using plant simulators. Some other firms that emphasize team learning are Federal Express, which invests heavily in teams for its quality effort, and Herman Miller, which stresses participative management and the Scanlon plan.

We view the seven learning orientations as a matrix. An organizational unit can be described by the pattern of its orientations in the matrix, which in turn provides a way to identify its learning style. Given the characteristics of the sites we studied and other sites we are familiar with, we believe it is possible to identify learning styles that represent a distinct pattern of orientations. Such styles may reflect the industry, size, or age of an organization, or the nature of its technology.

Facilitating Factors

The second part of our model is the facilitating factors that expedite learning. The ten factors are defined in the sidebar.

1. Scanning imperative.   Does the organization understand or comprehend the environment in which it functions? In recent years, researchers have emphasized the importance of environmental scanning and agreed that many organizations were in trouble because of limited or poor scanning efforts. Thus many firms have increased their scanning capacity. Five years into Motorola's quality program, a significant scanning effort showed it what others, particularly the Japanese, were doing. In reaction, Motorola substantially changed its approach and won the first Baldrige Award four years later. By contrast, the mainframe computer manufacturers (Cray, Unisys, IBM) and the U.S. auto companies in the 1970s failed to respond to developing changes that sound investigative work would have made painfully visible. Recent changes at Fiat result from a concerted scanning effort in which fifty senior managers visited the manufacturing facilities of world-class auto and other durable goods companies.

2. Performance gap.   First, how do managers, familiar with looking at the differences between targeted outcomes and actual performance, analyze variances? When feedback shows a gap, particularly if it implies failure, their analysis often leads to experimenting and developing new insights and skills. One reason that well-established, long-successful organizations are often not good learning systems is that they experience lengthy periods in which feedback is almost entirely positive; the lack of disconfirming evidence is a barrier to learning.

Secondly, is there a potential new vision that is not simply a quantitative extension of the old or goes well beyond the performance level seen as achievable in the old vision? One or more firm members may visualize something not previously noted. Awareness of a performance gap is important because it often leads the organization to recognize that learning needs to occur or that something already known may not be working. Even if a group cannot articulate exactly what that need might be, its awareness of ignorance can motivate learning, as occurred at Motorola after its 1984 benchmarking. Currently, this "humility" is driving Fiat's Direzione Technica to make a major study of what it needs to know.

In our findings, EDF provides perhaps the best instance of a performance gap leading to adaptive learning. Due to the nature of the nuclear power business, performance variations became the catalyst fore a learning effort to again achieve the prescribed standard. We also found that future-oriented CEOs encouraged performance-gap considerations related to generative learning at Motorola and MIC (parent company).

3. Concern for measurement.   Does the organization develop and use metrics that support learning? Are measures internally or externally focused, specific, and custom-built or standard measures? The importance of metrics in total quality programs has been well documented and is used in target-setting programs such as management by objectives.[12] Our interest is in how the discourse about measurements, and the search for the most appropriate ones, is a critical aspect of learning, almost as much as learning that evolves from responding to the feedback that metrics provide.

Motorola executives believe that concern for measurement was one of the most critical reasons for their quality program's success. At three or four critical junctures, reexamination of measurement issues helped propel a move to a new level of learning. They are applying this factor to new initiatives, a major concern of the executive groups we observed. At EDF, the value of metrics is clearly associated with the performance gap. Its nuclear power plants are authorized to operate at certain specifications that, if not met, may suggest or predict an unplanned event leading to shutdown. Each occasion becomes an opportunity for learning to take place.

4. Experimental mind-set.   Does the organization emphasize experimentation on an ongoing basis? If learning comes through experience, it follows that the more one can plan guided experiences, the more one will learn. Until managers see organizing for production at any stage of the value chain as a learning experiment as well as a production activity, learning will come slowly. Managers need to learn to act like applied research scientists at the same time they deliver goods and services.[13]

> Until managers see organizing for production at any stage of the value chain as a learning experiment as well as a production activity, learning will come slowly.

We did not see significant evidence of experimental mind-sets at our research sites, with some notable exceptions at Motorola. At its paging products operation, we observed the current production line for one product, a blueprint and preparation for the new setup to replace the line, and a "white room" laboratory in which research is now underway for the line that will replace the one currently being installed. Motorola University constantly tries new learning approaches; the two executive groups we observed at Motorola were also part of an experiment in executive education.

We have seen evidence of experimental mind-sets in reports about other firms. For example, on any given day, Wal-Mart conducts about 250 tests in its stores, concentrated on sales promotion, display, and customer service.

Although a traditional firm in many ways, 3M's attitude toward new product development and operational unit size suggests a strong experimental mind-set.

5. Climate of openness. Are the boundaries around information flow permeable so people can make their own observations? Much informal learning is a function of daily, often unplanned interactions among people. In addition, the opportunity to meet with other groups and see higher levels of management in operation promotes learning.[14] People need freedom to express their views through legitimate disagreement and debate. Another critical aspect is the extent to which errors are shared and not hidden.[15]

Perhaps the most dramatic example of openness in our findings is EDF, where abnormalities or deviations are publicly reported throughout the entire system of fifty-seven nuclear power plants. The company treats such incidents as researchable events to see if the problem exists anywhere else and follows up with a learning-driven investigation to eliminate it. It then disseminates this knowledge throughout the company. While this openness may be explained by the critical nature of problems in a nuclear power plant, we can only speculate as to what would be gained if any organization functioned as though a mistake is potentially disastrous and also an opportunity to learn.

> We can only speculate as to what would be gained if any organization functioned as though a mistake is potentially disastrous and also an opportunity to learn.

6. Continuous education. Is there a commitment to lifelong education at all levels of the organization? This includes formal programs but goes well beyond that to more pervasive support of any kind of developmental experience. The mere presence of traditional training and development activities is not sufficient; it must be accompanied by a palpable sense that one is never finished learning and practicing (something akin to the Samurai tradition). The extent to which this commitment permeates the entire organization, and not just the training and development groups, is another indicator. In many ways, this factor is another way of expressing what Senge calls "personal mastery."

MIC does an excellent job of exposing its young analysts to developmental experiences. Its chairman also seeks knowledge in many areas, not just direct financial matters. Motorola has a policy in which every employee has some educational experience every year; it has joint ventures with several community colleges around the country, joint programs with the state of Illinois for software competence development and training of school superintendents, and on-the-job and classroom experiences for managers up to the senior level. The company spends 3.6 percent of its revenues on education and plans to double this amount.[16] Among firms not in our study, General Electric, Unilever, and Digital Equipment Corporation have valued continuous education at all levels for many years.

7. Operational variety. Is there more than one way to accomplish work goals? An organization that supports variation in strategy, policy, process, structure, and personnel is more adaptable when unforeseen problems arise. It provides more options and, perhaps even more important, allows for rich stimulation and interpretation for all its members. This factor helps enhance future learning in a way not possible with a singular approach.

We did not see a great deal of variety at our sites. EDF, perhaps due to the importance of total control over operations, shows little variation. Fiat's Direzione Technica follows similar response routines, although the change to a new structure should lead to greater variation because of its independent design teams. An exception is MIC investment funds group, where we identified at least three different methods that fund managers used in making investment decisions. Senior management, although a bit skeptical about one of the methods, seemed willing to support all three as legitimate approaches.

8. Multiple advocates.   Along with involved leadership, is there more than one "champion" who sets the stage for learning? This is particularly necessary in learning that is related to changing a basic value or a long-cherished method. The greater the number of advocates who promote a new idea, the more rapidly and extensively the learning will take place. Moreover, in an effective system, any member should be able to act as an awareness-enhancing agent or an advocate for new competence development. In this way, both top-down and bottom-up initiatives are possible.

One of the authors participated in two significant change efforts that failed, largely because there was only one champion in each case. One highly frustrated CEO said, "It doesn't do me or the company any good if I'm the only champion of this new way of doing business." At Motorola, we found that a major factor in the quality effort's success was the early identification, empowerment, and encouragement of a significant number of advocates. In a current initiative we observed, Motorola is enlisting a minimum of 300 champions in strategic parts of the company. Digital Equipment Corporation has had learning initiators throughout the company since its early days. Digital's problem has been in assimilating and integrating the lessons of its myriad educational and experimental efforts, rather than in creating an environment that enables broad-scale initiation. MIC's investment funds group encourages many individuals to initiate their own learning but not to proselytize.

> The greater the number of advocates who promote a new idea, the more rapidly and extensively the learning will take place.

9. Involved leadership.   Is leadership at every organizational level engaged in hands-on implementation of the vision? This includes eliminating management layers, being visible in the bowels of the organization, and being an active, early participant in any learning effort. Only through direct involvement that reflects coordination, vision, and integration can leaders obtain important data and provide powerful role models.

At Motorola, CEO Bob Galvin not only drove the quality vision, he was a student in the first seminars on quality and made it the first item on the agenda at monthly meetings with his division executives. Much-admired Wal-Mart CEO David Glass spends two or three days each week at stores and warehouses; employees can call him at home and are often transferred to his hotel when he is in the field. Mike Walsh of Tenneco (formerly of Union Pacific Railroad) meets with groups of employees at all levels in what Tom Peters calls "conversation."[17]

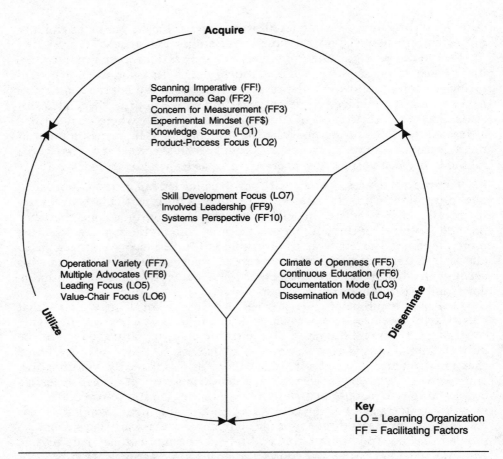

Figure 2. **Elements of an organizational learning system.**

10. Systems perspective.   Do the key actors think broadly about the inter-dependency of organizational variables? This involves the degree to which managers can look at their internal systems as a source of their difficulties, as opposed to blaming external factors. Research in the field of systems dynamics has demonstrated how managers elicit unintended consequences by taking action in one area without seeing its dynamic relationship to its effects.[18]

Do the key actors
think broadly about
the interdependency
of organizational
variables?

Despite its importance, this factor was relatively lacking at our research sites. MIC and Motorola are structured so that there are strong boundaries between groups and functions. Both have changed their perspectives recently, MIC as a consequence of unexpected internal problems related to the October 1987 stock market crash, and Motorola after experiencing difficulties in selling large-scale systems (as opposed to discrete products). In a 1992 survey of 3,000 Motorola employees that asked them to evaluate their unit based on Senge's five factors, they rated systems thinking the lowest and the one that required the most work to improve organizational learning. In contrast, Fiat's Direzione Technica took a systems approach to understanding the consequences of its structure on new product development. As a result, it changed the structure to establish mechanisms for simultaneous engineering. To reduce the new products' time to market, functions now work in parallel rather than sequentially.

General Directions for Enhancing Learning

We have divided the seven learning orientations and ten facilitating factors into three stages—knowledge acquisition, dissemination, and utilization. Figure 2 shows the orientations and factors within this framework. Within our two-part model, there are two general directions for enhancing learning in an organizational unit. One is to embrace the existing style and improve its effectiveness. This strategy develops a fundamental part of the culture to its fullest extent. For example, a firm that is a reflective imitator more than an innovator could adopt this strategy with heightened awareness of its value. A company that has benefited from heavy learning investments on the "make" side of the value chain would see the value of those investments and decide to build further on them. This approach builds on the notion that full acceptance of what has been accomplished is validating and energizing for those involved. It is similar to the appreciative inquiry numerous organizational change consultants advocate.[19] The task is to select two or three facilitating factors to improve on.

The second direction is to change learning orientations. The organizational group would make more learning investments at a different part of the value chain, try to be an innovator if it is now more of an imitator, and so on. These are different changes from those involved in enhancing the facilitative factors, and the tactics will be different. Some changes will be seen as an attack on the organization's basic values, and it may be possible to avoid this by moving toward balance between the two poles, so members of the organization will support the existing style and advocate the "new look" as a supplementary measure.

Supporting the Learning Orientations

In the second phase of our research, in which we worked closely with personnel from more than thirty *Fortune* "500" companies to identify their learning orientations, we validated our notion that organizations learn in varied ways. The singular "learning organization" should be a pluralistic model.

Looking at "what is" in a descriptive rather than normative way has another advantage in that you see better what you are *not* by examining better what you *are*. In the gestalt approach to dealing with resistance to organizational change, it has been well documented that change comes more readily if the targets of change first become more aware of and more accepting of their resistance.[20] In other words, it is important to gain full knowledge and appreciation of your organizational assumptions about learning whether you want to build on them or alter them.

This model may also be used to identify the complementarity of styles between coordinating organizations and to recognize that circumstances may dictate conditions and orientations in particular settings. For example, EDF's nuclear operations are constrained from transforming real-time operations due to the potentially dire consequences (e.g., the Chernobyl disaster) of operating under novel assumptions. However, at EDF, testing system assumptions is characteristic of its R&D division, which uses new technologies in the design of new plants. Thus changing one's style needs to be considered from a systems perspective; it may also be associated with the stage of organizational development.[21]

Strategies for Improving Organizational Learning Capability

When starting to improve its learning capabilities, an organization may decide to focus on any stage of the learning cycle—knowledge acquisition, dissemination, or utilization. While it may be possible or necessary to look at all three phases simultaneously, focusing on a single area is more manageable. The next task is to select an option for focus:

It is important to gain full knowledge and appreciation of your organizational assumptions about learning whether you want to build on them or alter them.

1. Improve on learning orientations. There are two reasons for selecting this option. First, the organization may decide to shift its position on one or more learning orientations. Second, the current pattern of learning orientations has resulted in identifiable strong competencies, so improving or expanding them may be the best way to enhance the unit's learning capabilities. This focus assumes that facilitating factors meet an acceptable standard and that more can be accomplished by adding to the strong base established by the learning orientations.
2. Improve on facilitating factors. In this option, the organization accepts its pattern of learning orientations as adequate or appropriate to its culture and decides that improving the systems and structures of the facilitating factors is the most useful course. This option assumes that maximizing the facilitating factors would add more to the organization's learning capabilities than enhancing or changing the current learning orientations.
3. Change both learning orientations and facilitating factors. An organization should select this option when it sees the other variables as inadequate. This option assumes that large-scale change is necessary and that changing one group of variables without changing the other will be only partially successful.

Each organizational unit or firm must make the decision to pursue one strategy or another for itself. While there are no rules for making this decision, the three options are incrementally more difficult to implement (i.e., one is the easiest to implement; three is the hardest). From the first to the third options, the resistance to change within the organization increases significantly. It is one thing to develop a plan for improving what is already done reasonably well; it is another to engage in nothing less than near-total transformation. It is one thing to stay within accepted, assimilated paradigms; it is another to replace institutionalized models.

Whatever the organization's choice, we offer three guidelines for developing and implementing a chosen strategy:

1. Before deciding to become something new, study and evaluate what you are now. Without full awareness and appreciation of current assumptions about management, organization, and learning, it is not possible to grasp what is being done well and what might be improved or changed.

2. Though the systemic issues and relationships in organizational life require that change be approached from multiple directions and at several points, organizations can change in major ways if people experience success with more modest, focused, and specific changes. As with many skills, there is a learning curve for the skill of managing and surviving transitions. Large-scale change requires that many initiatives be put into place in a carefully designed, integrated sequence.

3. Organizations must consider cultural factors in choosing and implementing any strategy, particularly when considering how it does specific things. For example, in a highly individualistic society like the United States or the United Kingdom, skill development focuses on individual skills; in comparison, more communitarian societies such as Japan or Korea have traditionally focused on group skill development. Moving from one pole to the other is a major cultural change; to simple improve on the existing orientation is much easier.

> Organizations must consider cultural factors in choosing and implementing any strategy.

To help managers better understand the learning capabilities in their own organizations, we have developed and are testing an "organizational learning inventory." This diagnostic tool will enable an organization's members to produce a learning profile based on our model. The profile can guide managers to their choices for improving learning capability. Through further research, we intend to show how learning profiles vary within and across different companies and industries.

Acknowledgments

The research in this paper was supported by a grant from the International Consortium for Executive Development Research, Lexington, Massachusetts, and by the MIT Organizational Learning Center. The authors would like to thank Joseph Rellin, Edgar Schein, Peter Senge, and Sandra Waddock for their helpful comments on an earlier version of this paper.

References

1. C. Argyris, "Double Loop Learning in Organizations," *Harvard Business Review*, September–October 1977, pp. 115–124; K. Weick, *The Social Psychology of Organizing* (Reading, Massachusetts: Addison-Wesley, 1979); B. Leavitt and J.G.

March, "Organizational Learning," *Annual Review of Sociology* 14 (1988): 319–340; P.M. Senge, *The Fifth Discipline* (New York: Doubleday, 1990); and E.H. Schein, "How Can Organizations Learn Faster? The Challenge of Entering the Green Room," *Sloan Management Review*, Winter 1993, pp. 85–92.

2. C.K. Prahalad and G. Hamel, "The Core Competence of the Corporation," *Harvard Business Review*, May–June 1990, pp. 79–91.

3. J. Child and A. Kieser, "Development of Organizations over Time," in N.C. Nystrom and W.H. Starbuck, eds., *Handbook of Organizational Design* (Oxford: Oxford University Press, 1981), pp. 28–64; and E.H. Schein, *Organizational Culture and Leadership* (San Francisco: Jossey-Bass, 1992).

4. J. Van Maanen and E.H. Schein, "Toward a Theory of Organizational Socialization," *Research in Organizational Behavior* 1 (1979): 1–37.

5. C. Argyris and D.A. Schön, *Organizational Learning: A Theory of Action Perspective* (Reading, Massachusetts: Addison-Wesley, 1978).

6. Senge (1990).

7. Huber identifies four constructs linked to organizational learning that he labels knowledge acquisition, information distribution, information interpretation, and organizational memory. Implicit in this formulation is that learning progresses through a series of stages. Our framework makes this sequence explicit and connects it to organizational action. Huber does not make this connection since to him learning alters the range of potential, rather than actual, behaviors. See: G. Huber, "Organizational Learning: The Contributing Processes and Literature, *Organization Science* 2 (1991): 88–115.

8. At Motorola, we observed and interviewed fifty senior managers, visited the paging products operations, and had access to about twenty-five internal documents. At Mutual Investment Corporation (a pseudonym for a large financial services company based in the United States), we observed and interviewed corporation employees in the investment funds group and the marketing groups. At Electricité de France, we observed and interviewed employees in the nuclear power operations. At Fiat, we observed and interviewed employees in the Direzione Technica (engineering division) in Torino, Italy.

9. A. Strauss, *Qualitative Analysis for Social Scientists* (Cambridge: Cambridge University Press, 1987).

10. For a discussion of "communities of practice" see: J.S. Brown and P. Puguid, "Organizational Learning and Communities of Practice," *Organization Science* 2 (1991); 40–57.

11. Argyris and Schön (1978).

12. W.H. Schmidt and J.P. Finnegan, *The Race Without a Finish Line: America's Quest for Total Quality* (San Francisco: Jossey-Bass, 1992).

13. For the idea of the factory as a learning laboratory, see: D. Leonard-Barton, "The Factory as a Learning Laboratory," *Sloan Management Review*, Fall 1992, pp. 39–52.

14. This skill has been referred to as "legitimate peripheral participation." See: J. Lave and E. Wenger, *Situated Learning: Legitimate Peripheral Participation* (Palo Alto, California: Institute for Research on Learning, IRL Report 90-0013, 1990).

15. C. Argyris, *Strategy, Change and Defensive Routines* (Boston: Putman, 1985).

16. See "Companies That Train Best," *Fortune*, 8 February 1993, pp. 44–48; and "Motorola: Training for the Millenium," *Business Week*, 28 March 1994, pp. 158–163.

17. T. Peters, *Liberation Management* (New York: Knopf, 1992).

18. Jay W. Forrester is considered to be the founder of the field of systems thinking.

19. S. Srivastra and D.L. Cooperrider and Associates, *Appreciative Management and Leadership* (San Francisco: Jossey-Bass, 1990).

20. E. Nevis, *Organizational Consulting: A Gestalt Approach* (Cleveland: Gestalt Institute of Cleveland Press, 1987).

21. W.R. Torbert, *Managing the Corporate Dream* (New York: Dow Jones-Irwin, 1987).

Edwin C. Nevis is director of special studies at the Organizational Learning Center, MIT Sloan School of Management. Anthony J. DiBella is a visiting assistant professor at the Carroll School of Management, Boston College. Janet M. Gould is associate director at the Organizational Learning Center.

The Learning Concept: How It's Being Implemented

Charlene Marmer Solomon

This article provides a good review of the idea of a learning organization and the value of viewing and managing an organization as a system. It includes a variety of examples from companies that have embraced this insight and how it has made a positive difference in their operations and ability to serve customers.

Laura Gilbert becomes passionate when she talks about her company as a *learning organization:* A place she defines as having a proactive, creative approach to the unknown, encouraging individuals to express their feelings, and using intelligence and imagination instead of just skills and authority to find new ways to be competitive and manage work. Because she's aware of fancy rhetoric around the topic, she's adamant that being a learning organization isn't a trend but a way people think about learning, relate to each other and connect to their organization.

As human resources manager at Minnesota Educational Computing Corp. (MECC), she and her colleagues have been thinking about learning—and learning new ways to think—since 1991. Undaunted by the magnitude of the changes they hope will evolve, Gilbert and colleagues try to make the concepts of the learning organization a reality in their company. In the book *The Fifth Discipline: The Art & Practice of the Learning Organization*, Peter M. Senge explains why: "As the world becomes more interconnected, and business becomes more complex and dynamic, . . . organizations that will truly excel in the future will be the organizations that discover how to tap people's commitment and capacity to learn at all levels in an organization."

These organizations create corporate structures where "people expand their capacity to create the results they truly desire, where new and expansive patterns of thinking are nurtured, where collective aspiration is set free, and where people continually are learning how to learn together."

MECC's approach to developing a vision statement illustrates this philosophy. In fall 1993, management came together at the company's annual

---

DEFINITION OF TERMS

Action Learning: Applying concepts on real time.

Collaborative Learning: The whole is greater than the sum of its parts.

Current Reality: Candid and forthright recognition of present circumstances.

Dialoguing: More than conversation, it strives to build the thought process by people adding insights and richness to the issue.

Learning Laboratories: A practice field where people can explore business issues in an open environment, offline.

Mental Models: (See "Senge's Five Disciplines for Learning Organizations, page 386.)

Personal Mastery: (See "Senge's Five Disciplines for Learning Organizations.)

Systems Thinking: (See "Senge's Five Disciplines for Learning Organizations.)

---

retreat. But instead of the CEO developing a mission statement and delivering it unilaterally to be received by everyone passively, senior managers got together and talked about what they wanted the company to look like at the turn-of-the-century. They then imagined themselves in the year 1998 and wrote an article fashioned for *The Wall Street Journal.* The story illustrated how the company's "phenomenal success" in 1998 drew its beginnings from the strong foundation it laid in 1993, spelling out the company's goals and mission.

Because the learning-organization notion involves everyone and the entire system, the managers returned to MECC's staff of 180 and said, "Here's the latest to hit the press about MECC. What's your department going to do to help us attain that vision? Why does your department exist and how do you fit in?"

Each department brainstormed answers to the questions. But, they didn't leave the answers in notebooks collecting grit on someone's highest shelf. Instead, every department wrote their visions on huge sheets of paper and taped them on the walls throughout the building. Some were written in script and calligraphy; some had artwork and illustrations; some were orderly with numbers and stats; some were colored and some were plain. Many departments took their messages and posted them in other areas of the company.

The enthusiasm was palpable, and even after a month, nobody wanted to take their messages off the wall. In fact, some of the ideas went directly into marketing campaigns and product development. "This kind of exercise can't help but affect the sense of connectedness, the sense of working as a whole system and the value that each provides towards a common goal," Gilbert says.

Exploring the concepts behind the learning organization. A prevalent notion of the learning organization is as MECC demonstrates: It's a system in

OPERATING PRINCIPLES OF THE LEARNING ORGANIZATION: UNDERSTANDING SOME OF THE PARAMETERS

- There's no such thing as a learning organization. This is because it's a vision that sees the world as interdependent and changing. A learning organization always is evolving.
- The learning organization embodies new capabilities beyond traditional organizations. It's based on a culture of human values of love and compassion. It's a way to practice conversation and coordinated action, and the capacity to see and work with the flow of life as a system. People within a learning organization use language as a way to connect and inquire into systemic consequences for their actions.
- Learning organizations are built by "servant leaders." Conventional ideas of leadership began with individual hero worship. This may block the emergence of leadership of teams. Servant leaders are people who lead because they choose to serve one another and the higher purpose.
- Learning arises from performance and practice. Learning is too important to leave to chance. People can't pick up what they need from training. Thus, learning centers (or virtual learning spaces) have grown as places viewed as managers' practice fields.
- Process and content are inseparable. Rather than look at content and process as fragments, viewing the two together enables new insights.
- Learning is dangerous. It occurs because we feel the need to change, yet we're afraid of the unknown. The learning required here is called "transformational learning," in which problems aren't separate from the way we think and the assumptions behind our ideas.

which everything is interrelated; people, production and procedures are part of a whole, each affecting and being affected by the others.

But it's more than that. Senge, who is the director of the Organizational Learning Center at Massachusetts Institute of Technology's Sloan School of Management, explains: "Really, when you look at what our work is about, it's trying to understand some of the core capabilities that might be necessary within organizations for them to thrive in the kind of world we live in today—a world where you can't predict things very precisely anymore and where you can't count on what worked in the past to work in the future . . . Ours is a world of increasing interdependency."

According to widely recognized pioneer thinkers such as Senge and Russell L. Ackoff, formerly of the Wharton School and chairman of the board at INTERACT, The Institute for Interactive Management in Bala Cynwyd, Pennsylvania, our traditional way of handling complexity prevents us from seeing the larger picture and from acknowledging our own connectedness to

THE EVOLUTION OF TRAINING IN A LEARNING ORGANIZATION

The learning organization requires organizational learning in addition to traditional training. Organizational learning is a set of processes and structures to help people create new knowledge, share their understanding, and continuously improve themselves and the results of the enterprise. It isn't a program or a project but a management philosophy.

Traditional Training

Employees receive skills training; executives receive development training
Training goals are based on requests by users
Training primarily addresses immediate needs or short-term plans
Needs assessments are done by the training group or by managers
Training is conducted locally or at an offsite classroom
Delivery of training is scheduled on a periodic basis
Training approach is a delivery of knowledge
Training is instructor driven; programs designed by specialists
Content is generalized; developed by training specialists; often prescriptive
Trainers develop and deliver content, trainees are recipients

Organizational Learning

All employees receive learning support, lifelong development
Learning goals are based on corporate strategy and users' needs
Learning focuses on core competencies and long-term strategic plans
Needs assessments are done jointly by individuals, managers and training groups
Education takes place at the workplace, job site or anywhere
Delivery of education is on real time, upon request
Education approach is to design learning experiences or workplace interventions
Education is self directed; process design involves participants
Content is specific and applied; developed jointly with trainees; trainees determine content
Educators facilitate process and coach learners, learners are joint developers

Source: *SRI Business Intelligence Program and Diane McGinty Weston,* Organizational Learning in Practice.

SENGE'S FIVE DISCIPLINES FOR LEARNING ORGANIZATIONS

These disciplines, or "component technologies" are elements that unite to begin to form a learning organization.

Personal Mastery: A special level of proficiency in which individuals become committed to their own lifelong learning.

Mental Models: Deeply ingrained assumptions that influence how we understand the world and how we take action.

Shared Vision Building: Sharing a picture of the future you want to realize

Team Learning: The ability for individuals collectively to produce extraordinary results and allow individual members to grow more rapidly than they could otherwise. Using dialogue and the suspending of assumptions, the team tries to think together. Team learning may be more important in a company than individual learning because without it, the organization can't learn.

Systems Thinking: A conceptual framework that sees all parts as interrelated and affecting each other. This fifth discipline is crucial so that all the elements develop together. It integrates all of the theory and practice; one can't be separated from the other.

Source: *The Fifth Discipline: The Art and Practice of the Learning Organization*, by Peter M. Senge.

it. People have a tendency to break problems down into smaller pieces so that they're more manageable. However, the difficulty with this reductionist type of thinking is that it assumes that the sum of the parts equals the whole. Furthermore, this approach dooms us to solving problems in the same way we've always tried to solve them. And proponents of the learning organization believe that unless we find radically new approaches to solve problems, we're doomed to failure. "The essence of a learning organization is that people are changing, people are developing ways of thinking and ways of interacting that are fundamentally different than the way most people operate most of the time in most organizations," Senge says.

The basic question then becomes, "What would be the core capabilities of organizations to be able to thrive in such a world?" Many organizations start with Senge' ideas about the five disciplines (see "Senge's Five Disciplines for Learning Organizations"). Eventually they ask, "What other ways could we think? What ways could we work together?"

But each organization has to find its own way. Even Senge acknowledges that the five disciplines are a foundation but don't actually tell you where to start. To be able to implement many of these ideas, experts say it's most important to create an environment in which people can learn.

Senge cites three key elements:

1. You need real commitment and a compelling business argument as to why it's vital to change. (In other words, people need to acknowledge that they're stuck. They need to be willing to direct a lot of energy and commitment toward something different.)

2. You need to have a domain in which to take action. Even if 10 people agree on a plan, it's pointless if they don't have a place in which they can take action. You didn't learn to walk by sitting around and contemplating it. Learning involves the willingness to experiment. A domain allows you to practice some of the ideas so that learning can become part of an ongoing process. The whole idea of *learning laboratories* is to create managerial practice fields where people come together and practice as well as devise new products and services. This is much like a sports team or a theater troupe rehearsing. Learning always involves taking action.

3. You need tools and methods so that you can put the ideas into practice. According to theorists, this element poses a big problem in trying to bring about innovation in the United States because there are very few tools we develop. "It's sobering to realize how long it takes new theories to get translated into practical tools," Senge says. One example of a tool is Toyota's philosophical commitment to quality management. When the company shifted the infrastructure of the factory so that people in the front lines were given methods to gauge quality, tools to conduct experiments and authority to stop the assembly line, the methods were made available to support the commitment and philosophy.

Finally, most theorists and practitioners in this field agree on three components: the change in mindset that's necessary for management to undergo; a creative orientation that encourages individuals to be proactive rather than reactive to situations; and an orientation toward systems thinking.

A learning organization is a philosophy, not a program. Because it's merely a concept, how do you translate the learning organization into everyday corporate life? How are companies working with the philosophy to implement change? And what role does human resources play in such an organization?

For most HR professionals, the very idea of considering *learning* as something separate from a training program is asking for a fundamental mindshift. But human resources isn't alone. This mindshift is a cornerstone of the whole idea, and is required by everyone.

For this reason, learning organizations don't just happen. In fact, many of the thinkers, researchers and practitioners say a company never becomes a learning organization because by definition it means always evolving, always being in flux, always learning. In addition, there are a variety of approaches that can be applied; there's a new, basic vocabulary to learn, with phrases such as *learning laboratories* and *dialoguing* (see "Definition of Terms," page 383); and no pat answers. And, it involves breaking down barriers in the ideas

> The very idea of considering *learning* as something separate from a training program is asking for a fundamental mindshift.

and assumptions—or *mental models*—we already possess, and in the way we talk to each other.

The learning organization is so radical that many human resources people (as well as others) feel uncomfortable with it. They say it's too soft; too amorphous. Some learning-organization advocates even worry that if the human resources staff gets involved in implementing the concept that they may attempt to turn it into a program, nullifying its benefits.

"It's hard for people to think differently about integrating new knowledge," says Susan Schilling, vice president of development and creative director at MECC. "It's a challenge to look differently at your customer, at your distribution and production methods, at the way you think about developing product." But, the organizations that can generate and quickly understand new information and effectively communicate it to the staff are going to have a competitive advantage, she says. "We have to keep raising the bar and improving the quality of our work and the timeliness of our decisions."

Given a chance, the learning-organization concept is powerful. It allows for greater productivity, efficiency and idea generation. "It smells like, looks like, and often feels like soft stuff, but when you cut through that and get to the core, it provides very solid, measurable and definable tools and processes that result in real live business results," says Ron Hutchinson, vice president of customer service for Milwaukee-based Harley-Davidson Motor Company Inc. Indeed, if you do it right you can save millions of dollars.

Take, for example, Deerborn, Michigan-based Ford Motor Co. "Because of behavioral changes that we attribute to the learning-organization concept, our team was more effective, which resulted in more up-front problem resolution," says Nick Zeniuk, business planning manager in Ford's Lincoln Continental Car Program.

"As a result, we'll be able to save $50 to $65 million that we would have spent correcting late designs or rebuilding production tools," says Zeniuk.

Business people such as Zeniuk believe in the learning-organization concept not just because it's the latest buzz word, but because they're discovering that its principles can make a difference in their work.

Ford Motor Co. is a place where systemic thinking works. Ford has been exploring the idea of organizational learning since the late 1980s. It's a place where *systems thinking, collaborative learning* and *action learning* come together. "There's a fundamental shift underway in the practice of management, and much of that is contained in the notion of systemic thinking and collaborative learning," says Victor Leo, Ford's liaison officer to MIT's Organizational Learning Center and program manager at Ford's Executive Development Center. "What's coming to the forefront is the ability to connect business functions, such as marketing, finance, product development and various staff-support activities, to see how they're interrelated and interdependent. It's causing a real shift in the way the values of the corporation are espoused and carried out."

The learning-organization philosophy began at a senior executive program in 1988 when management said it wanted to learn about thinking and how to think differently. Leo and his associates researched several of the top resources on systems thinking and collaborative learning. Within two years, 2,000 senior executives had gone through a week-long learning program that exposed them to the concepts, gave them a safe place to *dialogue* and opened their minds to the ideas. They accepted the concept as reasonable, but questioned how one would translate concepts into the workaday world. "We picked up the gauntlet and focused on moving from the concept to application," Leo says. He and a few other colleagues formed relationships with Senge, Ackoff and others, attended workshops and did a lot of reading. Then they looked for individuals who would begin work on applying the ideas.

Systemic thinking and collaborative learning didn't happen overnight. It required internalization of ideas and transformational change—and that required time. You can't move from machine age, or analytical thinking and individual performance, to a more systemic, collaborative view easily. You need an infrastructure where you can apply the theory, and an arena where you can practice the strategy and move away from fragmentation. In other words, you need to rehearse seeing the world (or the business) as a whole. As Leo puts it: "We constantly remind ourselves that the customer drives the whole vehicle. No one goes out and says, 'I bought this care because it had the best brakes.'" But it isn't easy to shift to that kind of holistic thinking.

Ford found several proponents who were willing to help create an arena for experimentation. One of the leading champions in the company is Zeniuk. He became interested because he believed the company could improve its product-development process. "We were managing in a stressful environment. We weren't able to get people to work effectively together until we entered into a crisis mode. We could produce excellent results, but the methods used weren't compatible with what I call learning."

Zeniuk wanted to enable more effective up-front product development to ensure the launch of a new Lincoln Continental. "When a company's style is crisis management, it tends to focus people's energies around a goal and eliminates distractions. When they're in crisis mode, people begin to understand their interrelationships and interdependencies and are able to produce incredible results. Crisis management does work, but we don't learn anything from the experience. And the future demands learning. If we can't learn, somebody else will pass us by."

Zeniuk began reading about the learning organization. In 1991, he met Peter Senge and, along with colleague Fred Simon, program manager, began working with the Organizational Learning Center. The center acted as a facilitator rather than a consultant, and insisted that Ford discover its own solutions—outsiders couldn't impose them.

Zeniuk and Simon rolled up their sleeves and with a small group (eight senior managers) worked two days at a time offsite every month for approximately eight months. They began to create situations (what they call learning labs) in which they could talk to each other about their *current reality*. They developed a vision of where they wanted to be and engaged the whole team

You can't move from machine age, or analytical thinking and individual performance, to a more systemic, collaborative view easily. You need an infrastructure where you can apply the theory, and an arena where you can practice the strategy and move away from fragmentation.

in developing prescriptions for getting there. "It took us approximately eight months for the bosses to learn how to quit being bosses," says Zeniuk. "Before we could engage a team and incorporate some of the new learning, we had to eliminate the conflict that naturally existed because we thought we already had the answers. We also had to eliminate the inability to listen to each other."

MIT's Organizational Learning Center introduced the group to a slew of techniques for breaking through those communication barriers and dialoguing with each other. The tools help individuals become conscious of their assumptions. These assumptions get in the way of communicating effectively because unconscious thinking colors the way we talk and the way that we see things.

Some of the tools the group used were left-hand/right-hand conversation (the problems that occur with unspoken messages), ladder of inference (a technique that helps to specify our assumptions behind our thinking through common understanding), balancing advocacy inquiry (the dual responsibility between espousing our own position and understanding the other person's position to create a situation both people can support), creative tension (a vision-driven action) and the system archetypes (diagramming techniques that reflect recurring system behavior and develop an understanding of the most effective place to take action). [Note: See Part 4, Quality References, for more on system archetypes.] They also began practicing techniques that forced them to face a lack of trust with each other, the inability to make decisions and the bias toward authoritarian management.

They discovered through the tools that these counterproductive behaviors were rooted in mistrust, fear and control. "When we began to realize this, we began to treat each other very differently. We learned to listen to each other. We got to do some serious dialoguing, which means talking to each other and not worrying about winning or losing," says Zeniuk.

After an intense eight months, they finally could ask each other what they thought—and began to feel truly comfortable to say what was really on their minds. Now that there was an effective learning team of bosses, the company designed a two-day learning lab for the rest of the people in the Lincoln Continental Car Program and trained them in groups of 25. Approximately 200 people now have experienced the learning lab, where cross-functional members of a team practiced using some of the tools to solve their day-to-day issues. According to Zeniuk, they came in with problems they couldn't resolve and walked out with new insight about how to resolve the issues.

One of the techniques the groups used is an aid to thinking systemically called *Shifting the Burden*. Here's an example of how it works. A group of development engineers were trying to lessen the noise, vibration and harshness *(NVH)* of a vehicle. They added reinforcements to help cut down the noise, but these added weight that increased forces on the braking system and the tires, which meant that those systems had to be redesigned. Upgrading the braking system increased the cost.

Essentially what happened was that the development engineers created a solution by *shifting the burden* to another group. "In the past, when one group acted to solve their issue, it usually caused a problem in another group. The resolution of these issues would be by whoever screamed the loudest, had the most clout or went to the boss the fastest." Using this technique to see how people ordinarily handled these situations, they saw that shifting the burden wasn't really helping the problem. They began to look at the systemic inter-relationship because everyone wanted the car to be quieter. Everyone agreed they needed to resolve the problem and not add any weight to the car, not add cost and not jeopardize the quality.

Once people realized their goal, they brought together the brake people, the development people and the chassis and suspension people and found they could revise the geometry to resolve the issue. "In other words, they got the perfect solution by thinking systemically instead of fighting among them-selves," says Zeniuk. "But, it takes time for us to become effective. It can take several years for us to not only use the tools but to become proficient at them and to get others around us to use them."

Another group within Ford leading learning-organization efforts is the Electronic Fuel Handling division. The reason? "We decided that if we were going to be competitive, we had to learn how to bring things to the customer faster than our competition. We're always trying to do the revolutionary things we need to do and figure we want to use all our energy making the best parts and not fighting over turf or back stabbing," says David Berdish, organizational learning specialist.

Berdish knows that you don't simply give people a copy of Senge's *Fifth Discipline* and say, "Voila, we're a learning organization. Instead, we have designed a model to look at different issues where we can practice some of the tools." They use a brainstorming technique that "forces us to surface the mental models and learn together as a team. It exhibits *personal mastery* as well because we have to be open and honest, which is difficult if your boss is there because you might say some things that put yourself at risk," says Berdish. "We find that it isn't always the hard stuff such as machinery break-downs or bottlenecks in the process that get in the way of our ability to per-form and learn. It's usually the soft and squishy stuff. We don't do a very good job relating to each other." So, rather than having traditional business meet-ings, the group spends a lot of time with people from different departments and functions trying to dialogue (speak openly). The dialogues can get intense.

For example, at one session an engineering manager said he couldn't un-derstand why the machinery always operated on Saturday. He really meant that he felt some of the line operators didn't mind if the machinery broke down during the week because they wanted overtime pay. A union em-ployee—one of the operators—wasn't happy about the inference and said that they wouldn't have so much trouble with the machinery if they stopped using inexperienced engineers and buying inferior material.

"It got very volatile and emotional," Berdish says. "And, we surfaced these feelings and talked and talked and talked about it." Certainly not a traditional

It isn't always the hard stuff such as machinery break-downs or bottlenecks in the process that get in the way of our ability to perform and learn. It's usually the soft and squishy stuff.

business meeting. They realized that although they didn't even know each other, they had a very strong relationship to each other.

After all the fireworks, they were able to work together to design equipment-maintenance specifications. They invited the suppliers and discovered that they were selling the division a lot of spare parts they might not need if the machinery was handled differently.

"All these things wouldn't have surfaced if we had just allowed the tension to exist," Berdish says. As it turned out, the division is saving "a ton of money" on spare parts, and the equipment-maintenance specifications that the three people designed are going to be the prototype for the entire company. And, says Berdish, it was all designed and developed just because three people finally began being honest with each other. They were able to surface the mental models (or assumptions), dialogue around it, and see their connectedness to each other.

Indeed, Berdish is such a passionate believer in the learning-organization concept that he and the Electronic Fuel Handling Division set up a joint venture with a local community college where the faculty works to help Ford, and Ford helps them learn about becoming a learning organization. Berdish's division started in 1992 with two groups that included 38 people. By September 1, 1994, Ford had 20 teams involved (400 people) plus classes at the community college.

Harley-Davidson and Chaparral Steel: Shared vision and commitment produce bottom-line results.   Harley-Davidson Motor Co. has clear objectives when it comes to the learning organization. Hutchinson puts it this way: "For this company to be effective long term, we must have an organization in place that understands what caused prior mistakes and failures—and most importantly what caused successes. Then, we need to know how we can inculcate the successes and inculcate the preventive measures to avoid additional failures."

Lofty goals, but ones shared by many in the organization. In fact, Harley-Davidson employees will tell anyone that the company wants the ability to develop processes and people that will ensure it has the capability for rapid, effective change based on an understanding of the whole business environment in which it operates.

To do that, they realize individuals have to have a shared vision of the values they espouse as a company—ideals such as intellectual curiosity, productivity, participation and flexibility. "We also operate on such values as telling the truth, being fair, keeping promises and respecting the individual," Hutchinson says.

The motorcycle company's story wasn't always so positive. It was on the brink of extinction in the years 1982 and 1983. However, due in part to its shared vision and learning philosophy, the company has had a phenomenal turnaround. During the last three years, it has sold out its model-year products prior to the start of the model year, despite the fact that the company doubled production in the last five years.

Hutchinson began working with such concepts as the learning organization approximately three years ago. A year later, during a major strategic planning process, the management group used some of the systems-thinking tools to discuss issues in ways that they'd never been discussed before. Using tools from the five disciplines and some of the dialogue processes, the managers reached consensus around strategic direction, and rapidly assimilated it into an organizational plan.

Furthermore, creating a shared vision enabled the company to solve a major problem with its assembly facility. Because Harley-Davidson was trying to increase the number of motorcycles it produces, the managers believed they would have to build another assembly plant. Through diagramming techniques and a decision-making process that helped to identify the impact a decision had on people, on capital and on quality—and understanding people's, capital's and quality's relationships to one another—they realized that they didn't need to build another assembly plant. They could use an existing one in a different way.

"That's a succinct example where applying the tools led to a much deeper understanding of the system and a better decision on a very strategic issue about the location of production facilities," Hutchinson says.

Midlothian, Texas-based Chaparral Steel Co. also has seen that learning produces clearly definable, bottom-line benefits. At least 80% of the company's 1,000 employees are in some form of education enhancement at any one time. And the education can range from psychology courses at the university to metallurgy. "When you're looking at a learning organization, you have to take a holistic approach," says Dennis E. Beach, vice president of administration. He says you must ask, "Does it lead to improving the bottom line?"

In Chaparral Steel's case, it does. The company can measure approximately how many employee hours it takes to produce a ton of steel. When the company started, it produced a ton of steel with approximately 2½ to three employee hours. During the company's 20-year lifetime, the employee hours to produce the same tonnage has decreased to approximately 1½. Even more dramatic, the average in the United States is six employee hours.

Many factors go into that productivity—education, participatory management, compensation structure, technology. It's all intertwined. However, a key factor is making a commitment to employees and developing trust between all employees at the company regardless of their positions. Managers must be coaches working toward the same goal.

Chaparral has been able to track its bottom-line benefits closely. For example, the company wasn't able to keep up with the demand for a product that comes off of a specific lathe so management determined that they needed two lathes to perform the same function. A manager approached the machinist who operated the lathe and gave him the authority and responsibility to find an additional one. This included traveling to Japan to see what they were doing, as well as traveling to other installations in the United States. The

Many factors go into that productivity—education, participatory management, compensation structure, technology. It's all intertwined.

machinist selected a used lathe that was on sale from another company and saved Chaparral approximately $300,000.

In addition to this kind of trust and shared vision, the company is committed to individual lifelong learning and operates without proposals, memos and the like around these issues. Instead, they communicate by talking to each other. "It just needs to make sense," says Beach.

Of course what makes sense in one company may not make sense in another. Every organization must find its own way. And the route may include other initiatives. For example, Harley-Davidson employed the learning-organization concept while reengineering. Others combine it with TQM efforts. "The fact that these popular theories or models have come to the forefront supports the concept that organizations truly are changing the way they think about the way to do business as we enter the new century," MECC's Gilbert says. "The main concepts of each—concern about quality, willingness to look at how all processes and work gets done, and an openness to learning at all levels of the organization and how they all work together—are critical to success of business in the coming years.

"That isn't to say that all of these models are right for all companies," Gilbert adds. "The essence of each of these is very important. However that doesn't mean that every company ought to go out and hire consultants to implement these ideas. Companies need to think about who they are and what's most important to them now as a priority. Know who you are and where to start. Know what's going to be most important in the organization."

Charlene Marmer Soloman is a contributing editor to Personnel Journal.

Quality Transformation
COMMUNICATION

Everything We Do Is Wrong

T.J. Larkin and Sandar Larkin

Top management often develops elaborate presentations to communicate with employees about corporate issues and work issues. For the most part, these communications don't really get the message out. This article explains why and provides some ideas for making communication work by developing a method that gets the word to supervisors in language they can understand and makes it easy to let line workers know what's going on.

It's time for the big announcement. Employees fill the cafeteria as senior management sits on a raised platform, each manager ready to communicate some part of the upcoming change. Uniting all the presentations is a new value and mission statement.

The speeches will be relayed live, via satellite, to plants and offices throughout the country. Two-way hookups will allow employees anywhere to raise their hands and ask questions.

Following the launch, a special edition of the company newspaper will be dedicated to the change. Posters displaying the new mission will hang in elevators and lobbies. The new logo will be everywhere.

This is a maximum effort. Nothing will be left undone.

And nothing will be right.

Not only will it fail—it will be positively harmful. Look at the assumptions in this communication plan:

- Source: The first words employees hear about the change should come from the lips of senior management.
- Medium: The best way to reach employees is through large meetings, videos, and print.
- Content: A new value or mission statement adds credibility to the proposed change.

If your instincts say this is not a good plan, you should listen to them. The scene described above is what is usually done, and it does not work. The Wyatt Co. investigated 531 U.S. companies undergoing major restructuring. When asked, "If you could go back in time and change one thing, what would it be?" CEOs answered, "The way we communicated with our employees."

But would it help if the CEOs could go back? Would they know what to do differently? Improving communication with frontline employees, the people making the products and delivering the service, means abandoning past ways and taking on three new principles:

- Target frontline supervisors—don't let executives introduce the change to frontline employees.
- Rely on face-to-face communication—don't rely on videos, print, or meetings.
- Communicate facts only—avoid value and mission statements.

Target Frontline Supervisors

The best way to improve communication is to reach frontline workers through their supervisors. The research on this is loud and clear.

Phillip Clampitt and Cal Downs asked employees to recall specific communication that increased their productivity, 70 percent mentioned communication with their supervisor, far surpassing communication with co-workers, meetings, memos, and companywide publications. When employees are asked how they most prefer to receive information, 90 percent say from their supervisor, according to research from TPF&C, a Towers Perrin company. Wyatt Co. studies show 76 percent of employees believe communication within their local work area is good, compared with only 47 percent believing communication from senior managers is good.

In general, research conducted with frontline employees (blue-collar or clerical workers) shows that communication with supervisors has the greatest impact on frontline performance, that supervisors are the preferred source for information, and that employees perceive supervisors as good communicators. As a result, any attempt to improve communication to the front line should devote 80 percent of its effort to improving communication with supervisors, and 20 percent to improving communication such as company newspapers, videos, and executive presentations. Two ways to target supervisors as privileged communicators are:

"If you could go back in time and change one thing, what would it be?" CEOs answered, 'The way we communicated with our employees."

- Supervisor briefing cards. Pocket-sized and fact-filled, these cards are printed up by a company's internal-communications department and distributed to supervisors so they can give the facts about any important issue to frontline employees.
- Supervisor advice forms. These force upward communications from supervisors to senior managers. Whatever the change—equipment purchases, department restructuring, or new operating procedures—supervisor advice forms require and document that the most critical communication actually happens.

A large manufacturing company faced a crisis when a competitor suddenly purchased 5 percent of their shares, and newspaper headlines began screaming of a hostile takeover. The communication plan for reaching the front line put supervisors as the No. 1 priority. Immediately following every major development supervisor briefing cards were prepared. Producing the cards involved writing, laminating, cutting the cards to pocket size, and air delivery to 5,000 supervisors around the country. This process usually took one day or less. Figure 1 on page 398 shows a typical card.

The supervisor briefing cards work because they respond to the reality of life on the front line:

Frontline worker stopping a supervisor as she passes: "Say, what's this I hear about the company being sold? Does this mean we could lose our jobs?"

Supervisor: "No, only 5 percent has been sold. We're probably OK until they purchase 15 percent; then we could have some serious problems."

Frontline worker: "Oh, thanks."

This is successful frontline communication, and it's made possible by targeting supervisors as privileged receivers.

The little conversation might not provide enough information for you. But then, you are a reader of *Across the Board* and they are not. Why do we persist in the fantasy that what frontline workers really want is a 3,000-word article published two weeks later in the company newspaper? Or that they yearn for a 45-minute speech from the CEO? The answer to their question is often buried in language they don't understand and served up with a heavy dose of platitudes about how we all need "to pull together as a team" and not "take our eye off the ball during this critical time."

Why can't we get it through our heads that what they really want is a short, straightforward answer to a short, straightforward question? And they want the answer now, not later, and in face-to-face conversation with their supervisors. Our communication efforts should be making sure that happens. Supervisor briefing cards make this possible.

A second example shows how improving the upward flow of communication should also target supervisors, this time as privileged senders of information through the use of supervisor advice forms.

A mining company worried about problems breaking in new machinery. Return-on-investment (ROI) targets were eventually reached, but much later than planned. The mine manager explained: "Implementing something new

The supervisor briefing cards work because they respond to the reality of life on the front line.

Why can't we get it through our heads that what they really want is a short, straightforward answer to a short, straightforward question? And they want the answer now.

SUPERVISION BRIEFING CARD

PRICE?
- rumors are EXT will offer our shareholders $32 a share
- current price is $28 a share

WHERE WOULD EXT GET THE MONEY TO BUY SHARES?
- borrow money from banks

HOW WOULD EXT REPAY THE BANKS?
- try to run us with a bigger profit
- probably break us up into pieces
- selling some pieces to other companies to repay loans

WHAT PARTS WOULD EXT SELL?
- We don't know

WHEN WILL WE KNOW WHAT'S GOING TO HAPPEN?
- EXT now owns 5% of our company
- They can sit on these shares or buy more
- EXT has said that if it buys more than 15% it promises to go all the way and get control of the company

---

Figure 1.   **Form for internal communication that keeps frontline employees in the loop.**

---

in this place is like doing root canal without Novocain.'' The problem, he believed, was due to poor communication between managers buying the equipment and the mine's supervisors. As a solution, he tried supervisor advice forms, requiring that they be used with all capital equipment requisitions: "If you can't document face-to-face communication with supervisors—you can't buy it.''

Engineers at the mine wanted to replace aging Caterpillar bulldozers with Komatsu dozers. The engineers submitted a dozen supervisor advice forms with the normal requisition paperwork (ROI projections, machine specifications, competitive bids, etc.). Figure 2 shows a supervisor advice form.

The supervisor advice forms revealed strong supervisor opposition to the proposed Komatsu bulldozers. Management responded by selecting supervisors with special communication skills and taking them to a neighboring mine that was having success with Komatsu dozers. Supervisors were able to operate the Komatsu equipment and speak face-to-face with the mine's operating and maintenance staff. In addition, Komatsu sales reps were brought in to explain to supervisors that their apprehensions were correct but old. Komatsu had improved their design, and most of their blade, track, and parts problems had been eliminated. Finally, supervisors learned that due to the

SUPERVISOR ADVICE FORM:
KOMATSU BULLDOZERS

supervisor: Ted McNeil

department: Maintenance

opinion

(check one)   ☒ do not purchase

☐ purchase with modifications

☐ purchase as described

comments

want CAT D-10s

Komatsus have problems

-blades hard to mount

-track has slippage problems

-Parts take too long!

Figure 2. **An example of a supervisor advice form.**

increasing number of customers, Komatsu promised to build a local warehouse providing eight-hour replacement for the most frequently needed parts.

This special supervisor communication is worth every ounce of the effort required because what must be avoided, above all else, is the lethal and highly dramatic supervisor tantrum. A tantrum whose audience is the frontline work force and whose intent is sabotaging investments made without supervisor input. When the first Komatsu dozers begin arriving, the absolute last thing you want is supervisors flip-flopping in disgust, draping the new investment in obscenities, and lamenting management's inability to distinguish good bulldozers from various parts of the human anatomy. Supervisors punish management for poor communication by poisoning the frontline work force, and this, in turn, plays havoc with implementation and ROI.

Purchasing a fleet of bulldozers carries a multibillion-dollar price tag; communicating directly with supervisors costs little more than a handful of dollars and hours. You need not always follow supervisor advice, but always show respect for their opinions, or be prepared for the consequences.

Above all else, the people in your internal communication department must know what they are doing. They must realize that all receivers are not

You need not always follow supervisor advice, but always show respect for their opinions, or be prepared for the consequences.

Where is it?	
Communications by budget size (most expensive first)	**Employees asking "where is it?"** (out of 40,000)
Your Bank (monthly video)	4
Transaction (twice monthly newspaper)	38
Teller-Talk (simplified annual report)	0
Personnel Report (montly listing of job bvacancies, promotions, and transfers)	2,112
Over-Time (monthly social committee publication)	890

Figure 3. **Employee responses to missing communications.**

created equal, that some are more important than others, that communication must be strategic, it must focus on where it can make a difference, it must focus on supervisors.

Go Face-to-Face

When trying to improve employee communication, almost always, the first impulse is to build a "program": video, print, electronic mail, briefing meetings, executives on a traveling road show. Strangely, we insist on doing so, all the time knowing that most important information moves by spoken word, face-to-face, in short informal interactions. We seem unable to grasp the truth before us: When it comes to reaching frontline employees, our greatest efforts should go into using the informal, not the formal, channels.

A large bank (1,200 branches and 40,000 employees) decided to audit the effectiveness of its communication program. Usually these communication audits involve long questionnaires, hundreds of questions, dozens of pages, where employees evaluate various types of corporate communication: company newspaper, video programs, bulletin boards, and newsflash sheets. This bank, however, discovered a faster, cheaper, easier, and much more valid way of measuring communication—they stopped all the communications without warning—and then counted the number of employees calling to ask, "Where is it?" (Figure 3).

The results gave a very clear indication of which communications were hitting their marks:

- One out of every 10,000 employees missed the *Your Bank* video program enough to call and ask "where is it?"
- A tiny fraction (0.09 percent) of employees inquired about the missing *Transaction* company newspaper.
- Overall, the bank spends big on the least noticed communication and small on the communication employees care most about—*Personnel Report*, the monthly listing of job vacancies, promotions, and transfers.

Pray this communication need never survive in a real market. Suppose *The Wall Street Journal* or *Financial Times* simply did not come out tomorrow. What percent of its subscribers would call asking about its absence, 20 percent? 30 percent? 50 percent? It seems fair to guess some number in excess of 0.09 percent would ask about the missing communication. Why? Because they want it. They value the information. The minuscule numbers missing the bank's formal communication show this communication does not play a major role in the day-to-day affairs of employees. Consequently, take some of these resources and redirect them to the communication that does play a major role: informal face-to-face communication between frontline employees and their supervisors.

A frontline worker sticks her head into the supervisor's office and asks, "Continuous annealing for our sheet-steel line? Is this some crazy R&D concoction, or will it really work?" This is the communication that matters: short, face-to-face interactions between supervisors and frontline employees. How supervisors answer these questions directly affects the performance of these companies. Putting continuous annealing into a plant will cost $200 million. The company will need every ounce of frontline cooperation it can get. Communication can help by making supervisors the top communication priority, by using the informal links between supervisors and their frontline workers to carry your most important messages. And spend time and money on formal communication only when your supervisor communication is running perfectly.

Think about how quickly some information moves through even large organizations.

Suppose that someone in your mailroom is having an affair with a member of your executive committee. Much as you may wish for this to stay secret, this information will rocket through the company. But how? Is the affair discussed in appropriately demure terms in a corporate video? Are the intimate details printed on newsflash sheets or posted on bulletin boards? Do supervisors attend training courses brushing up their affair-communication skills?

No, none of these things happen, but the news of the affair still moves like lightning throughout the corporation.

Rumors move so quickly because they travel on the ultimate "information superhighway," and we don't mean e-mail, video, print, or any other media. We mean the employee grapevine, a time-tested method of informal, face-to-face communication.

Stop Communicating Values

Nothing is more difficult than persuading executives to stop putting their corporate values into words. This despite the fact that in their hearts they know the best way to communicate a value is not in words but in action. Regardless, they hang on to the idea that the words will help it along.

This is wrong. Value pronouncements from the corporate center land on the front line and ring of insincerity.

Normal people in normal situations don't go about making value pronouncements: "I am a good corporate citizen!" "I pursue quality in everything I do!" "I treat others with respect and dignity at all times!" If a business contact spoke this way, his listeners would wonder just what it was he was trying to put over on them. We all know that values belong in actions, not words. A sincerely held value is something you deduce, not something you are told.

If you break the rule that values are best communicated in action, employees will punish you. We have seen employees twist *Quality—Our Mission* into *Quality's Gone Missin'*; *Hands-On Management* into *Wanking Managers*; and *Fast & Fussy*, used by a trucking firm, into names too obscene to print here. Employees rarely passively accept grand value campaigns. They know values belong in action, not words.

The very first time your values appear in words should be in an informal conversation between two frontline employees—"Say, have you noticed how serious this place is getting about 'customer service' "—and never in a company memo, poster, or executive speech.

Assume for a moment your value is innovation (it could be customer service, cost cutting, quality, or whatever). Then promotions, bonuses, hiring, and training should all stress innovation, and the company should frequently communicate the percentage of profit arising from new products or services. But don't create catchy slogans, frame your creed on office walls, and plaster your value on every flat surface in the company. A value taken seriously is put into action, not printed on pencils and coffee mugs.

Most important, don't force employees to talk about the value.

Ford Motor Co. ran a huge value campaign called *MVGP: Mission, Values, and Guiding Principles*. MVGP emphasized six values: quality, customer service, continuous improvement, employee involvement, partnership, and integrity. Ford printed these values everywhere and pushed them hard in publications, speeches, and videos. Meetings were held involving all of Ford's 185,000 employees. At these meetings employees were told to explain how the values were being implemented in their jobs. At one meting a stamping-plant manager testified to the impact of MVGP in his area:

"At the facility, we live by Mission, Values, and Guiding Principles. Both the union and management support the concepts totally. It's a way of life

> Value pronouncements from the corporate center land on the front line and ring of insincerity.

> A sincerely held value is something you deduce, not something you are told.

here: We know people and quality are No. 1, and every decision is based on that."

Please look at the plant manager's statement again—only this time forget you are reading an *Across the Board* article and read these words with your common-sense eyes: " . . . we live by Mission, Values, and Guiding Principles . . . union and management support the concepts totally . . . it's a way of life here . . . we know people and quality are No. 1 . . . every decision is based on that."

What's going on here? This is not the way plant managers normally speak. Peel away the surface words and listen for the meaning underneath. Our interpretation is:

"The bigwigs in corporate have climbed onto yet another management bandwagon. Tell these guys what they want to hear and get them the heck out of here, so we can go back to the real job of running a plant."

Employees mouthing slogans are not signs that communication is working. Just the opposite: They signify a breakdown in communication. Important channels are jammed with static. By communicating values, executives present themselves as out-of-touch bureaucrats, pacified by the sound of their own words repeated back to them. No matter how well intended, putting values into words is useless; forcing employees to talk these values is positively harmful.

> Employees mouthing slogans are not signs that communication is working. Just the opposite: They signify a breakdown in communication.

Think clearly before attempting to communicate these values. Employees will believe we have a particular value when they see it in our behavior; and they will adopt the value themselves only when they perceive this as essential to the attainment of their personal goals and ambitions. Propaganda does not help, and, as our example tries to show, can badly damage communication.

If we insist on communicating values, we will paint a picture of senior executives with both head and feet in the clouds. Better to keep those feet planted on terra firma, right next to the shoes of the frontline managers and employees.

TJ and Sandar Larkin are co-authors of Communicating Change *(McGraw-Hill, 1994) and directors of Larkin Communication Consulting. The company has offices in New York, London, and Melbourne, Australia.*

Pruning the Grapevine

Timothy Galpin

This article doesn't plow new ground—there isn't a lot to plow in communication—but it does provide some useful tools for planning communications. The author points that if managers do not take control of communication in an open and constructive fashion, the grapevine will flourish, perhaps the organization's detriment. However, when information is willingly shared and there is an accepted way for disseminating it, this diminishes the reason for the grapevine.

T*he company is being sold." "There will be massive cuts." "People will be let go."*

Unfortunately, those are familiar words to many employees. When you ask people where they first heard such statements, they often say, "in the lunchroom" or "at the coffee machine." In other words, they heard them through the grapevine.

People in the human resource department need to manage communications effectively—especially during organizational restructuring—so that the grapevine isn't the main source of information. One way is to adapt some traditional models of interpersonal communication for use in an organizational context.

Old Models, New Applications

Remember the Johari Window? This communication model—developed in 1969 by Joseph Luft and Harry Ingham—helps people improve interpersonal interactions through assessing the ways in which they give and receive information. The Johari Window is a grid divided into four regions that represent different types of information exchanged during communication. (See Figure 1).

The basic concept of the Johari Window is that open, two-way communication can enhance interpersonal effectiveness. Within the broader context of organizations, the Johari Window can help improve organizational effectiveness—also through open, two way communication. But first, it's important to understand how the model works on a personal level.

Region 1, the Arena, is the area of shared information. When people share information and understand each other, their interpersonal relationships tend

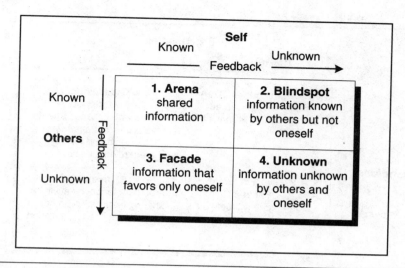

Figure 1. **The Johari Window.** This helps people assess how they communicate. Each region represents a different kind of information.

to be better. The larger the Arena (the more shared information), the more effective, productive, and mutually beneficial an interpersonal relationship is likely to be.

Region 2, the Blindspot, involves information that is known by others but not oneself. The Blindspot can damage interpersonal relationships because it's almost impossible to truly understand people's actions, thoughts, and feelings without knowing why they behave and think the way they do.

Region 3, the Facade, hinders interpersonal effectiveness in that the information in this area favors only oneself. Information in the Facade protects people from others knowing negative things about them. People might not share such information simply because they're apathetic. But more often, it can be because they desire power and control.

Region 4, the Unknown, involves information that is unknown by others and oneself. The area of the Unknown has the most potential for creativity, if all parties are willing to work together to gather information.

During organizational change, senior managers may try to keep information from those in lower-level positions for the same reasons that people keep information from each other in personal relationships: fear, power, and apathy. This creates a small organizational Arena and a large organization Facade.

A large Facade favors change agents and puts everyone else in the organization at a disadvantage. This often leads people to distrust, dislike, and even sabotage change initiatives. In addition, a Blindspot can form when change agents are unaware of others' thoughts and feelings.

The Johari Window can be adapted (see Figure 2) to help ease organizational change by enhancing communication. It's important to expand the

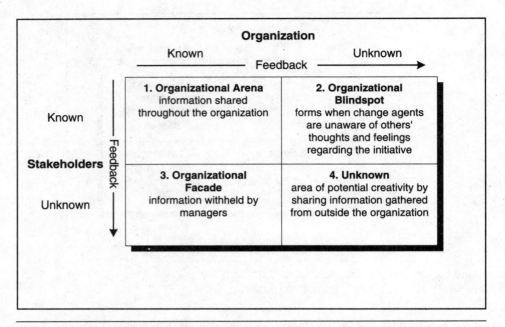

Figure 2. **The Organizational Johari Window.** The Johari Window can be adapted to improve organization-wide communication.

Arena along the two axes, Feedback and Exposure, which are pivotal to effective communication. Exposing more information to others expands the Arena along the vertical axis. Increasing feedback expands the Arena along the horizontal axis.

First, You Need a Plan

An effective communications plan is guided by several principles. First, make effective communication a priority. Then make sure that all messages are linked to the strategic objectives of the change effort.

Suppose that a goal of the change effort is to reduce costs. Any messages about the goal should communicate the reasons for the cost reduction, the specific reduction to be made, and the benefits of reducing costs. Messages should also identify the stakeholders, the people who will be affected most by the cost reduction.

All communications should be honest. It's best not to gloss over potential problems. People should be made aware of the realistic limits and goals. That way, they're less likely to jump to conclusions about worst-case scenarios. For example, if you tell people that the goal of a divisional cost reduction is 30 percent, they probably won't worry that the entire division will be shut down.

The emphasis should be proactive rather than reactive. Plan communications ahead and disseminate them early. Then you won't have to take a

All communications should be honest. It's best not to gloss over potential problems.

defensive position when things start happening—such as when people learn that they don't have the appropriate skills to deal with changes taking place.

All messages should be consistent and repeated through various channels such as videos, memos, newsletters, and regular meetings. Because of their personal "filters," people are more likely to misinterpret a one-time announcement from senior management. They might not hear the whole message. Or, they may focus only on certain aspects. Most of the time, people care only about how changes will affect them—at least, that's what they care about at first. Multiple, consistent communications can help people absorb and internalize the true content of the messages.

The communication also needs to establish mechanisms for two-way feedback. People should give and get feedback during the design, testing, and roll-out of all change efforts. Effective feedback focuses on stakeholders' concerns; work areas and processes that need improving; specific goals such as cost reduction, reduced cycle time, or improved customer service; and lessons that can be applied to future change efforts.

Many change efforts are poorly managed. Managers may think that withholding information ensures that people will learn what's happening only through official channels. But the grapevine is always in bloom.

Avoiding the Pitfalls

It may help to delegate to a special department some responsibility for organization-wide communication. The department can help formulate messages, set up delivery channels, create opportunities for communication, and conduct communication events. But final accountability still lies with management. When senior-level managers try to delegate ownership, they send a strong message that the change effort isn't worth their time. People interpret that as a lack of commitment, and they themselves become reluctant to commit.

Another pitfall is sending communications with unclear or incomplete descriptions of exactly what is happening. Later, implementation may break down as employees begin to question management's knowledge of the details.

Overall, poor communications planning can result in unclear roles, insufficient follow-up, and a lack of fine-tuning once implementation begins. But a well-designed plan breaks down the barriers to change and gets people's buy-in. In particular, insufficient communication from top management can lead middle managers to kill new initiatives.

Once a change effort is underway, it's important to keep open the channels of communication. By the time managers have set the direction of the effort, they've probably reconciled any concerns. They're also less likely to believe that they really have to communicate to others about what is happening. Yet, open communication is needed most as the changes cascade down through the organization to all levels. During roll-out, people will have questions. They need to feel that they're being listened to. They also may have helpful suggestions.

Managers may think that withholding information ensures that people will learn what's happening only through official channels. But the grapevine is always in bloom.

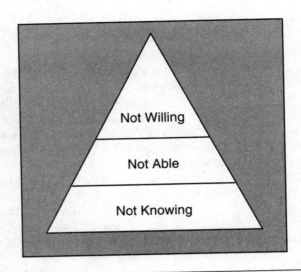

Figure 3.   **The Resistance Pyramid.** You can overcome people's resistance by giving them knowledge and skills so that they're more willing to change.

Possibly the biggest pitfall is underestimating people's resistance to change and their frustration. Employees may even exhibit dysfunctional behavior by sabotaging initiatives. The Resistance Pyramid shows how to overcome people's resistance to change (See Figure 3).

The Resistance Pyramid—developed by professors Nieder and Zimmerman at the University of Bremen in Hamburg, Germany—is similar to Abraham Maslow's Hierarchy. In Maslow's model, people's needs are arranged from low to high priority: physiological (lowest), safety, love and belongingness, esteem, and self-actualization (highest).

The Resistance Pyramid is made up of successive levels of resistance: not knowing, not able, and not willing. The degree to which resistance is overcome at each level reduces resistance at the next level.

The pyramid's first level, not knowing, is overcome through communicating information. The second level, not able, is overcome through training people in new skills—such as operating new equipment, working in teams, and following revised procedures. Once people have new knowledge and skills, they're more willing to change, and the top level—not willing—is overcome.

A four-phase process

Figure 4 depicts four phases of the communication process during a change effort. Phase 1 is announcing the effort to all employees and explaining the details. In Phase 2, the focus is on identifying any issues that may arise, such as employees worrying that there may be layoffs.

PHASE	SCOPE	PURPOSE
Phase 1 **Awareness Building** "This is what is happening."	**Corporate Wide**	• Line change initiatives with strategic plans. • Reaffirm the organization's values. • Give specific information about the process. • Announce senior management involvement and support.
Phase 2 **Project Status** "This is where we are going."	**Organization Specific**	• Demonstrate senior management's commitment. • Reaffirm the strategic rationale. • Identify managers' and employees' issues. • Gain information from pilot tests. • Provide the "big picture."
Phase 3 **Roll-Out** "This is what it means to you."	**Project Specific**	• Continue to show senior management's commitment. • Provide specific information on the changes being made and how they will affect people. • Provide training in new rules, skills, and methods.
Phase 4 **Follow-Up** "This is how we will make it work."	**Team Specific**	• Continue to show senior management's commitment. • Reaffirm the organization's values and strategic focus. • Listen to and act on managers' and employees' need to implement changes. • Refine changes to ensure success.

Figure 4. **The Communication Process.** The communication process in a change effort consists of four phases.

In Phase 3, the roll-out, communications should include information from any pilot tests on the proposed changes. At this stage, messages must be specific. They must focus on the implications of the roll-out for all employees and the organization as a whole. Phase 3 includes training in new skills, roles, and methods.

Phase 4 involves getting feedback and fine-tuning the implementation.

Stakeholders (who)	Objectives (why)	Key Messages (what)	Vehicles (how)	Timing (when and how often)	Accountability (ownership to deliver or implement)
middle management	• new roles • new methods • person impact	• meetings with the CEO and exectives • training	• meetings with the CEO and executives • training	• kickoff: week 1 • kickoff: month 1	• CEO and other executives • training dept
employees	• buy-in • understanding • new skills	• new roles • new methods • personal impact	• meetings with managers • training	kickoff: week 1 kickoff: month 1	• managers • training managers
customers	• information • awareness	• new methods • service impact	• meetings with sales reps	• kickoff: week 1	• sales reps
stakeholders	• information • awareness	• service impact • financial impact	• written information from CEO and CFO	• kickoff: week 1	• CEO and CFO
community	• information • awareness	• service impact • financial impact	• news releases	• kickoff: week 1	• CEO

Figure 5. **Communication-Strategy Matrix.** Here's an example of a communication strategy matrix of a change effort.

As the change effort takes shape, the communication process evolves. But some constants are necessary. The most important one is management support. Another is keeping people informed about how proposed changes will fit with the organization's values and strategic focus. This helps people view the change effort as essential to business success.

A communication-strategy matrix can help clarify who does what and how things are done. The matrix describes the stakeholders, goals, key messages, vehicles of communication, timing (when and how often information is disseminated), and accountability. (See Figure 5.)

The first step is identifying the key stakeholders inside and outside the organization. They can include senior managers, middle managers, lower-level employees, customers, suppliers, shareholders, and the community.

Once the stakeholders have been identified, it's important to know exactly what their stakes or interests entail. Most people want to know "what's in it for them." They want to know how their work will be affected, whether they'll have to relocate, and so forth. Once they know the particulars, they're more willing to listen to broader issues, such as increased market share.

Middle managers typically want to know whether they will manage the same people or report to the same boss. Shareholders want to know how changes will affect profits. Suppliers want to know whether orders will be cut or whether production should be stepped up. Members of the business community may want to know whether jobs will be lost or new jobs will open

Give people knowledge first and then new skills. A willingness to change will follow.

up. If stakeholders' questions aren't answered, the grapevine will provide its own, sometimes inaccurate, answers.

To help ensure the success of a change effort, it's important to get stakeholders' buy-in. It isn't enough just to tell them about planned changes. As in the Resistance Pyramid, give people knowledge first and then new skills. A willingness to change will follow.

All communications to stakeholders should describe the rationale for the change effort; people's new roles; and the benefits to employees, customers, shareholders, and the organization.

It's also important to identify the vehicles for communication—such as memos, speeches, meetings, videos, newsletters, electronic message boards, training sessions, news releases, posters, and so forth. The more consistent the communication is across those vehicles, the more credible it will be.

Even with effective communications, the grapevine won't ever wither and die. But you can prune the branches to keep them from growing wild.

Timothy Galpin is a principal in human resources and change management at Booz-Allen & Hamilton, McLean, Virginia.

PROCESS REENGINEERING

Will Participative Makeovers of Business Processes Succeed Where Reengineering Failed?

Thomas H. Davenport

Thomas Davenport explains how the standard approach to process reengineering often just doesn't work because it does not take into account the people who execute the processes. Davenport proposes a modified approach that includes the involvement of those affected by the changes. This is a thoughtful piece that adds to our understanding of what reengineering is all about.

Business process reengineering and information management initiatives often fail to live up to expectations. Some common rationalizations for poor results are:

- The process didn't have top management support.
- Middle management defeated attempts to implement major changes.

This article is reprinted from *Planning Review*, February 1995, with permission from the Planning Forum, the International Society for Strategic Management and Planning.

- The business environment changed before the new process could be adopted.
- The change initiative didn't fully enlist the cooperation of the people who were going to do the jobs.
- Because the initiatives were driven by an intent to cut costs rather than a strategic vision, they failed to promote the growth of the company.

However, my experience leads me to believe that we can't radically change the success rate of reengineering and information management initiatives if we see the problem merely in terms of a top-down or a bottom-up approach.

I am convinced that the real reason reengineering and information management initiatives fail so often is because they are wrongly assumed to be engineering projects. The engineering model emphasizes design, modeling, and advance planning. It deemphasizes the human skills needed to make a community out of a set of people working on the same process or sharing certain information.

For example, in most businesses' processes "reengineering" initiatives, a small design team decides on a radically better approach to work. For information systems, the dominant management paradigm is "information engineering," which involves modeling of information requirements leading to the development of applications and data bases.

In both cases, assumptions are made about human aspects of change that may be untenable. This is because, despite the appeal of engineering models of business change, we rarely have much success engineering human activities. We cannot understand business process or information environments sufficiently to have a tight coupling between design, implementation, and day-to-day practice. While creating engineering-oriented designs and models can be useful, we need to balance engineering with more bottom-up and emergent approaches to change.

Having been intimately involved with many reengineering projects during the last several years, I am increasingly convinced that the engineering model (or metaphor) is not the correct one. The reengineering concept can be traced to Frederick Taylor's mid-century approaches to industrial engineering and scientific management. Indeed, a coauthor and I called our first article on this topic "The New Industrial Engineering: Information Technology and Business Process Redesign."

The primary problem with Taylor's approach has always been that it separates the design of work from its execution. This flaw is repeated in "classical" reengineering, as defined in Michael Hammer's and James Champy's *Reengineering the Corporation:* "It is axiomatic that reengineering never, ever happens from the bottom up." This definition is most true when the issue is the politics of reengineering. Left to their own devices, middle managers don't normally strive to reengineer themselves out of power and line managers don't have the authority to instigate strategic reengineering. Top management

I am convinced that the real reason reengineering and information management initiatives fail so often is because they are wrongly assumed to be engineering projects.

must set the strategic direction for reengineering and demand implementation.

But in practice, the Hammer-Champy form of reengineering calls for a small group of people to design work processes for a much larger group. As a result, there is little participation in the design process by those who will actually do the work. These process engineers make implicit (or in some cases explicit) assumptions:

- There is one best way to organize work.
- I can easily and quickly understand how you do your work today.
- I can design your work better than you can design it.
- There is little about how you do your work now that is worth saving.
- You will do your work the way I specify.

These assumptions are problematic at best. First, while it is undeniable that most work arrangements can be improved upon, it is naive to assume that there is any "natural order" for a business process, as Hammer and Champy believe. Different observers of a process will often identify different improvements. Even where there is a clearly preferable work design, there frequently are valid reasons for not implementing it, such as excessive investment or high risk.

But more important, designing a business process isn't like designing a building, where the construction adheres precisely to the design specified in the blueprints. In business processes the couplings between design, implementation, and day-to-day execution are very loose. How could they be otherwise, given the following facts:

- Full implementation of a new process design may take several years.
- Those who implement and execute the process are usually different people from those who design it.
- The process design or formal procedure is only one factor determining how a worker will perform a process.
- It is impossible for designers to anticipate all of the daily contingencies that may affect how a process is performed.

I frequently visit firms that supposedly implemented a radical new process design several years earlier. When I ask how the new process is going, there is always a brief silence, then an admission that, "Things didn't turn out quite the way we planned."

There is also more rigorous evidence that implementation doesn't follow design. One study of 35 reengineering projects found that the revolutionary fervor of reengineering projects at the design phase usually dissipates into evolutionary change at the implementation phase. A detailed study of Xerox customer service processes found that it was impossible for any work design or procedure manual to anticipate some of the events that cropped up in the

While it is undeniable that most work arrangements can be improved upon, it is naive to assume that there is any "natural order" for a business process.

One study of 35 reengineering projects found that the revolutionary fervor of reengineering projects at the design phase usually dissipates into evolutionary change at the implementation phase.

field—for example, a peanut butter and jelly sandwich caught in the document feeder.

Overengineering Information

For more than 20 years the dominant management information paradigm has been that data streams could be designed architecturally and engineered. Also known as information engineering, or Business Systems Planning, the information architecture approach involves detailed modeling of information requirements and flows, and their relationship to business activities or processes. Thousands of such planning exercises have been carried out in firms with the primary goal of specifying which computerized information systems and data bases should be constructed within an organization.

Yet these approaches are problematic. Certainly information architecture is valuable in environments where the information to be managed is highly structured, where information needs vary little over time, and where there is a high level of consensus on key terms and meanings. Payroll and accounting applications are examples. But relatively few information environments have these characteristics. If we use architectural approaches to try to manage the entire information assets of an enterprise, we will almost certainly run into extreme difficulties.

This, in fact, has been the finding of several academic researchers who have investigated how enterprise-level information architecture works out in practice. Most such studies are never completed; they are canceled in favor of projects with more tangible benefits. Commonly, an enterprise model may take several years to complete. Those that are completed may be obsolete by the time they are finished. While there have been, to my knowledge, no studies of how information architectures actually changed information management and use practices, my guess is that the level of change is very low.

Oil company case.   The experience of a large oil company in building customer information architecture illustrates the problems with this approach. The firm had 80 million customers spread across 50 business units. The multi-year effort painstakingly categorized customers into 16 levels of a nested hierarchy. After three years, the sponsor realized that the firm's business strategy no longer emphasized sharing customer information across business units. In fact, several business units had been divested over the period, and four of the 16 customer levels were no longer relevant to the remaining units. The effort was abandoned.

The mounting evidence indicates that information is not well-suited to the fundamental assumptions that guide designers of buildings and bridges. Design engineers assume that the components will remain constant over time, that the designer controls the components, and that there is consensus on the purpose of the effort. But business information needs change rapidly; they are subject to a broad range of interpretation by those who use the information; and they are frequently the focus of dissenting views.

The mounting evidence indicates that information is not well-suited to the fundamental assumptions that guide designers of buildings and bridges.

Avoiding anarchy.   If full engineering is one extreme, the other extreme occurs when everyone's information needs are too disparate to allow for the imposition of any overall "system." This is much more rare a situation than those people who thrive on information anarchy would have us believe. While it's true that even the most common business processes have idiosyncrasies and great variation on how the meaning of a unit of information is assessed, nonetheless we see evidence every day of common processes and information environments.

More Workable Approaches to Process Design

In truth, neither top-down engineering nor bottom-up individualized processes and information best serves our business change purposes. What we need are intermediate solutions that allow for top-level direction while remaining sensitive to the fact that these are human processes. Fortunately, in the areas of both information and processes, middle-ground approaches are emerging. They combine some level of engineering discipline with the ability of employees to design their own work. Sometimes these solutions are a hard sell to senior executives, who don't like to admit that their deigns won't be implemented as planned. However, my argument is that it is better to plan and prepare for individual-level variation in work and information environments since it is inevitable that they will happen.

> What we need are intermediate solutions that allow for top-level direction while remaining sensitive to the fact that these are human processes.

Middle-road approaches to process management.   Some of the new business process reengineering approaches that are showing promise involve joint design of processes by design teams composed of either top managers or people appointed by them and execution teams composed of those who will do the work. One theoretical way to improve the effectiveness of such teams is to increase the size of the design team itself, or make its members more representative of those who will perform the work. In practice, however, this is difficult. In a large organization a major process may involve up to tens of thousands of people; one process being redesigned at IBM, for example, once had over a hundred thousand people in it. Given these numbers, expanding or "electing" a design team so that process workers feel they are adequately represented would be almost impossible.

But those who perform the processes can be asked to help the design team through interviews, surveys, and a telephone hotline, for example. In some companies this may be a valid means of giving workers a feeling that their ideas matter to the design of the new process. However, in companies with large numbers of workers involved in a process, their responses will be difficult to track, answer, and adopt as design suggestions.

A more feasible approach would be to parcel out the design task between design and execution teams. An executive design team would design the high levels of the process—its flows, performance objectives, inputs, and outputs, and the structure of the organization that performs it. Those who do the work would design the more detailed aspects of the process, such as how the work actually gets done on a day-to-day basis.

For this division of design labor to work, several circumstances must apply:

- There must be a clear delineation of processes and subprocesses that coordinate the design activity and communications.
- Managers must be willing to tolerate variations in how local sub-processes are performed since these will happen in any case!
- There must be clear performance objectives and measurement systems in order to confirm that lower level process design and performance are meeting higher level goals.

This is not a new idea. In the literature on socio-technical systems design, researchers recognized decades ago that participating in the design of work increased people's level of commitment to the new approach. They argued that the degree to which work should be specified by outsiders should be minimized, referring to the concept as "minimum critical specifications." Unfortunately, this crucial concept has been largely ignored in the reengineering movement.

I have personally observed this participative approach to reengineering in firms trying to redesign knowledge work processes. In such cases, managers are more likely to recognize that autonomous, creative knowledge workers do not want someone else to design their jobs. At a fast food firm, for example, the marketing reengineering team designed high-level flows for such subprocesses as promotions management, analysis of consumer information, and advertising. The team designed only the major steps and the deliverables to be produced, leaving it to the marketing professionals to design the details of their own work.

The method of observation and analysis during the design phase also has implications for how likely a design is to be implemented. In Michael Hammer's "Don't Automate, Obliterate" approach to reengineering, firms typically spend little time understanding how work is done in the present environment. This is a great mistake in my view. Instead, I advocate an "ethnographic" approach to studying the current work process. Like an anthropologist exploring a distinct culture, the analyst should act as an observer of the process. To truly understand some processes, designers must be willing to be participants. Such close observation of the process in action will give a design team a full understanding of the daily contingencies that affect how a process is performed. Further, only this type of participation is effective in demonstrating to people that the reengineering team really cares about how they do their work.

To truly understand some processes, designers must be willing to be participants.

The Implementation Phase

The search for alternatives to the engineering model of process redesign also should extend to the implementation phase. It can't be assumed that all parts of the organization for which a process is intended will implement it willingly.

Sell a new process as if it were a product. A more appropriate assumption, however, is that the targets of a new process are no more likely to buy a process redesign than a consumer is to buy a new product. The key is to market the process using all of the techniques for selling a process at one's disposal. In addition to such traditional tools as pricing, promotions, and publicity, these might include packaging the process design with other useful items, such as an information system to support the process, educational materials for necessary new skills, and role definitions for new positions.

Expect modifications.   Just as managers should assume that individuals will modify the processes they are supposed to perform, it also should be presumed that different regions, divisions, or offices will implement most processes with some variations. This is particularly true when implementations cross international boundaries, but occurs even in seemingly similar regions.

For example, when Pacific Bell designed a new circuit-provisioning process, it began to market it to five different regions within California. Each region eventually adopted the process and the associated information system, but their implementation approaches varied. One region felt that the roles envisioned in the process were too broad for their union environment. Another didn't believe that its customer support personnel would be able to use the system as designed. In short, although a single process might have been preferred, the ability of the regions to modify the designs probably increased their willingness to adopt them.

> Although a single process might have been preferred, the ability of the regions to modify the designs probably increased their willingness to adopt them.

Motivation for changing processes.   Finally, it should be noted that changes to business processes can occur through many means—not just through design and implementation. Business change happens because people want it to, so we need only look at the factors that lead people to want change. Changing how we compensate, evaluate, measure, and monitor individuals often creates a desire to do work differently. At a regional health insurance company, for example, simply measuring the consumption of time and cost across the process for underwriting a new policy led to 20 percent reductions in both. By manipulating these types of variables, we motivate individuals to design their own changes.

Middle-ground information solutions

To be successful, information management redesigns must recognize the role of individuals. Information only informs if there is a particular person who not only has access to the information, but also receives it at the appropriate time, focuses attention on it, interprets it, and acts on it. Information is thus as much a behavioral phenomenon as an engineering one, if not more so.

This approach to information management emphasizes the various roles that people play when they interact with information. For example:

- **Political.** Information, like any other resource, must be governed if it is to be used for maximum return on investment. And where there is government there is politics.
- **Support.** In my experience the best information environments are hybrids of both technology and human skill. People are much better than machines at categorizing, interpreting, and providing context for information.

- **Behavioral and cultural influences.** If we are going to succeed in creating the information environments we want and need, we will have to begin to manage information behaviors (engaging, sharing, and learning from information). The totality of an organization's information behaviors produces its information culture.
- **Process.** Like any other type of work, the activities involved in providing or using information can be viewed as processes that can be analyzed and improved.

Information Ecology

I call this new approach to information management "information ecology." Like the more familiar form of ecology, it involves establishing a context for analysis, an understanding of the interrelatedness of a number of different factors, the need for acute observation and description (instead of modeling and prediction), the valuing of diversity, and the recognition of continual flux and evolution.

But practicing information ecology does not make either technology or architecture irrelevant. Both the technology already deployed within the organization and the available technologies in the external technology marketplace, can drive planning and the day-to-day effectiveness of the information environment. Technology, in short, provides access to information, and while access is not sufficient, it is necessary.

There is also a place for information architecture and engineering. Architectural approaches are quite appropriate for certain types of information, particularly the more structured, quantitative information that dominated automation efforts in the early decades of information technology. However, even these architectural initiatives should be limited in scope, and the role of human or ecological approaches should not be forgotten. When the type of information being addressed is less structured and more knowledge-oriented, architectural approaches are less useful. However, when used together in a balanced fashion, these two approaches to information offer an intermediate approach similar to the one for business processes.

Several firms already have begun to apply the concepts of information ecology to their own information environments. For example, an insurance company in the U.K. is using the principles of information to adapt more effectively to its external environment, including customers and competitors. An aerospace firm is using the ecological approach, particularly as it applies to information politics and behavior, to try to better manage the scheduling of information. Two research organizations are focusing on increasing the sharing of information throughout the new product development process. While it is still too early to assess the results of these attempts at ecological management of information, early adopters are enthusiastic.

Thomas H. Davenport, professor of information systems at the University of Texas at Austin, is the author of Process Innovation: Reengineering Work Through Information Technology *(Boston: Harvard Business School Press, 1993).*

Is Reengineering Replacing Total Quality?

Joseph N. Kelada

We hear a lot about reengineering as if it were some new approach to management. This article correctly points out that this is not the case. Reengineering is one more approach to process improvement that companies that practice TQM might try. Kelada explains this point clearly and provides some additional useful direction for undertaking reengineering.

Business reengineering is everywhere. Many books and articles have stressed its importance and called it a must if an organization is to survive. President Clinton has been reinventing government, *Business Week* featured an article called "Rethinking IBM"[1] and others suggest that organizations redesign, reconstruct, or recreate themselves. It is the Re-revolution. Faced with drastic political, economic, social, and technological changes and the urgency to remain competitive, organizations must rethink the way they operate.

Business Reengineering and Total Quality

According to business reengineering proponents, radical changes must be made to business processes, instead of the incremental improvements that the total quality approach advocates. They suggest that radical changes are required to produce the significant improvement or breakthrough that is essential to surviving the present condition of world economics and fierce global competition. Some say that business reengineering is completely unrelated to total quality, while others view it as complementary. Should organizations abandon total quality and rush to reengineer themselves? Before jumping to conclusions, the situation deserves review.

Redefining Total Quality

Although practiced for almost a decade, total quality doesn't have the same meaning for everyone. For some, it is doing things right the first time or a combination of teamwork and participative management with strong leadership from the top. For others, it is defect-free products or doing things with excellence or perfection. For many, it is synonymous with customer satisfaction.

> Although practiced for almost a decade, total quality doesn't have the same meaning for everyone.

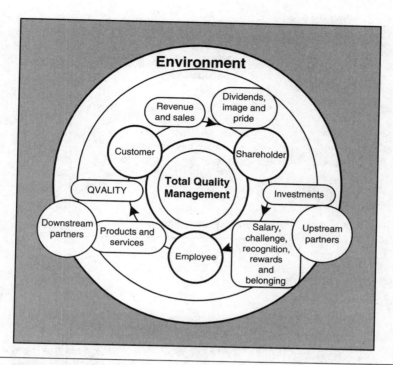

Figure 1. **The total quality triad.**

Total quality consists of simultaneously satisfying all of an organization's stakeholders: shareholders, customers, and management and nonmanagement employees. Shareholders look for a quality return on their investment, customers expect quality products and services, and employees strive for quality of life. This is also known as the total quality triad (see Figure 1). To satisfy the stakeholders by achieving the objectives of the triad, upstream partners (subcontractors and suppliers of raw materials and services) as well as downstream partners (distributors, wholesalers, retailers, carriers, installers, and repairers) must collaborate with all levels of the company's personnel. Moreover, in the current environmentally conscious society, companies must add protection, enhancement, and respect for the environment to their global objectives.[2]

Total quality management (TQM) has evolved to help achieve and maintain total quality, and it includes human, logical, and technical aspects (see Figure 2).

The human aspect is very important in starting and maintaining a total quality process in any organization. Top management must be convinced that it has to change its ways of doing business, exercise strong leadership, and mobilize both its employees and external partners. It must practice what it preaches and be committed and involved. Once the total quality process is

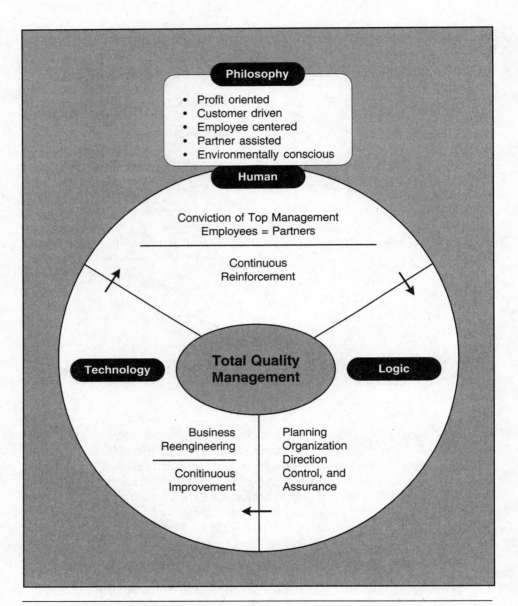

Figure 2. **Total quality management.**

under way, management must continuously reinforce it through its attitudes, behavior, rewards, recognition, and participative teamwork.

The logic of TQM is its ration aspect; it is realizing that total quality is not the product of sheer luck or an accident. It has to be managed, planned, organized, and controlled, and employees need direction, motivation, and empowerment.

Finally, it is not enough to be convinced that change and teamwork are prerequisites of success and progress, nor is it enough to know that total quality has to be planned and organized. Organizations must also know how to achieve total quality, hence the need to develop an elaborate technology. The technical aspect includes numerous methodologies, tools, and techniques for use at strategic or operational levels, such as business reengineering, quality function deployment, policy deployment, statistical process control, design of experiments, problem-solving techniques, ISO 9000, and many others.

Some people—including a number of total quality experts and business reengineering specialists—wrongly associate total quality exclusively with continuous improvement. In reality, both continuous improvement and innovation are needed to achieve total quality. A company cannot always improve because, at a given point, improvement is either impossible, infeasible, or extremely expensive. Therefore, it has to innovate. On the other hand, a company cannot always innovate or reengineer because generally after innovating it has to debug, improve, and fine-tune.

The two approaches neither contradict nor complement each other, because they are two parts of the same approach. AT&T illustrates this well in its *Reengineering Handbook*, which posits business reengineering as a fundamental component of the total quality approach.[3]

Therefore, total quality is an objective, TQM is the means to achieve it, and business reengineering is an important tool within the TQM technology (see Figure 3).

> Some people wrongly associate total quality exclusively with continuous improvement.

> Total quality is an objective, TQM is the means to achieve it, and business reengineering is an important tool within the TQM technology.

What Is Business Reengineering?

In general, business reengineering means an organization radically changes the way it thinks and the way it operates. More specifically, it involves changing processes, organizational structures, management style and behavior, compensation and reward systems, and the relationships with shareholders, customers, suppliers, and other external partners.

Thus, it is different from continuous improvement, which is gradually and incrementally doing better what is already being done. Business reengineering is synonymous with innovation because it is more than just automating or computerizing existing operations or processes. Progressing from handwritten to typed to computer-generated checks is not reengineering, but eliminating the necessity of a check altogether with direct deposits or withdrawals (see the "Reengineering at Work" sidebar).

How to Reengineer with Total Quality in Mind

When business reengineering is implemented, the objectives of total quality must always be at the forefront to ensure success; otherwise, implementation can be costly and still not yield acceptable and long-term results. Business reengineering emphasizes radically changing existing processes with the assumption that those changes will improve the company's global performance or performance of a specific process. To be effective, however, the company's

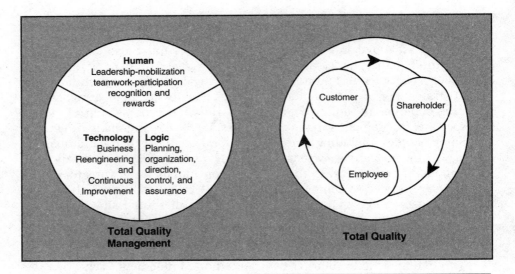

Figure 3. **Using total quality management to achieve total quality.**

internal structure and processes should be directly and formally linked to enhancing profitability through the fulfillment of its customers' needs. If this relationship is correctly and explicitly established from the start, business reengineering can be one of the best tools to achieve total quality and will significantly improve a company's performance.

For example, in a large company, people were complaining about their purchasing system. The purchase requisition process was too lengthy, cumbersome, and error prone. Managers attributed the organization's decreasing performance to this inefficient purchasing process, so a business reengineering team was set up. The team rethought the process from scratch. Cycle time was shortened, some procedures were eliminated, more sensible uses of computer systems were introduced, and errors were avoided. Despite these improvements, the general performance of the organization deteriorated still further. Errors made outside the purchasing department were now processed even faster and more efficiently than before. This reengineering project failed because it was assumed that changes in the purchasing process would significantly improve the company's performance. No effort had been made to specifically link this process to the company's profitability and customer satisfaction. Everyone had been working under an assumption rather than on facts.

This in no way means that business reengineering is inefficient or dangerous, nor does it mean that partial reengineering should be rejected or that only companywide projects are successful. It merely points out that, in the absence of a global diagnosis, it is possible to make the erroneous assumption that a given process adversely affects the performance of an organization. Any reengineering effort on that process, based on such an assumption, would obviously lead to failure.

When I visited a Japanese manufacturer some time ago, I witnessed an impressive feat of reengineering. Prior to the company's reengineering, customer delivery schedules were not being met and operating costs were running high, affecting either the price to the customer, company profits, or shareholders' dividends. After tracing these problems to different operations, it was noticed that the main cause was the company's dealings with its principal parts supplier. These included ordering from the supplier, issuing purchase orders, receiving parts, checking incoming parts against purchase orders, notifying the accounts payable department, issuing a check, and checking with the production control master schedule. At the supplier's end, each purchase order generated a work order, shipping order, delivery slip, invoice, receipt of the check, and deposit of the check at the bank. Transactions didn't stop there; once the bank had received the check, it had to credit the supplier's account, debit the customer's account, send statements to both, and then file the check. At the customer's end, these processes required the intervention of the manufacturing, production control, materials control, receiving, and accounting departments. At the supplier's end, various departments were involved, including order entry, manufacturing, materials control, production control, shipping, and accounts receivable. The bank also involved many departments in its processes.

To reduce time, cost, and errors, teams using a continuous improvement approach would have analyzed and improved each of these processes separately. But in this case, one reengineering team—with representatives from each of the departments involved, the supplier, and the bank—used the reengineering approach to group these activities into one all-encompassing process.

In the reengineered process, the supplier delivers a number of pallets containing parts and collects the ones that have been emptied. Attached to each empty pallet is a plastic card bearing a magnetic strip encoded with the part number and the quantity of parts initially transported on the pallet. The delivery person slides the cards one by one through a reader and removes the empty pallets. With one swipe of a card, a cascade effect is immediately triggered: An order for new parts is placed, a work order is issued at the supplier's end, feedback is provided to both the materials control and the production control departments as a follow-up to synchronize the ordering of parts and the production schedules, accounts payable is updated, and the bank gets a notice to pay the supplier (it credits the supplier's account, debits the customer's account, and updates the bank balance for both the customer and the supplier). Errors have been drastically reduced, time and costs have been saved, and the customer pays only when the parts are used rather than when they are received, which is an additional and welcome savings.

No attempt was made to improve the ordering, billing, accounts payable, or check-issuing systems; these were simply eliminated.

Introversive and Extraversive Management

Before beginning a total-quality-oriented reengineering effort, management must know the difference between introversive and extraversive management.

At a presentation about total quality before a hospital's top management team, the managers were asked about their roles in the hospital. Each defined his or her role in relation to his or her own specific department. For instance, the chief financial officer explained that he was responsible for accounting, financial statements, and budgets. None of the senior managers related their responsibilities to the hospital's patients.

In most organizations, people react similarly when asked how they perceive their roles: accountants count, buyers buy, and personnel departments hire and fire. If they all do their jobs correctly, and the company still goes bankrupt, obviously it is not their fault. This is how managers traditionally manage—a concept called introversive management (managers and employees only look inward at what they do in their departments). When top management evaluates the performance of a given department, it does so by measuring its output in terms of its mission: number of employees hired on time at a minimal cost, number of purchase orders processed, number of computer systems installed or updated, and number of error-free financial transactions. Action plans typically include objectives related to improving work conditions, introducing new technology, updating systems and procedures, reviewing the organizational structure and job descriptions, modifying the planning process, and so on. It is a mystery where the customers and shareholders fit in.

Achieving total quality requires extraversive management: measuring performance by not only looking outside a given department but also outside the organization. Every department and individual within a department must view his or her role as contributing to customers' needs. Fulfillment of these needs translates into revenues and dividends for shareholders who persuade top management to provide the employees with quality of life.

Achieving total quality requires extraversive management: measuring performance by not only looking outside a given department but also outside the organization.

How to Reengineer

In any reengineering project, management should start with the shareholders' needs. Generally, although not always, the organization's return on investment or dividends per share are established. (For some entrepreneurs, financial results are less important than their companies' image and reputation.) Management should look for trends rather that absolute figures, because the latter could point out that a company is the best in its field yet fail to indicate that its performance is on a rapid downtrend. Trends must be compared with industry averages and with the results of the company's main competitors.

The financial diagnosis should then be complemented with a study of customer satisfaction. The following model is very useful in assessing customer satisfaction. It contains seven main characteristics that influence customers' decisions:

1. Quality (Q): Customers look for products (i.e., goods and/or services) that suit their needs and are durable and reliable.
2. Volume (V): Customers require a certain quantity of a given product.
3. Administrative procedures (A): Customers face administrative procedures that might influence their decision to buy from a certain supplier. These are the procedures that buyers must go through to pay for the product (e.g., order entry, credit assessment, billing, and complaint processing), and they should be simple, rapid, and error-free to avoid any unnecessary inconvenience for the buyer.
4. Location (L): The location in which the product is available is important to the customer. Prominent factors include ease of access (e.g., proximity and parking facilities) and attractively arranged premises. Selling a wide variety of goods from a warehouse-type facility is a very successful recent trend.
5. Image and interrelations (I): The supplier's image and interrelations with its personnel constitute other factors that affect the decision to purchase. Image includes how the organization's behavior is perceived in areas such as protection of the environment and respect of human rights. Efficiency, promptness, and courtesy are highly appreciated in all interrelations with the company's personnel or representatives. An increasing number of organizations put significant effort into this area.
6. Time factor (T): Customers want to receive their products on time. Late deliveries might cause the loss of both sales and customers.
7. Yield (Y): The yield is the value, per dollar spent, that customers get from products. Customers are willing to pay higher prices for products that provide a better value. For example, more expensive brands of paint are bought because purchasers know that these brands will last longer.

The preceding factors spell QVALITY. The total quality diagnosis is a survey of present and potential customers that systematically examines these seven factors to find out what satisfies or dissatisfies customers and to what degree they value each factor.

When this two-part diagnosis of financial results and customer satisfaction is performed, the satisfaction of the employees, managers, and nonmanagers is evaluated. The business process, which includes the mainstream process and many supporting processes, is also mapped out. The mainstream process includes:

1. All operations that are undertaken, from perceiving customers' needs, fulfilling these needs, receiving the final payment, servicing the product until the guarantee expires, and replacing the

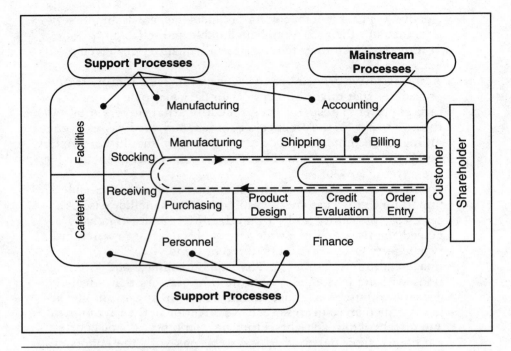

Figure 4. **The business process.**

product when the current one wears out, which starts the process again (see Figure 4)

2. Management activities that ensure operations are carried out effectively, on time, and at minimum cost, including planning, organizing, directing, and controlling

3. Information systems that ensure operations and management activities are carried out and completely effectively

The support processes are those that allow the mainstream process to function effectively by supplying it with necessary information, personnel or training, or capital and expenditures (see Figure 4).

By mapping the mainstream and support processes, those that need correction, improvement, or reengineering can be more easily identified. Examination of the seven QVALITY factors identifies:

■ The most frequent and/or the most critical problems
■ Late deliveries, which are classified by type of product, customer, area, and period of the year
■ Administrative problems, such as errors in billing, order entry, and customer credit evaluation or delays. Customer complaints can also help determine a number of problems.

Next, identified problems must be prioritized. The most critical and re-current problem should be traced back to specific activities or operations in the mainstream business process. At this point, this part of the process is thoroughly analyzed using problem-solving techniques such as flowcharting, brainstorming, nominal group technique, cause-and-effect diagrams, Pareto analysis, and scatter diagrams.

Before scrapping the existing process entirely, management should study the possibility of improving it by eliminating unnecessary operations, com-bining or modifying other operations, having someone else perform an oper-ation, or having the operation performed elsewhere, at a different time, or in a different sequence. If this preliminary investigation shows that the process cannot be improved effectively at a reasonable cost, it should be reengineered. The reengineering effort and its eventual direct impact are always closely linked with the end problem to be solved. This direct impact must, of course, translate into increased profitability for the organization and enhancement of whatever QVALITY factors are important to the customer.

The main cause of a problem might be traced to inadequacies in a support system, such as a lack of training or invalid information from the existing computer system. The processes are then analyzed in the same way as the components of the mainstream process. Next, the relevant process must be examined to determine whether it should be reengineered. Often, the cause of a problem is traced to outside partners, and it is solved with their collab-oration.

Orient Business Reengineering toward Total Quality

Increasingly, executives are adopting a global objective based on the total quality philosophy. This global objective simultaneously weaves together sat-isfaction for shareholders, customers, and employees; collaboration with out-side partners; and an overt desire to protect the environment.

TQM is used to achieve total quality because it embodies a human aspect, logic, and a new management technology. When continuous improvement is no longer effective, and the existing processes can no longer be modified or improved, the business process must be reengineered. When new processes replace the old, the company, in effect, is reinvented.

TQM is used to achieve total quality because it embodies a human aspect, logic, and a new management technology.

Business reengineering has to be oriented toward quality to be effective. When this is not the case, much effort, time, and money are spent to no avail and failure is wrongly attributed to the ineffectiveness of the approach.

References

1. Judith H. Dobrzynski, "Rethinking IBM," *Business Week*, Oct. 4, 1993, pp. 86–97.
2. Joseph Kelada, *Comprendre et réaliser la qualité totale*, second edition (Dollard Des Ormeaux, Quebec, Canada: Quafec Publishing, 1992).
3. *Reengineering Handbook*. AT&T Quality Steering Committee, 1991.

Joseph N. Kelada is a professor at the HEC Business School of the University of Montreal in Quebec, Canada, and a consultant in total quality and business reengineering.

Strategic Direction: Don't Reengineer Without It

Saul Berman

This article reminds managers that reengineering of various processes may cut costs and make processes more efficient in the short term. However, without connecting reengineering efforts to a more carefully considered strategy, they will not make that much of a difference in a company's growth and profitability. The article features three case studies demonstrating these points.

Many managers, on all levels, continue to believe in the necessity of strategy. But their influence has dwindled within some organizations, as requests for investment in long-term growth are vetoed by voices urging reengineering or restructuring as a quick-fix for poor earnings. Whatever the technique, the prescription is the same: Fix the processes, cut costs, restructure the corporation, find the technology to speed processes, and bump up the bottom line.

However, these efficiency techniques will not provide long-lasting financial health by themselves. In fact, senior executives in a number of organizations that have restructured or reengineered are beginning to express frustration about their long-term outlook for revenue generation.

Surveying satisfaction with reengineering. In a recent Price Waterhouse survey of the experience of *Fortune* 500 companies and large British companies with reengineering, we found that executives are only partly pleased with results. Reengineering had not helped them foster greater market growth or increase the speed with which new products and services come on the market, reported 63 percent of the executives.

Those top managers who expressed satisfaction with reengineering credited the process with achieving short-term benefits from cost cutting (in 61 percent of the cases), streamlining business processes (68 percent), increasing productivity (62 percent), and reducing headcount (57 percent.) However, most of them do not believe reengineering has helped them ensure the long-term survival of their companies.

Look long term before swinging the axe. In several recent assignments, Price Waterhouse has worked with executives who have elected to first draw

Most of them do not believe reengineering has helped them ensure the long-term survival of their companies.

This article is reprinted from *Planning Review*, November/December 1994 with permission from the Planning Forum, The International Society for Strategic Management and Planning.

a picture of both the long-term outlook for the company and the impact that efficiency initiatives might have, before reengineering. They believe that change management programs must be coherent with the firm's current or evolving strategic outlook. By relating the company's strategic direction to process efficiencies and cost reduction, they demonstrate how savings in one area can be used to pay for the investments needed to foster growth. Finally, through the use of quantitative-based tools such as shareholder value analysis, they are better prepared to quantify and predict the strategic impact of the reengineering process.

Three Cases

The following cases illustrate three change programs:

- A new business focus.
- A new technological outlook.
- An organizational overhaul.

Each example shows how company leaders focused their organizations first on strategy, and then linked it to the proposed efficiency programs. As a result, each company has enhanced its outlook for long-term revenue generation, while gaining short-term cost reductions as well.

Case 1: Risk Growth or Amble Off into the Sunset?

In the Eighties, a mid-sized independent entertainment company "Star Vault, Inc.," felt the competitive pressure in the industry mounting and embarked on a severe restructuring program. During the down-sizing, the company slashed its creative capacity, eliminating its internal production capability. Instead it concentrated on aggressively marketing its library of products in traditional and non-traditional channels. The short-term fix worked; Star Vault returned to profitability.

However, senior level management quickly realized that something else would have to be done. The profitability picture is more problematic than it looked. Since sales were increasingly coming from international distribution, the company could not depend on the domestic market. Star Vault's library was gradually becoming dated, and overexposed. While aggressive marketing and lack of investment in new products had temporarily buoyed profitability, this strategy was now threatening the company's future. Competition from other major studios for the most attractive product acquisitions was growing more intense. Production costs were escalating, especially for independent producers.

The challenge.   Senior management realized that the company had to think beyond efficiency to focus on the key driver of success in the entertainment industry—content. According to one industry expert, "Competition has intensified and companies need new product as a locomotive for future sales. Without it, it is difficult to sell the older, more profitable products through traditional channels."

The options weren't rosy.   From a creative standpoint, Star Vault was running on empty, and the costs of acquiring new products were escalating beyond its means. Star Vault was facing a sunset scenario: it could slim down further and continue to sell existing products. Or it could pursue a growth-oriented strategy, emphasizing its power in international distribution, and producing its own products for sale in niche markets that weren't attractive to its bigger rivals. However, even if management chose the growth strategy, it faced difficult questions:

- How should it build competitive advantage over the next five to ten years, given that traditional distribution channels would become increasingly saturated and more competitive?
- How specifically should the company differentiate itself in the marketplace, especially since it did not have many assets or much experience in non-traditional channels?
- How should this differentiation be set up down the road?
- Where should investment dollars be put?

Structuring the choices.   Uncertainty about how to compete in today's entertainment industry, as well as selling off its own creative capacity in the name of efficiency, had left Star Vault ill prepared for the future. But having to make a choice between these two alternatives—a sunset strategy or growth—clarified the strategic direction of the business.

Senior management realized it had to invest in growth to have a sustainable future. However, it first wanted to determine how the new product capacity would be paid for. To achieve this fundamental change in its business focus, Star Vault developed a plan for the company's strategic direction and position in the industry, plus a recommendation for a new strategic mission and the requisite capabilities.

Market focus.   Major companies in the entertainment business typically develop a valuable portfolio by making costly deals for new products that will appeal to the preferences of the mass market—a risky and competitive process. Star Vault decided to focus instead on acquiring new products for specific distribution channels and genres. This reduced the risk of big failures, while also enhancing the company's control over product marketing and distribution.

Quantification.   Management quantified the strategic plan's impact on both profitability and shareholder value. By estimating the present value of cash flows under different scenarios, and then comparing that against the cost of capital, management could also estimate value creation under all three scenarios (see Exhibit 1). The growth scenario was the clear winner. To create this future value, Star Vault elected to reengineer its business processes and use funds freed up by cost reductions to invest in the new strategy.

Management built detailed budgets to pinpoint needed cost savings. First, it analyzed actual costs, identifying incremental savings and establishing new cost baselines by department. Each department was categorized according to

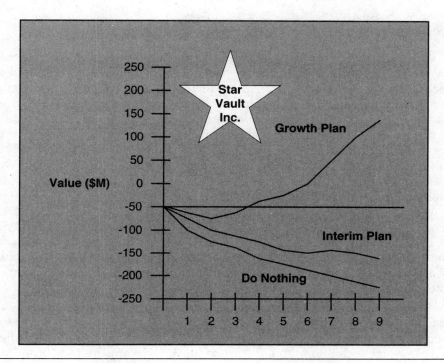

Exhibit 1.   **Shareholder value created under three scenarios.**

the significance of its total costs, its growth from the prior year, opportunities for cost savings, and most importantly, the impact the department had on the strategic objectives.

The cost investigation also helped identify some further avenues for changes in strategic direction. For example, in analyzing how to increase the productivity of its supplier relationship, the company determined that fostering strategic partnerships would ensure that its suppliers offered the company the best technical advice.

Instead of simply improving the processes, the company eliminated the non value-added expenses, and evaluated which organizational elements were relevant to the new strategy. Budget allocations were formulated based upon strategic importance. As a result, the company now has the opportunity to sustain and increase its market share.

Case 2: Designing a Technology Strategy Before Reengineering
A bold newcomer in the entertainment/communications industry, Star Maker, Inc., was at the height of its creative powers, enjoying continued good growth in both revenues and products. For the most part, the company was the brainchild of the CEO, who built the business from scratch by being the first with innovation after innovation. At the same time, however, the company was highly leveraged, and its profitability subject to large, short-term

fluctuations, depending on market events. As a result, it was an extremely cost-conscious institution.

Believing that a more sophisticated application of technology was necessary to help ensure the company's future, senior management recruited an executive from outside the company to be in charge of information systems. He realized immediately that while the technology of the external operations was the most sophisticated possible, internal business systems were behind the times. The company's internal communications were replete with duplicate and independent systems and processes. Because the organization had been so intensely cost conscious, investing in coherent company-wide systems had low priority. Over the years, the organization's internal systems had fallen further and further behind the state of the art.

When Star Maker's performance went through a downturn, senior management became intrigued by the prospect of reengineering the company to cut costs. At this point, however, the CIO stepped forward and persuaded senior management to first determine the correct role of technology—including a modernization of internal communications systems—in the company's strategic future.

The initial decision.   The sheer force of the CIO's intellectual leadership was enough to convince the rest of the executives that it was folly to ignore the importance of technology to their strategy. They formulated a plan to effectively leverage technology and, over time, push the company to the forefront of the industry, not just in the U.S., but on a global scale.

The search for success factors.   First, top management authorized a strategic analysis of the industry to determine what success factors would drive the company's future in each aspect of the business system. For example, to seize the opportunities arising from the proliferation of communications channels and outlets, it was important to have access to as many distribution channels as possible. Moreover, growth in foreign sales implied that international markets had to be expanded. For all markets, there was a clear need for new "content" and for top-notch customer service.

Strategy direction.   Next, management identified how technology could help the company's performance in these critical areas. Accessing multiple distribution channels, for example, would be facilitated by electronic product catalogues and customer interface standards to simplify accessing, marketing, and sales. Star Maker's international capabilities would require increasingly sophisticated use of technology to customize programming for local markets.

To improve program content, the company planned to expand into areas of production with higher costs and more risk. New electronic links enhanced strategic partnerships with content creators and producers.

Finally, in the area of sales and marketing, technology would also facilitate better customer service through more sophisticated electronic data links, while developing digital video technology would enable immediate on-site viewing of programming. In addition, the company would gradually develop the kind of databases necessary to increase customer service, while accentuating its capacity to analyze the market.

By first understanding the company's strategic direction and the implications for growth initiatives, Star Maker was finally ready to mount its reengineering effort. The cost reductions the company reaped from reengineering helped pay for the new technology it needed to drive growth.

By first understanding the company's strategic direction and the implications for growth initiatives, Star Maker was finally ready to mount its reengineering effort.

Case 3: A Mail-order/Retailer Adopts a New Organizational Structure

"Zendus, Inc.," started as a mail-order catalogue operation, grew into other catalogue areas, and finally built a chain of retail stores. All the Zendus managers realized that the company's organization had become a hodge-podge of functions and mismatched priorities. Some senior managers wanted to reengineer, others felt Zendus needed a new strategic direction. But without organizational coherence, how could the company effectively implement a strategy?

So Zendus decided that the first order of business was to get its organization into shape. An initial analysis concluded that a major problem was that the company was not leveraging its organizational strengths across all its lines of business. This is a chronic issue for organizations that have grown helterskelter. At Zendus there was no overarching accountability for the efficiency of the whole system.

For example, how could a marketing strategy work if the cross-functional planning and communication necessary for implementation was never even attempted? How could production become more strategic when operating personnel never saw sales projections?

The study found that there was inadequate accountability for actions, and confused lines of responsibility. Key deficiencies included limited cross-functional planning and communication, inconsistent cost methodologies, few linkages between sales forecasting and production, and little understanding of the source of budget variances.

While a key aim of the company's strategy was to increase the effectiveness of manufacturing, the study found that cultural differences between organizational units inhibited the company's ability to work toward a common goal. For example, marketing was adept with coming up with new product ideas, but manufacturing didn't have the capabilities to produce them.

However, the study also concluded that while Zendus had to efficiently share the physical and human assets of operating and marketing, its units also needed to maintain some independence of action because of the unique target market segments they were pursuing, and because of the differences in products and services they were offering.

The fork in the road. At this point, management identified two roads that could be taken:

- A large-scale shift toward a more functional organization.
- Separating the assets along a line of business organization.

Top management decided to pursue a modified matrix organization. Zendus would focus on the development of cross-functional teams and more effective processes.

Evaluating strategic alternatives. Management also began revising its strategy to take advantage of opportunities to use new and current capabilities. The study included an evaluation of existing businesses and specialty/spin-off opportunities, acquisition possibilities, expansion ideas, and alternative plans for changing the organization.

The study team found that there were opportunities to pursue core growth in the existing operations with little risk and capital outlays. At the same time, however, they also discovered they could grow even more by expanding and upscaling Zendus' current retail stores, and by acquiring additional mail order catalogues, first by spinning off some existing operations and then by buying new books.

However, before implementing its new organizational structure, management also determined that it had to be cost effective. The first step was to review the current administrative activities in order to identify key opportunities to improve effectiveness and efficiency.

Searching for areas of improvement. To make certain the organization had the capability to carry out this strategy, management was determined to perform an activity value analysis at the same time it was reengineering processes. The goal was to reduce costs without hurting morale or damaging the management capability that would soon be needed to support the revamped strategy.

Again, the key objectives of the cost study were built around Zendus' new organizational and strategic directions. The cost analysis was conducted department by department, bottom up, enlisting the whole organization in cost improvement.

Organizational change and cost control were accomplished simultaneously. Areas where costs were inconsistent with strategy were downsized. Positions and programs that didn't fit with the strategic direction were eliminated. The creative approval processes was streamlined, budget forecasting simplified, capital authorization procedures revised, and the content and frequency of certain production reports reduced.

Evaluating process improvements. Management identified new approaches to operating and financial planning in order to resolve real and perceived weaknesses before embarking on a new strategic course. It categorized the critical operating drivers in order to track the business against key financial measures and strategic initiatives, and to develop a more explicit understanding of the reporting system for the drivers and as well as more disciplined performance analysis. The result was an improved forecasting process.

The major innovation in this phase was identifying the company's operating drivers, which are distinct from normal financial measures. These operating drivers are quantitative measures linked to the strategic plan. They are based on fundamental forces and activities that drive performance—the ongoing processes and goals of the company rather than simply the results. Once the operating drivers were clear, it became much easier to link budgets to assumptions that could be quantified rather than simply stated. Variances in performance could be more quickly spotted, tracked, and acted upon.

Because of the work accomplished in this phase, two important organizational changes were implemented. First, management was able to link a systematic and disciplined performance analysis directly to its strategic and financial planning process. Second, the budgeting process was streamlined. This was facilitated by a more disciplined and thorough strategic planning process that focused the organization on high-level targets.

By the end of the first round of reengineering Zendus had become a simpler organization whose processes clearly supported its strategic objectives. For example, the company's new strategic planning process more thoroughly evaluates the relevant business environment, competitor activities, and market trends in order to quantify the impact of proposed initiatives and make budgeting more realistic. These quantitative assessments are then converted into three year P&Ls, which form the basis of the budgeting cycle.

This process, in turn, leads directly to better estimates of changes in sales and divisional spending and better calculation of corporate operating income. Budgeting can then be linked to strategy and become more realistic through the use of operating drivers. Forecasting has also become more realistic. Operating drivers are used as the basis for changes, with projection changes incorporated as soon as they are identified.

Finally, Zendus is now able to track its overall performance more closely. The P&L impact and cross-functional implications of significant events are immediately understood. Zendus is moving through the Nineties with a much more effective organizational structure in place, and thus has a greater capability to implement its new strategic direction.

> By the end of the first round of reengineering Zendus had become a simpler organization whose processes clearly supported its strategic objectives.

Lessons Learned

In each of these cases, new strategy was not the initial goal. Star Vault was content with its financial results after going through an arduous restructuring. Star Maker was cost conscious, skating on the margins of its industry, bent only on becoming as efficient as possible. Zendus wasn't looking to experiment either—it just wanted a more efficient organization.

What happened, however, was that certain members of each organization had the courage to urge a re-examination of strategy and strategic intent. As a result of this analysis, the management of all three companies learned these valuable lessons about how strategy and reengineering complement each other:

- **Make top management understand that reengineering is only an efficiency exercise.** It may temporarily bump up the bottom line. However, reengineering's lasting benefits result from its application to areas that enhance a company's strategic capabilities.

Since quick fix cost cutting can slash into an organization's muscle and bone, reengineer with the future in mind.

- **Learn to quantify strategy.** What will it cost? How much will it help the bottom line—and when? What are the milestones and what's the timetable—one year, two years, five years?
- **The whole organization must accept ownership of the strategy.** Get all levels of management to help make the plan. Senior management support needs to be ongoing, consistent, and visible.
- **Assess the organization's current capabilities and processes realistically.** Do they have to change before a new strategy can be executed?
- **Link strategy to the budgeting process.** Where will the money to pay for the strategy come from? How should the budgeting process change to track and promote the new strategy?

Saul Berman, is a regional managing partner of strategic consulting with the Management Consulting Services of Price Waterhouse LLP.

BENCHMARKING

The 10 Pitfalls of Benchmarking

Irving DeToro

Just as the title suggests, this article looks at various problems companies that undertake benchmarking might run into. It is a short piece but has a lot of good advice, which is why we've included it.

Benchmarking is accepted worldwide as a management technique to improve business performance. The concept is easy to understand, and many firms have proven that benchmarking provides added value. Yet, some organizations have failed in their attempts to implement this simple concept. To avoid mistakes in benchmarking, one must understand the types of common benchmarking miscues. What follows are 10 pitfalls that, if avoided, can help ensure benchmarking success:

Pitfall 1: Lack of Sponsorship

Like a successful sports team, a successful benchmarking team needs a leader. Unless a senior manager is aware of the project and has agreed to serve as the team's mentor, the project could fail. Often, the amount of time, effort, and resources needed to undertake a benchmarking project isn't understood. If a project is launched without sponsorship, team members might later be criticized for spending too much time away from their primary work.

A team that benchmarks without a manager might resemble an empowered team until it's time to present recommendations. The manager who must

Unless a senior manager is aware of the project and has agreed to serve as the team's mentor, the project could fail.

---

approve the recommendations might have no knowledge or appreciation of the project. Lacking a sponsor, a team's project could be unknowingly killed by an uninformed manager reallocating resources or changing priorities.

To avoid these problems, a team should submit to management a one- to four-page benchmarking project proposal that describes the project, its objectives, and potential costs. If the team can't gain approval for the project or get a sponsor, it makes little sense to proceed with a project that's not understood or appreciated or that is unlikely to lead to corrective action when completed.

Pitfall 2: Selecting the Wrong People for the Team

Who are the right people for a benchmarking team? Individuals involved in benchmarking should be the same ones who own or work in the process. It's useless for a team to address problems in business areas that are unfamiliar or where the team has no control or influence. While it might seem trite, an often-overlooked point is that those working in the process know the most about it and are the most capable of identifying and correcting problems.

Pitfall 3: Teams Not Fully Understanding Their Own Work

A benchmarking team often visits world-class organizations in the hope of learning how they achieved superior performance. After a friendly and insightful meeting, team members return to the office, but nothing happens as a result of the meeting. What went wrong?

It's likely that the team attempting to understand worldclass performance could not relate another company's performance to its own. If the benchmarking team didn't map, flowchart, or document its work process, and if it didn't benchmark with organizations that documented their processes, there can't be an effective transfer of techniques. The intent in every benchmarking project is for a team to understand how its process works and compare it to another company's process. The exchange of process steps is essential for improved performance.

> The intent in every benchmarking project is for a team to understand how its process works and compare it to another company's process.

Pitfall 4: Teams Taking on too Much

The task a team undertakes is often so broad that it becomes unmanageable. This broad area must be broken into smaller, more manageable projects that can be approached logically. A suggested approach is to create a functional flowchart of an entire area, such as production or marketing, and identify its processes. Criteria can then be used to select a process to be benchmarked that would best contribute to the organization's objectives. Thus, projects can be approached in order of importance and can be implemented and completed without large time lapses.

Pitfall 5: Managers Failing to Understand the Necessary Commitment

Teams will often begin a project knowing that the problems have long persisted and that some degree of time and effort will be required to correct them.

Managers, however, under the pressures of competition, improved performance, or demanding deadlines, need a faster solution. Since managers aren't as familiar with specific work issues as their employees, they tend to underestimate the time, cost, and effort required to successfully complete a benchmarking project. Managers should be informed that while it's impossible to know the exact time it will take for a typical benchmarking project, a rule of thumb is that a team of four or five individuals requires a third of their time for five months to complete a project.

Pitfall 6: Focusing on Metrics Rather Than Processes

There still are firms that focus their benchmarking efforts on performance targets (metrics) rather than processes. Even if a firm like this hits its performance target, it will have little idea how it can again achieve the same level of performance. Knowing that a competitor has a higher return on assets doesn't mean that its performance alone should become the new target (unless an understanding exists about how the competitor differs in the use of its assets and an evaluation of its process reveals that it can be emulated or surpassed).

Focusing on performance gaps is useful in identifying improvement opportunities. Seeing gaps might motivate a team to accelerate performance improvement in its area by mapping its process so it can effectively complete a benchmarking project.

Pitfall 7: Not Positioning Benchmarking within a Larger Strategy

Benchmarking is one of many total quality management tools—such as problem solving, process improvement, and process reengineering—used to shorten cycle time, reduce costs, and minimize variation. Benchmarking is compatible with and complementary to these tools, and they should be used together for maximum value.

For example, it's possible to aid problem solving by benchmarking potential solutions, aid process improvement by benchmarking proposed new processes, or aid reengineering by benchmarking completely redesigned processes. Benchmarking can also revitalize other quality tools. Process improvement, for example, is sometimes perceived as dry, hard work, while benchmarking is in vogue and more exciting.

To solve this problem, all benchmarking activity should be launched by management as part of an overall strategy to fulfill the organization's mission and vision.

Pitfall 8: Misunderstanding the Organization's Mission, Goals, and Objectives

To inform employees about company objectives and goals, most organizations hold meetings or distribute literature. More often than not, a couple of weeks later, everyone, including the managers, can't explain the objectives or goals. If this information is necessary to prioritize areas and processes that should be benchmarked, teams that can't explain the objectives and goals will be unable to select the organization's most critical processes.

To solve this problem, all benchmarking activity should be launched by management as part of an overall strategy to fulfill the organization's mission and vision by first attaining the short-term objectives and then the long-term goals.

Pitfall 9: Assuming Every Project Requires a Site Visit

When a benchmarking project is commissioned, the first reaction is to call a travel agent and arrange a trip. Meeting with well-managed organizations is always positive but not necessarily productive for either party. By this point, the notion that a team must be well prepared to discuss its specific work process should be appreciated. But experience has revealed that sufficient information might be available from the public domain, making a site visit unnecessary.

For example, a defense contractor, benchmarking a world-class maintenance project, identified Disney as a potential benchmarking partner. The team realized, however, that its client (the U.S. military) would not look favorably on the team traveling to Orlando, FL, in January. After completing its literature search on Disney, the team found sufficient information to improve its process, and it never had to leave town.

Pitfall 10: Failure to Inspect Benchmarking

Once benchmarking has been completed for a specific area or process benchmarks have been established and process changes implemented, managers should review progress in implementation and results. Failure to inspect, ask questions, or check for progress in implementing change and securing results will signal to everyone that benchmarking is not valued.

Conversely, a manager who involves his or her employees in benchmarking is giving the employees a chance to be empowered. To gain this empowerment, employees must know who their benchmarking partners are, the benchmark for the targeted process, the progress made in closing the gap, and how they can help this effort.

Avoiding the Pitfalls

Benchmarking is not rocket science. Much of it is common sense. By remembering and avoiding these 10 pitfalls, teams can benchmark more effectively and efficiently.

Irving DeToro, a benchmarking consultant and trainer, is the chief executive officer of The Quality Network Inc. in Rochester, New York.

Benchmarking: People Make the Process

Charles Goldwasser

This article, like the one by DeToro, includes practical advice on how to make benchmarking work. It provides additional advice on the importance of involving people to gain commitment to change and to make sure what is learned from the benchmarking process results in the improvements the organization is looking for. It includes one case study that shows how benchmarking can make a difference.

Let's face it: If benchmarking doesn't improve your company's bottom line, it is probably not worth doing.

After all, although talking and visiting with other companies can be enjoyable from an "industrial tourism" perspective, your company invests time and money in benchmarking to be more competitive and, ultimately, more profitable. So, if your benchmarking efforts are not producing positive results, it's important to understand what might be getting in the way.

Certain obstacles could result from deficiencies in various aspects of the benchmarking process. These include the strategic and operational significance of the areas you choose to benchmark, the level of understanding of your own business practices and processes, the relevance of your research and selection methods in identifying companies to learn from, the clarity of lessons and other information learned from benchmarking partners, or the level of real improvement potential this learning offers. A solid process is an important component of effective benchmarking.

But there's a lot more to it than the process itself. In fact, many benchmarking problems arise from a different set of variables that can have an even stronger impact on its bottom-line results. This second set of variables deals not with the benchmarking process, but with the issues that surface when benchmarkers try to implement change. For the people involved in benchmarking, their level of ability, their authority to drive change, the strength of their commitment to make change happen, and the general environment for change within their company all significantly impact the changes they can make and the results they can achieve.

This article is not about the benchmarking process. Its purpose is to highlight the importance of the second set of variables—the change-related variables—that impact what gets done with benchmarking information.

Traditional Benchmarking

The term benchmarking describes the overall process by which a company compares its performance with that of other companies, then learns how the strongest-performing companies achieve their results. Benchmarking is really a discovery process—discovering what truly strong performance is in a particular area of interest, which companies are getting the best results, and how they are doing so.

Given this focus, companies usually seek to accomplish three objectives with their benchmarking efforts: assess their current performance relative to other companies, discover and understand new ideas and methods to improve business processes and practices, and identify aggressive, yet achievable, future performance targets. The lessons to be learned have great potential for companies seeking to improve. However, even if the information exchange is successful, many benchmarking efforts do not reach their full potential for actually changing and improving companies.

Too often, information obtained through benchmarking studies sits idle. No matter how good the information is, benchmarking efforts can result in limited changes back at the office or plant unless people are willing and able to do something with it. Benchmarkers can easily find themselves stuck in the middle of "business as usual," unable to implement the real changes they seek to make.

Benchmarking efforts can result in limited changes back at the office or plant unless people are willing and able to do something with it.

The Bigger Picture

Benchmarking most effectively leads to bottomline improvements if it goes beyond information exchange to include one more crucial objective: to build desire, motivation and commitment among key individuals and groups to implement significant change. It is this additional objective that changes the benchmarking effort from a learning exercise into a vehicle for change. It causes benchmarking to be managed not as an end, but as a means to an end.

Benchmarking should be pursued with a specific purpose in mind. This purpose is usually related to continuous improvement efforts in companies seeking incremental changes or reengineering-type efforts in companies seeking more radical changes. Either way, gaining knowledge and learning lessons from other companies is not the deliverable. The deliverable is the implementation of real, meaningful change back at the workplace.

This linkage between benchmarking and change is important because it uncovers a number of issues that can keep good information from ever being used. Unless benchmarking efforts incorporate and are accompanied by effective change management, even the best ideas may be met by resistance and condemned to never-used benchmarking reports. On the other hand, by merging benchmarking and change management techniques, benchmarking can not only help overcome resistance to change, but even inspire creativity and motivate people to embrace change.

Unless benchmarking efforts incorporate and are accompanied by effective change management, even the best ideas may be met by resistance.

A benchmarking plan must include steps to build an effective support base for change, particularly if pivotal staff will be needed to implement change or if certain people can create significant obstacles to change. Potential change champions—people who are committed to driving change based on a positive benchmarking experience—should be informed and involved throughout the benchmarking process. These key people must be identified upfront. It starts with benchmarking planning:

- Is it your idea?
- Is the focus of the benchmarking effort within your area of authority and responsibility?
- Do you have the support of executives and managers whose areas of responsibility fall within the scope of the benchmarking effort?
- Do you need the support of others to get resources dedicated to benchmarking?

Areas of resistance or potential resistance should be noted and addressed before moving forward. This is critical because, at this point, you are just trying to get support to benchmark. Resistance to benchmarking at this stage is likely to develop into a strong change barrier once the information exchange is completed. On the other hand, potential opposition can be turned into support for change by involving the resistors in the benchmarking process.

Involved Selection

In the research phase of a benchmarking effort, you must determine which companies to talk with and/or visit. This is an important place to involve potential change champions and get their ideas on who is a strong performer in a particular area, or who they think should be included for some other reason.

Including others in the research process offers three main benefits. First, they may have important information about a company that may not surface through other research methods. In fact, they may have a contact at another company who can help gain entry to it for benchmarking purposes. Second, you want to eliminate potential excuses people may have for not trusting the information and ideas gained from benchmarking. To do this, you need to know what is important to others so you can address it upfront. You might include a company suggested by an employee not just because you may have missed something, but also to prevent your employee from later claiming that the benchmarking information is suspect because it did not include that company.

Third, including employees in this stage of the benchmarking effort gives them a chance to voice their ideas. Companies they may have been curious about can be identified for research. This builds excitement for the benchmarking effort itself and helps lead to greater ownership of the benchmarking findings.

The most critical place to involve potential change champions in benchmarking is during phone discussions and on-site visits with selected partners. In fact, you will likely want specific people to be involved with particular companies because of what you expect to learn from them. Strategic matches

Potential opposition can be turned into support for change by involving the resistors in the benchmarking process.

The most critical place to involve potential change champions in benchmarking is during phone discussions and on-site visits with selected partners.

THE LINK BETWEEN BENCHMARKING AND REENGINEERING

People often ask questions about how benchmarking relates to process reengineering. Are they the same thing? Are they in conflict with each other? The answer to both questions is "no." Benchmarking and process reengineering are two different but complementary methods for improving business performance.

Benchmarking involves learning about best practices from best-performing companies—how they are achieving strong performance. It is an effective tool for getting ideas to improve an existing activity, function or process. Process reengineering involves rethinking all aspects of a business process, including its purpose, tasks, structure, technology and outputs, then redesigning them from scratch to more efficiently and effectively deliver value-added process outputs. It is a valid concept for rethinking all types of business processes, but reengineering is usually applied to processes that are large and cross-functional.

Process reengineering consists of five phases:

- **Planning.** Get the project started by involving the right people, setting the scope and establishing objectives.
- **Internal learning.** Understand the current situation, current process flows, deliverables, delays, costs, problems, opportunities, etc.
- **External learning.** Expose the reengineering team to new ideas and experiences to bust their paradigms and stimulate creative thinking.
- **Redesign.** Apply internal and external learning to rethink the entire process from scratch, including the objectives, outcomes and process steps.
- **Implementation.** Put the right jobs, skills, structures and technologies in place to facilitate a successful shift to the new process.

Benchmarking is one step toward redesigning a process from scratch. Although benchmarking is an integral component of the external learning phase, other types of external learning could include attending seminars and conferences, and talking with key external constituencies (customers, suppliers, etc.). However, benchmarking is very effective in helping achieve the objectives of reengineering's external learning phase—stimulating new ideas and creative thinking. It is also a useful method for identifying continuous improvement opportunities and change ideas outside of process reengineering efforts. Benchmarking and process reengineering are two different business improvement techniques, but one can facilitate the success of the other.

between people and benchmarking companies can help overcome potential individual resistance to change or create champions for particular ideas. The strategic matching process also helps provide the greatest learning experiences by opening the minds and stimulating the creativity of knowledgeable people.

This involvement must be orchestrated to be effective. Key executives and managers should be responsible for specific areas of interest and fully prepared to address these areas in discussions or visits with other companies. They should also be active participants in debriefings of benchmarking visits.

Openly sharing findings, lessons learned and recommendations from site visits and other benchmarking activities can help build a wider understanding of the potential for change and the benefits of change. The audience should include anyone likely to be impacted by potential changes. Ultimately, change champions developed during benchmarking efforts can be very effective communicators to help build energy and support for implementing change.

A New Benchmarking Process

Benchmarking cannot lead to better performance and/or reduced costs unless it results in changes to current processes, practices and behaviors. Involving key people in benchmarking efforts can help bring about these changes by replacing feelings of resistance to change with feelings of excitement about change. Site visits can alter people's paradigms in a minute. If a picture is worth a thousand words, then seeing, touching and being able to ask questions is worth a million. Nothing can communicate the viability of concepts or ideas as well as examining them in action. For dramatic changes, viewing different processes and practices is especially important.

Involving people in benchmarking efforts also sends them a powerful message regarding the need and possibilities for change. It helps create a sense of urgency for improvement, sending a "wake-up" call to anyone who thinks that current ways are fine or that other ways will not work. In fact, it can generate momentum and challenge people to find ways to implement change. Seeing and talking with other companies can stimulate feelings of pride, competitiveness and jealousy that inspire people to make change happen. People often return from benchmarking site visits with a tremendous commitment to successfully implement change back in their companies. They believe that if other companies can do something, they can do it even better.

The excitement to begin implementing change can increase people's willingness to take action with minimum levels of supporting analysis. It can create an environment where "err on the side of doing" replaces "paralysis by analysis." Done effectively, benchmarking should create an energy and enthusiasm for change that will move people to put ideas into action.

Benchmarking also motivates and challenges those involved to stretch their vision of what is possible. Following successful benchmarking efforts, ideas for change often build and expand on what was learned from other companies.

> Done effectively, benchmarking should create an energy and enthusiasm for change that will move people to put ideas into action.

CASE STUDY: SOUTHERN CALIFORNIA GAS CO.

In 1993, Southern California Gas Co. was reengineering its materials management process. Earlier efforts in the late 1980s to significantly change this process were met with strong resistance and, ultimately, benefits were not realized. Implementation never went beyond a pilot program that was deemed "unsuccessful." Many people involved with that pilot were still with the company—several in key positions who could create significant obstacles to change this time around. People who remembered the pilot were skeptical that a similar change effort could work.

As part of the reengineering effort, a benchmarking study was conducted, resulting in site visits to six different companies in the healthcare supply, automobile manufacturing, truck manufacturing, chemical processing, appliance manufacturing and utility industries. Each company had some strategic match with Southern California Gas that could be used to help "sell" the validity of the benchmarking findings. Each company also had specific "enablers" that were helping them achieve superior results. Several companies had the same enabler—a material ordering and distribution process similar in concept to the one tried in the unsuccessful pilot of the late 1980s.

Site visit teams were carefully selected to allow key people to personally see this ordering and distribution process. Any lingering resistance was quickly replaced by excitement; the teams wanted to reconsider implementing a similar process at Southern California Gas. In fact, people returned from their site visits confident that they could not only implement, but possibly improve upon, what they saw at other companies. Process and implementation plans to deliver such results were quickly developed.

Ultimately, executives and managers involved in the reengineering and benchmarking efforts were so anxious to move ahead with the planned changes that they challenged the planning team to slash implementation time frames by as much as 75 percent for some plan elements. The reengineering team found a way to make it happen, but would only commit to such a rapid implementation roll-out if they got strong support and commitment from key executives. Due in large part to the energy and enthusiasm for change developed during the benchmarking effort, the executives supported the effort fully.

The strategic involvement of these key people made for a completely different implementation process this time around. There were numerous contributing factors, but the commitment and support for change by key individuals in various functions and at various levels throughout the company resulted in tremendous implementation success. Planned cost savings are being exceeded while service to material users throughout the company continues to improve.

Finally, involving key people in benchmarking efforts generates camaraderie, which, in turn, creates a team commitment to implement change. This commitment pays dividends when these change champions demonstrate ownership of change by playing significant roles in related communications efforts. It also helps provide the necessary ingredients to get past inevitable implementation problems and obstacles as they develop.

For benchmarking to truly be successful, it must go beyond information exchange to include effective change management. Remember, it isn't just the process—it's the people. This dual focus will help create motivation for meaningful change that delivers bottom-line results for your company.

Charles Goldwaser is a principal consultant in the production and process management practice at Price Waterhouse LLP Management Consulting Services.

Measuring up: Benchmarking Can Be Critical, but It Doesn't Have to be Expensive

Theodore B. Kinni

Here you'll find more practical advice for undertaking benchmarking studies and improvement projects. The author points out that benchmarking doesn't have to be expensive or complicated, and even small companies can take advantage of it. He briefly explains how to do this.

One of the most common of all business stories relates the woes of companies that leap unprepared onto the latest improvement bandwagon. Often they depart on these quests without a clue as to their current position in the marketplace and the areas in which they need improvement. They have only the vaguest vision of whatever pot of gold is offered by this newest fad. The result is invariably the same—wasted time, wasted energy, and wasted money. Their undoing? The gap between the way they see themselves and hard reality.

In case this seems an overstatement, consider the findings reported by Marie Jones of the Industrial Technology Institute, Ann Arbor, Mich. When manufacturers were asked to rank their companies within their industries, 50% of respondents placed themselves in the top 10%; 75% believed they were in the top 25%; and, 98% believed they ranked in the upper 50%. It doesn't take the mathematical genius of Einstein to discern the gap between perception and reality in these figures.

Benchmarking is a practice from which smaller businesses sometimes shy away from.

Continuous measurement, internal and external, is the way in which this gap is bridged. Companies need to base their superstructuring efforts on hard facts. Benchmarking, a measurement process that has been added to the corporate toolbox in the last decade, is one of the best ways to develop that picture. It is also a practice from which smaller businesses sometimes shy away, citing the high cost and time-intensive nature of the formal benchmarking studies conducted by their larger competitors.

There is some validity to this claim. When Houston-based International Benchmarking Clearinghouse (IBC) surveyed its corporate members in 1992, it found the average annual investment in benchmarking was $1,227,754 per member. The same survey revealed an average cost per benchmarking study of $67,657.

Figures, however, can be misleading. IBC's figures are most representative of full-blown studies undertaken by dedicated benchmarking staffs at large companies. Benchmarking can also be a relatively simple practice; it is easy to learn and offers a substantial payoff to smaller businesses. The difference between the high and low roads to benchmarking lies in the approach taken.

First, educate yourself.   Buying benchmarking expertise is a high-road practice that smaller businesses need not emulate. Learning to benchmark can begin with a call to your local bookstore. "I started with Bob Camp's book [*Benchmarking*, (ASQC Quality Press)], and once I saw that benchmarking could help us, I learned by the seat of my pants," recalls Tony Jachnycky of Tremco, Inc. "There isn't anything mystical about it."

Mr. Jachnycky, director of quality for the Beachwood, Ohio-based sealant and coating manufacturer, thinks 1 to 1½ days of formal training is adequate preparation for most people to conduct a benchmarking study. IBC members agree: In a member survey, 80% said study leaders needed two days or less of training, and almost 50% thought less than one day was enough.

Classroom training and seminars are widely available and, according to the experts, well worth the expense. The IBC, for example, offers three training modules: a two-day basic benchmarking seminar, a one-day managerial seminar, and a two-day, advanced-tools-and-techniques seminar. All cost well under $1,000, even for nonmembers, and for those anxious to avoid travel expenses the programs are regularly held at regional sites throughout the country.

Second, customize the methodology.   There are any number of benchmarking methodologies currently in use. A few of the more common are Motorola's five-step model, the seven-step process used by Westinghouse, and the 10-step Xerox model. All can be boiled down to an even simpler generic "meta-model" developed by the IBC and patterned after quality pioneer Walter A. Shewhart's PDCA (Plan-Do-Check-Act) cycle.

The four steps of IBC's meta-model are plan, collect, analyze, and improve. The planning step requires that the function or process to be studied, as well as the key data and information needed to measure it, be identified and the best benchmarking partners be located. During the collection step, information is gathered—both internally and externally—and, in turn, analyzed. This analysis phase reveals the performance gaps between "what is" and "what could be." This step also identifies best-practice enablers, which are defined by the IBC as "a broad set of activities that helps enhance the implementation of a best practice." Finally, in the improvement step, the practices uncovered in the benchmarking study are implemented and monitored.

The four steps of IBC's meta-model are plan, collect, analyze, and improve.

The key to using this process wisely is not so much carrying out each step in rote order, but understanding the intent of the process and modifying it to fit the unique needs of each organization. "Our benchmarking is not formalized," explains Ken Dooley, quality manager of Houston-based Syntron Inc., a manufacturer of marine seismatic exploration devices. "Small companies have different constraints than large companies. You have got to be able to mentally down-size the process to the point your budget can afford."

Mr. Dooley first used benchmarking to study the ISO 9000 standards and registration process before that knowledge was widely available in the U.S. He traveled to England and visited three U.S. companies doing business there. "We wanted to determine the future validity of the standards and learn the best process for successful registration," says Mr. Dooley. He learned well: Last month Syntron successfully passed its own ISO 9001 compliance audit without qualification on the first pass, an accomplishment that only about two in 10 companies can claim.

Third, use resources wisely.   Before benchmarking teams pack their bags and start racking up frequent-flyer miles, there are many sources of economical benchmarking information that can be utilized.

For instance, tap into the Industrial Technology Institute's (ITI) Performance Benchmarking Service to get a reality check before benchmarking. Currently, more than 800 manufacturers of discrete parts and assemblies with fewer than 500 employees are contributing to this benchmarking database, which is funded by the U.S. Dept. of Commerce. More than 40 key performance measures—ranging from value-added per employee to warranty costs as a percent of sales—are collected and tabulated by ITI. Together, the results paint a numerical portrait of world-class performance.

To participate, small manufacturers can contact ITI directly, complete a Performance Benchmarking Questionnaire for their own companies, and receive a 25-page report ranking their results against other companies in the same industry. The cost: $495 from ITI.

Even better, suggests Marie Jones, work through any of the 34 regional Manufacturing Technology Centers funded by the National Institute of Standards & Technology and receive the benchmarking report for free.

Once the decision to actively benchmark is made, seriously consider joining IBC. Not only does membership ensure the opportunity to network and benchmark with many of the country's most admired corporations, the range of services is comprehensive. Among others, IBC offers: Common Interest Groups—in areas such as ISO 9000, customer service, and new-product development—that explore best practices on an ongoing basis; the Electronic Network, an on-line conference and bulletin service to enhance dialogue between members; Consortium Studies, which link member companies in group-sponsored benchmarking studies that share costs and resources; and Information Services, which provides searches for data, partners, etc.

Understand that IBC membership costs can add up quickly, so it is probably not a good choice for casual practitioners. Initiation fees are $1,000 for companies with 200 or fewer employees and $3,000 for 201-to-500-employee organizations. Annual membership is $6,000, half of which covers fixed costs and services. The other half remains in a service account, from which Clearinghouse fees for training and such are deducted. Although service costs can range as high as $15,000 to participate in highly complex benchmarking studies, such as a best-practices study of the strategic-planning process, when compared with average study costs of more than $60,000, even that sounds like a bargain.

Finally, avoid the common pitfalls.   There are a few lessons that consistently pop up in the literature of benchmarking:

- Benchmarking is not a profit center. Understand its uses and pull it from the toolbox only when it is the best tool for the job.
- Start by benchmarking functions or processes that are critical to success. Don't waste time or money on insignificant studies.
- Benchmarking requires self-assessment. You cannot uncover performance gaps without first understanding and measuring your own processes.
- Gather the most cost-effective information first. The more you learn before an on-site visit, the more you will take away from it.
- Implement, implement, implement! Without implementation, a benchmarking study is an academic exercise with no value.

Theodore B. Kinni is a contributing editor to Industry Week *magazine.*

PROCESS MANAGEMENT AND MEASUREMENT

The Golden Rules of Process Redesign

Roger O. Rupp and James R. Russell

This is an extremely useful article for anyone looking at process management and improvement. It includes many tips and insights into what this is all about in a relatively small amount of space. We're confident this article will help you a lot in your process improvement activities.

Sustained high performance depends on how well a firm's processes satisfy customer needs. That's one reason there's so much discussion today about the need for companies to implement process improvement programs.

Process improvement is not a stand-alone concept. It exists as one of three steps of performance improvement: strategic planning, operational planning, and process improvement.

- *Strategic planning* considers customer needs and the business environment to establish overall strategies for customer satisfaction.

- *Operational planning* translates strategies into operational and financial requirements that are developed in a cooperative effort with customers and key operational managers at several levels.
- *Process improvement* focuses on implementing the best methods for translating valid operational requirements into finished products and services.

A Model for Process Improvement

Figure 1 outlines a methodology for process redesign. It begins with the identification of a reason for improvement followed by two distinct, though not mutually exclusive, improvement paths. By far, the most important and most-often neglected step is identifying a reason for improvement. In this step, a firm must identify a customer, select a valid measure of that customer's satisfaction, and determine whether one or more performance gaps exist between what the customer needs and what is currently being delivered. When drafting the reason for improvement, remember to keep the word "I" out of the need statements, for it can doom improvement efforts to failure before they begin. Instead, start out with the phrase "Our customer. . . . " After the reason for improvement is defined, the model offers two different improvement paths—problem solving and process restructuring—since performance gaps fall into two categories: process related and function related.

Some problems are caused by the process itself and seem to be built into the process. These process-related problems should be addressed using a process redesign approach in which the interactive aspects of the process are considered simultaneously. Problems best dealt with by using process restructuring are long cycle times, low-value activities, work flow, information processing, and decision making. Other performance gaps will have root causes that can best be addressed by stratification of the problem area and attacking the gap one small piece at a time. Problems amenable to root-cause analysis include errors, inconsistencies, functional problems, and excessive rework.

In practice, performance gaps that at first seem to stem from process problems might turn out to hinge on a single functional problem within the process. In that case, a shift from a process redesign mode to a root-cause analysis mode (to eliminate a single problem's underlying cause) is needed. Conversely, those seeking root causes to a specific problem might instead find they must deal with several related problems simultaneously. In that case, a team would shift from the problem-solving path to the process-restructuring path. Table 1 provides additional insight into which path might be more productive. Teams should always be willing to shift paths. Remember, the best approach is the one that yields the best results.

The Problem-Solving Path

This path requires a structured methodology to attain the discipline necessary to find and eliminate the root cause or causes of a problem. Without a structured methodology, there is a risk that only the problem's symptoms will be

When drafting the reason for improvement, remember to keep the word "I" out of the need statements, for it can doom improvement efforts to failure before they begin.

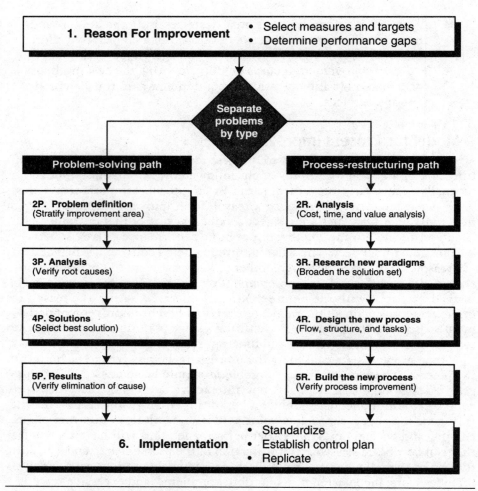

Figure 1. **The redesign process.**

alleviated. There are many structured approaches available, and all are based on the scientific method. These approaches rely on a series of hypotheses and verification using most of the seven basic problem-solving tools.

Once a reason for improvement has been established, the next step is to stratify the problem area into possible contributing factors to identify the specific problem that contributes most significantly to the problem area.[1]

The tendency of amateur problem solvers is to jump from problem area to analysis (or worse yet, to solutions) without defining the problem. After verifying, with data, that a problem exists, the next step is to apply analysis techniques, such as Ishikawa diagrams and statistical analysis, to get at the problem's root cause. Only after this analysis should solutions be proposed (see Figure 1). It is essential that the problem-solving discipline be continued

Table 1. **Which Path to Take**

Situation	Problem Solving	Process restructuring
Errors and defects	Best	Fixes here can have indirect effects
Cycle-time problem	Good	Best (especially for long complex processes)
Bureaucracy	Good	Best
Physical process	Good	Usually not effective
Nonphysical processes	Good	Best
Functional Problems	Best	Usually not effective
Multifunctional Problems	Usually not effective	Best
Workflow Problems	Good within a function	Usually best

into the final step to verify that the chosen solution had an effect on the customer's problem.

The Process-Restructuring Path

While problem solving seeks to understand root causes of deviation, process restructuring seeks to break down complexity into manageable pieces. Rather than focusing on a single problem, the process redesigner seeks to understand how whole sets of activities and problems are interrelated. When complexity itself is a problem, restructuring is probably the best path to pursue.

The heart of the restructuring path consists of four steps: analysis, investigation of new paradigms, process design, and process creation. Although some of the steps look like problem solving, a closer examination reveals important differences.

Rather than focusing on a single problem, the process redesigner seeks to understand how whole sets of activities and problems are interrelated.

Step 1: Analysis

The objective of analysis is to gather information that shows the causes of the identified process performance gaps. The key analysis activities are flowcharting, performing value analysis and complexity analysis, and determining the basic form of the process.

To begin, start with a high-level flowchart. Such a flowchart should show major supplier inputs (often they are in-house suppliers), three or four major transformation steps, and the products emerging from the transformation of

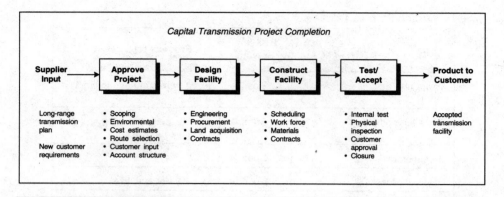

Figure 2.   **Example of a high-level flowchart.**

inputs. This high-level chart should be studied to draw broad conclusions about the process. Figure 2 is an example of such a flowchart. Notice that each transforming step includes notes describing the essential elements of the step without delving into the step's complexity. At this point, judgments can be made about where to look for improvements. For example, the high-level chart might indicate that 60% of the total cycle time for the process is consumed by a single operation or department.

Now comes the grueling work that many often omit: a detailed flowchart. Processes, like onions, are composed of many layers. Generally, the first pass at a detailed flowchart should uncover the next two layers of the process. Subprocesses that make up the "boxes" of the high-level chart must be detailed into flowcharts of their own. During this step, it is essential to get the workers involved in the study. How to achieve this cooperation is another matter, but experience has shown that if the workers don't want anyone to know how the process works, changes can't be implemented. That's why process improvement in a total quality environment is more likely to be successful than improvement in a traditional management environment.

A final verification of the resulting flowchart should be made. This can be accomplished by assembling a team of employees and asking them to walk through the process. This is an important step since it is likely that no one will have ever seen the entire process at once. The most common error uncovered during this review is the omission of rework, since it is difficult to recognize rework from within a single function.

The next analysis activity is a cost, time, and value exercise. The intent of this analysis is to compare the value of a step (in terms of customer satisfaction) to its cost (in terms of money and time). In essence, this is a return-on-investment analysis. Unlike other variables, such as cost or time, value is difficult to measure precisely. At best, the relative value of each process step can be established.

Value analysis begins by classifying activities into two categories: definite-value activities or suspect-value activities. Definite-value activities are

Table 2.   **Definite-Value or Suspect-Value Activity**

If any step fails on any question, its value is suspect.

Ask a Series of Hard Questions	Definite-Value Answers
Would the customer notice a loss of value if this step were missing?	Yes
Would the product or service be obviously incomplete without this step?	Yes
If you were forced to complete the product or service on an emergency basis, would you skip this step?	No
If you owned this business and could pocket the savings from skipping this step, would you skip it?	No
If this step is a review or inspection, is the reject rate significant?	Yes

those that directly contribute to satisfying customer expectations. They are the core of the process, and all other steps exist to support them. Table 2 presents a series of questions to determine whether a step is a definite-value or suspect-value activity. Typical suspect activities include reviews, signatures, formal approvals, status checks, coordination meetings, tracking, most types of inspection, rework, and filing.

Use the paired-comparison method to rank the process steps. In other words, compare each step to every other step and decide which step is more important. This method will force the steps into a top-to-bottom ranking. After ranking the steps, break them down into three to five categories of relative importance. Assign the steps in each category a numeric value, such as 5 for the most important steps, 3 for the steps of medium importance, and 1 for steps of least importance. Next, perform a similar ranking of steps based on their cost. A third ranking should be completed based on time consumption. Now the steps are ready to be plotted on a cost, time, and value profile as shown in Figure 3. For each step of the process, calculate the ratio of value to time and value to cost to arrive at a set of factors that should help in sorting the relative importance of the steps.

Definite-value activities are those that directly contribute to satisfying customer expectations. They are the core of the process.

Other Important Factors

A consideration of fragmentation, flexibility, complexity, and process type is important during the analysis step. Each must be documented for the existing process.

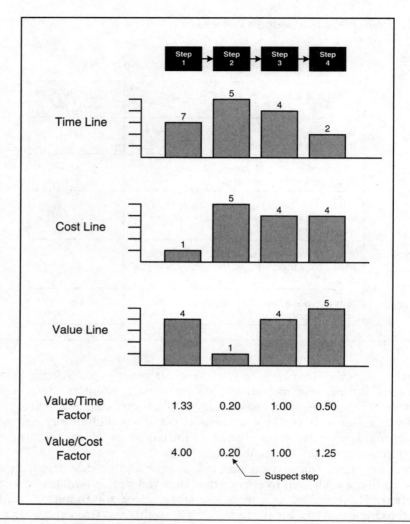

Figure 3. **Cost, time, and value analysis.**

Fragmentation. Frederick Taylor introduced the concept of segmentation and specialization of work activities.[2] This is the formula for assembly-line work, and it still works well for high-volume, low-flexibility work in which simple controls over the work are important. Unfortunately, little such work remains in the United States. To characterize fragmentation, simply count the number of times responsibility for a task changes hands. For example, in a typical hospital check-in process, the patient might be seen by a receptionist, admitting clerk, insurance specialist, lab technician, X-ray technician, and a nurse, for a total of five handoffs. Each handoff requires wasting time, coordination, and tracking and increases the risk of failed communication.

Flexibility. A process set in concrete makes things easy on the process owner, but what about the customers who are served by the process? It's not unusual to find processes that execute the same steps no matter what the input. For instance, does a procurement order for a $50 software package go through the same channels as a $50,000 procurement order?

Complexity. Processes should be checked for the number of places where logic diverges. If a large number of these branching points are found, the process designers might have tried to accomplish too much with one process. Also, try to gauge the extent of variability allowed in the process input. If a wide array of inputs are allowed, the process has probably been designed as a one-size-fits-all routine, or it has many branching points to accommodate the breadth of inputs. In either case, the process is probably too complex.

Process type. Processes can be categorized according to duration, complexity, frequency, and number of functions:

- **Type 1:** The first process type has long cycle times (months), many steps, occurs infrequently (monthly or yearly), and has many functional specialists. These processes are typically far removed from the product and customer. Examples include the annual budgeting process.
- **Type 2:** This process type accounts for the processes that are neither type 1 or type 3.
- **Type 3:** This process type has short cycle times (days or hours), few steps (less than five), occurs frequently (hourly or daily), and involves one or two functions.

How to Avoid Problems

There are two key points that can be used to help avoid pitfalls when identifying a process:

- Do not string several type-2 processes together and believe that they form a single process. They might be a collection of stand-alone processes that are invoked by a higher-level control process. In such cases, it's important to analyze each process separately. For example, a control-room operator might execute an emergency shutdown process if the overall operating process calls for it.
- Often, a related type-2 process (such as contract administration) is tacked onto a type-3 process (such as establishing a contract). It's important that these processes be uncoupled; otherwise, unnecessary complexity will be introduced into the process redesign.

Step 2: Investigating New Paradigms

At this point in process redesign, a detailed flowchart of existing processes—including supplementary information on time, flow rates, and handoffs—has been created, and some analysis has been performed to determine the factors

It's not unusual to find processes that execute the same steps no matter what the input.

that might be undermining performance. The next step requires breaking out of old thought patterns to discover new ways of operating.

One way to break out of old thought patterns is benchmarking. Benchmarking offers a structured look at how other organizations do things, and it helps companies generate new ideas and abandon old constraints. Benchmarking is an appropriate tool to use if time permits and there is a good possibility that other companies have superior processes.

The Xerox Corp. uses benchmarking as a corporate strategy. For example, when Xerox discovered that Fuji Xerox was selling copy machines for less than it cost Xerox to manufacture them, it believed it could do the same—so it did!

A second way to research new paradigms is to experiment with different internal process structures. This is an experiment of what-if scenarios. To begin, prepare several options for each part of the process being redesigned. The options can be modeled by preparing flowcharts for various combinations of activities and estimating the effect of cycle times and costs. Also consider information technology options. These technologies might totally revise one's perspective on how to design a process.

Step 3: Process Design

To facilitate process redesign, a set of process design rules keyed to cycle-time reduction has been developed. Activities that lengthen cycle time—rework, nonvalue-adding activities, poor or untimely performance feedback, handoffs of responsibility, and overall complexity—are bad for processes. It's estimated that cutting cycle times by 50% results in productivity increases of 20% to 70%.[4]

Since fast-cycle companies have an easier time reacting to changes in the marketplace, they also greatly reduce their risks by relying on fast reactions rather than shaky, long-term forecasts. Consider some of the things that make Toyota such a tough competitor. It processes dealer orders five times faster than the average for U.S. automakers; its production cycle for new car development is 40% as long as the three to five years for U.S. automakers; and it turns over inventory twice as fast.[5]

Process design rules fall into one of two categories—golden rules and simple commandments. The three golden rules are:

Golden Rule 1: Organize by product. Specialize in products rather than functions. Organizing processes by product allows a structure in which groups can work on a product or service from start to finish, thereby reducing fragmentation and inflexibility.

Golden Rule 2: Minimize the number of groups and individuals required to complete a product or service. This reduces the number of responsibility handoffs in the process and considerably shortens the performance feedback loops.

Golden Rule 3: Redesign the process flow, work-group structure, and individual duties at the same time. All three factors must work together. Redesigning one or two is not desirable.

The 16 commandments are:

Commandment 1: Design around core activities.

Commandment 2: Design for continuous flow of work.

Commandment 3: Avoid required or formalized activities.

Commandment 4: Combine steps. Integrate low-value steps (i.e., overhead) into direct-value steps.

Commandment 5: Avoid intraorganizational dependencies and shared responsibilities.

Commandment 6: Don't design assembly lines.

Commandment 7: Design activities to run in parallel paths.

Commandment 8: Don't mix process types.

Commandment 9: Design a modular organization—it should be composed of several stand-alone parts that can be redirected when needed.

Commandment 10: Locate individuals within a cellular unit in close physical proximity.

Commandment 11: Design work groups (modules) to be temporary.

Commandment 12: Create more multiskilled workers. Increase the scope of each job.

Commandment 13: Place specialists into the line organization.

Commandment 14: Give employees access to all the information they need to complete a product.

Commandment 15: If there are indirect support groups outside the line cellular units, they should have no daily control over processes that affect the cellular units.

Commandment 16: Give workers most of the decision-making authority.

Step 4: Process Creation

The new process is created using these steps:

Step 1: Based on benchmarking data and a knowledge of process types, select a basic process type.

Step 2: Using the golden rules and commandments, design the process organization, work flow, and activities.

Step 3: Document the design with flowcharts, organization charts, procedures, and process control charts.

Step 4: Pilot test the new operation if possible. Design specific data-gathering points into the pilot design for gathering data about the effectiveness and efficiency of the new process design.

The array of implementation activities is too large to address here. But, suffice it to say, if the stage isn't properly set for the new process, it will fail in production. Involving all affected parties—suppliers, process workers, and customers—throughout the redesign effort will help in the difficult implementation transition.

Planning Is Essential for Success

The process improvement model begins with documenting and measuring a customer need. Improvement activities can focus on solving specific problems (problem-solving path), a broader restructuring of major elements of the process (process-restructuring path), or a combination of the two. With both paths, a structured approach is taken to identify causes of performance shortfalls. In general, efficiency shortcomings will be dealt with by employee teams using a stratification approach to solve specific problems. Effectiveness shortcomings will more likely be dealt with by management teams using the process-redesign methodology. In either case, changes are driven by customer needs and process improvement is achieved through rigorous scientific methods.

References

1. "Quality Improvement Tools and Techniques," Total Quality Associates, 1992.
2. Frederick Taylor, *The Principles of Scientific Management* (New York, NY: Harper & Row, 1947).
3. David T. Kearns and David A. Nadler, *Prophets in the Dark* (New York, NY: HarperBusiness, 1992).
4. George Stalk Jr. and Thomas M. Hout, *Competing Against Time* (New York, NY: The Free Press, 1990).
5. Ibid.

Roger O. Rupp is the manager of quality support in the Resources Group of the Tennessee Valley Authority in Knoxville, Tennessee. James R. Russell is the manager of the Quality Resources Staff at the Tennessee Valley Authority in Knoxville, Tennessee.

Cycle Time and the Bottom Line

S. S. Cherukuri, R. G. Nieman, and N. C. Sirianni

This article, using a series of graphs, demonstrates how reducing cycle time results in higher profitability. Sometimes this is difficult to quantify. The methodology discussed here provides a concrete way to think about and understand the importance and value of time to the organization and to customers.

The Need

One of management's fundamental missions is to create profitable and sustainable competitive advantage. Business process improvement's objective is the implementation of an operating strategy that will result in competitive advantage. Corporate strategic questions such as, "What businesses should we be in?" and "How should we allocate our resources to those businesses?" are important. For most managers, however, two other questions of operating strategy are more relevant to their activities. "Given the business we are in, what should be our operating strategy for creating competitive advantage?" and "Having selected our operating strategy, how do we implement that strategy and achieve our goals?"

Arguably, there are only three basic operating strategies for competitive advantage. First, you can offer more value—better quality, better service than the competition is willing or able to provide—while maintaining proximity on cost. Another alternative is to be the low-cost producer but maintain proximity on value. The third alternative is a niche strategy, a hybrid of the first two. This strategy focuses on a segment of the market where either a value or cost strategy can be successfully implemented.

Whichever of the three you choose, the objective is to achieve significant operating performance—price, volume, mix, product cost, overhead cost, and investment. Investment, in particular, often is misunderstood and underemphasized in operating strategies. There is another influence on performance that may not be completely visible on an operating statement or balance sheet. This performance variable is cycle time—the time from concept to production—and it is critical to an organization's ability to create and sustain a competitive advantage. Major new insights will follow the realization that

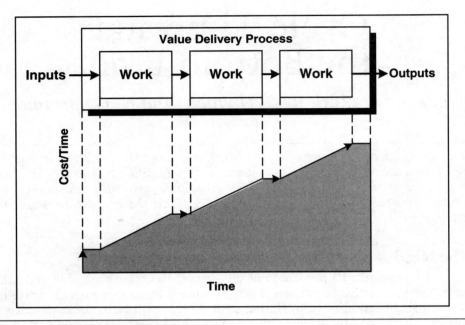

Figure 1. **Cost-time profiles and process.**

time can also be a powerful driving force for improvement. This may not be intuitively obvious. To appreciate this you must have an understanding of cycle time and its effects on customer satisfaction and quality.

The Obstacles

In a quest for improved financial performance, organizations often concentrate their energies on increased market share, price realization, and cost reduction. They often ignore another major quantitative influence on profit, the total investment in their business. Operating managers usually view investment as a static number. As a result, they often find investment difficult to manage. One example is inventories, which require extraordinary efforts to obtain even slight reductions. They usually leap up again as soon as attention turns elsewhere. This is a result of not understanding the difference between static and dynamic investments. Dynamic investments tend to change as business conditions and processes change. Static investments don't fluctuate in this manner.

There are two parts of dynamic investment. The first is "visible" in that it can be seen and measured on the balance sheet of the organization. There is an additional piece of the dynamic investment which can be said to be "invisible," because it is not on the balance sheet, having been treated as a period expense. Both of these, plus the static investment, make up the total investment in the business.

There is another obstacle to addressing the opportunities for performance improvement inherent in cycle time. It is the inability to visibly demonstrate the impact of cycle time on the performance of the organization. Physical volume, cost, static investment, and even price realization are relatively easy to measure and illustrate. But cycle time is an elusive variable; it is difficult to quantify. It is even more difficult to demonstrate its effects on financial performance.

The Solution

To understand cycle time and its relationship to cost and total investment, a methodology must be developed that illustrates these relationships in a way that will lead to process improvements in the business reengineering process. This methodology is "cost-time profiling." This innovative technique has been used by many organizations as a fundamental tool in their quest for bottom-line performance improvement.

Cost time profiles have been especially helpful in representing an organization's investments. Figure 1 illustrates a basic profile and demonstrates its relationship to the value delivery process.

Every cost-time profile has three components. The vertical lines in the figure represent purchased goods and services. The diagonal lines are labor or work performed. The horizontal lines are wait-time, when nothing is being done. Cost-time profiling is a way to illuminate, analyze, and improve the business processes shown in Figure 1. Every business process consists of people receiving inputs, adding value, and delivering outputs. The cost-time profile depicts those functions in terms of the cost and time required to complete the process. The vertical axis represents the buildup of costs, while the horizontal axis represents cycle time to perform the process. The area under the profile is an integration of cost over time. It's equal to the investment that has come about as a result of this process. This is a dynamic investment; that is, it changes with changes in the process. A static investment does not change with changes in cycle time. However, it can be a visible investment, which will appear on the balance sheet, or it can be invisible, having been charged-off as a period expense.

The entire value delivery process of the business, along with the resulting total investment, can be described with a macro cost-time profile (Figure 2).

The profile shows the sales and operating profit per period. The area within the boundaries of the profile is a measure of the total investment in the business, both dynamic and static. It also depicts the visible part of the investment as well as the invisible. This profile can be viewed as four pieces. Three of these pieces are above the baseline and represent dynamic investment. These three pieces are receivables, factory and distributions, and office. The office piece of the investment is the invisible investment. The costs associated with the office are not put into the inventory cost of goods sold, but are expensed monthly as they occur. As a result, they do not appear on the balance sheet. Instead, they are an investment in the business. If the cycle time for this portion of the process can be reduced, investment will be reduced

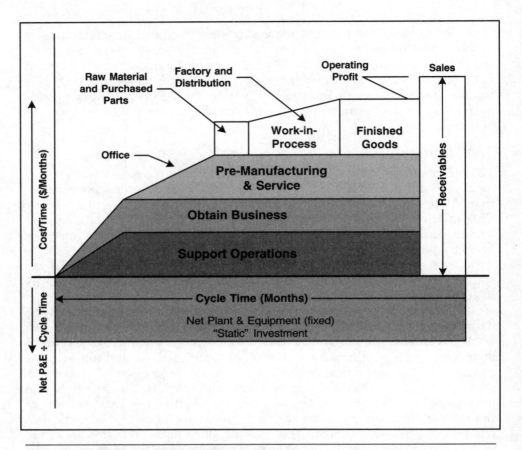

Figure 2. **Macro cost-time profile of the business.**

and the business will receive a one-time return of cash equal to the reduction of the area.

The factory and distribution piece of the investment has three parts: raw material and purchased parts, work-in-process, and shipping stock. This investment does appear on the balance sheet and is part of the visible investment.

Receivables also are visible on the balance sheet. The dimensions of the receivables area are the sales (height) and the average days outstanding (width or cycle time). These three—receivables, factory and distribution, and office—are dynamic since they will vary in size as sales, costs and cycle time change with changes in the value delivery process of the business.

The fourth piece of the investment is below the baseline. This piece is referred to as fixed investment. Nominally, its area represents the net (undepreciated) plant and equipment portion of the business. The protocol for displaying this requires that its height, multiplied by total cycle time equals its value. It's a static investment since it doesn't change as directly with cycle time as does the dynamic portion of the investment. However, displaying it in the fashion shown allows a valid comparison between this static portion of the investment and the dynamic portions. This display provides an excellent illustration of the major portions of the total investment of the business. It also provides an idea of the extent to which they are driven by cost and time.

In total, these four pieces make up the total investment of the organization. Three portions—office, factory and distribution, and receivables—are dynamic investments, as they are more directly impacted by changes in business processes. In addition, experience has shown that reducing cycle time will provide opportunities to reduce the fourth, static portion of the investment, since a business needs fewer storerooms, less factor and office space, and fewer machines. Of the four pieces, three are visible—receivables, factory and distribution, and net plant and equipment—as they appear on the balance sheet. The fourth portion, office, is invisible since it is not carried on the balance sheet, but is considered a period expense.

Three portions— office, factory and distribution, and receivables—are dynamic investments, as they are more directly impacted by changes in business processes.

Improving the Business Process

One objective of process improvement is to significantly reshape the top and bottom portions of the organization's cost-time profile in ways which will favorably impact the financial bottom-line. In general, the goal is to shrink the profile while increasing sales. This means the business process must be improved to reduce cycle time and costs in ways that will improve total perceived quality, which will result in increased sales. Figure 3 demonstrates what the profile might look like after such an improvement effort. The old profile is still shown as broken lines to provide a comparison.

Total cycle time has been reduced, the area of total investment lessened, and sales have increased. This increase in sales is accomplished without a commensurate increase in total cost. Factory and distribution costs increased, as might be expected with an increase in volume, but they have not increased as much as sales. However, the investment in this portion of the operation has decreased due to the reduction in cycle time. Office costs decreased, which results in increased operating profit both in total and as a percent of sales. The days outstanding of receivables decreased, lowering the investment even in the face of increased sales. Of course, the invisible portion of the investment has decreased in relation to the whole. Because the protocol of cost-time profiles causes the static or fixed investment to be aligned with total cycle time, this portion of the investment has changed shape. There is a reduction in cycle time, but it has not changed in its total area or value. The increase in sales produces an increase in turnover of this fixed investment. Total investment, dynamic and static, visible and invisible, has reduced significantly. When combined with the increase in operating margin, this results in a major increase in return on total investment.

An additional approach, cash efficiency conversion analysis, can extend the cost-time perspective into the more strategic decision-making processes of the business. This analysis is used to determine which plants or product

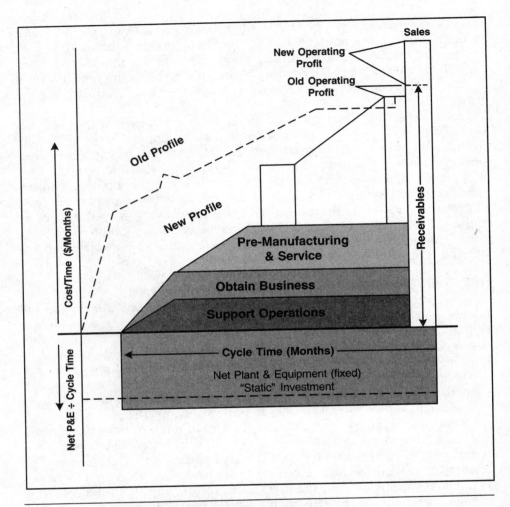

Figure 3.   **Macro cost-time profile of the business.**

lines have growth potential, and which ones should be divested. Using this analysis will establish acceptable profit levels for each component of the business and permit valid comparisons of performance.

Cash conversion efficiency analysis is based on developing cost-time profiles for individual product lines and plants, as well as for the business as a whole. These profiles provide information about the total investment—dynamic and static, visible and invisible—required for each entity. This information is displayed on the cash conversion efficiency chart (Figure 4).

The vertical axis of this chart is operating profit as a percent of sales. The horizontal axis is total investment as a percent of annual sales. The position of the total business is plotted on the chart as the median point. A target performance line for the business is established as shown. Any operation lying

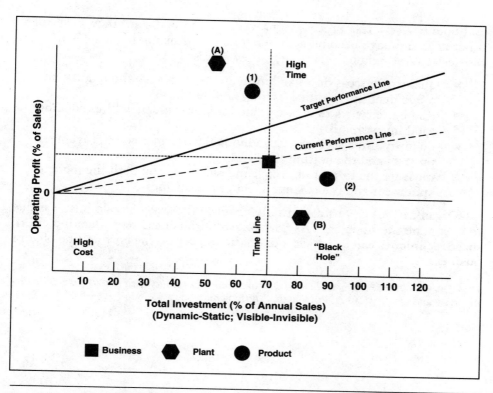

Figure 4. **Cash conversion efficiency.**

along this line is equal in performance relative to the use of total investment for the generation of profit. If located at the lower left of the line, the operation creates low profit margins, but does so with relatively low total investment. Conversely, those at the upper right of the line create higher profit margins, but require a relatively large amount of total investment to do so. The individual plants and individual product lines are located on the chart, with the size of the marker indicating relative size. By performing this evaluation, relative performance becomes self-evident. The overall goal is to drive each product and plant—and the total business—to the "northwest," into the value enhancement zone.

When performing an analysis using cost-time profiles, cash conversion efficiency is an excellent method for summarizing an analysis in a way which will lead to sound business decision making.

Summary

Cost-time profiling and its companion methodology, cash conversion efficiency, are powerful techniques for an organization that is serious about business reengineering. The techniques were developed to identify, understand

and quantify business process improvements. In addition, they have many other uses and have become a cornerstone of our business reengineering activities at Westinghouse. Currently, they are used to:

- quantify process flows and measure productivity and quality improvement in the office, factory, and field;
- find better ways to create value for stockholders while reducing total investment;
- quantify linkages between individual performance improvement projects and the bottom line; and
- measure the impact of cycle-time reductions on both the income statement and the balance sheet of the business.

Organizations have substantially changed the way they do business due to cost-time methodology. As part of a total business reengineering effort, these techniques can also have a dramatic impact on the bottom line of your business.

Nick Sinanni, Dick Nieman, and Cheri Cherukuri are consultants with the Westinghouse Productivity and Quality Center, Pittsburgh, Pennsylvania.

Creating a System for Continuous Improvement

D. Keith Denton

The author of this article suggests that continuous improvement comes from identifying ways to simplify or eliminate decision-making situations that complicate business and take time. This is a twist on what goes on when organizations improve their processes. Things get simpler and work better partially because we have eliminated sources of ambiguity that add variation and costs and not value.

When people speak of continuous improvement, they are really talking about continuous change. To have continuous change, there has to be some factor that binds people together. There must be a common purpose, and each member must understand his or her role. It is like a jigsaw puzzle in which everyone knows the location of the pieces and where they fit. If you want real, long-lasting change, then you must have a way of focusing people on the change—not as individuals, but as a cohesive unit.

Most of us fail to understand how we fit in and why we are important. We just do our job and wait for the next crisis to subside. Great things can happen only when change brings with it an understanding by *all* individuals, departments, and functions about their roles.

People are important to organizations, but the belief that people are *our most important* asset is a misconception. The most important asset of an organization is not its people, its technology, or even its highly paid managers. Each can be important, but each is simply a tool. Even the most gifted personnel will fail if they operate in a *system* that is designed to fail.

Thus, it is a firm's "system" of drawing people together for a common purpose that is the one crucial factor to success. If some great unifying factor draws normal, hard-working people together and helps them see their importance and their place in the organization, those people can do great things. On the other hand, a disjointed effort or approach to introducing change will likely fail. Even extraordinary people working extraordinarily hard will fail if they have no focus. Obviously, it would be best to have both extraordinary

> It is a firm's "system" of drawing people together for a common purpose that is the one crucial factor to success.

people and an extraordinary system of introducing change, but it is the latter that creates a great organization.

Systems of Work

Changes in the workplace have helped create unifying systems for continuous improvement in several firms. American Express made a significant change when it adopted a system built on "customer-based transactions." The company created a comprehensive delivery system around its external customer requests that would support key customer transactions. One of these networks is based on service "billing," another is "new accounts," and so on. Once American Express identified the key transactions, it proceeded to identify all of the critical functions needed to deliver quality service to those customers. The purpose was to create a logical system of information flowing from internal supplier to internal customer, rather than the haphazard approach common in many firms. Now every internal supplier and customer knows where it fits within the total customer transaction process.

American Express managers still maintain most of their old organizational structure, but they have been able to streamline customer response time, creating direct links between the performance of an action and the reaction of internal suppliers and customers. In most cases they can measure the outcome of a service employee's performance and the effect upon an individual customer.

Using customer transactions as a change agent is a powerful focal point because it becomes clear where each employee fits in. Another big advantage is the ability to directly and continually see the impact of one's decisions. The American Express system uses more than 100 customer transaction-related measures. This provides an important feature of change management: setting quantifiable benchmarks. For instance, American Express expects results to be better than 97 percent of that standard. Individuals and departments know at a glance how they are doing, where they fit in, and—perhaps best of all—*why* they are important.

Because American Express also knows that continuous improvement and continuous change do not occur unless the change is rewarded, it set up systems for rewarding those who exceed customer expectations. Included in the system are "great performer" awards and various monetary and nonmonetary incentives that are given for exceeded expectations. Obviously, there are flaws in any system, including that of American Express. But at least it has created a system for continuous change that tries to succeed.

Motorola provides another example of an exceptional company whose success is largely a result of its systematic approach toward implementing change. In Motorola's case, the unifying factor was not individual customer transactions, but rather the use of a *common language* to help unify its people. Functional areas and departments measure performance based on "defect per unit." Their objective, as they put it, is to "do it right the first time." In other words, no defects or errors is the ideal operating environment. This approach is referred to as six sigma. Statistically speaking, Motorola expects to have

Using customer transactions as a change agent is a powerful focal point because it becomes clear where each employee fits in.

fewer than four defects or defectives occurring in one million opportunities. Only four typos (or any other errors) in one million opportunities is pretty good quality in anyone's book!

Everyone must focus on the elimination of *variability* if the company hopes to reach its six sigma goal. It is only possible to produce at this level if people uniformly produce their products and deliver their services. To do this requires a lot of training. Motorola has made a major commitment to training, with about 2.4 percent of its budget going to help teach people to eliminate variability.

Changes as a Byproduct

Any systematic approach to change is better than the piecemeal approach often used by many organizations. Systematic application is good, but not all unifying approaches toward continuous change are equal. Even though American Express uses a systematic approach, much of its old hierarchy remains intact. It has simply overlaid a communication network over the old structure. As such, the network is somewhat superficial because it really does not change the way decisions are made or who makes them. Nor does it create a greater sense of ownership. It does, however, create stronger linkages between one functional area and another. Much of the same decision-making power over what will be changed is still centered at the top, but the operational people do know where they fit in.

An added advantage to American Express' unifying factor is the fact that it is positive rather than negative. Some companies attempt to create change by focusing on fear. It is acceptable to recognize threats, but the focus should not be on the negative. Those who use the "common enemy" tactic sometimes claim that foreign competition or budgetary restraints are the enemy and then attempt to unite their people against them. Often such an approach provides short-term improvements simply because there is power in the unifying factor. Creating dissatisfaction with the status quo is sometimes necessary, but it is not enough. Eventually, the negative aspects of constant fear and the lack of a positive and clearly focused vision of the future soon produce disillusionment and division. Many begin to feel that the common enemy is not outside but rather inside the company.

Despite the advantages of Motorola's and American Express' approaches, some serious drawbacks still remain. One of the most serious, as mentioned above, is that their systems do not really change the way decisions are made. Decisions may be faster, and people may have a clearer focus, but real decision making remains at the top. To implement true continuous improvement one must be able to focus and unify *all* of the organization. Everyone must feel a part of the change and accept ownership of the change. Unity of purpose does not mean equal decision making, but it does involve creating this sense of ownership.

Focusing people on external and internal customers and creating a common language used by all members certainly are big steps in unifying people, but they are not the ultimate way to unify. When people have a common

Unity of purpose does not mean equal decision making, but it does involve creating this sense of ownership.

sense of purpose, change is a natural outcome. It is a byproduct, not the product. To have a common purpose people must not only see the big picture, they must have some sense of control and ownership of the change process. They should be internal owners—not just internal customers.

An Extraordinary System of Work

One company that has been able to improve continually to meet competitive challenges is Springfield Remanufacturing Corporation (SRC). Improvement works so well at SRC because the firm creates that sense of ownership so essential to success. The corporation employs about 600 people and rebuilds gasoline and diesel engines—possibly better than anyone in the world. Although the company is not as widely known as Motorola or American Express, it has nevertheless received a lot of national attention. Its unqualified success and management practice made it a feature of the PBS series "Growing a Business." It has also been on the cover of *Inc.* Magazine and was featured on a segment of the "CBS Evening News." SRC's system for unifying its people's efforts involves using the income statement and balance sheet. The system teaches employees and managers alike to make changes based on the main objective of most organizations, whether the change makes money or controls costs.

Although most any company needs to make money, very few empower their people by teaching them how to do it and, specifically, where they fit in the process. A key difference between SRC's approach and the typical company is that other companies tend to believe their employees don't "need to know." SRC's approach is just the opposite. It believes its employees need to known *how* to make money, so it teaches people on even the lowest level about financial ratios, how to read income statements and balance sheets, and, most important, what they mean.

Training people to understand financial ratios is fine, but it would be meaningless if those same employees did not have some control over the numbers. SRC is employee owned and operated, but unlike most such companies there is open disclosure of its assets and liabilities. Jack Stack, the CEO, often says, "There's not a financial number we don't share with our people." This is because Stack recognizes it is the use of the income statement to create trust throughout the company that is SRC's unifying factor. The reason for any changes becomes obvious to employees; it is right there in black (or red) accounting ink. Every supervisor, department, and individual has a single line on the income statements. Employees know both what they contribute to and what they cost the organization. There is no place to hide, no doubt about what they need to do.

There is also no doubt as to whether change is effective. Quite simply, if it improves the income statement or balance sheet, it is a good change. SRC's approach works because it is logical and ties financial rewards to the financial health of the company. Individuals can receive a 10 percent bonus if they meet key financial goals, which are jointly set.

Employees know both what they contribute to and what they cost the organization. There is no place to hide, no doubt about what they need to do.

To make sure everyone keeps concentrating on making good decisions and changes, SRC conducts a weekly financial review meeting every Tuesday. Initially, these meetings are held between top management and mid-level personnel. Discussion revolves around variances on each line item of their projected monthly income statements. Any negative variance between projected and actual expenditures is the source of extended discussions. Later, members of this group meet with their respective departments and go through similar discussions with their personnel. Eventually every employee in the organization is informed.

Using the income statement as a unifying factor for change seems like the perfect tool for continuous change, but it does have a few flaws. There is no logical reason why organizations could not share their financial information except two: lack of trust and lack of commitment to extensive training. Unless they rethink the role of their people, there is no way organizations will be totally transparent and allow open disclosure of sensitive financial information.

Speed as a Change Agent

Making money is obviously a fundamental element in the success of most organizations, but it is not the only element. Reflecting the old adage, "Time is money," speed has become the competitive weapon of the 1990s. Study after study shows that those who get to a market first obtain and hold market share the longest. Some of the most successful organizations base their success on speed.

Citibank introduces three new financial services a week. A retailer called The Limited can take fashions off the drawing board and into stores in less than 60 days. Honda and Toyota can take a car from concept to market in three years, whereas it takes General Motors five years to do the same thing.

Most people need very little convincing of the importance of speed. What many fail to understand, though, is the importance of examining speed at its molecular level—namely, decision making. Although many talk about the need for change, little effort has been devoted to systematically examining how decisions are made and what needs changing.

When it comes to making decisions, two things are of utmost importance. First is the actual time it takes to resolve an issue. This does not mean the amount of time it *should* take to make a decision, nor the amount of time one would *like* it to take, but the *actual* or *real* time expended in making the decision.

Second, you need to know the minimum or ideal time it could take if things were perfect. The ideal would be no time at all; if you completely eliminate the need to make a decision, then you would have zero time. Assuming the decision has to be made, list all of the information that would be needed for the decision to be made quickly. Identify all pre-decision conditions. Then ask yourself, "What is the minimum time it would take to make the decision without error?"

Many decisions must move through several functional areas and up through several levels of the organization. Some are simple daily decisions requiring only a nod from one or more employees. This could include prioritizing a job as it comes into a work station. Other strategic or operational decisions require weeks, months, or even years to resolve. Some decisions are bottlenecked at key decision-making centers, such as corporate headquarters or product development areas.

Anyone wanting continuous improvement must prioritize the critical decisions that first need to be made: those that relate to the purpose of the organization. This involves analyzing a key decision to see what is actually occurring and how it can be improved. In the ideal situation one might expect the decision-making process to be linear as it moves through organizational levels. Theoretically, it might also be circular if the decision moves from one functional area to another. Unfortunately, neglect and acceptance of the status quo have changed these simple lines and circles of decisions into a tornado of activity that creates a lot of energy but brings about little effective decision making.

Change the Structure of Decisions

Untangling and streamlining the normally disjointed decision-making process of organizations or departments involves a step-by-step evaluation . The first step should be to challenge *why* the decision, or each step within the decision, needs to be made at all.

When it comes to change, elimination is the most powerful tool because it completely changes the way work is done. For instance, when organizations eliminate layers of management, they are structurally changing the way decisions are made. A natural outcome of this change is greater efficiency. Mike Walsh, CEO of Union Pacific, provides one example of what is occurring around the United States. When Walsh came on board at UP, there were nine layers of management between himself and those responsible for operations. So he set about eliminating six of those layers. He also increased the spending authority of his superintendents, thus eliminating the need for approval decisions and streamlining the decision making.

> When it comes to change, elimination is the most powerful tool because it completely changes the way work is done.

In another example, Pizza Hut asked its employees nationwide to make a change by redesigning their decision making. As a result, morale increased in their San Diego, St. Louis, and southern Florida stores when store managers helped decide what paperwork the parent company could eliminate. The managers recognized that to do that one must focus on eliminating bottlenecks and reducing mistakes and miscues.

Fortune reported that Sea Land went through restructuring by logically concentrating on work elimination, rather than job elimination. The aim was to get rid of unnecessary tasks, so the organization examined its job descriptions. As a result, many of those descriptions shrank from five pages to one. For example, salespeople no longer had to write overly detailed reports that nobody read anyway.

Of course, it is impossible to eliminate all decision making, but there are still ways of making changes through simplification. Union Pacific recognized the advantage of simplifying customer service decisions, so it installed new technology. Now when a customer calls, pertinent account information automatically flashes on the service representative's monitor, greatly simplifying asking questions and making decisions. UP also uses a mainframe to trace shipments and place orders, which means that nearly one-third of its bills can be sent electronically.

Du Pont provides a good example of how simplifying can help. In the 1980s Du Pont was forced to do more with less. One instance of where this occurred was in human resources, which had a pressing need to reduce the size of the department despite such emerging issues as child care, parental leave, flexible benefits, AIDS, and drug testing. To deal with this problem of decreasing size and increasing demand, the company decided to assess and prioritize the work it needed. In particular, it made a concerted effort to focus on several key changes, including eliminating tasks and adding value through technology. One of these initiatives was automation, particularly in the use of computer and video display equipment. Recognizing that the problems facing one plant or location and another were very similar, it decided to package advice in video format rather than send in experts in affirmative action or other areas. Now when one of its plants is facing a routine decision about an equal employment opportunity audit, plant managers can pull out a videotape that takes them step by step through the preparation process. By simplifying this process, Du Pont eliminated needless decisions and made permanent changes in the way work was done. Of course, someone with a question about the new system can still call corporate consultants for advice or explanation.

By simplifying this process, Du Pont eliminated needless decisions and made permanent changes in the way work was done.

Du Pont made use of other technology as well, including electronic mail and automated phone systems. By using numbers on a touch-tone phone a person can now dial a recording that provides specific details needed to fill out a form to receive additional information. The company also computerized its service manual so changes could be made electronically, eliminating the need to send updates to 800 manual holders throughout the company.

Of course, technology is not the only way to simplify. Du Pont also began to prioritize decision making. Low-priority decisions are fertile ground for elimination. In Du Pont's case, if the human resource people added something new to their list of assignments and responsibilities, they then looked closely at how they could eliminate, simplify, or reduce the low-priority decisions needed for the task. For instance, although they were not able to completely eliminate staff meetings, they did do away with weekly staff notes and scheduled the meetings every other week rather than weekly. One of the key strategies the company learned from this simplification process was that the solution to streamlining is to concentrate on predictable and repetitive tasks, such as OSHA inspections, benefit consultation, and training activities.

Simplifying delivery, production, and designs can also have a substantial payoff.

Simplifying delivery, production, and designs can also have a substantial payoff. At one time IBM made five medium-sized computers, each available in three cabinets for a total of 15 different boxes. Its new computers use only three cabinets between them. Simplification, as in this case, eliminates a multitude of decisions and overhead.

Combining

The final tool for continuous improvement of the decision-making process is through combining functions and knowledge. As with elimination or simplification, there are many ways to combine decision making. One is by using teams. For instance, concurrent engineering is a popular change that many companies have implemented. It involves the simultaneous design and development of both the product and the process. Combining the skills and knowledge of operational personnel can shift some decision-making authority from management to team members. The outcome is often the elimination of redundant activities.

Consider the case of Chaparral Steel's use of teams. Chaparral is one of the world's most productive steel companies. Its daily operations depend a great deal on effective team management. By giving teams the authority to make their own decisions, the firm eliminates the need for excessive management. Among other things, teams at Chaparral decide when to take their own coffee breaks and when to leave their machines.

The teams are also given a great deal of authority because they have been trained to understand the whole process of steelmaking. The company runs a training program that teaches members not only what happens to a piece of steel as it moves through their operation but also about finance, accounting, and sales. Because they are trained in this manner they know how their jobs relate to the welfare of the entire organization. Creating this understanding of how the company works enhances trust and unity. To reinforce the team system, Chaparral makes sure rewards are based on pay for skills, rather than on automatic raises, to encourage learning.

The hardest part of trying to change may be deciding where to focus your efforts. Continuous improvement can occur through such vehicles as American Express' single customer transaction, Motorola's zero defects per unit, or SRC's focus on creating company-wide understanding of how the business works, all of which have their advantages and limits. Another way to continuously improve and keep changes relevant is to concentrate on the speed of decision making.

GE's "Work Out" program is one of the more widely known cases of focusing on eliminating or simplifying decisions. In three-day sessions, participants examine simple and significant decisions, then break down problems into two categories—rattlers and pythons. Rattlers are simple problems, such as getting approval for needed work gloves; pythons are more complicated to unravel. The purpose of Work Out sessions is to eliminate work. Usually, a group of 50 or more people is involved in analyzing and changing a work area decision. In one of the meetings, for example, participants decided that the head of the computer lab should be allowed to spend petty cash without the approval of a superior, thereby eliminating that need to make a decision. Removing multiple approvals, unnecessary paperwork, excessive reports, routines, and even rituals is the focus of Work Out.

Anyone wanting to continue down the path of continuous improvement and implement successful change needs to create some systematic way to do it. Eliminating, simplifying, or combining decision steps are some ways that can be universally used.

References

Brian Dumaine, "Who Needs a Boss?" *Fortune*, May 7, 1990, p. 52.

Andrew Kupfer, "An Outsider Fires Up a Railroad," *Fortune*, December 18, 1989, p. 133.

Jeremy Main, "The Winning Organization," *Fortune*, September 26, 1988, p. 50.

Thomas A. Stewart, "Do You Push Your People Too Hard?," *Fortune*, October 22, 1990, p. 121.

D. Keith Denton is a professor of management at Southwest Missouri State University, Springfield.

SUPPLIERS AND PURCHASING

Crossing Company Lines

Robert J. Bowman

This article profiles efforts to measure the value added by each member of a supply chain in delivering final products to customers. The challenge has been to find metrics that are common to a wide variety of industries. The effort continues because such measures can enhance cooperation and reduce complexity and non-value-added work.

Imagine creating a tool for measuring quality that spans across the entire supply chain, is applicable to all major industries and is embraced by the biggest multinationals. In fact, a handful of companies are making steady progress toward that goal—with some major caveats.

3M, Xerox, AT&T Network Systems, Procter & Gamble and Nabisco Foods are among the participants in a new project to ensure quality throughout the supply chain, from suppliers to customers. They face the daunting task of crafting performance standards—known as "metrics"—that are general enough to apply to everyone but specific enough to be of practical use.

Other shippers involved in the project include Black & Decker, Levi Strauss, and Digital Equipment Corp. Rounding out the membership are three schools—M.I.T., Penn State, and Stanford University—and a consultant, Pittiglio, Rabin, Todd & McGrath of Weston, Mass.

Most members already have solid in-house programs for assessing vendor performance and for benchmarking themselves against others. But Don Pilgrim, supply chain management project manager with 3M, believes the companies can achieve even more through a group effort. "There's real power in leveraging across multiple companies that are facing the same issues and trying to manage change in their organizations," he says.

"We certainly have our own measurements," adds Paul Hicks, senior project manager with Procter & Gamble, "but benchmarking can be pretty difficult to do. You can throw a lot of money at it and not make a whole lot of progress."

Historically, each link in the supply chain has functioned separately, making decisions based on its own needs instead of the greater good, says Peter Metz, deputy director of M.I.T.'s Center for Transportation Studies. Companies have tended to consist of a series of fiefdoms battling one another for resources and supremacy. The result has been unacceptably high production costs.

Then there's the plethora of report cards and performance standards that quality-minded companies have devised over the past decade. Many have tantalizing similarities, but they're just different enough to be of little use to others—at least without major revisions.

Now comes the supply chain consortium to standardize those measurements and boil them down to a set of metrics that knows no industry bounds. Kara Kardon, the project manager at PRTM, says the project grew out of an informal discussion group following a Council of Logistics Management (CLM) meeting a couple of years back.

The consortium's first challenge was to define the term "supply chain," another in a seemingly endless series of logistics buzz-concepts. Indeed, few companies have a firm idea of who's responsible for fixing breaks in that mysterious chain.

"In many companies, it's either everyone's job or no one's job," says the consortium's initial report. "The supply chain is a process-oriented concept that does not conform to traditional organizational structures."

Phase one of the project, unveiled at CLM's 1994 annual conference in Cincinnati, involved the metrics and the framework to measure supply chain performance. The intent was to build a set of supply chain metrics that was common and consistent among participants. "It's a pretty good overall measure of supply chain performance," says Hicks.

Specific processes fall into the expected categories: planning, sourcing, production, order management, distribution, administration, customer accounting, product life cycle, and customer relations management.

Next, the consortium created a framework of primary and secondary metrics that can be found in just about any organization.

The first group consists of expected outcomes—order fulfillment, customer satisfaction, product quality, etc. The second relates to "diagnostics," or the factors behind those results. They include orders fulfilled by the committed date, warranty costs, customer inquiry response time, and product cycle times.

Some metrics may prove daunting to companies without a background in formal quality processes. Supply chain response time, for example, represents the number of days it takes to recognize a major shift in demand, replan production, and boost output by 20%. Others include formulas for nailing down

"There's real power in leveraging across multiple companies that are facing the same issues and trying to manage change in their organizations."

The consortium's first challenge was to define the term "supply chain," another in a seemingly endless series of logistics buzz-concepts.

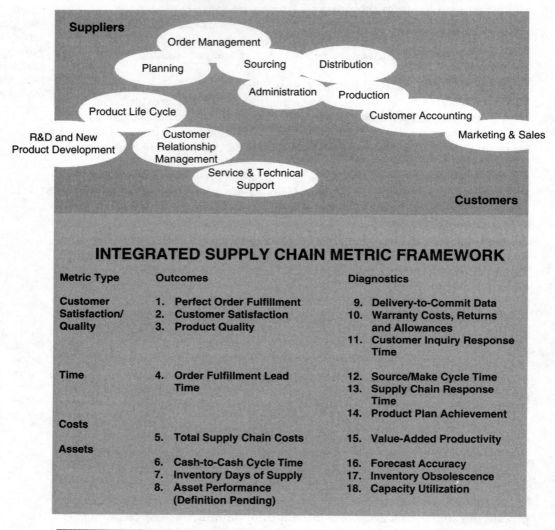

Figure 1. **The integrated supply chain process.**

"cash-to-cash" cycle time—the average time it takes to convert a dollar spent on raw materials into one collected for finished product.

Kardon says the list is similar to the style of individual shippers' report cards, although the elements are not weighted. There is no total score against which carriers are measured. The idea, she says, was to outline a series of elements that are common to multiple industries.

SUPPLY CHAIN MANAGEMENT AT WHAT COST?

An efficient supply chain should improve the corporate bottom line. Unfortunately, few accounting systems can accumulate or properly allocate supply chain costs, reports Systecon, the supply chain management practice of Coopers & Lybrand, Atlanta.

A recent Systecon report explains that logistics activities are typically reported under selling and administrative expense on the income statement. They are reviewed as individual functions. Few executives analyze service costs incurred at the customer, product or channel level. Also, management seldom links the costs of goods sold to such functions as purchasing, material requirements planning, and production scheduling and control.

Systecon recommends activity-based costing approaches to relate these fragmented facts into meaningful and manageable performance measures.

New View of the Supply Chain

The conclusions dovetailed somewhat with M.I.T.'s own supply chain integration program, which involves some of the same companies that are members of the new consortium. Yet the metrics aren't as simple as they seem, Metz says. In reality, they call for a whole new way of viewing an organization.

Companies involved in the project found the task harder than expected, Metz says. They quickly learned it takes more than a carrier report card to force managers to think as a team. In fact, he adds, carrier performance was only a small part of the effort.

Complicating matters is the changing role of carriers, the best of which are no longer content simply with transporting freight. They're moving into value-added tasks such as shelf stocking, equipment installation, training and packaging returns.

Striking a balance between the general and specific was equally tough. Standardized metrics can function only at the broadest possible level, such as measuring company response time from order placement to delivery.

Given the variety of industries represented by the consortium, Metz wonders how successful the effort can ultimately be. "I'm not sure we'll be able to come up with a common set of metrics for everybody," he notes.

Pilgrim says consortium members will pick and choose from among the metrics, discarding those that don't apply to their particular industries. "You don't try to force it," he says.

In the third and last phase—what Pilgrim calls "the final payoff"—they'll devise ways to incorporate their findings into everyday operations. Ideas will be bounced off an increasingly wide circle of companies, says Kardon.

The biggest problem may be limiting participation to a manageable number of companies. Kardon says response to the original CLM presentation was "overwhelming." The group is now evaluating which additional industries it wants to invite into the project.

The Door is Still Open

Hicks would like to see more manufacturers of consumer products. The group's original emphasis was on electronics because so many of its members came from that sector, he says.

So far, the effort has been concentrated in the United States, although the participants are all multinationals. A number of companies have expressed interest in starting a European consortium, Kardon says.

Whether they can come up with an effective means of measuring the global supply chain remains to be seen. At the very least, the consortium offers an unprecedented opportunity to talk about quality.

Robert J. Bowman is a contributing editor to Distribution *Magazine.*

How Scotsman Used Alliances to Solve a Design Problem

James Carbone

This is a good case study showing how a company can cooperate with its suppliers to design and develop new products that better meet customer and legal requirements much faster than the traditional approach. You'll read how Scotsman, a commercial refrigerator manufacturer, created a new CFC-free ice machine in record time.

In early 1991, executives at Scotsman Industries were feeling a little worried. Although Scotsman is the world's largest manufacturer of commercial ice making machines, the company had a regulatory deadline looming that potentially could devastate its business. Refrigerants that use chlorofluorocarbons (CFCs) would be banned by Jan. 1, 1996, because CFCs eat away the earth's protective ozone layer. Ice machines, air conditioners, and other cooling systems could no longer use Freon, because the refrigerant was CFC-based.

However, to roll out a product line before that deadline, Scotsman determined it had to design, build, and market a CFC-free machine by spring of 1993. That was no easy task because a Freon-free refrigerant and compressor had not yet been developed.

In addition to the CFC deadline, Scotsman had another problem: Customers perceived that Scotsman's quality was suspect. As part of a total quality management program, Scotsman conducted surveys and focus groups to learn what customers thought of Scotsman. The news wasn't good. Customers such as fast-food restaurants thought Scotsman's product quality and service quality left something to be desired.

"Customers said we needed to improve," says Darryl Hunter, director of purchasing. "For one thing, they wanted the product to last. But what we found out was we didn't even know what our customer's expectations were anymore. Fifteen or 20 years ago we knew what those expectations were, but we had not moved with the customer."

As part of a total quality management program, Scotsman conducted surveys and focus groups to learn what customers thought of Scotsman.

The challenge for Scotsman was to develop an ice machine that met the quality and performance requirements demanded by customers and still meet the government's CFC ban date. Scotsman decided it could not design such a machine by itself in that time-frame.

"We have learned that we cannot engineer every component in our product," says Hunter. "We don't have the knowledge. The expense of hiring such talent would be enormous and drive product costs to the point of uncompetitiveness," says Hunter.

Tapping supplier capabilities.   Beginning with the project, Scotsman went to a four-phase product development process that relied heavily on supplier involvement. The four phases include concept, feasibility, pre-production, and production.

At the concept stage, Scotsman determines which technology and which suppliers of that technology are needed to build a machine that meets customers expectations. Also at the concept stage, cross-functional teams are formed. Those teams—comprised of a purchaser, supplier quality manager, and an engineer—evaluate suppliers' capabilities to meet Scotsman's needs.

"We identify what technology we need, then we solicit the different suppliers of that technology and narrow it down," says Hunter. The team surveys suppliers and evaluates them on overall corporate philosophy, financial performance, ability to do just-in-time delivery, time-to-market performance, technical expertise, quality processes, and willingness to commit resources to a project. The team then discusses the evaluations and decides which suppliers to use.

In the feasibility stage, suppliers are placed on design teams. "We break suppliers into systems," says Hunter. "Our product breaks down into four systems: refrigeration, water system, electrical, and cabinet. We form teams of suppliers to develop these systems. We hold a big group setting with all suppliers involved. Then we break into sub teams that become working entities with our engineering department."

Also during this stage, the features and the cost of the product to be designed and built are discussed. "We start off with a statement of work," says Hunter. "For instance a customer would want an ice machine that produces a certain amount of ice per day with a lower energy and water consumption."

The customer may also want the machine to produce ice in certain geometric shapes that affect the dilution rate of the beverage. "If the ice dilutes quickly it waters down the drink and it doesn't taste as good," says Hunter. Most important is reliability. Customers want ice machines with a high mean time between failure (MTBF) rate.

"Our process involves the concept of 'target pricing' to arrive at the appropriate price level or make the appropriate design tradeoffs quickly," says Hunter. Scotsman and suppliers gather data to understand the component cost structure and to predict the capital costs.

Also during the feasibility phase, parts are ordered for concept model builds and prototypes. A bill of materials is constructed and target costs are filled in and compared against cost of goods target. Purchasers track the development of the project and make sure the suppler meets development schedules.

In pre-production, reliability testing begins. Purchasing works closely with the supplier on the documentation of control plans and statistical process control charts to ensure product quality is repeatable. Several production lot sizes are required prior to releasing the product for the pilot run. When the pilot run is held, the key suppliers are on site to deal with any issues that may arise.

When production begins, key suppliers are also on site. A review of the start up and the earlier phases is conducted, and a party is held to celebrate the launch.

Purchasers manage the project.   During the four-phase process, purchasers serve as the project managers, says Hunter. "They coordinate meetings with suppliers and coordinate target costs with engineering," says Hunter. The supplier quality manager works with the supplier and tries to find out where that product may fail. Purchasing and the supplier quality manager focus on control plans for the supplier on their processes.

With the CFC-free ice machine project, the key suppliers that were called in included DuPont (refrigerant), Copeland Corp. (compressor), Modine Heat Transfer (condenser), Alco (expansion valves), and Flexible Products (foam).

The Scotsman purchasers told suppliers what the total cost of the system had to be and what the price of the individual components of the machine should be. They also gave requirements for energy and water consumption, ice capacity, dilution rate, and mean time between failures (MTBF) that the system needed to meet.

The Scotsman purchasers told suppliers what the total cost of the system had to be and what the price of the individual components of the machine should be.

"The two most critical suppliers were DuPont and Copeland. We had never developed a product this way before, so we had three-way non-disclosure agreements," says Hunter.

DuPont tested refrigerants to find one that would be compatible. DuPont's job was to find an alternative to R 502, the CFC refrigerant that could be used in a compressor, says Bob Perhac, the project manager for DuPont.

"We looked at a number of alternative refrigerants to replace 502," says Perhac. "We tested different compounds and a number of different formulations and what we settled on was a product that had the closest match to 502 across the whole spectrum of operation characteristics." That product was a hydrofluorocarbon (HVC) compound called R404A (trade name SUVA).

While it was a close match, it was not identical; that posed problems for compressor manufacturer Copeland Corp. "The biggest issue for us was we were now dealing with a totally new refrigerant," says Howard Lanze, president of the refrigeration division of Copeland in Sidney, Ohio. "With the older refrigerants (CFC-based) we had 50 years of experience in applying and using them in our compressors. We understood how it would operate over the long run in system applications like ice machines."

Lanze says a key technical challenge with R404A was a lubricant that was needed. A mineral-based oil that was used in CFC compressors could not be used in a compressor that uses R404A.

"The biggest issue was the new lubricant," says Lanze. The mineral-based oil used with CFC refrigerants reacted with the chlorine in the refrigerant to provide the lubrication in the compressor. "In the absence of chlorine, the mineral-based oil did not work effectively. We had to work on several new types of oil. The one that was found to be most effective was a synthetic polyol ester oil," says Lanze.

The problem with the new oil was cost. "Mineral oil is priced at $1.50 to $1.80 per gallon, and synthetic oil is $50 to $55 per gallon," says Hunter. Through process improvements, the price dropped a little, "but not where we wanted it to be. Our initial target was just not obtainable and we had to go back to the customer and say to 'get rid of CFCs we have to increase our prices.' But we laid it all out, we put a spreadsheet together and showed them the cost breakdown. They accepted it," says Hunter.

The whole process to develop the new CFC-free machine took nine months. This would have been impossible if Copeland was not involved in the concept stage, says Lanze. The traditional approach of developing a compressor without working with a customer would have taken much longer.

The traditional approach of developing a compressor without working with a customer would have taken much longer.

"Typically what happens is we go to the customer and try to sell it, then find out it's not exactly what the customer wants and we have to make modifications. That process tends to take a lot longer," says Lanze. "If you want to reduce time to market you don't do things in series, you do things parallel."

Hunter says the toughest thing about the four-phase process was having to wait for the new compressor. "Without the compressor, the refrigerant system is nothing," he says. "They were developing the compressor about 30 to 60 days ahead of us as we worked on the ice machine. Every time Copeland would encounter a design problem, it would ripple back to our time schedule. If there was some variation that didn't look right, we would send Copeland back to the drawing board for a redesign."

For instance, Scotsman wants to further reduce product development time to just 10 months. To do so, it is working with some suppliers to share designs electronically.

Still, by involving Copeland and other key suppliers early in the design process, Scotsman introduced a CFC-free ice machine in April of last year, the first ice machine company to do so. Development of the machine took just 18 months. In the past, it took Scotsman 32 months to design a new machine, says Hunter.

"We could have released the product much earlier, but we had an extensive field test going on. We put 150 units into the field. We delayed the release of the product for four or five months. We improved mean time between failures two fold. They are higher priced than the old systems, but they last twice as long," according to Hunter.

While Scotsman has reduced its product development cycle and improved reliability, Hunter says it needs to continue to improve if it is to maintain its leadership position in the ice machine industry. For instance, Scotsman wants to further reduce product development time to just 10 months. To do so, it is working with some suppliers to share designs electronically.

For example, with injection molding, Scotsman formed a three-way design alliance. "We have our injection molding supplier and tool maker all tied together electronically," says Hunter. "We share designs. We phone modem drawings out to the tool maker direct instead of shipping it out FedEx to the injection molding supplier." He says that has cut the leadtime in sharing design changes from seven days to about 30 minutes.

Scotsman also is considering using a supplier bulletin board system of an on-line service that can download designs in real time, says Hunter.

Earlier supplier involvement with new products is affecting Scotsman's supply base. The company has 273 suppliers and has no plans to cut its supplier base. However, more business is being placed with fewer suppliers. "In 1991 we had 40 suppliers with 85% of the dollars we spent. Now we have 22 suppliers with 85% of the dollars," says Hunter.

Hunter says Scotsman's four-phase product development process has been a success and the company will continue to refine it. He said the process most recently was used to develop a new ice machine that will be introduced in May. "It will revolutionize the ice machine business in terms of production capability, aesthetic values, and overall reliability. And we couldn't have done it without our suppliers," he says.

James Carbone is senior editor for chemicals and electronics for Purchasing *magazine.*

INFORMATION MANAGEMENT

Restructuring the Purpose of IT In an Organization

Daniel P. Petrozzo

This article explores why IT is having such a hard time finding its role in organizations today and what the future may hold. It explores what corporate managers need to do to help create a new environment in which the IT department is an active partner in process improvement activities across the organization.

Not too long ago, the information technology (IT) organization was an internal cash cow that was holding its customers—the rest of the company—hostage. Systems were delivered when IT staff got around to it. Budgets were consistently overrun. The users just had to deal with it. After all, what choice was there?

Every manager knows the world has changed. The once mighty information systems departments are being pushed around by the business units. If the chief information officer (CIO) is lucky, he or she may stick around for more than a couple of years. Many firms are now outsourcing their entire systems operations to a third party that is thought to have the wisdom to do things faster, cheaper, and better. Software development is being treated like cafeteria service. This is indeed a brave new world.

All this change begs the question, what *is* the future of the IT department? Actually, the question needs to be rephrased to, what *should be* the future for the information systems department? Corporate management, senior information systems management, and information systems professionals will all have critical roles in shaping the future of this function. An examination of the forces tearing at information technology organizations reveals that several possible futures are likely. But first, how important is the role of technology anyway?

Information technology is intertwined with almost all corporate initiatives. Over the last few years, corporations and public-sector organizations have been using information technology to reengineer their operations and launch new strategic objectives. Mortgage companies are shrinking commitment intervals using advanced database and communications capabilities, quickly retrieving and compiling information about applicants. Securities firms are creating entirely new financial instruments; the inverse floaters that got Orange County into trouble are only the beginning. Police departments using wireless data technology as a crime fighting tool, accessing state and national crime databases without using their radios. Sales force automation systems are linking mobile salespeople with the home office to provide updated product information and faster, more reliable order entry. American Express is using America Online as a user interface to provide financial products and information to cardholders. These corporate initiatives and countless others are only possible because of sophisticated information technology.

Given the rising importance of information technology and its focus on improving businesses, it is surprising how far the star for the internal IT shop has fallen, the questioning of the role of IT, and the skepticism that surrounds technology efforts in many companies. One would think that all companies would view information technology and the central IT shops that provide it as vital to the existence of the corporation. But the stresses facing IT today are both different and more acute than they have every been.

What Does the IT World Look Like Today?

The world for the internal information technology organization is not the same as it once was. The primary reason for this is the change in the climate in which these organizations operate. Three external forces—business transformation, competition, and technology changes—are requiring the IT organization to evolve.

Business transformation consists of many "movements," such as reengineering, downsizing, and agility. The common thread is that the marketplace is pushing companies to examine the business that they are in and how they are executing core processes. Reengineering demands more of the information technology organization because it requires new skills, techniques, and resources. A 1994 Computer Sciences Corporation (CSC) Index survey of 600 companies reports that 54 percent of the respondents felt that "getting the information systems and technology infrastructure in place" was very or extremely difficult. Indeed, reengineering puts a strain on the IT organization

Given the rising importance of information technology and its focus on improving businesses, it is surprising how far the star for the internal IT shop has fallen.

in three ways. First, it requires that the personnel in the IT organization acquire in-depth knowledge of the business and technology enablers so that they can craft and implement a new vision of operations. Second, new methods such as rapid prototyping and simulation must be used to demonstrate and validate assumptions to the business units. Third, reengineering projects demand the analytical and problem-solving skills most often found in the information technology organization. These challenges take IT out of its usual comfort zone and force business-oriented technology innovation.

The new realities of the marketplace add to the strain brought on by change management movements. The volatile nature of business today requires firms to speed up product cycle times, which in turn creates a need for faster software development cycles. Also, as firms globalize, systems and data networks must have higher availability and increased performance. These new business realities are forcing IT to become better informed on corporate strategies, extremely focused on reducing cycle times, and on top of emerging technologies.

These new business realities are forcing IT to become better informed on corporate strategies, extremely focused on reducing cycle times, and on top of emerging technologies.

The competitive pressures on the internal information technology organization are just as daunting as the business pressures. In the book *Decline and Fall of the American Programmer*, author Ed Yourdon makes the claim that off-shore software development can be done faster, with better quality, and for less cost. This is not surprising, since 50 percent of the computer science Ph.D. students in the United States are foreign nationals. In fact, the India-based software programming group that Motorola uses earned the highest possible rating on a respected technical quality measure developed by Carnegie Mellon's Software Engineering Institute (SEI). In contrast, in measuring over 250 U.S. software houses, 74 percent measured according to the SEI standards achieved the lowest possible rating. Also, it is quite obvious that off-shore software houses are less costly. On Wall Street and in many R&D organizations, a fully loaded technical headcount costs approximately $150,000 per year. The same headcount in India costs $30,000 to $40,000. Given these cost comparisons alone, it is not surprising that business managers are looking off-shore for traditional IT functions.

At the same time, many companies are looking on-shore to rid themselves of the burden of managing an information technology organization altogether. The "outsourcing" craze has hit full swing. Recently, traditionally high-tech Hughes Aircraft and Xerox have handed over their entire information technology functions to CSC and Electronic Data Systems respectfully. Even the end-users are getting in on the act. Users are building their own powerful PC database, spreadsheet, and workgroup applications with products such as Microsoft's Access and Excel and Lotus's Notes. They are even designing their own jazzy screens with packages, like Visual Basic. With these options, a firm's IT shop no longer has a stranglehold on all technology initiatives.

Technology changes are also putting a strain on the information technology organization. In essence, technology itself is confusing IT because some technologies are rapidly maturing as others are emerging. The maturing process is evident because more often than before, IT is being faced with buy-versus-build decisions. While a large percentage of nonproprietary systems—

for example, payroll, human resources, and general ledger—are still developed internally, the focus is shifting to purchasing commercially available software in these areas. Many people believe that this was always the intent, but the harsh reality is that every company did things just differently enough so that a custom solution would be required. As long as the dollars were plentiful and competition was not as fierce, this mindset could prevail. Now the business need to develop software that provides a competitive advantage, coupled with the emergence of products that have matured, is forcing companies to reevaluate the traditional position to build instead of buy. PeopleSoft, a provider of human resource and financial service application products, is an excellent example of a company that has taken advantage of the trend of organizations seriously evaluating the buy-versus-build decision. PeopleSoft's revenues for 1994 increased 94 percent from 1993, to approximately $113 million. In addition, the latest round of turnkey products is another place where end-users can use their technical prowess. PeopleSoft products provide the capability to customize report writing and build applications without extensive assistance from a software development staff.

Although the client-server has been around several years, the migration to this architecture continues to have an effect on the IT organization. The change in skill sets required for the distributed computing model is proving difficult for many IT organizations to get a handle on. Just as important as the change in technology is the change in mindset for the IT professional away from centralized computing. As if this adjustment has not been enough, the emergence of workflow software, imaging, and desktop videoconferencing (with a plethora of computing applications built around it) will create a whole new set of technical challenges for the typical IT organization.

The New Roles for the IT Organization

IT organizations are facing changing customers, changing competitors, and changing tools. The status quo is certainly not acceptable. For IT organizations to survive, they must make fundamental changes in how they look and what they do. Similarly, a transformation must take place among information technology professionals.

Three new roles for the IT organization will emerge. But there is no guarantee that there will be a natural progression from one role to the next. In fact, elements of all three roles may exist in some companies. The role that an IT organization will play will largely depend on the talents of each organization, the culture of the firm, and the market forces within the vertical industry being supported. Although these roles have not been clearly distinguished for individual organizations, elements of each new role are being seen in many IT organizations across the United States. The three roles are described below.

Business Partners

Futurist Faith Popcorn coined the term "cocooning" to suggest that people will spend more quiet time at home and less time going out for entertainment. IT has done its own form of cocooning over the years with the "give me your requirement, I'll develop the code and throw it back over the wall" paradigm that had prevailed in most organizations. Since this model is now clearly unsatisfactory, IT professionals must become intimate with the business strategy and operations of the company where they work. In essence, they must break out of their cocoon. Much like managers who profess management by walking around, IT professionals must spend time in the business units so that they can understand the fundamental nature of the core business. For example, in several telecommunications companies, newly hired engineers and computer scientists spend time in operations learning how that department works. On Wall Street, many IT professionals are taking trader licensing exams so that they will become more acquainted with the business that they support.

Before IT can become a business partner, it must prove that it is a worthy one. IT leaders must overcome the myth that expenditures on information technology have not boosted overall productivity. They must do this by being able to clearly articulate the benefits of technology to the business, thereby dispelling the productivity paradox. Professor James Quinn of Dartmouth University explains that IT benefits are often best articulated by pointing out the opportunity costs that would be lost without the use of technology. Simply put, there are strategies, growth, and business opportunities that could never be realized without using information technology. For example, without sophisticated computer systems, the world's stock markets could never keep up with the number of trades. Point of sale and credit card verification technology are other examples of technology breakthroughs that have revolutionized the way many businesses run. It is difficult to imagine how fast food, supermarkets, and credit card companies would compete without using these technologies. Since they probably could not do so, IT has created a lowest common denominator market participation threshold. However, to gain a competitive advantage through the use of information technology, companies must far exceed this minimum threshold.

> IT leaders must overcome the myth that expenditures on information technology have not boosted overall productivity.

Without being so brash as to say that "you can't live without us," some IT organizations are creating disciplined approaches to justify why they are worthy partners. At Conoco, the oil concern, the IT organization worked with the business units to create value measurements. The value of a system solution is measured by how the technology positively affects different levels of the company—individual, department, and business unit.

Other IT organizations are measuring their value to the new business partnership by borrowing an often used reengineering concept. These companies are measuring the value of technology based on its impact on business processes. For example, Watkins-Johnson, an electronics firm, demonstrates the value of information technology by using an approach that ties value of technology to its impact on business processes in a cost/benefit approach. It looks at the cost of a given system function compared to the benefits to the process expected to be derived from implementing the system change.

Ultimately, for a partnership to develop, the remainder of a business must have a new outlook on IT. A 1994 article in the *Sloan Management Review* asked the question, "Is your CIO adding value?" The answers suggested that a CIO can only add value when senior corporate management views the use of information technology as strategic to the goals of the business. While some senior corporate managers are particularly enlightened in this area, others are only influenced when the CIO demonstrates an obsessive and continuous focus on business imperatives.

Change Agents

The Gartner Group reported that the business process reengineering market brought in $1.3 billion dollars to consultants in 1993. With an expected cumulative annual growth rate of 21 percent, reengineering consulting revenues in 1994 should exceed $1.5 billion. The Big Six firms continue to recruit heavily at the best business schools in the country for the next wave of reengineering consultants.

Fundamentally, companies are spending an unbelievable amount of money on the business of change. About all that most management scholars and gurus agree on is that the only certainty in the future is that change will be constant. Will companies continue to rely on external consultants to create change? If change is never ending, is there something preventing IT staff from becoming the new management consultants?

Today's emphasis on reengineering and change programs such as agility rely on technological innovation to enable companies to do things that they could not do without the use of technology. IT has the internal intellectual horsepower required to fuel these change initiatives. As IT personnel begin to bridge the skills gap in business acumen, they will become better qualified to execute business reengineering projects—not merely systems consolidations labeled as reengineering—than inexperienced business school graduates. It is easier to teach IT and other technical personnel about the business than it is to teach strictly business-oriented personnel about technology.

As IT personnel begin to bridge the skills gap in business acumen, they will become better qualified to execute business reengineering projects.

The addition of vertical industry business skills will not be enough for IT professionals to become the change agents of the future. Instead, they will need a wide variety of skills—process analysis, computer modeling and simulation, total quality management, and systems thinking—to complement their understanding of IT. Some of this orientation is already taking place. At a large telecommunications provider, IT professionals work hand-in-hand with operations personnel to simulate business processes and help introduce process improvements. Vendors are introducing products that couple workflow software or Computer-Aided Software Engineering tools with simulation software. The marketplace is starting to realize that technology and business processes are intertwined. The IT professional is in a perfect position to make this seamless web work.

A not-used-nearly-enough software development model may also assist the IT organization in its pursuit of becoming a change agent. Most managers are familiar with the use of prototypes to demonstrate software functionality. Less familiar is the concept of evolutionary software development. Instead of aiming for a complete specification, evolutionary development calls for getting some piece of the solution working in the production environment. The total solution is implemented rapidly via a series of incremental steps or software releases that build on the previous system release. Software "maintenance" is carried out in a similar fashion. Successful use of this model requires a much more intimate relationship between software designers and developers and the eventual end-users. Systems professionals must sit alongside the end-users as they develop systems. In this rapidly changing world, processes will constantly be in a state of flux. Therefore, technology support for enhanced processes must be introduced nearly simultaneously. The evolutionary development model best supports rapid business change, because as processes change the typical software requirements process will be unnecessary.

The evolutionary software model is in some sense the ultimate "anti-outsourcing" statement. If processes continue to change radically and technology needs to be delivered quickly, there will be no time to send systems development outside. Physical proximity will be advantageous to the process of system developers working closely with end-users. How will companies like Hughes Aircraft, which outsources its information systems to CSC, be able to make software changes quickly enough in this environment? It will be even more interesting to see how U.S. companies that outsource their developments to places such as India or Russia will meet this new pressure on cycle times.

CIOs can only become viable change agents when senior corporate management considers them experts in processes, technologies, and organizations. Many companies are forming internal consulting organizations with IT assuming the leadership role. One example is at Bankers Trust, where a strong CIO spearheads an internal consulting group of IT professionals that is structurally similar to many large consulting firms.

Plumbers and Garbage Collectors

"User-programmable" software could revolutionize the role of the IT organization. User-programmability means that end-users will be able to build meaningful applications from reusable software components built by systems developers or will use off-the-shelf software with its standard tools to build applications. The most dramatic possible effect is that the control of applications will shift from IT personnel to the end-users. Even if this takes place on a wide scale, IT will still have a vital and perhaps more important role.

The IT staff will become like plumbers. Plumbers make sure that the proper pipes are in place to support the appliances and fixtures that will need to be added later. In addition, plumbers fix problems with existing pipes, regardless of whether those problems are a result of normal wear and tear or negligence. In this spirit, IT professionals will shift their focus from application development and end-user support to infrastructure development. The IT infrastructure may consist of data layers, network layers, and software tools that can abstract applications from the nasty issues that hardware, databases, and communication protocols create. At the same time, IT will be responsible for the traditional role of ensuring that the hardware, operating systems, and communications networks remain in working order.

IT professionals will shift their focus from application development and end-user support to infrastructure development.

Much of the current thinking on software development stresses reuse. The emphasis has been on IT shops building reusable "code fragments." These fragments (or modules) can be reused to develop applications with similar functionality. They are also used when applications are replaced but a significant amount of functionality from the old application is still needed. To accomplish this, object-oriented design and development is stressed. In simple terms, objects are supposed to represent real-world items, such as customers, orders, and employees. Thus, object-oriented software focuses on the behaviors of objects. However, this software development model still puts the IT group at the center of the application development process. The evolution of reusable software will take us to the creation of software tools that a non-IT person can use to build applications.

Conceptually, users will be able to put application pieces together from high-level abstractions using software tools created specifically for this purpose. These tools will rely heavily on the automatic generation of the code needed to run the application. This software model does not stress reuse; rather, it stresses disposal and recreation. It should be quicker to throw out old systems and build the new without going through the painful specification and design stage. In many respects, this is exactly how Advanced Intelligent Network services work in the telecommunications world. In this environment, IT staff will act as garbage collectors: They will need to ensure that the old applications are disposed of properly so that they do not pollute the vital technology infrastructure. Leilani Allen, the head of information systems at PNC Mortgage Corporation, sees this model developing in such a way that IT will only have core technology competence and responsibility, and the tactical development—for example, applications—will be left to the end-users.

Others have even more outrageous visions of what the IT shop of the future will look like. The always controversial Tom Peters says, why not the one-person IT organization? Can this really happen? Peters notes that VeriFone, a credit card authorization company, has a CIO but no real central IT shop. The CIO scouts out and brings in new technologies, but the end-users incorporate it into the business themselves.

It is important for IT professionals to avoid falling into the same trap that the steelworkers did. Not so long ago, steelworkers were large in number and highly paid. As the industry changed due to competition and technology, many steelworkers lost their jobs. Those steelworkers that remain in the flourishing mini-mills of today are still highly paid but are getting paid for entirely different skills. Only the steelworkers who made the transition from the shovel to the computer remain. IT professionals must make the transition from being programmers and analysts to being business partners and change agents. They need to develop business and communications skills and pay attention to the bottom line.

The CIO scouts out and brings in new technologies, but the end-users incorporate it into the business themselves.

What Does the New IT Mean to You?

IT is obviously not going away. Almost every corporate decision now has a technology implication. Globalization, new product options, and even new billing mechanisms all require an upgrade or improvement to a company 's existing technology base. And it is obvious that IT needs to, and will, change dramatically. Of course, IT organization changes alone will not make the technology a strategic advantage for a company. The remainder of the business must embark on a journey of change that harmonizes with the changes in IT.

Corporate downsizing and cost controls have dismantled the old model in which IT received seemingly unlimited funding for initiatives that were only vaguely understood by business unit counterparts. Today, ferocious competition makes those employees that use IT to its fullest advantage only able to participate in the marketplace. Unfortunately, in most corporations, skeptical business unit managers try to squeeze IT to deliver even vaguer notions of the technological promised land: data warehouses, consolidated billing systems, and information architectures. While the business climate has changed considerably, many managers have not changed their basic paradigm for managing IT. Without a sweeping commitment from the business units, most companies will resign themselves to outsourcing all their IT. They will say that it saves them money because outsourcers can offer economies of scale. What they won't say is that they merely stopped trying because they were unable to manage IT, let alone make it a competitive advantage.

In the book *Post-Capitalist Society*, Peter Drucker examines the shift in the structure of the economic system from capital-based to knowledge-based. Drucker sees the successful companies in the world economy of the 21st century being deluged with knowledge workers—workers who are not only smart, but who want to continually learn; what will separate different companies is how they encourage and mobilize knowledge. Knowledge workers, according to Drucker, will have to completely overhaul their skills every three to four years. This is an interesting commentary, considering the fact that in spite of the technology revolution that has taken place over the last ten years and that is evolving rapidly in one-year time frames at this point, most managers in U.S. corporations have little more than a remedial knowledge of technology. If the status quo remains, managers that lack technology understanding and skills will not be the next century's knowledge workers.

The business units and IT organizations must develop an intimacy as customers of each others' products and services.

Fundamentally, this means that for the new IT paradigms to have a chance to be successful, the traditional internal customers of information technology need to become educated in technology. Initially, business partnerships will take place when the business units are capable of jointly developing solutions with their counterparts in IT. Just as IT personnel need to understand the business much better to craft better solutions, business unit personnel need to understand what the technology is and how it works, so that cost/benefits and strategic implications are better understood. To rephrase this in management parlance, the business units and IT organizations must develop an intimacy as customers of each others' products and services. This intimacy can only take place once the business units better understand what IT is all about—what it is capable of doing and why.

IT's transition from business partner to change agent will be possible only if IT makes a successful transformation in its capabilities and focus and if senior corporate management believes that this paradigm is one that can work successfully. IT personnel must assert themselves as change agents and convince senior management colleagues to consider them in lieu of prestigious management consults. Corporate management should believe and understand that the talent, intelligence, and focus is available internally to do what it traditionally had relied on consultants to do.

Even more education and knowledge will be required for the business units to support a world where IT staff become plumbers and garbage collectors. As older employees retire and newer employees take their place, the workforce will be injected with more technology-oriented business people. These new business unit employees will be the ones eventually developing applications. Their more senior bosses will have a whole new set of challenges to face. They will not only need to understand the role of IT in its traditional form as a supplier of products and services, but they also will need to manage a workforce of self-starting technology wizards. In addition, IT and business unit management will need to forge entirely new relationships with software vendors. They will need to force vendors of database management systems, such as Oracle and Sybase, turn-key system providers, such as PeopleSoft, and even desktop software providers like Microsoft to meet the functional and support needs of both the business unit application builders and the IT plumbers and garbage collectors. This will require quite a paradigm shift.

The IT organization is being forced to change because of a variety of factors. For a company to successfully incorporate the new IT, business units need to change how they perceive and use the IT organization. They also need to become better educated on the fundamentals of information technology. Although these changes are corporate in scope, they must be made individually. Perhaps the most telling quote on this point is from Daryl Plummer, division director of information systems for the State of Florida, who in response to the need for IT to change said, "We talk about legacy systems, but what we have is a lot of legacy people." The legacy people in IT and the business units will not have a role in forming the new IT; rather, the ones who learn and adapt will.

Daniel P. Petrozzo is President of Taylor Petrozzo Associates, a Bloomsbury, NJ-based consulting firm specializing in business reengineering and information technology. He is the coauthor of Successful Reengineering *(Van Nostrand Reinhold, 1994).*

Applications That Support Quality in an Enterprise

James W. Cortada

This excerpt, from co-editor James Cortada's book TQM for Information Systems Management, *briefly introduces some of the uses to which information technology may be used to assist in the implementation of process and quality improvement in many different types of organizations.*

The number of articles, books, and seminars available today on how to make IT a competitive tool for the enterprise is massive. IT executives are told how to deploy strategic initiatives, increase shareholder value, reduce costs, enhance global competitiveness, and facilitate downsizing or, in the elegant parlance of the mid-1990s, "streamline" the business, and to do all this with a customer/market focus. But as Deming, Crosby, Juran, and other experts on quality have long argued, how the processes of a company are managed is how things can be done most effectively and continuously improved. It turns out there are some applications of technology that, when implemented, facilitate quality management practices in other parts of the organization in a relatively dramatic fashion. What will be discussed below, therefore, are the enterprise-wide actions that an IT organization can take in the spirit of facilitating quality management practices.

Just looking at quality practices provides a clean rifle-shot view right through the enterprise because it is a process perspective. As Thomas H. Davenport has so effectively demonstrated, process innovation or reengineering is best done with a heavy dose of IT. However, the IS community can, in turn, offer to provide a bag of tools that extend beyond the "computer department" as a technology infrastructure in support of the goals of the company or agency.

> Process innovation or reengineering is best done with a heavy dose of IT.

How to Select Enterprise-Wide IT Applications

If IS has a responsibility to recommend to the rest of the enterprise applications that facilitate use of quality management practices, what criteria should be used? Business strategists tend to ignore the question, focusing instead simply on "big bang" applications that make companies competitive, change the rules of the game, or that cause significant declines in expenses—all good reasons for using IT, but they are all topics we will explore only as they enhance the practice of quality management principles. The question remains: Are there some applications that, if implemented, will encourage the use of such practices in general across the entire enterprise? The answer is definitely yes!

The selection process begins by establishing criteria for identifying applications. But first management should recognize that these applications in themselves facilitate competitive advantage. This is not new news. For example, in a survey of 71 health insurance company CEOs conducted in 1992, results indicated that the top five business strategies included better customer service and cost containment. IT plays a prominent role in both these areas. Why? Because IT provides technology that can help companies better serve customers, and it provides a way to collect and analyze data about business processes as well as control those processes. Don Tapscott and Art Carson, in articles and now in a book, have described in considerable detail how IT has broken down traditional walls between various organizations and serves as the glue that can hold the enterprise together.

The implication for quality management is that IT has to consider implementing applications that

- cover the entire enterprise
- are accessible by all process teams
- are relevant to process teams
- speed up transformation of processes
- foster teamwork
- promotes closer ties to customers
- make possible more customized services and products
- speed up work

Questions to ask include:

- To what extent will a project facilitate closer relations with customers such that they will buy more goods and services from us?
- To what extent will a project make it possible for our company to respond quicker and with greater effectiveness to changing market conditions (with more customized offerings)? Or cause these market conditions to change in favor of the company?
- To what extent will a project facilitate individuals and the organization as a whole to learn such that they can sustain innovation and the capability of improving constantly?
- To what extent will a project speed up the activities of the organization?

But first let us recognize what features of IT help individuals change processes and apply quality management tools and techniques. Figure 1 catalogs a variety of these characteristics that facilitate improvement of any process. To the extent that IT can either bring these to bear in specific process improvement projects or provide applications that make it possible for others

Characteristic	What IT Does	Significance
Transactional	Converts unstructured activities into routine ones	Drives down costs, errors and waste
Geographical	Moves data fast to wherever needed	Improves effectiveness, lowers costs, speeds response to situations
Automational	Reduces labor content	Lowers costs, increases consistency, and reliability
Analytical	Provides tools to facilitate fact-based decision making	Improves productivity, quality of decision making
Informational	Provides vast quantities of data in useable formats	Improves knowledge of teams, enhances fact-based management
Flexible	Can cause rapid changes in how tasks are performed	
Linking	Connects together various people and organizations	
Tracking	Will monitor and measure performance of processes, people, and resources	

Figure 1. **Characteristics of IT that facilitate use of quality management methods.**

indirectly to do process improvement work, so much the better. Essentially, the requirement for IT initiatives outside of IS is supportive, even passive, but necessary to facilitate others to practice quality management. Therefore, any enterprise-wide process that has characteristics listed in Figure 1 become candidates (e.g., E-mail and EDI).

A second way to look at the selection criteria is to respond to business-driven architectures, suggesting to the IS community how it must respond. Figure 2 is a graphical representation of this approach. The organization settles on a strategy, which the firm implements by designing processes and organizational structures that implement the strategy. Simultaneously, IT is requested to develop applications that support both the business strategy and the processes required. In turn, the IT community marshalls its resources to meet the requirements of the business. As it does that, IS staff ask themselves questions: What applications are needed both in and outside of IT? What data are needed? How will these applications and information be made available? Answers to those questions provide the linkage to the seven sets of activities normally evident in an IS organization (see bottom line of Figure 2) and how those activities influence what applications are developed. At the same time,

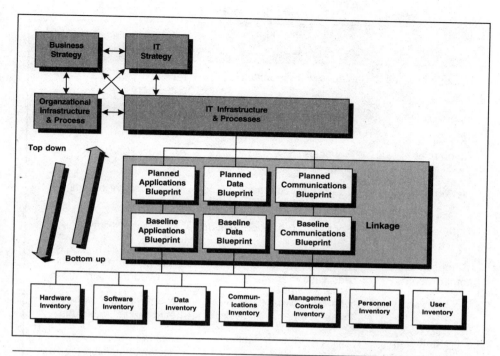

Figure 2. **Business-driven architectures must drive the IT process in the future.**

activities at these lower levels offer IS and planners an idea of what is technically relevant and possible for the entire enterprise to use in implementing quality practices.

The resulting list of possible applications can be long. For example, looking at the characteristics in Figure 1, it becomes obvious that good backbone telecommunications capabilities are crucial to a quality-focused enterprise.

Another way to look at establishing criteria for selecting applications is to mix IT characteristics with IT functions. Figure 3 catalogs some of the more obvious examples of this approach. You ask what is it that IT can do (e.g., provide modeling tools), determine what effect those should have (e.g., helping to identify what processes to change), and establish what benefits should accrue (e.g., lowering costs or making processes more effective in the eyes of the customer). This list is arbitrary; your IS organization should develop its own based on its core competencies, business strategy of the corporation, and realities of existing IT. The list does not have to be any longer than the example.

One expert, Thomas H. Davenport, has developed his own list of application types that support processes at a tactical level (see Figure 4) within a manufacturing operation. The list fits most manufacturing companies and is a nice twist to the suggestions in Figure 3 because it takes the list of selection criteria down to the functional level.

IT Effort	Effect on Quality Processes	Anticipated Benefits
Laptops in sales	Makes work mobile	Faster response to customers
Modeling tools	Identify what processes to change	Lower costs, more effective processes
Automation	Reduced steps, reduced or augmented human labor	Accuracy, productivity
Networking	Teamwork, communications	More effective results, employees
Databases	Fact-based decision making	Confidence, sapped, accuracy
Competitive/Customer records	More knowledge of rivals and customer needs	Become more competitive, improved decision making
Decision analysis	Improves "what if" and "what happens" analysis	Less risk of big mistakes; better quality decisions
Data gathering	Performance monitoring, measurements	Accurate, fact-based, improved decision making

Figure 3.   **Framework for exploiting IT as an enabler of quality management.**

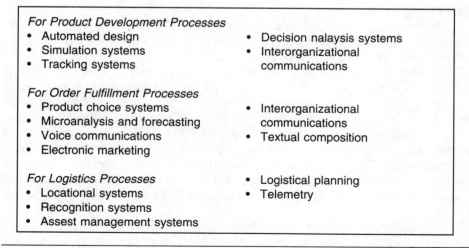

For Product Development Processes
- Automated design
- Simulation systems
- Tracking systems
- Decision nalaysis systems
- Interorganizational communications

For Order Fulfillment Processes
- Product choice systems
- Microanalysis and forecasting
- Voice communications
- Electronic marketing
- Interorganizational communications
- Textual composition

For Logistics Processes
- Locational systems
- Recognition systems
- Assest management systems
- Logistical planning
- Telemetry

Figure 4.   **Examples of generic processes of IT. Source: Adapted from Thomas H. Davenport,** *Process Innovation: Reengineering Work Through Information Technology* **(Boston: Harvard Business Review Press, 1993) pp. 50–63).**

Armed with a list of selection criteria, you can choose applications that have the potential of serving the widest number of employees across the entire organization, not just within IS. Each industry has its own unique opportunities that you should not ignore. For example, in the gas and electric utility business, reengineering manual meter-reading efforts (a popular activity at the moment) is dependent on state-of-the-art customer information databases with hooks into satellite communications and a billing system to which telecommunications can feed data. In the insurance industry, it is the capability of doing rapidly "what if" analysis in order to bring new products to market. In the credit card business, it is mass mailings, extensive marketing/demographics databases. IBM, with its far-flung development, manufacturing, and marketing activities in over 130 countries, needs the best E-mail and EDI systems, whereas Federal Express requires telemetric systems to track packages and trucks as they move around the world. All have in common the profound influence of base systems on such quality management practices as process reengineering, fact-based decision making, and process measurements.

Armed with a list of selection criteria, you can choose applications that have the potential of serving the widest number of employees across the entire organization.

Architecture for an Activity-Based Costing System

Patrick Howard

This is a well-written article, and will be valuable for those of you who have put the practice of activity-based costing to work in your organization. You will read here about how to effectively implement an ABC system and how to not let it be overwhelmed by more traditional finance costing systems.

In recent years, many major companies have conducted projects and studies to help them understand costs in terms of business process, customer segments, product, or other key organizational dimensions. The insights gained through activity-based costing (ABC) have proved invaluable.[1]

Today, many of these companies are beginning to implement ABC on a companywide basis, weaving together the principles of ABC with other major management systems such as budgeting, production forecasting, and financial reporting. Implementing ABC on a company wide basis is not as simple as A-B-C, however. In many companies, there are significant barriers to an ABC implementation project. These include the following:

- Entrenched cost management practices;
- Legacy systems;
- Inadequate procedures for managing information; and
- Difficulties of integrating ABC with other financial management systems.

This article describes a functional architecture for an ABC implementation project and how a well-documented architecture can help resolve these and other thorny issues. The four guidelines presented for developing an ABC architecture help ensure that the resulting processes will be integrated, where possible, with other major management systems.

Problems Begin with Approval for Implementation

Most companies approach the task of developing an ABC system with enthusiasm. They organize a series of projects and assign team members who optimistically begin the process. The team trains other managers and employees, examines design prototypes, and updates top management to gain approval for the implementation project—which is when the problems begin.

Practitioners who develop ABC systems agree that translating concepts into practice is a daunting task. Discussions on design and implementation issues quickly get side-tracked by a flurry of ideas, alternative approaches, and blind alleys. The most critical problem (and perhaps the most time-consuming) is resolving issues that are rooted in the established procedures of other management systems. These issues include the following:

> Practitioners who develop ABC systems agree that translating concepts into practice is a daunting task.

- Preserving flexibility in the definition of those business processes that swerve as measurement points for cost, operating volumes, and operating plans.
- Incorporating standards for continuous improvement that support the overall quality program of the company.
- Generating consistent activity volumes by production center for the annual budgeting, costing, and monthly closing cycles.
- Devising strategies to consolidate data maintenance (e.g., if new cost centers, processes, accounts, resources, or products are added, these elements must be defined and made available to all the company's management systems).
- Synchronizing the maintenance of data across all plants during the monthly and annual reporting cycles.
- Trapping errors in the process (e.g., what if the activity volumes generated for a cost center are incorrect? What if a product scheduled for production has no routings? What if raw materials structured to a bill of materials have no rates? When and where in the process are discrepancies and errors detected? How can the system be restarted?).
- Improving overall coordination of related, yet discrete, functions in the company (e.g., linking revisions in production forecasts to revisions in the variable component of product or process costs).

Functional Architecture

In large companies, the sheer magnitude and breadth of an ABC system demand that many organizational units participate in the development and operation of the system. However, having multiple constituencies for a single system often causes such obstacles as the following to arise:

- Competing objectives for system functionality;
- Varied levels of commitment to the project; and
- Mixed priorities in resolving issues.

For management and the project team, a framework is needed to give a balanced perspective of the ABC practices, procedures, and system functions that are common to, or in conflict with, other major management systems. This framework is the functional architecture. It organizes costing functions and shows in practical terms how ABC will operate and interact with other systems. A functional architecture translates "what" into "how" and gives management a concrete, top-level view of how the goals and objectives of ABC will be accomplished.

Exhibit 1 presents, in part, a high-level functional architecture that was developed for a major consumer products manufacturing company. As Exhibit 1 shows, introducing ABC to the company raised major issues, including issues related to management practices, application support, and organizational responsibilities. The development of the framework portrayed provided context and structure for achieving agreement on the best approach for resolving these issues and deploying ABC.

A conflict resolution process is also required as part of the project to break deadlocks and resolve issues quickly without compromising the ABC principles that have been adopted.

Key Guidelines

The following four guidelines should be considered in developing an architecture for ABC:

1. Don't just integrate: Consolidate.
2. If your data flows, stop it.
3. Make it relevant.
4. Demand excellence in the presentation.

Guideline 1: Don't Just Integrate: Consolidate

Developing a functional architecture for ABC is a progressive, incremental process. Cost functions must be designed and components of the system must be identified. Prototypes are built to provide visible demonstrations of how ABC costing works. Structured reviews of system components trigger discussions among the business specialists, who learn more about the costing functions and system processes needed for implementation. A well-structured approach to developing architecture can highlight opportunities to consolidate and simplify system processes for ABC.

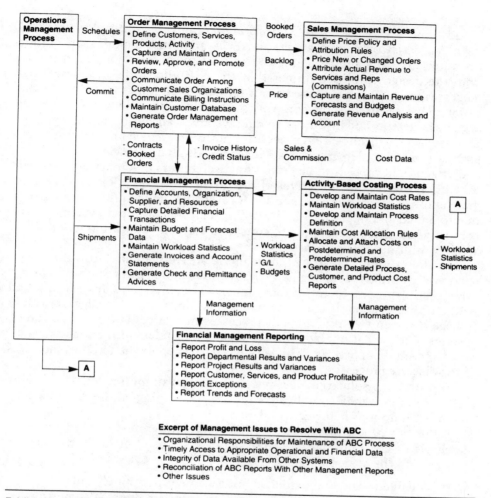

Exhibit 1. **High Level Functional Architecture: Integration of ABC With Other Management Systems.**

Functions common to ABC and other financial processes. For many companies that plan to improve their costing practices on a companywide basis, ABC must contend with legacy systems and practices that have evolved over many years. Often, ABC is designed and implemented as an enhanced management system rather than a replacement for existing cost or management reporting systems. The legacy systems often remain to serve regulatory or other reporting objectives that differ from those of ABC. To facilitate the implementation of ABC, a project team should look, where possible, to leverage functionality or data sources in existing systems without compromising management's objectives for ABC. Example 1 below illustrates coordination of ABC with existing systems.

Example 1: Consolidating allocation functions to support multiple costing objectives. Company A adopts an ABC system that includes sets of functions for allocating and attaching costs to cost objectives. On closer inspection, the design team determines that the cost allocation and attachment processes for ABC share common, but not identical, functions with the allocation processes used in the company's other financial management systems (e.g., its budgeting and inventory costing systems). The design team concludes that use of a single allocation process for multiple financial management systems is a viable implementation approach for ABC (i.e., a single cost allocation and attachment process to be driven by discrete sets of allocation rules that depend on the costing objectives of the financial system). Rather than integrate another cost allocation function for ABC (which would require separate maintenance and operation) into the financial management systems of the company, the designers choose to consolidate several allocation functions to support multiple costing processes.

As the example illustrates, developing an ABC architecture that is responsive to various reporting purposes requires more than merely adding another costing process on top of the company's other systems. Instead, a sound ABC architecture should encourage consolidation. Integration suggests a close linkage between two functions or processes in related, but clearly discrete, systems. Consolidation, by contrast, means that related functions are combined and implemented as a single function to support the unique objectives of the discrete processes.

However, consolidation does not always mean simplification. Combining system functions may complicate a process, depending on the difference between the functions being consolidated.

Definition of key information. ABC architecture must support a consolidated vie of key information across major systems of critical information. Data used in the system must be:

- Visible to and understood by management personnel; and
- Reconcilable with key information in other financial reporting systems in the company.

For example, if the definition of "resources" (i.e., labor, material, and overhead) is used consistently across the budgeting and financial reporting systems when ABC is implemented, confusion about how to interpret data can be reduced; as a result, more analysts can provide better responses to requests for special reporting.

Example 2: Defining and understanding key information. A plant manager asks an assistant to get information from the new ABC system about technicians who operate the newly installed, computerized production lines. The manager also asks for a schedule of direct material and overhead costs consumed in this manufacturing process. Given learning-curve problems on the shop floor, the manager anticipates relatively high resource costs on these lines. Under these circumstances, the assistant needs to understand two dimensions about the information to be gathered and reported.

The first dimension involves how labor, material, and overhead resources are defined and tracked. A fully deployed ABC system must be based on a uniform definition of resources that is consistently applied across—or at least reconciled with—all financial reporting systems. to begin the task, the assistant must understand fundamental points about how the company defines and tracks resources, including the following:

- The types of costs that are typically pooled under the general categories of labor, material, and overhead (e.g., Are employee benefits a labor cost or a direct overhead allocation?);
- The way costs are classified for allocation and reporting purposes (e.g., Are all labor costs treated as variable? Under what circumstances would a technician's cost be reclassified from direct labor to direct overhead in the ABC system?); and
- The method for assigning costs to processes (e.g., Does the method properly account for startup activities in the plant, or should adjustments be planned for such extraordinary circumstances as a startup operation?).

The second dimension concerns how resources are consumed. The plant manager wants to report labor costs for technicians separately from other direct labor costs that are attached to the process. Standard factors based on expected consumption must be established for each technician or class of technicians. These factors are tied to cost centers, operation centers, production processes, and products. Engineering change specifications must trigger changes in the standard factors recorded for the use of technicians.

As Example 2 illustrates, when ABC is introduced company wide, the definition of key information must be understood broadly, reconciled with other related management systems, and documented as part of the functional architecture.

Guideline 2: If Your Data Flows, Stop It

Processes change over time in response to changing business conditions, but data will remain relatively constant in a well-designed system. A cost database that is easy to understand, easy to manage, and free of redundant or conflicting information reflects a system that is built on sound architectural principles. A poorly designed database has implications for the entire company. Because the development of forecasts, budgets, and resource rates depends on data from many sources (e.g., bills of material and routings), a well-maintained database is crucial.

In an ABC system, product costs are generated based on the rates and standard factors entered for the product. But what happens when the underlying data used to generate product costs are revised? If, for example, product costs are generated on Day 1 and an engineer applies a change to the bill structure on Day 2, the relationship between the product cost and the product structure as reflected by the bill is no longer accurate. In other words, if a

> A fully deployed ABC system must be based on a uniform definition of resources that is consistently applied across all financial reporting systems.

plant accountant were to compare a product cost on-line at a computer terminal on Day 3 with the associated product bill, there would likely be confusion over the apparent discrepancy between product cost and the bill of material. Such discrepancies can occur in virtually every data relationship of an ABC system. These relationships must be resolved, not only for maintenance and reporting purposes, but to properly track and compute efficiency, material usage, and engineering change variances.

Some organizations respond to this problem by replicating the data and maintaining multiple files that reflect the weekly or monthly production cycles of the systems that they support. However, the redundancy of data creates new problems, such as discrepancies among various management reports that may use different versions of files. Information management breaks down. Data relationships are no longer constant, but appear to "flow" and change over time. Hence the guideline: "If your data flows, stop it."

Before proceeding with an ABC implementation, the integrity of the data design should be tested. Are the relationships understood and well documented? Are the same data defined consistently across financial systems? Are terms easy to understand?

Before proceeding with an ABC implementation, the integrity of the data design should be tested.

Guideline 3: Make It Relevant

The process of building a new system can be compared at times to an unanchored ship sitting at dock: If no one pays attention, the ship will drift away. Project management should incorporate appropriate checkpoints throughout the design phase to keep the system anchored to its intended business results. Four touchstones are particularly useful in testing the business relevance of ABC functional architecture.

1. *Design Reviews.* Periodic design reviews must be conducted on a peer relationship among business process owners, functional specialists, and system developers. The goal is to ensure that the system meets the business needs for quality management, continuous improvement, and other company initiatives. Every system function and every design point should be measured against the original goals for the project.
   Design reviews must be scheduled with all key constituents as an initial step in launching an ABC implementation. Without a fixed schedule, the reviews appear to lose priority given the crush of other activities in a project. Experience indicates that these sessions are fundamental to ensuring quality results in the final system.

2. *Timeliness.* System developers frequently misunderstand timeliness, which is one of the key attributes of sound ABC architecture. Timeliness is more than acceptable system throughput or response times of computer programs. The organizational scope of an ABC system means that timeliness must include the following:

   - *Business throughput.* The key functions of the architecture must be organized so that the steps to be completed and the time required are acceptable. If the system does not reinforce the company's ability to compete on time, stop the project; it is a poor investment. For example, is the cycle time of the organization improved with this new system? How long does it take to cost new product design, evaluate new customers, assess business segment performance, and identify abnormal scrap rates in production? Does the system help to mobilize the whole organization around the principles of business process, ensuring more focused and faster analysis of the company's key performance measures?

- *Error detection and restart.* The user's ability to detect errors, fix the problem, and quickly restart a process largely determines the perceived timeliness of the ABC system. In many systems, for example, product routings established by industrial engineers are used as a basis for generating production activity volume in plants. An error in a product standard entered during a month could be missed until unusual activity volumes are generated at the month-end closing. During a tight month-end closing, however, users are hard pressed to clean up all the data. Therefore, architecture must encompass appropriate tools for the industrial engineer to assess data integrity at the time of data entry.

- *Sequence of data maintenance.* The breadth of ABC systems obscures all the implications of sequencing data maintenance. An illustrative case at one large company involved the use of budgeted bills of material to generate cost rates. After the annual budgeting process started, plant locations sent in changes to the bills, but the changes were received too late to figure in computing production volumes. After investigating the situation, the corporate staff learned that plant employees could not perform bill maintenance any earlier. The sequence of data maintenance in other systems delayed the availability of data for ABC. Data modeling techniques can help users understand how the expected sequence of data maintenance affects timeliness and help resolve these issues during the design stage.

3. *Decision-Support Functions.* The architecture for ABC must encompass functions to support cost simulation, sensitivity analysis, and other decision-support activities. One high-priority requirement for an executive team may be modeling capabilities that support quick analysis of the numerous unpredictable issues that can arise.

4. *Business Performance Measures.* The final point in determining the relevance of the architecture has to do with taking a candid look at the company's key business performance measures. How will the ABC system help focus the organization on the performance goals established by management, and how will the ABC system help the company measure its progress against plan? ABC as a management discipline cannot be expected to measure and track against all key performance measures of the company, but

as part of an integrated financial management system, it should at least serve in a key reporting role.

Guideline 4: Demand Excellence in the Presentation

The old maxim of not judging a book by its cover does not apply in the realm of information system. As the complexity and breadth of a system increase, demands on "user presentation" also increase. User presentation—the look and feel of the screens that assist users in maintaining data, releasing jobs, or inquiring about results—is particularly important in ABC systems with their broad-scope processes.

A project team should take time to diagram or storybook the screen flow. To strengthen users' understanding of how ABC will work and look, screen flow can be organized by functional task. In other words, present the screens in the context of the organization's business practices.

For example, to compute cost rates and apply associated adjustments, show the order and set of screens that must be accessed to complete the work. Also describe navigation within the screen. What happens, for example, if a data-entry error occurs? What do users do if they cannot recall the value of a required field? What if they cannot recall the commands to commit information entered at the screen?

In architecture, details concerning user presentation may seem insignificant, but addressing them early helps determine the best software technology to implement the system. Developing "storyboards" about screen flow and navigation will also provide standards for screen navigation to guide developers in constructing the system.

The following basic tips on user presentation for ABC systems can save time and avoid confusion:

- *Provide on-line help at the screen and field level.* User procedures, including how to operate a screen and define a field, should be readily accessible through inquiry facilities.

- *Do not highlight errors, highlight solutions.* When a user enters an incorrect value at a screen, displaying an error message does not help identify valid values. The screen should present the valid set of available values from which the user can select the appropriate entry.

- *Do not simply show results; explain results.* The ability to implement this element for user presentation depends on the design of the data model. A user looking at a variance or activity volume may want to see details of the computations behind the numbers. Make it possible to display detailed data on how the result was derived.

- *Link screens to guide the user through data maintenance.* With scores of interdependencies in the data of an ABC system, the presentation must guide users through the process of adding new products, cost centers, resources, and so on. If key values are missing, a facility should present the appropriate screen that the user must complete before finishing the session.

Summary

Although the challenges for implementing ABC on a companywide basis are many, a functional architecture for ABC will help the project team navigate through difficult passages. The architecture provides a team with a balanced perspective of the ABC practices, procedures, and system functions that are common to, or in conflict with, the other major management systems. It serves to organize costing functions and show in practical terms how ABC will operate and interact with other systems. An architecture translates "what" to "how" and gives management a concrete, top-level view of how the goals and objectives of ABC will be accomplished. The four guidelines presented in this article will not make implementing an ABC system simple, but they may accelerate and ease the process of translating concept into practice.

Notes

1. Various articles and books on business process redesign have focused on benefits realized through improved organization speed or cost reduction. Although ABC is not specifically referenced by some authors writing on process redesign, the case studies in their articles and books assume an accurate understanding of process costs, which is fundamental to business case development. See, for example, Michael Hammer, *Reengineering the Corporation* (New York: HarperCollins, 1993): 150, 194; George Stalk, *Competing Against Time* (New York: The Free Press, 1990): 21–27. See also the case for reducing costs of accounting operations through improved efficiencies in Robert Gunn, "Shared Services: Major Companies are Re-Engineering Their Accounting Functions," *Management Accounting* (November 1993): 22–28.

Patrick Howard is a principal with the IBM Consulting Group in Chicago.

Merit Pay-Performance Reviews: They Just Don't Work

James L. Wilkerson

This is a very well done article that spells out how one company went through the development of a new pay system based on teamwork, systems goals, organizational goals, and the increased value employees can add as they become more skilled and experienced. If you are struggling with pay issues and the problems generated by invalid performance appraisals, this article can help you.

In late 1991, three powerful forces came together to foster change in my company, ABB Vetco Gray Inc., an oil field manufacturing and service company with worldwide headquarters in Houston, Texas. Those forces raised questions concerning one of the foundations of our human resource processes—pay for performance. At the time, we had a typical merit-pay and performance-review system, which we thought was working until we found out otherwise.

Force one.   We began a reengineering project in the United States to change the way we did our business fundamentally, that is, to focus more on our

> There was virtually no relationship between how we paid people and profitability.

customers. It wasn't long before we discovered that the cultural values associated with salary level and performance measurement—based on past performance—emphasized control, enshrined hierarchy, and were inconsistent with the reengineered environment of a customer-focused organization. There was virtually no relationship between how we paid people and profitability.

Force two.   The second reason we started to look seriously at our pay and performance system was the results of an employee survey. It was clear that our current merit-pay system was viewed as unfair, had no relationship to performance, and was considered an entitlement. In addition, as we began to supply our supervisors with new total quality management tools, Dr. W. Edwards Deming's list of Seven Deadly Diseases began to make sense. Deming's analysis of classic performance appraisal systems tells us they are deadly because they focus on individuals, not systems; they have too much variability; and they presume stable systems and processes exist. As a consequence, performance appraisals are not objective, consistent, dependable, or fair.[1] This analysis sounds a lot like what our employees told us about our pay-for-performance program when they were surveyed.

Force three.   The last impetus that we needed to make some adjustments in our pay system was our year-end financial analysis. The year-end results showed that even though our organization was going through a difficult market down-turn, which reduced revenues and put pressure on profits, our labor costs continued to rise at a compounding rate. It was time for a change.

Looking for a Better Way

We began our quest to find a better way. We were confident that someone must have a new and improved model for merit pay—one that would satisfy our employees and hook them into empowerment, please our supervisors by making their jobs easier, and make sense to our management by tracking our labor costs with the changes in the business cycle.

We started on a journey to find the perfect solution. And we did what most companies do when they are stuck—we turned to consultants. What a disappointment! They fell into three broad categories.

First, they were totally brain-dead with nothing new in their bag of tricks since shortly after World War II. Their approach was for us to improve the *administration* of merit pay because there was nothing wrong with the system. Their words reminded me of a quote by Captain E. J. Smith, vice president of the White Star line. He said, "This boat is unsinkable. I cannot imagine any condition which would cause this ship to founder." He was speaking, of course, about his new ship—the Titanic.

The second disappointing category of consultants consisted of Polly Parrots. They were great listeners who were willing to repeat any ideas you or your employees might have—as long as you were willing to pay.

The third and last category of consultants we talked to were Mystics from the Mist. They had no idea what it is like to run a business. Their concepts

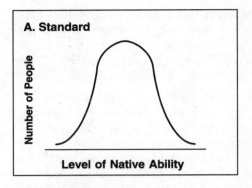
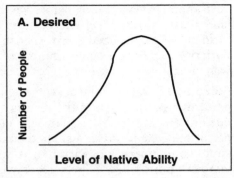

Figure 1. **Bell-shaped curve.**

were so bizarre they might be on an Oprah Winfrey show any afternoon. Instead of simplifying our system, their suggestions would have made it more complicated.

Flaws in the Standard Merit-Pay Model

To understand why our merit-pay system didn't work, we studied the development of individual pay for performance. We also studied the statistical and philosophical models on which most of today's systems are based. As we reviewed the information, we became convinced that even though industries and markets continue to evolve, the merit-pay or pay-for-performance process has been frozen in time.

So what's wrong with a standard merit-pay model? First of all, from a statistical viewpoint, it means serious problems for most of us unless we work for an extremely large organization. We are aware that merit pay is distributed based on a standard bell-shaped curve distribution of human performance (see Figure 1A). This historical paradigm has conditioned most managements to believe that there is a wide distribution of natural ability among people.

When merit pay is awarded this way, the assumption is that there will be a normal distribution—and complete randomness—with respect to selection of new employees, placement in jobs, and promotion. The normal distribution, which is like the general population, assumes no training, supervisory coaching, or any reinforcement system to increase performance.[2] This model assumes that human resource techniques are not useful and that the heart of a pay system is based on randomness. This randomness does not value reinforcement systems, such as pay-for-performance systems. The flaw here is that, in reality, not only are people's native abilities more alike in organizations because of the selection criteria, but companies strive to improve performance through human resources techniques such as training, education, and employee empowerment.

If we consider using the standard bell-shaped curve, we are "forcing" 50% of the performers to be rated below average. And for that curve to work, almost

We became convinced that even though industries and markets continue to evolve, the merit-pay or pay-for-performance process has been frozen in time.

70% of the company's employees must receive average or below-average pay increases. In reality, most organizations have a performance evaluation distribution that is skewed to the right (as in the *desired* bell-shaped curve shown in Figure 1B), which allows more employees to be rated above average, excellent, and exceptional. When the "desired curve" distribution happens, it creates a dilemma for supervisors because it is impossible to work within a budget based upon normal distribution.

It forces supervisors to:

- Rate employees lower than their actual performance to maintain the budget,
- Rate employees higher and have to explain why the increase doesn't match the rating, or
- Exceed their merit budget.

Edward E. Lawler III, a well-known authority on employee motivation and reward practices, is right on target with another problem with the traditional merit-pay system. From the employees' point of view, he says, "The difference in merit pay between the outstanding and poor performer is so small that there's no incentive value at all." He adds, "It's so unclear how a person got a higher or lower raise that it takes an enormous leap of faith, or stupidity, for an employee to decide that pay and performance are really related."[3]

Most of us believe that formal performance reviews systems are vehicles to relate pay to performance. But Aubrey C. Daniels says, "Apart from documentation for legal purposes, the annual performance appraisal is a waste of time. The managers who do the appraisals don't like them, nor do the performers receiving them. It is a masochistic and sadistic ritual of business. The way we appraise performance must change."[4]

Let's take a quick look at why most performance evaluations are not reasonable.

> Apart from documentation for legal purposes, the annual performance appraisal is a waste of time.

- The work of staff, as well as managers, is tied to many systems, processes, and people. But performance evaluations focus on individuals as if those individuals would be appraised apart from the systems, processes, or people with which they work. This focus encourages "lone rangers" and is a divisive influence.
- Performance evaluation presumes consistent, predictable systems. But systems and processes are subject to constant changes that often are beyond anyone's awareness or ability to predict.
- Performance evaluation requires a process of appraisal that is objective, consistent, dependable, and fair. Otherwise, the evaluations will be seen as capricious and based on favoritism. But such objectivity and consistency simply do not exist. We spend time— and a lot of money—training supervisors and attempting to develop systems that can convert human performance to some numerical grid. We have not been successful.

Peter Scholtes adds a final thought: "When all is said and done, the conventional performance evaluation system is more like a lottery than an objective observation process. It is distorted by evaluator bias and more often reflects the unpredictability and instability of the organization's systems."[5]

Although our employees might not have been as articulate or thoughtful as Peter Scholtes in their analyses, or the supervisors as concise in their complaints, their responses told us our system was ineffective. We were not rewarding or motivating leadership in our industry. At ABB Vetco Gray, merit pay and performance reviews had outlived their value.

A New Direction

At this point, management didn't have a quick fix. We were beginning to understand, however, why our pay-for-performance/merit-pay system didn't work and why its faults were magnified by the fundamental changes happening at our company. We had to make a hard and risky decision. Should we attempt to patch the system we had, knowing at best it would be neutral in reinforcing the culture changes we had going on, or should we throw it all out and start over?

Pritchett and Pound say, "If you don't make significant changes in the reward system, you'll actually reward resistance."[6] We experienced this resistance at the start of the process changes.

Our "new" organization had to focus on customers through partnerships, quality service, and quick responses; partner with suppliers; control costs; manage change; be strong globally while focusing on the local operation; and be innovative. Our challenge was to develop a system that communicated expected employee performance correlated with salary level. This system also would reinforce our organization's capabilities and competitive advantage. We knew that before designing the system we had to translate our organization's business strategy into the pay system's objectives. It is impossible to design a reward system that adds value to the organization without delineating the kind of people to be attracted and retained, the behaviors that are rewarded, and the desired organizational structure.[7]

We realized that to shift to the desired culture, management and employees must be provided with new processes to modify existing habits, perceptions, and knowledge that were barriers to change. We knew that one way to drive this desired change was to give employees the opportunity to link their pay to their value to the organization.

We settled on four objectives to align our employees' total pay and performance communication package:

- Shift employee focus to the organization's business results.
- Tie total pay to the cyclical nature of the business.
- Move to a "Career Management Process" that stimulates productivity instead of continuing an ineffective and negative performance appraisal system.

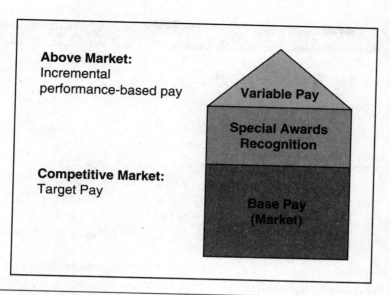

Figure 2.   **Our new program.**

■   Create an environment for high-performance employees where desired behaviors and qualities can grow.

A New Pay System

We decided to heed the advice given by Jack Welch in an article that appeared in *Fortune* magazine in which he stated, "The only way I see to get more productivity is by getting people involved and excited about their jobs."[8] We found that you get more productivity from people by involving them when you implement major change. To give our employees ownership and gain their acceptance for the new system, we selected a team of employees to help in its design. Their involvement helped drive the desired results for our new culture.

We developed a comprehensive model that eliminated individual merit pay (see Figure 2). The team decided that the pay rate per job would be determined by market comparison, if available, or internal comparison if market comparison were unavailable.

We also recognize that a longer-service employee has a network of contacts and more business savvy. This realization allowed us to pay employees for having acquired the potential for adding more value for our customers. We established three rates for each specific job to recognize the increasing value of an employee as he or she acquires definable competencies. We also wanted an extremely simple system that was flexible enough to keep our managers from being boxed in and straightforward enough so our employees would feel their base pay was "fair" in both external and internal comparisons. (For an overview of the steps in our new system, see sidebar, just below.)

A New Pay-For-Performance System

Step 1: Plan System Design

Change this element	From	To
Primary goal	Avoiding pay cost disadvantage	Competitive advantage
Organizational principles	Hierarchical control, stability	Fast, lean employee involvement, change
Level reinforced	Individual	Individual, team, unit
Role of market	Determinant of pay	Point of departure
Cost focus	Compensation pieces	Total pay cost—or total output cost
Who controls?	Staff; corporate	Line; business units
Administration	Precise, complex	Sloppy, simple[1]

Step 2: New System

The model has three distinct pay elements:

- A market-driven base pay for each job in the organization. The market midpoint becomes our point of departure, and employees have the opportunity to move to two higher levels within that particular job by demonstrating organizational capabilities and/or acquiring or demonstrating skills that will enable them to create additional value to the company in the future. As long as Sally and John are senior accountants, they will be paid exactly the same rate—unless they make improvements.
- "Fun" time to celebrate great and small successes through the President's Awards and the supervisor's discretionary rewards budget.
- A profit-sharing plan for all employees based on budgeted targets for our operations, with department targets to assist employees to see how they can affect our bottom line.

The elements of this model will:

- Help us accomplish the culture shift we launched with our reengineering program,
- Move us closer to an informed and empowered workforce, and
- Enable us to control labor costs without resorting to ongoing reductions in our labor force.

Continued—

A New Pay-For-Performance System (continued)

Step 3: Successful Implementation

In order for the change process to be successful, employees must have:

- Knowledge of the work, the business, and the total work system.
- Information about processes, quality, customer feedback, events, and business results.
- Power to act and make decisions about the work in all its aspects.
- Rewards tied to business results and growth in capability and contribution.

---

[1]E.E. Lawler, presentation at the ABB Inc. Human Resource Conference, May 1994.

Special Awards and Recognition

Because we were eliminating merit pay, we had to recognize outstanding individual performers or small teams that created breakthroughs to add value for our customers. We established two programs, one that was traditional and the other, as far as we know, unique.

Traditional recognition program.   Our traditional program benchmarks several high-tech companies that honor employees with celebrations recognizing their individual efforts. At ABB Vetco we established a President's Award that is given to four or five outstanding employees semiannually. The president or a representative travels to the employee's location and at a dinner with spouses or guests honors the employee, presents a plaque, and gives a significant monetary award.

Unique recognition program.   This unique program provides immediate rewards and recognition. Each supervisor is budgeted for one-half of 1% of the supervisor's direct-report salary budget. This amount is to be used at the supervisor's discretion—for recognition, celebration, gifts, and so forth. The key here is that management assumes that our supervisory staff are mature adults with the best interests of the company at heart. After all, supervisors make decisions every day that affect more money than is budgeted for the program. We are taking the risk that supervisors know what resources will energize and motivate their workforce.

As organizations adapt to more competitive environments, variable pay will become the primary way to link employees to their organizations.

Variable Pay

The last component of our new system—variable pay—is a powerful and flexible communication tool that can lead organization change or support an initiative for cultural change. We are convinced it will bring the organization's strategy and our employees' efforts into alignment for improved customer service. As organizations adapt to more competitive environments, variable pay will become the primary way to link employees to their organizations.[9]

Our variable pay is accomplished through a profit-sharing plan. Data show that at least one-third of all U.S. organizations have such plans.[10] Profit sharing usually is based on a formula that measures an organization's—in our case, ABB Vetco Gray-U.S.—overall financial performance. Our profit (earnings after financial items) is reported quarterly. After the budget is met, each employee not covered by an existing management incentive plan would receive a cash payment that would grow in proportion to profits. According to the recommendations of our employee team in the design process, all employees will share profits equally.

One of the major drawbacks to profit sharing is the difficulty employees have understanding how their efforts or changes in behavior can influence profit targets. To achieve goal congruence, each department establishes from one to three targets that would affect the bottom line. These targets are tracked graphically so employees can see the changes.

Career Management Process

Now that we have broken the chain between the pay process and the performance evaluation system we have a real opportunity for employees to add more value to the company. As part of our new Career Management Process (CMP), supervisors will become coaches for employees, helping them add value for the future rather than serving as appraisers reviewing past performance.

Instead of an immediate supervisor being the only person to "review" someone, other people affected by an employee's performance will have the opportunity to provide feedback about strengths and areas of improvement for the employee. Depending on the position being evaluated, this review could include supervisor(s), peers, internal customers, external customers, and suppliers. This multi-person review method is more objective, and its value is similar to that of a team effort. Specific measures, behaviors, skills, and competencies required for the person going through the CMP are identified. Part of the process is, of course, to establish and develop key competencies needed to perform each job. Then specific ways for an employee to grow—training needs, horizontal and vertical opportunities, and other continuous learning possibilities—are identified and put into a workable process for the employee.

In the last 18 months we have started learning how to change our ways of dealing with our employees. We have revised our base pay plan, implemented our Career Management Process model, and started our profit-sharing plan (January 1, 1995). We are recognizing our employees' successes, and we are finding innovative ways to add value to our company.

References

1. W.E. Deming, *Out of the Crisis*, MIT, Center for Advanced Engineering Study, Cambridge, Mass., 1986.

2. C. Cummings, "Linking Pay to Performance," *Personnel Administrator*, May 1988.

3. E.E. Lawler, G.E. Ledford, and S.A. Mohrman, *Employee Involvement in America*, American Productivity & Quality Center, Houston, Texas, 1989.

4. A.C. Daniels, *Bringing Out the Best in People*, McGraw-Hill, New York, N.Y, 1994.

5. P. Scholtes, *An Elaboration on Deming's Teaching on Performance Appraisal*, Joiner Associates Inc., Madison, Wis., 1987.

6. P. Pritchett and R. Pound, *High-Velocity Culture Change*, Pritchett Publishing Company, Dallas, Texas, 1993.

7. E.E. Lawler, *Strategic Pay*, Jossey-Bass Inc., San Francisco, Calif., 1990.

8. J. Welch, "Jack Welch's Lessons for Success," *Fortune*, January 25, 1993.

9. J.R. Schuster and P.K. Zingheim, *The New Pay*, Lexington Books, New York, N.Y., 1992.

10. Lawler, et al, *op cit*.

James L. Wilkerson is vice president of Human Resources, ABB Vetco Gray Inc., Houston, Texas.

Ten Reasons You Should Be Using 360-Degree Feedback

Robert Hoffman

This article profiles what 360-degree feedback is and its advantages over more traditional performance review techniques. It is an approach designed to help people improve rather than make them defensive about actions that are more the result of how the system functions than from what any individual does. This article is a good introduction to this technique.

The use of 360° feedback is increasing every day. Many companies have turned to this popular diagnostic and assessment tool to increase employee participation and to demonstrate a commitment to their workforce. The process identifies behaviors nurtured by the corporation and teaches techniques to align personal focus with organizational expectations.

Also known as full-circle appraisal, multi-rater assessment or group performance appraisal, 360° feedback is an approach that gathers behavioral observations from many layers within the organization and includes employee self-assessment. The individual employee completes the same structured evaluation process that managers, direct reports, team members, peers and, in many cases, external clients use to evaluate his or her performance.

Summary results are compared against organizational strategies, values and business objectives. The feedback is communicated to the employee and interpreted with the assistance of the company's human resource department or an outside consultant. The technique can be used for team-based work groups and for traditional working hierarchies.

> The objective of the 360° process is to identify areas for both organizational and individual improvement.

The objective of the 360° process is to identify areas for both organizational and individual improvement. Some companies use the tool solely as a developmental mechanism. Others incorporate 360° feedback as a key part of the performance appraisal process. The technique is used by a growing number of firms including General Electric, AT&T, Digital Equipment Corporation, Nabisco and Warner-Lambert.

Incorporating 360° feedback into the performance assessment cycle has proved valuable as a tool for providing insight into the entire organization.

Jim Gemmell of Mobile Oil embraces the process, "Until we implemented 360° feedback, we were only focusing on issues related to managing upwards. We would typically neglect other critical aspects of our business objectives. Currently, with 360° feedback we show concern for employees at all levels, in addition to emphasizing the external client focus of Mobil."

Implementing 360° feedback is relatively simple. Outlined below are 10 facts about this evaluation process that you can use to persuade your company to begin now.

1. Defines corporate competencies.   Many companies are wrestling with the problem of identifying their organization's true mission. What must be done to meet the demands of the marketplace? How can companies link the critical factors that bond job requirements with business objectives? What these organizations need is an instrument that determines the relationship between their strategic plan and performance expectations.

When 360° feedback is used, contrasting the results of self-evaluation against organizational norms illuminates areas of the business plan that need more attention from the employee. As Roger Baguley, an organizational development consultant to Digital Equipment of Canada explains, "The evolution of performance appraisal is exemplified by the 360° feedback instrument. A properly designed and executed process will determine the continuity of product delivered at the level above and below the individual. You can truly determine if the results required by the strategic plan are filtering throughout all organizational levels." Once the differences are known, senior management can more effectively communicate the skills, knowledge and experiences necessary to align individual goals with overall corporate strategy.

2. Increases the focus on customer service.   Many organizations today emphasize meeting the needs of both internal and external customers. A 360° feedback program can reinforce total quality management (TQM) and continuous process improvement programs. Customers of the employee or work group assess key variables that contribute to the cornerstone of quality program. A sample question measuring customer service skills might be, "How effectively does the employee get things done without creating unnecessary adversarial relationships?" The validity of the TQM program is determined by the extent of positive survey responses. Incorporating customer feedback in the evaluation process emphasizes the importance of client expectations in determining company focus.

3. Supports team initiatives.   The shift from individual to team-based initiatives is spiraling. More companies have realized that a team-based culture can be a catalyst for attaining business objectives. Regardless of whether an organization is just beginning to involve employees or has migrated completely to self-directed work teams, the multi-rater process promotes team-building. The traditional approach of relying on feedback from an employee's manager becomes only part of the overall assessment process. Incorporating feedback from direct reports, peers and higher organizational levels fosters the transition to teams. Employees are more inclined to consider factors beyond the bosses' expectations when exhibiting behaviors and striving for results.

4. Creates a high-involvement workforce. In a highly involved workforce, front-line associates are given responsibility for taking initiative, making decisions, questioning historical routines and developing plans. Although many organizations support greater participation at all employee levels, the move to a high-involvement culture induces many changes.

Shifting accountability to employees expedites their "buy-in" to company initiatives. Including employees from multiple layers in the feedback process is concrete evidence that their opinions, observations and evaluations are valued by the organization. Creating an atmosphere that accents involvement can foster voluntary collaboration, an element sometimes sacrificed in traditional, striated cultures.

Shifting account-ability to employees expedites their "buy-in" to company initiatives.

5. Decreases hierarchies, promotes streamlining. Corporations continue to use downsizing as a method for becoming more competitive. The flattening and decentralization of organizations is an outgrowth of corporate streamlining. After downsizing, supervisors and team leaders may see their roles evolve, leading to positions with broader responsibility and expanded jurisdiction. It is not unusual for a supervisor who in the past had six to eight direct reports to have 12 to 15 reports, or more, today. Moving rating responsibilities to a mixed group of employees reinforces the new corporate structure that shifts accountability to many. Consequently, multi-level feedback promotes the streamlining initiative.

6. Detects barriers to success. The concept of 360° feedback can be threatening to even the most progressive managers. The idea that direct reports and peers will have significant impact on a supervisor's overall evaluation and organizational future can be truly intimidating. As William McKiernan of Colgate-Palmolive explains, "We think we know how we are viewed by colleagues and subordinates; however, when we receive the results, many of us are shocked."

Feedback sometimes indicates that a manager perceived as a hurdle by his or her reports is stalling strategic growth. Success can be limited by such restrictive behaviors as inflexibility, refusing to give information, lack of initiative and inappropriate leadership style. McKiernan added, "Three hundred sixty-degree feedback on a departmental basis is an effective method that determines how we can be better as individuals and as an organization. We use the results to plan departmental training needs. How can we expect people to meet our objectives if the necessary skills are underdeveloped?"

7. Assesses developmental needs. Many 360° feedback programs emphasize employee development. Some organizations use the mechanism as a needs-assessment device. Steve Craig of Mobil Oil explained his company's use of 360° feedback as a developmental tool, "The primary focus of our process is identifying areas where the employee can be more effective in the long run. To be successful in the Mobil organization you need to prepare yourself for future challenges, in addition to attaining consistent performance on an ongoing basis.''

Feedback received during the process allows for easy assessment of current effectiveness and the need to develop critical skills. Unlike traditional development tools, the process focuses on skills across organizational boundaries. Identifying a realistic developmental plan can make the difference between an employee that merely survives within the company and one that prospers. Once a developmental plan is created, improvement can be measured during subsequent feedback evaluations.

8. Avoids discrimination and bias. Historically, performance assessments have been fertile grounds for legal scrutiny. Appraisals may be the centerpiece of a complaint alleging discrimination, wrongful termination of unfair treatment. Unskilled evaluators tend to evaluate factors that may be inappropriate, unrelated to the position or not representative of job success. Failure to eliminate evaluation errors may raise employee concerns and increase the probability that a dissatisfied worker will go outside the company for relief.

In 360° feedback, the role of evaluator is shared. Shifting this responsibility from one individual reduces the severity of any one person's shortcomings as an evaluator, including errors of leniency, personal bias and subjectivity. Using multi-rater feedback reduces the potential for personal bias and thus legal exposure.

9. Identifies performance thresholds. The behaviors measured during the assessment process allow individuals to understand their strengths and weaknesses. Profiles of both high-potential employees and those needing corrective action are developed during the feedback cycle. When the link between organizational values and current behavior is explained, employees can focus on developing approaches that lead to career growth. The predictive ability of the 360° feedback process highlights long-term success factors.

Using multi-rater feedback reduces the potential for personal bias and thus legal exposure.

Potential defects and high-potential attributes are used as baseline performance measures. Through the identification process, linkages are formed creating action plans. The final analysis identifies behaviors connected with high growth potential and those associated with career derailment.

10. Easy to implement. Introducing a 360° feedback program to an organization can be accomplished with relative administrative ease. Completing the feedback instrument, evaluating and communicating results, forming developmental plans and following-up can all be done by the human resource staff or an outside consultant.

To maximize the potential benefits of 360° feedback, a well-formulated plan should be devised. Some issues to consider include the following:

- How will the new process be communicated to team leaders, managers and employees?
- Should only 360° feedback be used or should the process be combined with other appraisal systems?
- How will staff be trained to use the instrument effectively?

- Should an outside consultant be used?
- Can a program be purchased off-the-shelf or should the process be customized for the organization?
- Is a computer-based evaluation or a paper-and-pencil form best for the organization?

While creating a high-involvement culture, 360° feedback provides a proactive system that truly aligns behavior with organizational expectations.

Organizations responding fully to these issues can expect smooth implementation. While creating a high-involvement culture, 360° feedback provides a proactive system that truly aligns behavior with organizational expectations. Adherence to these principles promotes the corporate vision, enhances relationships between employees, and provides the constructive feedback most employees crave.

Robert Hoffman is a senior human resource professional and president of ORBOB Consulting, Inc., a firm specializing in organizational diagnostics, feedback and innovative solutions.

If Empowerment is So Good, Why Does It Hurt?

Lawrence Holpp

Anything involving people and what they control or are responsible for can get complicated. This seems to be especially true when empowering employees and teams to become self-managing. This article talks about why empowerment is difficult and how to make it work. It is a thoughtful piece and provides practical advice with some good examples.

In a robotics lab deep in the bowels of the Massachusetts Institute of Technology, there squats an ungainly collection of nuts and bolts that looks like an ancestor of Luke Skywalker's little buddy R2D2. Students have programmed it to wander around the lab at night picking up empty soda cans and depositing them in the recycling bin. At the end of its rounds, the industrious gizmo parks itself in the corner and shuts down. All rather sophomoric, except for one thing: Without a central program, human intervention, or constant redoing of its program, the robot manages its routines flawlessly each night.

To do more with less, to do it without tight controls, to instill the principles of outstanding and consistent performance. . . . If we substitute "teams" for that robot and any number of tasks for the chore of picking up cans, we could be talking about the goals underlying the present corporate drive for employee empowerment.

In many companies, though, empowerment goes down like organizational castor oil. What it has in common with that old panacea is that we think it's good for us even though it tastes terrible. We take it when we're bloated and need to lean out fast. It treats the symptoms while ignoring the causes. Holding our noses, we swallow it all at once, glance obliquely at the outcome, and try to forget it until the next time we'll need it.

Nobody wants to admit they have a problem with the complex process of empowering teams, but nearly everybody does. The causes are legion:

- A large health care organization decides to create self-directed teams but fails to involve the physicians. Result: The docs don't

> Nobody wants to admit they have a problem with the complex process of empowering teams, but nearly everybody does.

---

show up for case-management reviews, decisions are postponed, patients wait for service, and the teams are discouraged to the point that they disband.

- ■ The president of a bank holding company falls in love with the idea of empowerment and tells his training manager to get on with it. Six months later teams have been formed, training begun, and the roles of supervisors challenged. Problem: Vice presidents weren't brought into the picture, and now they're resisting, with questions and suspicions, the changes proposed by the teams. The teams can't tell if the empowerment campaign has any real support. Suddenly all sorts of problems have been created where none existed before.

- ■ With the best of intentions, a start-up manufacturing plant devotes a great deal of time and money to selecting the "right kinds" of employees, teaching them to work in teams, and training managers to operate in a team environment. The missing link: The plant fails to measure team progress. Instead of setting goals for their teams and holding them to achieving those goals, managers close their eyes, cross their fingers, and hope that everything will work out. It doesn't. Finally, an old-school executive from corporate headquarters has to be called in to take control.

In each case, management wanted to do the right thing. The decision-makers understood that empowerment involves more than lip service—that it requires both commitment and resources. The errors were not strategic, but tactical. These organizations failed to think through the process, reflect on potential problems, ask a few hard questions about their goals, and spend the time to consider how these goals would be received and interpreted by employees.

For many trainers and consultants, the intuitively correct solution is to go back to the cultural drawing board. With rulers, markers, charts and tape, we want to work with executive groups, boards and management teams in order to reengineer not processes, but visions, goals, missions and values. We want to tinker with executive teams until they are running like clocks, aligned and on time. We want to involve the work force through focus groups in which we can enlist their spirits, plunge our hands into their historical experience, and come away with confirmation of our grand plan. We then want to roll out this plan with fanfare, free lunches, a video, and an inspiring speech by the CEO.

But welcome to the '90s. Life's not like that anymore—at least, not in my experience. I haven't facilitated a vision workshop in four years that's lasted longer than a day. I can't get managers to sit through any kind of training session more than two days long. I'm forced to employ every gram of persuasion I have to get work-team members to drag themselves away from their computers and sit down to meet once a week. When I say that empowerment takes years, eyes cloud over and someone from Cincinnati pipes up that his team was totally empowered in a week, everyone was very happy, and what's the big deal?

Maybe things are different in your company. But assuming they're not, perhaps we need a new paradigm for the kind of intervention that makes empowerment work in unfavorable or indifferent environments. The old models of realigning organizational cultures through a kind of long-term therapy are out the window. What we need is a simpler approach.

Which brings us back to the robot janitor at MIT. The deep thinkers at that university have abstracted a set of principles that govern the error-free, yet simple programming that propels this tin heap:

- Do the basics first.
- Learn to do things flawlessly.
- Add new tasks only as previous tasks are mastered.
- Make the new tasks work as flawlessly as the basic ones.
- Repeat, ad infinitum.

I submit that those principles offer a good outline for making empowerment work.

Do the Basics First

Begin with a definition and a set of goals. Have a plan that is clearly articulated to the teams involved.

It's amazing how many organizations simply skip this step or leave it to the human resources department to take care of. Try as they might, HR people are not up to the task of relieving management of its basic responsibilities.

Empowerment requires a specific, operational definition. Here's one that has proven useful to a number of organizations:

Empowerment is a process for helping the right people at the right levels make the right decisions for the right reasons.

This definition asks a lot but it also provides a lot. For one thing, it suggests a number of questions that need to be asked and answered to the satisfaction of everyone involved.

Empowerment is a process for helping the right people at the right levels make the right decisions for the right reasons.

Right people.   Who should we target to begin an empowerment effort? Is there some way to determine which groups are best suited for empowerment and self-direction? Can anyone be empowered or only certain people? How do we deal with those who don't seem to want to take responsibility?

Right levels.   What kinds of decisions should people be making on their own? What are the boundaries? How much authority can we push down the line, and how quickly can we do it? How do we track the effectiveness of delegation? How do we make sure things are getting done? If we're forming a team, who does the team report to? What are the differences between managing team performance and managing individual performance? How do we deal with people's expectations to be recognized and promoted as individuals? Can responsibility and authority be an adequate substitute for a management job title? If so, how?

THE PREMATURE TEAM

What happens when you uncork a team before its time? Some years ago, at a pharmaceutical plant, a long-time supervisor on the third shift finally retired. Since he'd had the reputation of being an autocrat, everyone felt that here was an opportunity to try out some new ideas about teams and participation. Management decided to get this retiring supervisor's crew of four maintenance mechanics to operate as a team without a supervisor.

The plant manager, the production manager and I (the consultant in the picture) met with the mechanics to discuss the situation. We collected all the problems and obstacles they saw in this new arrangement. We listed the issues, one at a time, until they were all on the table. Then the plant manager addressed as many of their concerns as he could. When he or the production manager couldn't provide an immediate answer, they promised a quick follow-up. Thus ended the meeting. We congratulated ourselves on having established an empowered, self-managed work group (though we didn't use that expression), in one quick and efficient meeting.

Within a month, the four men on the third shift, who used to work, play and socialize together, were at each other's throats. Crisis followed crisis, with managers being called in, often out of their sleep, to resolve issues that would only crop up again and again in slightly altered forms. For instance, a dispute would arise over who should clean the tool crib. Using our flip chart and calendars, we laboriously worked out a three-month schedule. The next week the mechanics would complain that they couldn't agree on who would write up parts orders.

After several months of this, the second-shift supervisor began to give the third-shift team its instructions for the evening, and the first-shift supervisors reviewed the night's activity with them. After a while, one of the mechanics was appointed "lead" and functioned as a supervisor in nearly all respects. They were still called a team, but the mechanics were supervised, their work was controlled by others outside the "team," and the responsibility for most significant functions remained in the hands of management.

Having told this little story many times, I've gotten lots of excellent advice: We went wrong in not following up with the crew, in failing to train them and so on.

But the real lesson, I think, is that the popular bromide about how workers make many "management decisions" in their private lives, and therefore can easily take over management responsibilities on the job, is a vast oversimplification. Yes, most workers can balance a checkbook, mow the lawn when the grass gets high, and select a contractor to put on a new roof. But in reality, those skills do not translate easily into the ability to work as a team to coordinate budgets, plan preventative maintenance, deal with vendors and suppliers, or select new team members. These represent a new set of tasks being done in an unfamiliar environment. Ensuring flawless performance, or performance of any quality at all, takes time, planning, and a measurement system that tracks each step of the learning process.

Right decisions.   What are the right decisions? What are the boundaries of decision-making? What should people be tackling right now? Three months from now? A year from now? What role will management play in decision-making? What if we see a team making a bad decision? Can we intervene without sinking the team?

Right reasons.   How much knowledge and education does the team really need to make good decisions? What's our investment in training going to be? Can we really afford it? Is this a long-term business strategy and are we willing to make a commitment to not jerking people around? Do we really understand what we're proposing to do, and do we seriously believe in it?

By answering these questions, managers can begin to get their hands around the scope of their empowerment strategy. They can avoid a lengthy and perhaps redundant sociotechnical analysis while nonetheless airing the key issues and making some important preliminary decisions. It may be impossible to get empowerment right the first time, the maxims of total quality notwithstanding; but it's inexcusable to avoid asking the right questions.

Learn to Do Things Flawlessly

Treat every delegation of some new area of authority and responsibility as if it's your last. Don't move on until the team has got the new task down cold.

There's no great mystery in handling the basics: housekeeping, vacation planning, shift coverage, even phone coverage. But the team will find it more difficult to manage things like rotating jobs, maintaining standards, and taking responsibility for results. Allowing the team to move on to the next task before it has mastered the present one condones half-baked performance and lowers standards.

At GE Capital Mortgage Insurance in Raleigh, NC, team-development coordinator Robert Phillips has devised a system to ensure that each department responsible for pushing empowerment into the ranks has a written plan in place. It's neither complicated nor even particularly demanding, but it does require each manager to think through the tasks that will be delegated, explain how that task is currently handled, and set a goal for when it will be assumed by the team.

"We don't want to dictate what each team should be doing and when," says Phillips, "but we feel that each team should have its own plan for empowerment and that it should be a written plan, not just a general goal."

The GE scheme consists of a matrix that lists the kind of tasks that teams will be asked to assume during the next few years. A generic list is provided that helps managers think through a broad range of actions, but each list must be customized by management and staff working together to build the final document. Once the list is built, management needs to ask itself two questions: Who is currently responsible for this task? And what role will the team play in this task when the empowerment process is complete?

For instance, in a newly formed team, hiring currently would be the responsibility of management. The goal might be that one year from now, the

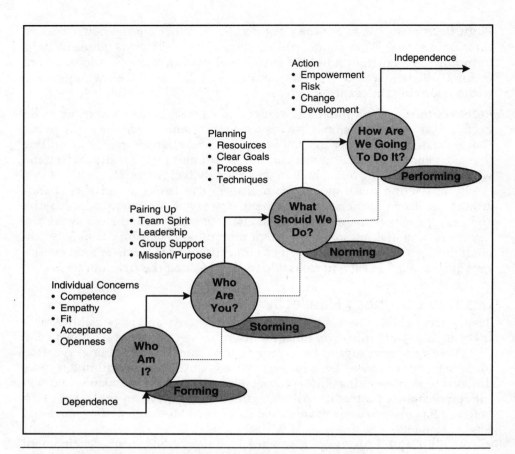

Figure 1. **Team Development: Who Am I and Who Are You?**

team will make hiring decisions entirely on its own. As an intermediate step, six months from now the team and management should be sharing joint responsibility for hiring new members. Firing, on the other hand, will remain permanently a management responsibility. By charting out such plans for all of the tasks the team will (and will not) be expected to take over, everyone understands from the beginning what the "empowerment" process will mean and how it will work.

Add New Tasks Only as Previous Tasks Are Mastered

Until the team has demonstrated competence in a task, new tasks should be delayed. Mastery, consistency, control, uniformity and direction are words seldom associated with either self-managing teams or empowerment. Nevertheless, to ensure that empowerment goals are met and that the process moves along at a steady pace, performance management is critical.

When your teams start complaining because management doesn't want them hiring, firing, budgeting, or doing the company's strategic plan until they are capable of getting their day-to-day work done with consistency and quality, you may interpret that to mean that they do not, as yet, have a realistic sense of what performance management is all about.

At Thrall Car, a manufacturer of railroad cars in Cartersville, GA, the importance of managing team performance became clear after a year of letting teams feel their way. At that point, some teams had made significant progress while others foundered, still uncertain of their mandate and expectations. The lagging teams needed some sort of structure to help them move ahead.

Thrall Car's steering committee drafted a set of job descriptions that clearly laid out duties and responsibilities in each of several key areas: quality, administration, safety and housekeeping, team function, production, and tools and materials. For instance, under "team function," a catch-all category covering such things as meetings, self management and communications, the basics were spelled out in detail: "Teams will meet weekly, for no longer than 60 minutes, to address team duties and problem-solving issues. An approved agenda and structured meeting format are required. . . . Teams will address and counsel any team member whose performance or conduct (such as attendance, quality, safety, work habits, etc.) violates company rules or hampers the smooth function of the team." And so on.

If this sounds a bit draconian—or even contradictory, since the point of the whole effort is supposed to be to get people to manage themselves instead of just following rules—consider the common alternatives: frustration, poor performance, and, sometimes, the dissolution of the empowerment vision itself. A good maxim of empowerment is that it's always easier to loosen up than to tighten up. Power delegated all at once is more difficult to take back than when it's given piecemeal, connected to performance and achievement.

A good maxim of empowerment is that it's always easier to loosen up than to tighten up.

Make the New Tasks Work as Flawlessly as the Basic Ones

As levels of empowerment build up, the speed at which the process moves increases. Maybe there's a physical principle that accounts for this, something associated with Newton's laws of motion. It isn't nearly as difficult to get maturing teams to take responsibility for complex assignments as to get beginning teams to do their timekeeping or basic office management in the first place.

The figure below depicts the process by which a group of people develop into a team. As the figure suggests, team development is a matter of personal development as well. Each team member has to get some positive feedback from the others during the initial "forming" stage, for instance, or the team will be reluctant to proceed through the other stages.

A great deal has been written about the difficulties of moving a team through the forming/storming/norming/performing process. But the good news is that once any *task* has moved through this process, it will be easier to move another one through. This is because the personal relationships, including trust and cooperation, already have been cemented. In other words, once you have made the journey from isolation and individuality to team performance, even on a simple task, it becomes easier and faster to repeat the journey with subsequent tasks—including more complex ones.

Repeat, Ad Infinitum

The real benefits of empowerment are seldom felt early on in the process. In fact, the costs of hiring the right people, training them, and working closely with them long enough to get them comfortable with the range of management duties they are expected to perform can be costly. The payoff comes later on when, with little supervision, they are able to take a task and make it part of their work.

To maintain this process is, for management, a lot like dancing with a 500-pound gorilla: You don't stop when you're tired, you stop when the gorilla is tired. Teams don't get tired of having control over their work, and a process of empowerment, once begun, is difficult to withdraw.

Lawrence Holpp heads Quality Partners, a consulting firm in Chapel Hill, NC.

Peer Review Drives Compensation at Johnsonville

Shannon Peters Talbott

Johnsonville Foods has been a leader in implementing quality management techniques and self-managing teams. This article profiles how employees developed a new compensation system based on peer reviews of skills acquired and meeting goals.

At Johnsonville Foods, employees are talking about each other. But they aren't gossiping near the watercooler or spreading rumors in the lunchroom. This talk is encouraged by management: It's peer review.

More than a decade ago, as part of an improvement effort, Johnsonville Foods incorporated a team structure into its work environment. Within this framework, open communication and coworker feedback became vital to the functioning of the business. As employees learned to work together as part of high-performance teams, they began to incorporate the essentials of peer review into their day-to-day jobs.

Today, Johnsonville's employee feedback isn't informal, as it was in the 1980s. Instead, the Sheboygan, Wisconsin-based sausage manufacturer uses a structured peer-review process in practically all areas, including not only performance, development and dispute resolution, but also compensation.

Peer review's move into the compensation arena began four years ago at Johnsonville, with the company's approximately 400 hourly employees, or *members*. Tim Lenz, an employee in Johnsonville's manufacturing facility, was one of many who were frustrated with the company's hourly compensation strategy.

"There really wasn't a system anymore," says Lenz, who's now assistant coordinator for Johnsonville's Riverside, Wisconsin, plant. "When I came to the company in 1979, we had several wage scales for positions throughout the facility. These slowly deteriorated, and it had gotten to the point where no one knew how to get a raise."

Leah Glaub, member services (equivalent to human resources in many companies) coordinator at Johnsonville, agrees that the company's hourly compensation strategy wasn't ideal: "We had a system in which the squeaky wheel got the oil," Glaub says. "People would pick up different responsibilities, then go to their coaches and get salary increases. There wasn't really an established system, and this caused frustration among people."

A team of employees leads the design process.   Instead of simply complaining about the haphazard process, Lenz decided to do something about it. In 1990, he went to the vice president of manufacturing and proposed that a group of employees work together to rethink the hourly compensation system. The vice president not only approved Lenz's suggestion, he also agreed to work with the team as needed throughout the design process.

Having obtained this support, Lenz hung a note on the plant bulletin board, inviting other employees to help him try to improve the hourly compensation system. He says that approximately 12 people signed up to help. After several introductory meetings, eight of these volunteers made the commitment to be members of the hourly compensation design team.

During one of the initial meetings, the team members decided that they needed some assistance from member services. "We invited a member of our company's [HR] department to join the team, because we knew that those skills would be necessary, and knowledge about compensation would help us determine the right system for our company," says Lenz. Because the team members had little or no expertise in the compensation area, this HR person (later replaced by Glaub) was able to conduct initial research for the team and gather useful data to assist them in the compensation system's design.

As part of the research process, team members also conducted focus groups of employees at Johnsonville to determine their needs and expectations, benchmarked other companies to evaluate different types of compensation systems and talked with consultants to generate ideas.

Lenz says that one particularly helpful research project was a site visit and one-day seminar on skill-based pay sponsored by Aid Association for Lutherans, a fraternal benefits society in Appleton, Wisconsin. This seminar helped the team determine what type of compensation structure would work within Johnsonville's culture, he says.

Cumulatively, this research led the team to develop four primary philosophies for Johnsonville:

1. Employees need to know exactly what they have to do to get a raise.
2. Employees should have responsibility for compensation. They should be able to request a pay increase when they feel they're ready.
3. Employees should be involved in the review process.
4. Base pay should equal the average market rate based on traditional internal and external values.

Once these goals were articulated, the team set about to meet them. But this didn't happen overnight. In fact, because the team met and discussed the project only once every two weeks on average, the final proposal wasn't introduced until 1992. "If I were to do this again, I'd like to see the team move faster," says Glaub. She adds that part of the problem was the team's determination to introduce a flawless program: "Sometimes, you can't just sit there and [try to] make something perfect. You just have to go try it out and then start tweaking it from there."

The process was a long one, but the result was strong. After two years of work and cooperation, the team members presented management with a compensation system that directly responded to the four philosophies they had established for Johnsonville.

Lenz says that as a whole, the senior ranks approved of the team's proposal. Because he had kept management updated along the way and because the vice president of manufacturing worked with the team off and on throughout the process, there weren't any surprises during the final presentation. "A few were skeptical, but the majority were supportive," Lenz says. Therefore, after presentations to employees and a vote by all members of the work force, the new compensation system was introduced.

Peers review performance to determine pay increases.   Overall, the compensation system is what Lenz describes as "pay-for-performance." Although grounded in a traditional evaluation structure—a point factor—it's also heavily reliant on a peer-review process.

The system centers around *result blocks* for each of approximately 80 positions. These blocks each comprise as many as 15 separate criteria, which highlight the key requirements for each job. Lenz says that most positions have two or three result blocks that are completed in progression, but some positions have as many as five. "Our belief is that you start out with the tasks that you must accomplish to do the basic parts of your job," he says. "These make up the first result block. Once you know how to do these tasks, you progress to the skills you need to know to perform at a higher level. Finally, you go on to the results that you should be able to achieve because of the competencies that you have."

Going along with this belief is a philosophy that people should be paid for what they do, and shouldn't be restricted from learning and growing. Therefore, the company sets no limits on how quickly employees can move through their result blocks. "If someone is doing the job, we don't want to hold them back," Glaub explains. "We want to pay them what the job's worth." She adds, however, it takes employees months—and sometimes years—to work through most of the blocks: "If you have them set up right, people are going to be challenged and won't test through them too quickly."

The company sets no limits on how quickly employees can move through their result blocks.

When employees are ready to be evaluated on a result block, they must follow specific steps. On the bulletin board in each plant, there's a form to initiate this compensation change process. When an employee feels prepared to "pass" an evaluation of all eight to 15 results, he or she fills out the form, which includes the employee's name, title and team, as well as the result block to be evaluated. This completed, the employee passes the form on to his or her supervisor, or *coach.*

Together, the employee and supervisor select some of the employee's peers who already have completed the result block being evaluated and also are in a position to see the employee's work on a regular basis. These employees—plus the employee's team leader and supervisor—become the peer-review team. Glaub says that usually this number comes to four or five, but "it depends on the job and how many people that person really interacts with day to day."

For each result in the block, there is a different measurement—evaluations that range from written quizzes to timed demonstrations. "They're supposed to be as objective as possible," says Glaub. "We really are looking for proof of new competencies." She admits, however, that some results—especially in the highest result blocks—need to be quite subjective in nature. "For example, I have payroll coordinators on my team," she explains. "One of the things that they have on their last result block is that they must make meaningful contributions to project teams." Understandably, "meaningful contributions" aren't easily measured. Therefore, the peers reviewing the result block must analyze the employee's past meeting participation and come to a consensus on whether he or she met the criterium.

Glaub says that for most supervisors, this peer-review process is refreshing. "They get a lot of input," she says. This makes the performance review and salary decision easier: "The decision isn't based only on their observations—it's based on a number of different people's observations. They feel more like facilitators and less like judges."

But what do employees think about it? Lenz says that they like having more control over their salary increases. "We don't have the good-old-boy system anymore," he says. "People, for the most part, don't mind honestly evaluating their peers, because that means that they will be evaluated fairly, too, when it comes time for their result-block test."

Glaub says that if employees are uncomfortable participating in the peer review, she does what she can to make it easier for them. "If someone is having a tough time, we make them responsible for an area that's easier to measure so that they don't feel they're getting into personal issues," she says. But—in the end—peer review is required of everyone. "Since the 1980s, we've been a very team-oriented company," Glaub says. "People are used to giving a lot of feedback and being involved. If it's uncomfortable for some people, they have to get used to it if they want to work here. That's just the way we operate."

Peer review is required of everyone.

Monthly contract fulfillment determines individual bonus. As the hourly team was completing its task, another team of approximately 35 employees began looking at Johnsonville's bonus system. Working closely with Glaub and the member services department, the team developed a monthly companywide bonus system that also requires that employees talk openly with—and about—their peers.

According to this plan, Johnsonville employees followed designated steps to receive their bonuses. The process begins with all teams, salaried members and coaches writing six-month contracts, stating their six-month goals and the ways they plan to meet them. The goals must fall into the framework of four overriding company *endstates:* a noticeably better product, outstanding financial results, outstanding customer service and outstanding people.

In addition, the six-month contract contains professional-development goals. These ensure that each employee continually is challenging himself or herself to learn more and provide increasing value to his or her customers, says Gene Rech, southwest regional sales coach for Johnsonville. "If you aren't at fair market value, you want to work on the skills that will get you there," he says. "If you are already at fair market value, you should include actions that will move you further ahead." Glaub says that these professional-development actions vary greatly from job to job and month to month, but examples might include reading a specific book or learning a new computer skill. "It's any action that will help you to move your position forward," she explains.

At the beginning of every month, each employee writes a contract that includes his or her actions that will help accomplish that month's goals—and eventually, the six-month goals as well. "The whole purpose is to help people focus, prioritize and manage their time," Glaub says. "The contracts really keep [employees] moving on long-term actions."

To obtain feedback on this performance, individual employees select three internal *customers*—or people who will be affected by the employee's work—as feedback providers each month. Through the company's electronic bulletin board system, employees send their contracts to the three customers. At the end of the month, these customers respond through surveys that provide detailed information on employees' performance.

Employees also post their contracts to a companywide bulletin board so anyone can read others' monthly goals and actions and comment on them. "We realize that people have more than three customers each month," Glaub says. "This allows for more feedback from others who may be interested. People do get comments on their contracts through this system."

Glaub says that the company teams meet at the beginning of the month to review contracts and ensure that the employees' goals are attainable. "It's the team members' role to say up front, 'Hey, I don't think you're doing enough for your bonus this month,' or 'Hey, I think it would work out better if you focused on some different activities,' " she says.

At this same meeting, the team discusses the customer feedback from the previous month's contracts. "If you do something for someone and the team thinks you could have done it better or differently, you'll receive feedback that will help you improve your performance next time," Glaub explains. Lenz adds: "If there was an honest effort and constant communication, then we use the attempt as a learning experience." This isn't always the case, however. "If you don't complete a project, your team may not give you your whole bonus," Glaub says.

This is an important aspect of the system. As it is set up, bonuses—which are based on the company's performance—are distributed monthly to teams

> Goals must fall into the framework of four overriding company *endstates:* a noticeably better product, outstanding financial results, outstanding customer service and outstanding people.

as a whole. Each individual has a bonus *target* for the year, which Glaub says usually makes up 10% to 25% of an employee's base pay. However, the monthly responsibility for dividing the bonus is left to the team members, who must decide collaboratively if the individual members have fulfilled their contracted obligations. "Sometimes, employees come in below target at the year's end; sometimes they get 110% of their targeted bonus," Glaub says. "The target is established so individuals can measure their performance against a pre-established dollar amount."

Glaub says that in the event that contracts aren't complete, the team usually knows before the month's end. "Team members are supposed to come tell us halfway through the month if they're having some difficulties or if something came up of higher priority," Glaub says. "In those instances, the customers must say that it's OK that the member didn't finish the work [and fulfill the contract]." Usually, in these circumstances, Glaub says the employee will continue to work with the same customer the following month.

Lenz says that there have been cases in which team members didn't receive the bonuses expected: "We've had team members who lost some of their dollars because they didn't fulfill some of their contract obligations." This is rare, however. Why? Not only is there a financial incentive to complete tasks, but the contract also encourages hard work. "You're making a commitment when you write your contract, so you have to plan well and organize your time to get your work done," Glaub says. "People don't like to go to others and say, 'I didn't get finished.' "

> You're making a commitment when you write your contract, so you have to plan well and organize your time to get your work done.

The peer-review process builds bonds between workers.   As Johnsonville enters its third year of peer review for compensation, everyone agrees that the benefits are evident. For management, the process alleviates some of the pressure caused by performance reviews and salary decisions. And for employees, it creates structure and needed challenge. "It can be stressful because the bar always is raised, and you can't get into those comfort levels where you can just coast," Lenz explains. "But, there's always a lot expected of you, and your contributions are valued. Plus, everyone knows what needs to be done to get a salary increase."

In addition, Rech says that there's a better bond between employees as a result of the review process. "People know what's being done throughout their areas. Everyone knows what others are working on, and each member is accountable to his or her peers." Overall, says Rech, the peer-review structure improves employee communication regarding job descriptions, work flow, accountability, and productivity. Or, in other words, peer review helps this sausage company create more than one type of link.

Shannon Peters Talbott is the staff writer at Personnel Journal.

The Impact of QS-9000

Perry L. Johnson

This brief article introduces readers to the new QS-9000 standards, developed by the automobile industry to supplement the more generic ISO-9000 standards. The goal is to assure that suppliers to the automobile manufacturers are certified in specialties unique to this industry.

Literally thousands of manufacturing suppliers around the world have heard the monumental news about the Big Three's decision to standardize their quality system requirements. Now they wonder how it will impact them.

QS-9000—the new quality system standard that has been jointly adopted by Chrysler, Ford and GM—is expected to spark changes and ignite new challenges for every company that supplies production materials and service parts to the Big Three.

QS-9000 combines the internationally recognized quality standard ISO 9000 with Chrysler's "Supplier Quality Assurance Manual," Ford's "Q-101 Quality System Standard" and GM's "Targets for Excellence." Under the guidelines of the new QS-9000 standard, Big Three suppliers need to pay close attention to two major changes.

First, manufacturing suppliers must establish, document and implement effective quality systems based on the new requirements spelled out in the QS-9000 quality manual. Second—and more importantly—suppliers must comply with ISO 9000: the standard for world-class quality. In their commitment to ensure customer satisfaction and build quality automobiles, the Big

Three have made ISO 9000 the foundation of their new quality system standard.

ISO 9000 is a generic series of quality assurance and quality management standards designed to help companies maintain efficient quality systems. The International Organization for Standardization created the standards in 1987. The Geneva-based international consortium consists of more than 100 different countries. The American National Standards Institute represents the United States.

The ISO 9000 standards were invented to facilitate the international exchange of goods and services through the enforcement of uniform quality systems. In the last seven years, these standards have had an enormous impact worldwide—especially in the European Union, where ISO 9000 registration has virtually become a requirement for doing business.

ISO 9000's real strength lies in the criteria it gives companies for pinpointing deficiencies and defining and measuring their quality systems. By conforming to the ISO 9000 quality-system requirements, companies receive the guidelines to build quality into their products. They can look forward to increased satisfaction among customers, less product rework and fewer product returns, which ultimately leads to cost savings.

To become registered to ISO 9000, companies must adopt one of three core quality system models: ISO 9001, 9002 or 9003. Companies become certified to the model that most closely fits the scope of their operations.

ISO 9001, the most comprehensive model, assures quality in the areas of design, development, production, installation and servicing. It is typically used by manufacturing companies that design and build their own products, thus it is the standard most Big Three suppliers will have to adopt. ISO 9001 is comprised of 20 quality system requirements covering a broad scope of elements:

- Management responsibility (4.1)
- Quality system (4.2)
- Contract review (4.3)
- Design control (4.4)
- Document and data control (4.5)
- Purchasing (4.6)
- Control of customer-supplied product (4.7)
- Product identification and traceability (4.8)
- Inspection and testing (4.10)
- Control of inspection, measuring and test equipment (4.11)
- Inspection and test status (4.12)
- Control of nonconforming product (4.13)
- Corrective and preventive action (4.14)
- Handling, storage, packaging, preservation and delivery (4.15)
- Control of quality records (4.16)
- Internal quality audits (4.17)
- Training (4.18)

- Servicing (4.19)
- Statistical techniques (4.20)

ISO 9002 is the standard Big Three suppliers adopt if a subcontractor designs and services their products. It requires 19 of the 20 elements listed above (there are no design-control requirements).

ISO 9003, the most limited standard, is the one for which companies least often apply. It only requires conformance to final inspection and test procedures (16 of the 20 elements listed above), and is typically used by testing laboratories and equipment distributors that inspect and test supplied products.

Initially, suppliers to the Big Three will only be required to comply to one ISO 9000 quality-system model. But, eventually, they will have to seek formal registration. GM requires its suppliers to be registered by 1997.

While ISO 9000 forms the main building block of QS-9000, suppliers should be aware of additional requirements. They must fully comply to sector-specific requirements. These revolve around the production part-approval process, continuous improvement and manufacturing capabilities.

Moreover, QS-9000 addresses customer-specific requirements—additional guidelines suppliers must meet that address the specific, characteristic needs of Chrysler, Ford and GM. For example, suppliers and subcontractors who provide heat-treating services to Ford will be assessed against the "Ford Heat-Treat System Survey Guidelines."

As a measure of protection to ensure that suppliers conform to the new QS-9000 quality-system requirements, suppliers will have to schedule on-site audits or assessments of their facilities.

According to the QS-9000 quality manual, the audits can be performed by either a second party (the customer) or a third party (an accredited independent company called a registrar) at the supplier's discretion. However, once a company becomes registered to ISO 9000, third-party audits are no longer optional—they are mandatory.

Through QS-9000 and ISO 9000, the Big Three will be able to assure the quality of their products and provide better customer satisfaction. For the suppliers, conformance to the new quality-system requirements should bring significant competitive advantages.

While implementing a quality system is a difficult task that can take many months to complete, firms that become registered to QS-9000/ISO 9000 will be considered to have higher standards and better quality products. This should give Big Three suppliers a competitive edge over nonregistered companies.

Perry L. Johnson, president and founder of Perry Johnson Inc., is an educator and consultant on the theories and practices of total quality management. Johnson also is the author of Keeping Score: Strategies and Tactics for Winning the Quality War *and* ISO 9000: Meeting the New International Standards.

Managing Records for ISO 9000 Compliance

Eugenia K. Brumm

ISO 9000 certification requires that you have sound records of your proce-dures and that you have followed these procedures, as documented in your records. This article explains the whys and hows of doing this. It is excerpted from the book of the same title. For more on ISO 9000, see Part Four, Quality References, which includes "ISO 9000 for Beginners" and "How to Select an ISO 9000 Registrar."

All activities that affect quality, including developing a quality plan, prod-uct design, processing materials, manufacturing, and distribution, must be recorded. It is the only requirement in the ISO 9000 series of standards that must be adhered to in every facet and activity. If there is a link throughout the standards, it is the emphasis on recording information that pertains to all quality aspects.

ISO 9000 Sections That Require Records

Often, the only evidence of product quality is in the records. In many cases, because it is impossible to determine product quality by looking at the prod-uct, records are required to determine whether the product has the quality level required by the customer and promised by the manufacturer. As a result, many decisions regarding product quality are based solely on data.

Quality records provide strong inferential evidence; this evidence should not be underestimated. If records are sloppy, it could be assumed that the process and product are sloppy. If quality records are in disarray, maintained poorly, or difficult to retrieve, by implication, the quality system and product quality could be questioned. In most cases, the state of the records will reflect the state of the quality system and product, because records reflect the level and depth of control and order that exist in the quality system. Records are also inferential in that it is assumed that if certain conditions are in place and information is recorded accurately about those conditions, the manufactured product has a certain quality level. Table 1 provides examples of inferential quality records.

> Quality records provide strong infer-ential evidence; this evidence should not be underestimated.

Table 1. **Types of Inferential Quality Records**

Category	Inferential Role	ISO 9000 Record Type
Employees	Indicates that employees were trained in activities that they were required to perform	Training records
	Indicates that employees received correct and current instructions to perform their activities	Document control records
Procedures	Reveals that instructions were written by knowledgeable individuals	Document control records
	Provides evidence that instructions have been distributed	Document control records
Manufacturing	Provides evidence that processes are being monitored	Process control records
	Proves that processes are being conducted within specified limits	Process control records

The Need to Understand Terms

There is a great deal of confusion about the definitions of records, documents, documentation, and document control within ISO 9000 records requirements. To compound the confusion, the standards use the terms interchangeably. Without understanding the following terms, it is impossible to develop strong quality records systems and tight document-control systems:

Records. The following definitions for records are equally valid:

1. Recorded information, regardless of medium or characteristics, made or received by an organization that is useful in the operation of the organization[1]
2. Any information captured in reproducible form that is required for conducting business[2]

Examples of quality records include corrective-action requests; nonconformance, disposition, audit, and material reports; project-status minutes; or calibration-data, deviation-request, receipt, supplier, final, or visual-inspection records.

Documents. Documents is a term that denotes an organization's written or graphical procedures, policies, or instructions. Documents explain what an

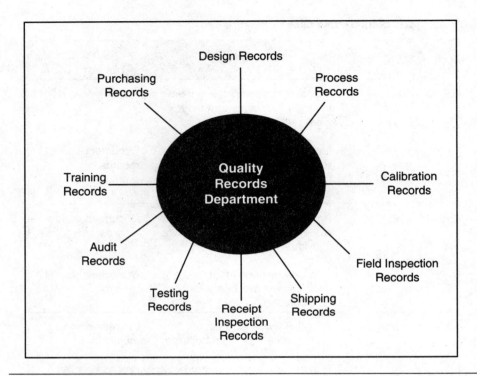

Figure 1. **Quality records department.**

Documents provide guidelines, explanations, and instructions about how to operate. Records contain information about the activity.

organization plans to do and how it will be accomplished as well as instruct employees how to perform their tasks. Documents are part of the larger organizational framework of operating information. Unlike records, documents exist before the fact; they provide guidelines, explanations, and instructions about how to operate. Records contain information about the activity, and thus do not exist until after the activity has been performed. Controlled quality system documents include quality manuals; raw materials specifications; and procedures on marketing, quality assurance, hazardous waste handling, document control, and internal quality audits.

Documentation. As it relates to ISO 9000, documentation encompasses both records and documents. Sometimes, documentation is used when the standards refer to records requirements. In other instances, it is used when the standards refer to documented procedures.

Document control. This is a *system* of managing, distributing, and keeping records on the documents created by an organization as part of its overall quality system. Document control and records management are often confused because a complex series of records must be maintained about the document control system. Also, records are the only proof that a tight document control system has been established and is operational.

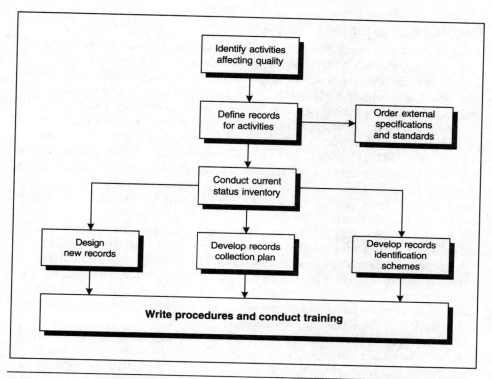

Figure 2.   **Beginning the ISO 9000 records process.**

Implied vs. Specified Records

Reading the standards and deciphering the records' requirements are not straightforward tasks. Many people wrongly assume that focusing on the records, document, and data control sections of the standards will satisfy the requirements and be sufficient for compliance. Remember that the standards' wording is condensed and distilled and that familiarity with all sections in the standard in which one is working is mandatory to glean the records' requirements.

Throughout the standards is the concept of implied-records sections indicating that activities be documented, even though the sections do not specify a record requirement. Here is an example of an implied record: "Repaired and/or reworked product shall be reinspected in accordance with the quality plan and/or documented procedures."[3]

This statement does not explicitly require that records be created, but how can an organization prove that it has reinspected the reworked product if not by creating and maintaining records? Also the standards do not list the data that should be collected and recorded. When one is reading requirements, it is good practice to pose the question, "How and by what means can this be proven?" Satisfying many sections of the standards often revolves around records.

Records Management Program

A records management program (RMP) forms the foundation for successful compliance with ISO 9000 records requirements. The standards' concise statements that list elements pertaining to records actually contain major components of a complete RMP, each of which (depending on the organization's size, age, and complexity) can take several years to develop and implement. Grounded in orderly methods and proven approaches, records management provides a recipe for what to do, how to do it, and where to begin. Section 4.16 of *ANSI/ASQC Q9001* has several records management components: records creation management, records retention development, vital records security, filing systems management, records centers management, development of organizing schemes, indexing, and knowledge of how and when to dispose of quality records.

Section 4.16 states: "The supplier shall establish and maintain documented procedures for identification, collection, indexing, access, filing, storage, maintenance and disposition of quality records. . . . All quality records shall be legible and shall be stored and retained in such a way that they are readily retrievable in facilities that provide a suitable environment to prevent damage or deterioration and to prevent loss. Retention times of quality records shall be established and recorded."[4]

Depending on the types of media and technologies used to organize, store, and retrieve quality records, this section (by implication) can also include knowledge and management of micrographics, optical disk technology, and the integration of information technology tools.

Quality Records Department

Since records are a part of an organization's quality functions and the same activities must be carried out on all quality records, it makes good business sense to coordinate quality records management under the auspices of a quality records department (QRD). When each quality function is responsible for creating, maintaining, identifying, retaining, storing, and disposing of its own records, duplication of effort can occur, along with gaps in records and information.

Generally, records expertise does not reside in each quality function. Records management activities can diffuse the energies of those whose main purpose is to manage their quality activities. Also, a lack of dedicated management of quality records can result in chaotic quality records and procedures and poor records-related decisions. The QRD should function as a hub around which activities revolve; this will help ensure uniformity in records appearance, identification, and organization (see Figure 1). Figure 2 outlines a plan an organization can use to address the records portions of ISO 9000.

It is important to have a qualified professional records manager spearhead the records compliance process. This manager is needed because of the time and knowledge required to develop and manage quality records. (To understand the breadth of quality records, see the sidebar "Questions to Ask About

A records management program (RMP) forms the foundation for successful compliance with ISO 9000 records requirements.

It makes good business sense to coordinate quality records management under the auspices of a quality records department (QRD).

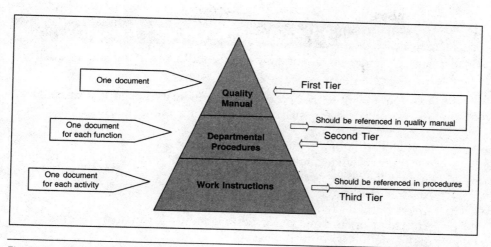

Figure 3.   **Three tiers of quality documents.**

Quality Records.") How records are handled, identified, and accessed influences the compliance activities of each section of the standards.

Identify Current Activities

Before developing new records for a quality-related function, one must identify current records for the activities listed in the standards. This current-status inventory of record types should be conducted against a checklist of record types that has been prepared from going through the standards. This inventory is different from the conventional records-management inventory in that its aim is not to develop an entire records management program. Its purpose is to identify the records that already exist compared against those that need to be developed. Conducting this inventory is valuable because it reveals gaps and overlaps in records, format problems, missing data elements, and information on how records are organized and stored. It also provides information that can be used to develop records-collection and identification schemes.

Most likely, the results of a current-status inventory will be:

- Designing or redesigning forms and records
- Developing and writing a records-collection procedure
- Creating a records-identification scheme and procedure

External Specifications and Standards

Complying with ISO 9000 records requirements expands beyond an organization's internally created records and documents. Part of beginning a records process is identifying external (industry) specifications and standards that must become part of an organization's collection of documents. For example, the organization might use an ASQC sampling procedure and reference it in

QUESTIONS TO ASK ABOUT QUALITY RECORDS

Here are 15 questions an organization should ask itself about quality records:

1. Are there documented procedures for identifying, collecting, indexing, filing, accessing, storing, maintaining, and disposing of all quality records?
2. Is the location of all quality records known?
3. Is it known what quality records are being created and retained in each of the quality-related functions?
4. Are the quality records clearly identified?
5. Are the quality records legible?
6. Are there organizing and access schemes for quality records that make them easy to retrieve?
7. Is there a retention schedule for the quality records?
8. Are quality records disposed of as dictated by the retention schedule?
9. Are the quality records stored in appropriate equipment?
10. Are the quality records maintained in an environment that protects them against deterioration or destruction?
11. Is there back-up for the quality records?
12. Are the quality records filled out accurately and completely, and does anyone check this?
13. Do departments and individuals understand how to route quality records?
14. Are the quality records collected in each department, in a centralized record department, or not at all?
15. Are the appropriate signatures and stamps affixed to the quality records?

an internal controlled document. In such cases, it is necessary to have the ASQC procedure in-house and readily retrievable.

The QRD should be responsible for organizing and providing access to external specifications and standards. To aid the department in this area, a technical-information subscription service can be used. If this type of service is not used, the QRD is still responsible for indexing and organizing external specifications and standards. Lists of in-house standards should be generated (via a data base index) and provided to each department that needs them. One must keep abreast of updated editions of the external specifications and standards, since they will be examined by auditors.

ISO 9000 Records Requirements by Sections of Q9001

Sections 4.1 (Management Responsibility) and 4.2 (Quality System) of *ANSI/ ASQC Q9001* provide the essence of the entire required quality system and the rationale for establishing the Q9000 standard's requirements. The purpose

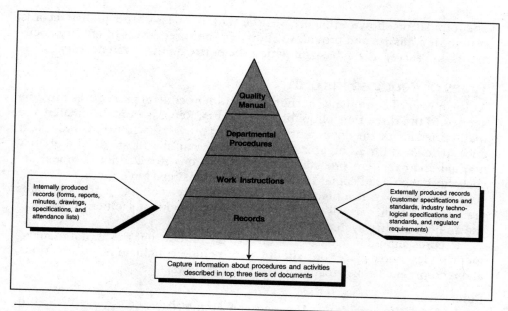

Figure 4.   **Fourth tier: quality records.**

of these sections is to ensure that the organization addresses each facet affecting quality and that everything is put in writing. This is often referred to as having a documented quality system. The requirements in the previously mentioned sections are:

- Develop an overall quality plan or policy.
- Delineate departmental responsibilities through procedures.
- Give this information to those actually performing the operations through specific work instructions.
- Record that these requirements have been met.
- Review the system to ensure that it works.

The Role of Records

The three-tier approach to documenting the quality system is often used to depict the different types of documents that an organization must produce to address the required aspects of the standards (see Figure 3). As the pyramid model depicts, the documents become more specific as one progresses from the top to the bottom of the pyramid. What is missing in this depiction is the fourth tier, which is shown in Figure 4. Records provide data and information on the work that has been performed throughout the entire quality loop.

Records reveal that all aspects of a documented quality system are in place. They are an integral part of the documented system and provide evidence to demonstrate conformance to specified requirements, indicating effective quality-system operation. Quality records form the base of the pyramid. If no records were kept of any work, there would be no quality system.

The foundation shown in Figure 4 is the thoroughness of the quality records system. It supports and provides validity to the three levels of quality documents and serves as the base on which the entire quality system rests.

Types of Required Records

At the outset of compliance activities, document control procedures must be applied to the three tiers of quality documents. Records must be created and maintained about the documents' creation, approval, distribution, and use. It does little good for an organization to prepare and distribute a solid quality manual and excellent procedures and instructions if it cannot demonstrate that those who need copies (and subsequent revisions) have them.

Other types of records required in these early sections of the standards are: internal audit records of the quality system and management reviews of the audited quality system.

Records should be created not only to document that the actual management review took place, but should also include conclusions, observations, and recommendations emanating from the reviews.

References
1. *Association of Records Managers and Administrators Glossary*, (Prairie Village, KS: ARMA International, 1989).

2. Ira Penn, Gail B. Pennix, and Jim Coulson, *Records Management Handbook* (Cambridge, England: Gower, 1994).

3. *ANSI/ASQC Q9001*, Section 4.13.2, Nonconforming Product Review and Disposition (Milwaukee, WI: ASQC, 1994).

4. *ANSI/ASQC Q9001*, Section 4.16, Control of Quality Records (Milwaukee, WI: ASQC, 1994).

Eugenia K. Brumm is the president of Quality Records Institute in Austin, Texas. She received a doctorate in information resources management from the University of Illinois in Champaign-Urbana. Eugenia K. Brumm's Managing Records for ISO 9000 Compliance (order number H0870) is available through ASQC Quality Press.

BALDRIGE CRITERIA/ QUALITY AUDITS

Why Not a Do-It-Yourself Baldrige Award?

Mike Herrington

The Baldrige criteria aren't just for those applying for the reward anymore (in fact, they never were just for applicants). This article spells out how various companies have used the award criteria to do an internal self-assessment. The criteria provide an excellent base on which to learn how well your processes are managed and how you are doing at understanding and satisfying customers. This piece can help you get started.

You've heard all the arguments against the Baldrige Award:

- "It's too bureaucratic."
- "I can't understand the criteria."
- "I'm too busy running my business to waste time on a contest."

Many disdain the competition for the Malcolm Baldrige National Quality Award (MBNQA), but companies increasingly are using the Baldrige criteria for self-assessment—one of the reasons why hundreds of thousands of copies of the criteria have been distributed.

The Baldrige Award process is designed, of necessity, to accommodate a vast array of businesses—large and small, service and manufacturing. But individual companies, divisions, or businesses can customize the process to get the assessment's real value: accelerating business-performance improvement.

Why do a self-assessment at all? For the same reasons that budgets and strategic plans are done. But budgets and strategic plans are accepted parts of the landscape, while Baldrige's newness—the first awards were given in 1988—raises the customary resistance to change. Also, some would argue that a Baldrige internal-assessment process is redundant in an organization with well-developed budget and strategic-planning processes. But experience has shown that, while there can be overlap, the Baldrige criteria's broader scope brings into full view important areas of the business not typically subject to systematic evaluation.

> The Baldrige criteria's broader scope brings into full view important areas of the business not typically subject to systematic evaluation.

Internal assessment is about improving business performance, a point often lost in all the talk about scores or contests. A self-assessment *process* begins with two or more self-assessments. In addition to business improvement, organizations that have done internal assessments for several years have found other, unanticipated benefits:

- stronger alignment of the organization around business processes, customers, and results;
- strengthened common language of quality, change management, and business improvement;
- significant management education; and
- a high level of personal growth and development of those involved in the process.

So how are these results achieved with the least possible effort and resource demand? No one has arrived at the ideal solution, but companies are trying various approaches—and they appear to be working.

The MBNQA Process

As a point of reference, let's look briefly at the MBNQA process. A written application of up to 85 pages (70 for small businesses) is evaluated by five to eight examiners, each working independently. Their work is submitted to a panel of judges who decide if the application is strong enough to continue to the next step, the consensus step.

This step is the first time the examiners work together as a team and leads to agreement on strengths, areas for improvement, and scores. They submit a conclusion to the judges, who this time decide which applications are strong enough to warrant a site visit by the examiner team.

The cycle time for the process varies from about four months for those applicants who do not make it to the consensus step, to six to nine months for those strong enough to go through all the steps.

A key challenge for most organizations is the first self-assessment. Initial efforts can be awkward; recall the patience required the first time you used a personal computer, or your first attempt at golf. This is when the frustration level is high, and so, too, can be the dropout rate. Compounding the matter in the Baldrige process is the fact that the criteria are designed for evaluation of a world-class business. It's sort of like starting your golf career by playing the Masters Tournament, or learning to dive by trying a full twisting one-and-one-half. Often, too, since this is an internal process, little coaching or expertise is available to ease you through the rough spots.

One approach to simplifying the initial effort is to use only some of the Baldrige criteria. A number of companies have limited their first efforts to the Results category and the Customer Focus and Satisfaction category. These two of the seven Baldrige categories comprise only about 35 percent of the criteria items but make up nearly 50 percent of the points, or weight, of the criteria. Of the 10 items in these categories, six call for data that can be presented as charts and graphs, with minimal need for extended written narrative.

By limiting training to these two categories or some other customized subset of the criteria, the content, time, and resources required for management education is reduced significantly. Similar reductions also occur in training the self-assessment team and the examiner team. Such initial approaches build a solid foundation of understanding, so that future expansion to the full criteria goes more smoothly.

> One approach to simplifying the initial effort is to use only some of the Baldrige criteria.

The Examiner Team

A properly composed examiner team is the critical leverage point for effective and credible self-assessment. The initial tendency is to staff the team with quality professionals; however, while these individuals serve an important role in understanding the criteria and guiding the process, they don't always bring sufficient "business sense" to the process.

Thus, in most companies, the majority of the examiner-team members are line managers. For them, the process's scope and comprehensiveness make it a tremendous developmental experience. Many companies believe that the strengthened on-the-job performance of line managers who've served as examiners easily justifies their time away from their normal duties.

The need for education and training of the examiner team is unavoidable: In addition to understanding the criteria, they must know how to develop strengths and areas for improvement and to conduct the site visit or oral evaluation. A great deal of material, including elaborate case studies (with company identities disguised, since actual applications are confidential), is available from the people who run the Baldrige Award. This forms the core training materials.

In their initial efforts at internal assessment, many companies use consultants or training organizations, either hiring them or borrowing them from other companies. As organizations mature and develop experience in their process, this training often is brought in-house.

Another common practice for companies just beginning internal assessment is to employ MBNQA examiners in the evaluation, site visit, and feedback process. This compensates for initial lack of experience and provides

HOW CARRIER DOES IT

For several years Syracuse, N.Y.-based Carrier Corp. has used the Malcolm Baldrige National Quality Award criteria as the cornerstone for awarding the in-house Willis H. Carrier Global Quality Award. All its activities, whether training, customer surveys, employee surveys, or process-improvement/reengineering programs, are linked consciously to the seven Baldrige categories.

The first notable feature of Carrier's process is that it is global. The company has translated the criteria into five languages, including Chinese. All assessments include site visits. Site-visit examiners can be from not only another business within Carrier but another country. While different countries' cultures have presented challenges familiar to those active in the global marketplace, the process is surprisingly uniform, and has given Carrier a common language of quality, and common metrics, to integrate its operations.

Carrier has developed comprehensive training materials. Beginning with publicly available information from the American Society for Quality Control, including some case studies, company officials have since customized the materials a great deal and have even prepared their own case study for internal training. Workbooks further explain the criteria and help structure the documentation process.

Over several years, Carrier has cut the cycle time for the process. Each business is required to do a self-assessment before a companywide review. Examiner training, evaluation of the written document, scoring, and site-visit preparation are concentrated into a two-week period, with a site visit conducted for each assessment. To give people time to prepare, seven days before the visit they are given a list summarizing what the team will be looking for.

The team gives verbal feedback before leaving the site. The actual feedback report is completed in two weeks. The cost of the visit—travel, hotel, etc.—is borne by the business being evaluated.

The entire process is overseen by a Carrier panel of judges, similar to that of the MBNQA. While Carrier does not link its internal-assessment results to compensation, the William Carrier award is its most prestigious internal recognition. Awards are also given for best-in-class performance by category. Carrier credits the award process with being a key element in its recent business-performance improvement.

training for examination teams throughout the entire process. Again, as companies mature in their process, they become more self-sufficient, and the need for outsiders diminishes. Where internal-assessment scores are linked strongly to rewards and compensation, however, the use of experienced MBNQA examiners tends to be ongoing.

Most companies follow the national-award practice of having a five-to-eight-person evaluation team, which allows for a balanced evaluation from a variety of perspectives. Then, too, since this team approach reduces the visibility of individuals (and pressure on them), there is less likelihood of shooting an entire examiner team than one or two messengers.

Self-assessment and examiner teams can be composed of the same people. However, as an examiner team they evaluate a business other than their own. For example, let's say there are two businesses in the company, A and B. Each appoints a self-assessment team to prepare whatever documentation is needed. Then, in conducting the evaluation, site visit, and scoring, the team from business A evaluates business B, and vice versa. In addition to getting an unbiased evaluation, when these people return to their normal duties they bring a fresh set of new ideas learned from the other business.

As internal assessments are repeated from year to year, it is common practice to "roll over" anywhere from one-third to two-thirds of the examiner team. The returning examiners, often designated senior examiners or team leaders, provide consistency from year to year, while the newly appointed examiners expand the number of people who benefit from the MBNQA process.

The Site Visit

Some Baldrige winners have reported spending enormous amounts of time and money—one winner bragged about spending $800,000—in preparing their application and hosting the site visit. Such efforts are not required for internal assessment, since you're writing it for yourself rather than outsiders.

Thus, you don't have to define and explain you unique characteristics. Use the jargon and language of your own business, and don't bother prettifying charts and graphs. The final document is a means to the end, not the end itself.

While most companies follow the MBNQA process of limiting the site-visit step to those with strong written applications, others have made it a required part of each business's internal assessment. The site visit goes to the facts without filtration or interpretation, reducing the dependency on the written document to describe the business in great detail.

There is a trade-off between these two complementary efforts. When you know that there is going to be a site visit, the role of the document changes, from being the sole tool for evaluation to simply being a high-level description of the business, designed to guide the site visit. The combination of the two allows a complete evaluation to be made. Some companies that have made the site-visit step a required part of the process actually limit the number of pages to as few as 50, compared to the MBNQA's 85.

Knowing that a site visit always will be conducted also reduces the inclination to "gild the lily" in the document. At first many people think of the site visit as an audit, with an "inspection" mentality, and a wasteful redundancy. Soon, though, most see the difference: One hopes that an audit will

Since this team approach reduces the visibility of individuals, there is less likelihood of shooting an entire examiner team than one or two messengers.

If the goal of internal assessment is business improvement, then the site visit becomes the ultimate search for the facts on which the improvement plan is based.

How Weyerhaeuser Does It

Some units within Washington-based Weyerhaeuser Co. have done self-assessment since 1989, with emphasis on making it a line instead of a staff process, emphasizing improvement planning rather than scoring, and minimizing the time commitment.

The Wood Products and Timberland Business Sector, building on this experience, has completed one self-assessment cycle. Within this sector, each of the 10–15 people on the business-leadership team is assigned specific items among the 28 in the Baldrige criteria, for which they will be responsible throughout the entire self-assessment process. Eight to 16 hours of prework involving one of the MBNQA case studies precedes one day of training, during which the team members evaluate and score the specific items of the case study that they have been assigned.

Next, the team members are given four to six weeks to gather information within their own Weyerhaeuser business. They are asked, though, to devote no more than eight hours to this process, the wisdom being that if information can't be found in this time, it either doesn't exist or isn't actually being used. Each individual then evaluates his findings and prepares a one-page summary of strengths, areas for improvement, and suggested improvement plans. These are presented to the entire self-assessment team in a one-day meeting during which all items are discussed.

Using an electronic scoring system, everyone scores each item as it is presented, and the average score becomes the final score. The scores are for the private knowledge of the business team and are kept confidential. However, the results of the self-assessment become apparent to upper management through each department's revised business plan.

The entire self-assessment process occurs over about a two-month period, and requires 30 to 35 hours of time from each member of the business-management team. The process is facilitated by the company's quality department, but the work and decisions rest with line management. Wood Products and Timberland Business Sector management expects that all its businesses will repeat the self-assessment within 12 to 18 months, and plans are being developed now for a companywide quality-award process.

produce no findings, while an effective site visit produces voluminous findings.

Experience has shown that the visit is the process's most valuable step. If the goal of internal assessment is business improvement, then the site visit becomes the ultimate search for the facts on which the improvement plan is based. Such visits can last as long as five days, though for internal assessments one to three days is more typical.

The critical element in a successful site visit is a well-trained and -prepared examiner team. From evaluating the application, the team members have a good sense of what additional information they need to give meaningful and actionable feedback. The team is free to go anywhere and talk to anyone at the site. In a continuing effort to shorten the cycle time, oral feedback of major findings sometimes is given at the end of the site visit, though commonly a final written summary is prepared.

The site visit is a mutually rewarding experience: The people at the site benefit from having their operation evaluated by a team of knowledgeable businessmen, and the site-visit team comes away having the rare opportunity to see in detail how another business operates. For the company as a whole, this learning and cross-pollination raises the expectations and standards of performance across the entire organization.

A few companies have evolved to a point where in some of their businesses the site visit is the *entire* process and no prior document is prepared. In effect, the assessment becomes an oral presentation to the examiner team. This typically happens after several cycles of internal assessment, when the criteria and process are well-understood. At that point the business is beyond the "audit" mentality and the process is accepted as a natural and valuable part of business-improvement activities.

Cycle-Time Reduction and Scoring

The national Baldrige procedure can take from four to nine months, depending on how far in the process the applicant goes. If a similarly performed internal assessment is to be done annually, which is the common practice, this leaves little time to act on the conclusions before the next assessment cycle.

The best way to shorten total cycle time is to eliminate delays between steps. Carrier Corp. has come close to this ideal: Training, evaluation, scoring, and site-visit *planning* all are accomplished within two weeks. Carrier holds the site visit a short time later and in another two weeks presents feedback to the business-leadership team. Such a concentrated effort has the added benefit of getting the undivided time and attention of the examiners and minimizing their time away from day-to-day work.

Feedback, in the National MBNQA process, is not prescriptive. In other words, while areas for improvement are identified, no recommendations are made as to how to actually make the improvements.

In internal assessment, however, prescriptiveness can be desirable. By this stage in the process we have well-trained, highly capable examiners whose suggestions on what and how to improve should be welcomed.

An internal assessment usually brings to the surface more opportunities and ideas for improvement than can be implemented in one assessment cycle. Recall that Xerox Corp., when winning the Baldrige award, still identified nearly 500 areas for improvement that it subsequently distilled into a five-year improvement plan. The final decision on which improvements to undertake typically is made by the business-leadership team. This allows them to take other ideas into account and avoid overloading the organization with

Xerox Corp., when winning the Baldrige award, still identified nearly 500 areas for improvement.

BALDRIGE AND BLUEPRINTING

By Michael E. Berkin

The real skeleton of value of the Malcolm Baldrige National Quality Award model is the *integration of the parts* of a business in a manner that logically translates customer needs into product and service features and into process designs. That "translation," when done well, in turn results in customer satisfaction. This is the heart of the Baldrige model, the primary benefit from its use.

When a stock-car racer uses, let's say, a small-block Chevrolet engine, it might look like an ordinary Chevrolet engine. It's not. Instead, it is an engine that has been "blueprinted," a long, tedious, expensive process. During that process, the engine is disassembled, and every component part is calibrated closely and precisely to fit and align perfectly with every other part of the engine. All the "looseness" is drained out of it, so that it tightly functions at the top level of its potential power.

As master mechanic Harry Hyde once said of stock cars: "They might look like your jackass, go-to-the-grocery car, but they are thoroughbreds. They are put together piece-by-piece, all by hand. We use the best metal available and we build these things by blueprints.

In an analogous fashion, we formed a cross-functional team and set out to blueprint our company, Dun & Bradstreet Information Services, to make sure not only that we all spoke the same language in the same way, but also that each work unit had a much clearer understanding of the needs and tolerances for the work units that provided the "inputs" for them, and for the internal customers to which they sent their "outputs."

In short, we wanted to make sure that everyone on the team understood the differences among a valve, a wrist pin, and a connecting rod, as well as how they worked together. And we wanted to blueprint those engine components so that when we fired the engine and tuned it through using the Baldrige model, it would have a better chance of outperforming competitors.

Because in business, as in auto racing, alignment and integration translate into speed and maneuverability. As David A. Garvin, Harvard Business School professor and former member of the Baldrige board of overseers, put it in *Harvard Business Review:* "Speed is a particularly good measure of integration because it reflects the tightness of the coupling with the organization. Sharply reduced cycle times are both a result and a key indicator of organizational integration."

Michael E. Berkin is Dun & Bradstreet Information Services senior vice president for performance quality and customer service, and an examiner for the Malcolm Baldrige National Quality Award committee.

too many projects. It is not unusual, however, for the assessment to lead to a reshuffling of strategic priorities.

Scoring is an integral part of the process, valuable in gauging progress from one self-assessment to the next, and nearly all companies include it. However, the scoring process is not precise. Because of this variability, the National Award process does not provide the applicants with a specific score. Instead, the 1,000-point scoring system is broken into eight scoring ranges, and the applicants are told only the range in which their score fell. Many companies follow a similar practice.

Concern over scoring accuracy is somewhat dependent on how the score is to be used. The options range from including self-assessment scores in the formula for executive compensation to providing the basis of a companywide recognition process to being kept completely confidential.

Obviously, the higher the stakes associated with the score, the greater management's concern for precision. Also, the higher the stakes, the more pressure the examiners feel they are under, and the greater the danger that the process will turn into a beauty contest rather than a search for facts.

One source of scoring variability is the MBNQA scoring guidelines themselves. These must be quite general to accommodate the range of applicant size and the mix of manufacturing and service businesses. To reduce scoring variability, companies such as Carrier, McDonnell Douglas Corp., and Whirlpool Corp. have developed tailored, more-detailed scoring guidelines.

Management's understanding of the scoring process is important. Individual items are scored on a percentage basis. Though most of us have a mental model of 70 percent as an average score and 50 percent as an embarrassment, in the Baldrige process a 50 percent score reflects a sound, systematic business engaged in continuous internal improvement and incorporating some level of benchmarking in its key processes. In other words, 50 percent is quite good. A 70 percent score is within the range of Baldrige winners.

Two caveats: Don't change or rewrite the criteria or modify the weight or point distribution. Experience has found the criteria to be sound and comprehensive, and changing the criteria means losing a considerable, and growing, body of available Baldrige information, not the least of which is training materials and case studies.

Some companies, though, stress key or unique priorities not represented in the Baldrige criteria, and therefore add items to the criteria. Johnson & Johnson, for example, added a Business Results category to incorporate more strategic and financial measures. When additions are made, the usual practice is to add points, so that the overall total exceeds the 1,000 points of the Baldrige criteria. Beware, though: Tinker with the existing measurements at your own risk.

Some companies use point levels to reward high achievers. In a 1993 Conference Board survey of self-assessment practices, 12 of 36 responding Total Quality Management Center member companies mentioned some form of recognition. These are rarely competitive, winner-take-all processes. More commonly they are gold, silver, and bronze award levels (typically signified

To reduce scoring variability, companies such as Carrier, McDonnell Douglas Corp., and Whirlpool Corp. have developed tailored, more-detailed scoring guidelines.

with a plaque) with no limit to the number of each award that can be given. The typical threshold for the bronze level is 500 points, or 50 percent. Some companies also recognize levels of improvement, and, to further expand the amount of recognition, a few companies also recognize levels of achievement for each of the seven categories of the criteria.

In all cases, recognition is a mechanism for identifying internal benchmarks and best practices, with the hope that they will spread to other parts of the company to accelerate their learning and improvement.

Mike Herrington is a consultant in quality and business-process improvement in Fairfield, Conn. He was formerly vice president for quality improvement at Olin Corp.

PART FOUR

Quality
References

We have created *The Quality Yearbook* for your use as an anthology and reference to the quality management movement. Parts One to Three are the anthology part of the book. Part Four is the reference part. Several sections make up this reference. Some include lists where you can find more information. Some include how-to information, and some provide background for better understanding total quality management. Specifically, you'll find:

- **Comprehensive Annotated Bibliography.** We have ordered this in a similar way to the book's organization. It lists hundreds of articles and books on quality management from a large number of sources. This bibliography is current through the fall of 1995, and it should serve as the first place to turn to find more information on any aspect of quality management in which you have interest.

- **A Quality Management Library, Part 2.** In the 1995 yearbook, we included a listing and review of 25 books we thought might make up the core of a library in quality management. Here you will find installment 2, with 25 more titles.

- **Directory of Magazines and Journals.** This section lists over 60 different publications that focus on or regularly include articles on quality management. This list rates the magazines according to their usefulness to managers learning about quality.

- **On-Line Quality Services.** This is substantially expanded over the section we established in the 1995 yearbook. There is much available on quality on the internet and other sources, and we have included a good list of resources to get you started.

- **Understanding Systems Thinking.** This is a special section. In this edition of the yearbook, we have put more emphasis on the idea of systems thinking. Reproduced here is a chapter from Peter Senge's book, *The Fifth Discipline*, that clearly explains the difference between traditional linear thinking and systems thinking,

a more powerful and realistic way to understand and improve organzational behavior patterns.

- **How To Partner.** More and more companies are seeking partners in the development of products, in logistics, and in marketing and selling. This short piece
  provides some practical advice on how to effectively undertake and manage partnerships to the mutual benefit of all parties.

- **ISO 9000 for Beginners.** ISO certification is becoming common more and more
  for many companies. Just what this is all about remains somewhat unclear to
  many managers. This original article, prepared for this yearbook by a highly regarded consultant, tells you just what ISO is all about.

- **How to Select an ISO 9000 Registrar.** This is an article we found that offers very
  practical advice on selecting and working the company that will audit and make
  the decision whether you will achieve certification or not.

- **Quality Quotes.** We have included a selection of around 200 quotations from
  many different people, including business writers, philosophers, poets, and practicing managers. These are food for thought and can be helpful when planning a
  speech or writing a report.

- **The 1995 Baldrige Award Winners and the 1996 Baldrige Criteria.** Despite the
  fact that the winners and criteria are announced less than three months prior to
  the publication of this book, we felt it was vital to be able to provide our readers
  with this information. By special arrangement with our production staff and the
  publisher, we are able to include this information for you.

- **Index.** We have prepared a detailed index to supplement the table of contents.
  This should be valuable in helping you find more information on many topics
  covered throughout this book.

Annotated Bibliography of Quality Books and Articles

This year's bibliography is organized very much as in earlier editions. We have included bibliographic citations that appeared after we went to press for the previous edition, so you will see some material published late in 1994. In this edition, you will find references to publications that have appeared through early September 1995.

This year the literature continued to discuss case studies of quality practices. We saw a dramatic increase in publications concerning cost justification of quality practices, specific "how-to" on quality tools and techniques, and about ISO 9000. The amount of material on reengineering and benchmarking is down, although the quality of reengineering literature has improved greatly. You will notice a few new sections, such as "Concepts" and "Tools," that simply reflect a refinement of our organization of bibliographic citations. We have tried to give a good balance between articles from a wide variety of magazines and journals along with as many books as we could track that came out in 1995. As in past years, this bibliography is not definitive; it is selective and, we think, represents between 40 and 50 percent of what appeared on the topic.

TOTAL QUALITY MANAGEMENT IN GENERAL

Cortada, James W. and Woods, John A. *McGraw-Hill Encyclopedia of Quality Terms & Concepts*, New York: McGraw-Hill, 1995.

A comprehensive reference of the technical and nontechnical terms that cover all aspects of managing processes to improve quality and customer satisfaction. Includes more than 600 terms.

Hodgetts, Richard M. *Implementing TQM in Small and Medium Sized Businesses*, New York: AMACOM, 1995.

A hands-on guide with lots of examples to help companies of any size get started on the quality journey.

Hradesky, John L. *Total Quality Management Handbook*, New York: McGraw-Hill, 1995.

This is an attempt to give managers a comprehensive and practical guide to many of the techniques and tools involved in quality management.

William J. Latzko and David M. Saunders. *Four Days with Dr. Deming*, Reading, MA: Addison-Wesley, 1995.

Just as its title states, this is a description of the experience and the insights gained from taking Dr. Deming's four-day seminar.

Swift, J.A. *Introduction to Modern Statistical Control and Management*, Delray, Beach, FL: St. Lucie Press, 1995.

Covers material on control charts, but also includes information of quality function deployment, benchmarking, ISO 9000, and other quality management topics.

Voehl, Frank et al. *Deming: The Way We Knew Him*, Delray Beach, FL: St. Lucie Press, 1995.

A contributed volume of personal stories about Deming and his contribution to helping everyone better appreciate his contributions to improving management practices.

Woods, John A. and Cortada, James, W. *QualiTrends: Seven Quality Secrets that Can Change Your Life*, New York: McGraw-Hill, 1996.

A short book designed to introduce some basic concepts that provide the foundation for quality management and include teamwork, process management, customer focus, the use of statistics, and others. Useful for any company as a tool to orient employees to the basics of quality management.

MANUFACTURING SECTOR
General Trends

Crosby, Philip B. *Quality Is Still Free: Making Quality Certain in Uncertain Times*, New York: McGraw-Hill, 1995.
Crosby's continuing discussion of the ideas he introduced in his original book, *Quality Is Free.*

Jasinowski, Jerry. "America's Manufacturing Revolution," *Vital Speeches of the Day* 61, no. 11 (March 15, 1995): 348–352.
Reports on how U.S. industry became the most competitive in the world again. Key success factors included: leadership managing change, application of TQM, investment in IT, empowering employees, product innovation, and competing around the world. Continous improvement will be key to future success.

Johnston, Richard, Cahill, Gerry, and Smith, Bruce. "SPC Enhances TQM," *Appliance Manufacturer* 42, no. 11 (November 1994): 54–55.
Describes the value of using statistical process control in a manufacturing setting. Offers a very high level definition of when this tool should be used.

Kasul, Ruth A. and Motwani, Jaideep G. "Total Quality Management in Manufacturing: Thematic Factor Assessment," *International Journal of Quality and Reliability Management* 12, no. 13 (1995): 57–76.
Offers a synthesis of TQM literature on eight critical factors and supporting performance measurements as applied to manufacturing.

Port, Otis. "Custom Made, Direct from the Plant," *Business Week* (November 18, 1994): 158–159.
Describes the growing trend in manufacturing of deploying mass customization and why this is becoming an attractive strategy for many companies.

Schriener, Judy, Angelo, William J., and McManamy, Bob. "Total Quality Management

Struggles Into A Low Orbit," *ENR* 234, no. 19 (May 15, 1995): 24–28.
Reports on various surveys done about the use of TQM in the construction industry. About half still do not use TQM. Customers of this industry have been the ones insisting that this industry apply TQM. There remains much confusion about the subject here.

Staniforth, David. "To Restructure Or Not? That Is The Managerial Question," *TQM Magazine* 6, no. 5 (1994): 28–31.
Presents results of survey of 52 British manufacturing companies. 66 percent are organized by function, downsizing an flattening is extensive. 45 percent report having gone through major changes, another 35 percent moderate reorganization. In part this has been done to share responsibility for the success of the organization with more employees.

Automotive

Anonymous. "Quality: A Way of Life in the Motor City," *Quality* (March 1995): 22–24, 26, 28.
Reviews the Deming-style quality inspection practices in the U.S. automotive industry. This is a detailed look at how this is done today, with examples. The ideas are applicable in many industries.

Johnson, Marv. "Toyota's Quality Standard," *Transportation and Distribution* 36, no. 4 (April 1995): 106.
Toyota has long been an innovative manufacturer, using its own processes similar to but different than ISO and TQM driven. This is a case study of its operations at Columbus, Indiana, where it manufactures forklifts.

Electronics, Computers, Telecoms

Anand, Vineeta. "TQM Cuts Manager Ranks at Bell Atlantic," *Pensions and Investments* 23, no. 1 (January 9, 1995): 3, 26.
Describes how Bell Atlantic reduced the number of money managers in half, trimming costs by 60 percent, while risk levels stayed the same. Returns on investments have remained very good.

Anonymous. "Reengineering the Telco," *Communications Week International* (April 10, 1995): 18ff.
Describes the before and after experience of the New Zealand telco (1987–1995). How it responded to competition, its downsizing efforts, and what was reengineered are explained. Then it describes the experiences

of other telcos in various countries in Europe and Asia and the United States; an important article.

Basinger, R.G. et al. "Total Quality Management in the Switching Systems Business Unit," *AT&T Technical Journal* 73, no. 6 (November/December 1994): 7–18.

This describes AT&T's quality policy and how it is applied in the Switching Systems Business unit at Bell Labs in Naperville, Ill. Includes a useful discussion of how the company is dealing with the evolving concept of customer value add.

Catlow, Geraldine and Cryer, David. "A Case Study of Process Improvement," *Management Accounting* 73, no. 1 (January 1995): 28–29.

Describes TQM at Texas Instruments. Describes how process improvement is done at TI by using a specific project at the company.

Dambach, Barry F. and Allenby, Braden R. "Implementing Design for Environment at AT&T," *Total Quality Environmental Management* 4, no. 3 (Spring 1995): 51–62.

This is a fascinating look at the application of TQM principles in such areas as pipe waste management and TQEM. AT&T has been one of the most effective of the major corporations in applying quality management practices, which are outlined in this case study.

Eisman, Regina. "Eyes on the Prize," *Incentive* 169, no. 1 (January 1995): 43–47.

Discusses how AT&T has been transforming itself since 1988, the role of prizes in that change (e.g., internal quality awards and the Baldrige), and what it is currently focusing on.

Kim, Gary. "Core Competence Adds Value to Quality Service," *America's Network* 99, no. 12 (June 1995): 88.

Expresses that the application of core competencies improves quality of service. Argues how that is the case in the telcom industry.

Law, K.Y., Choi, Y.M. and Cheng, L.L. "TQM in The Electronics Industry: The Hong Kong Experience," in *Third International Symposium on Consumer Elecronics 1994*, vol. 2, pp. 535–541.

This is a history of the application of TQM in this industry in Hong Kong. Carefully states why some have been successful and others have not.

Ludeman, Kate. "Waving the White Flag," *Quality Progress* 28, no. 5 (May 1995): 35–40.

Tried and failed to create a semiconductor industry survey in an attempt to identify points of cooperation in this industry. Describes cooperative and competitive conditions in this industry, one that is an extensive user of quality management practices.

Robbins, Renee M. "Reengineered Support: An Interview with IBM's Buell G. Duncan III," *Systems Management 3X/400* 22, no. 11 (November 1994): 35–42.

Duncan is the vice president of sales for IBM's AS/400 Division. He describes IBM's service and support strategy and how it is working to be consistent in delivery. Comments on how the company is also reengineering other aspects of its sales operations.

Shields, Malcolm. "Total Quality Management: Another Mast to String Your Flag To, Or A Means to Change A Company's Culture?" *TQM Magazine* 6, no. 5 (1994): 45–46.

Explains how Microtech Ltd. began implementing TQM in August, 1993. This small company invested in training, communication, and involvement. Describes their customer survey. Specific benefits are cited along with the approach taken by the firm.

Various Manufacturing Industries

Anonymous. "A Picture of Quality," *Quality* 34, no. 1 (January 1995): 42–46.

Describes how Polaroid used SPC in the design and assembly of its Captiva camera. Details how TQM was used, targets set, and results obtained; a very useful little case study on the use of SPC in a manufacturing setting.

Anonymous. "Wedgwood's Approach to TQM in Manufacturing," *Ceramic Industry* (March 1995): 39.

Wedgwood Group has implemented quality control procedures for 500 years and today ISO 9000, TQM, and JIT, all of which are briefly described.

Byrne, Art. "How Wiremold Reinvented Itself with *Kaizen*," *Target* 11, no. 1 (January/February 1995): 8–14.

CEOs rarely write about quality practices; this article is an exception to that rule. He describes how the leading U.S. producer of wire management systems transformed its business practices over the past three years applying continuous improvement strategies.

Clutz, Ron. "Competitive Edges," *Canadian Manager* 19, no. 4 (December 1994): 17–19.

Describes the changing nature of quality practices and technology in the printing industry. Includes review of the role of TQM, business process reengineering, and activity-based costing.

McKim, R.A. and Kiani, H. "Applying Total Quality Management to the North American Construction Industry," *Cost Engineering* 37, no. 3 (March 1995): 24–28.

Provides a case study of TQM being applied by a rough framing subcontractor with primary focus on how field activities were organized. Careful measurements were taken of the process and the results presented.

Pitman, Glenn A., Motwani, Jaideep G., and Schliker, Doborah. "Total Quality Management in the American Defense Industry: A Case Study," *International Journal of Quality and Reliability Management* 11, no. 9 (1994): 101–108.

Describes the U.S. Department of Defense's emphasis on TQM and how it is expanding TQM into its suppliers. A case study of an aerospace defense contractor is used to illustrate the implementation process.

Various Process Industries

Anonymous. "Benchmarking Goes Global," *Chemical Marketing Reporter* (April 10, 1995): 16ff.

Reports that chemical companies are moving away from just cost cutting to best practices in product development and globalization. A tool being used to facilitate this change is benchmarking. Quotes many consultants on what is going on and how. This also describes specific examples from the chemical industry.

Anonymous. "TQM Scores Vary Among Printers," *American Printer* 214, no. 4 (January 1995): 76.

Presents results of a survey: 65 percent of printers had TQM programs; 68 percent of those that do not intend to within the next two years. Over half said they got benefits; 28 percent said not really.

Gibson, W. David. "Under One Umbrella," *Chemical Marketing Reporter* 246, no. 18 (October 31, 1994): PSR12–SR13.

Discusses how TQM is being applied by chemical companies. Cites why it is being used by many companies, including Union Carbide. This is a good introduction to TQM in the chemical industry.

Pitts, Colin. "Is It Spring or Autumn for TQM?" *TQM Magazine* 6, no. 5 (1994): 35–37.

Discusses TQM at BP Chemicals International, Ltd. Details many successes at BP, a significant case study. What is of particular value is the fact that this company

has been implementing TQM for a number of years so that we can track its evolution over time.

Thayer, Ann. "Chemical Companies Extend Total Quality Management Boundaries," *Chemical & Engineering News* 73, no. 9 (February 27, 1995): 15–23.

Reports on how the chemical industry has embraced TQM and includes examples from Eastman Chemical Co., Union Carbide Corp., Praxair Inc., and Rhone Poulenc. This is an important industry case study covering major TQM initiatives and results over the past 10 years.

SERVICES SECTOR

Anderson, Kristin and Zemke, Ron. *Knock Your Socks Off Answers*, New York: AMACOM, 1995.

This is another title in the "Knock Your Socks Off" series. It includes lots of stories and advice on making customer service the priority of your business.

Berry, Leonard L. *On Great Service: A Framework for Action*, New York: The Free Press, 1995.

Berry is a leading thinker in the area of service quality, and this book talks about why service is important and how your company can develop customer service that promotes growth, profitability, and happy customers. (Berry has written the article that opens this yearbook.)

Sanders, Betsy. *Fabled Service: Ordinary Acts, Extraordinary Outcomes*, Erlanger, KY: Pfeiffer & Company, 1995.

A down-to-earth review and practical guide to offering great service.

Stamatis, D.H. *Total Quality Service: Principles, Practices, and Implementation*, Delray Beach, FL: St. Lucie Press, 1995.

Reviews in detail how to make a commitment to customer service a central part of organizational efforts and how to use quality principles to continuously improve service efforts.

Banking and Finance

Allen, Paul H. "Comment: Process Reengineering Can Put the Industry's House in Order," *The American Banker* (August 16, 1995): 15ff.

Argues that reengineering does reinvigorate bank personnel when they are allowed to make changes. Explains how this works, with process examples; a useful piece for the banking community to read.

Anonymous. "Bank's 'Quality' Effort Makes Sound Business Sense," *Health Manpower Management* 20, no. 4 (194): 21–22.

Describes the experience with TQM at American Express Bank after two years of effort. Defines progress and areas of expected improvement. It focuses on how this bank started from ground zero.

Anonymous. "The Bank That Likes Its Customers To Say 'Yes'," *Health Manpower Management* 20, no. 4 (1994): 23–24.

This is the case study of how TQM was implemented at TSB, the 6th largest bank in Great Britain, beginning in 1989. The objectives, strategies, and approaches implemented are described. The centerpiece of the effort was focusing on satisfying customers.

Dignan, Wyn. "Business Process Reengineering at the Cooperative Bank: Improving Personal Customer Service," *TQM Magazine* 7, no. 1 (1995): 42–45.

This is a case study of a bank that used reengineering methods to improve customer service. This is an important article; the case occurred in an industry slow to appreciate the value of customer-driven practices. It has specifics, including benefits; an excellent article.

Fullerton, Paul. "Customer Service," *Banking World* 13, no. 1 (January 1995): 22–25.

Describes customer service at the Yorkshire Bank in the U.K. It has grown market share by 5 percent in three years due to its customer service strategy, which is described in this article. Its strategy essentially is to build relationships with customers.

Harker, Patrick T. and Hunter, Larry W. "Engineering Products for Customer Value," *Bank Management* 71, no. 2 (March/April 1995): 52–57.

Argues that bankers talk about customer service, but their practices are far from reflecting that rhetoric. This is based on a study of bank practices of two business school professors. Yet found exceptions in banks willing to provide high-performance customer service.

Hotchkiss, D. Anne. "What Do Your Customers Really Think?" *Bank Marketing* 27, no. 3 (March 1995): 13–20.

Describes how to have customer-focused banking: customer retention, hiring the right people, and various customer-related policies. The article is prescriptive on what should be done.

Macdonald, John. "Quality and the Financial Service Sector," *Managing Service Quality* 5, no. 1 (1995): 43–46.

Reports on growing interest in TQM in the banking community but also wide variance on how people define it. Describes how a British arm of the Prudential Assurance Co., is applying it.

Morrall, Katharine. "Building the Bank on Total Quality Management," *Bank Marketing* 27, no. 3 (March 1995): 64–68.

Provides two case studies of how banks are beginning to apply quality management practices: what they are doing, the issues they are dealing with, and the role of management.

O'Keefe, Michele. "TQM: More Than Alphabet Soup," *Bank Systems and Technology* 32, no. 4 (April 1995): 68.

Calls on banks to take quality and TQM seriously by providing more customer-focused services. Provides an example of one that did: KeyCorp.

Distribution (Wholesale/Retail)

Mathews, Ryan. "Does Re-engineering Really Work?" *Progressive Grocer* 74, no. 2 (February 1995): 32–38.

Says the jury is still out. However, at Spartan Stores, Inc., expects to try it. Gives an explanation of expectations and about how TQM could apply in the grocery business.

Hotels

Anonymous. "Hyatt Focuses on Personalized Service That Set Itself Apart," *Travel Weekly* (January 19, 1995): 12.

Hyatt Key West Resort and Marina is a case study of a hotel making money with good customer service, which is described here. A variety of creative services are described.

Bond, Helen. "Frequent Guest Programs Build Loyalty," *Hotel & Motel Management* 210, no. 3 (February 20, 1995): 23, 25.

Frequent guest programs are now a sophisticated marketing effort. Describes how this customer retention strategy is being deployed and why it is effective.

Callan, Roger J. "Quality Assurance Certification for Hospitality Marketing, Sales and Customer Services," *Service Industries Journal* 14, no. 4 (October 1994): 482–498.

Quality assurance approaches should be extended to marketing and customer services. Discusses the extent to which quality practices have been applied in the hospitality industry. Marketing and sales represents the next logical step in the implementation of quality practices.

Insurance

Allio, Michael K. and Allio, Robert J. "Selective Insurance Corporation: Uniting Reengineering and Strategy," *Planning Review* (May/June 1995): 28–30, 45.

This is a case study of Selective Insurance's experience conducting process reengineering to drive business growth. Lessons learned: set strategy first, reengineer second; commit to leading and managing change, and be proactive by starting before the crisis hits.

Miller, Mike. "Customer Service Drives Reengineering Effort," *Personnel Journal* 73, no. 11 (November 1994): 87–91.

Describes reengineering at Metropolitan Property and Casualty Insurance Company begun around 1991. Began with how old and new policies were delivered to customers, then on aligning customer service and employee satisfaction, with details on employee surveys and other feedback mechanisms.

Transportation and Travel

Sullivan, David. "Benchmarking: Case Studies in Success," *NPN: National Petroleum News* 87, no. 2 (February 1995): 46.

Reports a benchmarking study of a chain of service stations of an oil company. This reports on a comprehensive analysis covering all aspects of this kind of retail operation. This describes an effective benchmarking effort.

Utilities

Fiksel, Joseph. "Metrics, Decisions, and Strategies: Environmental Performance Measurement in the Electric Utility Industry," *Total Quality Environmental Management* (Winter 1995): 63–70.

Describes how utilities and industrial companies can develop an environmental performance framework, integrate it into their strategic and operating business practices, and use it for evaluation of alternative environmental strategies.

Other Services

Ghosh, B.C. and Ling, Mak Tzi. "Total Quality Management in Services: The Case of Singapore's Advertising Industry," *TQM Magazine* 6, no. 4 (1994): 34–41.

Describes how to use TQM in advertising agencies in Singapore. Reports on how TQM can help in this industry.

Samborn, Hope Viner. "Total Quality Management," *Legal Assistant Today* 12, no. 2 (November/December 1994): 40–43.

Argues that paralegals are playing a growing role in the implementation of TQM in law offices because they understand the processes involved in running such a firm. Defines TQM as it exists in a law office environment.

PUBLIC SECTOR
Federal, State, and Local Government

Attaran, Mohsen and Fitzgerald, Heather D. "Implementing TQM in the Delivery of Government Contracted Healthcare," *Industrial Management* 37, no. 2 (March–April 1995): 9–14.

More than just about health care, this article is about the application of TQM in a government-regulated service environment. Argues that it can be adapted to public sector use.

Berman, Evan M. "Implementing TQM in State Welfare Agencies," *Administration in Social Work* 19, no. 1 (1995): 55–72.

This surveys how it is done across various government agencies; 30 state welfare agencies practice TQM, half began in 1991, and most are reporting successes. Applied most commonly in field operations, IT, income maintenance programs, and in AFDC programs. This is an important article.

Berman, Evan M. and West, Jonathan P. "Municipal Commitment to Total Quality Management: A Survey of Recent Progress," *Public Administration Review* 55, no. 1 (January/February 1995): 57–66.

Presents results of a survey sent to all city managers in cities of over 25,000 inhabitants concerning TQM. 11 percent of all the surveyed cities have made a substantial commitment to TQM. TQM appears most in police, parks and recreation, streets, and personnel services. Says it is too early to make any conclusions about results of TQM in municipalities.

Bruno, Gerard. *The Process Analyis Workbook for Government: How to Achieve More with Less,* Milwaukee: Quality Press, 1995.

This is intended to identify and eliminate waste and errors in paper-intensive processes. Defines a seven-step process to do this within a public sector environment. Also includes a substantial discussion of quality management principles.

Dobbs, Matti F. "Continuous Improvement as Continuous Implementation: Implementing TQM in the City of Santa Ana," *Public Productivity and Management Review* 18, no. 1 (Fall 1994): 89–100.

This is a case study of how a local government implemented TQM and lessons learned. The key was employee empowerment and worker satisfaction with collaboration among various departments. They focused on prevention of problems and measuring against goals. A wonderful case study!

Emison, Gerald A. "Total Quality Management and Strategic Change: The Pacific Northwest Experience," *Engineering Management Journal* 7, no. 2 (June 1995): 35–41.

Describes TQM activities in the Seattle, Washington office of the U.S. Environmental Protection Agency (EPA) over the previous four years.

Galloway, Robert A. "Quality Management in Police Services," *TQM Magazine* 6, no. 6 (1994): 4–8.

Using the example of the police department in Brighton, Colorado, the author looks at customer-oriented policing, arguing that this approach is viable.

Hunt, Michele. "Freeing the Spirit of Public Service in All of Us," *Public Productivity and Management Review* 18, no. 4 (Summer 1995): 397–406.

Argues that the public's expectations require U.S. government agencies to initiate fundamental changes in how they operate. The option of applying customer-focused strategies is no longer an option. Also lists why TQM commonly fails.

Hunt, Robert A. "On the Road to Quality, Watch Out for the Bumps," *Journal for Quality & Participation* 18, no. 1 (January/February 1995): 24–28.

Describes TQM at Incline Village General Improvement District where service problems were eliminated and performance improved practicing TQM.

Jenkins, Sarah, Noon, Mike, and Lucio, Miguel Martinez. "Negotiating Quality: The Case of TQM in Royal Mail," *Employee Relations* 17, no. 3 (1995): 87–98.

Describes the application of TQM in the British postal service, how it was done, and the results achieved.

Jones, Christopher R. and Hampton, Donald J.W. "Excellence in NZ Local Government," *Management Services* 39, no. 7 (July 1995): 22–25.

Describes some of the quality management practices in governments in New Zealand. Describes the work of one city council, based on the experiences they learned from the city of Madison, Wisconsin, USA.

Kaufman, Roger T. and Rusell, Raymond. "Government Support for Profit Sharing, Gainsharing, ESOPs, and TQM," *Contemporary Economic Policy* 13, no. 2 (April 1995): 38–48.

Relates that these programs increase productivity of employees but that they have not worked yet in government. Offers reasons for that circumstance so that failures of the past are not repeated by public officials.

Kelly, Laurel and Spina, Lori. "Total Quality Management and Organizational Change: The Martin County, Florida Model," *Assessment Journal* 2, no. 1 (January–February 1995): 28–31.

This is a case study, covering the implementation of TQM at the Property Appraiser's Office to improve service, reduce costs, and raise self-esteem of employees. Describes how these goals were achieved.

Kim, Pan S., Pindur, Wolfgang, and Reynolds, Keith. "Creating A New Organizational Culture: The Key to Total Quality Management in The Public Sector," *International Journal of Public Administration* 18, no. 4 (April 1995): 675–709.

Describes the kinds of organizational changes required in the public sector for TQM to work based on the experience of the private sector. Calls for fundamentally rethinking public administration's culture.

Levine, David I. and Helper, Susan. "A Quality Policy for America," *Contemporary Economic Policy* 13, no. 2 (April 1995): 26–37.

Describes the benefits of TQM and then argues it should be part of a national quality policy consisting of three parts: implementing TQM throughout the U.S. government, creating national certifications for employee quality skills, and creating nationally recognized supplier quality certifications.

Lowerre, Jim. "If At First You Don't Succeed," *Quality Progress* 27, no. 12 (December 1994): 51–54.

Discusses how TQM and Deming's 14 Points were applied at the U.S. Army Command and General Staff College's School of Corresponding Studies at Fort Leavenworth, Kansas. First round was Deming-based with presentations and that faded; second round was TQM and that worked.

Mahler, Julianne G. "Evolution of a Quality Management Program," *Public Productivity and Management Review* 18, no. 4 (Summer 1995): 387–396.

How TQM evolves is a function of how new organizational patterns evolve. Describes a public sector culture and how its evolution influenced the introduction and application of TQM.

Mani, Bonnie G. "Old Wine in New Bottles Tastes Better: A Case Study of TQM Implementation in the IRS," *Public Administration Review* 55, no. 2 (March–April 1995): 147–158.

Touts the success of the IRS applying TQM principles as relevant to other public administration agencies. It is a case study with positive results.

McGowan, Robert P. "Total Quality Management: Lessons from Business and Government," *Public Productivity and Management Review* 18, no. 4 (Summer 1995): 321–331.

Discusses how TQM was applied at a regional office of a large U.S. federal agency and at a large private firm, both involved in environmental management, comparing the two experiences. Draws some comparisons.

Nagel, James R. "TQM and the Pentagon," *Industrial Engineering* 26, no. 12 (December 1994): 57–59.

The U.S. military buys more than any other organization in the world, and its military systems are of the best quality. TQM and other quality-related programs and guidelines to insure this level of performance are critical. These are briefly described along with the Pentagon's overall quality strategy. It is a leader in this area.

Nyhan, Ronald C. and Marlowe Jr., Herbert A. "Performance Measurement in the Public Sector: Challenges and Opportunities," *Public Productivity and Management Review* 18, no. 4 (Summer 1995): 333–348.

TQM and performance measurements must be linked together, although measurements remain problematic in the public sector. Argues that TQM facilitates the implementation of such measures in the public sector.

Romancik, David J. "Partnership Toward Improvement," *Project Management Journal* 26, no. 2 (June 1995): 14–20.

Describes the TQM initiative called Program Oriented Contract Administration Services (PROCAS) used by the U.S. Defense Logistics Agency (DLA) for continuous improvement in relations with suppliers to the defense agencies.

Scheidt, Anthony and Amsler, Gordon M. "Military Pharmacy Looks to TQM to Satisfy Its Customers," *National Productivity Review* 14, no. 2 (Spring 1995): 47–56.

Presents a case study of a military pharmacy that was audited to see why customer complaints were high and to determine what to do differently. The case study focuses on how the study was done and recommendations for improvement were made.

Scully, John P. "How to Lead the Way to TQM," *National Productivity Review* 14, no. 2 (Spring 1995): 13–18.

This is a case study about the implementation of TQM at Management Operations Directorate (MOD), an organization supporting scientists and engineers at the Goddard Space Flight Center. This covers three years of experience.

Spencer, Michael S. and Loomba, Arvinder, P.S. "Uncovering Implementation Problems Keeps TQM on Track at Iowa's Department of Employment Services," *National Productivity Review* 14, no. 2 (Spring 1995): 37–46.

Describes how Iowa did an organizational assessment before beginning to implement TQM to determine attitudes of employees. Documented some frustrations due to a top-down approach to implementing TQM, rather than a bottoms-up strategy.

Williamson, Vicki and Schwarzkopf, A.B. "Total Quality Management in State Government," *Oklahoma Business Bulletin* 63, no. 3 (March 1995): 6–15.

This reports on the use of TQM in all 50 states of the United States. On how it all started, the answer was various: governor drove it, or legislature insisted on it while in some states it is driven centrally and in others on an agency-by-agency basis.

Health Care

Bellile, Susan K. "Benchmarking Sets Standards for Clinical Improvements," *Health Care Strategic Management* 13, no. 2 (February 1995): 15–16.

Discusses the benefits and actions taken when doing clinical benchmarking. Focuses on the definition of benchmarking.

Bender, A. Douglas and Krasnick, Carla J. "Total Quality Management: Lessons Learned from the

Medical Practice Environment," *Health Care Supervisor* 13, no. 4 (June 1995): 70–76.

Lessons concentrate on creating motivation and understanding the potential value of TQM, appreciating what are the barriers created by institutional and industry cultures, stating the operating principles of TQM, figuring out what tools to use, then allowing employees to try it.

Benneyan, James C. and Kaminsky, Frank C. "Another View on How to Measure Health Care Quality," *Quality Progress* 28, no. 2 (February 1995): 120–124.

Continues the debate in this journal about health care measurements. Discussion centers around the use of SPC methods in managing process variation.

Binsham Lin & Jennifer Clousing. "Total Quality Management in Health Care: A Survey of Current Practices," *Total Quality Management* 6, no. 1 (1995): 69–76.

Presents results of a survey of TQM practices in hospitals in northern Louisiana, USA. Nearly half have TQM programs. Concludes quality is still not the driving force in care of patients. TQM programs are not fully deployed while focusing on satisfying patients remains a goal yet to be achieved.

Counte, Michael A. et al. "Improving Hospital Performance: Issues In Assessing the Impact of TQM Activities," *Hospital & Health Services Administration* 40, no. 1 (Spring 1995): 80–94.

Says the jury is still out on whether TQM is making a difference in hospital administration. Suggests an approach by which a health care organization can define the kinds of benefits it could expect from the practice of TQM.

Dolan, Thomas C. "Supporting Continous Quality Improvement," *Healthcare Executive* 10, no. 4 (July–August 1995): 3.

Announces courses on the topic being taught by the American College of Healthcare Executives—a model of the kind of industry offerings should exist elsewhere as well.

Hutchison, Doug. "Chaos Theory, Complexity Theory, and Health Care Quality Management," *Quality Progress* 27, no. 11 (November 1994): 69–72.

Discusses the value of TQM in health accounting, use of SPC, application of chaos theory for some applications, and when to develop complexity theory-based processes. The article is very original in its thinking but focuses on processes.

Joss, Richard. "What Makes for Successful TQM in the NHS?" *International Journal of Health Care Quality Assurance* 7, no. 7 (1994): 4–9.

Reports the results of an evaluation of a British health organization, demonstrating that you can predict factors for successful implementation of TQM. For instance, success depends on making line management and staff responsible for continuous improvement results. Provides a methodology for determining customer requirements.

Kaldenberg, Dennis O. and Gobeli, David H. "Total Quality Management Practices and Business Outcomes: Evidence from Dental Practices," *Journal of Small Business Management* 33, no. 1 (January 1995): 21–33.

The theme is the relationship between organization outcomes and TQM, using the Baldrige criteria. Results of a survey suggest a strong correlation between the two using dental operations as the example.

Koumoutzis, Nick. "Make Behavioral Considerations Your First Priority in Quality Improvements," *Industrial Engineering* 26, no. 12 (December 1994): 63–65.

Argues that in their search to improve patient care, hospitals are turning to TQM. Describes what these means, e.g., patient centered and less efficiency dominant. Offers details on how this is being done today.

Meyer, John W. and Feingold, Moira G. "Integrating Financial Modeling and Patient Care Reengineering," *Healthcare Financial Management* 49, no. 2 (February 1995): 32–40.

To reduce costs and increase quality, many hospitals are reengineering patient care processes by employing standardization, with increased awareness by staff as to the financial implications of their day-to-day decisions while taking care of patients.

Pescod, W.D.T. "Effective Use of a Common Problem Solving Process as an Integral Part of TQM," *International Journal of Health Care Quality Assurance* 7, no. 7 (1994): 10–13.

Argues that having systems and ways to identify problems and solve them within organizations is crucial to the successful implementation of modern management practices (i.e., TQM). Problem-solving processes are critical to success.

Shaw, Diana V., Day, Denni O., and Slavinskas, Elizabeth. "Learning from Mistakes," *Quality Progress* 28, no. 6 (June 195): 45–48.

Using the University of Rochester Strong Memorial Hospital Medical Center, the authors describe how they have applied TQM over the previous several years. Emphasis was on enhancing problem-solving methods so that improvements could be made; results reported are very positive.

Sluyter, Gary V. and Barnette, John E. "Application of Total Quality Management to Mental Health: A Benchmark Case Study," *Journal of Mental Health Administration* 22, no. 3 (Summer 1995): 278–285.

Presents a case study of implementation of TQM in a mental health institution. The case is the Shawnee Hills Mental Health Center in Charleston, West Virginia, USA.

Swinehart, Kerry and Green, Ronald F. "Continuous Improvement and TQM in Health Care," *International Journal of Health Care Quality Assurance* 8, no. 1 (1995): 23–27.

Argues that the U.S. health industry is in deep crisis and that it needs to control costs and quality better. Suggests TQM can help and why. This is a tough message to an industry in trouble.

Van Court, Mari. "Redesign of a Credentialing Process," *Journal for Quality & Participation* 18, no. 1 (January/February 1995): 84–86.

The Joint Commission on Accreditation of Healthcare Organizations (JCAHO) requires credentialing hospitals every two years. The process for a hospital to go through that process is documented as applied at St. Joseph's Hospital and Healthcare Center at Tacoma, Washington.

Yank, G. "Quality Improvement in Health Care Organizations: A General Systems Perspective," *Behavioral Science* 40, no. 2 (April 1995): 85–103.

TQM methods require effective feedback regulations of key organizational performance parameters. Describes how quality practices can be effective in a hospital environment and uses the case of the University of Virginia's teaching hospital. This is a well-balanced, useful overview.

Education (K–12)

Anfuso, Dawn. "Intel Brings TQM to the Business of Education," *Personnel Journal* 74, no. 1 (January 1995): 77.

Describes how Intel taught TQM tools to a school district and to its students.

Arcaro, Janice. *Creating Quality in the Classroom*, Delray Beach, FL: St. Lucie Press, 1995.

Explains successful lesson plans and methods to bring about positive change in the classroom, outlined by a practicing teacher.

Arcaro, Jerome. *The Baldrige Award for Education: How to Measure and Document Quality Improvement*, Delray Beach, FL: St. Lucie Press, 1995.

This book explains how to use the Baldrige criteria to assess and improve educational systems.

Langford, David P. and Cleary, Barbara A. *Orchestrating Learning with Quality*. Milwaukee: Quality Press, 1995.

Discusses how educator and student can work together in a learning/classroom environment. Applies quality practices, such as understanding variation, schools as systems, quality and learning theory, and suggests a strategy. (See excerpt from this in the K–12 Education section of this edition of the yearbook.)

Smialek, Mary Ann. "Total Quality in K–12 Education," *Quality Progress* 28, no. 5 (May 1995): 69–72.

Says schools are about to change dramatically and that leaders in this industry must be ready to apply TQM practices. Quality practices will be the enablers to change in K–12 education.

Weller Jr., L. David. "Principals and Quality Performance: Getting in the Back Door," *TQM Magazine* 7, no. 1 (1995): 20–23.

Criticizes tactics used by schools to implement Deming's principals, tactics which are often dull and thus promoting failure. However, the author also reports that the process of seminars, roundtables, and discussion groups ultimately works in schools.

Higher Education

Anderson, Elizabeth. "High Tech. v. High Touch: A Case Study of TQM Implementation in Higher Education," *Managing Service Quality* 5, no. 2 (1995): 48–56.

This presents the experience with TQM at the University of Houston within the Business School, along with IT tools, such as SERVQUAL, to assess student perceptions of services.

Balderston, Frederick E. *Managing Today's University: Strategies for Viability, Change, and Excellence,* San Francisco: Jossey-Bass, 1995.

The original book was published in 1974 and subsequently became a minor classic, an early attempt to address, among many topics, the role of quality and excellence. This edition is a rewrite and thus is up-to-date, an extraordinarily important book for higher education executives.

Buch, Kimberly and Shelnutt, J. William. "UNC Charlotte Measures the Effects of Its Quality Initiative," *Quality Progress* 28, no. 7 (July 1995): 73–77.

The University of North Carolina at Charlotte has a quality program that is described in this article. Includes measures of progress.

Chen, Al Y.S. and Rodgers, Jacci L. "Teaching the Teachers TQM," *Management Accounting* 76, no. 11 (May 1995): 42–46.

Reports on the successful implementation of the University Challenge Program put together by several companies (IBM, Motorola, Proctor & Gamble) to encourage universities to apply, study, and teach TQM practices.

Denning, Peter J. and Medina Mora, Raul. "Completing the Loops," *Interfaces* 25, no. 3 (May–June 1995): 42–57.

Describes a method for mapping, measuring, tracking, and managing commitments in business processes as applied at George Mason University.

Ermer, Donald S. "Using QFD Becomes an Educational Experience for Students and Faculty," *Quality Progress* 28, no. 5 (May 1995): 131–136.

Defines QFD—a tool that uses customer input in design of products—and then how students used it in three projects within the Mechanical Engineering Department at the University of Wisconsin at Madison. Results are also presented.

Fram, Eugene H. and Camp, Robert C. "Finding and Implementing Best Practices in Higher Education," *Quality Progress* 28, no. 2 (February 1995): 69–73.

Describes a benchmarking model that colleges and universities can use; an excellent overview of what high education executives will have to do.

Mihaly, Mary. "Arthur Taylor: Taking TQM To School," *Industry Week* 244, no. 5 (March 6, 1995): 48–54.

Describes his work at president of Muhlenburg College where for years he has taught and implemented TQM

principles. This is an important case study of successful implementation of TQM in higher education. (Reproduced in this edition of the yearbook.)

Queeney, Donna S. *Assessing Needs in Continuing Education.* San Francisco: Jossey-Bass, 1995.

Although intended for a corporate audience, this really needs to be read by continuing education executives in higher education because it provides a detailed approach on how to assess how a company can identify what training its people need and, hence, what higher education can provide.

Schonberger, Richard J. "TQM: What's in It for Academics?" *Business Horizons* 38, no. 1 (January/February 1995): 67–70.

Explains why TQM should be used in academia, even though it barely is today. Describes where higher education is using TQM: marketing, business policy and strategy, accounting and auditing, organizational behavior, information systems, and engineering. (Reproduced in this edition of the yearbook.)

Walker, H. Fred. "Texas Instruments' and Iowa State University's Experience with the University Challenge Program," *Quality Progress* 28, no. 7 (July 1995): 103–106.

This is an update of the initial startup of implementing quality practices at ISU. Reports some faculty resistance to TQM as applied to teaching. ISU is using the Baldrige Criteria tailored to higher education.

Wambsganss, Jacob R. and Kennett, Danny. "Defining the Customer," *Management Accounting* 76, no. 11 (May 1995): 39–41.

Universities should think of future employers, not students, as their customers. Admonishes the accounting departments of universities to do this, applying TQM. Briefly suggests how this would play out. (Reproduced in this edition of the yearbook.)

Nonprofit Associations

Pappas, Alceste T. *Reengineering Your Nonprofit Organization.* New York: John Wiley & Sons, 1995.

This is the first book published on quality and reengineering of nonprofits. This takes proven business practices and makes them applicable in this environment; an important book, should become the guidebook for nonprofit executives.

QUALITY TRANSFORMATION
Leadership

Griffiths, David. *Management in a Quality Environment.* Milwaukee: Quality Press, 1995.

Discusses how a manager can operate in quality-focused organizations: philosophy and attitude, tasks, working in cross-functional situations, coordinating, coaching role, personal practices, and many other issues.

Groth, John C. "Total Quality Management: Perspectives for Leaders," *TQM Magazine* 7, no. 3 (1995): 54–59.

A clear vision becomes the basis for goal setting. Need a clearly stated TQM philosophy too. TQM efficiency can increase as guidelines for implementation are laid out.

Kouzes, James M. and Posner, Barry Z. *The Leadership Challenge*, San Francisco: Jossey-Bass, 1995.

A revision of a leading title on leadership, it offers a broader scope of leaders in every industry and walk of life, including education and nonprofit. Includes lots of anecdotes to back up the authors' conclusions.

Main, M. Jeremy. "Fixing the CEO's Quality Vision," *Executive Excellence* 12, no. 7 (July 1995): 8.

Implementing TQM forces CEOs to rethink many issues; therefore, it is tough going. Boils down to the CEO making his or her TQM vision part of the corporate culture.

McHale, Hank. *Actual Experiences of a CEO: How to Make Continuous Improvement in Manufacturing Succeed for Your Company.* Milwaukee: ASQC Quality Press, 1995.

This is the first book written by a CEO on the subject and includes a great deal on leadership, not just about TQM in manufacturing.

Mears, Peter and Voehl, Frank. *The Executive Guide to Implementing Quality Systems*, Delray Beach, FL: St. Lucie Press, 1995.

As its title says, this provides a step-by-step approach to establish and carry through the implementation of quality management practices in any organization.

Powell, James Lawrence. *Pathways to Leadership: How to Achieve and Sustain Success*, San Francisco: Jossey-Bass, 1995.

Aimed at nonprofit executives, this book offers tips for becoming a successful nonprofit leader.

Pritchett, Lou. *Stop Paddling & Start Rocking the Boat*, New York: HarperBusiness, 1995.

Pritchett is the former VP of sales for Procter & Gamble who set up the partnership between P&G and Wal-Mart. This book is all about partnering to the benefit of both partners. Includes many, many stories from the author's 36 years with P&G.

Shapiro, Eileen C. *Fad Surfing in the Boardroom*, Reading, MA: Addison-Wesley, 1995.

American businesses are always looking for the latest "right answer." This book looks at several of the management "fads" of the past few years and explains how, whenever we ignore the fundamentals and look for panaceas, we set ourselves up for failure. The idea of management insights, such as TQM, as being fads rather than insights, is symptomatic of the superficiality of management in many organizations.

Tippett, Donald D. and Waits, David A. "Project Management and TQM: Why Aren't Project Managers Coming on Board?" *Industrial Management* 36, no. 5 (September/October 1994): 12–15.

Reports result of a study indicating 70% of large U.S. companies use TQM; 33% report positive results. Upper management, however, continues to be focused just on cost, schedule, and performance, thus project managers have to also. This narrow focus leaves out many other ways of looking at success (e.g., feedback from processes).

Yates, Ronald. "Total Quality Leadership," *Vital Speeches of the Day* 61, no. 7 (January 15, 1995): 211–213.

Argues the case for executive leadership beginning with establishing a vision for the enterprise and how that relates to the quality practices of the firm. Visions build involvement and commitment on the part of employees for the corporate game plan.

Zairi, Mohamed. "Leadership in TQM Implementation," *TQM Magazine* 6, no. 6 (1994): 9–16.

Reviews the literature on leadership and management within a TQM environment. Identifies key ingredients for effective quality leadership; a nice introduction to the topic.

Cultural Transformation

Bickham, William. *Liberating the Human Spirit in the Workplace*, Burr Ridge, IL: Irwin Professional Publishing, 1995.

Using lots of vignettes, the author shows readers how to take full advantage of their own human capabilities to unlock their own creativity and that of other employees to the benefit of the company and all stakeholders.

Bolman, Lee G. and Deal, Terrence E. *Leading with Soul: An Uncommon Journey of the Spirit*, San Francisco: Jossey-Bass, 1995.

A kind of parable or story that conveys several lessons on leading transformation.

Brooke, Carole. "Information Technology and the Quality Gap," *Employee Relations* 16, no. 4 (1994): 22–34.

This is a case study of what happened to 30 programmers within an IT organization when a gap formed between espoused philosophy and TQM implementation techniques. Failed to be personable enough; an excellent case study on the value of paying attention to cultural and personnel issues and not just focusing on reengineering processes.

Carr, David K., et al. *Managing the Change Process: A Fieldbook for Change Agents, Team Leaders, and Reengineering Managers*, New York: McGraw-Hill, 1995.

A practical review of strategies and techniques for proactively facilitating change in today's organizations.

Edosomwan, Johnson A. *Organizational Transformation and Process Reengineering*, Delray Beach, FL: St. Lucie Press, 1995.

Claims to cover all aspects of reengineering, use of IT, and cultural change. It is the authors' own methodology for organizational change, offering useful models, tools, and some methodologies, some new and others familiar.

Gouillart, Francis J. and Kelly, James N. *Transforming the Organization*, New York: McGraw-Hill, 1995.

This book explains the organization as a biological system, a useful metaphor for understanding how to facilitate the success of the entire organization: employees, customers, suppliers, and all stakeholders. (An excerpt from this book is included in this yearbook.)

Gull, Gregory A. "In Search of TQM Success," *Executive Excellence* 12, no. 7 (July 1995): 17–18.

Root cause of failure of TQM is frequently due to a lack of understanding that is then reflected in bad implementation. Argues the case for incremental improvement in the implementation process in an organization continuously changing. Adapting to quality principles is key to corporate success.

Handfield, Robert and Ghosh, Soumen. "Creating a Quality Culture through Organizational Change: A Case Analysis," *Journal of International Marketing* 2, no. 3 (1994): 7–36.

Provides an overview of what is quality management, using case studies of 13 North American and European companies. Results: those first with TQM had significant competitive advantage over rivals.

Galbraith, Jay R. *Designing Organizations*. San Francisco: Jossey-Bass, 1995.

Describes how to design effective organizations working with forces that influence organizations: buyer power, variety, change, and speed. Emphasis is on developing institutions that are customer focused.

Haines, Stephen. *Sustaining High Performance: The Strategic Transformation to a Customer-Focused Learning Organization*. Delray Beach, FL: St. Lucie Press, 1995.

Divided into four parts: re-inventing strategic management, developing a strategic plan, mastering strategic change, and getting started; it is written by a strategic planning expert.

Higginson, Thomas and Waxler, Robert P. "Communication, Commitment and Corporate Culture: The Foundation for TQM and Reengineering," *Industrial Management* 36, no. 6 (November/December 1994): 4–7.

Argues the case for communication, leadership, teamwork, training, and corporate culture all being components of successful implementation of TQM. They emphasize cultural issues and the value of effective communications with employees.

Kotter, John P. "Leading Change: Why Transformation Efforts Fail," *Harvard Business Review* 73, no. 2 (March–April 1995): 59–67.

All the various forms of change, e.g., TQM, reengineering, and right sizing, collectively have tended to be less successful. Conclusions: can't skip steps, it takes a long time and second, a critical mistake along the way can be devastating to the entire process.

Long, Carl and Vickers Koch, Mary. "Is It Process Management and, with or Instead of TQM?" *Jour-*

nal for Quality and Participation 18, no. 3 (June 1995): 70–74.

Argues that process management must embrace innovation and improvement of strategic level processes, not just daily operational ones. Provides a list of keys of successful application.

McArthur, C. Dan and Womack, Larry. *Outcome Management: Redesigning Your Business Systems to Achieve Your Vision*, New York: AMACOM, 1995.

A sleeper, but a well-done book that includes lots of practical advice for making vision a reality. A good explanation of the idea of an organization and why this is important.

Marquardt, Michael. *Building the Learning Organization*, New York: McGraw-Hill, 1995.

Designed for trainers to help them help organizations transform themselves into learning organizations. (See Nevis article in the systems thinking/learning organizations section of the yearbook for more on this idea.)

McNabb, David E. and Sepic, F. Thomas. "Culture, Climate, and Total Quality Management: Measuring Readiness for Change," *Public Productivity and Management Review* 18, no. 4 (Summer 1995): 369–385.

Describes results of a study done in a U.S. federal agency concerning organizational culture, operating climate, and organizational policies as they effected TQM.

Milakovich, Michael E. *Improving Service Quality: Achieving High Performance in the Public and Private Sectors.* Delray Beach, FL: St. Lucie Press, 1995.

This is a general guide to the discussion of how to change organizations, especially in the public sector and with a health industry view too. Comments on how to do this in nonprofits, utilities, and insurance companies.

O'Toole, James. *Leading Change: Overcoming the Ideology of Comfort and the Tyranny of Custom.* San Francisco: Jossey-Bass, 1995.

Describes how management can adopt moral strategy and earn the trust of employees in order to guide an empowered workforce.

Randall, Robert M. "How to Reshape Your Busines to Fit the Future," *Planning Review* (January/February 1995): 6–11, 45–46.

This is an interview with Gary Hamel, co-author of *Competing for the Future.* He urges management to seek breakthrough strategies for creating markets for to-

morow. Provides descriptions of how such companies function and what their cultures are like.

Revenaugh, D. Lance. "Implementing Major Organizational Change: Can We Really Do It?" *TQM Magazine* 6, no. 6 (1994): 38–48.

Describes why BPR projects fail, using two models to illustrate the issues involved. Emphasis on strategic and cultural issues that must be taken into account.

Sohal, Amrik and Morrsion, Michael. "Is There a Link Between Total Quality Management and Learning Organizations?" *TQM Magazine* 7, no. 3 (1995): 41–44.

Measures activities in 3 TQM-oriented organizations with some standard building blocks for calculating if an organization is a learning one or not. Concludes that TQM tends to make it possible for an organization to become and operate as a learning one.

Customer Focus

Brecka, Jon. "Quality Executives See Rising Customer Expecations, *Quality Progress* 28, no. 5 (May 1995): 18.

Reports results of a survey of quality executives, 93 percent of whom said their customers will have higher expectations of their suppliers over the next three years. The message is get ready by improving your own quality of goods and services.

Brown, Stanley A. *What Customers Value Most*, New York: John Wiley & Sons, 1995.

This is a practical guide on what to reengineer concerning customers, covering all aspects of relations with customers; excellent and practical.

Brown, Stanley A. "You Can Get Satisfaction," *Sales and Marketing Management* 147, no. 7 (July 1995): 106–107.

Describes how AMP Inc. looked at customer satisfaction for guidance on what to reengineer within the company. Describes their effective customer feedback process.

Carpenter, Phil. "Customer Lifetime Value: Do the Math," *Marketing Computers* 15, no. 1 (January 1995): 18–19.

Describes how to take a quantitative view of the value of a customer. Actually takes you through the math. Then he takes you through a case study of this method being applied by Jandel Scientific. This is an outstanding piece that should be read!

deJong, Jennifer. "Turbocharging Customer Service," *Inc.* 17, no. 9 (1995): 35–39.

Describes how Stoneyfield Farm Inc., solicits and tracks customer opinions concerning its yogurt. Cites other similar cases of rigorous customer feedback processes and their benefits to the firms that do this.

Jamieson, David. "Customer Retention: Focus or Failure," *TQM Magazine* 6, no. 5 (1994): 11–13. Describes how to focus attention on their needs and wants and what topics to focus on (e.g., service levels, competition, priorities for improvements, etc.). Complains that many companies are still not doing this right.

Lapidus, Richard S. and Schibrowsky, John A. "Aggregate Complaint Analysis: A Procedure for Developing Customer Service Satisfaction," *Journal of Services Marketing* 8, no. 4 (1994): 50–60. Outlines a defensive marketing strategy that deploys use of complaint analysis and the House of Quality as used in quality function deployment (QFD). This is a fascinating and original way of combining two sources of information to understand better common customer complaints and to understand various combinations of service attributes.

LeNoble, Philip Jay. "What Price Will Client Pay for Service?" *Marketing News* 29, no. 15 (July 17, 1995): 4. Does not answer the question! However, it has been asked frequently and, although this article does not answer the question, other studies suggest it is up to 5 percent more for comparable products or services.

Lowenstein, Michael W. *Customer Retention: An Integrated Process for Keeping Your Best Customers.* Milwaukee: Quality Press, 1995. Compares retention with satisfaction strategies, arguing the case for customer retention approaches being more effective. This short book then details how to implement such approaches.

Naumann, Earl. *Creating Customer Value: The Path to Sustainable Competitive Advantage.* Cincinnati, OH: Thomson Executive Press, 1995. This is a practical presentation of an approach an organization can use to improve and pressure customer satisfaction. Includes diagnostic steps based on the Baldrige criteria and includes case studies.

Ovenden, Anthony. "Keep Your Customers Happy and Your Competition Will Slowly Fade Away," *TQM Magazine* 7, no. 1 (1995): 46–49. This is a convenient summary of the business philosophy of taking care of customers, with examples of key processes: complaints, polling customer attitudes, and providing quality services.

Ridley, Jeffrey. "Does Quality Control Services?" *TQM Magazine* 6, no. 6 (1994): 17–18. Discusses the importance of quality in a marketplace controller, then focuses on the issue of the extent to which service providers adequately measure their performance. Discusses future trends.

Royal, Weld F. "Cashing in on Complaints," *Sales and Marketing Management* 147, no. 5 (May 1995): 86–92. Reports on how to use an effective customer complaint process to retain business and build customer loyalty; a nice summary of the process.

Spreng, Richard A., Harrell, Gilbert D., and Mackoy, Robert D. "Service Recovery: Impact on Satisfaction and Intentions," *Journal of Services Marketing* 9, no. 1 (1995): 15–22. This is one of the first wide-spread studies that validates the importance of recovering well from a problem with a customer to insure the customer's continued loyalty. Findings included: interaction with claims personnel is more influential on customer satisfaction than the problem (damage) itself. Good recovery leads to positive relations with customers.

Toombs, Ken and Bailey, George. "How to Redesign Your Organization to Match Customer Needs," *Managing Service Quality* 5, no. 3 (1995): 52–56. Explains how marketing data on what customers value is being used by companies to redesign their organizations. Conjoint and focus groups are two popular techniques for getting to information about what customers value. Many comments are presented on what customers value.

Quality Implementation Strategies and Planning

Ahire, Sanjay L. and Rana, Dharam S. "Selection of TQM Pilot Projects Using an MCDM Approach," *International Journal of Quality and Reliability Management* 12, no. 1 (1995): 61–81. Argues that since selecting the right pilots early in the implementation stages of using TQM is important, a methodology would be useful. Introduces a pilot selection process called the multiple criteria decision making (MCDM) model, with a hospital case study.

Anonymous. "TQM: The Experiences of Ten Small Businesses," *Business Horizons* (January 1995): 71.

Tells how 10 small companies successfully implemented TQM.

Aubrey, Robert and Cohen, Paul M. *Working Wisdom: Timeless Skills and Vanguard Strategies for Learning Organizations.* San Francisco: Jossey-Bass, 1995.

Describes five mentoring skills that make it possible for organizations to improve.

Buhler, Patricia. "The Quality Journey: A Road Worth Traveling," *Supervision* 56, no. 3 (March 1995): 24–26.

States the importance of good communications as part of the process of implementing quality practices. First, communicate the benefits; second, have management build a vision; third, expose everyone continuously to the concepts involved.

Cook, E. and Dale, B.G. "Organizing for Continuous Improvement: An Examination," *TQM Magazine* 7, no. 1 (1995): 7–13.

Reports on a study of six organizations about what they did to organize for quality improvements. Key was the use of a TQM Steering Committee and improvement facilitators, both organized in ways that changed over time. As people took responsibility for improving their work, a quality support structure became less critical for success.

Corrigan, James P. "The Art of TQM," *Quality Progress* 28, no. 7 (July 1995): 61–64.

Describes why TQM sometimes fails: lacks constancy of purpose, lacks adequate leadership, lacks failure to pilot improvement teams. Places strong emphasis on executive leadership to make TQM work.

Covey, Stephen R. "Quality Relationships," *Executive Excellence* 12, no. 7 (July 1995): 20.

Argues the case for a total approach to TQM implementation involving relationships of trust and empowered people to move from inspection to prevention. Calls quality a new style of working.

Dawson, Patrick. "Implementing Quality Management: Some General Lessons on Managing Change," *Asia Pacific Journal of Quality Management* 4, no. 1 (1995): 35–46.

Advocates a processual strategy for implementing TQM. Lessons: there is no one best way, accept TQM blues, don't go overboard on measurements, don't try to do everything at once, train people just in time, tailor your programs to your needs, and seek support everywhere. This is a good article.

Dawson, Patrick. "Quality Management: Beyond the Japanese Model," *International Journal of Quality and Reliability Management* 11, no. 7 (1994): 51–59.

Argues that the Japanese model for quality management may not apply as effectively in Australia as in Asia. Uses a case study involving the Pirelli Cables to make his point.

Ehresman, Terry. *Small Business Success Through TQM: Practical Methods to Improve Your Organization's Performance.* Milwaukee: Quality Press, 1995.

Emphasizes how to train employees about TQM, then discusses how to implement TQM in a company. It is high level yet specific enough to be actionable.

Early, John F. and Godfrey, A. Blanton. "But It Takes Too Long . . .," *Quality Progress* 28, no. 7 (July 1995): 51–55.

TQM requires a complete transformation of a corporate culture and reducing the time it takes to do things is the way to get results. Reports on a study done by the Juran Institute to look at the causes of delay. Time wasters included spending only part-time on projects, executives who delay confronting resistance to change, vague mission, not sticking with the vital few, too much flow diagramming, poor training, premature reaching conclusions, and poor implementation. This is an important article.

Feinberg, Samuel. "Overcoming the Real Issues of Implementation," *Quality Progress* 28, no. 7 (July 1995): 79–81.

GEC Plesey Semiconductors based its TQM on customers, teamwork, and improvement. Describes measures of each (e.g., number of active and completed team, savings from team projects, etc.). This is a well-done tactical approach to understanding the progress of TQM.

Foster, Morris, Smith, Start, and Whittle, Susan. "Reengineering Your TQM Effort: What to Do When It Runs Out of Steam?" *TQM Magazine* 6, no. 4 (1994): 42–47.

Study results in an attempt to answer this question are reported. Typically problem programs have changed implementation approaches more than once. Four TQM approaches were identified: planning mindset, learning mindset, visionary mindset, and transformation mindset. Each are described.

Godfrey, A. Blanton. "10 Quality Trends," *Executive Excellence* 12, no. 7 (July 1995): 10–11.

Presents 10 trends: expansion of TQM concepts, quality improvement at revolutionary pace, partnering, training for all, self-directing workteams, I/T for quality, process management and reengineering, customer focus, benchmarking, strategic quality management.

Harvey, Tom. "Service Quality: The Culprit and the Cure," *Bank Marketing* 27, no. 6 (June 1995): 24–28.

Begin by understanding the organization's commitment to service quality, and why—due to cultural barriers—then suggests that banks conduct surveys to measure customer wants and attitudes. Gaps between views and services is what gets fixed.

Kaye, Michael M. and Dyason, Marilyn D. "The Fifth Era," *TQM Magazine* 7, no. 1 (1995): 33–37.

Presents results of research in 13 organizations about why they fail to evolve their quality practices over time to better forms, e.g., to strategic quality management. Presents an organizational profile and key characteristics against which other organizations can judge themselves.

Lund, Klaus and Thomsen, Claus. "How to Sustain the Total Quality Management Process after the First 12 Months," *TQM Magazine* 6, no. 5 (1994): 47–49.

Describes 11 things that can be done based on the experience of these authors over 8 years. The steps are the ones other articles and companies have reported as being successful; useful introduction to implementation issues.

Mann, Robin and Kehoe, Dennis. "Factors Affecting the Implementation and Success of TQM," *International Journal of Quality and Reliability Management* 12, no. 1 (1995):11–23.

Presents the results of a survey of some 200 companies to identify the key factors affecting implementation of TQM. These are: process factors, types of employees, shared values, management style, organizational structure, number of employees, and industrial relations. Best practices here involves considering all seven when developing a TQM implementation plan.

Mohrman, Susan Albers et al. "Total Quality Management: Practice and Outcomes in the Largest U.S. Firms," *Employee Relations* 17, no. 3 (1995): 26–41.

Presents the results of a survey of some 1,000 firms concerning TQM practices. Companies reported benefits in three areas: work performance, competitiveness and profitability, and employee outcomes.

Rice, Judy C. "U.S. Business: Guilty As Charged," *National Productivity Review* 14, no. 1 (Winter 1994/1995): 1–8.

Critical of how management has implemented TQM but then discusses the need for total transformation. Then describes the attributes of a dedicated TQM manager and what he/she does.

Roehm, Harper A., Klein, Donal, and Castellano, Joseph F. "Blending Quality Theories for Continuous Improvement," *Management Accounting* (February 1995): 26–32.

This is a case study of how Grand Rapids Spring & Wire Products combines quality concepts from various gurus to create a profitable competitive business. Includes action plans, process work, key indicators of success, leading to a learning organization.

Shadur, Mark A. "Total Quality: Systems Survive, Culture Changes," *Long Range Planning* 28, no. 2 (April 1995): 115–125.

Offers two Australian case studies of implementation, one an automobile manufacturing operation, the other an airline. He concludes that setting up standards of performance should come first, cultural changes can follow second.

Shea, John and Gobeli, David. "TQM: The Experiences of Ten Small Businesses," *Business Horizons* 38, no. 1 (January/February 1995): 71–77.

Presents what is going on with TQM in 10 businesses with less than 50 employees each. Validates that TQM does add value in this size organization.

Troy, Kathryn and Schein, Lawrence. "The Quality Culture: Manufacturing versus Services," *Managing Service Quality* 5, no. 3 (1995): 45–47.

A Conference Board survey suggests it takes 3 to 4 years for TQM to be accepted by employees and 8 to 10 for it to be fully implemented. Compares and contrasts implementation in manufacturing and service organizations.

Westbrook, Jerry D. and Utley, Dawn R. "TQM: The Effect of Culture on Implementation," *Engineering Management Journal* 7, no. 2 (June 1995): 31–34.

Looks at the factors that influence the implementation of TQM. Offers six attributes of TQM, e.g., customer focus, continuous improvement, etc. Offers the results of assessments done in various organizations.

Communication

Quirke, Bill. *Communicating Change.* London: McGraw-Hill, 1995.

This is a detailed description of the role of communications in an organization. It describes the processes involved, how they are deployed and includes examples. This book also has a short bibliography on the topic.

Training

Harshman, Carl and Phillips, Steve. *Team Training: From Startup to High Performance,* New York: McGraw-Hill, 1995.

Lots of information and lesson plans to use training to turn a traditional hierarchically based department to one where teams and teamwork prevail.

Mendosa, Rick. "Is There a Payoff?" *Sales and Marketing Management* 147, no. 6 (June 1995): 64–71.

Argues that it is important to measure the effects of training on the bottom line. Presents criteria used by such companies as AT&T, R.R. Donnelley, and Microsoft to understand the value of training.

Niehoff, Brian P. and Whitney-Bammerlin, Donita L. "Don't Let Your Training Process Derail Your Journey to Total Quality Management," *SAM Advanced Management Journal* 60, no. 1 (Winter 1995): 39–45.

Blames bad training as one reason why TQM sometimes fails. Proposes that companies use Bloom's 1956 taxonomy to insure courses are on track to produce results. Describes this approach, one of 6 levels of skills, and how to use it.

Quakkelaar, Arnold J. "Tools for Success," *Total Quality Review* 5, no. 2, May/June 1995.

A review of on-site competency-based training programs that allow individuals to take charge of their own training.

Szekely, Peter. "Investing in Workers Ups Company Profits Study," *Reuters,* June 5, 1995.

This is the first comprehensive study conducted on the effects of innovative workplace practices on the bottom line. It was published by the U.S. Labor Department. This article describes this very important study. It strongly defends the value of investing in employee training by the nation and companies. The study also found that 85 percent of the Fortune 1000 companies use TQM.

Tunis, Cyril J. "Linking Capability 97 to Our Business," *Training and Development* 49, no. 2 (February 1995): 26–28.

Describes how employees are trained at Pacific Bell, describing its seven-step process that insures linkage between training and business results. Used TQM tools to build skills.

Around the World

Anonymous. "Beyond ISO: European Chemical Manufactures Are Increasingly Seeing the ISO Process as Only the First Step Toward Improvement," *Chemical Marketing Reporter* (April 10, 1995): 18ff.

Argues that ISO certification has helped West European chemical companies be profitable and that they are now expanding on that initial wave of certification to improve operations even further. Also discusses the role of the British BS 7750 quality standards. Includes quotes and case studies; is very specific.

Barker, Brendan (ed). *Quality Promotion in Europe.* Brookfield, VT: Gower Publishing Co., 1994.

This is an excellent and detailed look at what is going on with quality in the twelve member nations of the European Union. In each chapter there is a discussion of the origin of quality practices, how they are organized to do it, major issues and programs.

Chang, Pao Long and Lu, Kuen Horng. "Current Status of Total Quality Management Implementation in Taiwan Companies," *TQM Magazine* 7, no. 1 (1995): 14–19.

Presents an overview of local TQM practices, citing eight practices and pointing out the extraordinary role of training and inspection that takes place.

Lam, Simon S.K. "Total Quality Management Programs and Job Satisfaction in Hong Kong," *International Journal of Management* 12, no. 1 (March 1995): 96–101.

A survey was done of 221 front liner supervisors concerning their satisfaction working in a TQM environment. TQM caused their work to become more complicated, required greater skill and accuracy, and did not make their jobs more interesting or important. TQM did not improve their pay or promotion rates.

McKenna, Steve. "The Cultural Transferability of Business and Organization Reengineering: Examples from Southeast Asia," *TQM Magazine* 7, no. 3 (1995): 12–16.

Looks at how effective reengineering works in two organizations, one in Thailand the other in Singapore. Concludes that it is impossible to introduce in a non-western culture as proposed by Champy and Hammer.

Redman, Tom, Snape, Ed, and Wilinson, Adrian. "Is Quality Management Working in the UK?" *Journal of General Management* 20, no. 3 (Spring 1995): 44–59.

Presents survey material suggesting that TQM is relatively healthy in the UK but that there were also concerns about implementation and results. It is more widespread in manufacturing and production industries and less so in the service sector, in large rather than smaller companies, and in private rather than publicly held companies. Foreign companies practiced it more than British firms.

QUALITY TOOLS AND TECHNIQUES
Concepts

Bemowski, John. "TQM: Flimsy Footing of Firm Foundation?" *Quality Progress* 28, no. 7 (July 1995): 27–28.

Reports on 13 papers sent to his journal defending or attacking TQM. Bottom line report from these papers: yes there are problems with TQM but it is worthy of defending. It is a firm foundation.

Choppin, Jon. "Total Quality Management: What Isn't It?" *Managing Service Quality* 5, no. 1 (1995): 47–49.

Success with TQM is linked to developing a strategy for implementation that fits your organization. Thus one might focus on teamwork, another organization on customer satisfaction, etc. Defines what TQM is.

Cusins, Peter. "Understanding Quality Through Systems Thinking," *TQM Magazine* 6, no. 5 (1994): 19–27.

Presents systems theory followed by quality management applications. This is a useful introduction to systems thinking and theory in a business context (e.g., as applied to organizations, people, quality, processes, etc.).

Dobbins, Richard D. "A Failure of Methods, Not Philosophy," *Quality Progress* 28, no. 7 (July 1995): 31–33.

Defines TQM's purposes then argues that the debate over success and failure is confusing. Reports successful implementations are the result of a variety of approaches. Senior management must be committed and continuous improvement a way of life.

Drummond, Helga. "Beyond Quality," *Journal of General Management* 20, no. 4 (Summer 1995): 68–77.

Argues that TQM is the apotheosis of scientific management *a la* F.W. Taylor's management precepts.

Evans, Rob. "In Defense of TQM," *TQM Magazine* 7, no. 1 (1995): 5–6.

Discusses widely held misconceptions of TQM, e.g., it is not everything you need to run a business, nor is it part of BS 5750, and cites a Harvard study that says TQM used with other management practices leads to success.

Hackman, J. Richard and Wageman, Ruth. "Total Quality Management: Empirical, Conceptual, and Practical Issues," *Administrative Science Quarterly* 40, no. 2 (June 1995): 309–342.

Assesses coherence, distinctiveness and likely perseverance of TQM as a new management movement.

Lakhe, R.R. and Mohanty, R.P. "Total Quality Management: Concepts, Evolution, and Acceptability in Developing Economies," *International Journal of Quality and Reliability Management* 1, no. 9 (1994): 9–33.

The value of this article is less because it announces that TQM is being accepted around the world but more because it offers a useful account of how quality practices have evolved over time. It also offers a nice overview of the basic concepts of quality management.

Latzko, William J. and Saunders, David M. *Four Days with Dr. Deming: A Strategy for Modern Methods of Management.* Reading, MA: Addison-Wesley, 1995.

This is a useful review of Deming's famous four day course plus quotes from him and other material that introduces the reader to his ideas in a thorough manner.

McConnell, Charles R. "Total Quality and the Shifting Management Paradigm," *Health Care Supervisor* 13, no. 3 (March 1995): 71–79.

Concepts behind TQM have been around, and each time they fail they come back in an organization and do better than the previous occasion. This increasing rate of success is due to changes in management attitudes and roles.

Sanderson, Michael. "Future Developments in Total Quality Management: What Can We Learn from the Past?" *TQM Magazine* 7, no. 3 (1995): 28–31.

Offers a brief history of quality, driven over time by competition from ancient times to the present. Offers a four-part model of TQM drawn from history.

Voehl, Frank et al. *Deming: The Way We Knew Him,* Delray Beach, FL: St. Lucie Press, 1995.

This summarizes his 14 Points, with each of his points written about by a key expert on Deming, e.g., Mary

Walton, Myron Tribus, and others with personal stories about him; fascinating.

Benchmarking

Boone, Louis E. and Wilkins, Dianne. "The Role of Benchmarking in Total Quality Management," *International Journal of Management* 12, no. 1 (March 1995): 123–131.

Once an organization has a unity of purpose, benchmarking becomes a useful tool. It can facilitate customer focus and sound management practices while improving overall quality practices.

Harrington, H. James, and Harrington, James S. *Benchmarking Implementation Guide*, New York: McGraw-Hill, 1996.

This guide covers the full spectrum of industries and activities: products, services, processes, equipment, and benchmarking. The book includes a five-phase structure that has worked for many prominent companies.

Mentzer, John T., Bienstock, Carol C., and Kahn, Kenneth B. "Benchmarking Satisfaction," *Marketing Management* 4, no. 1 (Summer 1995): 40–46.

Looks at customer satisfaction measurements and practices in 124 firms. That is the basis for defining who were the market leaders; common patterns of leaders emerged. They include: sales and marketing designs the customer feedback questions, top management and marketing support feedback processes, qualitative and quantitative measurements are deployed, evaluation of these data is done, and customer satisfaction is woven in the company's strategies.

Russell, J.P. *Quality Management Benchmark Assesment*. Milwaukee: ASQC Quality Press, 1995.

Russell fills in a relatively new gap in the benchmarking literature by presenting one of the first books to assess quality management as a benchmarking candidate.

Zairi, Mohamed and Hutton, Rob. "Benchmarking: A Process Driven Tool for Quality Improvement," *TQM Magazine* 7, no. 3 (1995): 35–40.

Successful TQM initiatives are fosted by the use of stretch goals created from benchmarking. Explains how TQM and benchmarking are linked to the philosophy of continuous improvement.

Reengineering and Improving Processes

Alavi, Maryam and Yoo, Youngjin. "Productivity Gains of BPR: Achieving Success Where Others Have Failed," *Information Systems Management* 12, no. 4 (Fall 1995): 43–47.

Is a useful summary of what business processing reengineering is all about.

Anonymous. "What Are the Risks of Undertaking a Major Reengineering Project?" *The American Banker* (July 10, 1995): 18ff.

Presents a half dozen comments by executives in this industry with their views on the subject, primarily about how to avoid the risk of failure; short and to the point.

Bennis, Warren and Mische, Michael A. *The 21st Century: Reinventing Through Reengineering*, Erlanger, KY: Pfeiffer & Co., 1995.

This short book is designed to give readers a clear sense of what reengineering is all about in a short time. Includes a procedure for undertaking reengineering efforts.

Berman, Saul. "Strategic Direction: Don't Reengineer without It," *Planning Review* (November/December 1994): 18–23.

Argues through three case studies that you have to select the strategic direction you want to take an organization before you can do meaningful reengineering. This is a useful brief on the relationship between strategic planning and process reengineering.

Brandt, John R. "Reengineering Must Be Radical," *Industry Week* 243, no. 21 (November 21, 1994): 72.

Reports on a recent speech by James A. Champy, a leading proponent of process reengineering, essentially repeating the same message he had been arguing for the past two years. Includes some of the concepts from his 1995 book, *Reengineering Management*.

Carr, David K. and Johansson, Henry J. *Best Practices in Reengineering: What Works and What Doesn't in the Reengineering Process*, New York: McGraw-Hill, 1995.

This is a well-informed book with a great deal of practical information about best practices in reengineering written by two consultants. It is a practical, street-wise discussion of the issue and how to go about reengineering, or at least avoiding obvious problems; a solid book.

Champy, James. *Reengineering Management: The Mandate for New Leadership*, New York: Harper Business, 1995.

In this book Champy argues that reengineering will not be successful unless the role of management is also reengineered. He discusses the role of management and provides examples of successful work.

Cresto, George, Mabe, Jay, and O'Malley, Bryan. "Meeting the Challenges of BPR," *Bobbin* 36, no. 6 (February 1995): 72–78.

When doing reengineering, it is critical to involve employees who have a deep understanding of how your business does the process being redone. Provides advice on what are the right things to do to get the effort launched.

DuBrin, Andrew J. *Reengineering Survival Guide: Managing and Succeeding in the Changing Workplace*, Cincinnati, OH: Thomson Executive Press, 1996.

Emphasizes the human side of reengineering and how to help people deal with the changes, including downsizing, that come with reengineering efforts. Includes lots of material on how reengineering should help release the talents and power of individuals to contribute to organizations.

Hammer, Michael and Stanton, Steven A. *The Reengineering Revolution: A Handbook*, New York: Harper Business, 1995.

This is actually a better book than his *Reengineering the Corporation*. It provides a large body of material on how to do reengineering, key success factors, and examples of well done and failed efforts.

Hyde, A.C. "A Primer on Process Reengineering," *Public Manager* 24, no. 1 (Spring 1995): 55–68.

This is an overview of what process reengineering is about, why it is done, and the kinds of results to expect. It is a useful introduction to the topic.

Jackson, David. "BPR: Hype or Reality?" *TQM Review* 6, no. 6 (1994): 19–22.

Business process reengineering has much in that it is not new, but the need for change is very high. Argues that it is more important to determine what to change rather than how to change before diving into the details of a reengineering effort.

Johann, Bernard. *Designing Cross-Functional Business Processes*, San Francisco: Jossey-Bass, 1995.

This describes a step-by-step approach for creating business processes.

Kind, John. "Fostering Creativity," *TQM Magazine* 6, no. 5 (1994): 9–10.

Argues the case for pursuing creativity as a way to improve differentiation and superiority. Links that to process improvement and reengineering activities. Recommends that data be presented graphically rather than just in text or numerically.

Macdonald, John. "Together TQM and BPR Are Winners," *TQM Magazine* 7, no. 3 (1995): 21–25.

Provides a general introduction to business process reengineering and how it relates to TQM; they work together.

Pappas, Alceste T. *Reengineering Your Nonprofit Organization*, New York: John Wiley & Sons, 1995.

Shows how to analyze, develop, and implement the best practices of the nonprofit world for improving organizational performance.

Revenaugh, D. Lance. "Business Process Re-engineering: The Unavoidable Challenge," *Management Decision* 32, no. 7 (1994): 16–27.

The author explores why many reengineering projects fail, looking at two widely used models of organizational analysis. These are the IT strategic grid and the corporate tribes model. Gives advice on how to avoid identified problems.

Weisz, M. "BPR Is Like Teenage Sex," *American Programs* 8, no. 6 (June 195): 8–15.

Business process reengineering is like teenage sex, argues the author. Everyone is talking about it, everyone thinks everyone else is doing it, few are, and those that are not will. Hype raises expectations of BPR to unreasonable levels. But like sex, it does not appear to be going away.

Wright, Brett M. "Leveraging Re-engineering Through TQM," *TQM Magazine* 7, no. 3 (1995): 50–53.

Offers a case study to demonstrate how reengineering leveraged one organization's positive implementation of TQM. Says they are both very closely related.

Zairi, Mohamed and Sinclair, David. "Business Process Reengineering and Process Management: A Survey of Current Practice and Future Trends in Integrated Management," *Management Decision* 33, no. 3 (1995): 3–16.

Reports on the use of BPR in the United Kingdom, finding that companies are as various in their application as people are in what they mean by reengineering. There appears to be no common strategy evident.

Measurements

Anonymous. "Best Practice, Better Profitability," *New Zealand Manufacturer* (April 1995): 9.

Presents an example of a comprehensive analytical system that offers manufacturing firms a way to conduct an evaluation of their organization, and use of TQM, woven back into financial measures.

Fanjoy, Bruce S. "Bringing Financial Discipline to Service Quality," *TQM Magazine* 6, no. 6 (1994): 57–61.

Describes annuitized valuation, a tool for measuring the asset value of a customer, i.e., potential cash flow of a customer over time.

Lavinsky, David. "In CSM Study, You Don't Always Get What You Expect," *Marketing News* 29, no. 1 (January 2, 1995): 6.

Describes the value of customer satisfaction measurements, and what the value is of a good CSM. It also describes what are some important questions to ask customers, e.g., what is the value of something to them as opposed to "Did we meet your needs."

Webster, Calum and Hung, Li Chu. "Measuring Service Quality and Promoting Decentring," *TQM Magazine* 6, no. 5 (1994): 50–55.

Describes two questionnaires used to measure service quality, derivatives of the work done by Parasuraman, Zeithaml, and Berry in 1988. Describes how to conduct the surveys and what information you get. Relies on SERVQUAL software tool, which is also described.

Zairi, Mohamed and Letza, Steve. "Performance Measurement: A Challenge for Total Quality and the Accounting Professions," *Asia Pacific Journal of Quality Management* 3, no. 2 (1994): 26–41.

Presents a range of issues associated with performance measurements and TQM. Explains what is needed and then presents what is used by Federal Express. Concludes with suggestions on how to implement new measurements.

Tools

Brewer, Geoffrey. "The Best Meeting I Ever Ran," *Performance* (March 1995): 51–54.
Five executives were interviewed on what makes for a useful meeting. Getting results is the answer. It is a wonderful little piece with war stories and practical advice. Includes comments on quality and teamwork.

Forsha, Harry I. *Show Me: The Complete Guide to Storyboarding and Problem Solving*, Milwaukee: Quality Press, 1995.

Describes how to use storyboarding techniques for developing presentations and understanding problems and issues. This is the definitive description of this tech-

nique with over 300 pages of text. In addition, the author has published *Show Me: Storyboard Workbook and Template* (Milwaukee: Quality Press, 1995), 70 aid to creation of storyboards with plans and practice guide.

Hradesky, John L. *Total Quality Management Handbook*, New York; McGraw-Hill, 1995.

This is a massive anthology of all the quality management practices that have evolved over the past 20 years in one book. It includes reengineering, the seven quality tools, etc.

Hupp, Toni, Polak, Craig, and Westgaard, Odin. *Designing Work Groups, Jobs, and Work Flow.* San Francisco: Jossey-Bass, 1995.

Provides various checklists, reusable worksheets, flow charts, and other aids for controlling and changing work activities.

Kathawala, Yunus and Motwani, Jaideep. "Implementing Quality Function Deployment—A Systems Approach," *TQM Magazine* 6, no. 6 (1994): 31–37.

Discusses how to implement QFD and how it can be used as a competitive tool. Provides some examples of where QFD has been used.

Kendrick, John J. "SPC on the Line," *Quality* 34, no. 1 (January 1995): 35–39.

Describes how best to enjoy a successful SPC program, complete with discussion of the merits of software tools. This is very much a discussion of approach, however.

Locks, Mitchell O. *Reliability, Maintainability, and Availability Assessment, Second Edition.* Milwaukee: Quality Press, 1995.

Discusses quantitative reliability assessments for quality assurance and reliability engineers. It is a detailed discussion of four widely deployed parametric reliability models, with examples.

Neblett, B. "The Role of Test in Total Quality Management," *IEEE Aerospace Electronics Systems Magazine* 10, no. 5 (May 1995): 26–34.
This paper provides metrics of quality estimation and how to implement a system for measuring defect levels and capabilities of processes; useful for large projects and manufacturing environments. Provides a good discussion of Process Potential Index (Cp) and Process Capabilities Index (Cpk).

Rigby, Darrell K. "Managing the Management Tools," *Planning Review* 22, no. 5 (September/October 1994): 20–24.

Presents results of a survey to see what management tools were being used and how effective these were. Companies used 12 of 25 tools on average. Most popular were Mission Statements, Customer Satisfaction Survey, and TQM. Least used were Value Chain Analysis, and Technology S curves. All used tools delivered benefits. Concludes with advice on how best to pick and deploy tools.

Roth, Philip L., Schleifer, Lydia L.F., and Switzer, Fred S. "Nominal Group Technique: An Aid in Implementing TQM," *CPA Journal* 65, no. 5 (May 1995): 68–69.

Defines NGT as a tool to maximize number of ideas generated by a group and how it can be used in TQM. Discusses the pros and cons of this tool and when to use it.

Shirose, Kunio, Kimura, Yoshifumi, and Kaneda, Mitsugu. *P-M Analysis: An Advanced Step in TPM Implementation,* Portland, OR: Productivity Press, 1995.

This describes a tool used by manufacturing for implementing zero defects. This describes what it is, how to implement it, what tools to use, and gives examples; best publication available on the subject.

Stamatis, D.H. *Failure Mode and Effect Analysis: FMEA from Theory to Execution.* Milwaukee: Quality Press, 1995.

This is a comprehensive look at FMEA, and about how to implement it with examples. It is the definitive work on the subject.

Stephens, Kenneth S. *Volume 2: How to Perform Continuous Sampling, Second Edition.* Milwaukee: Quality Press, 1995.

This 75 page book shows how to do acceptance sampling and nine different approaches. It is detailed and comprehensive and includes new methods since publication of the original edition.

Tague, Nancy R. *The Quality Toolbox.* Milwaukee: Quality Press, 1995.

Discusses more than 50 basic quality tools: what they are, how and when to use them; useful for training people on quality improvements. This is an important publication for those interested in implementing quality practices and, in particular, process improvement and reengineering.

Teams and Teamwork

Atkinson, Cyril. "The Total Teamwork Way," *TQM Magazine* 7, no. 3 (1995): 32–34.

Uses a soccer team as an analogy to describe how TQM operates in a team-based approach.

Augenstein, David M. "The Power of Teamwork," *Fleet Equipment* 21, no. 6 (June 1995): 12.

Successful companies have deployed TQM and focus on people issues. Give them the right tool, e.g., training, education, and equipment, and let them participate in decision making. Give them the opportunity to succeed.

Coyle Shapiro, Jackie. "The Impact of a TQM Intervention on Teamwork: A Longitudinal Assessment," *Employee Relations* 17, no. 3 (1995): 63–74.

Studies the effect of TQM on teamworking in manufacturing environments. One important result was that intervention proved a better indicator of teamwork than participation in the intervention.

DuBrin, Andrew J. *The Breakthrough Team Player: Becoming the MVP on Your Workplace Team,* New York: AMACOM, 1995.

Though the idea of an MVP may seem contradictory, here it means how to learn how to enhance your ability to work with others to create a high-performance team.

Fisher, Kimball, et al. *Tips for Teams: A Ready Reference for Solving Common Team Problems,* New York: McGraw-Hill, 1995.

Just as its title says, this book includes over 400 tips for dealing with all aspects of implementing teams. It also includes other material to help teams succeed.

Guzzo, Richard A. *Team Effectiveness and Decision Making in Organizations,* San Francisco: Jossey-Bass, 1995.

Investigates the internal processes and external factors that affect critical decision making in teams and presents tested models and methods for improving team effectiveness in any organizational context.

Kennedy, Carol. "Managing Without Managers," *Director* 48, no. 3 (October 1994): 48–52.

Describes how self-directed teams function and their role in both the United States and in the United Kingdom. Describes the right mix of complimentary skills needed to be successful. A useful introduction to the topic.

Losoncy, Lewis E. *The Motivating Team Leader,* Delray Beach, FL: St. Lucie Press, 1995.

The author is a noted psychologist. He presents 43 approaches that leaders can use to help support and motivate team members to perform.

Mohrman, Susan Albers, Cohen, Susan G., and Moharman, Jr., Allan M. *Designing Team-Based Organizations,* San Francisco: Jossey-Bass, 1995.

Describes how to create organizations that rely primarily on team-based activities.

Motta, Richard A. "How to Build on Team Momentum," *Bobbin* 36, no. 10 (June 1995): 114.

This is a case study of the Harodite Finishing Company's use of teams. Their key to success was an effective team recognition process, creating Recognition Day programs which are described.

O'Brien, Maureen. *Who's Got the Ball (and Other Nagging Questions About Team Life),* San Francisco: Jossey-Bass, 1995.

Covers all aspects of helping teams succeed, including setting the "noble purpose," making meeting worthwhile, making team decisions, eliminating gridlock, and more.

Ray, Darrel and Bronstein, Howard. *Teaming Up: Making the Transition to a Self-Directed, Team-Based Organization,* New York: McGraw-Hill, 1995.

This is a good introduction to what self-managed teams are about, how they work, and how to move your organization in this direction.

Robbins, Harvey and Finley, Michael. *Why Teams Don't Work: What Went Wrong and How to Make It Right,* Princeton, NJ: Pacesetter Books, 1995.

This is an example of contemporary team literature in that it moves on from simply defending the need to use teams to a look at how and where to apply this approach to organizing workers and work.

Swanson, Roger C. *The Quality Improvement Handbook: Team Guide to Tools and Techniques,* Delray Beach, FL: St. Lucie Press, 1995.

Provides quality improvement teams and team leaders with a comprehensive set of tools and techniques to solve problems and improve processes. Includes coverage of more advanced quality tools as well as the basics.

Temme, Jim. "Calling a Team a Team Doesn't Mean That It Is: Successful Teamwork Must Be A Way of Life," *Plant Engineering* 49, no. 1 (January 9, 1995): 108, 112.

Argues that management must mean it if they want to use teams, a way of life and that is prepared for. Discusses key traits of real teams (e.g., empowerment, trust, etc.)

Weller, L. David. "Quality Teams: Problems, Causes, Solutions," *TQM Magazine* 7, no. 3 (1995): 45–49.

Looks at teacher teams in schools. Suggests how facilitators can identify problems and get them fixed as they crop up.

FUNCTIONAL PROCESSES
Planning

Bohan, George P. "Focus the Strategy to Achieve Results," *Quality Progress* 28, no. 7 (July 1995): 89–92.

Identifies as problems in implementing TQM: the process has insufficient focus, and there is not enough change in business systems. In short, managers do not always have a good plan for implementation of TQM. Argues the case for building such a plan.

Butz Jr., Howard E. "Strategic Planning: The Missing Link in TQM," *Quality Progress* 28, no. 5 (May 1995): 105–108.

Argues the case for linking TQM to business strategy to make quality work and that is done by weaving TQM in the firm's strategic planning process.

Davenport, Thomas H. "Will Participative Makeovers of Business Processes Succeed Where Reengineering Failed?" *The Planning Forum* (January/February 1995): 24–29.

An expert in process reengineering argues the need for combined information systems and business processes that combine top-level direction and business processes. Descibes how to bring this about.

Powell, Thomas C. "Total Quality Management As Competitive Advantage: A Review and Empirical Study," *Strategic Management Journal* 16, no. 1 (January 1995): 15–37.

Treats TQM as a strategic resource that needs to be studied by those concerned about strategic management. Views TQM as a potential source of competitive advantage, offering ideas on how to do that. Possible advantages derive from open culture, employee empowerment, and executive commitment.

Simpson, Daniel. "How to Identify and Enhance Core Competencies," *Planning Review* (November/December 194): 24–26.

Moderates a discussion on the topic with planners from Clorox, Owens Corning Fiberglas, American Exress, Shell, IBM, and 3M.

Simpson, Daniel. "The Planning Process and the Role of the Planner," *Planning Review* (January/February 1995): 20–23.

This reports comments by chief planning officers in response to the question: How can companies optimally balance the planning process? This is very much a collection of best practices comments by experienced planners from Owens Corning Fiberglass, American Express, Shell, IBM, and 3M.

Toombs, Ken and Bailey, George. "How to Redesign Your Organization to Match Customer Needs," *Planning Review* 23, no. 2 (March–April 1995): 20–24.

Describes how some companies are now taking marketing information about their internal and external customers and are applying that data to the redesign of parts of their organizations. Usually what gets reorganized is the product and services sides of the house. Results: lower costs, improved profitability and customer satisfaction. Three case studies are provided.

Sales and Marketing

Anonymous. "Selling a Relationship from Field Sales Forces to Cross-Functional Teams," *Sales and Marketing Management* (January 1995): 14.

Announces the case of Dendrite International that was making its sales organization a cross-functional team, with sales personnel working with experts in communications, customer service, and high-tech development to make "the sale." This is a significant new approach to direct sales.

Blair, Margaret Henderson. "Measure for Measure, Advertising's Eluded Total Quality Management Model," *Brandweek* 36, no. 25 (June 19, 1995): 17.

Says TQM has not been used in advertising; the missing piece is a rigorous measurement process. It can be done, however: tools for seeing the effects of an advertisement on television, persuasion test scores to in market sales results, etc.

Carey, Robert. "Rewards of a TQM Program," *Sales and Marketing Management (Performance Supplement)* (November 1994): 11.

Reports results of a recent survey that demonstrates that when you link compensation to performance you get results. Second, that this is being done more frequently. Third, that various forms of reward compensation are being tried and implemented.

Docter, Eric. "Leveraging Customer Information to Improve Customer Satisfaction," *Telemarketing* 13, no. 9 (March 1995): 86–91.

Describes the emergence of the customer information resource, a database of many pieces of information about customers. Describes the nature of the IT involved in supporting this kind of customer focus.

Donohue, C.B. and Miles, F.M. "Total Quality Management in the Marketing Organization," *APEC '95 Tenth Anual Applied Power Electronics Conference and Exposition. Conference Proceedings 1995*, vol. 1, pp. 252–256.

Discusses the difficult task of implementing TQM in marketing and sales, particularly in getting marketing to take a leadership role with quality management practices.

Fram, Eugene H. "Not so Strange Bedfellows: Marketing and Total Quality Management," *Managing Service Quality* 5, no. 1 (1995): 50–56.

Forming strong partnerships with marketing helps firms to implement TQM because it leads to integration of customer requirements into company operations. Today such partnerships vary in success and implementation; suggests how they should operate.

Goffin, Keith. "Understanding Customers' Views: An Example of the Use of Repertory Grid Technique," *Management Research News* 17, no. 10, 11 (1994): 17–28.

The technique was used in a case study to identify how customers perceived support for a technology product in the medical field. Lessons: interviews have to be very carefully designed; the technique has to work; and the answers obtained can be unequivocal, which is ideal for product support management to work with.

Johnson, William C. and Chvala, Richard J. *Total Quality in Marketing*, Delray Beach, FL: St. Lucie Press, 1995.

Designed to help managers implement total quality management principles and techniques in the marketing processes.

Lowther, Nancy. "Total Quality Sales," *American Printer* 214, no. 3 (December 1994): 57–59.

Provides reasons why sales people resist TQM, arguing that they have an elitist attitude that must change. This is brought about by training. The article is rather innocent.

McCloskey, Larry A. *Selling with Excellence: A Quality Approach for Sales Professionals*, Milwaukee: Quality Press, 1995.
Describes four ways sales organizations can improve continuously. This very short book discusses such processes as customer feedback, use of data, and action plans. While the topics are very traditional, they are described in a quality-focused context.

Rudick, Judi. "Are You Treating Your Customers Like a One Night Stand?" *American Salesman* 40, no. 2 (February 1995): 23–26.
This presents the argument for customer retention strategies; don't ignore them. Other articles in this issue deal with related issues, such as value-added services.

Smith, George A. *Sales Productivity Measurement*, Milwaukee: ASQC Quality Press, 1995.
This 119-page book provides a methodology for measuring productivity in sales within the context of quality management practices, continuing a series of publications on sales practices from this press.

Welch, Cas and Geissler, Pete. *Applying Total Quality to Sales*, Milwaukee: Quality Press, 1995.
This is a 53-page pamphlet that provides five case studies of how to implement TQM tools and process improvement in sales operations. Particulary useful is the discussion on how to measure total quality in a sales function.

Zeller, Thomas L. and Gillis, Darin M. "Achieving Market Excellence Through Quality: The Case of Ford Motor Company," *Business Horizons* 38, no. 3 (May–June 1995): 23–31.
Ford has left behind many old business models in order to develop a strong market-focused strategy for growing its business. For example, its supplier relations strategy is designed to support its long-term market goals. Touts Ford as a successful model.

Logistics and Supplier Relations

Anonymous. "The Missing Ingredient?" *Health Manpower Management* 20, no. 4 (1994): 32. Presents the results of a recent survey of 100 senior executives in Fortune 500 manufacturing and service companies. 62 percent reported that they would like to see suppliers take quality initiatives and that customers are often left out of the picture in implementation of quality practices.

Anonymous. "Preferential Treatment," *Small Business Reports* 19, no. 11 (November 1994): 23–32.
Describes how companies are becoming preferred suppliers to large organizations. These programs are based on the application of TQM principles, described in detail. Really is a useful article on supplier relations strategies.

Avery, Susan. "Xerox Winners Exceed ISO 9000," *Purchasing* 118, no. 1 (January 12, 1995): 111–113.
Describes how Xerox qualifies its suppliers (uses ISO 9000 standard). Xerox also requires its suppliers to do continuous improvement, not just document their processes. Describes the benefits to Xerox of having their suppliers operate in a complete TQM environment.

Ayliffe, Roy. "Partnering: Will It Deliver for You?" *Logistics Focus* 3, no. 2 (March 1995): 7–9.
Describes the application of partnering strategies in the United Kingdom, citing the work of Partnership Sourcing Limited, set up in 1990 to support use of partnering strategies. Describes best practices of this process, an approach that was in great demand.

Morgan, Jim. "Value Added Turns Legit," *Purchasing* (April 6, 1995): 47, 51–52. Presents the results of a survey on the role of value added, describing its growing importance and how to use the concept in corporate purchasing practices.

Quayle, Michael. "Change Partners and Dance," *Purchasing and Supply Management* (February 1995): 32–35.
Describes the positive desire many have for this approach but also two barriers: lack of commitment and lack of understanding. Citing a Japanese automotive manufacturing model, an approach for developing true partnership sourcing is described.

Richards, Lee. "Empowerment and Trust Key to Partnerships," *TQM Magazine* 7, no. 1 (1995): 38–41.
Describes how SGS Thomson Microelectronics deals with its suppliers. 15 suppliers work very closely with the firm over many years as they provide services, and both sides improve operations. This is a wonderful example of how it is done right.

Product Development and Manufacturing

Anonymous. "Software Is One Segment of TQM Big Picture," *American Machinist* (March 1995): 16. Statistical process control software is an important tool in improving production quality. Argues the case how such software can help integrate all manufacturing steps to improve quality all up and down the line.

Bowman, Robert J. "Supply Chain: Crossing Company Lines," *Distribution* (February 1995): 24–26, 30.

Describes how the use of standard quality measurements that know no industry bounds are being used by several companies to ensure quality from product entry to final delivery. Describes in detail the measurements being deployed by 3M, Xerox, AT&T Network Systems, Proctor & Gamble, and Nabisco Foods.

Carbone, James. "How Scotsman Used Alliances to Solve a Design Problem," *Purchasing* (February 16, 1995): 36–40.

Describes how the use of suppliers helped Scotsman Industries design rapidly a new ice machine that met government regulations. It is a useful case study of the role of purchasing agents in the design of a product.

Chase, Victor D. "In Virtual Reality, Customers Help Product Design," *Appliance Manufacturer* 43, no. 5 (May 1995): 14.

Matsushita Electric Works Ltd. uses virtual reality applications in showroom in Japan to allow customers to customize their kitchens by selecting from 30,000 products in a variety of layouts. Virtual reality is expected to expand in many industries as a selling tool.

Curtis, Steven L. "Safety and Total Quality Management," *Professional Safety* 40, no. 1 (January 1995): 18–20.

Discusses how unplanned variation causes waste and inefficiency in a production environment. Use of TQM can eliminate variation. Safety managers can use SPC to improve safety, explaining how.

Levy, P. et al. "Developing Integration Through Total Quality Supply Chain Management," *Integrated Manufacturing Systems* 6, no. 3 (1995): 4–12.

Interest on the part of manufacturing companies is increasing in developing programs that involve customer supplier relationships. Benefits of taking a quality approach are becoming more widespread and obvious. Describes what the current trends are.

McHale, Hank. *Actual Experiences of a CEO: How to Make Continuous Improvement in Manufacturing Succeed for Your Company*, Milwaukee: Quality Press, 1995.

This provides many specific suggestions on how to implement CI in manufacturing, with examples. This short book discusses a wide variety of tools and methods, ranging from such tools as root cause analysis to CI implementation strategies. The audience is the executive.

Mills, John, Platts, Ken, and Gregory, Mike. "A Framework for the Design of Manufacturing Strategy Processes," *International Journal of Operations and Production Management* 15, no. 4 (1995): 17–49.

Documents the factors important in the design of manufacturing strategy processes, weaving in TQM and JIT, and cellular manufacturing methods, into the process. This is a practical framework.

Miltenburg, John. *Manufacturing Strategy: How to Formulate and Implement a Winning Plan*, Portland, OR: Productivity Press, 1995.

This is a step-by-step description of how to create a strategy for implementing a manufacturing strategy, complete with worksheets, examples, and tools.

Moore, Lila. "Quality Automation," *Apparel Industry Magazine* 56, no. 4 (May 1995): 56–60.

This is a case study of how the Virginia Apparel Corporation applied TQM in its production processes with the following results: 50 percent reduction in process defects, fabric defects down by over 30 percent, reduced 2nd runs by 70 percent, while improving relations with customers, suppliers, and processors. Has seven audit points on the production floor to track quality. Presents a very strong case in favor of TQM in this industry.

Oakland, J.S. and Aldridge, A.J. "Quality Management in Civil and Structural Engineering Consulting," *International Journal of Quality and Reliability Management* 12, no. 3 (1995): 32–48.

Surveys how the construction industry applies quality management. Also does a literature review.

Peck, Babbi. "Tools for Teams Addressing Total Customer Satisfaction," *Industrial Engineering* (January 1995): 30–31, 34.

Describes a case of using QFD methods to develop new products, also applying IE methods to design to a specific price range as required by customers. This is a case of an expanded use of House of Quality techniques; clearly written.

Price, R.C. "TQM in the R&D Function," *Quality Progress* 28, no. 7 (July 1995): 109–111.

Two concepts to apply here are customer supplier chains and process management model. Describes how these two elements must be managed in an R&D situation, using, for example, simultaneous engineering,

ISO 9001 management system, and quality function deployment.

Robinson, Charles J. and Ginder, Andrew P. *Implementing TPM: The North American Experience*, Portland, OR: Productivity Press, 1995.

This is the best book now available on productive maintenance practices. Describes how TPM was developed in Japan, used in the United States in manufacturing environments, results you can get, and presents examples and strategies.

Survant, T. Greg. "Changing the Way We Think Is Key to Successful New Product: How Lexmark Invented a New Product Design and Delivery Process," *Target* 11, no. 2 (March/April 1995): 9–15.

A product development manager at this PC printer company describes how his firm was able to design an effective product design process that now leads to the successful introduction of many new products each year. Emphasizes the positive role of employee empowerment.

Voss, C.A. "Significant Issues for the Future of Product Innovation," *Journal of Product Innovation Management* 11, no. 5 (November 1994): 460–463.

Acknowledges the interdependency of such processes as product innovation, development, process, technology acquisition, industrial design, TQM, and QFD. Calls for closer linkages for a "total innovation management."

Willmott, Peter. "Total Quality with Teeth," *TQM Magazine* 6, no. 4 (1994): 48–50.

Describes total productive maintenance (TPM) or the application of quality principles to maintenance of equipment in manufacturing and processing industries. Defines the aim and benefits of TPM. As a concept and practice, it has been around for just 20 years.

Yee, E.C. and Sotak, R.C. "Implementing Total Quality Management for World Class Product Development," *APEC '95 Tenth Annual Applied Power Electronics Conference and Exposition. Conference Proceedings 1995*, vol. 1, pp. 72–75.

TQM as applied at AT&T Power Systems is described as a positive experience.

Youssef, Mohammed A. "Measuring the Intensity Level of Just in Time Activities and Its Impact on Quality," *International Journal of Quality & Reliability Management* 11, no. 5 (1994): 59–80.

The study was based on data from 165 manufacturing companies in industrial machinery equipment, electronic and electric machinery equipment, and transport equipment, all American. Concludes there is a wide difference in quality among firms with various intensity levels of JIT; offers many details on such issues as manufacturability, time-based strategies, TQM, design and engineering workmanship, and vendor quality.

Information Technology

Aggarwal, Rajesh and Lee, Jong Sung. "CASE and TQM for Flexible Systems," *Information Systems Management* 12, no. 4 (Fall 1995): 15–19.

Argues that CASE tools are the best available for applying TQM in systems development. Criticizes problems in other approaches, e.g., poor planning and documentation, inadequate analysis and design, lack of user involvement, etc.

Bartel, Timothy and Finster, Mark. "A TQM Process for Systems Integration: Getting the Most from COTS Software," *Information Systems Management* 12, no. 3 (Summer 1995): 19–29.

COTS stands for commercial off-the-shelf software, the article is about how to apply TQM to the implementation of such systems. Presents a model that can be used to perform the required systems integration by project teams. Argues the benefits for using TQM techniques in systems integration.

Beckley, Glen B. "Metrics for Continuous Improvement: Tapping the Potential of Legacy Systems," *Journal of Systems Management* 45, no. 12 (December 1994): 20–21.

Announces that existing "legacy" software applications normally capture a great deal of information about their performance. These transaction performance data can be used by TQM teams; suggests how they can use such information to improve performance and lower costs.

Cortada, James W. "Eight Steps to Justification," *Beyond Computing* (July/August 1995): 38.

Lists eight ways to cost justify information processing, the result of research on best practices in this area. Takes a highly holistic approach.

Cortada, James W. *TQM for Information Systems Management: Quality Practices for Continuous Improvement*, New York: McGraw-Hill, 1995.

This is a comprehensive review of how TQM is being applied in information processing organizations covering such issues as strategic planning, application developments, process reengineering, personnel practices, and assessment of organizational performance.

Dekkers, C.A. "Stand Up and Be Counted (IS Software Metrics and Total Quality Management),"

Management Systems Development 15, no. 3 (March 1995): 1–5.

Argues the case for using software metrics to improve quality in IS.

Eom, Sean, Karathanos, Demetrius, and Stough, Stanley. "Executive Support Systems: A Key for Enhancing Senior Executive Leadership in Total Quality Management," *Information Strategy: The Executive's Journal* 11, no. 2 (Winter 1995): 27–34.

Uses Baldrige criteria to assess information needs where TQM is used. Drivers of senior executive information needs are the requirements for fact-based decision making. Recommends that executives develop a small list of key performance indicators (KPIs). Shows how these can be organized using the Baldrige criteria.

Hendrick, Rebecca. "An Information Infrasctructure for Innovative Management of Government," *Public Administration Review* 54, no. 6 (November/December 1994): 543–555.

Says that with all the quality transformation going on in the public sector, it needs an IT plan to support all of that. Then she offers a proposed framework, with such quality elements incorporated as feedback and organization. The model is useful for other industries as well.

Kanakovsky, R. "A Proposal for TQM in Software Development," *Autom.tech. Prax.* 37, no. 4 (April 1995): 32–35, 38–41.

Declares TQM in software development has not yet yielded positive results, due to the complexity of the task of programming. Proposes for how TQM could be applied in software development in which for each step of development, quality targets are set and realized.

McManus, John. "TQM: Lessons To Be Learned From Failure," *Managing Service Quality* 4, no. 6 (1994): 8–9.

Presents the results of a survey done within an IS shop in a British corporation regarding TQM. Describes the survey instrument. Results suggested the staff knew little about TQM but strongly endorsed it anyway!

McConnell, Patrick and Ciotti, Vincent G. "Applying TQM/CQI Principles to Information System Selection," *Healthcare Financial Management* 49, no. 6 (June 1995): 48–56.

Describes how management at North Valley Hospital in Whitefish, Montana, applied TQM to the process. An end user team selected the system.

Pastore, Richard. "CIO 100: Best Practices: All for the Best," *CIO* 8, no. 19 (August 1995): 26–30.

Reengineering, TQM, and best practice benchmarking helps organizations, but to sustain competitive advantage, the firm must have interdependent best practices across the entire organization.

Rouse, Anne and Watson, David. "Applying TQM to Information Systems Quality: The Role of Culture," *Asia Pacific Journal of Quality Management* 4, no. 1 (1995): 12–23.

Argues that a supportive organizational culture is required to make TQM work in IS. An Australian case study demonstrates how the lack of such a culture undermines implementation of TQM. Concludes with a model of how to go about building the required culture.

Research and Development

Dellana, Scott A. and Wiebe, Henry A. "An Exploration of Total Quality Management Practices in U.S. R&D Organizations," *Engineering Management Journal* 7, no. 2 (June 1995): 23–29.

Presents the results of a study of the application of TQM in 31 U.S. R&D organizations. Progress was shown to be a function of how TQM was measured in these organizations.

Mori, Teruo. *Taguchi Techniques for Image and Pattern Developing Technology*, Englewood Cliffs, NJ: Prentice-Hall, 1995.

This is a detailed, technical treatise that well applies Taguchi methods in R&D and IT environments.

Roberts, George W. (ed). *Quality Planning, Control, and Improvement in Research and Development*, New York: Marcel Dekker, 1995.

This is an anthology of papers on theory and practice of quality in an R&D environment. This is a large and useful book, given the fact that there is little on the subject available to R&D organizations.

Tottie, Magnus and Lager, Thomas. "QFD: Linking the Customer to the Product Development Process As a Part of the TQM Concept," *R&D Management* 25, no. 3 (July 1995): 257–267.

Describes how Luossavaara Kiirunavaara AB, a leading supplier of iron ore products in Europe, applies quality function deployment to improve responsiveness to customers. Describes what is QFD and how it is applied; argues that it has improved business results.

Accounting, Finance, and Cost Justification

Eisman, Regina. "Progress on the Quality Road," *Incentive* 169, no. 4 (April 1995): 7.

Reports results of survey by Zenger Miller Achieve, saying majority of companies are reporting positive results with TQM. 74 percent use it, 80 percent of the manufacturing companies, and 66 percent of the service companies.

Ernst & Young. *After Reengineering: Measuring Profit Through Real-Time Cost Management*, New York: John Wiley & Sons, 1995.

Combines activity-based costing and process control systems to illustrate how to measure profits; a how-to book.

Forrest, Edward. *Activity-Based Management: A Comprehensive Implementation Guide*, New York: McGraw-Hill, 1995.

This book is designed as a hands-on resource suppling detailed procedures for planning, organizing, and implementing a total ABM initiative.

Grant, Vince. "Total Quality Challenges the Management Accountant," *Management Accounting* 73, no. 6 (June 1995): 40–41.

Explains how TQM can help this profession add value. Describes developments in the world of quality in the British accounting community, particularly about current research underway.

Hawkes, Lindsay C. and Adams, Michael B. "Total Quality Management and the Internal Audit: Empirical Evidence," *Managerial Auditing Journal* 10, no. 1 (1995): 31–36.

This is a study of how auditors functioned in manufacturing companies and found that in TQM focused firms, one-third did not use auditors, the other two-thirds had them active in quality programs, hence reducing concerns about financial integrity. Argues that the role of auditors is changing fundamentally in companies that apply TQM.

Howard, Patrick. "Architecture for an Activity-Based Costing System," *Cost Management* (Winter 1995): 14–21.

Describes a functional architecture that can be used to implement ABC while overcoming significant obstacles. This is a "hands-on how-to" article by a real expert!

Lederer, P.J. and Seung, Kyu Rhee. "Economics of Total Quality Management," *Journal of Operations Research* 12, nos. 3–4 (June 1995): 353–367.

Presents two economic models demonstrating the economic value of total quality management practices. In the first, sunk investments are made in quality to reduce cost and improve quality—an investment in technology usually—and the second, in customer satisfaction strategies. The consequences of both approaches are described.

Letza, Steve R. and Gadd, Ken. "Should Activity Based Costing Be Considered as the Costing Method of Choice for Total Quality Organizations?" *TQM Magazine* 6, no. 5 (1994): 57–63.

Introduces the concept of ABC and its focus on cost drivers. Describes ABC in a total quality context and its appropriateness. It is a useful introduction to the debate, favoring its use in a quality-focused environment.

Marshall, Brent. "Activity Based Costing at Wavin," *Management Accounting* 73, no. 5 (May 1995): 28–30.

This is a British case study that began in 1990 with TQM implemented. ABC was then applied to profitability management and is now part of the day-to-day management of the company. It is given a thumbs up as a management tool.

Mavrinac, Sarah C., Jones, Neil R., and Meyer, Marshall W. *The Financial and Non-Financial Returns to Innovative Workplace Practices*, Boston: Ernest & Young, March 1995.

This is an important study commissioned by the U.S. Department of Labor to look at the returns on innovative practices in the workplace such as TQM. It presents some evidence of solid returns and also is an excellent summary of all the research done on cost justification and returns done by academics, companies, and consultants; perhaps the most important quality publication of 1995.

Monden, Yasuhiro. *Cost Reduction Systems: Target Costing and Kaizen Costing*, Portland, OR: Productivity Press, 1995.

Presents ideas that have profoundly influenced Japanese manufacturing in the past decade. Target costing is used during the design and testing of new products by planning quality into products. Kaizen costing is for reducing the cost of existing products already in production. This is a detailed, well-organized survey of the subject, with examples.

Ruhl, Jack M. and Yang, Roger Y.W. "Continuous Process Improvement in Small CPA Firms," *CPA Journal* 65, no. 6 (June 1995): 24–28.

Argues the case for continuous improvement of practice and administrative processes in such firms: internal accounting and administrative functions, client service and communications, practice development, specific procedures to reduce audit cycle time, and tax department practices.

Singhvi, Virendra. "Reengineering the Payables Process," *Management Accounting* 76, no. 9 (March 1995): 46–49.
This describes how to reengineer the accounts payable process, with details on what a new process should look like.

Human Resources

Anonymous. "Total Quality Management: A Good Thing for Safety," *Industrial Relations Review and Report* no. 573 (December 1994): PSSSS11–SSSS13.
Reports on a study of accidents in five organizations, detailing their costs. Then argues that TQM can help reduce accidents.

Blackburn, Richard and Rosen, Benson. "Does HRM Walk the TQM Talk?" *HRMagazine* 40, no. 7 (July 1995): 69–72.
Calls on the human resource community to champion TQM through educational and communications programs. Describes other actions the HR professional can take to promote and support TQM.

Boyle, Daniel C. *Secrets of a Successful Employee Recognition System*, Portland, OR: Productivity Press, 1995.
Describes the author's 100Club gift rewards process for employees as implemented at various U.S. companies. This short book describes how this kind of recognition system is implemented. Includes material on how to link this to suggestion processes.

Carnell, Bob. "Panacea? Not Even a Placebo: Performance Related Pay," *Management Accounting* 73, no. 1 (January 1995): 32–33.
Describes how one organization dropped performance-related pay bcause it was incompatible with TQM due to incompatible cultures and modes of operation.

Conti, Robert F. "TQM and Incentive Pay in Unionized Firms Don't Mix," *Journal for Quality and Participation* 18, no. 3 (June 1995): 40–44.
Says there are conflicts between individual incentive pay and TQM. Add union-management combat and the problem gets worse; explains the issues. Presents results of two studies about the results of TQM in unionized plants.

Eckes, George. "Practical Alternatives to Performance Appraisals," *Quality Progress* 27, no. 11 (November 1994): 57–60.
While TQM and traditional appraisals are at odds, they will not go away. Argues the case for two alternatives: customer supplier appraisals and process appraisals.

Eckhardt, Robert. "Introducing Quality Principles into Safety Regulatory Strategies," *Professional Safety* 40, no. 5 (May 1995): 34–36.
Employees should be treated as customers by people in the field of safety; endorses how TQM can be used to improve safety management.

Harrington, H. James. "Eliminate Performance Appraisals? Ridiculous!" *Total Quality Review* 5, no. 2, May/June 1995.
Harrington's rebuttal to the idea that performance appraisals of individuals are not a sound way to manage people. (Compare this with Peter Scholtes' article noted below.)

Hill, Stephen and Wilkinson, Adrian. "In Search of TQM," *Employee Relations* 17, no. 3 (1995): 8–25.
Argues that there are partial and full implementation of TQM by companies, with great variation. For UK firms, the issue is how to introduce TQM or maintaining it in the face of downsizing.

Japan Human Relations Association (ed.). *The Improvement Engine: Creativity and Innovation Through Employee Involvement, The Kaizen Teian System*, Portland, OR: Productivity Press, 1995.
Describes how to get employees involved in continuous improvement in companies; includes practical examples and worksheets. Also useful for implementing effective employee suggestion processes, a key strategic initiative.

Knouse, Stephen B. *The Reward and Recognition Process in Total Quality Management*, Milwaukee: Quality Press, 1995. This is a useful introduction to these two processes as applied within a quality-focused environment, with case studies. Includes both theory and advice on how to implement.

Knouse, Stephen B. "Variation on Skill Based Pay for Total Quality Management," *SAM Advanced Management Journal* 60, no. 1 (Winter 1995): 34–38.

For many companies, their compensation plans do not reinforce TQM-based behavior. The answer is probably to implement skill-based compensation approaches. Suggests how you move to such systems and their best characteristics.

Lam, Simon S.K. "Quality Management and Job Satisfaction," *International Journal of Quality & Reliability* 12, no. 4 (1995): 72–78.

Presents results of a survey of 220 supervisors in Hong Kong to see what was the perceived impact of TQM. TQM had no effect on pay or promotions, made jobs more demanding, not more interesting.

Levine, David I. *Reinventing the Workplace: How Business and Employees Can Both Win*, Washington, DC: Brookings Institute, 1995.

This is an excellent book on recent management/employee relations, practices and trends in the workplace. This is a must-read for senior management.

Moe, Jeffrey L. "What Does 'Employee Involvement' Mean?" *Quality Progress* 28, no. 7 (July 1995): 67–71.

Describes TQM activities at Glaxo, Inc., including improving communications and leadership. Describes how to improve and understand the range of types of relations between employees and their managers.

Petrick, Joseph A. and Furr, Diana S. *Total Quality in Managing Human Resources*, Delray Beach, FL: St. Lucie Press, 1995.

Explains the whats and hows of taking advantage of quality management principles and techniques to continuously improve the HR department in any organization.

Randolph, W. Alan. "Navigating the Journey to Empowerment," *Organizational Dynamics* 23, no. 4 (Spring 1995): 19–31.

This is an important article on empowerment—what it is, how it works successfully—and is based on research conducted with 10 companies in various industries. Discusses information sharing, role of trust, and effects on organization.

Scholtes, Peter R. "Performance Without Appraisal," *Total Quality Review*, 5, no. 2, May/ June 1995.

A summary of the arguments against performance appraisal by a respected teacher of Deming's ideas. Thoughtful and thought provoking.

Simmons, David E., Shadur, Mark A., and Preston, Arthur P. "Integrating TQM and HRM," *Employee Relations* 17, no. 3 (1995): 75–86.

The two approaches are compared and contrasted with a case study of Tubemakers Australia, winner of Australia's quality award. Key here was the company's ability to centralize strategic elements of TQM while delegating enough so that local needs of workers could be addressed.

Snape, Ed. et al. "Managing Human Resources for TQM: Possibilities and Pitfalls," *Employee Relations* 17, no. 3 (1995): 42–51.

Implications of TQM on the management of people is the subject of this article. Poor employee relations strategies doom TQM, but once implemented, they will have resulted in major changes in human resource strategies and policies.

Wood, Stephen and Peccei, Riccardo. "Does Total Quality Management Make a Difference to Employee Attitudes?" *Employee Relations* 17, no. 3 (1995): 52–62.

Presents results of a study of a British factory, demonstrating that those people whose attitudes changed the most were more likely to have participated in TQM activities while those who did not were more negative.

STANDARDS AND ASSESSMENTS
ISO 9000

Anonymous. "ISO Expands: Most Large Companies Have Adopted ISO 9000 and Now the Standard Is Moving Down to All Levels," *Chemical Marketing Reporter* (April 10, 1995): 12ff.

First it was large companies being certified, but now suppliers to those companies are being certified. Describes ISO and has many quotes about it from those who have gone through the process. By the end of 1996, 12,000 U.S. companies will have been certified as compared to 100 in 1990. Includes estimates of cost to be certified.

Anonymous. "Life After ISO: Canada: Growing Number of Processors Have Obtained ISO Registration," *Canadian Plastics* (February 1995): 21ff.

Describes who has been certified, the effort they went through and why. ISO has influenced positively the effectiveness of management, teamwork, and communications while also improving customer satisfaction. This is a useful, well-done article on implementation steps with case studies.

Beardsley, Jeff. "One Company's Journey to ISO 9000 Registration," *Journal for Quality and Participation* 18, no. 2 (March 1995): 66–71.

Kind & Knox Gelatine obtained its certification in order to enhance internal controls, improve operations, and discipline. Results have been positive and are described in this case study.

Brumm, Eugenia K. *Managing Records for ISO 9000 Compliance*, Milwaukee: Quality Press, 1995.

Describes how best to keep the large number of records required of an ISO 9000 certified organization. Focuses on each record requirement of ISO 9001 in tremendous detail. Includes a great deal about the audit process and what is required in the form of documentation to navigate through that effort.

Ho, Samuel K.M. "Is the ISO 9000 Series for Total Quality Management?" *International Journal of Quality and Reliability Management* 11, no. 9 (1994): 74–89.

Around the world ISO 9000 and TQM are being seen as "passports to success. Offers an implementation framework for both approaches to be applied by businesses. Reprinted in *the International Journal of Physical Distribution and Logistics Management* 25, no. 1 (1995): 51–66.

Keeney, Kent A. and Tsiakal, Joseph J. *The Audit Kit*, Milwaukee: Quality Press, 1995.

Contains 26 audit packets for use in assessing ISO 9000 operations, with all the forms and templates needed. Should be used in conjunction with the 50-page booklet these authors published, *The ISO 9000 Auditor's Companion* (Milwaukee: Quality Press, 1995).

Mauch, Peter, Stewart, James, and Straka, Frank. *The 90-Day ISO Manual*, Delray Beach, FL: St. Lucie Press, 1995.

This is a 150-page introduction to the implementation of ISO; includes discussion of benefits of registration.

Sharp, Alan. "Alternative Schemes for ISO 9000 Harmonization in Europe," *TQM Magazine* 6, no. 5 (1994): 14–18.

This is an important report about how European certification and auditing standards for ISO 9000 are being managed. Discusses what the European Accreditation of Certification (EAC) is doing to improve standardization of the certification and auditing processes.

Taylor, W.A. "ISO 9000 and the Small Business: What Really Is the Problem?" *IEE Colloquium on ISO 9000 and The Small Business* (1995): P3, 1–5.

Addresses the lack of quantitative research on ISO 9000 in presenting some survey results from certified companies. Over 700 Irish companies were surveyed on costs, purpose for registration, and results; an important article.

Zuckerman, Amy. *ISO 9000 Made Easy: A Cost-Saving Guide to Documentation and Registration*, New York: AMCAOM Books, 1995.

This is an easy-to-read, simple review of the topic, a useful "how-to" book, particularly useful for companies just beginning the ISO 9000 process.

Awards, Other Standards and Issues

Anonymous. "Evaluating the Operation of the European Quality Award (EQA) Model for Self Assessment," *Management Accounting* 73, no. 4 (April 1995): 8.

This British journal reports that UK companies are increasingly using an EQA approach for evaluating their quality operations; documents benefits of this approach.

Anonymous. "The Straining of Quality," *Economist* 334, no. 7897 (January 14, 1995): 55–56.

Announces that fewer organizations applied for the Baldrige Award in 1994 and attributes this decline to corporate America's increasingly wrangling with TQM.

Myers, Dale H. and Heller, Jeffrey. "The Dual Role of AT&T's Self Assessment Process," *Quality Progress* 28, no. 1 (January 1995): 79–83.

Describes how AT&T found a systematic way to assess its progress in applying quality management practices and in matching its business strategy up with its customers' needs. This is an important case study since AT&T has won so many quality awards.

Stevenson, David. "Quality Awards: A Means to an End or an End in Themselves?" *TQM Magazine* 6, no. 5 (1994): 7–8.

Argues that winning an award is no substitute for achieving profit and happy customers. Discusses the role and effect of quality awards on British firms.

Assessments

Knutton, Peter. "A Model Approach to Self-Assessment," *Works Management* 47, no. 12 (December 1994): 12–16.

Some European manufacturing firms are now using as their assessment model the European Model for Total Quality as their way of measuring progress on quality and world-class excellence. Takes you through the case of Compair Broomwade, a British manufacturer of compressors, which uses this model as part of its strategy for continuous improvement.

Tamimi, Nabil and Gershon, Mark. "A Tool for Assessing Industry TQM Practices Versus the Deming Philosophy," *Production and Inventory Management Journal* 36, no. 1 (First Quarter 1995): 27–32.

Offers a Deming-based tool that can be used to self-audit a firm's use of TQM. Offers a survey instrument and comments on how to use it.

Wilson, Paul F. and Pearson, Richard D. *Performance-Based Assessments: External, Internal, and Self-Asessment Tools for Total Quality Management*, Milwaukee: Quality Press, 1995.

This is a relatively detailed introduction to the concept of performance-based assessments, how to get started, doing one, and presenting the results.

A Quality Management Library, Part 2

In putting together *The Quality Yearbook*, we have to keep abreast of the literature of this field and make judgments about what we feel are worthwhile materials to include. While the yearbook includes the best pieces we could find, mostly from magazines and journals, we also want to share with you some of the books we have discovered. That was the purpose of establishing this section of the yearbook. Last year we recommended 25 books that might help you establish or add to your library on quality management. This year, in quality management library part 2, we have chosen 25 more books you might consider. This year's list includes an eclectic collection of titles, from works by Deming and Feigenbaum to new books that came out in 1995. There are books on technical subjects and on the soft side of quality, dealing with culture, teams, and empowering people. For each selection, we include basic information about the book, its focus, and then a list of chapters. We think including the contents is the most useful way to help you determine if each of these is a book that you might like to have in your quality management library.

We have listed each title directly below in alphabetical order by the last name of the author. This is followed by a more detailed description of each one in the section that follows this list.

1. Yoji Akao, Editor, *Quality Function Deployment*
2. Leonard L. Berry, *On Great Service: A Framework for Action*
3. Christopher E. Bogan and Michael J. English, *Benchmarking for Best Practices*
4. James C. Collins and Jerry I. Porras, *Built to Last: Successful Habits of Visionary Companies*
5. James W. Cortada and John A. Woods, *McGraw-Hill Encyclopedia of Quality Terms and Concepts*
6. W. Edwards Deming, *The New Economics for Industry, Government, Education*, Second Edition
7. Armand V. Feigenbaum, *Total Quality Control*, Third Edition, Revised
8. Francis J. Gouillart and James N. Kelly, *Transforming the Organization*
9. H. James Harrington and James S. Harrington, *Total Improvement Management*
10. Jon R. Katzenbach and Douglas K. Smith, *The Wisdom of Teams: Creating the High Performance Organization*
11. David T. Kearns and David A. Nadler, *Prophets in the Dark*

12. Alfie Kohn, *No Contest: The Case Against Competition*
14. Charles C. Manz and Henry P. Sims, Jr., *Business Without Bosses*
15. C. Dan McArthur and Larry Womack, *Outcome Management*
16. Eugene H. Melan, *Process Management: Methods for Improving Products and Service*
17. Earl Naumann and Kathleen Giel, *Customer Satisfaction Measurement and Management*
18. Hy Pitt, *SPC for the Rest of Us*
19. Hal F. Rosenbluth and Diane McFerrin Peters, *The Customer Comes Second*
20. Eberhard E. Scheuing and William F. Christopher, Editors, *The Service Quality Handbook*
21. Shoji Shiba, Alan Graham, and David Walden, *A New American TQM*
22. Jay W. Spechler, *Managing Quality in America's Most Admired Companies*
23. Jack Stack, *The Great Game of Business*
24. James P. Womack, Daniel T. Jones, and Daniel Roos, *The Machine That Changed the World*
25. Ron Zemke with Dick Schaff, *The Service Edge*

Descriptions of Recommended Books

Yoji Akao, Editor, *Quality Function Deployment: Integrating Customer Requirements into Product Design*, 369 pages, Productivity Press, 1990.

Quality function deployment (QFD) is, to give a precise definition, "a highly structured methodology for identifying, classifying, and ranking customer requirements and expected benefits from a product or service, then correlating these to design features and production requirements." This book explains QFD in detail. It features chapters by various Japanese practitioners, who explain the various aspects of this subject with plenty of illustrations. QFD can be time-consuming, but it is one of the key methods that the Japanese use to maintain their ability to deliver goods and services that truly meet customer needs and often evoke true delight from customers. The book requires some work to get through, but if you are interested in this tool, it is worth the effort.

TABLE OF CONTENTS: 1. An Introduction to Quality Function Deployment; 2. Using the Demanded Quality Deployment Chart; 3. Using and Promoting Quality Charts; 4. Using Quality Deployment Charts: Subsystems, Parts Deployment, Quality Assurance Charts; 5. Using Quality Control Process Charts: Quality Function Deployment at the Preproduction Stage; 6. Quality Function Deployment and Technology Deployment; 7. Quality Deployment and Reliability Deployment; 8. Quality Deployment and Cost Deployment; 9. Quality Function Deployment in Process Industries; 10. Quality Deployment in the Construction Industry; 11. Quality Function Deployment for the Service Industry; 12. Quality Function Deployment for Software Development.

Leonard L. Berry, *On Great Service: A Framework for Action*, 292 pages, The Free Press, 1995.

This book explains in concrete terms how to make service excellence the center of your business. It describes a framework for delivering great service, to the mutual benefit of customers and the company. It is loaded with examples of businesses whose approach to service is to continuously outdo themselves in their ability to delight customers. Of course this is great for customers, but these are also among the most successful of American companies. For a preview of Berry's approach to this subject, see his original article that introduces this year's edition of the yearbook.

TABLE OF CONTENTS: 1. A Framework for Great Service; 2. Nurture Service Leadership; 3. Build a Service Quality Information System; 4. Create a Service Strategy; 5. Commit to the Principles of Great Service; 6. Organize for Great Service; 7. Embrace Technology; 8. Compete for Talent; 9. Develop Service Skills and Knowledge; 10. Empower Servers to Serve; 11. Work at Teamwork; 12. Measure Performance, Reward Excellence; 13. The Artistry of Great Service.

Christopher E. Bogan and Michael J. English, *Benchmarking for Best Practices: Winning Through Innovative Adaptation*, 312 pages, McGraw-Hill, 1994.

Written by two respected practitioners, this book is one of the best we have seen on understanding and using benchmarking to improve your processes, often dramatically. The goal in all this is to learn how to learn from others to innovate in your own company. The book shows how to design a benchmarking approach that nearly guarantees success. It talks about how to manage best practice information throughout the company. It includes a series of exercises called *Steal This Idea*®. Benchmarking is an economic and intelligent way to learn how to improve without reinventing the wheel. This book provides a foundation for starting up a benchmarking study and keeping it going.

TABLE OF CONTENTS: 1. Benchmarking for Best Practices: Winning Through Adaptive Innovation; 2. Fast Learning Through Innovative Adaptation; 3. Benchmarks and Performance Measurement; 4. The Secrets of Successful Benchmarking; 5. Design for Implementation Success; 6. Integrating Benchmarking into Your Organization; 7. Putting Benchmarking to Work in the Executive Office and Boardroom; 8. Benchmarking and Strategic Planning; 9. Benchmarking and Business Process Reengineering; 10. Benchmarking and Time-Based Competition; 11. Benchmarking and Change Management; 12. International Benchmarking; 13. Benchmarking in the Public Sector; 14. Managing Best Practice Knowledge; 15. Benchmarking and the Twenty-First Century Organization; **Appendices:** Steal This Idea®—The Art of Innovative Adaptation: How Can Your Organization Apply these Ideas; Steal this Idea® Exercise; Developing the Culture: Executive Exercise.

James C. Collins and Jerry I. Porras, *Built to Last: Successful Habits of Visionary Companies*, 322 pages, HarperBusiness, 1994.

Great companies are not accidents. They have great cultures that foster excellence throughout the organization. These are cultures that are not dependent on the CEO to either set or perpetuate. These companies have well-articulated values out of which emerge the decisions, actions, and teamwork necessary to not only survive but thrive in today's competitive environment. This book, based on extensive research by the authors, profiles many such companies like Hewlett-Packard, Johnson & Johnson, 3M, Marriott, and many others. It is written in a down-to-earth style. Highly recommended.

TABLE OF CONTENTS: 1. The Best of the Best; 2. Clock Building, Not Time Telling; **Interlude:** No "Tyranny of the OR" (Embrace the "Genius of the And"); 3. More Than Profits; 4. Preserve the Core/Stimulate Progress; 5. Big Hairy Audacious Goals; 6. Cult-Like Cultures; 7. Try a Lot of Stuff and Keep What Works; 8. Home-Grown Management; 9. Good Enough Never Is; 10. The End of the Beginning; **Epilogue:** Frequently Asked Questions; **Appendix 1:** Research Issues; **Appendix 2:** Founding Roots of Visionary Companies.

James W. Cortada and John A. Woods, *McGraw-Hill Encyclopedia of Quality Terms and Concepts*, 400 pages, McGraw-Hill, 1995.

By the authors of the yearbook, this is a comprehensive review of terms that cover quality management with definitions, explanations, and examples. It is aimed at executives who are involved with both the hard and the soft sides of quality implementation. It includes over 600 terms, has 82 figures, and has references for more information following most entries. It is an easy-to-use reference that anyone involved in quality management will find useful.

TABLE OF CONTENTS: Encyclopedia of Quality Terms and Concepts; **Appendix 1:** Quality References; **Appendix 2:** Magazines and Journals on Quality Management; **Appendix 3:** Major Quality Organizations.

W. Edwards Deming, *The New Economics for Industry, Government, Education*, Second Edition, 247 pages, MIT Center for Advanced Engineering Study, 1994.

This is Deming's last book, a kind of summary of his thinking on the issues of understanding an organization as a system, his "profound knowledge," leadership, and variation. It is easy to read and is actually quite short because there are not that many words per page. To get a good sense of Deming's insights into effective management, this book is well worth your time.

TABLE OF CONTENTS: 1. How Are We Doing? 2. The Heavy Losses; 3. Introduction to a System; 4. A System of Profound Knowledge; 5. Leadership; 6. Management of People; 7. The Red Beads; 8. Shewhart and Control Charts; 9. The Funnel; 10. Some Lessons in Variation; **Appendix:** Continuing Purchase of Supplies and Services.

Armand V. Feigenbaum, *Total Quality Control*, Third Edition, Revised, 863 pages, McGraw-Hill, 1991.

This is one of the premier reference works available for those implementing quality control in their organizations. First published in 1951 (!), it is written by one of the founders of the quality movement. While there are parts that are technical, it is understandable by most of us and covers nearly everything you could want to know about quality control methodology, including their implementation.

TABLE OF CONTENTS: **Part One. Business Quality Management** 1. The Quality of Products and Services and Total Quality Control; 2. The Buyer, the Producer, and the New Marketplace Demands for Quality; 3. Productivity, Technology, and the Internationalization of Quality; 4. What are the Factors in Controlling Quality and What are the Jobs of Quality Control? **Part Two. The Total Quality System** 5. The Systems Approach to Quality; 6. Establishing the Quality System; 7. Quality Costs—Foundation of Quality Systems Economics **Part Three. Management Strategies for Quality** 8. Organizing for Quality; 9. Achieving Total Commitment to Quality; **Part**

Four. Engineering Technology of Quality 10. Quality-Engineering Technology; 11. Process-Control-Engineering Technology; 12. Quality Information Equipment Engineering Technology; **Part Five. Statistical Technology of Quality** 13. Frequency Distributions; 14. Control Charts; 15. Sampling Tables; 16. Special Methods; 17. Product Reliability; **Part Six. Applying Total Quality Control in Your Company** 18. New-Design Control; 19. Incoming-Material Control; 20. Product Control; 21. Special Process Studies; **Part Seven. The Total Quality Imperative for the 1990s** 22. The Total Quality Imperative; 23. The Benchmarks of Total Quality Control for the 1990s; 24. Four Management Principles of Total Quality; **Epilogue:** The Principles of Total Quality Control: A Summary.

Francis J. Gouillart and James N. Kelly, *Transforming the Organization: Reframing Corporate Direction, Restructuring the Company, Revitalizing the Enterprise, Renewing People,* 323 pages, McGraw-Hill, 1995.

In this new and thoughtful book, the authors propose a model of the organization as a living entity where all the parts are necessary for the whole to thrive. Transforming organizations has to do with continuously learning more about the relationships among the parts so you can practice the four Rs of transformation: Reframe, Restructure, Revitalize, and Renew. The book is thoughtfully written and provides a useful metaphor for managers who want to make their companies better for employees, more responsive to customers, and more efficient in their processes. An excerpt from the introduction to this book is included in this yearbook in the section on Cultural Transformation.

TABLE OF CONTENTS: Introduction: A Framework for Transformation **Part One. Reframing** 1. Achieving Mobilization; 2. Creating the Vision; 3. Building the Measurement System; **Part Two. Restructuring** 4. Constructing an Economic Model 5. Configuring the Physical Infrastructure; 6. Redesigning the Work Architecture; **Part Three. Revitalization** 7. Achieving Market Focus; 8. Inventing New Businesses; 9. Changing the Rules Through Information Technology; **Part Four. Renewal** 10. Developing the Reward System; 11. Building Individual Learning; 12. Developing the Organization.

H. James Harrington and James S. Harrington, *Total Improvement Management: The Next Generation in Performance Improvement,* 488 pages, McGraw-Hill, 1994.

Jim Harrington's book *Business Improvement Management* is one of the largest selling books ever on how to implement process improvement in organizations. This new book is its successor. It suggests that there is no single right way to implement continuous improvement in an organization. It must be a combination of several methodologies and tools, including total quality management, total productivity management, total cost management, total resource management, and total technology management. When you properly balance all of these, then you have a strategy of Total Improvement Management that pulls them together. The strength of Harrington's books are their practicality. This provides a fine introduction to all these areas.

TABLE OF CONTENTS: Introduction; Overview; 1. Top Management Leadership: The People Who Need to Change First; 2. Business Planning Process: Aligning the Organization and the People; 3. Environmental Change Plans: Best Practices for Improvement Planning and Implementation; 4. External Customer Focus: Best Practices for Outstanding Customer Relationships; 5. Quality Management Systems: ISO 9000 and More; 6. Management Participation: Management Must Set an Example; 7. Team Building: Bringing Synergy to the Organization; 8. Individual Excellence: Going Beyond Teams; 9. Supplier Relations: Developing a Supply Management Process; 10. Process Breakthrough: Jump-Starting Your Process; 11. Product Process Excellence: The Production Side of All Organizations; 12. Service Process Excellence: How to Best Serve Your

Customers; 13. The Measurement Process: The Balance Score Card; 14. Organizational Structure: Restructuring the Organization for the 21st Century; 15. Rewards and Recognition: Rewarding Desired Behavior.

Jon R. Katzenbach and Douglas K. Smith, *The Wisdom of Teams: Creating the High Performance Organization,* 317 pages, Hardback: Harvard Business School Press; Trade Paperback: HarperBusiness, 1993.

In a down-to-earth fashion with lots of examples, the authors of this book explain the why and how of teams and the relationship of effective teams and teamwork and high organizational performance. They demonstrate that when you focus on work processes rather than the individuals doing tasks, teams just make sense. To quote from early in the book: "Teams outperform individuals acting alone or in larger organizations, groupings, especially when performance requires multiple skills, judgments, and experiences. Most people recognize the capabilities of teams; most have the common sense to make teams work. Nevertheless, most people overlook team opportunities themselves." This book is about how to avoid that and how to implement teams in any organization.

TABLE OF CONTENTS: **Prologue:** A New About What to Expect; **Part One. Understanding Teams** 1. Why Teams? 2. One Team: A Story of Performance; 3. Team Basics: A Working Definition and Discipline; 4. High Performance Teams: Very Useful Models; **Part Two. Becoming a Team** 5. The Team Performance Curve; 6. Moving Up the Curve: From Individual to Team Performance; 7. Team Leaders; 8. Teams, Obstacles, and Endings: Getting Unstuck; **Part Three. Exploiting the Potential** 9. Teams and Performance: The Reinforcing Cycle; 10. Teams and Major Change: An Inevitable Combination; 11. Team Performance at the Top: A Difficult Challenge; 12. Top Management's Role: Leading to the High-Performance Organization; **Epilogue:** A Call to Action; **Appendix A.** The Teams Question and Answer Guide; **Appendix B.** Teams Researched for the Book.

David T. Kearns and David A. Nadler, *Prophets in the Dark: How Xerox Reinvented Itself and Beat Back the Japanese,* 334 pages, HarperBusiness, 1992.

This is just what the title says. Xerox was a successful American company playing according to American rules when it was confronted by a raft of Japanese companies who built and sold copiers every bit as good as Xerox for a lot less money. The company assessed and then reinvented itself using the principles of process management, operating to optimize the entire organizational system to reduce costs and increase quality. This book is the story of how that happened by the man who led it: David Kearns. It is candid and interesting to read. A good lesson on the wrong and right ways to get things done, it concludes with a number of lessons relevant to any organization.

TABLE OF CONTENTS: 1. A New Vista; 2. The Unwanted Product; 3. Xerox Grows Up; 4. Life with the Ford Men; 5. Stormy Times; 6. The Coyote Eats the Road Runner; 7. The Odd Couple; 8. Pushing A Wet Noodle; 9. Another Prophet; 10. The Meeting in Virginia; 11. Dining at the Quality Restaurant; 12. A Backward Step; 13. The Blooming of Quality; 14. The Race with No Finish Line; **Lessons:** The Lessons of Experience; A Book for Decline; What is Quality Anyway? Managing Organizational Change; Beyond the Magic Leader; The CEO and His Consultant; A Uniquely American Solution; From Decline to Competitiveness.

Alfie Kohn, *No Contest: The Case Against Competition,* Revised Edition, 245 pages text (plus 78 pages of references and notes), Houghton Mifflin, 1992.

This is a controversial yet very thoughtful book. The basic premise is that unless we practice win-win, we compromise the quality of our performance. Win-lose competition is a recipe for failure, he argues and demonstrates through many different studies. The point is that cooperation is the way to bring out the best in people, keep them focused on the right goals, and in succeeding such that everyone feels a winner. Not everyone agrees with Kohn. His second book, *Punished By Rewards*, is equally controversial and suggests that rewards for individual performance are a short-term solution that cause people to work for the reward rather than for the intrinsic pleasure of doing a job right. Both of these are important books.

TABLE OF CONTENTS 1. The "Number One" Obsession; 2. Is Competition Inevitable? 3. Is Competition More Productive? 4. Is Competition More Enjoyable? 5. Does Competition Build Character? 6. Against Each Other; 7. The Logic of Playing Dirty; 8. Women and Competition; 9. Beyond Competition; 10. Learning Together; Afterword.

Thomas D. Kuczmarski, *Managing New Products: The Power of Innovation,* Second Edition, 304 pages, Prentice Hall, 1992.

The author of this book, a leading consultant in new product development, contends, with some validity, that the adjective "innovative" is the proper descriptor of companies that will develop a sustainable competitive advantage in the global economy. He emphasizes the importance of investing in innovative new products as the correct long-term strategy for organizations over the short-term orientation of acquisitions. And he provides detailed instructions on how to go about developing a strategy that emphasizes innovation, as practiced in companies like 3M and Rubbermaid. This is a thoughtful book on an important subject in the quality arena.

TABLE OF CONTENTS: 1. Introduction; 2. Applauding the Key Success Factors; 3. Conducting a Diagnostic Audit; 4. Developing a New Product Strategy; 5. Managing the New Product Process; 6. Structuring and Leading the Organization; 7. Rewarding and Motivating Champions; 8. Innovating for the Future; 9. Creating Newness for Nonprofit Organizations.

Charles C. Manz and Henry P. Sims, Jr., *Business Without Bosses: How Self-Managing Teams Are Building High-Performing Companies,* 238 pages, John Wiley & Sons, 1993.

This book provides a clear rationale for a company to move to self-managed teams. It describes how to do this, why it works, what the pitfalls are, and what resistance managers face, and it includes several examples from real companies. The book is written in a down-to-earth fashion with many anecdotes and how-to lists throughout. Research shows that when people truly feel they are responsible for their own success and have the authority to make decisions concerning their work, this brings out the best in them. They become committed to the company because they feel the company is committed to them. Self-managed teams are not a panacea, but with the proper training, access to information, and a supportive culture, they work better than the alternative. This book can help any manager better understand what all this is about.

TABLE OF CONTENTS: Introduction: Tyrannosaurus Rex: The Boss as Corporate Dinosaur; 1. On the Road to Teams: Overcoming the Middle Management Brick Wall; 2. The Day-to-Day Team Experience: Roles, Behaviors, and Performance of Mature Self-Managing Teams; 3. The

Good and the Bad of Teams: A Practical Look at Successes and Challenges; 4. The Early Implementation Phase: Getting Teams Started in the Office; 5. The Illusion of Self Management: Using Teams to Disempower; 6. Self Management Without Formal Teams: The Organization as a Team; 7. Teams and Total Quality Management: An International Application; 8. The Strategy Team: Teams at the Top; 9. Business Without Bosses Through Teams: What Have We Learned? Where are We Going? **Appendix:** How to Get What You Want From Your Job.

C. Dan McArthur and Larry Womack, *Outcome Management: Redesigning Your Business Systems to Achieve Your Vision*, 242 pages, AMACOM, 1995.

This is a new and insightful book that helps managers better understand the full implications of managing organizations as the systems they are. The authors take their title from Deming's admonishment "Manage outcomes. Let the people manage themselves!" This book provides a synthesis of the principles of systems thinking and TQM to more effectively manage the changes necessary to remain competitive in today's fast-changing world. It fully acknowledges the human side of organizations and provides many ideas for taking full advantage of people as components of the organizational system. These comments make the book sound somewhat theoretical, but it is written in an inviting fashion that will help you better understand what Deming and the other pioneering thinkers in quality management had in mind.

TABLE OF CONTENTS: Introduction: The Essentials of Successful Management; **Section I. Ready? Beyond Conventional Thinking** 1. The Changing Targets of Commerce; 2. Aiming the Arrows of Time—Leadership; 3. Drawing the Bow—Organization; 4. Better than One—The Dual-Track Approach; 5. Big Bangs—System Redesign; 6. Before You Start—Deploying Outcome Management; **Section II. Aim. The Basis of Unconventional Thinking** 7. Integrating—Unconventional Thinking; 8. Putting It All to Work—Integrated Action; 9. Technology and Time are of the Essence; 10. Quality and Knowledge—Roots and Wings; 11. Fitness and Facts—Winning Through Preparation; **Section III. Fire! Most Excellent Formula** 12. The Ultimate Strategy—$E = mc^2$; 13. Predicting the Future—Outcome Management; 14. Reference Point—Transforming the Future; 15. Being is More Powerful than Becoming; Epilogue: Dreams of the Future; **Appendix:** Getting Started—A Guide to Launching Outcome Management.

Eugene H. Melan, *Process Management: Methods for Improving Products and Service*, 262 pages, McGraw-Hill (co-published with ASQC Quality Press), 1993.

This is a very practical and complete step-by-step explanation of how to manage and improve processes in any type of organization. This books provides one of the best overviews of what process management you'll find anywhere. It starts at ground zero and takes you through all the basics. It includes methods for evaluating and assessing a process, guidelines for designing a process, how-to information for implementing process management in a TQM environment, and lots more. Highly recommended.

TABLE OF CONTENTS: **Part 1. Fundamentals of Process Management** 1. Introduction; 2. Origins and Characteristics of a Process; 3. Fundamentals of Process Management: Process Initialization; 4. Fundamentals of Process Management: Defining the Process; 5. Fundamentals of Process Management: Process Control; 6. Analyzing the Process: The Classical Method; 7. Analyzing the Process: Modern Methods; 8. Assessing and Evaluating a Process; 9. Process Management in Practice I: Putting It All Together; 10. Process Management in Practice II: Implementing Process Management for TQM; **Part 2. Cases in Process Management Applications** 11. Process Management in Staff/Service Operations; 12. Process Management in Financial Operations; 13. Process Management in a Laboratory; **Part 3. Processes: Present and Future** 14. Designing a Process; 15. Future Trends.

Earl Naumann and Kathleen Giel, *Customer Satisfaction Measurement and Management: Using the Voice of the Customer*, 456 pages, Thomson Executive Press, 1995.

If you want to have a reference and guide to collecting, analyzing, and using data about customers, this is about the most comprehensive and practical book we have encountered. It takes you step by step through the processes involved in figuring out what to ask your customers about their needs and wants, how to ask it, and what to do with the information after you collect it—specifically making improvements that are good for the company and its customers. It even includes a chapter on using these methods to collect information about internal customers. The book includes lots of examples, as well. If you are looking for a book that includes some theory and lots of how-to on this important subject, this is a good one.

Hy Pitt, *SPC for the Rest of Us: A Personal Path to Statistical Process Control*, 429 pages, Addison-Wesley, 1994.

For many, SPC is the technical part of Total Quality Management that sometimes is just forgotten or not put into practice except on the factory floor. Statistics, the tool by which to best understand the measurements of process outputs, is not easy. However, statistics are not so difficult to understand either, if you put a little time in. And managing to reduce variation and improve quality depends on the use of statistical measurements to understand your system and its capabilities. This is the best book we have found for those who want to know something about SPC but aren't engineers or technicians. SPC for the rest of us properly describes this book. It is a clear, not difficult, yet accurate review of the basic statistics involved in undertaking SPC in any area of a business, including the front office, the shop floor, or measuring customer satisfaction.

Hal F. Rosenbluth and Diane McFerrin Peters, *The Customer Comes Second and Other Secrets of Exceptional Service*, 240 pages, Quill (William Morrow), 1992.

This is not a theory book. It is a profile of Rosenbluth, Inc., one of the largest travel agencies in the world, and how it got that way. David Kearns' *Prophets in the Dark* profiles how a manufacturing company made itself competitive again by implementing total quality management methods and principles. This book, shorter and more informal, shows how a service company used these techniques not to become competitive again but to grow from a regional travel agency headquartered in Philadelphia to a national company booking over $1.5 billion dollars in business annually. If you want to know what removing fear from the workplace is all about, this book is a good place to start. It also shows what results when you do it right—meaning you create a great place to work, you look out for customers, and you focus on getting better and better at this. A short, but insightful book.

TABLE OF CONTENTS: 1. Cultural Metamorphosis; 2. How It All Begins; 3. Happiness in the Workplace; 4. Inventing the Future; 5. Finding the Right People; 6. Perpetual Training: A Secret Weapon; 7. Technology as a Tool; 8. Service Is an Attitude, an Art, and a Process; 9. The Creation of a Culture; 10. The Birth and Nurturing of Ideas; 11. The Gardening Process; 12. Look Around You; 13. Open Partnerships; 14. Blazing New Trails; 15. A Lot to Digest.

Eberhard E. Scheuing and William F. Christopher, Editors, *The Service Quality Handbook*, 550 pages, AMACOM, 1993.

This book includes 57 articles by a wide variety of experts in the area of customer service and quality. The list of contributors is virtually a who's who of the major writers and practitioners in this area, including Curt Reimann, Karl Albrecht, Paul Allaire, Robert Camp, Ron Zemke, Chris Hart, Patrick Townsend and Joan Gebhardt, Stew Leonard, Jr., and several others, equally qualified if not as well known. This is a comprehensive review of all aspects of managing for service quality. It includes articles that explain why you should do it, how to do it, and war stories of those who are doing it and the success they have enjoyed. In the table of contents, we just list the part. Under each part there are four or five chapters, each by a different contributor.

TABLE OF CONTENTS: Part I. The Evolution of the Service Quality Movement (4 chapters); Part II. Creating the Quality Vision (5 chapters); Part III. Creating the Service Quality Framework (5 chapters); Part IV. Deploying Quality Service (4 chapters); Part V. The Role of Employees in Service Quality (4 chapters); Part VI. Implementing Service Quality (4 chapters); Part VII. Delivering Service Quality (4 chapters); Part VIII. Measuring Service Quality (4 chapters); Part IX. Reinforcing Service Quality (5 chapters); Part X. Managing Quality In Government Services (2 chapters).

Shoji Shiba, Alan Graham, and David Walden, *A New American TQM: Four Practical Revolutions in Management*, 574 pages, Productivity Press, 1993.

This book is specifically oriented toward the development of TQM in the United States. The fact that one author is from Japan is especially valuable because it allows for a contrast between the way they do it in Japan and the way it's done in the United States. What are the four practical revolutions of the subtitle? From the preface, the authors answer this question: "We believe that companies cannot succeed in the long run without systems and practices that support customer focus [1], continuous improvement [2], total participation [3], and societal networking [4]." These "revolutions" are certainly not unique. In fact, writer after writer keeps coming up with them. (Maybe there really is something going on here.) Anyway, this book proceeds step by step through each of these four areas with detailed explanations, replete with lots of figures that capture the points being made. Fundamentally, this is a comprehensive and basic textbook on the principles of quality management. If you wanted to recommend a book to someone who was a beginner that would take them far along the road to understanding what managing to deliver quality is all about, this would be a good choice.

Jay W. Spechler, *Managing Quality in America's Most Admired Companies*, 421 pages, Barrett-Koehler Publishers, 1993.

This book, by a former senior examiner for the Malcolm Baldrige National Quality Award, provides a basic understanding of what managing for quality is all about. It then provides 32 case studies from a wide variety of industries that provide brief overviews of how these companies did it. There are loads of useful ideas in this book, and it's especially valuable for showing how others may be going about what you want to do. It may be useful for finding companies you can benchmark. You will note that some of the companies profiled are not necessarily thriving these days, but, for this author, there was still some part of their operations worth noting.

Jack Stack, *The Great Game of Business: The Only Sensible Way to Run a Company*, 252 page, Doubleday Currency, 1992.

Have you heard of the Springfield Remanufacturing Company? It's a company in Springfield, Missouri where they refurbish and sell engines of all sorts for use in machinery. Jack Stack, CEO and author of this book, has made his company famous for its open-book management approach. In this approach, all employees are trained to understand the numbers, know exactly what and how much value they add to the company, and are compensated based on this. This book explains this approach to information sharing and how it brings people together in any organization. A basic tenet of TQM is that teamwork is important and that an open environment that eliminates fear is important. Stack has intuitively appreciated this and created an environment and management approach that affirms this. Their success speaks for itself. The company's remanufactured engines are highly regarded in the marketplace. His ideas are spreading as SRC has become a mecca for other companies seeking to understand this idea of open-book management.

TABLE OF CONTENTS: 1. Why We Teach People How to Make Money; 2. Myths of Management; 3. The Feeling of a Winner; 4. The Big Picture; 5. Open-Book Management; 6. Setting Standards; 7. Skip the Praise—Give Us a Raise; 9. The Great Huddle; 10. A Company of Owners; 11. The Highest Level of Thinking; 12. The Ultimate Law: The Message to Middle Managers.

James P. Womack, Daniel T. Jones, and Daniel Roos, *The Machine That Changed the World: The Story of Lean Production*, 323 pages, Hardback: Rawson Associates, Trade Paperback: HarperPerennial, 1990.

When this book came out in 1990, *Business Week* called it "the best book on the changes shaping manufacturing and the most readable." This is a very influential book on the history and implementation of lean production in the automobile industry. The book contrasts lean production with mass production and shows why the latter is on the way out. This is a book about theory, but it is a story at the same time, with special emphasis on NUMMI, the joint venture between Toyota and General Motors in Fremont, California. The partnership turned a plant that produced average GM cars into one that produced cars of world-class quality for a lot less money and with less rancor with the UAW. If you are interested in the future of manufacturing (any type of manufacturing), this book about its evolution is one you will want to review.

TABLE OF CONTENTS: Before You Begin this Book; 1. The Industry of Industries in Transition; **Part One. The Origins of Lean Production** 2. The Rise and Fall of Mass Production; 3. The Rise of Lean Production; **Part Two. The Elements of Lean Production** 4. Running the Factory; 5. Designing the Car; 6. Coordinating the Supply Chain; 7. Dealing With Customers; 8. Managing the Lean Enterprise; **Part Three. Diffusing Lean Production** 9. Confusion about Diffusion; 10. Completing the Transition; Epilogue.

Ron Zemke with Dick Schaff, *The Service Edge: 101 Companies that Profit from Customer Care*, 584 pages, A Plume Book, 1989.

Ron Zemke, a consulting editor for *The Quality Yearbook* is widely known for the "Knock Your Socks Service" series of books. Those books talk about the whys and hows of service delivery. The book we're recommending here can be especially useful in understanding how attending to customer service can pay big dividends in terms of growth and profitability. The book includes a 76-page beginning part that talks about the principles of distinctive service, then goes on to provide the 101 case studies of the title. These are companies that understand the importance of customer service in building long-term customer relationships. They know that it's much cheaper to hold onto a current customer than to find a new one. They also know that a solid base of repeat customers is the key to sustained growth in a competitive marketplace. This book provides the principles and examples that can help companies in any industry begin to make service to customers a primary focus on their business strategy. In reviewing the contents, check the number of different industries from which the examples are drawn.

TABLE OF CONTENTS: Part 1: The Principles of Distinctive Service The Customer Service Dilemma; Creating Distinctive Service: A Will Management Act; Operating Principle #1: Listen, Understand, and Respond to Customers; Operating Principle #2: Define Superior Service and Establish a Service Strategy; Operating Principle #3: Set Standards and Measure Performance; Operating Principles #4: Select, Train, and Empower Employees to Work for the Customer; Operating Principles #5: Recognize and Reward Accomplishment; **Part 2: The Service 101** Travel: Airlines, Services; Hotels; Health Care: Hospitals, Support; Financial: Personal, Banking, Brokerage, Insurance; Wheels: Automotive, Trucking; Food Service: Restaurants, Fast Food; Food Sales: Retail, Wholesale; Retailing: General, Specialty, Catalog; Technology: Electronics, Support, Communications; Manufacturing; Business-to-Business: Delivery, Expertise, Duplicating, Support; Pacesetters: Entertainment, Information, Public, Care; Suggested Readings and Bibliography.

Directory of Magazines and Journals

This section includes a comprehensive (though not exhaustive) listing of publications that regularly cover issues on quality management. Some of them are dedicated to quality issues, and some of them cover quality as part of their regular editorial policy. We have included several newsletters not described in earlier editions of the yearbook. If you have an interest in one of these, you can usually call and get a sample issue to see if it's something you would like to read regularly. Many quality organizations, such as the American Society for Quality Control and others, include a variety of newsletters of interest to members. Most local quality organizations also publish their own newsletters. Those publications are not listed here as they are available only to members. You can find out more about those organizations in the 1994 and 1995 editions of *The Quality Yearbook* where we have included a directory of organizations devoted to quality management issues.

We have organized this listing into three categories:

1. Magazines, journals, and newsletters dedicated to quality
2. General business magazines, journals, and newsletters that often include articles on quality
3. Industry and special interest magazines, journals, and newsletters that often cover quality issues

All magazines, journals, and newsletters included have something of value to anyone interested in TQM, depending on background and specialty. However, to help you sort through these in terms of their value in learning about and implementing quality, we have developed the following ratings:

★★★ = Highest recommendation, regularly includes very useful information on quality management
★★ = Highly recommended, frequently includes useful articles
★ = Recommended, includes some useful articles

Note: In establishing these ratings, they do not apply to the overall "quality" of the magazines, but to their coverage of quality management topics.

Magazines, Journals, and Newsletters Dedicated to Quality
Critical Linkages II Newsletter
Published by Sager Educational Enterprises five times a year (Jan., Mar., May., Sept., and Nov.), 21 Wallis Road, Chestnut Hill, MA 02167, phone: (617) 469-9644, fax: (617) 469-9639.

Subscriptions: United States: 1 year $30; outside United States: 1 year $36.

This newsletter is designed to help managers understand the interconnections among people, departments, customers, suppliers, schools, and the community and how that understanding can help them manage better. Special emphasis on education. Rating: ★★

Customer Service Manager's Letter

Published monthly by Bureau of Business Practice (Division of Simon & Schuster), 24 Rope Ferry Road, Waterford, CT 06386, (800) 876-9105.

Subscriptions: United States: 1 year $144, 2 or more subscriptions 1 year $130 each; international: call or write.

This is an 8-page, full-color newsletter with advice aimed at customer service managers. Emphasizes issues involved in implementing TQM both in terms of teamwork and empowerment and in terms of service excellence. Rating: ★★

Eye On Improvement

Published 24 times a year by the Institute for Healthcare Improvement, P.O. Box 38100, Cleveland, OH 44138-0100, (800) 895-4951. (Note: the IHI also publishes *Quality Connection* out of Boston.)

Subscriptions: United States and Canada: 1 year $120; international: 1 year $140.

A newsletter designed to quickly spread the word to frontline health systems leadership of useful information on quality management techniques and practices. Most of the articles are short digests of material that has appeared in many other publications that would be of interest to health care professionals. Edited by Donald Berwick, M.D., a leading figure in implementing TQM in the delivery of health care. Rating: ★★★

Healthcare Quality Abstracts

Published monthly except July by COR Healthcare Resources, P.O. Box 40959, Santa Barbara, CA 93140, phone: (805) 564–2177, fax: (805) 564–2146.

Subscriptions: U.S. and Canada: 1 year $98; all other countries: 1 year $110.

This is just what it says it is—a newsletter format abstracting of current articles from a variety of journals all dealing with quality management in health care. The listing is broken up by topic, and the sources for all articles are listed on the back page with addresses and phone numbers of publishers. Rating: ★★

Joint Commission Journal of Quality Improvement

Published monthly under the editorial direction of the Joint Commission by Mosby–Year Book, Inc., 11830 Westline Industrial Drive, St. Louis, MO 63146–3318, (314) 453–4351 or (800) 453–4351.

Subscriptions: $115 per year for U.S., all other countries, $125 per year.

This journal replaced the former journal published by The Joint Commission, the *Quality Review Bulletin*. The goal of this refereed journal is to publish articles that emphasize the improvement of health care quality, which includes the measurement, assessment, and/or improvement of performance in health care quality and delivery. The journal includes how-to articles and case studies. Rating: ★★★

Journal for Quality and Participation

Published seven times a year (January/February, March, June, July/August, September, October/November, and December) by the Association for Quality and Participation, 801-B West 8th Street, Suite 501, Cincinnati, OH 45203, (513) 381-1959.

Subscriptions: Available as part of membership in AQP. Nonmembers: $52 per year in the United States and $75 for international orders.

Most issues are centered around a theme with several articles on that theme, plus the inclusion of other pieces that cover topics related to quality management. Some themes for 1996 include joy in work, measuring success, taking full advantage of IT, quality service, and quality for the knowledge worker. The journal often includes articles by well-known consultants and writers. This is one of a handful of journals that anyone really interested in quality management practices should be reading. Rating: ★★★

Journal of Quality Technology

Published quarterly by the American Society for Quality Control, 611 East Wisconsin Avenue, P.O. Box 3005, Milwaukee, WI 53201-3005, (414) 272-8575.

Subscriptions: For ASQC members, annual subscription is $20 in the United States, $38.50 in Canada, and $36 for other international; for nonmembers, $30 annually in the United States, $40 for other international subscriptions.

A technically oriented journal, with heavy use of statistics, emphasizing the practical applicability of new techniques, instructive examples of the operation of existing techniques, and results of historical researches. Useful only to those involved in quality control technology. Rating: ★★

National Productivity Review

Published quarterly by John Wiley & Sons, Inc., 605 Third Avenue, New York, NY 10158, (212) 850-6479.

Subscriptions: United States, Canada and Mexico, 1 year $175; other countries, 1 year $225. Discounts available on multiple copy subscriptions.

A journal that includes practical articles focusing on the implementation of quality in all types of organizations. The articles are often written by the people who did the work. The writing is uneven, but the content is nearly always valuable. The articles tend to be long, so they require some time to read and reflect on. Divided into three sections: Ideas and Opinions, Features, and Reviews. Rating: ★★★

PI Quality

Published bimonthly by Hitchcock Publishing Co., 191 Gary Avenue, Carol Stream, IL 60188–2292, phone: (708) 665–1000, fax: (708) 462–2225.

Subscriptions: Free to qualified individuals in process industries, or $40 per year in the U.S. and $100 per year for all other countries.

Because it is aimed at qualified circulation, this magazine includes a variety of articles dealing with the use of various technology in the process industries (which include food, beverages, chemicals, pharmaceuticals, soaps, textiles, papers, petroleum, rubber, plastics, stone, clay, glass, leather, and primary metal processing). Articles tend to be short and technology oriented. Rating: ★

Quality

Published monthly by Hitchcock Publishing Company, One Chilton Way, Radnor, PA 19089.

Subscriptions: United States, 1 year $70. Canada and Mexico, 1 year $85. International, 1 year $160.

Includes articles that focus mainly on the technical aspects of implementing total quality management in production and manufacturing environments. Includes reviews and event calendar. Especially of interest to engineers and quality technicians. Rating: ★★★

The Quality Connection

Published quarterly by the Institute for Healthcare Improvement, One Exeter Plaza, Ninth Floor, Boston, MA 02116, phone: (617) 424-4800, fax: (617) 424-4848.

Subscriptions: This newsletter is distributed free of charge to anyone interested in quality management in health care.

This newsletter includes interviews, commentaries, and other topics of interest on implementing quality management in health care. Donald Berwick, one of the leaders in this area, is the president and CEO of IHI, and this newsletter is part of their effort to spread the word. Since it is free, it won't get a rating, but it is definitely worth receiving if you have an interest in this area.

Quality Digest

Published monthly by QCI International, 1350 Vista Way, P.O. Box 882, Red Bluff, CA 96080, phone (800) 527-8875 or (916) 527-8875, fax: (916) 527-6983.

Subscriptions: 1 year $49, 2 years $78, 3 years $107; $69 for international orders.

Includes a variety of how-to articles and pieces on how various organizations implement quality, especially in people management. Also includes monthly columnists such as Tom Peters, Karl Albrecht, and Ken Blanchard, plus book reviews and other information. Rating: ★★★

Quality Engineering

Published quarterly by the American Society for Quality Control and Marcel Dekker, Inc. Subscriptions available through Marcel Dekker Journals, P.O. Box 5017, Monticello, NY 12701-5176.

Subscriptions: 1 year $35; add $14 for surface mail and $22 for airmail to Europe and $26 for airmail to Asia.

Dedicated to quality management articles that deal with this message: "What the problem was, how we solved it, and what the results were." Articles tend to be detailed and moderately technical, but quite relevant to quality professionals. Rating: ★★

Quality and Reliability Engineering
Published bimonthly by John Wiley & Sons Ltd., Baffins Lane, Chichester, Sussex PO19 1UD, England.

Subscriptions: 1 year $495.

A technical journal with articles designed to fill the gap between theoretical methods and scientific research on one hand and current industrial practices on the other. Highly specialized and mathematical. Recommended only for corporate or university libraries for use by engineers in this area. Rating: ★★

Quality Management in Health Care
Published quarterly by Aspen Publishers Inc, 7201 McKinney Circle, Frederick, MD 21701, (800) 638-8437.

Subscriptions: $134 per year in the U.S. and Canada. For international subscriptions, contact: Swets Publishing Service, P.O. Box 825, 2160 SZ Lisse, The Netherlands.

This is a refereed journal with the purpose of providing a forum to explore the theoretical, technical, and strategic elements of quality management, and to assist those who wish to implement TQM in health care. Articles tend to be practical, somewhat technical, and oriented toward specific tasks in health care management. Rating: ★★

Quality in Manufacturing
Published bimonthly by Huebcore Communications, Inc., 29100 Aurora Road, Suite 200, (216) 248-1125.

Subscriptions: 1 year $75; Canada and Mexico 1 year $95; international 1 year $155. Available free to qualified people in manufacturing (call for sample copy).

A closed circulation large format four-color magazine devoted to reviews and articles about quality technology in manufacturing. Rating: ★

Quality Management Journal
Published quarterly by the American Society for Quality Control, 611 East Wisconsin Avenue, P.O. Box 3005, Milwaukee, WI 53201-3005, (414) 272-8575.

Subscriptions: Available to members of ASQC in the United States at $50 annually, to nonmembers at $60; Canada: $74 to members and $84 to nonmembers; international: $74 to members and $84 to nonmembers.

A peer-reviewed journal designed to present academic research on quality management in a style that makes it accessible to managers in all fields. Rating: ★★★

Quality Management Update

Published 24 times a year by Faulkner & Gray, Inc., 11 Penn Plaza, New York, NY 10001, (800) 535-8403.

Subscriptions: United States: 1 year $325; outside United States: 1 year $355.

This is a semimonthly newsletter for the health care industry, especially aimed at operational managers who are charged with implementing quality management practices. Just as its title says, it is an update on what's going on at various institutions around the country, as well as from the Joint Commission on Accreditation of Healthcare Organizations, and so on. Rating: ★★

Quality Progress

Published monthly by the American Society for Quality Control, Inc., 611 East Wisconsin Avenue, P.O. Box 3005, Milwaukee, WI 53201-3005, (414) 272-8575.

Subscriptions: Available as part of membership in the ASQC. $50 per year for nonmembers in the United States and $85 for first class to Canada and international airmail.

This is the foremost magazine dealing with quality management topics. Every issue is devoted to a theme but also includes several other articles dealing with a broad spectrum of issues. The articles are nearly always practical and provide perspectives that anyone interested in quality management will find valuable. It is the source of more articles in *The Quality Yearbook* than any other. Includes event calendars, reviews, and many other regular features. Rating: ★★★

Re-Designing Customer Service

Published monthly by Organizational Development Corporation, P.O. Box 312, Mukwonago, WI 53149, (800) 634-1884.

Subscriptions: United States: 1 year $144, 2 years $222; international: call or write.

This is an 8-page, two-color newsletter that covers a variety of topics having to do with improving customer service. It includes short articles that describe what leading companies are doing and how-to advice. Rating: ★★

The Systems Thinker

Published 10 times a year by Pegasus Communications, Inc., P.O. Box 120, Kendall Square, Cambridge, MA 02142, phone: (617) 576-1231, fax: (617) 576-3114.

Subscriptions: All subscriptions: 1 year $167.

A thoughtful and important newsletter for anyone interested in the systems view of organizations and in using this insight to better understand and improve organizational processes. It includes articles that help you recognize various patterns of behavior and case studies of systems thinking implementation. Systems thinking is the foundation of the learning organization, and this newsletter can help you create your own learning organization. (See the excerpt from Peter Senge about systems thinking in the reference section of this edition of the yearbook.) Rating: ★★★

Strategies for Healthcare Excellence

Published monthly by COR Research Inc., P.O. Box 40959, Santa Barbara, CA 93140–0959, (805) 564–2177.

Subscriptions: U.S. and Canada: 1 year $197; all other countries: 1 year $210.

This is a 12-page, two-color newsletter that includes detailed case studies on how specific health care facilities and managers are implementing quality principles in their organizations. Each issue usually includes one long piece followed by other short articles on this subject. Rating: ★★

Target

Published bimonthly by the Association for Manufacturing Excellence, 380 West Palatine Road, Wheeling, IL 60090, (708) 520-3282.

Subscriptions: Available to members of AME as part of membership. Cost of annual membership: $125.

Includes many practical articles on how various industries and companies are implementing TQM in manufacturing and management. Also includes reports from regional chapters, book reviews, and event calendar. Practical, accessible, and well-done. Rating: ★★★

The Center for Quality Management Journal

Published quarterly by the Center for Quality Management, 70 Fawcett Street, MS 15/4B, Cambridge, MA 02138, (617) 873-2152.

Subscriptions: $70 per year.

This is a new journal, started in 1992, and it includes a selection of practical articles focusing on the implementation of TQM in different organizations. Rating: ★

The Quality Observer

Published monthly by The Quality Observer Corporation, 3505 Old Lee Highway, P.O. Box 1111, Fairfax, VA 22030, (703) 691-9295.

Subscriptions: 1 year $53, 2 years $90, and 3 years $130; overseas, 1 year $68, 2 years $120, and 3 years $175; libraries, 1 year $90 (2 copies each issues sent to same address); corporations, 1 year $180 (5 copies each issue sent to same address).

Billed as the "International News Magazine of Quality," this is a three-color tabloid-sized publication, with case studies, international news, interviews, and regular columns on quality topics. Rating: ★★

The Total Quality Review

Published bimonthly by Cambridge Strategy Publications, P.O. Box 26007, Alexandria, VA 22313–6007.

Subscriptions: Introductory subscription in the U.S. available at $135 (regular rate: $165) per year; international: introductory subscription $165 (regular rate: $195) per year.

Organized around differing themes each month, it includes a variety of how-to articles, case studies, and background pieces for understanding the implementation of TQM. Also includes regular news from the Council for Continuous Improvement. Rating: ★★

Total Quality Environmental Manager

Published quarterly by John Wiley & Sons, Inc., 605 Third Avenue, New York, NY 10158, (212) 850–6479.

Subscriptions: U.S., Canada, Mexico 1 year $159; other countries 1 year $209.

While aimed at managers and, to some degree, engineers in the environmental area, its articles are practical and cover a broad spectrum in the application of TQM principles to this field. Worth having in the library of any company interested in this field. Rating: ★★★

Total Quality Management

Published three times a year by Carfax Publishing Company, P.O. Box 25, Abington, Oxfordshire OX14 3UE, United Kingdom or P.O. Box 2025, Dunnellon, FL 32630.

Subscriptions: Information available by writing to either of these addresses.

An academic journal with a practical bent, it includes articles of practical interest to managers and academics. It covers all aspects of quality management. Rating: ★★

TQM in Higher Education

Published monthly by Magna Publications Inc., 2718 Dryden Drive, Madison, WI 53704-3086, (608) 246-3580 or (800) 433-0499.

Subscriptions: $138 per year with discounts available for additional subscriptions to the same location.

A monthly eight-page, two-color newsletter covering ideas on applying TQM principles, case studies, information on TQM tools, and other practical articles on quality management in colleges and universities. Rating: ★★

General Business Magazines, Journals, and Newsletters That Include Coverage of Quality

Across the Board

Published ten times annually (January/February and July/August combined issues) by The Conference Board, Inc., 845 Third Avenue, New York, NY 10022, (212) 759-0900.

Subscriptions: $20 annually for Conference Board Associates and $40 annually for nonassociates.

A thoughtfully edited magazine on issues of interest to all managers. Includes columns, commentaries, how-to and company profiles, and issue-related articles. Articles occasionally directly related to quality, but nearly all are indirectly related. Rating: ★★★

Business Ethics

Published bimonthly by Mavis Publications, Inc., 52 South 10th Street, #110, Minneapolis, MN 55403-4700, (612) 962-4700.

Subscriptions: $49 per year in the United States and $59 for international subscriptions; available to first-time subscribers for $29.

Includes articles on topics of ethical and social concern to business, all of which are arguably related to quality in one way or another. Occasionally includes articles specifically on quality management and its implementation in socially responsible organizations.
Rating: ★★

Business Horizons

Published bimonthly by JAI Press, Inc., 55 Old Post Road, No. 2, P.O. Box 1678, Greenwich, CT 06836-1678, (203) 661-7602.

Subscriptions: $60 per year in the United States; outside the United States add $20 for surface mail and $30 for airmail.

Published out of the Indiana University Graduate School of Business, there is a diversity of articles of interest to managers, often shorter and more practically oriented than found in the *Harvard Business Review*. Seems to deal with quality management issues on a regular basis. Rating: ★★

Business Week

Published weekly by McGraw-Hill, Inc., 1221 Avenue of the Americas, New York, NY 10020, (212) 512-2000.

Subscriptions: Official subscription rate: 1 year $44.95, 2 years $74.95, and 3 years $99.95. Widely available at discounted subscription rates.

The leading business newsweekly in the United States. Gives special attention to quality in one or two issues per year and includes articles on quality management as appropriate during the year. Rating: ★★

California Management Review

Published quarterly by the University of California, Walter A. Haas School of Business, 350 Barrows Hall, University of California, Berkeley, CA 94720, (510) 642-7159.

Subscriptions: 1 year $45, 2 years $80, and 3 years $115; international subscriptions 1 year $68, 2 years $126, and 3 years $184.

An academic journal with a practical orientation, often including in-depth articles on quality management theory and implementation. Rating: ★★

Executive Excellence

Published monthly by Executive Excellence Publishing, 3507 North University, Suite 100, Provo, UT 84604-4479, (800) 371-7716.

Subscriptions: United States and Canada: 1 year $129, 2 years $199, 3 years $297; other countries: 1 year $169, 2 years $279, 3 years $407.

This is the newsletter from Stephen R. Covey's group. It bills itself as "The magazine of leadership development, managerial effectiveness, and organizational productivity." It is usually 20 pages long, beautifully designed, and printed in full color. The articles are usually around one to two pages each, contributed by well-known consultants and executives. All the articles are fundamentally based on quality management principles. Well done, but basically designed to get you thinking about issues. Rating:★★

Fortune

Published biweekly by Time Warner, Inc., Time & Life Building, Rockefeller Center, New York, NY 10020, (800) 621-8000.

Subscriptions: Official subscription rate: $52.95 1 year, United States and $53.75 1 year, Canada. Widely available at discounted subscription rates.

Provides in-depth reviews of management and other business topics and profiles of executives. Articles do not often focus on quality per se, but they are useful as benchmarks for understanding quality management practices in relation to traditional perspectives on managing. Rating: ★★

Harvard Business Review

Published bimonthly by the Harvard Business School, Boston, MA 02163, (617) 495-6800.

Subscriptions: $75 per year, United States, $95 per year in Canada and Mexico, and $145 in all other countries.

Includes in-depth articles on management techniques in all functional areas by highly regarded researchers and executives. Often includes articles of direct or indirect relevance to those interested in quality. Rating: ★★★

Inc.

Published monthly by *Inc.*, 38 Commercial Wharf, Boston, MA 02110, (617) 248-8000 or (800) 234-0999 for subscription information.

Subscriptions: Available at various rates, often discounted. Currently being offered at $19 for 1 year or $38 for 3 years.

The premier magazine covering issues of interest to small- and medium-sized businesses. Loaded with practical how-to techniques and articles and company and executive profiles. Sometimes covers issues directly related to quality management issues, though it only occasionally uses the word quality to describe this approach. Rating: ★★

Industry Week

Published biweekly by Penton Publishing Company, 1100 Superior Avenue, Cleveland, OH 44114-2543, (216) 696-7000.

Subscriptions: Distributed as a closed circulation magazine to qualified executives in administration, finance, production, engineering, purchasing, marketing, and sales. To those who do not qualify, it is available by subscription in the United States at $60 for 1 year, $95 for 2 years; Canada $80 for 1 year, $140 for 2 years; Mexico $90 for 1 year, $160 for 2 years; all other countries $100 for 1 year, $180 for 2 years.

Includes articles, columns, and reviews of timely interest to managers. Recently got a new editor, and the emphasis has been less on topics directly relating to quality management. It also tends to feature more profiles of individual managers. Still a good magazine. Rating: ★★

Journal of Business Strategy
Published bimonthly by Faulkner Group, Inc., 11 Penn Plaza, New York, NY 10001, (212) 967-7000.

Subscriptions: $98 per year in the United States and Canada and $128 per year in all other countries.

Each edition includes a Special Focus section that provides an in-depth look at one topic of interest in strategic planning and thinking, plus additional articles, columns, and features. Often covers topics on quality management. Rating: ★★

The Lakewood Report
Published by Lakewood Publications, Inc., 50 S. Ninth Street, Minneapolis, MN 55402, phone: (800) 328-4329, fax: (612) 333-6526.

Subscriptions: United States: $128 annually; Canada: add $10 plus 7% GST (#123705485); other international: $148 annually.

This is the successor to two newsletters that were merged: *The Service Edge* and *Total Quality Newsletter*. It is a 12-page, two-color newsletter with lots of short, practical items that readers can use, perhaps immediately. It also features descriptions of what various companies are doing to implement quality-oriented practices. Very useful and easy to read. Rating: ★★★

Management Review
Published monthly by the American Management Association Publications Division, Box 408, Saranac, NY 12983-0408.

Subscriptions: $45 per year in the United States; non-U.S. subscriptions $60 per year.

The official magazine of the American Management Association, it includes a variety of articles of interest to managers and often includes items on quality issues. Rating: ★★

Nation's Business
Published by the U.S. Chamber of Commerce, 1615 H Street NW, Washington, DC 20062-2000, (202) 463-5650.

Subscriptions: 1 year $22, 2 years $35, and 3 years $46; Canadian and international subscriptions add $20 to each rate.

Includes articles of interest to small- and medium-sized business, with frequent coverage of quality management issues. Rating: ★★

Sloan Management Review
Published quarterly by the MIT Sloan School of Management, 292 Main Street, E38-120, Cambridge, MA 02139, (617) 253-7170.

Subscriptions: $59 per year; $79 for Canada and Mexico, and $89 for all other international subscriptions.

Includes practical yet thoughtful, well-researched articles on a variety of issues of direct interest to managers interested in quality topics. Articles tend to be long, but they will help you better understand the subjects they cover. Authors are usually academics but sensitive to the needs of managers. Rating: ★★★

Supervisory Management

Published monthly by the American Management Association, 135 West 50th Street, New York, NY 10020, phone: (800) 759-8520, or (212) 903-8075, fax: (212) 903-8083.

Subscriptions: United States: 1 year $65, 2 years $110.50; all other countries add $10 per year.

This is a 12-page, two-color newsletter oriented especially toward the needs of first-line supervisors. It regularly deals with issues related to quality management, with special regular sections on teams and teamwork. Lots of short pieces; practical and down-to-earth. However, it is heavy on principles and light on examples from real companies. Rating: ★★

Tom Peters On Achieving Excellence

Newsletter published monthly by TPG Communications, P.O. Box 2189, Berkeley, CA 94702-0189, (800) 959-1059.

Subscriptions: United States: 1 year $197 and 2 years $244. Call for international rates.

A slick, readable, and practical 12-page two-color newsletter in the Peters style. Each issue has a theme with lots of short pieces on what different companies and people are doing to solve various business problems. Rating: ★★

Industry and Special Interest Magazines, Journals, and Newsletters that Cover Quality

APICS-The Performance Advantage

Published quarterly by the American Production and Inventory Control Society, Inc., 500 West Annandale Road, Falls Church, VA 22046-4274, phone (800) 444-2742 or (703) 237-8344, fax: (703) 237-1071.

Subscriptions: Included as part of membership package. Nonmembers subscriptions available at $30 per year; $40 in Mexico and Canada, and $50 for all other international subscriptions.

Covers the latest manufacturing principles and practices, case studies, columns, and news. Often includes articles on quality management in its field. Rating: ★★

Bank Management

Published bimonthly by Bank Administration Institute, One North Franklin, Chicago, IL 60606, (800) 655-2706.

Subscriptions: United States: 1 year $59; international: 1 year $89.

Oriented toward strategic issues in bank management. Attractively produced magazine that occasionally covers quality management topics. Rating: ★

Change

Published bimonthly by Heldref Publications, 1319 Eighteenth Street NW, Washington, DC 20036-1802, (212) 296-6267 or (800) 365-9753 for subscriptions.

Subscriptions: United States: $31 per year; outside the United States, add $12 per year.

Billed as the magazine of higher learning, it addresses issues of interest to the administration of colleges and universities, and occasionally carries articles on quality management topics. Rating: ★

Educational Leadership

Published monthly September through May, except bimonthly December/ January issue, by the Association for Supervision and Curriculum Development, 1250 North Pitt Street, Alexandria, VA 22314–1453, phone: (703) 549–9110, fax: (703) 549–3891.

Subscriptions: Part of membership package in ASCD. For nonmembers: 1 year $36. Call or write for international subscriptions.

Popular journal for educators and administrators. Occasionally includes articles covering quality principles in teaching and administration. Rating: ★

Healthcare Executive

Published bimonthly by the Amercian College of Healthcare Executives, 840 North Lake Shore Drive, Chicago, IL 60611–9842.

Subscriptions: Write to Processing Center, 1951 Cornell Avenue, Melrose Park, IL 60160. 1 year $45, 2 years $80. For subscriptions outside the U.S., add $15 per year.

Aimed at health care managers, this journal regularly covers quality management issues. Most articles are relatively short and basic. Rating: ★★

Healthcare Forum Journal

Published bimonthly by The Healthcare Forum, 830 Market Street, San Francisco, CA 94102, (415) 421–8810.

Subscriptions: Available as part of membership in The Healthcare Forum or 1 year $45, 2 years $80, 3 years $115. Canada and Mexico add $15 per year; 1 year all other countries $90.

A well-done journal that regularly includes articles on TQM. Articles are often in-depth yet down to earth and readable. Includes many ads on resources for health care managers looking to implement TQM. Rating: ★★

Health Care Management Review

Published quarterly by Aspen Publishers Inc, 7201 McKinney Circle, Frederick, MD 21701, (800) 638–8437.

Subscriptions: $110 per year in the U.S. and Canada. For international subscriptions, contact: Swets Publishing Service, P.O. Box 825, 2160 SZ Lisse, The Netherlands.

A refereed journal that regularly includes articles in the field of health care management. Articles tend to be five to ten pages with references, but nontechnical in nature. Rating: ★★

HR Focus

Published by the American Management Association, 135 West 50th Street, New York, NY 10020, (212) 903-8389.

Subscriptions: 1 year $51.75, 2 years $88, and 3 years $132. Add $10 per year for outside the United States.

Newsletter-like publication, but longer than the average newsletter. Covers a variety of issues and news items of interest to HR managers. Sometimes includes articles on quality subjects. Rating: ★

HRMagazine

Published monthly by the Society for Human Resource Management, 606 North Washington Street, Alexandria, VA 22314, (703) 548-3440.

Subscriptions: Members of SHRM receive magazine as part of their membership. Nonmember subscriptions available in the United States, Canada, and Mexico at 1 year $49, 2 years $79, and 3 years $119. Write for information on international subscription rates.

Dedicated to human resource issues, with occasional articles on quality issues related to HR. Rating: ★

Industrial Engineering

Published monthly by the Institute of Industrial Engineers, 25 Technology Park, Norcross, GA 30092, phone: (404) 449–0461, fax: (404) 263–8532.

Subscriptions: Included as part of membership. Subscriptions available in the U.S. to non-members for 1 year $49, 2 years $82, and 3 years $115; Canada and international subscriptions: 1 year $70, 2 years $120, and 3 years $170.

While aimed at engineers, its articles are nontechnical and oriented toward the application of TQM principles. Includes a regular monthly column on quality. Rating: ★★★

Industrial Management

Published bimonthly by the Institute of Industrial Engineers, 25 Technology Park/Atlanta, Norcross, GA 30092, (404) 449-0460.

Subscriptions: 1 year $32, 2 years $54, and 3 years $80; international subscriptions 1 year $40, 2 years $68, and 3 years $94.

A serious journal with an academic bent that includes quality-oriented articles that are accessible to practitioners. Rating: ★

Integrated Manufacturing Systems

Published monthly by MCB University Press Ltd., 60/62 Toller Lane, Bradford, West Yorkshire, England BD8 9734, phone: 44 274 499–821, fax: 44 274

547–143. In the U.S.: P.O. Box 10812, Birmingham, AL 35201–0812, phone: (205) 995–1567 or (800) 633–4931, fax: (205) 995–1588.

Subscriptions: Call or write for subscription information.

A British journal dedicated to articles relating to the integration of production, design, supply, and marketing functions of manufacturing enterprises. Includes news and review center insert in each edition. Technical, but nonmathematical. Rating: ★★

Journal of Health Care Marketing
Published quarterly by the American Marketing Association Publishing Group, 250 South Wacker Drive, Chicago, IL 60606, (312) 648–0536.

Subscriptions: $50 per year in the U.S., $60 in other countries.

Regularly covers quality issues, especially with regard to customer satisfaction and service quality. Rating: ★★

Management Accounting
Published monthly by the Institute of Management Accountants, 10 Paragon Drive, Montvale, NJ 07645–1760, phone: (201) 573–1760, fax: (201) 573–0639.

Subscriptions: Free to members, nonmembers: $125 per year.

Frequently includes articles on activity based accounting and other subjects related to the implementation of quality principles in accounting processes. For accountants interested in TQM, highly recommended. Rating: ★★★

Manufacturing Engineering
Published monthly by the Society of Manufacturing Engineers, P.O. Box 930, Dearborn, MI 48121, (313) 271-1500.

Subscriptions: Closed circulation magazine sent free to members of the society and others involved with manufacturing. Personal subscription information available by contacting SME.

Covers articles on manufacturing, with some coverage of quality issues, including a monthly column, "The Quality Adviser." Rating: ★

Modern Healthcare
Published weekly by Crain Communications Inc., 965 East Jefferson, Detroit, MI 48207-3185, (800) 678-9595.

Subscriptions: 1 year $110 and 2 years $200; add $48 for all non-U.S. subscriptions.

A health care industry weekly magazine including news articles plus a variety of articles on managing health care facilities. Occasionally includes articles on quality management. Rating: ★

Performance and Instruction
Published monthly except for combined May/June and November/December issues by the National Society for Performance and Instruction, NSPI Publications, 1300 L Street NW, Suite 1250, Washington, DC 20005, (202) 408-7969.

Subscriptions: Available as part of membership; annual subscriptions available to nonmembers for $50.

Includes detailed articles on practical training techniques that will be of direct use to TQM trainers, though the orientation of the journal is not directed to TQM. Rating: ★★

Personnel Journal

Published monthly by ACC Communications, 245 Fischer Avenue, B-2, Costa Mesa, CA 92626.

Subscriptions: $55 per year. For multiyear and international subscriptions, write to the publishers.

An exceptionally well-done journal that regularly includes articles related to quality issues in the area of human resources, including teams and compensation. Regularly includes articles profiling practices at various companies. Rating: ★★★

Phi Delta Kappan

Published monthly except July and August by Phi Delta Kappa, Inc. (professional educators fraternity), 408 North Union, P.O. Box 789, Bloomington, IN 47402, (812) 339–1156 or (800) 766–1156.

Subscriptions: 1 year $35; other countries: 1 year $38.50.

Publishes articles on educational research and leadership with emphasis on trends and policies in education. Occasionally includes thoughtful articles directly relating to quality principles in education. Also includes articles indirectly related. Rating: ★

Planning Review

Published bimonthly by The Planning Forum, 5900 College Corner Pike, P.O. Box 70, Oxford, OH 45056–0070.

Subscriptions: $95 per year in the U.S. and Canada; $115 for all other countries.

Not dedicated to TQM, but many articles are related to TQM principles or discuss their application. Many issues include a theme such as reengineering or mass customization. Most issues include cases studies of real companies. Rating: ★★

Research in Higher Education

Published bimonthly by Human Sciences Press, Inc., 233 Spring Street, New York, NY 10013–1578.

Subscriptions: For individuals in the U.S.: 1 year $65; other countries: $76.

A refereed journal aimed at planners, faculty, and higher education administrators to better understand how to efficiently and effectively manage these institutions. Articles frequently cover case studies in a particular area at various colleges and universities, with occasional articles on applying TQM. Somewhat technical. Rating: ★

The School Administrator

Published monthly by the American Association of School Administrators, 1801 North Moore Street, Arlington, VA 22209, (703) 875-7905.

Subscriptions: Included as part of membership.

Dedicated to the problems and opportunities of school administrators, occasionally including articles on quality in schools. Rating: ★

The Service Edge

Published monthly by Lakewood Publications, 50 South Ninth Street, Minneapolis, MN 55402, phone: (800) 328–4329 or (612) 333–0471, fax: (612) 333–6526.

Subscriptions: 1 year U.S.: $147; Canada add $100 plus 7% GST; other countries add $20 to U.S. rate.

This is an eight page, two-color newsletter covering specific issues in the delivery of quality to customers and creating company environments where service and quality thrive for everyone. Lots of practical ideas. Edited by Ron Zemke. Rating: ★★

Training

Published monthly by Lakewood Publications, Inc., 50 South Ninth Street, Minneapolis, MN 55402, (612) 333-0471.

Subscriptions: U.S.: 1 year $68, 2 years $116, and 3 years $150; Canada and Mexico: 1 year $78; international: 1 year $89.

Includes articles on issues of interest to corporate trainers, with frequent articles on quality management and training. Articles are practical, well-written, and of interest to all involved in quality management. Often includes articles on quality management.
Rating: ★★★

Training & Development

Published monthly by the American Society for Training and Development, Inc., 1640 King Street, Box 1443, Alexandria, VA 22313-2043, (703) 683-8100.

Subscriptions: Members of ASTD receive this magazine as part of their membership. Nonmember subscriptions available in the United States at $75 per year. International subscription: $135 for surface mail and $165 for airmail.

Includes articles on training, human resources, and management issues, with frequent coverage of quality management topics in these areas.
Rating: ★★

Quality Resources On-line
(Quality@Online.TQY)

There has been an explosion in the amount of material on quality management topics available via computer on-line services. In fact, there is more than can be covered in this section of the yearbook. However, we want to give you a taste and a reasonable overview of what is available and how to access these resources. Most of the material below involves the internet. However, there are some other on-line quality information providers that we describe as well.

Some Background Information about Quality on the Internet

The internet is more complicated to explain than to do. Once you have access to the internet via a server (a computer that you dial into to get you onto the internet) or a commercial provider, such as CompuServe, America Online, Prodigy, or Delphi, and have a web browser, such as Netscape, you can easily access sites that are concerned with quality issues (or many other subjects, for that matter).

If you didn't have the list we provide below, you could still find site after site using something called a "search engine." These allow you to key in certain words, and then these engines will list all the sites that match those words. For example, using the Yahoo (that's its name) or Web Crawler search engines, you could key in *Process Reengineering* or *Total Quality Management*, and you will get a long list of sites that have something to do with this subject—some directly related, some not. Using your mouse, you can then click on one of those listed, and the web browser automatically will find and bring it up on your computer. The site you find may then have other sites it lists that seem of interest. You can click on these and see if they are related to what you are looking for. Doing this may, in turn, lead you to other sites, and on and on. This is, in essence, what "web surfing" is all about. To save you some time, we provide you with a place to start your search and to help you identify some specific areas in which you may have an interest.

Types of On-line Services

There are four basic types of on-line services available. There are (a) discussion groups, (b) information sources, (c) commercial and nonprofit organizations (such as universities) offering consulting and training services, and (d) bulletin board services. Here is more on each:

- **Discussion Groups.** These are services that facilitate discussion of whatever their subject matter concerns, for example ISO 9000, process reengineering, and so on. These are also called, in the parlance of the internet, *listservs*. To become involved, you must subscribe (meaning to sign up) to the service. After that you will receive via E-mail all the submissions from other members. This can range from a few to more than 30 per day. If you want to respond to one, you can do that, and it will go out to everyone on the list. Below you'll find a list of discussion groups and what you have to do to subscribe to them.

- **Information Sources**. These are sites on the internet (a site is a company or a university or an individual that you can access via the internet) that have stored on their computers lots of information that you can read by clicking on the items in which you have an interest. Some commercial sites also give you access to free information or direct you to sites where you can find material.

- **Commercial Organizations.** These are companies that have developed sites that explain their services—such as training; consulting; or selling various books, software, or similar materials that you may find valuable. These sites often have links to other sites that may be valuable to you. Another type of commercial site now on the internet is one that may include various articles available for free, links to other sites that sell things, and links to other sites that are related to the subject matter. These commercial sites may have more extensive databases of information available, but you can only access these with a password. The way you get a password is by paying a fee. The site will explain how to pay and obtain access. These sites may also include ads (you click on the name to see the ad) from consulting companies and others that deal with the subject matter at hand. These companies pay the commercial site a fee for allowing them to have their information available at this site.

- **Bulletin Board Services.** These are private services that you access through a special number (sometimes an 800 number, sometimes via long distance). They are literally electronic bulletin boards, each dedicated to a particular topic. They are like discussion groups, except instead of everyone getting individual postings to your E-mail, they are maintained on a central computer that you call into. If you are interested in a particular subject, you can add your comments. You can also download information and, sometimes, software that is available via the bulletin board.

What follows now is a listing of on-line services in these various categories.

Discussion Groups

Joining a discussion group requires that you send an E-mail message to the person that manages or moderates the distribution list. For each of the groups below, we give you the E-mail address of the list moderator and what you should say in the message. Usually you just write in the body of the message "Subscribe [name of list] and your [first name, last name]." Sometimes you don't include your name. Sometimes you just put the word "Subscribe" in the subject line of the message and that's all. Note that upper and lower case should be used as shown in our listings. We tell you exactly what to say for each list. When you subscribe, you will usually receive an introductory message that describes the service, what you can expect, and how to participate. This message will also tell you how to stop your subscription if you don't find it of value. The name of the list describes its subject matter. Also, some of these are maintained in the UK—you can tell which ones by the E-mail address that ends in uk.

Malcolm Baldrige Quality Award
Message to: majordomo@quality.org
In body (of message): subscribe baldrige

Business Process Management and Improvement
Message to: majordomo@quality.org
In body: info bpmi

Business Process Reengineering 1
Message to: listserv@is.tgwi.tudelft.nl
In body: sub BPR-1 [] [] (Note: [] [] means include your first name and last name—without brackets.)

Business Process Reengineering 2
Message to: mailbase@mailbase.ac.uk
In body: join BPR [] []

Change (Deals with initiating and sustaining changes in organizations)
Message to: majordomo@mindspring.com
In body: info change

CQEN (Community Quality Electronic Network)
Message to: cqen.list-request@deming.eng.clemson.edu
In subject line: subscribe

CQI-L (Continuous Quality Improvement, with special emphasis on this subject in universities)
Message to: listserv@mr.net
In body: subscribe CQI-L [] []

DEN (Deming Electronic Network)
Message to: den.list-request@deming.eng.clemson.edu
In subject line: subscribe

Empowerment
Message to: majordomo@world.std.com
Subject: subscribe

In body: SUBSCRIBE
         EMPOWERMENT
         END

ISO 9000
Message to: listserv@vm1.nodak.edu
In body: subcribe ISO9000 [] []

ISO 9000-3
Message to: majordomo@quality.org
In body: info iso9000-3

ISO 14000
Message to: listserv@vm1.nodak.edu
In body: subscribe quest [] []

Learning Organizations (Deals with systems thinking and learning organization issues as developed by Peter Senge and colleagues at MIT)
Message to: majordomo@word.std.com
In body: Line 1: info learning-org
Line 2: end

MIL-QUAL-D (Military Quality Discussion List)
Message to: majordomo@quality.org
In body: subscribe mil-qual-d

QFD-L (Quality Function Deployment Discussion List)
Message to: majordomo@quality.org
In body: subscribe qfd-l

QF-Health (Quality Issues for Health Care Professionals)
In body: info qp-health

PUBAOM (Academy of Management Public and Non-profit Division)
Message to: majordomo@mailer.fsu.edu
In body: subscribe pubaom

Quality (Deals with broad variety of issues on quality management)
Message to: listserv@pucc.princeton.edu
In body: Subscribe Quality

Quality Management (Based in the UK)
Message to: mailbase@mailbase.ac.uk
In body: join quality-management [] []

REGOnet (Re-inventing Government)
Message to: listserv@pandora.sf.ca.us
In body: information REGO-L

The four following relate to the federal government:

REGO-QUAL (Creating Quality Leadership and Management)
REGO-ORG (Transforming Organizational Structures)
REGO-DOD (Department of Defense)
REGO-EOP (Executive Office of the President)
Message to: Listproc@gmu.edu
In body: subscribe REGO-XXX [] [] (where 'XXX' is QUAL, ORG, DOD, or EOP (taken from the list above).

TEAMNET-L (Research on teams)
Message to: roquemor@terrill.unt.edu
In body: join Teamnet [] []

TOC-L (Theory of Constraints—a special approach to systems management)
Message to: listserv@netcom.com
In body: subscribe TOC-L [] []

Total-Quality-AsiaPac (Total Quality in the Asia Pacific)
Message to: Mailbase@mailbase.ac.uk
In body: Join Total-Quality-AsiaPac [] []

Total-Quality-EcoSys (Total Quality in environmental systems)
Message to: Mailbase@mailbase.ac.uk
In body: Join Total-Quality-EcoSys [] []

Total-Quality-ISOStds (ISO Standards)
Message to: Mailbase@mailbase.ac.uk
In body: Join Total-Quality-ISOStds [] []

Total-Quality-Statistics (Statistics for continuous improvement)
Message to: Mailbase@mailbase.ac.uk
In body: Join Total-Quality-Statistics

TQM-D (An unmoderated version of Quality list above very active)
Message to: majordomo@quality.org
In body: subscribe tqm-d

TQM-L (Total Quality Management In Higher Education)
Message to: listserv@ukanvm.bitnet
In body: subscribe TQM-L [] []

TQMLIB (Implementing TQM in libraries)
Message to: listserv@cms.cc.wayne.edu
In body: subscribe TQMLIB [] []

TQM (Another quality discussion maintained at Clemson University)
Message to: tqm.list-request@deming.eng.clemson.edu
In subject: subscribe

TQMEDU-L (Quality issues in education)
Message to: listserv@humber.bitnet
In body: subscribe TQMEDU-l [] []

Information Sources

At these locations, accessible through the worldwide web, you can find a great deal of information and links to other sites too numerous to include here. However, one of the great things about the internet is that once you access sites like these we are about to list, you can find nearly anything you are interested in by following various links.

QUALITY.ORG

This is probably the best single place to start in searching for information about quality resources on the internet. It has more information and links to other sites than any other site we know about.
Access: Via WWW: http://www.quality.org/qc; via FTP: ftp://quality.org/pub/qc; via gopher: gopher://quality.org

CLEMSON UNIVERSITY The next best place to find quality resources on the internet. A lot of information, bulletin boards, and links to other sites.
Access: Via WWW: http://deming.eng.clemson.edu/; via ftp: deming.eng.clemson.edu/pub/tqmbbs; via gopher: gopher://deming.eng.clemson.edu:70/1

Babson College Babson's site includes various documents on quality issues, including the implementation of quality management at this school.
Access: Via gopher: gopher://info.babson.edu:70/11/:quality

CQEN (Community Quality Electronic Network) Includes information on community quality efforts across the globe. There is an archive (a collection of the postings) of the CQEN mailing list and articles to view on-line.
Access: via WWW: http://deming.eng.clemson.edu/pub/cqen

DEN (Deming Electronic Network) Includes information on efforts to keep Deming's message circulating. There is a list of Deming User Groups across the globe and an archive of the DEN mail list.
Access: via WWW: http://deming.eng.clemson.edu/pub/den

FEDWORLD Includes a large amount of government information concerning quality-related subjects plus telnet links to the TQM BBS, OPM Mainstreet.
Access: via WWW: http://www.fedworld.gov

HEPROC Education-focus site
Access: via gopher: gopher://www.digimark.net/1/educ/dirs/tqm via WWW: http://www.digimark.net:801/educ/www/quality/index.html

ISO Online Includes information and links on ISO 9000
Access: via WWW: http://www.iso.ch/welcome.html

NIST (National Institute of Standards and Technology) Information about the Baldrige Award and related subjects.
Access: via WWW: http://www.nist.gov:8102

NPR (National Performance Review) Information on what's going on in different goverment agencies as they go about reinventing government.
Access: via WWW: http://www.npr.gov or send E-mail to:
almanac@ace.esusda.gov, in body of message say: send npr catalog. The response will provide current information plus instructions to get E-mail documents.

Public Sector Continuous Improvement Page Includes various links to other sites; has a section on ASQC Public Sector Network.
Access: via WWW: http://deming.eng.clemson.edu/pub/psci/

QFD Includes information and links dealing with quality function deployment.
Access: via WWW: http://mijuno.larc.nasa.gov/dfc/qfd.html

QFD Institute More information on quality function deployment and links to other sites.
Access: via WWW: http://nauticom.net/www.qfdi/

Theory of Constraints Deals with the version of systems management. Includes information and links.
Access: via WWW: http://www.lm.com/~dshu/toc/cac.html

UNIV OF WISCONSIN Includes the Madison Area Quality Improvement Network newsletter and the Center for Quality and Productivity Improvement Reports.
Access via gopher: gopher://gopher.adp.wisc.edu/11/.facstf/.tqm

U.S. Department of Labor's Best Practices Clearinghouse A lot of stuff, but if you know what you're looking for, you might find it.
Access: via WWW: http://athena.itl.saic.com:80/fed/uscompanies/labor/

Commercial Organizations

This includes on-line resources on the internet and offered privately.

ASQC This is the page of the American Society for Quality Control. It includes detailed information about the society, its services, publications, quality news, and links to other sites. Access: via WWW: http://www.asqc.org/lynx.html

American Productivity and Quality Center and the International Benchmarking Exchange This is the page of this member organization. It includes information about the organization, its services, reprints from its magazine *The Quality Journey*, and links to other sites.
Access: via WWW: http://www.apqc.org/

QualiNet This is one of those sites where companies that have training, consulting, books, and so on to sell can pay to have them included here. This site also has links to many other sites dealing with quality.

Access: via WWW: http:///www.qualinet.com/

International Quality Network (QualNet) This is another service that in-cludes paid ads as part of its offerings. These ads include résumés of quality professionals and other companies that offer services and products in the area of TQM. There are various articles and other material available. Many links to other sites are included as well.
Access: http;://www.pacification.net/~qualnet/

Quality Wave This is another service similar to QualiNet. It includes a lot of links and is worth visiting.
Access: via WWW: http://www.xnet.com/~creacon/Q4Q/index.html

WARIA (Workflow and Reengineering International Association) This site features paid-for ads along with articles and other resources and listing of many other sites dealing with quality issues. Worth checking out.
Access: via WWW: http://vvv.com.waria/

The Benchmarking Exchange This is a commercial company that supplies a broad selection of information on-line, but available only by paid subscription. Users can gain access to TBE via both the internet or directly, by using any communications software package. Material available on TBE includes a best practices database, as well as articles, presentations, and other information from a wide variety of sources.
Access: via WWW: http://www.benchnet.com, where you can learn more about TBE; via communication software: configure your modem in this way: Data bits 8, Parity none Stop bits 1, Echo off, Duplex full, Emulation ANSI, and Baud rate up to 115,400 bps. Then dial 408 662-9813 and register. If you want information prior to signing up, call 800 662-9801 or 408 662-9800 and talk to a real person. The cost of a subscription is $255 for 3 months, $495 for 1 year, and $745 for 2 years. Corporate rates are available.

ISO Online This is the page of the International Standards Organization. It includes a lot of information on ISO 9000–related topics.
Access: via WWW: http://www.iso.ch/welcome.html

Quality Online Forum This is another subscription service developed by American Informatics, Inc. This includes many different resources, including E-mail with other subscribers, articles from *Quality Digest* and the *Journal for Quality and Participation*. It also includes directory of listings from com-panies that pay to be included and also has on-line ads paid for the placing company. QOF includes a variety of catalogs on-line from which you can purchase books, videos, and other materials. Cost is $60 per year. This gives you 2 hours per day access and free software to take full advantage of the system. It will also be available via the internet, but no address is available at time of publication. To subscribe, call via voice mail to 913 379-5590 or send an E-mail message to info@qof.com.

Phoenix Systems Synectics This is a company that maintains a page on the internet, mainly dedicated to TQM and business process reengineering. It includes various articles and other information that may be useful. It also includes several links to other sites. Worth checking out.
Access: via WWW: http://www.phoenix.ca/bpr/

Bulletin Board Services

TQM BBS This is run by Tom Glenn. You can access it using any communication software. It includes nearly 500 files on TQM topics, all of which are available for downloading. This service is run by Tom Glenn. It is small and can handle only a few calls at a time. There are no fees other than a long distance call.
Access: via any communications package: Data bits 8, Parity none, Stop bits 1, ANSI, up to 9600 bps. Call 301 585-1164 to connect with the service. Once you connect, press escape key twice, and answer questions on screen. You can also call Tom Glenn at 301 565-8882 or connect via E-mail at tom.glenn@tqm.permanet.org for more information.

OPM Mainstreet This is a free bulletin board service maintained by the federal government.
Access: call 202 606-4800 and follow directions on screen.

TQL BBS This is a free service maintained by the U.S. Navy to distribute and share information regarding total quality leadership.
Access: call 703 602-9094.

Acknowledgment

We want to thank Bill Casti, who serves as coordinator for much of what goes on in the internet concerning quality management issues. He was very helpful in preparing this section. You can learn more about Bill by checking his home page, which you can get to via the Quality.Org service, which he maintains.

Understanding Systems Thinking

Peter M. Senge

In The Quality Yearbook *this year, we have been emphasizing the idea of systems thinking. The reason is that understanding organizations as systems is the foundation of implementing TQM. TQM is about continuously improving systems processes to create a mutually beneficial relationship between organizations, customers, and other stakeholders. Learning how to view an organization as a system, to make sense of its system processes, provides the foundation for identifying the points where you will have the greatest leverage when you make imrprovements. This is the value of systems thinking. This view of the world is one that looks at the pieces and the whole in terms of how the pieces interact to create the whole. And then how to manage it successfully.*

At some level, we all practice systems thinking. We have some vague assumptions about how things relate together, and these affect how we behave in various situations. Often, these assumptions go unspoken or, even, unacknowledged. But they're still there. Systems thinking is about bringing these assumptions out into the open, looking at their value in terms of serving customers and improving processes and then abandoning those that don't help you do this. It is about making changes that will improve an organization's efficiency and effectiveness for those on the inside and the outside.

The best single description of how to do this that we have come across is in Peter Senge's book The Fifth Discipline: The Art and Practice of the Learning Organization. *Thus, we requested and received permission to reproduce here chapter 5 from that book, which Senge called "A Shift of Mind." You probably know about this book. It has been very successful, though more people have purchased it than read it. Of all the chapters in that book, this is the one that provides the insights that all the others are based on. Senge carefully takes us through how to understand a system, how to analyze interactions, and what this means for successful management decisions and actions.*

One thing you start to see once you understand organizational systems and processes is that certain patterns of behavior start to emerge. People who deal with systems call these patterns archetypes. We can think of these archetypes as being like personality types. Some people are impulsive, some are shy, some are agressive, some are thoughtful, and so on. These person-alities or archetypes help explain people's behavior and what happens to them. Organizational processes have patterns as well. Senge and his col-leagues have identified several basic systems archetypes. Using the infor-mation in this chapter, we can make sense of these archetypes and, in so doing, figure out how to make changes that will give help us make the most improvement for the efforts we put forth. Following this chapter, we have included Senge's list and description of nine different systems archetypes. Think about them in terms of your organization's processes.

Seeing the World Anew

There is something in all of us that loves to put together a puzzle, that loves to see the image of the whole emerge. The beauty of a person, or a flower, or a poem lies in seeing all of it. It is interesting that the words "whole" and "health" come from the same root (the Old English *hal*, as in "hale and hearty"). So it should come as no surprise that the unhealthiness of our world today is in direct proportion to our inability to see it as a whole.

Systems thinking is a discipline for seeing wholes. It is a framework for seeing interrelationships rather than things, for seeing patterns of change rather than static "snapshots." It is a set of general principles—distilled over the course of the twentieth century, spanning fields as diverse as the physical and social sciences, engineering, and management. It is also a set of specific tools and techniques, originating in two threads: in "feedback" concepts of cybernetics and in "servo-mechanism" engineering theory dating back to the nineteenth century. During the last thirty years, these tools have been applied to understand a wide range of corporate, urban, regional, economic, political, ecological, and even physiological systems. And systems thinking is a sensi-bility—for the subtle interconnectedness that gives living systems their unique character.

Today, systems thinking is needed more than ever because we are becom-ing overwhelmed by complexity. Perhaps for the first time in history, hu-mankind has the capacity to create far more information than anyone can absorb, to foster far greater interdependency than anyone can manage, and to accelerate change far faster than anyone's ability to keep pace. Certainly the scale of complexity is without precedent. All around us are examples of "sys-temic breakdowns"—problems such as global warming, ozone depletion, the international drug trade, and the U.S. trade and budget deficits.—problems that have no simple local cause. Similarly, organizations break down, despite individual brilliance and innovative products, because they are unable to pull their diverse functions and talents into a productive whole.

Complexity can easily undermine confidence and responsibility—as in the frequent refrain, "It's all too complex for me," or "There's nothing I can do. It's the system." Systems thinking is the antidote to this sense of helplessness that many feel as we enter the "age of interdependence." Systems thinking is a discipline for seeing the "structures" that underlie complex situations, and for discerning high from low leverage change. That is, by seeing wholes we learn how to foster health. To do so, systems thinking offers a language that begins by restructuring how we think.

I call systems thinking the fifth discipline because it is the conceptual cornerstone that underlies all of the five learning disciplines of this book. All are concerned with a shift of mind from seeing parts to seeing wholes, from seeing people as helpless reactors to seeing them as active participants in shaping their reality, from reacting to the present to creating the future. Without systems thinking, there is neither the incentive nor the means to integrate the learning disciplines once they have come into practice. As the fifth discipline, systems thinking is the cornerstone of how learning organizations think about their world.

There is no more poignant example of the need for systems thinking than the U.S.-U.S.S.R. arms race. While the world has stood and watched for the past forty years, the two mightiest political powers have engaged in a race to see who could get fastest to where no one wanted to go. I have not yet met a person who is in favor of the arms race. Even those who regard it as absolutely necessary, or who profit from it, will, in their quieter moments, confess that they wish it were not necessary. It has drained the U.S. economy and devastated the Soviet economy. It has ensnared successive administrations of political leaders, and terrified two generations of the world's citizens.

The roots of the arms race lie not in rival political ideologies, nor in nuclear arms, but in a way of thinking both sides have shared. The United States establishment, for example, has had a viewpoint of the arms race that essentially resembled the following:

$$\text{U.S.S.R. ARMS} \longrightarrow \text{THREAT TO AMERICANS} \longrightarrow \text{NEED TO BUILD U.S. ARMS}$$

At the same time, the Soviet leaders have had a view of the arms race somewhat resembling this:

$$\text{U.S. ARMS} \longrightarrow \text{THREAT TO SOVIETS} \longrightarrow \text{NEED TO BUILD U.S.S.R. ARMS}$$

From the American viewpoint, the Soviets have been the aggressor, and U.S. expansion of nuclear arms has been a defensive response to the threats posed by the Soviets. From the Soviet viewpoint, the United States has been the aggressor, and Soviet expansion of nuclear arms has been a defensive response to the threat posed by the Americans.

But the two straight lines form a circle. The two nations' individual, "linear," or nonsystemic viewpoints interact to create a "system," a set of variables that influence one another:

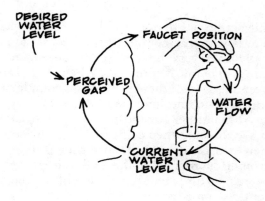

The systems view of the arms race shows a perpetual cycle of aggression. The United States responds to a perceived Threat to Americans by increasing U.S. arms, which increases the Threat to the Soviets, which leads to more Soviet arms, which increases the Threat to the United States, which leads to more U.S. arms, which increases the Threat to the Soviets, which . . . and so on, and so on. From their individual viewpoints, each side achieves its short-term goal. Both sides respond to a perceived threat. But their actions end up creating the opposite outcome, increased threat, in the long run. Here, as in many systems, *doing the obvious thing does not product the obvious, desired outcome.* The long-term result of each side's efforts to be more secure is heightened insecurity for all, with a combined nuclear stockpile of ten thousand times the total firepower of World War II.

Interestingly, both sides failed for years to adopt a true systems view, despite an abundance of "systems analysts," sophisticated analyses of each others' nuclear arsenals, and complex computer simulations of attack and counterattack war scenarios. Why then have these supposed tools for dealing with complexity not empowered us to escape the illogic of the arms race?

The answer lies in the same reason that sophisticated tools of forecasting and business analysis, as well as elegant strategic plans, usually fail to produce dramatic breakthroughs in managing a business. They are all designed to handle the sort of complexity in which there are many variables: *detail complexity. But there are two types of complexity.* The second type is *dynamic complexity*, situations where cause and effect are subtle, and where the effects over time of interventions are not obvious. Conventional forecasting, planning, and analysis methods are not equipped to deal with dynamic complexity. Mixing many ingredients in a stew involves detail complexity, as does following a complex set of instructions to assemble a machine, or taking inventory in a discount retail store. But none of these situations is especially complex dynamically.

When the same action has dramatically different effects in the short run and the long, there is dynamic complexity. When an action has one set of consequences locally and a very different set of consequences in another part of the system, there is dynamic complexity. When obvious interventions produce nonobvious consequences, there is dynamic complexity. A gyroscope is a dynamically complex machine: If you push downward on one edge, it moves to the left; if you push another edge to the left, it moves upward. Yet, how trivially simple is a gyroscope when compared with the complex dynamics of an enterprise, where it takes days to produce something, weeks to develop a new marketing promotion, months to hire and train new people, and years to develop new products, nurture management talent, and build a reputation for quality—and all of these processes interact continually.

The real leverage in most management situations lies in understanding dynamic complexity, not detail complexity. Balancing market growth and capacity expansion is a dynamic problem. Developing a profitable mix of price, product (or service) quality, design, and availability that make a strong market position is a dynamic problem. Improving quality, lowering total costs, and satisfying customers in a sustainable manner is a dynamic problem.

Unfortunately, most "systems analyses" focus on detail complexity not dynamic complexity. Simulations with thousands of variables and complex arrays of details can actually distract us from seeing patterns and major interrelationships. In fact, sadly, for most people "systems thinking" means "fighting complexity with complexity," devising increasingly "complex" (we should really say "detailed") solutions to increasingly "complex" problems. In fact, this is the antithesis of real systems thinking.

The arms race is, most fundamentally, a problem of dynamic complexity. Insight into the causes and possible cures requires seeing the interrelationships, such as between our actions to become more secure and the threats they create for the Soviets. It requires seeing the delays between action and consequence, such as the delay between a U.S. decision to build up arms and a consequent Soviet counter-buildup. And it requires seeing patterns of change, not just snapshots, such as continuing escalation.

Seeing the major interrelationships underlying a problem leads to new insight into what might be done. In the case of the arms race, as in any escalation dynamic, the obvious question is, "Can the vicious cycle be run in reverse?" "Can the arms race be run backward?"

This may be just what is happening today. Soviet General Secretary Mikhail Gorbachev's initiatives in arms reduction have started a new "peace race" with both sides eager to keep pace with the other's reductions in nuclear arsenals. It is too early to tell whether the shifts in policy initiated by the Soviets in 1988 and 1989 will initiate a sustained unwinding of the U.S.-U.S.S.R. arms race. There are many other factors in the global geopolitical system beyond the pure U.S.-U.S.S.R. interaction. But we appear to be witnessing the first glimmer of a genuinely systemic approach.

The essence of the discipline of systems thinking lies in a shift of mind:

> - seeing interrelationships rather than linear cause-effect chains, and
> - seeing processes of change rather than snapshots

The practice of systems thinking starts with understanding a simple concept called "feedback" that shows how actions can reinforce or counteract (balance) each other. *It builds to learning to recognize types of "structures" that recur again and again:* the arms race is a generic or archetypal pattern of escalation, at its heart no different from turf warfare between two street gangs, the demise of a marriage, or the advertising battles of two consumer goods companies fighting for market share. Eventually, systems thinking forms a rich language for describing a vast array of interrelationships and patterns of change. Ultimately, *it simplifies life* by helping us see the deeper patterns lying behind the events and the details.

Learning any new language is difficult at first. But as you start to master the basics, it gets easier. Research with young children has shown that many learn systems thinking remarkable quickly. It appears that we have latent skills as systems thinkers that are undeveloped, even repressed by formal education in linear thinking. Hopefully, what follows will help rediscover some of those latent skills and bring to the surface the systems thinker that is within each of us.

Seeing Circles of Causality

Reality is made up of circles but we see straight lines. Herein lie the beginnings of our limitation as systems thinkers.

One of the reasons for this fragmentation in our thinking stems from our language. Language shapes perception. What we *see* depends on what we are prepared to see. Western languages, with their subject-verb-object structure, are biased toward a linear view. If we want to see systemwide interrelationships, we need a language of interrelationships, a language made up of circles. Without such a language, our habitual ways of seeing the world produce fragmented views and counterproductive actions—as it has done for decision makers in the arms race. Such a language is important in facing dynamically complex issues and strategic choices, especially when individuals, teams, and organizations need to see beyond events and into the forces that shape change.

To illustrate the rudiments of the new language, consider a very simple system—filling a glass of water. You might think, "That's not a system—it's too simple." But think again.

From the linear viewpoint, we way, "I am filling a glass of water." What most of us have in mind looks pretty much like the following picture:

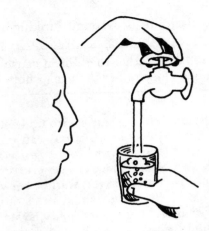

But, in fact, as we fill the glass, we are watching the water level rise. We monitor the "gap" between the level and our goal, the "desired water level." As the water approaches the desired level, we adjust the faucet position to slow the flow of water, until it is turned off when the glass is full. In fact, when we fill a glass of water we operate in a "water-regulation" system involving five variables: our desired water level, the glass's current water level, the gap between the two, the faucet position, and the water flow. These variables are organized in a circle or loop of cause-effect relationships which is called a "feedback process." The process operates continuously to bring the water level to its desired level:

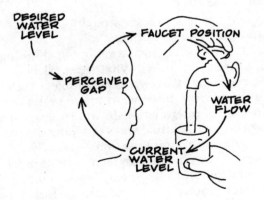

People get confused about "feedback" because we often use the word in a somewhat different way—to gather opinions about an act we have undertaken. "Give me some feedback on the brewery decision," you might say. "What did you think of the way I handled it?" In that context, "positive feedback" means encouraging remarks and "negative feedback" means bad news. But in systems thinking, feedback is a broader concept. It means any reciprocal flow of influence. In systems thinking it is an axiom that every influence in both *cause* and *effect*. Nothing is ever influenced in just one direction.

Though simple in concept, the feedback loop overturns deeply ingrained ideas—such as causality. In everyday English we say, "I am filling the glass of water" without thinking very deeply about the real meaning of the statement. It implies a one-way causality—"I am causing the water level to rise." More precisely, "My hand on the faucet is controlling the rate of flow of water into the glass." Clearly, this statement describes only half of the feedback process: the linkages from "faucet position" to "flow of water" to "water level."

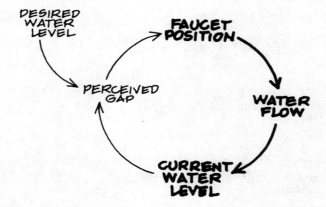

But it would be just as true to describe only the other "half" of the process: "The level of water in the glass is controlling my hand."

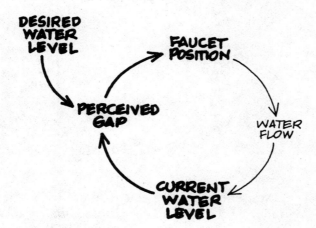

Both statements are equally incomplete. The more complete statement of causality is that my intent to fill a glass of water creates a system that causes water to flow in when the level is low, then shuts the flow off when the glass is full. In other words, the structure causes the behavior. This distinction is important because seeing only individual actions and missing the

HOW TO READ A SYSTEMS DIAGRAM

The key to seeing reality systemically is seeing circles of influence rather than straight lines. This is the first step to breaking out of the reactive mindset that comes inevitably from "linear" thinking. Every circle tells a story. By tracing the flows of influence, you can see patterns that repeat themselves, time after time, making situations better or worse.

From any element in a situation, you can trace arrows that represent influence on another element:

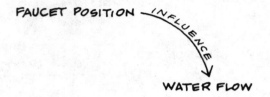

Above, the faucet position arrow points to water flow. Any change made to the faucet position will alter the flow of water. But arrows never exist in isolation:

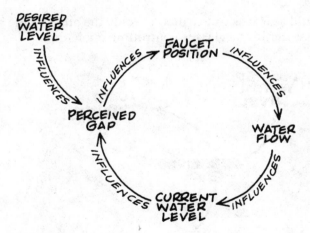

To follow the story, start at any element and watch the action ensue, circling as the train in a toy railroad does through its recurring journey. A good place to start is with the action being taken by the decision maker:

I set the faucet position, which adjusts the water flow, which changes the water level. As the water level changes, the perceived gap (between the current and desired water levels) changes. As the gap changes, my hand's position on the faucet changes again. And so on . . .

Continued—

How to Read a Systems Diagram (continued)

When reading a feedback circle diagram, the main skill is to see the "story" that the diagram tells: how the structure creates a particular pattern of behavior (or, in a complex structure, several patterns of behavior) and how that pattern might be influenced. Here the story is filling the water glass and gradually closing down the faucet as the glass fills.

structure underlying the actions lies at the root of our powerlessness in complex situations.

In fact, all causal attributions made in everyday English are highly suspect! Most are embedded in linear ways of seeing. They are at best partially accurate, inherently biased toward describing portions of reciprocal processes, not the entire processes.

Another idea overturned by the feedback perspective is anthropocentrism—or seeing ourselves as the center of activities. The simple description, "I am filling the glass of water," suggests a world of human actors standing at the center of activity, operating on an inanimate reality. *From the systems perspective, the human actor is part of the feedback process, not standing apart from it. This represents a profound shift in awareness.* It allows us to see how we are continually both influenced by and influencing our reality. It is the shift in awareness so ardently advocated by ecologists in their cries that we see ourselves as part of nature, not separate from nature. It is the shift in awareness recognized by many (but not all) of the world's great philosophical systems—for example, the *Bhagavad Gita*'s chastisement:

All Actions are wrought by the qualities of nature only. The self, deluded by egoism, thinketh: "I am the doer."

In addition, the feedback concept complicates the ethical issue of responsibility. In the arms race, who is responsible? From each side's linear view, responsibility clearly lies with the other side: "It is their aggressive actions, and their nationalistic intent, that are causing us to respond by building our arms." A linear view always suggests a simple locus of responsibility. When things go wrong, this is seen as blame—"he, she, it did it"—or guilt—"I did it." At a deep level, there is no difference between blame and guilt, for both spring from linear perceptions. From the linear view, we are always looking for someone or something that must be responsible—they can even be directed toward hidden agents within ourselves. When my son was four years old, he used to say, "My stomach won't let me eat it," when turning down his vegetables. We may chuckle, but is his assignment of responsibility really different from the adult who says, "My neuroses keep me from trusting people."

In mastering systems thinking, we give up the assumption that there must be an individual, or individual agent, responsible. The feedback perspective suggests that *everyone shares responsibility for problems generated by a system.* That doesn't necessarily imply that everyone involved can exert equal leverage in changing the system. But it does imply that the search for scapegoats—a particularly alluring pastime in individualistic cultures such as ours in the United States—is a blind alley.

Finally, the feedback concept illuminates the limitations of our language. When we try to describe in words even a very simple system, such as filling the water glass, it gets very awkward: "When I fill a glass of water, there is a feedback process that causes me to adjust the faucet position, which adjusts the water flow and feeds back to alter the water position. The goal of the process is to make the water level rise to my desired level." This is precisely why a new language for describing systems is needed. If it is this awkward to describe a system as simple as filling a water glass, *imagine our difficulties using everyday English to describe the multiple feedback processes in an organization.*

All this takes some getting used to. We are steeped in a linear language for describing our experience. We find simple statements about causality and responsibility familiar and comfortable. It is not that they must be given up, anymore than you give up English to learn French. There are many situations where simple linear descriptions suffice and looking for feedback processes would be a waste of time. But not when dealing with problems of dynamic complexity.

Reinforcing and Balancing Feedback and Delays: The Building Blocks of Systems Thinking

There are two distinct types of feedback processes: reinforcing and balancing. *Reinforcing* (or amplifying) feedback processes are the engines of growth. Whenever you are in a situation where things are growing, you can be sure that reinforcing feedback is at work. Reinforcing feedback can also generate accelerating decline—a pattern of decline where small drops amplify themselves into larger and larger drops, such as the decline in bank assets when there is a financial panic.

Balancing (or stabilizing) feedback operates whenever there is a goal-oriented behavior. If the goal is to be not moving, then balancing feedback will act the way the brakes in a car do. If the goal is to be moving at sixty miles per hour, then balancing feedback will cause you to accelerate to sixty but no faster. The "goal" can be an explicit target, as when a firm seeks a desired market share, or it can be implicit, such as a bad habit, which despite disavowing, we stick to nevertheless.

In addition, many feedback processes contain *"delays,"* interruptions in the flow of influence which make the consequences of actions occur gradually.

All ideas in the language of systems thinking are built up from these elements, just as English sentences are built up from nouns and verbs. Once we have learned the building blocks, we can begin constructing stories: the systems archetypes of the next chapter.

Reinforcing Feedback: Discovering How Small Changes Can Grow

If you are in a reinforcing feedback system, you may be blind to how small actions can grow into large consequences—for better or for worse. Seeing the system often allows you to influence how it works.

For example, managers frequently fail to appreciate the extent to which their own expectations influence subordinates' performance. If I see a person as having high potential, I give him special attention to develop that potential. When he flowers, I feel that my original assessment was correct and I help him still further. Conversely, those I regard as having lower potential languish in disregard and inattention, perform in a disinterested manner, and further justify, in my mind, the lack of attention I give them.

Psychologist Robert Merton first identified this phenomenon as the "self-fulfilling prophecy." It is also known as the "Pygmalion effect," after the famous George Bernard Shaw play (later to become *My Fair Lady*). Shaw in turn had taken his title from Pygmalion, a character in Greek and Roman mythology, who believed so strongly in the beauty of the statue he had carved that it came to life.

Pygmalion effects have been shown to operate in countless situations. An example occurs in schools, where a teacher's opinion of a student influences the behavior of that student. Jane is shy and does particularly poorly in her first semester at a new school (because her parents were fighting constantly). This leads her teacher to form an opinion that she is unmotivated. Next semester, the teacher pays less attention to Jane and she does poorly again, withdrawing further. Over time, Jane gets caught in an ever-worsening spiral of withdrawal, poor performance, "labeling" by her teachers, inattention, and further withdrawing. Thus, students are unintentionally "tracked" into a high self-image of their abilities, where they get personal attention, or a low self-image, where their poor class work is reinforced in an ever-worsening spiral.

In *reinforcing processes* such as the Pygmalion effect, a small change builds on itself. Whatever movement occurs is amplified, producing more movement in the same direction. A small action snowballs, with more and more and still more of the same, resembling compounding interest. Some reinforcing (amplifying) processes are "vicious cycles," in which things start off badly and grow worse. The "gas crisis" was a classic example. Word that gasoline was becoming scarce set off a spate of trips to the local service station, to fill up. Once people started seeing lines of cars, they were convinced that the crisis was here. Panic and hoarding then set in. Before long, everyone was "topping off" their tanks when they were only one-quarter empty, lest they be caught when the pumps went dry. A run on a bank is another example, as are escalation structures such as the arms race or price wars.

But there's nothing inherently bad about reinforcing loops. There are also "virtuous cycles"—processes that reinforce in desired directions. For instance, physical exercise can lead to a reinforcing spiral; you feel better, thus you exercise more, thus you're rewarded by feeling better and exercise still more. The arms race run in reverse, if it can be sustained, makes another virtuous circle. The growth of any new product involves reinforcing spirals. For example, many products grow from "word of mouth." Word of mouth about a product can reinforce a snowballing sense of good feeling (as occurred with the Volkswagen Beetle and more recent Japanese imports) as satisfied customers tell others who then become satisfied customers, who tell still others.

Here is how you might diagram such a process:

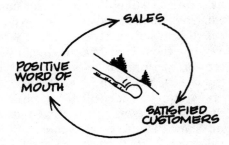

The behavior that results from a reinforcing loop is either accelerating growth or accelerating decline. For example, the arms race produces an accelerating growth of arms stockpiles:

Positive word of mouth produced rapidly rising sales of Volkswagens during the 1950s, and videocassette recorders during the 1980s. A bank run produces an accelerating decline in a bank's deposits.

Folk wisdom speaks of reinforcing loops in terms such as "snowball effect," "bandwagon effect," or "vicious circle," and in phrases describing particular systems: "the rich get richer and the poor get poorer." In business, we know that "momentum is everything," in building confidence in a new product or within a fledgling organization. We also know about reinforcing spirals running the wrong way. "The rats are jumping ship" suggests a situation where, as soon as a few people lose confidence, their defection will cause others to defect in a vicious spiral of eroding confidence. Word of mouth can

HOW TO READ A REINFORCING CIRCLE DIAGRAM

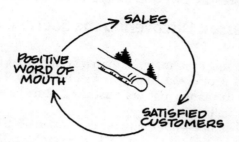

Reinforcing Sales Process Caused by Customers Talking to Each Other About Your Product

This diagram shows a reinforcing feedback process wherein actions *snowball*. Again, you can follow the process by walking yourself around the circle:

If the product is a good product, more sales means more satisfied customers, which means more positive word of mouth. That will lead to still more sales, which means even more widespread word of mouth . . . and so on. On the other hand, if the product is defective, the virtuous cycle becomes a vicious cycle: sales lead to less satisfied customers, less positive word of mouth, and less sales; which leads to still less positive word of mouth and less sales.

easily work in reverse, and (as occurred with contaminated over-the-counter drugs) produce marketplace disaster.

Both good news and bad news reinforcing loops accelerate so quickly that they often take people by surprise. A French schoolchildren's jingle illustrates the process. First there is just one lily pad in a corner of a pond. But every day the number of lily pads doubles. It takes thirty days to fill the pond, but for the first twenty-eight days, no one even notices. Suddenly, on the twenty-ninth day, the pond is half full of lily pads and the villagers become concerned. But by this time there is little that can be done. The next day their worst fears come true. That's why environmental dangers are so worrisome, especially those that follow reinforcing patterns (as many environmentalists fear occurs with such pollutants as CFCs). By the time the problem is noticed, it may be too late. Extinctions of species often follow patterns of slow, gradually accelerating decline over long time periods, then rapid demise. So do extinctions of corporations.

But pure accelerating growth or decline rarely continues unchecked in nature, because reinforcing processes rarely occur in isolation. Eventually, limits are encountered—which can slow growth, stop it, divert it, or even reverse it. Even the lily pads stop growing when the limit of the pond's perimeter is encountered. These limits are one form of *balancing feedback*, which, after reinforcing processes, is the second basic element of systems thinking.

Balancing Processes: Discovering the Sources of Stability and Resistance

If you are in a balancing system, you are in a system that is seeking stability. If the system's goal is one you like, you will be happy. If it is not, you will find all your efforts to change matters frustrated—until you can either change the goal or weaken its influence.

Nature loves a balance—but many times, human decision makers act contrary to these balances, and pay the price. For example, managers under budget pressure often cut back staff to lower costs, but eventually discover that their remaining staff is now overworked, and their costs have not gone down at all—because the remaining work has been farmed out to consultants, or because overtime has made up the difference. The reason that costs don't stay down is that *the system has its own agenda*. There is an implicit goal, unspoken but very real—the amount of work that is expected to get done.

In a balancing (stabilizing) system, there is a self-correction that attempts to maintain some goal or target. Filling the glass of water is a balancing process with the goal of a full glass. Hiring new employees is a balancing process with the goal of having a target work force size or rate of growth. Steering a car and staying upright on a bicycle are also examples of balancing processes, where the goal is heading in a desired direction.

Balancing feedback processes are everywhere. They underlie all goal-oriented behavior. Complex organisms such as the human body contain thousands of balancing feedback processes that maintain temperature and balance, heal our wounds, adjust our eyesight to the amount of light, and alert us to threat. A biologist would say that all of these processes are the mechanisms by which our body achieves *homeostasis*—its ability to maintain conditions for survival in a changing environment. Balancing feedback prompts us to eat when we need food, and to sleep when we need rest, or—as shown in the diagram above—to put on a sweater when we are cold.

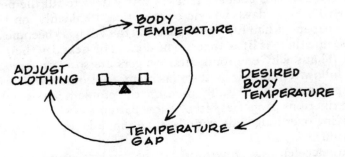

As in all balancing processes, the crucial element—our body temperature—gradually adjusts itself toward its desired level:

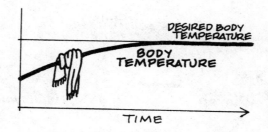

Organizations and societies resemble complex organisms because they too have myriad balancing feedback processes. In corporations, the production and materials ordering process is constantly adjusting in response to changes in incoming orders; short-term (discounts) and long-term (list) prices adjust in response to changes in demand or competitors' prices; and borrowing adjusts with changes in cash balances or financing needs.

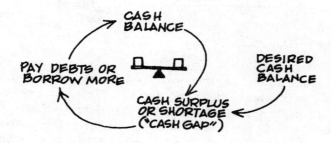

Planning creates longer-term balancing processes. A human resource plan might establish long-term growth targets in head count and in skill profile of the work force to match anticipated needs. Market research and R&D plans shape new product development and investments in people, technologies, and capital plant to build competitive advantage.

What makes balancing processes so difficult in management is that the goals are often implicit, and no one recognizes that the balancing process exists at all. I recall a good friend who tried, fruitlessly, to reduce burnout among professionals in his rapidly growing training business. He wrote memos, shortened working hours, even closed and locked offices earlier—all attempts to get people to stop overworking. But all these actions were offset—people ignored the memos, disobeyed the shortened hours, and took their work home with them when the offices were locked. Why? Because an unwritten norm in the organization stated that the *real* heros, the people who really cared and who got ahead in the organization, worked seventy hours a week—a norm that my friend had established himself by his own prodigious energy and long hours.

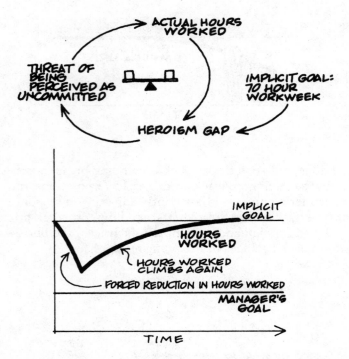

To understand how an organism works we must understand its balancing processes—those that are explicit *and* implicit. We could master long lists of body parts, organs, bones, veins, and blood vessels and yet we would not understand how the body functions—until we understand how the neuromuscular system maintains balance, or how the cardiovascular system maintains blood pressure and oxygen levels. This is why many attempts to redesign social systems fail. The state-controlled economy fails because it severs the multiple self-correcting processes that operate in a free market system. This is why corporate mergers often fail. When two hospitals in Boston, both with outstanding traditions of patient care, were merged several years ago, the new larger hospital had state-of-the-art facilities but lost the spirit of personal care and employee loyalty that had characterized the original institutions. In the merged hospital, subtle balancing processes in the older hospitals that monitored quality, paid attention to employee needs, and maintained friendly relationships with patients were disrupted by new administrative structures and procedures.

Though simple in concept, balancing processes can generate surprising and problematic behavior if they go undetected.

In general, balancing loops are more difficult to see than reinforcing loops because it often *looks* like nothing is happening. There's no dramatic growth of sales and marketing expenditures, or nuclear arms, or lily pads. Instead, the balancing process maintains the status quo, even when all participants want change. The feeling, as Lewis Carroll's Queen of Hearts put it, of needing "all

HOW TO READ A BALANCING CIRCLE DIAGRAM

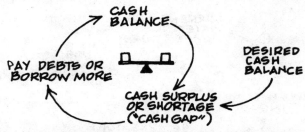

Balancing Process for Adjusting Cash Balance to Cash Surplus or Shortage

This diagram shows a balancing feedback process.

To walk yourself through the process, it's generally easiest to start at the gap—the discrepancy between what is desired and what exists:

Here, there is a shortfall in cash on hand for our cash flow needs. (In other words, there's a gap between our desired and actual cash balances.)

Then look at the actions being taken to correct the gap;

We borrow money, which makes our cash balance larger, and the gap decreases.

The chart shows that a balancing process is always operating to reduce a gap between what is desired and what exists. Moreover, such goals as desired cash balances change over time with growth or decline in the business. Regardless, the balancing process will continue to work to adjust actual cash balances to what is needed, even if the target is moving.

the running you can do to keep the same place," is a clue that a balancing loop may exist nearby.

Leaders who attempt organizational change often find themselves unwittingly caught in balancing processes. To the leaders, it looks as though their efforts are clashing with sudden resistance that seems to come from nowhere. In fact, as my friend found when he tried to reduce burnout, the resistance is a response by the system, trying to maintain an implicit system goal. Until this goal is recognized, the change effort is doomed to failure. So long as the leader continues to be the "model," his work habits will set the norm. Either he must change his habits, or establish new and different models.

Whenever there is "resistance to change," you can count on there being one or more "hidden" balancing processes. Resistance to change is neither capricious nor mysterious. It almost always arises from threats to traditional norms and ways of doing things. Often these norms are woven into the fabric of established power relationships. The norm is entrenched because the distribution of authority and control is entrenched. Rather than pushing harder

HOW TO READ A DELAY

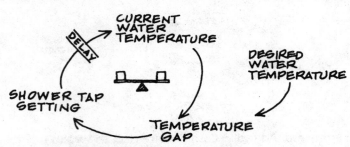

Balancing Process with a Delay: A Sluggish Shower

Here's our earlier "water faucet" feedback diagram again— but this time, with antiquated plumbing. Now there's a significant delay between the time you turn the faucet, and the time you see change in the water flow. Those two cross-hatch lines represent the delay.

Arrows with cross-hatch lines don't tell you how many seconds (or years) the delay will last. You only know it's long enough to make a difference.

When you follow an arrow with a delay, add the word "eventually" to the story you tell in your mind. "I moved the faucet handle, which eventually changed the water flow." Or, "I began a new construction project, and eventually, the houses were ready." You may even want to skip a beat—"one, two"—as you talk through the process.

to overcome resistance to change, artful leaders discern the source of the resistance. They focus directly on the implicit norms and power relationships within which the norms are embedded.

DELAYS: WHEN THINGS HAPPEN . . . EVENTUALLY

As we've seen, systems seem to have minds of their own. Nowhere is this more evident than in delays—interruptions between your actions and their consequences. Delays can make you badly overshoot your mark, or they can have a positive effect if you recognize them and work with them.

"One of the highest leverage points for improving system performance," says Ray Stata, CEO of Analog Devices, "is the minimization of system delays." Stata is referring to an increasing awareness on the part of American manufacturers that while they have worked traditionally to control tightly the amount of inventory in warehouses, their Japanese counterparts have concentrated on reducing delays—a much more successful effort. "The way leading companies manage time," says George Stalk, vice president of the Boston

Consulting Group, "—in production, in new product development, in sales and distribution—represents the most powerful new source of competitive disadvantage."

Delays between actions and consequences are everywhere in human systems. We invest now to reap a benefit in the distant future; we hire a person today but it may be months before he or she is fully productive; we commit resources to a new project knowing that it will be years before it will pay off. But delays are often unappreciated and lead to instability. For example, the decision makers in the beer game consistently misjudged the delays that kept them from getting orders filled when they thought they would.

Delays, when the effect of one variable on another takes time, constitute the third basic building block for a systems language. Virtually all feedback processes have some form of delay. But often the delays are either unrecognized or not well understood. This can result in "overshoot," going further than needed to achieve a desired result. The delay between eating and feeling full has been the nemesis of many a happy diner; we don't yet feel full when we should stop eating, so we keep going until we are overstuffed. The delay between starting a new construction project and its completion results in overbuilding real estate markets and an eventual shakeout.

Unrecognized delays can also lead to instability and breakdown, especially when they are long. Adjusting the shower temperature, for instance, is far more difficult when there is a ten-second delay before the water temperature adjusts, than when the delay takes only a second or two.

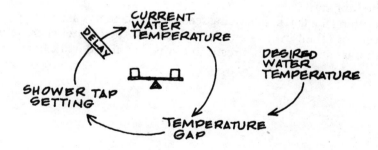

During that ten seconds after you turn up the heat, the water remains cold. You receive no response to your action; so you *perceive* that your act has had no effect. You respond by continuing to turn up the heat. When the hot water finally arrives, a 190-degree water gusher erupts from the faucet. You jump out and turn it back; and, after another delay, it's frigid again. On and on you go, through the balancing loop process. Each cycle of adjustments compensates somewhat for the cycle before. A diagram would look like this:

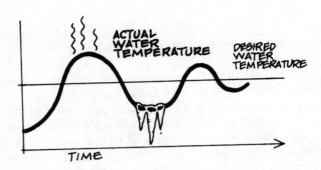

The more aggressive you are in your behavior—the more drastically you turn the knobs—the longer it will take to reach the right temperature. That's one of the lessons of balancing loops with delays: that aggressive action often produces exactly the opposite of what is intended. It produces instability and oscillation, instead of moving you more quickly toward your goal.

Delays are no less problematic in reinforcing loops. In the arms race example, each side perceives itself as gaining advantage from expanding its arsenal because of the delay in the other side's response. This delay can be as long as five years because of the time required to gather intelligence on the other side's weaponry, and to design and deploy new weapons. It is this temporary perceived advantage that keeps the escalation process going. If each side were able to respond instantly to buildups of its adversary, incentives to keep building would be nil.

The systems viewpoint is generally oriented toward the long-term view. That's why delays and feedback loops are so important. In the short term, you can often ignore them; they're inconsequential. They only come back to haunt you in the long term.

Reinforcing feedback, balancing feedback, and delays are all fairly simple. They come into their own as building blocks for the "systems archetypes"—more elaborate structures that recur in our personal and work lives again and again.

Systems Archetypes

Now we come to the archetypes we mentioned in the introduction to the above chapter. These are patterns of recurring behavior we encounter in every organization. In reading about and considering these archetypes and the kinds of results that come from these process patterns, remember this: every system will have elements that will cause problems of one sort or another. We tweak the system here to fix something, and it causes problems somewhere else.

Those who know that organizations are systems appreciate that management is a constant balancing act, where your role is to keep making improvements, large and small. Then you have to deal with the results of those improvements, not all of which will be positive. In other words, we can never really get things right, we can just get them pretty good for now and keep doing that over and over. The fact is that if you ever finally think things are "just right," you can be sure that's when something will start to go wrong. The archetypes can help you make continuous improvements and to get better at balancing the productive and destructive forces at work in all organizations.

Balancing Process With Delay

Structure:

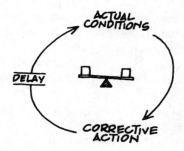

Description: A person, a group, or an organization, acting toward a goal, adjusts their behavior in response to delayed feedback. If they are not conscious of the delay, they end up taking more corrective action than needed, or (sometimes) just giving up because they cannot see that any progress is being made.

Early Warning Symptom: "We thought we were in balance, but then we overshot the mark." (Later, you may overshoot in the other direction again.)

Management Principle: In a sluggish system, aggressiveness produces instability. Either be patient or make the system more responsive.

Business Story: Real estate developers keep building new properties until the market has gone soft—but, by then, there are already enough additional properties still under construction to guarantee a glut.

Other Examples: A shower where the hot water responds sluggishly to changes in the faucet positions; production/distribution glut and shortage cycles; cycles in production rates and in-process inventory due to long manufacturing cycle times; the Tiananmen Square massacre, in which the government delayed its reaction to protest, and then cracked down unexpectedly hard; sudden, excessive stock market soars and crashes.

LIMITS to GROWTH

Structure:

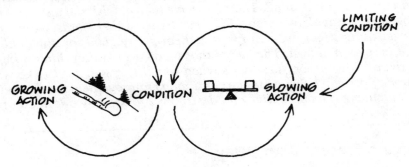

Description: A process feeds on itself to produce a period of accelerating growth or expansion. Then the growth begins to slow (often inexplicably to the participants in the system) and eventually comes to a halt, and may even reverse itself and begin an accelerating collapse.

The growth phase is caused by a reinforcing feedback process (or by several reinforcing feedback processes). The slowing arises due to a balancing process brought into play as a "limit" is approached. The limit can be a resource constraint, or an external or internal response to growth. The accelerating collapse (when it occurs) arises from the reinforcing process operating in reverse, to generate more and more contraction.

Early Warning Symptom: "Why should we worry about problems we don't have? We're growing tremendously." (A little later, "Sure there are some problems, but all we have to do is go back to what was working before." Still later, "The harder we run, the more we seem to stay in the same place.")

Management Principle: Don't push on the reinforcing (growth) process, remove (or weaken) the source of limitation.

Business Story: A company instituted an affirmative action program, which grew in support and activity as well-qualified minority employees were successfully introduced into work teams throughout the company. But eventually resistance emerged; the new staffers were perceived as not having "earned" their positions over other qualified aspirants. The harder individual teams were pressured to accept the new members, the more they resisted.

Other Examples: Learning a new skill, such as tennis, you make rapid progress early on as your competence and confidence builds, but then you begin to encounter limits to your natural abilities that can be overcome only by learning new techniques that may come "less naturally" at first.

A new startup that grows rapidly until it reaches a size that requires more professional management skills and formal organization; a new product team that works beautifully until its success causes it to bring in too many new members who neither share the work style nor values of the founding members; a city that grows steadily until available land is filled, leading to rising housing prices; a social movement that grows until it encounters increasing resistance from "nonconverts"; an animal population that grows rapidly when its natural predators are removed, only to overgraze its range and decline due to starvation.

Shifting the Burden

Structure:

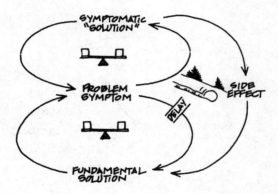

Description: A short-term "solution" is used to correct a problem, with seemingly positive immediate results. As this correction is used more and more, more fundamental long-term corrective measures are used less and less. Over time, the capabilities for the fundamental solution may atrophy or become disabled, leading to even greater reliance on the symptomatic solution.

Early Warning Symptom: "Look here, this solution has worked so far! What do you mean, there's trouble down that road?"

Management Principle: Focus on the fundamental solution. If symptomatic solution is imperative (because of delays in fundamental solution), use it to gain time while working on the fundamental solution.

Business Story: A dramatic new circuit board technology can be used to develop unique functionality and cost savings in a great many new product applications, but it can also be substituted for existing boards in current products. Salespeople can try to sell to "specialty customers" who appreciate the special properties of the technology and will eventually design new products which exploit it fully (the "fundamental solution") or sell to "commodity customers" who do not care about its special properties and will simply substitute it for other boards (the "symptomatic solution"). Given management pressures to meet quarterly sales targets, salespeople sell to whoever is ready to buy, which usually will be commodity customers since there are more of them and delays in the selling cycle are shorter. Over time, the dramatic new technology fails to develop a loyal customer base and becomes subject to the price and margin pressures that characterize commodity products.

Other Examples: Selling more to existing customers rather than broadening the customer base; paying bills by borrowing, instead of going through the discipline of budgeting; using alcohol, drugs, or even something as benign as exercise to relieve work stress and thereby not facing the need to control the workload itself; and any addiction, anywhere, to anything.

Special Case: Shifting the Burden to the Intervenor

Structure:

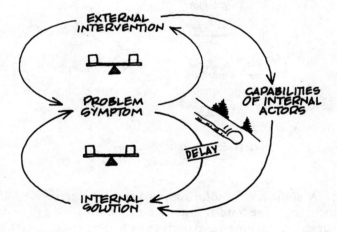

One area where shifting the burden structures are so common and so pernicious that it warrants special notice is when outside "intervenors" try to help solve problems. The intervention attempts to ameliorate obvious problem symptoms, and does so successfully that the people within the system never learn how to deal with the problems themselves.

Management Principle: "Teach people to fish, rather than giving them fish." Focus on enhancing the capabilities of the "host system" to solve its own problems. If outside help is needed, "helpers" should be strictly limited to a one-time intervention (and everyone knows this in advance) or be able to help people develop their own skills, resources, and infrastructure to be more capable in the future.

Business Story: An innovative insurance company was committed to the concept of independent local offices that would call on headquarters staff only for occasional help. Initially the concept worked well, until the industry went through a crisis. Facing sudden severe losses, the local offices called in the more experienced central management for help in rewriting rate structures— a process which took months. Meanwhile, the local managers focused their attention on managing the crisis. The crisis was resolved, but the next time rate structures were called into question, the local offices had lost some of their confidence. They called in the central managers as "insurance." After several years of this behavior, the local offices found themselves without underwriters who could manage rate structure changes independently.

Other Examples: Dependence on outside contractors instead of training your own people. Numerous forms of government aid that attempt to solve pressing problems only to foster dependency and need for increasing aid: welfare systems that foster single-family households; housing or job training programs that attract the needy to cities with the best programs; food aid to developing countries which lowers deaths and increases population growth; social security systems that reduce personal savings and encourage the breakup of the extended family.

Eroding Goals

Structure:

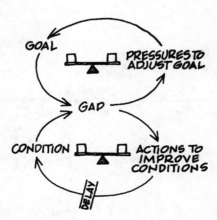

Description: A shifting the burden type of structure in which the short-term solution involves letting a long-term, fundamental goal decline.

Early Warning Symptom: "It's okay if our performance standards slide a little, just until the crisis is over."

Management Principle: Hold the vision.

Business Story: A high-tech manufacturer finds itself losing market share, despite a terrific product and ongoing improvements. But the firm, oriented toward its design "geniuses," had never gotten production scheduling under control. An outside investigator discovered that customers were increasingly dissatisfied with late schedules, and were turning to competitors instead. The company stood on its record: "We've maintained a consistent 90 percent success in meeting the delivery time quoted to the customer." It therefore looked elsewhere for the problem. However, every time the company began to slip its schedules, it responded by making the quoted delivery time a little longer. Thus, the quoted delivery time to customers was getting lengthier, and lengthier, and lengthier . . .

Other Examples: Successful people who lower their own expectations for themselves and gradually become less successful. Firms that tacitly lower their quality standards by cutting budgets rather than investing in developing a new higher quality (and perhaps lower cost) ways of doing things, all the while proclaiming their continued commitment to quality. Lowered government targets for "full employment" or balancing the federal deficit. Sliding targets for controlling dangerous pollutants or protecting endangered species.

Escalation

Structure:

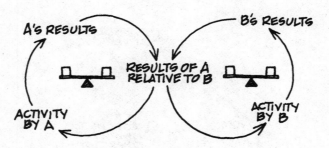

Description: Two people or organizations each see their welfare as depending on a relative advantage over the other. Whenever one side gets ahead, the other is more threatened, leading it to act more aggressively to reestablish its advantage, which threatens the first, increasing its aggressiveness, and so on. Often each side sees its own aggressive behavior as a defensive response to the other's aggression; but each side acting "in defense" results in a buildup that goes far beyond either side's desires.

Early Warning Symptom: "If our opponent would only slow down, then we could stop fighting this battle and get some other things done."

Management Principle: Look for a way for both sides to "win," or to achieve their objectives. In many instances, one side can unilaterally reverse the vicious spiral by taking overtly aggressive "peaceful" actions that cause the other to feel less threatened.

Business Story: A company developed an ingenious design for a stroller, which carried three toddlers at once, yet was light and convenient for travel. It was an immediate hit with families with several young children. Almost simultaneously, a competitor emerged with a similar product. After several years, jealous of the other company's share of the market, the first company lowered its price by 20 percent. The second company felt a decline in sales, and lowered its price too. Then the first company, still committed to boosting share, lowered its prices still further. The second company reluctantly did the same, even though its profits were beginning to suffer. Several years later, both companies were barely breaking even, and survival of the triple carriage was in doubt.

Other Examples: Advertising wars. Increasing reliance on lawyers to settle disputes. Gang warfare. The breakup of a marriage. Inflating budget estimates: as some groups inflate their estimates, others find themselves doing likewise in order to get "their piece of the pie," which leads to everyone inflating his estimates still further. Battle for the "ear" of the president of a company. And, of course, the arms race.

Success to the Successful

Structure:

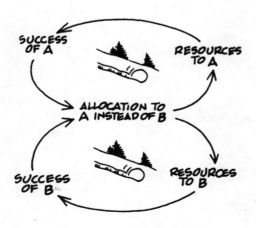

Description: Two activities compete for limited support or resources. The more successful one becomes, the more support it gains, thereby starving the other.

Early Warning Symptom: One of the two interrelated activities, groups, or individuals is beginning to do very well and the other is struggling.

Management Principle: Look for the overarching goal for balanced achievement of both choices. In some cases, break or weaken the coupling between the two, so that they do not compete for the same limited resource (this is desirable in cases where the coupling is inadvertent and creates an unhealthy competition for resources).

Business Story: A manager has two protégés, and wishes to bring both along equally in the firm. However, one of the two ends up getting preferential treatment because the other is out sick for a week. When the second protégé returns to work, the manager feels guilty, and avoids the person, thereby giving still more opportunity to the first protégé. The first protégé, feeling the approval, flourishes, and therefore gets more opportunity. The second protégé, feeling insecure, does less effective work and receives even fewer opportunities, although the two people had equal ability in the beginning. Eventually, the second protégé leaves the firm.

Other Examples: Balancing home and work life, in which a worker gets caught working overtime so much that relationships at home deteriorate and it gets more and more "painful" to go home, which, of course, makes the worker even more likely to neglect home life in the future. Two products compete for limited financial and managerial resources within a firm; one is an immediate hit in the marketplace and receives more investment, which depletes the resources available to the other, setting in motion a reinforcing spiral fueling growth of the first and starving the second. A shy student gets off to a poor start in school (perhaps because of emotional problems or an undetected learning disability), becomes labeled a "slow learner," and gets less and less encouragement and attention than his or her more outgoing peers.

Tragedy of the Commons

Structure:

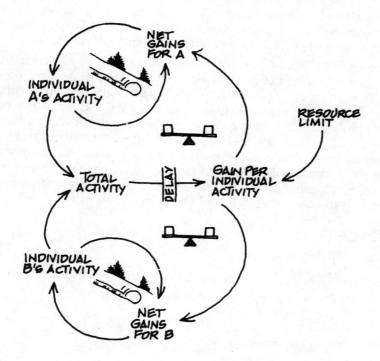

Description: Individuals use a commonly available but limited resource solely on the basis of individual need. At first they are rewarded for using it; eventually, they get diminishing returns, which causes them to intensify their efforts. Eventually, the resource is either significantly depleted, eroded, or entirely used up.

Early Warning Symptom: "There used to be plenty for everyone. Now things are getting tough. If I'm going to get any profit out of it this year, I'll have to work harder."

Management Principle: Manage the "commons," either through educating everyone and creating forms of self-regulation and peer pressure, or through an official regulating mechanism, ideally designed by participants.

Business Story: Several divisions of a company agreed to share a retail salesforce. Each district manager was initially concerned that the shared salesforce wouldn't give enough attention to his or her particular business, and that volume would decline. One particularly aggressive manager advised all his account managers to set higher sales targets than were truly needed, so that the salesforce would at least give them the minimum support they needed. The other divisions saw this division pushing for extra work, and decided to employ the same strategy. The new salesforce's managers wanted to accommodate all of their "clients," so they continued to accept the higher requests from the divisions. This created a tremendous overburden of work, lowered performance, and increased turnover. Pretty soon, joining the retail salesforce was only slightly more popular than joining the French Foreign Legion, and each division had to go back to maintaining its own salesforce.

Other Examples: Exhaustion of a shared secretarial pool. Deteriorating reputation for customer service after customers have had to listen to six different salespeople from six different divisions of the same corporation pitching competing products. (The "shared resource" in this case was the firm's positive customer reputation.) A highly successful retail chain gives up on joint sales promotions with manufacturers after being deluged with proposals by enthusiastic manufacturers, or establishes terms for joint ventures that leave little profit for the manufacturers. Depletion of a natural resource by competing companies which mine it. And, of course, all manner of pollution problems from acid rain to ozone depletion and the "greenhouse effect."

Fixes That Fail

Structure:

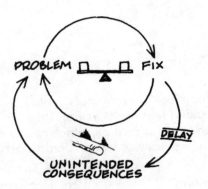

Description: A fix, effective in the short term, has unforeseen long-term consequences which may require even more use of the same fix.

Early Warning Symptom: "It always seemed to work before; why isn't it working now?"

Management Principle: Maintain focus on the long term. Disregard short-term "fix," if feasible, or use it only to "buy time" while working on long-term remedy.

Business Story: A manufacturing company launched a new set of high-performance parts, which were wildly successful at first. However, the CEO was driven by maximizing his ROI, so he deferred ordering expensive, new production machines. Manufacturing quality suffered, which led to a reputation for low quality. Customer demand fell off dramatically over the ensuing year, which depressed returns and made the CEO even more unwilling to invest in new production equipment.

Other Examples: People and organizations who borrow to pay interest on other loans, thereby ensuring that they will have to pay even more interest later. Cutting back maintenance schedules to save costs, which eventually leads to more breakdowns and higher costs, creating still more cost-cutting pressures.

Growth and Underinvestment

Structure:

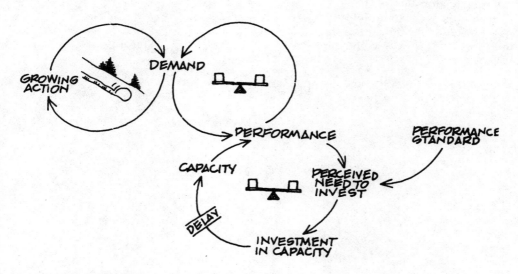

Description: Growth approaches a limit which can be eliminated or pushed into the future if the firm, or individual, invests in additional "capacity." But the investment must be aggressive and sufficiently rapid to forestall reduced growth, or else it will never get made. Oftentimes, key goals or performance standards are lowered to justify underinvestment. When this happens, there is a self-fulfilling prophecy where lower goals lead to lower expectations, which are then borne out by poor performance caused by underinvestment.

Early Warning Symptom: "Well, we used to be the best, and we'll be the best again, but right now we have to conserve our resources and not over-invest."

Management Principle: If there is a genuine potential for growth, build capacity in advance of demand, as a strategy for creating demand. Hold the vision, especially as regards assessing key performance standards and evaluating whether capacity to meet potential demand is adequate.

Business Story: People Express Airlines found itself unable to build service capacity to keep pace with exploding demand. Rather than putting more resources into training or growing more slowly (for example, through raising prices somewhat), the firm tried to "outgrow" its problems. The result was deteriorating service quality and increased competition, while morale deteriorated. In order to keep up with the continued stress, the company relied more and more on the "solution" of underinvesting in service capacity, until customers no longer found flying People Express attractive.

Other Examples: Companies which let service quality or product quality of any sort decline, simultaneously blaming competition or their sales management for not pushing hard enough to maintain sales. People with grand visions who never realistically assess the time and effort they must put in to achieve their visions.

How to Make Partnerships Work

James W. Cortada

"**P**artnering" and "partnerships" are terms used as loosely today as are "quality" and "reengineering." Ask managers what those terms really mean, and they have to pause, often thinking for the first time about their definitions. Yet partnering is a part of corporate strategies, and their success or failure may depend on how well they go about it. This problem is similar to the misunderstanding of what TQM is about and the subsequent complaints about TQM not being all it's cracked up to be. Of course, the problem in these situations is not with TQM, but our understanding of what it is all about. Well here we go again; this time not with process management or benchmarking or even with ISO 9000 or the Baldrige criteria. Now the problem is with partnering and what it means or doesn't mean.

Harvard Business School professors have spoken about the "virtual corporations," while other scholars at the Sloan School explain the application of strategic IT planning to link us intimately to other companies and agencies creating, in effect, seamless connections without institutional borders. Executives are quick to declare these connections as partnerships. Proponents of "best practices" in purchase processes embrace the idea as well. However, many vendors would call these partnerships more like the fidelity required of medieval serfs to their lords while other institutions would more kindly say they are victims of begging and one-sided relationships.

So how are you to apply the concept of partnerships effectively? After all, long before the articulation of quality management principles and practices, there were partnerships, both in legal and moral forms, of advantage to all involved and that focused the best of an organization's skills and assets. There are clearly advantages to partnering up with other companies. However, doing it right begins with a clear understanding of what partnerships are and why you use them. Then comes the how-to of implementation.

What Is A Partnership?

Dictionaries and lawyers provide the definition that a partnership is "a legal relationship between two or more persons contractually associated as joint principals in a business." Put another way, it is a 50/50 ownership of a project or company with all owners sharing equally the profits and risks of the venture. Partnerships are formed to gain benefits not obtainable in the absence of such an arrangement. Partnerships are formed to go after three types of benefits: (1) financial gain, (2) reduced risk taking, and (3) rapid and dramatic innovation. This explanation is about as far as any lawyer or business school will take you. But for centuries, business people have known there was more to it.

For one thing, effective partnerships invariably reflect a sincere commitment to the success of the partners. This is reflected in personal and emotional involvement and the allocation of sufficient resources by all parties. This commitment of resources is vital. Some managers will use the term partnership without committing the resources to make it succeed. For example,

- By our description, can a university president speak of a partnership with a corporation in which the expectation is that the business will contribute money to the university without specific benefits in exchange (for example, well-defined research undertaken, people trained, or products developed)?
- Is it a partnership when a manufacturing company declares its critical few suppliers as partners when the manufacturer dictates the terms of sales?
- Is it a partnership when the president of a country says he or she is working in partnership with a legislature dominated by an opposing party to get an economic reform program implemented?

Possibly, but not very likely since, in each instance, there are uneven contributions to the project and often ill-defined or even opposing objectives between the so-called partners.

The point is that a good partnership is one in which there is equality of expectations, investments of time, funding, effort, and commitment to make it work. In short, it is a win/win for all involved in which everyone benefits because the whole is greater than its sum. Common goals and incentives exist that insure behavior designed to achieve these objectives. Commitment is often the hardest part of making a dictionary definition of a partnership work, but that is the first step to the successful exploitation of a strategy of partnering.

What Makes for a Good Partnership?

Trust: A confidence that all parties in the partnership believe in and support mutual goals and value the opinions, motives, and skills of partners. Trust comes about from long discussions and an understanding of what everyone wants to get out of the relationship. Nobody's objectives are in severe conflict with anybody else's.

Mutual support: Everyone taking care of each other. The Three Musketeers said it best: "All for one, and one for all." Like the Three Musketeers, partners come to depend on each other to make the partnership successful.

Shared assumptions: Through dialogue, experience, and study, the partners have figured together where they want to take the project or business and have views on what the opportunities are and how to resolve problems and seize upon opportunities.

Equality of Contributions: Each partner has put up as many resources as the others to make the deal work. The contribution does not have to be exactly the same (that is, the same amount of money or people). It just must be seen by all involved as being a fair and equal contribution for the risk and returns expected. This is not the time to talk about such legal forms as limited partnerships or full partnerships. Any partnership essentially calls for an equitable contribution to the project by all the partners involved. The idea is simple and does not need to be complicated by fine details. In addition to equity of contribution, there also has to be the sense that the investment by all partners is substantial enough such that it is in everyone's interest to make the partnership work because failure would be too expensive. The Three Musketeers would argue that failure could be the loss of their lives; for you, it is the failure of the project or bankruptcy of the business.

How Do Successful Partnerships Work?

You already know part of the answer: make sure all the partners go into the deal with a clear understanding and agreement as to what each needs to get out of the relationship to make it a win/win situation. Partnerships that work well take some common steps regardless of the legal or practical nature of the partnership:

1. **Partners clearly define the objectives to be attained.** These objectives are stated numerically and on a time line. For example, statements can be of sales volumes attained by certain dates or project milestones achieved by specific dates. It is normal to see changes in objectives over time, but the principle remains the same: clearly stated and agreed-to objectives. That way expectations are realistic and do not get out of hand.

2. **Partners clearly define the commitments they must make to the partnership.** These commitments can range from money, people, buildings, to other assets committed to the partnership. The commitments are defined at the start of the relationship and, like objectives, are constantly revisited to make sure they still make sense or need to be modified.

    Often each partner is coming to the table with something the other does not have (for example, special skills or equipment); these should be appreciated for what they will contribute to the success of the partnership. This is yet another form of clearly understanding expectations, roles, and responsibilities.

3. **Communications remains a central great quality of the partnership.** Much as you would with a well-run process, partners share with each other all pertinent information regarding the progress of the partnership. Often this sharing of information and sound communications occurs on a frequent and planned basis. Thus reports are issued on schedule, and a variety of communication tools are used: shared E-mail, staff meetings, and strategic planning sessions.

4. **Team practices often represent the "best practices" in a partnership.** Increasingly, it is becoming evident that the most successful

partnerships also act like teams. People with the greatest knowledge of the partnership's objectives and actions make decisions and are empowered to do the work their way. Incentives, rewards, and measurements of performance are increasingly skewed in the direction of team-based behavior.

5. **Partnerships often develop their own culture apart from that of the partnership organizations.** This often happens when two companies decide to set up a subsidiary owned 50 percent by each. An example might be the New United Motor Manufacturing Incorporated (NUMMI), a partnership between GM and Toyota that has its own unique labor agreement and culture. In this case, the subsidiary is given the leeway to create its own corporate culture in order to be effective. That means the partnership companies have to be very careful not to smother the new organization with their own culture (e.g., heavy reporting requirements or conformance to a partner's personnel practices).

The following include other more tactical steps that partnerships can take to improve the probability of success:

Education: Take the time to learn from each partner and from the activities of the partnership. More than simply sharing information, this calls for formal processes for understanding what the partnership is doing and how to improve its work.

Planning: Spend time planning at both the tactical and strategic levels. More than a good management practice, it is a crucial element of success since more than one organization is involved. It is irrelevant whether the partnership is a legal or practical one, planning is very critical in all relationships.

Performance measurements: Create and then modify as needed a set of performance measures of the partnership's activities. These measures can be of functions (organizations) or processes and can include departmental or project report cards, balanced score cards, or various process measurements.

People: Make sure that employees assigned to the partnership are being paid and compensated in ways that are consistent with the objectives of the partnership. It is not uncommon, for example, in a new partnership to see employees from multiple companies thrown together who are being measured differently, even in conflict with the objectives of the partnership. Sort those issues out quickly and early in the relationship so that everyone is aligned together.

Technology: Take advantage of computers and telecommunications to facilitate the partnership. Information technology can facilitate the sharing of information and coordination of activities across multiple organizations. E-mail facilitates reporting and communicating, EDI the transfer of data (for example, orders for goods and services), and databases the sharing of information used in different ways by partners. Well applied, information technology blurs the borders between organizations. For example, a database of engineering drawings shared between a subcontractor working on part of a project and others working on different components is a common illustration of sharing.

Other Quality Management Practices That Can Be Applied in a Partnership

For years now, manufacturing companies have used ISO 9000 as a way of standardizing work across their own organizations and those of their suppliers. This strategic use of a quality tool can be applied in any partnership where ISO practices make sense for individual partners themselves because ISO facilitates the best practices cited above: communications and setting of realistic expectations.

A second tool is the Baldrige criteria for the same reasons as ISO 9000: These criteria encourage use of common standards and a unified focus on what is important. Baldrige assessments can offer the same advantages in a partnership as experienced within any company. Such assessments cause important questions to be asked and answered concerning how customers are treated, how well the organization (for example, a partnership) uses information, and how effective it is over time. Both Baldrige and ISO cause partnerships to become learning organizations teaching the partners what works and fails and why. The common language of a Baldrige assessment or an ISO 9000 audit are transferrable across organizations.

Process management and process reengineering can be critical to the success of a partnership. It is not uncommon, for instance, for a process to begin in one organization, pass through one or more partners, and end in yet other organizations (vendors or customers for example). Often the reengineering of a process facilitates the formation and use of partnerships to get things done quickly and in radically new ways. For example, various technical standards found in information technology can often be consolidated and standardized in forms that make sense to customers. This can be done through the use of wholly owned subsidiaries established for the purpose of merging activities.

A systems view of how a variety of organizations can work together is crucial. Total quality management has built into its beliefs the notion that things operate in a holistic manner, that is to say, activities in one part of an organization influence those in another, much like a sore toe makes you feel bad all over. When management applies TQM-like or systems perspectives, the various components of a collection of organizations and partnerships can be brought together in some rational whole. Hence the debate and enormous interest in recent years in such organizational constructs as the "virtual organization," "borderless companies," and "learning enterprises." These are all variations on a common theme: multiple enterprises working in concert together. Making all of that work is often best done by dipping into the bag of TQM tricks, many of which have already been discussed above.

Where to Learn More about Partnerships

One of the best sources of information is the quality literature because so many of the detailed practices discussed above come from this body of activities. Books on reengineering, such as Michael Hammer and James Champy's

Reengineering the Corporation (HarperCollins, 1993) are useful. For an on-going update on quality materials, see the bibliography in different editions of *The Quality Yearbook*.

A second source of information are business management journals, typically those that focus on strategic issues. The key journals are the *Harvard Business Review, Sloan Management Review, California Management Review*, and the *Journal of Business Strategy*. These provide both examples and "rules of the road."

There is also a growing body of articles and books emerging from purchase process reengineering that discusses how various organizations can work together. This literature is extensive. For a quick listing of recent articles and books, see any of the *Quality Yearbooks* that have bibliographies specifically on supplier relations. Your own industry magazines and journals also carry articles on partnerships (usually successful ones) that are also instructive. But do not hesitate to read about partnerships in other industries since it may be that partnerships you want to form are with companies outside your SIC code! Look what happened in 1993–1994 with telephone companies, Hollywood studios, and television and cable companies as they all rushed to position themselves for a ride on the information highway!

Some Final Thoughts

There has been almost no discussion above about legal issues, such as the contractual relationships involved in various forms of partnerships, or how to expand or collapse such relationships. After all, legal relationships are important and should be entered into for many sound reasons. In no way are we suggesting that legal considerations are irrelevant. But, more to the point, legal relationships are merely the byproduct of a strategic intent. You first have to decide that you want some form of partnership to get at some business advantage. Thus the first decision is a business one, not a legal issue. Once you have decided that a partnership is the way to go, then you still have other business decisions to make: what kind of management style do you want, what kind of practices are appropriate, and who should you partner with? Once those decisions are made, then the legal relationships can be defined.

CEOs acquiring companies or forming partnerships, while they will consult lawyers all along the way to a partnership, ultimately decide what to do based on their perception of what a potential partner can bring to the table and what they themselves can offer as well. Then they turn to the lawyers to "draw up the papers." Normally it is at that point that the lawyers are told what the purpose and style of the partnership should be as a guide to their work in crafting the partnership contracting documents.

Outsourcing has become a very popular strategy for companies and government agencies in the 1990s. Are these partnerships? In many cases, they have the appearance of a partnership because one organization is dependent on another for a service (for example, for providing computing) and in fact many of the behaviors of these organizations with their outsourcers are partnerlike. But they are not necessarily a formal partnership, merely a long-term relationship with a supplier. The distinction is important because one remains the customer or supplier to the other, lacking equality in the relationship both legally and practically. Ask any supplier to an automotive manufacturer who hears constantly that he or she is a partner of Ford Motor, Toyota, or General Motors and you will understand very quickly the difference. The morale is quite simple: there is a difference between a partnership and an outsourced relationship even though the rhetoric used by both parties is often that of partnership.

Finally, like a good marriage, a good partnership can bring profound benefits to the couple, but it requires a lot of work to be successful. Just as nearly half the marriages end in divorce, so too many partnerships fail and for the same reasons. If you want a partnership to work, practice the steps suggested above and model your behavior like a good spouse.

ISO 9000 for Beginners

Alan K. Lund

ISO 9000 certification is becoming more and more important as businesses go global. Doing business with a certified company means that that company has carefully documented its processes and follows that documentation with discipline. More simply, it means a company says what it does and does what it says. ISO 9000 is still new to many people. This original article has been prepared by consulting editor Alan K. Lund to explain just what ISO is all about and why certification makes sense. Lund is president of The Ironbridge Group, a highly regarded ISO 9000 consulting company. After reading this article, check the one that follows it. It is about the practicalities involved in selecting an ISO 9000 registrar. These two articles should provide you with a basic understanding of what certification is all about and how to get started.

Background of ISO 9000

In less than a decade since they were initially published, the international quality standards known as ISO 9000 have surged to worldwide recognition. Initially published in 1987, ISO 9000 can be classified as a generic set of quality standards that provide specific guidelines for establishing and maintaining a quality management system. The ISO standards may be applied to any organization and are for manufacturers and service entities alike. The ISO standards were developed on a consensus basis (over 40 countries) and have been structured as a set of Best Business Practices. The intent of the standards is to provide an international benchmark for in-house quality practices and to allow at least some degree of comparison on a global basis. Over 90 countries, including the United States, have formally adopted the ISO 9000 Standards.

The ISO standards are likely to have a more-defined impact on quality practices throughout the world than any other quality concept. Since the mid-1980s, over 70,000 sites have been registered to one of the ISO 9000 standards. U.S. companies were slow to adopt the standard, but customer pressure, potential for lost sales, demands for higher quality, and the need to reduce costs have forced many firms to seek ISO 9000 registration. As of June 1995, over 6,800 U.S. sites have achieved ISO 9000. Market studies indicate that over 100,000 sites will become registered in the next 3 to 5 years (Figure 1).

The ISO 9000 standards are coordinated on a worldwide basis by the International Organization for Standardization, which is based in Geneva, Switzerland. The International Organization for Standardization (ISO) is a worldwide federation of national standards bodies made up of more than 100 countries. This organization was formed with the objective to promote the

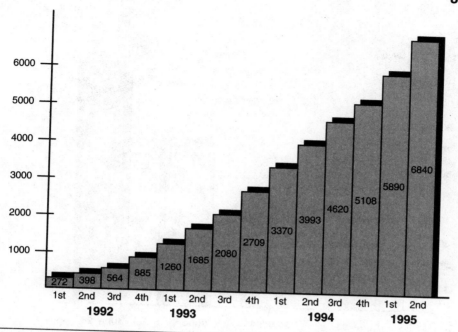

Figure 1.   **United States registration growth by quarter: 1992–1995.**

development of standardization and related activities throughout the world. The basic goal of the ISO organization is to facilitate the international exchange of goods and services. These goals are addressed through the efforts of some 180 technical committees. These committees did not simply create a new set of standards but, based upon experience with a range of military and manufacturing regulations, set out to compile a "directory" of Best Business Practices. In other words, the goal was to create a set of generic standards that would provide specific guidelines for establishing and maintaining a quality system. Further, the ISO process would provide for a means of verification by objective, third-party observers (termed registrars) that the quality system was in place and was a part of the day-to-day business activities of the company.

On a worldwide basis, registration to the ISO 9000 series of standards continues to grow (Figure 2).

The United Kingdom leads the ISO activity with nearly 37,000 registrations, followed by the rest of Europe with 18,500 registrations. As of June 1994, ISO 9000 registrations had occurred in 76 different countries.

In the United States, the ISO 9000 standards are coordinated by ANSI (American National Standards Institute) and ASQC (American Society for Quality Control) and are published as the ANSI/ASQC Q9000 series. Accreditation of registrars (organizations that perform the verification activities at the company's site) and auditors is handled by the RAB (Registrar Accreditation Board), a subset of ASQC.

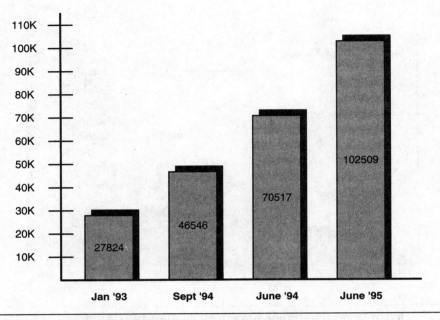

Figure 2. **ISO 9000 registrations, worldwide basis.**

The Role of ISO 9000 in Quality Systems: From the Company's Perspective

There has been, and continues to be, a state of confusion that surrounds the ISO standards. Questions such as Why were they developed? What is the impact on the way a company operates? Is a company required to be ISO registered? How are the specific requirements of the ISO standard applied on a company-by-company basis? How does the verification process work? are prevalent throughout the industry. The core of ISO 9000, as with a wide variety of business, process, and/or customer improvement programs, such as total quality management (TQM), continuous improvement process (CIP), total quality system (TQS), quality circles, plus a host of other initiatives, can be stated in one word—*quality*. The fundamental issues that separate ISO 9000 from each of these initiatives is the depth and scope of the quality requirements. A quick review of the dictionary will define a "standard" as— "something established for use as a rule or basis of comparison in measuring quantity, quality, value, etc." The majority of quality programs lack a solid foundation that includes all functions of a company's operations. ISO 9000 not only requires that a company define its customer requirements and obligations but also define, develop, implement, and maintain a quality system involving all personnel (from executive management to staff and line-level personnel) in the reduction and/or elimination of process variables that affect the quality of the product or service delivered.

The purpose of ISO 9000 was not to develop another quality standard that companies would use as the ultimate or only measuring tool for improving quality. As previously identified, the ISO standards merely provide a basic set of guidelines that seek to help the individual company to establish a quality management system that will provide a *framework* or a *foundation* for the interactions that occur between each of the company's business operations and their customer. As a stand-alone document, the ISO standards define a basic set of requirements that must be apparent, available, and implemented. Requirements such as a documented quality manual, documented procedures for a limited number of specific processes (such as management review, purchasing, contract review, calibration, etc.), and the availability of specific quality records that provide objective evidence that the quality system works are included in this basic set of requirements. Past these fundamental issues, the ISO standard lets the company, and/or the company's contract with its customer(s), decide what is to be included, documented, and maintained in the company's defined quality management system.

The most critical piece of the ISO implementation puzzle is for the individual company to identify and document their processes as they actually occur, not the way they would like the process to happen, but in reality—the way the company's processes operate in the real world. Past the specific ISO standard and contractual requirements, the primary focus of ISO 9000 is for a company to consistently do what they have documented and to be able to show that the implemented quality system has established a continuous improvement discipline that is based on preventive measures.

ISO 9000 is a voluntary, self-imposed quality management system that does not prescribe "how" a company should operate, only that the company be able to meet the customer's requirements, as defined in the customer's order; that the implemented quality system meet the **intent** of the ISO standard; and that objective evidence be **readily** available to prove that the company is in control of their processes. Implementing the basic requirements of ISO 9000 will provide a common reference point for the company and for its customers. An effective ISO quality system is characterized by the following:

- Consistent processes that can be verified through quality records and internal audits results.
- Useful documentation that mirrors the way the processes occur on a regular basis.
- Committed executive-level management personnel who understand the strategic importance of quality planning, quality involvement, and the integration of the ISO requirements into each and every business function.
- A high level of customer satisfaction that is continuously measured and assessed for ways to improve both the customer's stated and implied quality needs.

- A quality management system that seeks to identify and eliminate the root cause for nonconformance by understanding the variations in processes and establishing counter measures to prevent their reoccurrence.
- Trained and confident employees who understand the company's policy on quality and their role in ensuring that processes remain in control.

For a quality program to have value (both internal and external to the company), long-term stability, and a measurable return-on-investment, the system must address each segment of the business operations and must become a part of the day-to-day operations. From a company perspective, the key to an effective and successful ISO quality management system will not be found by creating and implementing documentation (quality manual, procedures, work instructions, etc.) but through the realization that the ISO 9000 process will help a company to improve customer satisfaction, uncover process inconsistencies, and strengthen the quality foundation through a structured program of continuous improvement.

The Role of ISO 9000 Systems: From the Customer's Perspective

The typical supplier/customer relationship centers on a series of common elements that generally revolve around the company's ability to deliver a quality product or service within the time specified and at the agreed upon price; added to these issues will be the customer's expectation regarding stated and implied support. The majority of customer/supplier relationships operate on a contractual agreement between the two parties; the majority of problems stem from unclear or ambiguous contractual requirements, misunderstandings of what was truly required, variations in the process from the supplier's operations, and miscommunicated changes in specifications or requirements as requested or communicated from the customer. Each of these issues typically revolves around an undefined level of trust. ISO 9000 provides a framework for this supplier-to-customer relationship by providing the assurance that the supplier has a quality management system that is both documented and implemented, certified by an independent third party, and built around a program that targets continuous improvement, preventive action, and customer satisfaction. An effective ISO 9000 program should, and does, add "value" to the customer/supplier relationship by providing both parties with a common reference point.

The ISO 9000 Standards

The ISO 9000 standards provide a company with a set of guidelines and requirements for establishing and maintaining a system for quality. The intent is to provide a benchmark for the company's in-house quality practices and to allow some degree of comparison on a worldwide basis.

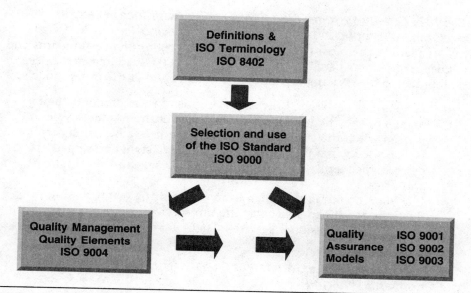

Figure 3. **ISO 9000 standards.**

The basic ISO 9000 series is comprised of five standards: *ISO 9000, ISO 9001, ISO 9002, ISO 9003,* and *ISO 9004.* In the United States, the ISO standards are identified as ANSI/ASQC Q9000-1-1994, ANSI/ASQC Q9001-1994, ANSI/ASQC Q9002-1994, ANSI/ASQC Q9003-1994, and ANSI/ASQC Q9004-1-1994. The standards are of two types:

Guidance Standards
Conformance Standards

ISO 9000 (Q9001) and ISO 9004 (Q9004-1) are guidance standards. This means they are *descriptive* documents, not *prescriptive* requirements. Companies do not register to either ISO 9000 or ISO 9004. Instead, they register to one of the conformance standards, ISO 9001, ISO 9002, or ISO 9003. These are models for quality systems.

In descriptive form, the ISO 9000 standards can be visualized as shown in Figure 3.

Conformance Standards

ISO 9001, ISO 9002, and ISO 9003 are models used for external quality assurance. Each standard contains a set of necessary quality system elements. ISO 9001 is the most comprehensive standard while ISO 9003 is the least comprehensive. Each model is a complete, independent document. A company should select the appropriate conformance model after a thorough assessment of its quality system needs.

ISO 9001: *Quality Systems: Model for Quality Assurance in Design, Development, Production, Installation, and Servicing*

This standard is the most comprehensive of the conformance standards and includes all elements listed in ISO 9002 and ISO 9003. It addresses the design, development, and servicing capabilities not addressed in the other models.

- ISO 9001 is used when the supplier must ensure product conformance to specified needs throughout the entire product cycle. It is used when the contract specifically requires a design effort. It is also used when product requirements are stated principally in performance terms that are a function of design and development activities.
- ISO 9001 commonly applies to manufacturing or processing industries, but it can also be applied to services, such as construction, or to professional services, such as architecture and engineering.

ISO 9002: *Quality Systems: Model for Quality Assurance in Production, Installation, and Servicing*

ISO 9002 addresses the prevention, detection and correction of problems during production, installation , and servicing.

The main distinction between ISO 9001 and ISO 9002 is that ISO 9002 does not include the design function.

- ISO 9002 applies to a wide range of industries whose work is based on technical designs and specifications provided by their customers. It is relevant for products that do not involve a design aspect and is used when the specified product requirements are stated in terms of an already established design or specification.

ISO 9003: *Quality Systems: Model for Quality Assurance in Final Inspection and Test*

ISO 9003 is the least comprehensive standard. It addresses only the requirements for detection and wqcontrol of problems during final inspection and testing.

- ISO 9003 applies to organizations whose products or services can be adequately assessed by testing and inspection. Generally, this refers to less complete products or services.

Table 1 compares the quality system elements contained in each model.

Guidance Standards

ISO 9000: *Quality Management and Quality Assurance Standards: Guidelines for Selection and Use*

ISO 9000 explains fundamental quality concepts. It defines key terms and provides guidance on selecting and using, as well as tailoring, ISO 9001, ISO 9002, and ISO 9003 for external quality assurance purposes.

Table 1. **Comparison of the Quality System Elements**

ISO 9000 Series Clause Comparison Table	ISO 9000 Number 1994		
Title of ISO Clause	ISO 9001	ISO 9002	ISO 9003
Management Responsibility	4.1	4.1	4.1
Quality System	4.2	4.2	4.2
Contract Review	4.3	4.3	4.3
Design Control	4.4		
Document and Data Control	4.5	4.5	4.5
Purchasing	4.6	4.6	
Customer Supplied Product	4.7	4.7	4.7
Product Identification & Traceability	4.8	4.8	4.8
Process Control	4.9	4.9	
Inspection & Testing	4.10	4.10	4.10
Control of Inspection, Measuring, and Test Equipment	4.11	4.11	4.11
Inspection and Test Status	4.12	4.12	4.12
Control of Nonconforming Product	4.13	4.13	4.13
Corrective and Preventive Action	4.14	4.14	4.14
Handling, Storage, Packaging, Preservation, and Delivery	4.15	4.15	4.15
Control of Quality Records	4.16	4.16	4.16
Internal Quality Audits	4.17	4.17	4.17
Training	4.18	4.18	4.18
Servicing	4.19	4.19	
Statistical Techniques	4.20	4.20	4.20

■ ISO 9000 offers guidance in selecting the appropriate model for quality assurance. It also provides guidance on using ISO 9004 for internal quality management purposes. It is the *road map* for use of the entire series.

The choice of which model to select depends on the functional or organizational capability required of a supplier (defined by the ISO standards as the company seeking ISO registration). After a company consults ISO 9000, it should consult ISO 9004 to develop and implement a quality system and to determine the extent to which each quality system element is applicable. ISO

9004 can help every company develop a thorough internal quality assurance system.

ISO 9004: *Quality Management and Quality System Elements: Guidelines*

ISO 9004 provides guidance to all organizations for internal quality management purposes, without regard to external contractual requirements of quality assurance. ISO 9004 addresses the primary quality system elements contained in ISO 9001, ISO 9002, and ISO 9003 in greater detail and helps an organization to determine the extent to which each quality system is applicable.

ISO 9004 covers the following general topics:

- Management Responsibility (4.0)
- Quality System Elements (5.0)
- Financial Considerations of Quality Systems (6.0)
- Quality in Marketing (7.0)
- Quality in Specification and Design (8.0)
- Quality in Purchasing (9.0)
- Quality in Processes (10.0)
- Control of Processes (11.0)
- Product Verification (12.0)
- Control of Inspection, Measuring, and Test Equipment (13.0)
- Control of Nonconforming Product (14.0)
- Corrective Action (15.0)
- Post-Production Activities (16.0)
- Quality Records (17.0)
- Personnel (18.0)
- Product Safety (19.0)
- Use of Statistical Methods (20.0)

The ISO Implementation Process

The key to approaching ISO 9000 registration is to understand that the company's quality system must demonstrate the following:

Intent: Evidence that the company intends to implement the provisions of the ISO standard and that executive management has established the commitment necessary to achieve this task.

Implementation: An awareness throughout the organization that the elements and requirements of the ISO standard are understood and being adequately followed.

Effectiveness: Proof—via "readily available" records, documents, and other objective evidence—that the intent of the ISO standard has been fully implemented and is an essential part of management review, quality records, day-to-day operations, etc.

The key word for achieving compliance is *documentation*. ISO registration requires that you document all quality system processes as they relate to each of the clauses of the ISO standard. What the ISO audit team looks for is a consistent response that satisfies the requirements. The best approach for

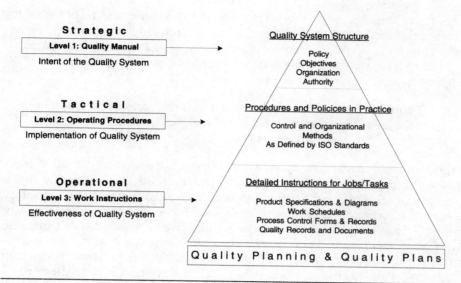

Figure 4. *Documentation levels described.*

a company is to develop and implement documentation based strictly on the way the company operates:

- Document processes as they are truly performed.
- Compare what is done to the requirements established by the selected ISO standard.
- Establish documentation, records, procedures, etc. where the quality system has a void.
- Implement the documentation and . . . *consistently do what was documented.*

There are three basic levels of documentation required:

- The first level is a quality manual that highlights the organization's quality policy.
- The second level is a set of procedures, typically one for each department or business function, that define how the processes are handled within these areas.
- The third level is a set of work instructions, operational or process procedures (where appropriate) that provide task-level instruction for personnel.

In descriptive form, the levels of documentation are as shown in Figure 4.

Each level of documentation must interlock with every other level and provide evidence of consistency of the process performed. If the policy manual states that the manager of the manufacturing department is responsible for ensuring the quality of the widgets, the manufacturing department's procedures must back up this statement and show how that quality is attained.

Studies have indicated that companies choose to go through the ISO 9000 registration process for three primary reasons:

- **To maintain current market position or to gain access to additional markets, particularly on a global basis, where ISO 9000 has become the accepted quality standard.**

In the European market, there are two classes of products to consider: *regulated* and *unregulated*. With unregulated products, such as paper and furniture, mutual recognition of national standards governs free trade for nonsafety aspects of a product. Regulated products are those for which the European Union (EU) has named a new directive for standardization and set a timetable for its implementation. There are 23 laws establishing the new approach directives, which today cover such areas as machinery, personal protection equipment, telecommunications, and medical devices. Each of these regulated categories has its own requirements.

ISO 9000 promises to offer a single system for meeting product regulations in all the EU countries because it provides a route to gaining approval to use the CE (Communaute Europeene) mark. The CE mark is becoming the passport for selling regulated products in Europe. Product cannot be sold in Europe after the date of a directive's implementation unless it has the CE mark.

- **To meet contractual and/or specified requirements stipulated by a customer that requires ISO 9000 for continuing contracts.**

As the benefits associated with ISO registration continue to become apparent, more organizations are using the ISO standards as a means to verify quality from existing subcontractors and as a selection criteria to compare the expected performance on requests for quotes. Specific clauses within the ISO standards (i.e., 4.6.2—Evaluation of Subcontractors) stipulate that subcontractors must be selected and evaluated on the basis of their ability to meet subcontract requirements. ISO registration is rapidly becoming one of the most noted means of gauging-expected subcontractor performance and provides the supplier with a recognized measure of assurance that the subcontractor meets a defined set of quality requirements.

- **For the competitive value (increased market share, reduced costs, etc.) to be gained from improved quality.**

While market pressure is the main driving force behind U.S. companies becoming registered, many companies implementing the standards begin to identify and address non-value-added internal processes and are able to achieve quality improvements as a result. The effective implementation of the ISO standard requires that an organization review, assess, and define the processes associated with meeting the customer requirements: how marketing, sales, engineering, production, administration, etc., transform the customer's order into a deliverable product or service that meets the contractual requirements.

ISO 9000 Registration Process

To achieve ISO 9000 registration, companies must seek the services of a registrar:

- The registrar is an accredited, independent third party who evaluates the firm's quality system for conformity to ISO 9001, 9002, or 9003.
- Identification of the most appropriate registrar should be based on:

  The registrar's knowledge of your specific industry.

  The accreditation of the registrar (including current status of the accreditation and in what countries the accreditation is recognized).

  Specific recommendations from customers.

- The registrar's evaluation includes a review of the quality policy, documentation system, and records, along with a thorough on-site audit. The registrar, once convinced that a quality system conforms to the selected standard, issues a certificate describing the scope of registration.
- Fundamentally, third-party registration under the ISO 9000 standards means that a company has demonstrated that it has an *appropriate quality system* for the products or services it offers. Moreover, standardized registration means that a single audit can assure customers throughout the world that a supplier's quality system meets a specific set of requirements.
- Registration is usually granted for three years, with periodic on-site surveillance in the interim (typically every 6 months).

  Currently, there are over 50 registrars in the United States. Some have direct ties to EU countries, some are organizations that have formal agreements with EU registrars, and some are approved by the U.S. accreditation agency, the Registrar Accreditation Board (RAB) in Milwaukee.

It is important to remember that the early stages of the design, development, and implementation of the quality management system will require substantial time and attention on the part of executive management (10–15 percent during the first 6 months of system review and implementation). The amount of time invested will be directly proportional to the overall success of the implemented quality management system.

Key points worth noting are

- ISO 9000 should not be viewed as a *"registration"* process, but rather as a model for continuous improvement.
- ISO 9000 is the first standard that establishes an unending, continuous improvement process that incorporates assessments by an unbiased, third party.
- The process of semi-annual and annual assessments will provide the company with the internal objective evidence (through management reviews, internal auditing, corrective action, customer interaction, etc.) and external reviews (registrar) on which to base strategic business and operational plans.
- Registration to the ISO standard will focus increased attention on identifying and implementing needed employee training.
- The basis of the ISO standard is its ability to be tailored to the way a company does business.

What does the customer require?
How is the appropriate information communicated throughout the organization?
Where do the majority of problems occur?
When does a company implement and/or upgrade current processes?

Future of ISO 9000

Criticism against the ISO standards is mainly directed at the issues of bureaucracy, documentation requirements, and the end quality of the product or service delivered:

- The bureaucracy element comes from the requirement that a company must contract for the services of a registrar to perform the formal registration audit to verify that the company's established quality management system is implemented and effective and that the system meets both the intent and the base requirements of the ISO standard. The registrar maintains a high degree of trust in the company's intentions and assumes that the company is in compliance with its own documented processes.

  The registrar is looking at the company's quality management system and is looking for the fundamental elements of a quality strategy that structures the company's operations for continuous improvement. Periodic surveillance audits (typically every 6 months) by the registrar's audit team provides the registrar, the company, and the outside world with confidence that the audited quality system is maintained and that the quality improvement efforts are "preventive" versus "reactive" in scope.

- The issue of documentation is a two-edged sword—the company defines when and where the majority of documentation is needed.

For basic requirements, the ISO Standard defines specific areas where documented procedures must be established and maintained, when records must be maintained, and when quality planning activities must occur. Aside from these specific requirements, the ISO standard and the registrar approach a company's documentation from the aspects of ***Intent—Implementation—Effectiveness.***

If the company (or customer contract) specifically creates, implements, or otherwise establishes the need for documentation, the registrar's audit team merely assesses the documentation and subsequent process for consistency and effectiveness.

If the company establishes documented procedures, the registrar assumes the company follows the procedure on a consistent basis, i.e., if the company states all or every widget is packed in a red box with blue tape, the registrar will verify that this occurs.

In the vast majority of cases, documentation already exists, process reviews occur on a regular basis, personnel understand the steps associated with their specific task, and processes are routinely monitored, but these issues are informal, not controlled, and/or not effectively communicated throughout the organization.

The ISO standards do not require a complicated structure of documentation—only that the documentation established be effectively implemented and appropriately controlled.

- The objective of the ISO standard is to ensure consistency of quality-critical processes. The ISO standards define a product as hardware, software, processed material, or service. In short, the ISO standard does not care what product or service the company provides. ISO 9000 does not contain a clause that requires a company to produce a quality product or service—only that processes be appropriately documented, fully implemented, and that there is objective evidence of process consistency throughout the organization. As in all cases, the customer ultimately defines the quality of the product or service provided.

The ISO standards are more than a set of prescriptive quality clauses; this set of quality system elements was designed to provide a framework of "Best Business Practices" and does not specify how any company should specifically implement the ISO requirements. A quick review of ISO 9004 details that the primary emphasis of the ISO standards, as well as the registrar, and more importantly, the company and its customers, is meeting the customer's requirements (internal and external customers) and providing consistent quality of the product or service. The marketplace and customers define the level of quality needed for competitive purposes. A company's success in the marketplace is achieved when processes, costs, procedures, systems, etc., are in control and production of the product or service is consistent. ISO 9000 cannot assure that the company will be profitable; it's up to management to control the system that in effect will ultimately help to control the cost of production.

Summary

During the past two years, the benefits associated with ISO 9000 have become apparent to such organizations as the Big 3 auto makers, major truck manufacturers, the Department of Defense, NASA, the Federal Aviation Authority, and the Food and Drug Administration. Each of these entities, along with over 70,000 ISO 9000 registered sites, have adopted the ISO standards and are passing the requirements downstream to end users and subcontractors. The Big 3 auto makers' adoption of QS 9000 and T/E 9000 (ISO 9000 in its entirety plus additional automotive-specific requirements) will impact over 60,000 first-tier and tooling/equipment suppliers to Ford, General Motors, and Chrysler. The Department of Defenses' phased program to eliminate the MIL-Q-9858 standard by mid-year 1996 begins the shift of responsibility for quality system verification and assessment from military inspection to the company's responsibility and will affect several thousand additional suppliers to the defense industry.

The process of ISO registration takes time, allocation of resources (dollars and personnel), a commitment from executive management, and a method whereby all affected employees have both an awareness of the company's quality system and an understanding of how they contribute to the prevention of quality problems. Businesses that have achieved registration report that the most important external benefits include higher perceived quality, improved customer satisfaction, and a competitive edge, all leading to improved quality, reduced costs, and a foundation for increased market share.

How to Select an ISO 9000 Registrar

C.W. Russ Russo

This is a complete review of how to go about choosing an ISO 9000 registrar. The author takes you through all the steps and tells you what questions to ask so you will find the registrar your company can work with best.

When a company decides to seek ISO 9000 registration, it faces many interesting decisions and challenges. One primary question a company must answer is: "Who is the right registrar for us?" During the past two years I have developed a list of questions that companies might use to interview and select a registrar. I have asked trainees and management representatives what questions they thought were important or would be helpful to them when interviewing potential registrars. I have also asked registered companies about their experiences with registrars and what questions they wished they had asked. And recently, the Kansas City ISO 9000 Support Group completed a series of presentations by several different registrars to help our membership (businesses who are currently preparing for ISO 9000 registration) learn about different registrars and how they conduct audits.

During the past two years I have learned several things. The most important revelation was that no two registrars do things exactly alike. All registrars do perceive that they provide a service to their customers: the companies they register. And they all understand that they must live within the diversely interpreted requirements of their individual accreditation bodies. However, beyond those two similarities, there are significant differences in approach and personality among registrars. The net result of this past two years' effort is the following compilation of ideas about this important topic.

Seeking Registration

A company that decides to seek ISO 9000 registration should organize a project or implementation plan. The project plan should include initial research into potential registrars, interviews with several potential candidates and, finally, a contract with a registrar. Usually, an implementation plan will take about 18 months or more, and the research work to select a registrar should

---

begin early in the process. Then the list of potential registrars should be narrowed, and a final selection made four to six months before the proposed date to achieve registration.

A company seeking ISO 9000 registration establishes a long-term relationship with its registrar. This relationship starts when the company reveals detailed background information (usually in the form of an application) to the registrar. More information comes through a preaudit, then the registration audit, and follow-up or surveillance audits every six months.

The initial contract arrangement is usually for three years and can be renewed for additional three-year periods. Establishing a successful long-term relationship with a registrar requires a systematic and careful approach. Your management representative should develop a list of interview questions to ask each of several potential candidates. The list should be an evolving document, and as the company prepares for the registration audit and new questions and concerns arise, the list should be updated.

The registrar will ask company management to provide detailed background information about the company before a contract is signed. Usually this information relates to company size, products made, number of employees, site locations and other factual information. Underlying all these questions are several concerns. First, the registrar wants your company to succeed in registering to the ISO 9000 standard. However, registrars must also always satisfy the requirements of their accreditation agencies so they can protect their accreditation and the status of the other companies they have registered.

Therefore, your company's relationship with the registrar is a two-way street. The registrar wants to make sure you are happy with them and that they can work for you. Your company also needs to work hard to make sure the selected registrar is a good fit and that you can work with them. The following suggested questions can help your management representative and ISO 9000 project implementation team begin to gather information about potential registrars. This list is not intended to be all-inclusive; rather, it is an idea starter and a basis for your company to begin to develop your own list of questions and concerns.

Money

One of the most important questions is the matter of fees. An ISO 9000 implementation project requires a significant resource commitment, and the registrar's fees represent a noticeable portion of those costs. Registrars are sensitive to this issue and will work with you to make sure you clearly understand their fee schedule and anticipated future expenses. Your company should not be shy about asking for a detailed explanation of these costs. Registrars want you to understand all of the costs, and they prefer to have these matters settled early in the relationship so they can get on with the business of providing their service to you. These questions can help your company predict and budget for registrar-related costs:

- What are your annual fees and total anticipated costs?

- What is included in the original fee?
- Is a pre-assessment included in your price?
- What are your billing arrangements and timetable for payments due?
- Can you predict costs for expenses, such as transportation, lodging and per-diem for assessors?
- Will we see the bills for expenses, or is there a flat-rate schedule?
- If we do not achieve registration on the first attempt, what expenses will we incur for a follow-up audit (in addition to assessors' travel expenses)?
- What are the costs if we need to postpone the initial audit?
- What are the ongoing costs for surveillance audits?
- What are the renewal costs for subsequent three-year periods?

The Registrar's Experience

The second category of questions to ask registrars relates to their experience and reputation. These four questions will give your company an idea of the registrar's experience level and what kind of companies they register.

- How long have you been a registrar?
- Who accredited you?
- How long have you been accredited?
- What is the scope of your accreditation?

Many registrars started in the United States by establishing relationships with European registrars and using their European counterparts' experience as a foundation to build their client base. Your company should not be put off by a registrar that does not have a long history of activity in the United States. ISO 9000 is a relatively new process here, and most U.S. registrars have not been in practice for more than a few years. In response to the question about scope, the accreditation agency will specify the industries and types of businesses for which the registrar is authorized to provide registration services. Usually the industries are identified by their SIC codes.

- Can you provide us with a list of companies that you have registered?

This is public information. The CEEM Guide to Registered Companies, as well as the American Society for Quality Control, has extensive registrar information, including the SIC codes of companies that have been registered and the number of audits a registrar has performed. This information is routinely updated and will give you a good sense of the kind of companies the registrar has worked with. Also, the registrar might be willing to provide you with contact names of other clients.

- Do you have memoranda of understanding, or do you have multiple accreditations?

- If you have memoranda of understanding or multiple accreditations, with whom are they?
- What are the additional costs if memoranda of understanding are necessary?

Memoranda of understanding are agreements between two registrars that they will accept the result of each others' audits and will recognize companies that they each register. Memoranda of understanding are a particularly important issue for companies doing business in several countries. Some registrars take pride in not having memoranda of understanding; they prefer to do all of their own registration work by having multiple accreditations through various national accreditation bodies. However, they allow U.S. registrations to be recognized in foreign countries.

- What is your success rate for registering companies on the first registration audit? On the second attempt? What is the average number of attempts to achieve registration?

Registrars' goal is to see companies succeed in becoming registered. Therefore, they try to make sure the company is prepared before they conduct an ISO 9000 registration audit. If the average number of audit visits is one or two, it is a good indication the registrar has done an effective job of determining whether their companies are prepared for the audit.

The Auditors' Experience

An issue related to the registrar's experience is the background and reputation of assessors who will actually perform the ISO 9000 audit.

- What is the assessors' audit experience, how long have they been involved with ISO 9000, and how many years have they been in the quality business?
- What is the work knowledge and experience of these individuals in my company's industry?

Registrars seek the most qualified assessor team members possible. One team member must be certified as a lead assessor, and most or all other team members should have an assessor certification. It is also appropriate to raise the question of the assessors' actual experience in your industry. This question has two parts:

- What quality assurance experience do the assessors have in our industry?
- Second, and as important, what experience do the assessors actually have working in our industry?

Some companies prefer to have assessors with actual production experience in their industry in addition to quality assurance experience. So registrars find themselves seeking a balance between industry experience and quality assurance auditing experience. Each assessor will be able to provide a list of

SIC codes for industries in which he or she has experience (both quality assurance and actual production work).

- How many new or less-experienced individuals will be on the team in a learning status?

One or two observers or new auditors may be on the team. Registrars need to build their cadre of assessors, and they accomplish this by closely monitoring new auditors in actual audit situations. However, that does not mean that your company must support the costs of this endeavor. Usually registrars will bear costs for these individuals and will not charge the company for their time or expenses.

- Are your assessors employees, or do you use contract assessors?
- If you use contract assessors, have you used them before? How do you know their experience level?

There are valid arguments for both sides of this question of which is better, having assessors who are the registrar's full-time employees or are contractors. Some registrars promote the fact they use only their own employees as assessors, with the advantage that they can train their auditors to conduct audits one way. Registrars who use their own employees, however, may not be able to staff the team with assessors who have qualifications in your particular industry. Using contract assessors allows the registrar to find individuals experienced in your industry, with your product and with your company size.

Registrars have more employee-related expenses when they maintain a cadre of employee assessors. Generally, however, the customer does not see a difference in cost because registrars charge about the same for either an employee or a contractor assessor.

Contract assessors also have an opportunity to work for more than one registrar and may bring a broader perspective to the audit activity. Most important, the contract assessor understands the nature of his or her relationship with the registrar and the registrar's relationship with the company as a supplier of a service to a customer. Contract assessors must work to maintain their reputations with the registrar if they expect future work.

Experience in Your Industry

The final element of experience and reputation has to do with the registrar's experience in your industry and with your product line, as well as with companies your size.

- Are you familiar with my product?
- How many people on the audit team have experience with my product and processes?

The registrar should attempt to load the team with as many subject-matter experts as possible. The audit team should consist of at least one individual who is a subject-matter expert, has worked in your particular industry or related industry and understands your processes. The ISO 9000 standards are subject to much interpretation, and you will want the auditors' interpretations to be similar to your own. This is more likely to happen if the auditors have experience (either quality assurance or actual production) in your industry and with companies your size.

Several arguments relate to this issue. Some companies are concerned that assessors with industry experience might be limited by their own perceptions of "how it ought to be done," i.e., these auditors will try to compare how your company completes a process with how they used to do it. On the other hand, the company does not want to spend a lot of time teaching auditors about their specific business.

- Have you worked with companies my size?

This is an important question. Many assessors come from quality assurance backgrounds in large to very large companies. Smaller companies may be less formal and structured in how they achieve their goals. For example, some small companies, particularly those with long-term employees, frequently do not require as detailed or as many procedures as do larger companies. Assessors need to be able to adapt their thinking to understand a small company's operation.

- Do you have a local office in my area? Do you have assessors in my region?

You could save some travel expenses if the registrar has an office nearby. However, this issue should be the last on a list of determining factors.

The Registrar's Approach

Like individuals, registrars have their own personality, style and philosophical approach. Because usually you are establishing a relationship of at least three years, your company needs to find a comfortable fit with a registrar. Here are some basic questions that will help your company begin to understand how registrars conduct an ISO 9000 audit and registration process:

- Do you recommend a pre-audit?
- Do you prefer to do the pre-audit yourselves, or may we have an outside consultant do the pre-audit?
- Can the individual(s) who perform the pre-audit also perform the ISO 9000 audit?

Registrars will most frequently recommend a pre-assessment and suggest they perform it because a pre-assessment is an opportunity for the registrar to confirm there are no major gaps between your system and ISO 9000's requirements. Usually the pre-assessment is a systems audit, i.e., an audit to make sure required documentation is in place. In a systems audit, the assessment is limited to "what you say." The actual ISO 9000 registration audit is a compliance audit in which the assessors evaluate that you have implemented your system. A compliance audit provides an opportunity to demonstrate that "you do what you say."

More than anything else, both you and the registrar want to avoid finding a major nonconformance during the registration audit. The pre-assessment allows both you and the registrar to gain a level of confidence in your system. It provides a dry-run with less stress than a full audit. It also presents an excellent opportunity for the registrar to establish personal contact with members of your company.

One drawback, however, is that your registrar cannot offer you consultation services, which means they cannot help you fix problems that might be found in a pre-assessment audit. You may decide to hire an outside consultant to conduct a gap or delta audit (an evaluation of your system against the standard and/or your implementation against your procedures). In contrast to the registrar, the consultant can suggest how to resolve problem areas.

The advantage of having the same individuals who performed the pre-assessment also serve on the registration audit is they come to the audit with basic knowledge about your company and its quality assurance system. Scheduling is often an issue, however, and registrars cannot guarantee you will have the same assessors on both the pre-assessment and the registration audits. Nevertheless, registrars will attempt to work with you and have the same individuals do both audits if schedules permit.

- How do you help your clients decide on which standard to register to?
- If our company has a design function, can we be registered under ISO 9002?

The registrar will follow the guidance contained in ISO 9000-1 when helping you decide which standard is appropriate. In general, companies that have design functions should register to ISO 9001, and those companies that do not should register to ISO 9002. However, ISO 9000-1 is a guideline, not a standard, and some differences of interpretation exist among registrars. Most registrars prefer you register to ISO 9001 if you have a design function.

- Are you able to review a procedure and comment on whether it meets the standard's requirements?

Registrars may be willing to review a procedure for adequacy; however, your management representative should clearly understand that such an evaluation is generally a yes/no call and there should be no consultation or suggestions on how to improve the procedure. If you have a question about adequacy of procedures or their implementation, it may be more expeditious to have a consultant review the procedures and their implementation.

- Do you stop an audit if you discover a major nonconformance?

A major nonconformance indicates a significant gap in your process. Some registrars will stop an audit if they find a major nonconformance. However, most registrars dislike taking this action because it creates enormous dissatisfaction and upheaval. Also, such action adds considerable expense to your company because the team then leaves and must be rescheduled. Your representative needs to discuss this issue with the registrar so you understand the implications and costs involved.

- If a nonconformance is found during an audit, can that part of the audit be delayed for a quick fix?
- Will the audit team accept an "on-the-spot" fix or delete a nonconformance if the fix is in place before the end of the audit?

Generally, the audit team will not accept last-minute fixes, nor will they delete a found nonconformance. Companies need to understand that registrars believe this issue reflects on their credibility. Their thinking is that the nonconformance existed and they found it and, therefore, they must report it. Some registrars will report the nonconformance as found and fixed. Companies should understand that the audit team will find nonconformances and the company will correct them. Nonconformances are part of the process, and the overall outcome does not hinge on a few nonconformances.

- What are your most frequently found nonconformances, and on average, during a registration audit, how many nonconformances do you report?

Most nonconformances are found in the areas of documentation and data control, and record keeping. A typical registration team, on a three-day audit of a medium-sized company, may find nine to 15 nonconformances and about 150 observations. This average was taken from several registrars who responded to this question. There is probably no "average" other than to say that registrars will find some nonconformances. Audit teams rarely, if ever, find no nonconformances. No one is perfect, and audit teams do not want anyone to suspect they are not doing a thorough job. Therefore, the company should be prepared to receive some nonconformances.

- What percentage of companies that you audit receive their registration on the first try? Is there an improved rate of first-time success if you conduct a pre-audit?

The answer to the first part of this question can be from 50 percent to 75 percent. Again, this average was taken from registrars who responded to this question. However, as more resources, such as consultants and publications on the topic, have become available to help companies and as registrars have gained experience in doing audits, the rate of first-time successes seems to be improving. The answer to the second part is that companies generally will experience a better chance of a first-time success if they have a pre-assessment.

- Can a registration certificate be issued if outstanding nonconformances are waiting to be resolved?

The answer depends on the severity and number of nonconformances. Generally, the registrar will ask the company to address all issues and resolve them or, at a minimum, have a workable plan underway to resolve them before issuing a certificate.

- Does the registrar need a controlled copy of the quality manual?
- Do we need to notify the registrar or get permission to make changes in our quality manual?
- What is the process if our company needs to change our quality manual?

Usually the answer to the first two questions is no. Regardless, your management representative and implementation team need to carefully construct the quality manual so that frequent changes become unnecessary. One of the simplest structural solutions is to explain the process in the body of the quality manual and then attach lists and data as appendixes to the manual. For example, a list of company procedures might be given in an appendix rather than be referenced by the number in the main quality manual. Updating an appendix is simpler than updating the entire manual.

The answer to the third question is that each registrar uses its own set of rules and administrative procedures when accepting updated/changed quality manuals. The registrar may elect not to be notified about updates.

- How does the registrar handle a situation in which some function is not located at our facility? For example, if purchasing or engineering is not located at our facility, does the audit team need to go to their physical location?

This is a company-specific issue. Generally the registrar wants to be assured these functions are adequately addressed to meet the standard. Your management representative must ensure that the registrar understands how these functions are organized and where they are located. The representative must also ensure off-site company functions are ready if an audit visit is required.

- Are follow-up audits scheduled or pre-announced?
- Does the registrar specify which of the elements in the ISO 9000 standard they will be looking at during each surveillance visit?

Usually follow-up visits are pre-announced, and the registrar will tell you which elements they will be looking at. Registrars are not playing games; they want your company to know about and be able to schedule these audits. Of course, the assessors will always refer to prior nonconformance reports and observed weaknesses in the systems.

And an auditor will always be at liberty to follow a lead or go beyond the preplanned areas of the audit when evidence suggests that is appropriate. You should routinely expect auditors to look at management review, internal audits and corrective actions during every surveillance audit. Auditors know they can judge the commitment to and effectiveness of a quality assurance system by looking at these three areas.

Preparing for the Audit

The next series of questions will help your company understand the coordination necessary to prepare for an audit. Your management representative and the implementation team must work with the selected registrar to ensure schedules are set for the team visit. Your company wants to schedule the audit to occur as soon as you are ready for it; however, because your company is continuing its implementation process, you don't want the audit before you are ready.

- Once we have a contract, what is the wait-time before we will schedule a registration audit?

Two years ago, long wait-times were common. Now that more registrars have entered the market and gained additional experience, these wait-times have been significantly reduced. Still, registrars will want as much lead time as possible to enable them to have the resources available to conduct your audit.

- Can you describe a typical timetable of events from initial contract to issuance of the registration certificate?
  Most registrars can give you a fairly representative schedule of when these activities and events occur.
- How long should my quality assurance system be operational before you can conduct the audit?

The registrar would prefer not to see "wet ink" on your procedures, but at the same time, they understand you are working on your implementation plan and that some of your procedures will have been updated recently. The most important considerations for the registrar are the status of your management review, internal audit and corrective action procedures. These procedures and systems should be put into operation early in the implementation process so you have time to use them, gain experience with them, and have had time to allow them to support your quality assurance system. Typically, and particularly for these three procedures, a registrar will want to see a minimum of four to six months of records after these systems are in place.

- How much time generally elapses between initial audit and corrective actions and the issuance of the registration certificate?
- What is the average timetable to fix nonconformances?
- Will the registrar accept written verification of corrective actions, or must an assessor revisit to verify the corrective action before a registration certificate is issued?

- Do we have to wait a certain amount of time after fixing the non-conformance before we can reschedule another try?

Since there is little chance your company will escape with zero nonconformance reports, how they are resolved is a primary concern for companies that are under market-driven pressure to achieve registration. Every registrar handles these issues differently, and your management representative should discuss them in detail with the registrar.

- How many days will the assessment take, and how many assessors will be on the team?
- How long after the audit will we be notified of the results?

Once the registrar understands your company and its operation, they should be able to provide a fairly accurate estimate to answer these questions. Your company should understand that the audit team does not make the final registration decision. The team leader will make a recommendation to the registrar, and the registrar's senior board will meet to evaluate the team's report and recommendation. This process will take some time. However, at the end of the registration visit, the team leader should provide the company with copies of all nonconformance reports and will usually tell the company what the recommendation will be.

- Will you send us a copy of the audit report?

Usually the answer is yes; however, some registrars provide only the non-compliance reports. They will often send a letter with an explanation of the status of the process and what you must accomplish to achieve registration.

- At the end of three years, do you do a complete audit, or can you simply do continuing surveillance audits?

Some registrars want to do a complete compliance audit at the end of the first three-year period. Others believe that since they have established an on-going relationship with your company, they understand the effectiveness of your quality assurance system. A positive relationship over the three years, positive surveillance visits and evidence that you maintain your system may lead registrars to forego the complete audit and continue with only surveillance visits or a shortened form of a complete audit. Regardless of the kind of audit conducted at the end of the first three-year period, the company will need to assess its ISO 9000 and future registrar needs. If the experience has been useful and productive, your company may elect to continue with the same registrar and to sign another three-year contract.

- How long after the audit will we receive our certificate and ISO 9000 registration number?

Another way to approach this issue is to ask the registrar to provide a checklist of exactly what must be accomplished in order to receive a certificate. It is useful to have a comprehensive list of goals and expectations and a reasonable timetable for each. Your company should work with your registrar to establish such a timetable and have a clear understanding of the activities and time necessary to accomplish your goals.

Administrative Questions

The first six series of questions were designed to help your company select a registrar. Once the registrar is selected, the contract is signed and the registration audit is scheduled, several administrative details will help the scheduled audit proceed smoothly. Once the audit team arrives at your company, the assessors have a significant amount of work to do in the short time (typically three or four days) available for the audit. They will value a well-organized effort by the company to be ready to participate in the audit. Several dozen items and questions probably should be addressed before the team arrives. Here is a start on the list of questions to ask:

- Who is our contact person at the registrar's office to take care of the routine administrative functions for setting up the audit visits?
- What level of accommodations and hotels do you require for your assessors?
- Should meals be brought in, or do you prefer to go away from the company for them?
- Who arranges transportation, and how many rental cars will be necessary?
- What kind of facilities and set-up do you require at the company site during the visit? This question addresses office space, maps, phones, access to copy machines, etc.
- How many auditors will be at the initial audit?
- How many auditors will be at surveillance audits?

Planning Ahead

Two major points can be gleaned from the questions and issues discussed in this article. The first point is that the process will vary by registrar and by company. The second point is that, in addition to all of the tasks your management representative must accomplish, helping the company select the right registrar will take significant organization and effort.

An ISO 9000 implementation project is a complex and resource-intensive undertaking. An important part of the project is selecting a registrar who can work successfully with your company. Registrars have personalities, like individuals, and have their own approach to interpreting the standards and establishing and maintaining relationships with their clients. Just as in the ISO 9000 registration process, there is no "right way" to do it, and there is no requirement for consistency across registrars. Registrars operate under the requirements of their accreditation bodies and ISO 10011 series. These series, like the ISO 9000 series, remain open to interpretations.

Since the relationship with a registrar usually lasts for three or more years, companies must implement a careful and systematic plan for finding and selecting a registrar with whom they can feel comfortable and who will be able to work well with them. The seven categories of questions and issues listed above provides a start to tailoring a list of questions that your management representative can use to interview prospective registrars. Such a systematic approach will improve the probability that your company will select the right registrar.

C.W. Russ Russo is managing partner of The Trainers Workshop, a consulting firm in Lawrence, Kansas, that provides consulting, training and support in quality management, continuous improvement and ISO 9000.

Quotes on Quality

The purpose of these quotes is to provide inspirational insight into what total quality management is all about, to get you thinking about this approach in new ways, and to offer material useful in speeches and presentations. The quotes below are organized loosely by topic. Several of the quotes might have fit in several categories. We tried to put them in the most logical one. But in looking for thoughts on a particular topic, we suggest you still scan the entire section.

The quotes come from eclectic sources, including philosophers, poets, and scientists as well as business writers and managers. There is a reason for this. The ideas of quality management are not unique to this field. They naturally emerge in a variety of forms and contexts whenever people contemplate excellence and high performance in any human endeavor. We may come to see that quality management is ultimately about bringing out the best in all of us to facilitate our mutual success and prosperity. Wise people have appreciated such notions from time immemorial. Consider that as you read these quotes.

The categories we have chosen include the following: Quality Defined, Quality Management, Quality Leadership, Culture of Quality, Customers, Training, Teams and Teamwork, Process Management, Measurement, Human Resources, Continuous Improvement, and "The Wrong Stuff." Some categories include many more quotes than others. It just seems people have said more quotable statements about leadership, for example, than about measurements.

Finally, if there are quotes you especially like, we would be pleased to have you send them to us. We will use them in future editions and credit you with their submission.

Quality Defined

Includes thoughts on what quality means to different people.

The good of man is the active exercise of his soul's faculties. This exercise must occupy a complete lifetime. One swallow does not make a spring, nor does one fine day. Excellence is a habit, not an event.

—Aristotle

Value equals benefits received for burdens endured.

—Leonard L. Berry

If you're going to put your name on all your products, you should never produce a bad product. If you make a mistake, you'll hurt your whole company.

—Bruno Bich, Bic Pen Company

Good wares make good markets.

—Nicholas Breton, English Poet, 1555–1625

I am easily satisfied with the best.

—Winston Churchill

The ultimate victory in competition is derived from the inner satisfaction of knowing that you have done your best and that you have gotten the most out of what you had to give.

—Howard Cosell

Good, better, best
Never let it rest
Until the good becomes the better
And the better becomes the best.

—Elementary school rhyme

Quality is never an accident; it is always the result of high intention, sincere effort, intelligent direction, and skillful execution; it presents the wise choice of many alternatives.

—Willa A. Foster

Good is not good where better is expected.

—Thomas Fuller

If a man is called a streetsweeper, he should sweep the streets even as Michelangelo painted, or Beethoven composed music, or Shakespeare wrote poetry. He should sweep streets so well that all the hosts of heaven and earth will pause to say, here lived a streetsweeper who did his job well.

—Martin Luther King, Jr.

It's a funny thing about life: If you refuse to accept anything but the very best you will very often get it.

—W. Somerset Maugham

I think "quality control" is an oxymoron. True quality needs space to breathe. If quality is built in, then where's the need for control? Why on earth would you want to control quality? It should be allowed to run rampant.

—Hal F. Rosenbluth

What is essential is invisible to the eye.

—Antoine de Saint-Exupéry

Quality Leadership

Includes thoughts on individual leadership behaviors that bring about the success of all.

Desire is the key to motivation, but it's the determination and commitment of an unrelenting pursuit of your goal—a commitment to excellence—that will enable you to attain the success you seek.

—Mario Andretti

A wise man sometimes changes his mind, but a fool never.
—Arabic Proverb

A leader must have the courage to act against an expert's advice.
—James Callaghan

I should rather men should ask why my statue is not set up than why it is.
—Cato the Elder (quoted by Plutarch)

If you lead the people with correctness, who will dare not to be correct?
—Confucius

It ain't braggin' if you can do it.
—Dizzy Dean

You do not lead by hitting people over the head—that's assault not leadership.
—Dwight D. Eisenhower

Our chief want in life is somebody who will make us do what we can.
—Ralph Waldo Emerson

It was high counsel that I once heard given to a young person, "Always do what you are afraid to do."
—Ralph Waldo Emerson

Would you persuade, speak of interest, not of reason.
—Benjamin Franklin

Leaders have a significant role in creating the state of mind that is society.
—John Gardner

The humility which comes from others having faith in you.
—Dag Hammerskjöld

The greatest thing in this world is not so much where we are, but in what direction we are moving.
—Oliver Wendell Holmes

You cannot manage men into battle. You manage things; you lead people.
—Grace Murray Hopper

Leadership has a harder job to do than just choose sides. It must bring sides together.
—Jesse Jackson

Example is always more efficacious than precept.
—Samuel Johnson

The probability that the bowman's arrow hits the deer does not lie in the arrow or the deer. It lies in the bowman's mind.
—Bart Kosko

If you wish to hit the center of the target, you must aim a little above it; all arrows are subject to the earth's gravity.

—Henry Wadsworth Longfellow

The most important wings on an airplane are on the pilot.

—T. Allen McArtor (FAA Administrator)

I am a big believer in the "mirror test." All that matters is if you can look in the mirror and honestly tell the person you see there, that you've done your best.

—John McKay (football coach)

The means prepare the end, and the end is what the means have made it.

—John Morley

By asking for the impossible, we obtain the best possible.

—Giovanni Battista Niccolini

Being a visionary leader is not about giving speeches and inspiring the troops. How I spend my day is pretty much the same as how any executive spends his day. Being a visionary leader is about solving day-to-day problems with my vision in mind.

—Bill O'Brien

Unless you try to do something beyond what you have already mastered, you will never grow.

—Ronald E. Osborn

The best leaders . . . almost without exception and at every level, are master users of stories and symbols.

—Tom Peters

Enquire often, but judge rarely, and thou wilt not often be mistaken.

—William Penn

Where example keeps pace with authority, power hardly fails to be obey'd.

—William Penn

You take people as far as they will go, not as far as you would like them to go.

—Jeannette Rankin

People ask the difference between a leader and a boss. . . . The leader leads, and the boss drives.

—Theodore Roosevelt

All things are ready, if our minds are so.

—William Shakespeare

Some men see things as they are and say "Why?" I dream things that never were, and say "Why not?"

—George Bernard Shaw

They say you can't do it, but sometimes it doesn't always work.
—Casey Stengel

I know how to listen when clever men are talking. That is the secret of what you call my influence.
—Hermann Sudermann

Managing for Quality

Includes thoughts on the concerns of any manager who wants to facilitate quality and on managerial decision making.

Shelving hard decisions is the least ethical course.
—Adrian Cadbury

Deliberate with caution but act with decision and promptness.
—Charles Caleb Colton

There are only two ways to be quite unprejudiced and impartial. One is to be completely ignorant. The other is to be completely indifferent. Bias and prejudice are attitudes to be kept in hand, not attitudes to be avoided.
—Charles P. Curtis (Attorney and Member, The Harvard Corporation)

It is useless to make a formal decision with which group members informally disagree.
—William G. Dyer

In every affair, consider what precedes and what follows, and then undertake it.
—Epictetus

Indecision is often worse than wrong action.
—Gerald Ford

Nothing chastens a planner more than the knowledge that he will have to carry out the plan.
—General James Gavin

Reengineering never proceeds bottom-up. It is a top-down phenomenon. And without top-down leadership, reengineering failure is a foregone conclusion. However, the failure may not occur right away.
—Michael Hammer

Seize the day and put the least possible trust in tomorrow.
—Horace (Roman Poet)

A good rule in organizational analysis is that no meeting of the minds is really reached until we talk of *specific actions or decisions*. We can talk of who is responsible for budgets, or inventory, or quality, but little is settled. It is only when we get down to the action words—measure, compute, prepare, check, endorse, recommend, approve—that we can make clear who is to do what.
—Joseph M. Juran

To cherish traditions, old buildings, ancient cultures, and graceful life-styles is a worthy thing—but in the world of technology to cling to outmoded methods of manufacture, old product lines, old markets, or old attitudes among management and workers is a prescription for suicide.

—Sir Leuan Maddock

What the Japanese mean by "democracy" is a system that should take the side of, or give consideration to, the weaker or lower; in practice any decision should be made on the basis of a consensus which includes those located lower in the hierarchy.

—Chie Nakane

One of life's most painful moments comes when we must admit that we didn't do our homework, that we are not prepared.

—Merlin Olsen

If you put off everything till you're sure of it, you'll get nothing done.

—Norman Vincent Peale

Always use your chain of command to issue orders, but if you use the chain of command for information, you're dead.

—Admiral Hyman Rickover

Planning is action laid out in advance.

—G.C. Sawyer

A leader is not an administrator who loves to run others, but someone who carries water for his people so they can get on with their jobs.

—Robert Townsend

Knowledge of his own conditions but not the conditions of the enemy has an even chance of winning and losing a battle. He who has neither a thorough knowledge of his own conditions nor of the enemy is sure to lose every battle.

—Sun Tzu

The art of progress is to preserve order amid change and to preserve change amid order.

—Alfred North Whitehead

Seek simplicity and distrust it.

—Alfred North Whitehead

You don't make decisions; you understand situations and act completely in accord with that understanding.

—John Woods

Whom God would sorely vex, he endows with abundant good sense.

—Yiddish Proverb

Culture of Quality

Includes thoughts that suggest the attributes of a quality culture.

It's probably not love that makes the world go around but rather those mutually supportive alliances through which partners recognize their dependance on each other for the achievements of shared and private goals. . . . Treat employees like partners, and they act like partners.

—Fred Allen (Former Chairman, Pitney-Bowes)

Do not seek to follow in the footsteps of the men of old; seek what they sought.

—Matsuo Basho (16th Century Japanese Poet)

Excellence nourishes the soul.

—Leonard L. Berry

For most organizations, restructuring into service delivery teams involves a major cultural change from the accustomed ways of operating.

—Leonard L. Berry

Management creates an empowered state of mind in the organization by treating employees as part-owners of the business and expecting them to act like owners.

—Leonard L. Berry

All actions are wrought by the quality of nature only. The self, deluded by egoism, thinketh: "I am the doer."

—The Bhagavad Gita

The great law of culture is: Let each become all that he was created capable of being.

—Thomas Carlyle

If I understood too clearly what I was doing, where I was going, then I probably wasn't working on anything very interesting.

—Peter Carruthers (Physicist)

The form of a meeting is simply a reflection of the culture.

—Terrence Deal and Allan A. Kennedy

Criticism has few terrors for a man with a great purpose.

—Benjamin Disraeli

In order for me to look good, everybody around me has to look good.

—Doris Drury

Why is that I always get a whole person when what I really want is a pair of hands?

—Henry Ford

You've got to have an atmosphere where people can make mistakes. If we're not making mistakes, we're not going anywhere.

—Gordon Foward (President, Chapparal Steel)

Two roads diverged in a wood, and I—
I took the one less traveled by,
And that has made all the difference.

—Robert Frost, "The Road Not Taken"

God, to me, it seems,
is a verb
not a noun,
proper or improper.

—R. Buckminster Fuller

The ability to learn faster than your competitors may be the only sustainable competitive advantage.

—Arie P. de Geus

Treat others as ends not as means.

—Dag Hammerskjöld

The productivity of a work group seems to depend on how the group members see their own goals in relation to the goals of the organization.

—Paul Hersey and Ken Blanchard

Great minds have purposes, others have wishes. Little minds are tamed and subdued by misfortune; but great minds rise above them.

—Washington Irving

Great innovations should not be forced on slender majorities.

—Thomas Jefferson

True artists ship.

—Steven Jobs

Civility is not a sign of weakness, and sincereity is always subject to proof.

—John F. Kennedy

You don't have to preach honesty to men with a creative purpose. A genuine craftsman will not adulterate this product. The reason isn't because duty says he shouldn't, but because passion says he couldn't.

—Walter Lippmann

The price of success is hard work, dedication to the job at hand, and the determination that whether we win or lose, we have applied the best of ourselves to the task at hand.

—Vince Lombardi

There is no security on this earth; there is only opportunity.

—Douglas MacArthur

Our goal should be minimum standardization of human behavior.

—Douglas McGregor

The gods cannot help one who loses opportunities.

—Mencius

Strategies grow initially like weeds in a garden, they are not cultivated like tomatoes in a hothouse.

—Henry Mintzberg

Creativity, by definition, rearranges established categories. Planning, by its very nature, preserves them.

—Henry Mintzberg

One of the rules of caution is not to be too cautious.

—Bahya ib Paquda

Excellent firms don't believe in excellence—only in constant improvement and constant change.

—Tom Peters

Most hierarchies were established by men who now monopolize the upper levels, thus depriving women of their rightful share of opportunities for incompetence.

—Laurence J. Peter

Do not wish to be anything but what you are, and try to be that perfectly.

—St. Francis de Sales

Linus: In life you win some and you lose some.
Charlie Brown: That would be nice.

—Charles Schulz

Do as adversaries in law, strive mightily,
But eat and drink as friends.

—William Shakespeare

Men are wise not in proportion to their experience, but to their capacity for experience.

—George Bernard Shaw

It is very difficult to get someone to believe something when his salary depends on his not believing it.

—Upton Sinclair

There's no evidence that you can keep an organization creative, although I think it is possible with a lot of time and energy.

—Walter Ulmer

New ideas . . . are not born in a conforming environment.

—Roger von Oech

Customers
Includes thoughts on the idea of serving customers.

The first time former customer research is done, executives frequently are surprised by the sizeable percentage of customers who defect for service-related reasons.

—Leonard L. Berry

Reengineering posits a radical new principle: that the design of work must be based not on hierarchical management and the specialization of labor but on end-to-end processes and the creation of value for the customer.

—Michael Hammer

Customers' needs do not remain static. There is no such thing as a permanent list of customers' needs.

—Joseph M. Juran

The purpose of a business is to create and keep customers.

—Theodore Levitt

Treat the customer as an appreciating asset.

—Tom Peters

Remember, some customers will want to be chauffeured, others will want the wheel themselves. Some will speed, others will take it slow. One way or another, all will be in the driver's seat. It's just a question of which companies they will pay for the ride.

—Faye Rice

No great marketing decisions have been made on quantitative data.

—John Sculley

Never underestimate the power of apology. The importance of apologizing for unmet expectations cannot be overstated.

—Ron Zemke

Training
Includes thoughts on the value of training.

When an archer misses the mark, he turns and looks for the fault within himself. Failure to hit the bull's-eye is never the fault of the target. To improve your aim—improve yourself.

—Gilbert Arland

The truth can never be told so as to be understood and not be believ'd.

—William Blake

We are forced to rely on our people, which is why we put so much emphasis on training them.

—Henry Block

When asked what learning was most necessary, he said, "Not to unlearn what you have learned."

—Diogenes

The significant problems we face cannot be solved at the same level of thinking we were at when we created them.

—Albert Einstein

Experience teaches slowly, and at the cost of mistakes.

—J.A. Froude

You must learn from the mistakes of others. You can't possibly live long enough to make them all yourself.

—Sam Levenson

Never chide with anger, but instruction.

—William Penn

First study the science, and then practice the art which is born of that science.

—Leonardo da Vinci

Believe one who has tried it.

—Virgil

Experience is the name everyone gives to his mistakes.

—Oscar Wilde

It's what you learn after you know it all that counts.

—John Wooden

Things are hard before we know how to do them; afterwards, they are easy.

—John Woods

Teams and Teamwork

Includes thoughts on working together to achieve common goals.

Nothing creates more self-respect among employees than being included in the process of making decisions.

—Judith Bardwick

Participative management is, simply stated, involving the right people at the right time in the decision process.

—Wayne Barlow

Competition, which is the instinct of selfishness, is another word for dissipation of energy, while combination is the secret of efficient production.

—Edward Bellamy

The ratio of We's to I's is the best indicator or the development of a team.

—Lewis D. Eigen

A competitive culture endures by tearing people down.

—Jules Henry

For people to treat each other as teammates, they have to believe it is in their best interests to cooperate; they must be more concerned with how the system as a whole operates than with optimizing their own little piece.

—Brian L. Joiner

Contrary to what you think, your company will be a lot more productive if you refuse to tolerate competition among your employees.

—Alfie Kohn

When a team outgrows individual performance and learns team confidence, excellence becomes a reality.

—Joe Paterno

"Great people" don't equal "great teams."

—Tom Peters

Competition is just a particular form of cooperation.

—John Woods

Process Management/Reengineering

Includes a variety of ideas on the idea of processes, their management, and some thoughts on reengineering.

The unfinished is nothing.

—Henri Frédérick Amiel

The value of an idea lies in using it.

—Thomas Edison

No great thing is created suddenly.

—Epictetus

It is not enough to take steps which may some day lead to a goal; each step must be itself a goal and a step likewise.

—Goethe

Detect and fix any problem in a production process at the lowest stage possible.

—Andrew S. Grove

Reengineering: The fundamental rethinking and radical redesign of business processes to bring about dramatic improvement in performance.

—Michael Hammer

Reengineering eliminates work, not jobs or people.

—Michael Hammer

It is profitable wisdom to know when we have done enough: Much time and pains are spared in not flattering ourselves against probabilities.

—William Penn

Almost all quality improvement comes via simplification of design, manufacturing, layout, processes, and procedures.

—Tom Peters

All materials handling is waste.

—Shigeo Shingoiu

The difference between failure and success is doing a thing nearly right and doing a thing exactly right.

—Edward Simmons

Measurement

Includes ideas on making measurements, collecting data, and understanding and misunderstanding them.

It seems to be a rule of wisdom never to rely on memory alone . . .

—Ralph Waldo Emerson

The professional's grasp of the numbers is a measure of the control he has over the events that the numbers represent.

—Harold Geneen

Facts do not cease to exist because they are ignored.

—Aldous Huxley

Measures are an innovation that changed a world of innocent and noble simplicity into one forever filled with dishonesty.

—Flavius Josephus

You get what you measure. Measure the wrong thing and you get the wrong behaviors.

—John H. Lingle

When dealing with numerical data, approximately right is better than precisely wrong.

—Carl G. Thor

A fact may blossom into a truth.

—Henry David Thoreau

Few things are harder to put up with than the annoyance of a good example.

—Mark Twain

Continuous Improvement

Includes several thoughts on change and improvement.

On corporate change: Sacred cows make great burgers.

—Anonymous

Every organization has to prepare for the abandonment of everything it does.

—Peter F. Drucker

The future never just happened. It was created.

—Will and Ariel Durant

Yesterday's miracle is today's intolerable condition.

—Lewis D. Eigen

In this world the passage of time brings increasing order. Order is the law of nature. If time is an arrow, that arrow points to order. The future is pattern, organization, union, intensification; the past randomness, confusion, disintegration, dissipation.

—Albert Einstein

Businessmen go down with their businesses because they like the old way so well they cannot bring themselves to change . . . Seldom does the cobbler take up with a new fangled way of soling shoes and seldom does the artisan willingly take up with new methods in his trade.

—Henry Ford

At the end of every day of every year, two things remain unshakable, our constancy of purpose and our continuous discontent with the immediate present.

—Robert C. Goizueta

If we are to perceive all the implications of the new, we must risk, at least temporarily, ambiguity and disorder.

—J.J. Gordon

Whoever is winning at the moment will always seem invincible.

—George Orwell

Winners in business must learn to relish change with the same enthusiasm and energy that we have resisted it in the past.

—Tom Peters

One should recognize and manage innovation as it really is—a tumultuous, somewhat random, interactive learning process linking a worldwide network of knowledge sources to the subtle unpredictability of customers' end uses.

—James Brian Quinn

To climb steep hills
Requires slow pace at first.

—William Shakespeare

I accost an American sailor, and inquire why the ships of his country are built so as to last but for a short time; he answers without hesitation that the art of navigation is every day making such rapid progress that the finest vessel would become almost useless if it lasted beyond a few years.

—Alexis de Tocqeville

He only is exempt from failures who makes no efforts.

—Richard Whatley

If you always expect the unexpected, you will never be disappointed.

—John Woods

Communication

Thoughts on the importance of communication and on its nature.

Managers who are skilled communicators may also be good at covering up real problems.

—Chris Argyris

You must call each thing by its proper name or that which must get done will not.

—A. Harvey Block

An individual without information cannot take responsibility; an individual who is given information cannot help but take responsibility.

—Jan Carlzon

Let thy speech be better than silence, or be silent.

—Dionysius the Elder

Knowledge is power. In post-capitalism, power comes from transmitting information to make it productive, not hiding it.

—Peter F. Drucker

How well we communicate is determined not by how well we say things but by how well we are understood.

—Andrew S. Grove

A social collectivity is patterned communicative behavior; communicative behavior does not occur *within* a network of relationships but is that network.

—Leonard C. Hawes

The right to be heard does not automatically include the right to be taken seriously. To be taken seriously depends entirely upon what is being said.

—Hubert Humphrey

From listening comes wisdom; from speaking comes repentance.

—Italian proverb

True words are not fine. Fine words are not true.

—Lao Tzu

Whenever one has anything unpleasant to say, one should always be quite candid.

—Oscar Wilde

Vision

Includes quotes on what vision means and what it is.

Thinking is not simply the description—by perception or recall—of something which is there. It is the use of information . . . to get somewhere else.

—F.C. Bartlett

It is the very essence of intelligence to coordinate means with a view to a remote end, and to undertake what it does not feel absolutely sure of carrying out.

—Henri Bergson

The empires of the future are the empires of the mind.

—Winston Churchill

Objectives are not fate; they are direction. They are not commands; they are commitments. They do not determine the future; they are a means to mobilize resources and energies of the business for the making of the future.

—Peter F. Drucker

What makes life weary is the want of a motive.

—George Eliot (Mary Ann Evans)

I skate to where I think the puck will be.

—Wayne Gretzky

I find the great thing in this world is, not where we stand, as in the direction we are moving.

—Oliver Wendell Holmes

The obscure we see eventually; the completely apparent takes longer.

—Edward R. Murrow

Learning Organizations

Includes comments on the nature of learning and its place in managing and in life.

You don't learn anything the second time you're kicked by a mule.

—Anonymous

True wisdom is plenty of experience, observation, and reflection. False wisdom is plenty of ignorance, arrogance, and impudence.

—Josh Billings (Henry Wheeler Shaw)

Often a liberal antidote of experience supplies a sovereign cure for a paralyzing abstraction built upon a theory.

—Benjamin Nathan Cardozo

Information's pretty thin stuff unless mixed with experience.

—Clarence Day

Sensible people find nothing useless.

—Jean de La Fontaine

Desire to know why and how, curiosity, which is a lust of the mind, that by a perseverance of delight is the continued and indefatigable generation of knowledge, exceedeth the short vehemence of any carnal pleasure.

—Thomas Hobbes

Experience is not what happens to you; it's what you do with what happens to you.

—Aldous Huxley

The great tragedy of science—the slaying of a beautiful hypothesis by an ugly fact.

—Thomas H. Huxley

It is the customary fate of new truths to begin as heresies and to end as superstitions.

—Thomas H. Huxley

The uncreative mind can spot wrong answers, but it takes a creative mind to spot wrong questions.

—Anthony Jay

Experience is a hard teacher because she gives the test first, the lesson afterwards.

—Vernon Law (baseball pitcher)

No man's knowledge here can go beyond his experience.

—John Locke

Learning and visionary approaches appear to be superior to planning as means for creating strategy.

—Henry Mintzberg

. . . by chance you will say, but chance only favors the mind which is prepared.

—Louis Pasteur

If people don't have their own vision, all they can do is "sign up" for someone else's. This result is compliance, never commitment.

—Peter M. Senge

It can be no dishonor to learn from others when they speak good sense.

—Sophocles

A man should never be ashamed to own he has been in the wrong, which is but saying, in other words, that he is wiser today than he was yesterday.

—Jonathan Swift

And others' follies teach us not,
Nor much their wisdom teaches.
And most, of sterling, is what
Our own experience preaches.

—Alfred, Lord Tennyson

Does he have 17 years of experience or one year of experience 17 times.

—Paul R. Weisenfeld

We are living in the first period of human history for which the assumption that the time-span of major cultural change is greater than the life-span of an individual is false. Today this time-span is considerably shorter than that of human life, and accordingly our training must prepare individuals to face a novelty of conditions.

—Alfred North Whitehead

The Wrong Stuff

Includes a variety of thoughts that suggest what happens when people do a poor job of practicing quality management and what the wrong stuff includes.

Torture the data long enough, and they will confess to anything.

—Anonymous

Ineffective leaders often act on the advice and counsel of the last person they talked to.

—Warren Bennis

The first job of a leader is define the vision for the organization—but without longevity of leadership, you can have the "vision of the month club."

—Warren G. Bennis

The first corruption in a society that is still alive is that the end justifies the means.

—Georges Bernanos

No passion so effectually robs the mind of all its power of acting and reasoning as fear.

—Edmund Burke

The maxim, "Nothing prevails but perfection" may be spelled, PARALYSIS.

—Winston Churchill

Many of the obstacles for change which have been attributed to human nature are in fact due to the inertia of institutions and to the voluntary desire of powerful classes to maintain the existing status.

—John Dewey

Carelessness is worse than theft.

—Gaelic proverb

Many companies expect that after this round of downsizing is over, they will be able to resume their regular management practices. It was these management practices, however, that created the need for downsizing.

—Ronald L. Heilmann

If you do not expect the unexpected, you will not find it.

—Heraclitus

Irrationally held truths may be more harmful that reasoned errors.

—Thomas H. Huxley

Dogmatism is puppyism come to its full growth.

—Douglas Jerrold

Fanaticism: Redoubling your efforts after your objective has been forgotten.

—Joseph M. Juran

Goal setting has traditionally been based on past performance. This practice has tended to perpetuate the sins of the past.

—Joseph M. Juran

He uses statistics as a drunken man uses lampposts—for support rather than illumination.

—Andrew Lang

All men are liable to error; and most men are, in many points, by passion or interest, under temptation to it.

—John Locke

A boss's mere expression of an opinion can be interpreted as a decision—even a direct order—by a staff member caught in the clutches of risk avoidance.

—Alec Mackenzie

Dreadful things are just as apt to happen when stupid people control a situation as when definitely ill-natured people are in charge.

—Don Marquis

The greatest disservice that Harvard Business School has ever played on corporate America is management by objectives.

—James McManus

He who knows only his own case, knows little of that.

—John Stuart Mill

An obsession with control generally seems to reflect a fear of uncertainty.

—Henry Mintzberg

The prime occupational hazard of a manager is superficiality.

—Henry Mintzberg

Apparently our society, not unlike the Greeks with their Delphic oracles, takes great comfort in believing that very talented 'seers' removed from the hurly-burly world of reality, can foretell coming events.

—Leonard Sayles

The hardest knife ill-used doth lose its edge.

—William Shakespeare

One of the greatest diseases is to be nobody to anybody.

—Mother Teresa

1995 Malcolm Baldrige National Quality Award Winners

In 1995, two companies received Baldrige Awards recognizing their outstanding efforts to improve processes and satisfy customers—they were both in manufacturing:

- **Armstrong World Industries' Building Products Operation**, headquartered in Lancaster, Pennsylvania. The BPD is the world's largest manufacturer of acoustical ceiling systems.
- **Corning Telecommunications Products Division**, located in Corning, New York. This is a division of Corning, Incorporated and manufactures optical fibers used in modern electronic communications.

There were no recipients in the services or small business categories this year.

In 1995, there were 47 applicants for the Baldrige Award, down from 1994's 71 applications. There were 13 site visits, seven in manufacturing, four in services, and two in small business. The smaller number of applications does not reflect on the importance of the award or the esteem in which it is held in American business. It does, however, reflect on the fact that there are now many state awards (see the 1995 yearbook for a review of these) and that many companies are investing effort in becoming ISO 9000 certified.

An especially important consideration in choosing the winning companies is their position as role models for others to emulate. Given the stiff competition and the judges' desire to select those companies that they view as the best role models, these two companies stood out above all other applicants in 1995.

The Real Value of the Baldrige Award

While receiving the Baldrige is a visible and public payoff for companies actively implementing total quality management as a philosophy and mode of operating, this is only the frosting on the cake for those firms involved in the process. The real value of the Baldrige Award is its use as a set of guidelines for transforming a company. Thousands of organizations of all types use the Baldrige criteria to help them proceed down the road to a more realistic, customer-oriented, efficient, and effective management process. Further, the award helps publicize the importance of doing this, and the winners become benchmarks to help others in their quality journey.

Since Baldrige winners become benchmarks, we present the following overviews of 1995's winners to give you a sense of what the Baldrige judges determined were outstanding examples of companies that practice managing for continuous process improvement and total quality. In doing this, we reproduce the announcement from the National Institute of Standards and Technology, citing their reasons for selecting each recipient. We then provide an edited version of the recipient companies' explanations of their quality efforts. Finally, we give you names you can contact to get additional information on these companies and their individual approaches to managing for total quality.

1995 Baldrige Award Winner, Manufacturing Category: Armstrong World Industries, Inc. Building Products Operations

The following is an edited version of the press release from the National Institute of Standards and Technology announcing that Armstrong Building Products Operations had received a Baldrige award for 1995.

Armstrong World Industries' Building Products Operation (BPO) is the world's largest manufacturer and marketer of acoustical ceiling systems for commercial and residential markets. Sales in 1994 totaled $628 million. BPO has 2,500 employees working at its headquarters in Lancaster, Pennsylvania, and in seven manufacturing facilities: Beaver Falls and Marrietta, Pennsylvania; Hilliard, Ohio; Macon, Georgia; Mobile, Alabama; Pensacola, Florida; and St. Helens, Oregon. For 10 years, BPO has maintained a close association with its 45 key suppliers through a Supplier Quality Management Program and with 11 key carriers through its Quality Motor Carrier Program. BPO serves two major markets. The first is commercial, such as health care facilities and offices, which are served through distributors, contractors, and specifiers. The second is do-it-yourself customers, who buy BPO products primarily through wholesalers, lumberyards, and large building supply stores.

The following gives some examples of BPO's quality management efforts:

- In its manufacturing process, BPO uses a significant amount of waste materials from other industries, including scrapped newsprint and mineral wool, a byproduct of steel production. In addition, most of the scrap generated during manufacturing is reused in the process.
- Each year for the past five years, BPO has had more than 300 improvement teams operating at any given time. "Best practices" generated by these teams are shared among plants through conference calls, computer networks, and through "Functional Excellence" conferences.

- Output per manufacturing employee and annual sales per manufacturing employee are critical measures for performance for BPO. As a result of employee involvement, recognition, and gain sharing and eliminating "non-value-added" activity, since 1991 output per manufacturing employee has improved by 39 percent and annual sales per manufacturing employee have risen by 40 percent.
- BPO continuously monitors its carriers' on-time delivery performance, a key customer satisfier, and provides them with monthly "report cards." Since 1992, on-time delivery has improved from 93 percent to 97.3 percent while BPO carriers reduced their arrival time window from four hours to 30 minutes.
- Safety is integrated into BPO's improvement process. In 1994, BPO employees worked over 3 million hours without a lost-time injury, a company and industry record.

The following is excerpted from Armstrong's press releases sent out shortly after receiving the award.

Armstrong's Quality Evolution

Armstrong World Industries was founded in 1860 when Thomas Morton Armstrong bought a cork bottle-stopper business in Pittsburgh, Pennsylvania, for $300. At the time, most manufacturers worked under the premise "let the buyer beware." Armstrong thought differently. He put his name on every bag of corks he sold, along with a written guarantee of quality. His motto: "Let the buyer have faith." If a customer complained about Armstrong corks, those corks were quickly replaced. What Armstrong did was unheard of in those days: correcting a defect after the product was sold. Thomas Armstrong's commitment to customer value has had a prevailing influence in his company's philosophy and values through the years.

Armstrong's rich heritage of customer service and quality kicked into high gear when the company embraced the concepts of quality management in 1983—even though it was already a leader in most of its markets. Today, BPO's quality improvement process has matured and been refined into the business excellence process. Its operations are among the most effective, integrated improvement processes in any American company. The company's processes have evolved through several improvement cycles, taking advantage of customer and employee feedback as well benchmarking, competitive comparisons, and the use of the Baldrige criteria.

Corporate "non-negotiables" and key business drivers focus each operation on developing high performance in value-adding functions. Detailed human resources strategies are linked to overall business strategies through gain-sharing, training, and recognition programs. Capability development and a documented change process are examples of tools used to develop and leverage a high-performance organization. Strategies and action plans are reviewed by BPO's Quality Leadership Team, and business results are built into every employee's compensation by various reward plans.

A documented New Product Delivery Process (NPDP) incorporates techniques and information inputs to reflect the changing needs and expectations of each customer segment. NPDP has been through several cycles of improvement and refinement, and results include an increasing percent of sales coming from new products.

To get products to customers more efficiently, BPO uses its Quality Motor Carrier Services program, introduced in 1989. The program has made an impact by dramatically reducing the number of carriers BPO uses as well as improving on-time delivery.

Overall Results

Trends and overall performance levels important to BPO show constant improvement and are superior to industry competition. Of special note are trends and levels of key productivity measures, such as manufacturing output per employee and sales per employee. Safety has reached outstanding levels—among the best in any industry. Gainsharing payouts, recognition, training, and education all show improving trends. Financial results also demonstrate the success of this management approach including earnings growth, profit, return on assets, cost of quality, and breakeven points.

Close to Customers

BPO uses a variety of approaches to keep close to their customers and build relationships. These include customer advisory meetings, 800 numbers, visits, TechLine, a sales force specialized by segments, market research, and convention attendance.

Customer satisfaction is measured by segment. Overall levels of satisfaction are very high, and BPO is developing more and more sophisticated measures, such as from the customer composite satisfaction index and the customer value analysis. Satisfaction levels compare very favorably with competitors and show that BPO has been in a leadership position for many years.

BPO strives to set the standard for excellence, to keep raising the bar. The organization has used the tools of quality management to successfully transform itself from a tradition-bound, heavy manufacturer into a highly capable global competitor.

* * *

For more information on BPO quality efforts, contact John M. Scheldrup, Manager, Corporate Communications, Armstrong World Industries, 313 W. Liberty Street, Lancaster, PA, 17603; Phone (717) 396-2766, fax (717) 396-2555.

1995 Baldrige Award Winner, Manufacturing Category: Corning Telecommunications Products Division

The following is an edited version of the press release from the National Institute of Standards and Technology announcing that Corning Telecommunications Products Division had received a Baldrige award for 1995.

Using technology developed and patented by its parent, Corning Telecommunications Products Division was formed in 1983 to manufacture optical fiber that uses pulses of light to carry large amounts of information over great distances at low cost. With sales in 30 different countries, Corning TPD is the largest optical fiber manufacturer in the world. The company has formed joint ventures with companies in Europe and Australia to manufacture optical fiber. The following gives some examples of Corning TPD's quality improvement efforts:

- TPD uses a formal, documented process management system to control and continuously improve over 800 processes throughout its business and manufacturing operations. Fifty of these processes are designated Core Business Processes and are owned and managed by TPD's key business leaders.
- Corning TPD tracks 220 in-process and finished product attributes—optical or mechanical parameters that characterize optical fiber performance. Process capability for key parameters, such as glass diameter and fiber curl, has improved steadily over the last three years.
- One measure of satisfaction is the quality of products shipped to customers, expressed as parts per million product returns. In 1994, returns were at or below 250 ppm level—meaning that only 250 reels of fiber cable out of every one million reels were returned (0.025 percent).
- Productivity, as measured by kilometers of fiber produced per employee, doubled from 1987 to 1994 as a result of reducing manufacturing processing steps, developing new manufacturing equipment, and making technological improvements to existing equipment.
- TPD uses diverse tools to measure the satisfaction of its customers. 92 percent of TPD's customers rate them "excellent" to "very good." Over 80 percent of the company's customers cite TPD as the best overall supplier.
- TPD uses its "goal sharing" variable compensation system to directly link the compensation of employees at all levels of the organization to key division performance measures, including indicators of customer satisfaction.

* * *

The following is excerpted from Corning TPD's background information, sent out by the company shortly after receiving the award.

The Corning Telecommunications Products Division designs and manufactures optical fiber products that are used in the transmission of voice, video, and data signals in telecommunications systems worldwide. The hair-thin optical fiber designed and commercialized at TPD's facilities in Corning, New York, and manufactured in the Wilmington, North Carolina, manufacturing plant is a key component of the information superhighway. TPD is the world's largest manufacturer of optical fiber and has maintained or grown market share against major competitors over the past four years.

TPD's Quality Approach

From the beginning, TPD's manufacturing and delivery processes have been supported by an integrated system of controls that assure product consistency and high-performance levels, exceeding customer expectations. All manufacturing processes are operated under closed-loop computer control, which is essential to achieving product consistency, which is measured in microns. TPD's use of quality architecture, a means of building quality into the manufacturing process, often calls upon use of the Cpk parameter to make control decisions so that processes are adjusted on-line. This assures that outputs remain within very strict specifications and with minimum variation.

The purity and reliability of raw material and purchased parts are critical to optical fiber performance, and high-impact suppliers are managed under TPD's Supplier Total Value process. This process uses evaluations of supplier quality systems, their technology contributions to optical fiber, the price/value relationship, and fulfillment of ongoing requirements to sustain and drive improvement in the relationship. TPD's experience with suppliers in this process has driven the customer total value process, which TPD uses with its key customers to evaluate itself as a supplier.

Of TPD's three foundation values—people, process, and technology—people has consistently been identified as the most important. Through rigorous, disciplined management of processes, TPD has established a culture of continuous improvement that produces the lowest optical fiber manufacturing costs and highest productivity in the industry. TPD's innovative product and process technologies have established it as the technology leader in optical fiber manufacturing. However, the company acknowledges that none of these accomplishments would have been realized without continued investment in TPD's people as valued individuals and critical players in building business success. TPD has invested heavily in improving the systems used to select the right people and help them grow and adapt to the changes associated with rapid business growth and a culture of continuous improvement. TPD has made a long-term commitment to development of high-performance work systems on the manufacturing floor. It is using employee-designed work teams to address redesigned work areas, multiple job-task flexibility, cross-training, multiple skill levels, and simplification of job classifications.

Customer Focus

TPD serves a two-tiered market, selling optical fiber to domestic and international cable manufacturers who then create optical fiber cable for use by communications companies. TPD considers the cablers to be direct customers and the owners of the communication systems to be end-user customers. Additionally, TPD supplies optical fiber product and manufacturing technology to joint venture fiber-making operations in key international markets and formed with local cablers.

TPD uses its Customer Response System (CRS) to identify, collect, and address cabler and end-user customer expectations. Three different processes within CRS are used to gain comprehensive insight into customer requirements and measure customer satisfaction performance. The Customer Report Card and Customer Total Value processes are administered by customer contact teams assigned to each cabler and provide quarterly feedback on their expectations and near-term satisfaction levels. The Customer Total Value process mirrors TPD's own Supplier Total Value process, and requires interactive discussion between the customer and TPD's account team followed by joint development of a Corrective Action/Initiative Plan as needed. A refinement to these two processes is the Customer Value Assessment, a third party assessment of TPD's customer satisfaction performance. This process is conducted annually, although the focus alternates between direct and end-user customers each year.

Another key component of CRS is the customer database (CDB), a state-of-the-art computer repository for direct feedback from customers. The CDB treats customer requirements, complaints, compliments, and competitor offerings as data sets and allows teams and individuals who own the data to retrieve and use the data as needed. The teams use TBD's corrective action and customer initiative processes, the final components of CRS, to convert customer feedback data into customer priorities.

Use of the CRS has enabled TPD to lead the industry in customer satisfaction. Over 80 percent of its worldwide customers have ranked TPD as their number-one supplier. Among TPD's end-user customers, 99 percent view TPD as the technical leader in the industry, and 94 percent rate TPD's optical fiber the best for overall quality compared with that of any competitor. Shipping reliability and delivery responsiveness has been greater than 99 percent since 1993.

Results

TPD's investment in people, processes, and technology and its focused and well-deployed strategy have driven improvement in all aspects of its operations. Product returns have been reduced 10-fold in the last 10 years and are now 250 ppm. Manufacturing costs are the lowest in the industry, and by using a theory of constraints analysis, productivity at the bottleneck manufacturing process step has been doubled. TPD has been able to share these gains with customers with significant price reductions over the past eight years.

TPD has increased the information-carrying capacity of its single-mode products by a factor of 13 since 1983, enabling larger and larger volumes of information to be transmitted over the same or fewer number of fibers. Manufacturing process improvements and new product innovations have improved optical fiber reliability, enabling fiber to better withstand the stresses of cabling and installation.

OSHA recordable incidents and lost time accidents have been driven well below the expected performance within its standard industry code. Hazardous waste generation has been minimized such that the pounds shipped off-site for disposal per kilometer of fiber manufactured has decreased 90 percent in eight years.

*   *   *

For more information, contact Gerald J. McQuaid, Vice President, Business Systems Corning Incorporated, Telecommunications Products Division, Corning, NY 14831; phone (800) 525-2524 or (607) 974-7528, fax (607) 974-7648.

1996 Malcolm Baldrige National Quality Award Criteria

This section provides you with a summary of the 1996 Baldrige Award Criteria, including changes from the 1995 Criteria, with points given for each category. You can receive a complete copy of the 1996 Criteria and the 1996 Application Forms and Instructions (Criteria and Application are two separate documents) by writing to:

Malcolm Baldrige National Quality Award
National Institute of Standards and Technology
Route 270 and Quince Orchard Road
Administration Building, Room A537
Gaithersburg, MD 20899-0001
  Phone (301) 975-2036
Fax (301) 948-3716
Internet: oqp@micf.nist.gov

1996 Award Criteria: Values, Concepts, and Framework

Award Criteria Purposes

The Malcolm Baldrige National Quality Award Criteria are the basis for making Awards and for giving feedback to applicants. In addition, the Criteria have three important roles in strengthening U.S. competitiveness:

- to help improve performance practices and capabilities;
- to facilitate communication and sharing of best practices information among and within organizations of all types based upon a common understanding of key performance requirements; and
- to serve as a working tool for managing performance, planning, training, and assessment.

Award Criteria Goals

The Criteria are designed to help companies enhance their competitiveness through focus on dual, results-oriented goals:

- delivery of ever-improving value to customers, resulting in marketplace success; and
- improvement of overall company performance and capabilities.

Core Values and Concepts

The Award Criteria are built upon a set of core values and concepts. These values and concepts are the foundation for integrating customer and company performance requirements within a results-oriented framework. These core values and concepts are:

Customer-Driven Quality

Quality is judged by customers. All product and service features and characteristics that contribute value to customers and lead to customer satisfaction and preference must be a key focus of a company's management system. Value, satisfaction, and preference may be influenced by many factors throughout the customer's overall purchase, ownership, and service experiences. These factors include the company's relationship with customers that helps build trust, confidence, and loyalty. This concept of quality includes not only the product and service characteristics that meet basic customer requirements, but it also includes those features and characteristics that enhance them and differentiate them from competing offerings. Such enhancement and differentiation may be based upon new offerings, combinations of product and service offerings, rapid response, or special relationships.

Customer-driven quality is thus a strategic concept. It is directed toward customer retention, market share gain, and growth. It demands constant sensitivity to emerging customer and market requirements, and measurement of the factors that drive customer satisfaction and retention. It also demands awareness of developments in technology and of competitors' offerings, and rapid and flexible response to customer and market requirements.

Success requires more than defect and error reduction, merely meeting specifications, and reducing complaints. Nevertheless, defect and error reduction and elimination of causes of dissatisfaction contribute significantly to the customers' view of quality and are thus also important parts of customer-driven quality. In addition, the company's success in recovering from defects and errors ("making things right for the customer") is crucial to building customer relationships and to customer retention.

Leadership

A company's senior leaders need to set directions and create a customer orientation, clear and visible values, and high expectations. Reinforcement of the values and expectations requires personal commitment and involvement. The leaders' basic values and commitment need to address all stakeholders and include areas of public responsibility and corporate citizenship. The leaders need to guide the creation of strategies, systems, and methods for achieving excellence and building capabilities. The systems and methods need to guide all activities and decisions of the company. The senior leaders need to commit to the development of the entire work force and should encourage participation and creativity by all employees. Through their personal involvement in planning, communications, review of company performance, and employee recognition, the senior leaders serve as role models, reinforcing the values and building leadership and initiative throughout the company.

Continuous Improvement and Learning

Achieving the highest levels of performance requires a well-executed approach to continuous improvement. The term "continuous improvement" refers to both incremental and "breakthrough" improvement. Improvement needs to be "embedded" in the way the company functions. Embedded means: (1) improvement is part of the daily work of all work units; (2) improvement processes seek to eliminate problems at their source; and (3) improvement is driven by opportunities to do better, as well as by problems that must be corrected. Sources of improvement include: employee ideas; R&D; customer input; and benchmarking or other comparative performance information.

Improvements may be of several types: (1) enhancing value to customers through new and improved products and services; (2) reducing errors, defects, and waste; (3) improving responsiveness and cycle time performance; (4) improving productivity and effectiveness in the use of all resources; and (5) improving the company's performance in fulfilling its public responsibilities and serving as a corporate citizen role model. Thus, improvement is intended not to provide better products and services, but also to be responsive and efficient—both conferring additional marketplace advantages. To meet these objectives, continuous improvement must contain cycles of planning, execution, and evaluation. This requires a basis—preferably a quantitative basis—for assessing progress and for deriving information for future cycles of improvement. Such information should directly link performance goals and internal operations.

Employee Participation and Development

A company's success in improving performance depends increasingly on the skills and motivation of its work force. Employee success depends increasingly on having meaningful opportunities to learn and to practice new skills. Companies need to invest in the development of the work force through education, training, and opportunities for continuing growth. Such opportunities might include classroom and on-the-job training, job rotation, and pay for demonstrated skills. Structured on-the-job training offers a cost-effective way to train and to better link training to work processes. Work force education and training programs may need to utilize advanced technologies, such as electronic support systems, computer-based learning, and satellite broadcasts. Increasingly, training, development, and work organizations need to be tailored to a diverse work force and to more flexible, high performance work practices.

Major challenges in the area of work force development include: (1) integration of human resource management—selection, performance, recognition, training, and career advancement; and (2) aligning human resource management with business plans and strategic change processes. Addressing these challenges requires acquisition and use of employee-related data on skills, satisfaction, motivation, safety, and well-being. Such data need to be tied to indicators of company or unit performance, such as customer satisfaction, customer retention, and productivity. Through this approach, human resource management may be better integrated and aligned with business directions.

Fast Response

Success in competitive markets increasingly demands ever-shorter cycles for new or improved product and service introduction. Also, faster and more flexible response to customers is now a more critical requirement. Major improvement in response time often requires simplification of work organizations and work processes. To accomplish such improvement, the time performance of work processes should be among the key process measures. There are other important benefits derived from this focus: response time improvements often drive simultaneous improvements in organization, quality, and productivity. Hence it is beneficial to consider response time, quality, and productivity objectives together.

Design Quality and Prevention

Business management should place strong emphasis on design quality—problem and waste prevention achieved through building quality into products and services and efficiency into production and delivery processes. In general, costs of preventing problems at the design stage are much lower than costs of correcting problems that occur "downstream." Design quality includes the creation of fault-tolerant (robust) or failure-resistant processes and products.

A major issue in competition is the design-to-introduction ("product generation") cycle time. Meeting the demands of rapidly changing markets requires that companies carry out stage-to-stage coordination and integration ("concurrent engineering") of functions and activities from basic research to commercialization. Increasingly, design quality also includes the ability to incorporate information gathered from diverse sources and data bases, that combine factors such as customer preference, competitive offerings, marketplace changes, and external research findings and developments.

From the point of view of public responsibility, the design stage is a critical decision point. Design decisions affect process waste streams and the composition of municipal and industrial wastes. The growing demands for a cleaner environment mean that companies' design strategies need to include environmental factors.

Consistent with the theme of design quality and prevention, improvement needs to emphasize interventions "upstream"—at early stages in processes. This approach yields the maximum overall benefits of improvements and corrections. Such upstream intervention also needs to take into account the company's suppliers.

Long-Range View of the Future

Pursuit of market leadership requires a strong future orientation and a willingness to make long-term commitments to all stakeholders—customers, employees, suppliers, stockholders, the public, and the community. Planning needs to anticipate many types of changes including those that may affect customers' expectations of products and services, technological developments, changing customer segments, evolving regulatory requirements, community/societal expectations, and thrusts by competitors. Plans, strategies, and resource allocations need to reflect these commitments and changes. A major part of the long-term commitment is developing employees and suppliers and fulfilling public responsibilities.

Management by Fact

Modern business management systems depend upon measurement, data, information, and analysis. Measurements must derive from the company's strategy and encompass all key processes and the outputs and results of those processes. Facts and data needed for performance improvement and assessment are of many types, including: customer, product and service performance, operations, market, competitive comparisons, supplier, employee-related, and cost and financial. Analysis refers to extracting larger meaning from data to support evaluation and decision making at all levels within the company. Such analysis may entail using data to reveal information—such as trends, projections, and cause and effect—that might not be evident without analysis. Facts, data, and analysis support a variety of company purposes, such as planning, reviewing company performance, improving operations, and comparing company performance with competitors' or with "best practices" benchmarks.

A major consideration in the use of data and analysis to improve performance involves the creation and use of performance measures or indicators. Performance measures or indicators are measurable characteristics of products, services, processes, and operations the company uses to track and improve performance. *The measures or indicators should be selected to best represent the factors that lead to improved customer, operational, and financial performance. A system of measures or indicators tied to customer and/ or company performance requirements represents a clear basis for aligning all activities with the company's goals.* Through the analysis of data from the tracking processes, the measures or indicators themselves may be evaluated and changed. For example, measures selected to track product and service quality may be judged by how well improvement in these measures correlates with improvement in customer satisfaction and customer retention.

Partnership Development

Companies should seek to build internal and external partnerships to better accomplish their overall goals.

Internal partnerships might include those that promote labor-management cooperation, such as agreements with unions. Agreements might entail employee development, cross-training, or new work organizations, such as high performance work teams. Internal partnerships might also involve creating network relationships among company units to improve flexibility and responsiveness.

External partnerships may be with customers, suppliers, and education organizations for a variety of purposes, including education and training. An increasingly important kind of external partnership is the strategic partnership or alliance. Such partnerships might offer a company entry into new markets or a basis for new products or services. A partnership might also permit the blending of a company's core competencies or leadership capabilities with complementary strengths and capabilities of partners, thereby enhancing overall capability, including speed and flexibility. Internal and external partnerships should seek to develop longer-term objectives, thereby creating a basis for mutual investments. Partners should address the key requirements for success of the partnership, means of regular communication, approaches to evaluating progress, and means for adapting to changing conditions. In some cases, joint education and training initiatives could offer a cost-effective means to help ensure the success.

Corporate Responsibility and Citizenship

A company's management should stress corporate responsibility and encourage corporate citizenship. Corporate responsibility refers to basic expectations of the company—business ethics and protection of public health, safety, and the environment. Health, safety, and environmental considerations include the company's operations as well as the life cycles of products and services. Companies need to address factors such as resource conservation and waste reduction at their source. Planning related to public health, safety, and the environment should anticipate adverse impacts that may arise in facilities management, production, distribution, transportation, use and disposal of products. Plans should seek to prevent problems, to provide a forthright company response if problems occur, and to make available information needed to maintain public awareness, safety, and confidence. Inclusion of public responsibility areas within a performance system means meeting all local, state, and federal laws and regulatory requirements. It also means treating these and related requirements as areas for continuous improvement "beyond mere compliance." This requires that appropriate measures of be created and used in managing performance.

Corporate citizenship refers to leadership and support—within limits of a company's resources—of publicly important purposes, including areas of corporate responsibility. Such purposes might include education improvement, improving health care value, environmental excellence, resource conservation, community services, improving industry and business practices, and sharing of nonproprietary quality-related information. Leadership as a corporate citizen also entails influencing other organizations, private and public, to partner for these purposes. For example, individual companies could lead efforts to help define the obligations of their industry to its communities.

Results Orientation

A company's performance system needs to focus on results. Results should be guided by and balanced by the interests of all stakeholders—customers,

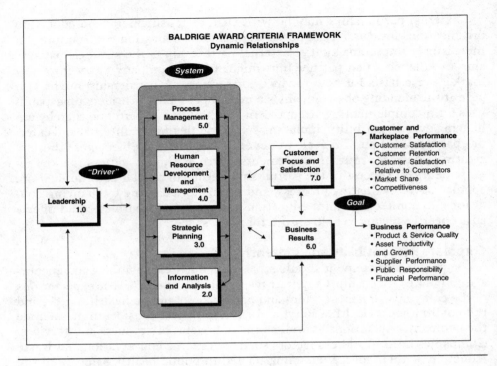

employees, stockholders, suppliers and partners, the public, and the community. To meet the sometimes conflicting and changing aims that balance implies, company strategy needs to explicitly address all stakeholder requirements to ensure that actions and plans meet the differing needs and avoid adverse impact on the stakeholders. The use of a balanced composite of performance measures offers an effective means to communicate requirements, to monitor actual performance, and to marshal support for improving results.

Award Criteria Framework

The core values and concepts are embodied in seven Categories, as follows:

1. Leadership
2. Information and Analysis
3. Strategic Planning
4. Human Resource Development and Management
5. Process Management
6. Business Results
7. Customer Focus and Satisfaction

The framework connecting and integrating the Categories is given in the figure below.

The framework has three basic elements:

Driver
Senior executive leadership sets directions, creates values, goals, expectations, and systems, and pursues customer and business performance excellence.

System
The system comprises the set of well-defined and well-designed processes for meeting the company's customer and performance requirements.

Goal
The basic aims of leadership and the purposes of the system are two-fold:

Customer and Marketplace Performance
Customer and marketplace performance means delivery of ever-improving value to customers, high levels of customer satisfaction, and a strong competitive position.

Business Performance
Business performance is reflected in a wide variety of financial and non-financial results, including human resource development and corporate responsibility.

The seven Criteria Categories shown in the figure are subdivided into Items and Areas to Address:

Items
There are 24 Examination Items, each focusing on a major requirement. Item titles and point values are given on page 750.

Areas to Address
Items consist of one or more Areas to Address (Areas). Information is submitted by applicants in response to specific requirements of these Areas.

Changes from the 1995 Award Criteria
The Criteria continue to evolve toward comprehensive coverage of performance, addressing the needs and expectations of all stakeholders—customers, employees, stockholders, suppliers, and the public. The Criteria for 1996 further strengthen and integrate the high performance and competitiveness improvement themes emphasized in 1995. The most significant changes made in the Criteria and in the Criteria booklet are summarized as follows:

- Although the number of Items remains at 24, one Item has been added to the Business Results Category, and two Items from the Customer Focus and Satisfaction Category (Items 7.4 and 7.5 in 1995) have been combined.
- The number of Areas to Address (Areas) has been reduced from 54 to 52.

- A Message to Executives has been added to provide a broad perspective on the meaning of performance in the Award Criteria and on the larger benefits from participating in the Award process.
- A Glossary of Key Terms has been added to better define and to help tie together the major performance themes in the Criteria.
- A separate section, Preparing the Business Overview, has been added to highlight the particular importance of this Overview to writing, reviewing, and evaluating an application. Applicants are encouraged to prepare the Business Overview *first*. This recommendation is made for two reasons: (1) to help ensure that responses to the Criteria Items focus on what is relevant and important to the business; and (2) to bring about better consistency among responses to different items.
- The Award Criteria Response Guidelines have been revised. The purpose of this revision is to help applicants and other users of the Criteria to prepare responses that make possible better feedback. Particular emphasis is placed on helping applicants provide clearer and more complete information on deployment.
- The Criteria Framework diagram has been revised to better reflect the results goals and the meaning of performance.
- The section on Item Descriptions has been revised and updated.

Applicants and other users of the Award Criteria are cautioned to note that some changes in wording have been made in many Items and Item Notes. Changes, by category, are:

Leadership
- Item 1.2 now has two Areas compared with three in 1995. Areas 1.2a and 1.2b from 1995 were combined, thus better integrating communications with other related organizational requirements. In addition, the company performance review Area (1.2b in 1996 and 1.2c in 1995) is now much more explicit in its requirements. The Area now calls for nonfinancial and financial data related to the needs of all key stakeholders. It also calls for information on the tracking of progress relative to plans, competitive performance, and productivity in the use of assets.

Information and Analysis
- Item 2.1 (Area 2.1a) now includes a requirement to provide information on the design of the company's performance measurement system. This change is intended to enhance the diagnostic value of the Item and strengthen the feedback to applicants.

Strategic Planning
- Major planning concepts, most notably, "key business drivers," have been included in a Glossary of Key Terms.

Human Resource Development and Management

- The meaning of "high performance work," the focus of Item 4.2, has been included in the Glossary of Key Terms.
- An Item has been created in Category 6.0 (Item 6.3) for reporting all human resource results.

Process Management

- The meaning of "process" has been included in the Glossary of Key Terms.

Business Results

- A new Item, Human Resource Results (Item 6.3), has been created. This Item is intended to provide a better focus on and a more comprehensive treatment of the human resource results required by the Human Resource Development and Management Category and previously included in the Company Operational and Financial Results (Item 6.2 in 1995).

Customer Focus and Satisfaction

- Two Items from 1995 (Customer Satisfaction Results and Customer Satisfaction Comparison) have been combined. The new Item (Customer Satisfaction Results) integrates the requirements included in the two 1995 Items.

1996 Award Criteria—Item Listing

1996 Categories/Items	Point Values

1.0 Leadership   **90**

    1.1 Senior Executive Leadership 45
    1.2 Leadership System and Organization 25
    1.3 Public Responsibility and Corporate Citizenship 20

2.0 Information and Analysis   **75**

    2.1 Management of Information and Data....................................... 20
    2.2 Competitive Comparisons and Benchmarking............................ 15
    2.3 Analysis and Use of Company-Level Data 40

3.0 Strategic Planning   **55**

    3.1 Strategy Development 35
    3.2 Strategy Deployment... 20

4.0 Human Resource Development and Management   **140**

    4.1 Human Resource Planning and Evaluation 20
    4.2 High Performance Work Systems 45
    4.3 Employee Education, Training, and Development...................... 50
    4.4 Employee Well-Being and Satisfaction................................. 25

5.0 Process Management   **140**

    5.1 Design and Introduction of Products and Services...................... 40
    5.2 Process Management: Product and Service Production and
        Delivery 40
    5.3 Process Management: Support Services 30
    5.4 Management of Supplier Performance 30

6.0 Business Results   **250**

    6.1 Product and Service Quality Results.................................... 75
    6.2 Company Operational and Financial Results............................110
    6.3 Human Resource Results 35
    6.4 Supplier Performance Results 30

7.0 Customer Focus and Satisfaction   **250**

    7.1 Customer and Market Knowledge 30
    7.2 Customer Relationship Management 30
    7.3 Customer Satisfaction Determination................................... 30
    7.4 Customer Satisfaction Results 160

    TOTAL POINTS   **1000**

Index

1996 *Quality Yearbook* Feedback Survey

Please cut this form out, fill it in, and mail it to us. We need your feedback. On a scale of 1 to 5 (1 = poor, 5 = outstanding), please respond to the following questions:

1. Overall, how would you assess the value of this book to you? ＿＿ (Rate 1–5)

   Please describe how it has been valuable or not valuable to you. ＿＿＿＿＿＿＿

   ＿＿＿＿＿＿＿＿＿＿＿＿＿＿＿＿＿＿＿＿＿＿＿＿＿＿＿＿＿＿＿＿＿＿＿＿＿

   ＿＿＿＿＿＿＿＿＿＿＿＿＿＿＿＿＿＿＿＿＿＿＿＿＿＿＿＿＿＿＿＿＿＿＿＿＿

   Why? ＿＿＿＿＿＿＿＿＿＿＿＿＿＿＿＿＿＿＿＿＿＿＿＿＿＿＿＿＿＿＿＿＿

   ＿＿＿＿＿＿＿＿＿＿＿＿＿＿＿＿＿＿＿＿＿＿＿＿＿＿＿＿＿＿＿＿＿＿＿＿＿

2. How would you assess the value of Part One to you? ＿＿ (Rate 1–5)

   What did you find valuable about this part and why? ＿＿＿＿＿＿＿＿＿＿

   ＿＿＿＿＿＿＿＿＿＿＿＿＿＿＿＿＿＿＿＿＿＿＿＿＿＿＿＿＿＿＿＿＿＿＿＿＿

   ＿＿＿＿＿＿＿＿＿＿＿＿＿＿＿＿＿＿＿＿＿＿＿＿＿＿＿＿＿＿＿＿＿＿＿＿＿

3. How would you assess the value of Part Two to you? ＿＿ (Rate 1–5)

   What did you find valuable about this part and why? ＿＿＿＿＿＿＿＿＿＿

   ＿＿＿＿＿＿＿＿＿＿＿＿＿＿＿＿＿＿＿＿＿＿＿＿＿＿＿＿＿＿＿＿＿＿＿＿＿

   ＿＿＿＿＿＿＿＿＿＿＿＿＿＿＿＿＿＿＿＿＿＿＿＿＿＿＿＿＿＿＿＿＿＿＿＿＿

4. How would you assess the value of Part Three to you? ＿＿ (Rate 1–5)

   What did you find valuable about this part and why? ＿＿＿＿＿＿＿＿＿＿

   ＿＿＿＿＿＿＿＿＿＿＿＿＿＿＿＿＿＿＿＿＿＿＿＿＿＿＿＿＿＿＿＿＿＿＿＿＿

   ＿＿＿＿＿＿＿＿＿＿＿＿＿＿＿＿＿＿＿＿＿＿＿＿＿＿＿＿＿＿＿＿＿＿＿＿＿

5. How would you assess the value of Part Four to you? ＿＿ (Rate 1–5)

   What did you find valuable about this part and why? ＿＿＿＿＿＿＿＿＿＿

   ＿＿＿＿＿＿＿＿＿＿＿＿＿＿＿＿＿＿＿＿＿＿＿＿＿＿＿＿＿＿＿＿＿＿＿＿＿

   ＿＿＿＿＿＿＿＿＿＿＿＿＿＿＿＿＿＿＿＿＿＿＿＿＿＿＿＿＿＿＿＿＿＿＿＿＿

6. What changes and improvements would you like to see in the 1997 yearbook?

   ＿＿＿＿＿＿＿＿＿＿＿＿＿＿＿＿＿＿＿＿＿＿＿＿＿＿＿＿＿＿＿＿＿＿＿＿＿

   ＿＿＿＿＿＿＿＿＿＿＿＿＿＿＿＿＿＿＿＿＿＿＿＿＿＿＿＿＿＿＿＿＿＿＿＿＿